D0140731

THE CHRISTIAN TRADITION

THE CHRISTIAN TRADITION

A HISTORICAL AND THEOLOGICAL INTRODUCTION

Peter Feldmeier

UNIVERSITY OF TOLEDO

NEW YORK   OXFORD
OXFORD UNIVERSITY PRESS

Oxford University Press is a department of the University of Oxford.
It furthers the University's objective of excellence in research, scholarship,
and education by publishing worldwide. Oxford is a registered trade mark
of Oxford University Press in the UK and certain other countries.

Published in the United States of America by Oxford University Press
198 Madison Avenue, New York, NY 10016, United States of America.

© 2017 by Oxford University Press

For titles covered by Section 112 of the US Higher Education
Opportunity Act, please visit www.oup.com/us/he for the
latest information about pricing and alternate formats.

All rights reserved. No part of this publication may be reproduced,
stored in a retrieval system, or transmitted, in any form or by any
means, without the prior permission in writing of Oxford University
Press, or as expressly permitted by law, by license, or under terms
agreed with the appropriate reproduction rights organization.
Inquiries concerning reproduction outside the scope of the above
should be sent to the Rights Department, Oxford University Press,
at the address above.

You must not circulate this work in any other form
and you must impose this same condition on any acquirer.

Library of Congress Cataloging-in-Publication Data

Names: Feldmeier, Peter.
Title: The Christian tradition : a historical and theological introduction /
    Peter Feldmeier, University of Toledo.
Description: 1 [edition]. | New York, NY : Oxford University Press, 2016.
Identifiers: LCCN 2015041647 (print) | LCCN 2016013125 (ebook) | ISBN
    9780199374380 | ISBN 9780199374397 ()
Subjects: LCSH: Christianity.
Classification: LCC BR121.3 .F45 2016 (print) | LCC BR121.3 (ebook) | DDC
    230—dc23
LC record available at https://lccn.loc.gov/2015041647

9 8 7 6 5 4 3 2

Printed by Webcom Inc., Canada

LOAVES AND FISHES
© 2003 by John August Swanson
Serigraph 24″ by 36″
www.JohnAugustSwanson.com
Los Angeles artist John August Swanson is noted for his finely detailed, brilliantly colored
paintings and original prints. His works are found in the Smithsonian Institution's
National Museum of American History, London's Tate Gallery, the Vatican Museum's
Collection of Modern Religious Art, and the Bibliothèque Nationale, Paris.
Web site: www.JohnAugustSwanson.com

BRIEF CONTENTS

CONTENTS

MAPS

TIMELINES

PREFACE

I have been teaching an introductory course in Christianity for twenty years, and in all those years I have never been completely satisfied with a textbook. Some offer excellent historical material, while others focus on doctrine. Several, as is the case with this book, have attempted to unite both, but these are fewer and farther between. None that I could find was able to convey the tenor or feel of the Christian tradition in a way that avoided either losing scholarly objectivity or outright religious advocacy. I am convinced that it is crucial to meet all of these objectives in a way that is engaging, is interesting, and allows students to appreciate something of how Christianity understands itself. None of the texts I have reviewed or used help students get inside the theological and spiritual values and perspectives that ground important Christian figures and movements, and few engage students in what these teachings or developments imply. Thus, students often get the big picture of the history of the church without understanding the theological or spiritual values that undergird various developments. Students ought to see why these issues mattered and may still matter.

What I have found is that a typical textbook chapter on, say, the Protestant Reformation may convey the knowledge that Martin Luther led the German Reformation, objected to indulgences, believed in justification by faith alone, and held there were only two sacraments. It may teach students that Ulrich Zwingli and John Calvin led the Swiss Reformation, that Zwingli did not believe in the real presence of Christ in the Eucharist, and that Calvin believed in double predestination. But such a chapter typically does not get underneath the religious imagination of these figures to see why these beliefs would have been important to them, how they understood the working of God's grace or providence, and what kind of Christian faith emerged from their influences. Rarely are students led to consider what kind of spirituality or faith posture was being advanced by such individuals, nor are they helped to consider the implications of such stances.

My experience as a teacher led me to desire a textbook that is academically honest and meets the standards of both religious and secular scholars in the field, that tells the history of the development of Christianity in a fair and compelling way, that shows how and why theological and historical developments happened and what these mean, and that portrays how the Christian tradition has been experienced within Christianity itself. It is certainly not a text that advocates the Christian faith. This book is for any student who wishes to understand Christianity, whether that student holds no religious belief or is even hostile to belief, or whether he or she identifies with any of the other religious traditions of the world, is personally Christian, or self-identifies as spiritual but not religious. Students and professors alike will find it to be balanced. The data I provide and interpretations I give to those data represent scholarly consensus, as is appropriate in a broad survey textbook.

Christianity has been part of Mediterranean culture for 2,000 years, and European culture for 1,500 years. It has influenced (and been influenced by) politics, economics, education, literature, morality, art, and architecture—indeed, everything that makes up culture. On a fair assessment, Christianity has been responsible for the development of Western society's hospitals, schools, orphanages, and tradition of social justice. Christianity has also been responsible for the Crusades, political power grabs, and witch hunts. One cannot understand Western history and culture without understanding the Christian tradition; for a well-educated person it is an imperative.

This textbook intends to remedy such a lack of understanding, at least to the degree that a survey work can do such a thing, and it intends to do so in a holistic, integrated, and balanced way. Readers will come to understand the breadth of Christianity, from its Jewish roots and the ministry of Jesus to its development as an independent religious movement and its eventual evolution into the world's largest religion. Toward this aim, we have adopted the following format:

Chapter One: Students will be introduced to Christianity and its sources of authority, particularly the Bible and responsible approaches to the Bible.

Chapter Two: Students will encounter the Old Testament; its history, foundational persons, and fundamental themes; and developments that are particularly important to Christianity.

Chapter Three: Students will discover the person and ministry of Jesus in the New Testament, including his religious and political setting, and particular interpretations of his ministry in each of the four Gospels.

Chapter Four: Students will engage the rest of the New Testament, particularly the Acts of the Apostles and the crucial ministry and writings of the apostle Paul.

Chapter Five: Students will discover how and why the early Christian movement became a separate religion from Judaism, and how it experienced itself in opposition to the Roman Empire that persecuted it.

Chapter Six: Students will get underneath the institutional life of the church to discover its outlook, worship and community life, and moral tenor.

Chapter Seven: Students will see how Christianity went from being a persecuted church to being a publicly favored church, how and why Christian leaders convened to create universal dogmas, and how dissenting Christians broke communion with the majority church.

Chapter Eight: Students will be introduced to some of the great theological and spiritual leaders of the patristic church and how they influenced theology, doctrine, and spirituality.

Chapter Nine: Students will learn about major developments in the settled church's spiritual life, including the growth of monasticism and other forms of Christian piety that grounded the church's practice and self-understanding.

Chapter Ten: Students will find out how the church spread throughout southeast Africa, the Middle East, and eastern European countries, with the baptism of whole masses of peoples and the conversion of their leaders.

Chapter Eleven: Students will discover the missions and development of Christianity in Europe as Charlemagne's conquests transformed much of the continent into the Holy Roman Empire. Students will also discover the increasingly major importance of the bishop of Rome, the pope, who became a power player in the Western world, and will be introduced to the Crusades and the complexity of the relationship between Christianity and war.

Chapter Twelve: Students will learn about the cultural and economic shifts that occurred during the Middle Ages in Europe and how they affected religious movements inside and outside the church. They will also discover new forms of Christian piety and spiritual imagination and examine how the Middle Ages produced a different kind of theological discourse.

Chapter Thirteen: Students will encounter the great figures and cultural changes that came from the Renaissance, when a new kind of humanism and calls for reform of the church emerged.

Chapter Fourteen: Students will encounter the great persons of the Reformation, how and why they challenged Roman Catholicism, and how European Christianity broke up into several factions.

Chapter Fifteen: Students will find out how the Roman Catholic Church responded institutionally to the Reformation in response to both external events and internal demands for change that had been brewing for a century or more.

Chapter Sixteen: Students will see how the breakup of Christianity in the West influenced the wars that ravaged European countries for almost a century. They will also see how the Enlightenment challenged Christianity and the assumptions traditionally made regarding religious authority.

Chapter Seventeen: Students will learn about the worldwide expansion of European colonialism and how Christian missions were involved both in bringing the Christian faith to masses of peoples in the Americas, Africa, and the Far East and in the exploitation of many of these peoples.

Chapter Eighteen: Students will discover the religious dynamics that were part and parcel of the development of the United States and created the conditions for the massive expansion of denominations and the first-ever separation of church and state.

Chapter Nineteen: Students will learn about how the modern world has challenged religious faith and Christianity in particular, and how Christianity has variously responded.

Chapter Twenty: Students will see how the widespread development of Evangelical and Pentecostal Christianity happened, particularly in the United States, and how this has affected culture, politics, and Christian self-understanding.

Chapter Twenty-One: Students will see how Christianity is growing and changing worldwide, its dramatic expansion in Africa and parts of Asia, theological initiatives of the modern church, and what history might anticipate for the future of the Christian Tradition.

To facilitate this more holistic approach to learning about the Christian tradition, we have also made sure to provide numerous images that will give students visuals of some of the persons, places, and dynamics being discussed. Visualizing a monastery, an icon, or an image of an important saint or theologian both inspires the imagination and helps lock into memory what is being discussed. We also have included timelines in virtually every chapter, as well as a number of maps. It is one thing to read about the spread of Islam or the size of the Holy Roman Empire, and another to see a visual of it.

A book such as this simply has to include a number of facts and concepts to learn, and toward this end, we have included key terms in bold, with a glossary in the back of the book as a helpful reference. Furthermore, we have included at the end of each chapter Summary Questions, which assist both teacher and student in identifying the most important parts of the chapter, and Discussion Questions, which challenge the reader to consider his or her own values, interpretations, and perspectives in concert with the chapter's material. They are ways of asking: What does it mean? What do you make of it? Where would you side on this controversy, and why? In this way students will not just learn facts, but will process the material for themselves. This can generate great classroom discussion as well as individual critical thinking skills and personal value making.

ACKNOWLEDGMENTS

There are many persons to thank for this book. First and foremost, I want to thank Robert Miller, executive editor of Oxford University Press. I have never experienced so much diligence and professionalism in getting a book together than I have from Robert in preparing *The Christian Tradition*. The book would not have happened without his confidence in the project, his robust vetting process, and his broad-scale review process. At the University of Toledo, I'd like to thank my chair, John Sarnecki, who has been consistently supportive, and graduate assistants Zach Zschaechner, Kyle Novak, Liz Johnson, and Ethan Deitrich. I would also like to thank Dr. Marie Pannier Feldmeier, whose editorial support substantially improved a number of chapters. Finally, and most importantly, I'd like to thank colleagues, personally known and unknown to me, who were gracious enough to comment on, challenge, praise, and offer corrections to either my proposal or the manuscript. It would have been a very different book without them, and certainly a less professional one. They are: Marlin Adrian (Salem College), Candy Gunther Brown (Indiana University), Maeve Callan (Simpson College), Rose Caraway (Northern Arizona University), Rose Ann Christian (Towson University), Christian A. Eberhart (University of Houston), James Ramon Felak (University of Washington), H. Ashley Hall (Creighton University), Meira Kensky (Coe College), Aaron Ketchell (University of Kansas), John Knight (Marist College), Marian Maskulak (St. John's University), Frederick Parrella (Santa Clara University), Anthony Petro (Boston University), Christina Remer (Bishop's University), Marcia Robinson (Syracuse University), and Myles Werntz (Baylor University). I also benefited from several anonymous critiques from scholars to whom I am most grateful.

A CHRISTIAN TIMELINE

3000–2000 BCE	Beginnings of civilization in the ancient Near East
c. 1850–1750 BCE	Abraham migrates to Canaan; beginning of the patriarchal period
c. 1250 BCE	Moses leads the Exodus from Egypt; the Israelites make a covenant at Sinai
c. 1220–1020 BCE	Joshua leads the invasion of Canaan; the period of the Judges (tribal confederacy)
c. 1000–961 BCE	David reigns as king
922 BCE	Kingdom divides into two kingdoms: Israel (north) and Judah (south)
721 BCE	The northern kingdom of Israel is defeated by the Assyrians
597 BCE	The southern kingdom of Judah is defeated by the Babylonians
538 BCE	Return to Palestine (Temple rebuilt 520–515 BCE)
c. 500 BCE	Beginning of compilation of Hebrew Bible
334–326 BCE	Alexander the Great conquers the Near East, institutes the process of hellenization
167 BCE	Maccabean Revolt; Jewish control of Palestine
63 BCE	Romans conquer Palestine and capture Jerusalem
37–4 BCE	Rule of Herod the Great
c. 27–30 CE	Ministry of Jesus
c. 33 CE	Conversion of Paul of Tarsus
c. 65–110 CE	New Testament texts are written
c. 200 CE	Christians arrive in India
313 CE	Co-emperors Constantine and Licinius issue the Edict of Milan
325 CE	Council of Nicaea defines the full divine nature of Jesus and condemns teachings of Arius
391 CE	Emperor Theodosius declares Christianity the official religion of the Roman Empire
451 CE	Council of Chalcedon adopts the dogma that Christ is "one person with two natures"; dissent leads to breakup of the church and establishment of Eastern Christian churches in Armenia, Syria, Egypt, Ethiopia, Eritrea, and India

481–511 CE	Clovis unites Gaul (France) and adopts Christianity
c. 500s CE	Christians spread into China eventually
570–632 CE	Life of Muhammad
638–711 CE	Jerusalem, North Africa, and Spain come under Arab Rule
723 CE	Boniface sent as a missionary to Germanic tribes
756 CE	Rise of the Papal States
787 CE	Council of Nicaea II defends the veneration of icons
800 CE	Charlemagne crowned
1054 CE	Schism between Eastern Orthodox and Roman Catholic
1096–1099 CE	First Crusade
1202–1204 CE	Fourth Crusade; Western soldiers pillage Constantinople
1309–1377 CE	Avignon papacy in France
1347–1351 CE	Bubonic plague (Black Death) decimates much of Europe
1414–1418 CE	Council of Constance ends rival papal claims and pronounces conciliarism
1440 CE	Invention of the printing press
1492 CE	Christopher Columbus lands in the Americas
1517 CE	Martin Luther writes his Ninety-Five Theses challenging indulgences
1519 CE	Conquest of Mexico by Hernán Cortés
1523 CE	Ulrich Zwingli leads reform movement in Zurich
1533 CE	Copernicus publishes *On the Revolutions of the Heavenly Spheres*, advancing heliocentrism (planets revolving around the sun)
1534 CE	King Henry VIII creates separate Church of England
1536 CE	Calvin leads reform movement in Geneva; Tyndale's English Bible is printed
1540 CE	Jesuits founded by Ignatius of Loyola and companions
1542–1552 CE	Francis Xavier leads missions in India and Japan
1545–1563 CE	Council of Trent reforms the Roman Catholic Church
1555 CE	Peace of Augsburg signed, allowing German princes to establish Lutheranism or Catholicism in their realms
1582 CE	Matteo Ricci brings missions to China
1609 CE	First Baptist church established in Amsterdam
1611 CE	King James Bible completed
1618–1648 CE	Thirty Years' War, ended by the Peace of Westphalia (1648)
1620 CE	Puritans arrive in North America on the *Mayflower* and establish a colony at Plymouth
1636 CE	Roger Williams founds the colony of Providence (Rhode Island), the first American colony with religious liberty

1675 CE	Philipp Jakob Spener publishes *Pia Desideria*; beginnings of Pietism
c. 1726 CE	Beginning of the First Great Awakening in America
1775 CE	Beginning of the American Revolution
1789 CE	Beginning of French Revolution; Catholicism is largely suppressed
1789 CE	John Carroll is made first Catholic bishop in America
1801 CE	Beginning of the Second Great Awakening at Cane Ridge, Kentucky
1859 CE	Charles Darwin publishes *On the Origin of Species*
1869–1870 CE	Vatican I declares papal infallibility
1885–1887 CE	Holiness churches formed in the United States
c. 1900 CE	Social Gospel Movement becomes influential
1906 CE	Azusa Street Revival; beginnings of American Pentecostal movement
1919 CE	William Riley founds the Christian Fundamentals Association
1948 CE	World Council of Churches established in Amsterdam
1949 CE	Billy Graham launches his national career with a three-month revival in Los Angeles
1962–1965 CE	Vatican II updates the Catholic Church
1978 CE	Religious Right emerges in U.S. political life
1990 CE	Russia allows for freedom of religion
1999 CE	Catholic Church and Lutheran World Federation sign Joint Declaration on the Doctrine of Justification; World Methodist Council adopts it in 2006
2005 CE	United Church of Christ allows same-sex marriages, followed by ELCA Lutheran Church in 2011 and Presbyterian Church U.S.A. in 2014
2015 CE	Anglican Church ordains Libby Lane as first woman bishop in the Church of England
2015 CE	Historic high killing of Christians at 7,100 that year with the highest tolls from Nigeria, Central African Republic, Syria, Kenya, and North Korea
2016 CE	First meeting in history between the bishop of Rome (Francis I) and the Moscow patriarch (Kirill I)

Introduction

Sociologist Peter Berger once famously remarked that if India is the world's most religious country and Sweden the least, then the United States is a nation of Indians ruled by Swedes. This is to say that the American population is very religious, but its cultural and political leaders are not. While Berger's proclamation is pithy, it is not very accurate. For one thing, many American political leaders have been quite religious. Modern presidents such as Jimmy Carter, George H. W. Bush, Bill Clinton, George W. Bush, and Barack Obama have all been practicing Christians. Ronald Reagan regularly spiced up his speeches with religious rhetoric and even proclaimed 1983 the "Year of the Bible." In addition, the American citizenry, while broadly claiming to be religious, is in fact rather ignorant about religion. Just over 70 percent of Americans identify themselves as Christians, but few of them know even the basics of the Bible, Christian history, or even what their specific church teaches. In his book *Religious Literacy*, Steven Prothero points out that only half of American adults can name even one of the Gospels, fewer can name the first book of the Bible, only a quarter know that the Acts of the Apostles is in the New Testament, and, humorously, 10 percent believe that Joan of Arc was

Noah's wife.[1] Ironically, the vast majority of these Christians also believe that the Bible is the word of God.

Upon completing an in-depth study of religious beliefs among adolescents in 2005, sociologist Christian Smith concluded that most American youth and their parents know so little about the specifics of their religion, Christian or otherwise, that they embrace a broad generic worldview he has labeled "moralistic, therapeutic deism." On this view, there is a God who wants people to be good and fair, the goal of life is to be happy and feel good about oneself, God is not much involved in our lives except perhaps when needed to solve a problem, and nice, good-hearted people go to heaven when they die.

One of the reasons for religious illiteracy is that religion has been virtually eliminated from public schools and common discourse. In order to respect the separation of church and state and to avoid controversial religious themes, high school textbooks avoid religion altogether. As Prothero writes, "these world history texts may actually skip altogether the life of Jesus, the Protestant Reformation, and even the Holocaust—all on the theory that religion is too hot to handle in the public schools. The result, according to a report released by the Association for Supervision and Curriculum Development, is 'massive ignorance of any faith besides one's own (and sometimes even one's own).'"[2] How many students are taught that the Great Awakening in the eighteenth century cemented American colonists' national imagination as a prelude to the Revolutionary War? How many realize that the American abolitionist, suffragist, and prohibitionist movements were all religiously inspired?

Another reason for religious illiteracy in the United States is that religious traditions in contemporary American society often ask very little from their adherents. Consider, for instance, the massive demands in money, energy, and time made on U.S. youth by schools and extracurricular activities such as sports and compare these demands to those made by religious institutions—the latter are far fewer, if they exist at all.

Nevertheless, knowing about religion and its impact on history and culture is arguably critically important. Without understanding religion, we cannot understand culture or history. Western civilization has been formed in large part by religion, particularly Christianity. Without knowledge of the Bible and Christian history, much of the Western world, including its music, art, literature, and values, is unintelligible. So, even for atheists and agnostics, knowledge about religion is crucial for understanding society and the world.

It can also be argued that religion has intrinsic value. Sociologist Mircea Eliade describes human nature as *homo religiosus*, that is, our very nature is to be religious. According to Eliade and others, humans share a transcendental mental structure that is essentially religious. We seek answers to fundamental questions about what grounds our very being. Who are we at the core? What counts as a meaningful life? What grounds morality? Where did the world come from, and why does it exist? What determines the destiny of human beings? These are all ultimately religious questions.

Religion responds by communicating an all-embracing horizon of meaning. It guarantees supreme values and highest ideals, and it gives its adherents a sense of home, trust, strength, and hope. Religion also tends to create the kinds of people that are good for society in various ways. Robert Putnam and David Campbell, in *American Grace: How Religion Divides and Unites Us*,[3] found a high correlation between religious observance and what they call "good neighborliness." Religiously observant Americans, they reported, donate more money, volunteer more, and are more civically engaged. It is less the specific religion that matters, and more the depth of engagement that makes all the difference. However, even as religious people in general tend to be particularly good citizens, religions and their adherents can also be divisive. A problem with adhering to such an all-embracing horizon of meaning with such surety is that those outside one's religion can be dismissed or even attacked. Thus, religion can also operate as a source of social and political conflict. And, of course, adherents to a given religion can act divisively within their own ranks. Given this, it seems all the more imperative to be well educated about religions and their dynamics.

INTRODUCING CHRISTIANITY

Thus far we have been discussing religion as a whole. This book, however, is about Christianity, a crucially important religion to understand, particularly for Westerners. Not only has Christianity shaped much of what has grounded Western culture for well over 1,000 years, but it is the largest world religion today, boasting about 2.2 billion adherents. Christianity is the dominant religion in Western Europe, as well as in Russia, central and eastern Europe, and Latin America, and it is burgeoning in Africa too. Consider this fact: In 1900, there were 7 million Christians in Africa. Today, there are over 400 million. Christianity is a force to be reckoned with.

This book will examine the history and theological development of Christianity. In some ways, it takes the posture of an outsider. It will look at the tradition from the perspective of social science, particularly using historical and phenomenological analyses. It is assuredly not a book that assumes the reader is religious. The facts are what the facts are, and this book will attempt to interpret them fairly and in ways that represent the best scholarship. It is meant to inform religious and nonreligious believers alike and will pass the test of secular scholarship. In another sense, however, it is indeed an insider's book in that it will also seek to examine Christianity as Christianity understands itself, that is, from its own religious intuitions and sensibility.

To appreciate the insider/outsider approach, we might imagine two architects describing a house, the second of whom happens to live in it. Both have the ability to accurately describe the structure, foundation, materials, and so on. The one who inhabits the house, however, has an additional resource. He knows how it *feels* to live there. He experiences the sunrise through the window, feels the warmth of the fireplace when it is ablaze, and hears the house creak in the wind. He knows the house on an intimate, visceral level. On the other hand, he may have become so used to living there that he no longer recognizes the basement's moldy smell or the incongruity between the landscape and the home's design. Here the outsider might see problems that escape the insider's notice. Both play essential roles in fully describing the home. In the same way, this book attempts to adopt both an insider and outsider approach. It takes advantage of the experience of a lived religious faith as articulated by that faith while simultaneously drawing on secular scholarship that may offer fresh and illuminating interpretations.

In *Religion in the Making*, Alfred North Whitehead observes that "Christianity . . . has always been a religion seeking a metaphysic, in contrast to Buddhism which is a metaphysic generating a religion."[4] This is a fascinating insight. The Buddha purported to discover the nature of the universe, its causes and conditions (metaphysics), and then created a religious movement around these teachings. Christianity, however, formed as a community of believers in Jesus of Nazareth, through whom they experienced God's

salvation. The development of theological and philosophical doctrines about him, his relationship to God, and, indeed, the very nature of God as the Trinity came centuries later.

Christianity claims that adherents encounter the saving presence of God in Jesus Christ. For Christians, he is the revelation of God. The Catholic Church reflects Whitehead's insight in a document on revelation that conveys a perspective broadly shared by Christian Protestant, Catholic, Orthodox, and Evangelical academics. The first chapter on divine revelation begins thus:

> It pleased God, in his goodness and wisdom, to reveal himself and to make known the mystery of his will. His will was that men should have access to the Father, through Christ, the Word made flesh, in the Holy Spirit, and thus become sharers in the divine nature. . . . The most intimate truth which this revelation gives us about God and the salvation of man shines forth in Christ, who is himself both the mediator and the sum total of Revelation. . . . Hence, Jesus speaks the words of God, and accomplishes the saving work which the Father gave him to do. As a result he himself—to see whom is to see the Father—completed and perfected Revelation and confirmed it with divine guarantees (*Dei Verbum*, nos. 2–4).[5]

One sees in this teaching that for Christians Jesus is central to both salvation and revelation. In this tradition revelation focuses not on doctrines to believe, but on a figure to believe in and know. Christianity formed a religion around Jesus.

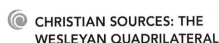 ## CHRISTIAN SOURCES: THE WESLEYAN QUADRILATERAL

In studying the works of John Wesley, the eighteenth-century founder of the Methodist movement, Albert Outler, a twentieth-century Methodist theologian, discovered four interrelated dynamics or sources in Wesley's theology. Officially formulated in 1968 by the United Methodist Church, these four concepts are known collectively as the **Wesleyan Quadrilateral**, a framework that the Anglican Church also formally embraces as the "Four Pillars." The Quadrilateral looks to the creative interplay of (1) reason, (2) experience, (3) tradition, and (4) scripture to make sense of the faith. While Roman Catholics might say that authority comes from scripture, tradition, and the magisterium (the teaching authority of bishops), and many Evangelicals might say that authority comes from scripture alone, an analysis of Christian theology and practice consistently reveals Wesley's Quadrilateral. Let us consider each of these four elements in turn.

First, most Christians believe that faith ought to be reasonable. Christianity views its doctrines as intellectually compelling, and theology about doctrine is sometimes called *systematic theology*, as it attempts to make coherent the collective body of Christian beliefs. Second, Christian faith is decidedly grounded in lived experience. Christianity, like all religions, is shaped by every culture it encounters. This ongoing molding of the tradition is not problematic, since faith is made relevant in part through its lived experience within a particular culture. Today, that lived experience also incorporates the insights of the social sciences. Third, tradition involves the religious continuity of the faith lived out by adherents as well as of the authoritative voices held up by Christians. In the Roman Catholic, Eastern Orthodox, and Anglican churches, these authoritative voices are represented by bishops, who are understood to assume the ongoing role of the apostles. In the Lutheran Church, doctrinal authority is conveyed through representatives who participate in regular Lutheran Conventions. In the Southern Baptist Church, representatives meet yearly to formally articulate doctrine and policies for the Southern Baptist Convention. Fourth, most Christians give the Bible a pride of place in their faith (Wesley assuredly did). Christians broadly refer to the Bible as the "word of God." Here we find the source of the early understanding of God as working throughout the histories of ancient Judaism and the early Jesus movement.

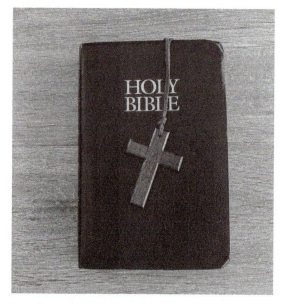

FIGURE 1-1 The Bible is one of the most, if not the most, authoritative sources for Christians.

The remainder of this chapter focuses on the Bible and various ways to understand its nature and authority. The Bible is the text beyond any other text that grounds the Christian story and on which Christians rely for self-understanding. The following sections will also help ground us for the next three chapters.

THE BIBLE AS AUTHORITY

Virtually all Christians locate a great deal of authority in the Bible. It represents the written—and thus consistent and unalterable—expression of the original experiences of God's saving presence in the ancient Jewish (Old Testament) and early church (New Testament) contexts. For this reason it is Christianity's core reference text. What does it mean to say that the Bible has authority? The Bible did not come out of thin air, nor was it discovered on some bishop's desk. It is a collection that was many years in the making. Many Christian texts disseminated in the early church declared themselves to be letters or gospels by apostles, but over time the larger church ultimately rejected most of these, determining which texts were representative of the authentic faith and which were not. This means that early Christian leaders were grounded first and foremost in a tradition. Why choose the Gospel of Matthew but not the Gospel of Philip? Or the Gospel of John but not the Gospel of Thomas? The short answer is that church leaders did not recognize the latter as representing authentic tradition, but saw the former as doing so. There are intrinsic connections between scripture and tradition, between texts and the remembered witness of the apostles, the ongoing experience of the church, the church's prayer, and its growing theological commitments. There is also a relationship between church leaders and the tradition. Bishops created canonical lists of approved texts by judging which texts reflected the authentic tradition as they understood it.

The Bible is authoritative, but what does this mean? The word "authority" comes from the Latin *auctoritas*, which means "origination" or "source." It is related to *auctorare*, meaning "to bind." Thus, to say that the Bible is *a* or *the* source of authority for Christians suggests that it is a source book that has binding power over believers. One of the few places that the Bible speaks of itself is found in Second Timothy, referencing the Old Testament: "All scripture is inspired by God and is useful for teaching, for reproof, for correction, and for training in righteousness" (3:16). This is a strong statement, although it doesn't claim that scripture is "dictated" by God or that there are no other important authoritative resources.

Authority has a domain. Regarding any authority, we must ask: Over what sphere is this person or text authoritative? With respect to the Bible, over what domain or domains does the Bible have authority? Certainly not over scientific matters, as the authors did not have access to modern scientific insights. But does the relevant sphere encompass only doctrinal matters, or could the Bible be brought to bear on contemporary social policy? Does the text reveal authoritative *data* about religious matters, or does it provide authoritative *ways to think* about religious issues? Do some parts of the Bible perform one or the other of these functions better than other parts? How can the Bible deal with issues unrelated to the time, place, or cultural assumptions in which it is grounded? The Bible's authority is intimately wedded to issues of interpretation.

APPROACHES TO THE BIBLE

Secular scholars who study Christianity along with other religions recognize that the Bible plays an essential role in Christian self-understanding, but they do not see the text as divinely and uniquely inspired. Alongside the Bible's relationship to Christianity, they may assess other religious texts' relationships to their respective traditions, be they the Vedas for Hinduism, the Qu'ran for Islam, or the Sutras for Buddhism. They may regard some parts of these texts as inspiring, interesting, fascinating, or even spiritually wise, but they do not embrace a particular religion's canon as decisively different from other religions' canons, and they do not discuss whether these texts reveal something true about God. Call this the secular approach to the Bible. The secular approach simply cannot represent Christianity as it sees itself.

Another approach to the Bible adopts what is called a **biblicist** point of view. Biblicists believe that the Bible was essentially dictated by God, a perspective sometimes referred to as the *golden typewriter theory*. In *The Bible Made Impossible*, Christian Smith argues that biblicists embrace most or all of the following claims:

1. **Divine writing.** The Bible contains God's very speech and is thus inerrant.
2. **Total representation.** The Bible represents the totality of God's communication to humanity.
3. **Complete coverage.** The Bible conveys the totality of God's will in all issues related to Christianity.

4. **Easily intelligible.** Reasonable people can understand what the Bible teaches.
5. **Common sense.** The Bible is best read in the most obvious, literal sense.
6. *Sola scriptura.* The Bible is the only trustworthy religious authority.
7. **Internal harmony.** The Bible is internally consistent.
8. **Universal applicability.** Whatever the biblical authors wrote is valid for all places and eras.
9. **Inductively clear.** All belief and practice can be discerned from clear biblical truths.
10. **Handbook model.** The Bible is a manual for everything, including science, economics, health, politics, and so on.

Smith argues persuasively that biblicism cannot work because it ignores the pervasive interpretive pluralism in Christianity, even among biblicists themselves. These differences of opinion encompass such crucial matters as the nature of atonement, the meaning of baptism, views of hell, the nature of law, divorce and remarriage, salvation for non-Christians, gender roles, the Rapture, free will, predestination, revelation, eternal security—the list could go on and on. Smith also shows that some biblical texts are simply incompatible with others and thus require biblicists to make arbitrary determinations about which texts should be emphasized and which ignored, which texts are merely culturally relative and thus can be set aside and which are universal claims for all time. Nor can biblicism account for odd passages. If everything in the Bible came from God's mind, what ought one to make of Paul claiming that "Cretans are always liars" (Titus 1:12) or the statement in Psalms that "happy shall they be who take your little ones and dash them against the rock" (Ps. 137:9)?

Because biblicism imagines that there are no problems in the Bible, it provides a kind of intellectual pass from addressing hard questions about one's method of interpretation. Few scholars are bona fide biblicists, even including Evangelical scholars who represent institutions whose formal positions sound like biblicism. Renowned Evangelical biblical scholar Kenton Sparks, for example, writes, "The Bible does not offer a single, well-integrated univocal theology; it offers instead numerous overlapping, but nonetheless distinctive theologies. . . . The literary, historical, ethical, and theological diversity in Scripture . . . scholars have documented a thousand times over."[6]

The greatest concern about biblicism in scholarship, however, is that many regard it as philosophically naïve. God, as absolute spirit, transcends human concepts. To reduce God to human categories diminishes God to a creature, albeit a big one, one who thinks and talks like human beings. Moreover, ascribing human language to God fails to appreciate how human language works. Human words are both inherently limited and relevant principally to the cultural milieu in which they are used. This doesn't mean, of course, that one cannot gain insight from discourse from another place or time. But it does mean that any articulation must suffer from the limitations of human language. A text may be relevant to another place or time, but bringing out its relevance requires an interpretive lens that is necessarily provisional and fallible.

Consider the following texts, each of which is widely ignored or rejected by the vast majority of Christians, biblicists or not: Paul proclaims that a man with long hair or praying with his head covered is a disgrace, while women may *only* pray with their heads covered (1 Cor. 11:1–5, 11); Jesus promises that believers can drink poison without harm (Mark 16:17–18); Paul forbids women from speaking in church (1 Cor. 14:34–35); Paul forbids Christian women from braiding their hair or wearing jewelry (1 Tim. 2:9); Paul proclaims that women will be saved through childbearing (1 Tim. 2:15); Paul instructs all unmarried men against looking for wives (1 Cor. 7:27).

If one way to approach the Bible is through a secular lens, in which the Bible is simply not the word of God, and another way is through a literalist lens, in which the Bible is close to the actual speech of God, a third way is through a faithful and critical analysis of the text and its relationship to tradition. This is not a middle way between the other two perspectives. Rather, it imagines the Bible as containing various expressions of authentic encounters with God given the context and limitations of the biblical authors. In this approach the Bible is still understood as the word of God and as revelation that conveys a saving faith, but this revelation is seen as contextual, complex, and reflective of the limitations of the human authors as well as their specific historical location. What makes this text a revelation for Christians is that Christians believe it articulates God's plan of salvation.

First and foremost, biblical scholars engage the Bible through appreciation of literary genres (*form criticism*). Some parts of the Bible are mythic, some are poetic, others narrative, others historical, and so on. Scholars interpret a given text using rules associated with the genre to which it belongs. Take Genesis 2:4b–11:9: here we find a mythical garden where God strolls in the evening, serpents walk around and talk, and sons of God have intercourse with human women to create a race of giants. To view this as a scientific text is to impose a modern framework onto a narrative not designed for that purpose. Instead, by allowing the genre to be itself, one is invited to enter into the imagination of the story to discover essential truths about humanity and its relationship to God. Taking the genre seriously actually helps the text come alive and convey its revelatory truth.

Besides sensitivity to literary genre, scholarship incorporates historical analysis (the *historical-critical method*), perhaps the most important part of authentic interpretation. In this approach scholars examine what the original language meant in its historical context. They identify cultural assumptions operative within this context, and they seek to discern the conditions that gave rise to the text. They also focus on whether and how the text was edited (*redaction criticism*). For example, Mark's Gospel has two

endings. The original Gospel almost certainly ended at 16:8; the following verses 9 through 20 augment and partially contradict the original ending. One can also see where Matthew and Luke seem to cite portions of Mark's Gospel, sometimes verbatim, only to change or add to the text. This phenomenon is not seen as scandalous by Christian scholars, but as part of the revelatory dynamics of the Bible. Why was the change made, and what was the point? What's being revealed in that editorial choice?

To these scholarly engagements we could add a plethora of other necessary lenses through which to understand the Bible. *Source criticism* focuses on where the text or tradition came from. *Rhetorical criticism* focuses on how the text functions for its audience. *Narrative criticism* looks at how the text is structured, its plot development, themes, and motifs. *Psychological criticism* considers how the text affects hearers and readers. *Ideology criticism* examines how the text imagines power relations and whose voices are left out. *Canonical criticism* investigates why the church chose certain texts and abandoned others. The list could continue.

Within Christian scholarship, the purpose of diverse forms of biblical criticism is not to reduce or exhaust the Bible's contents, but to appreciate its bottomless depths and draw as much insight as possible from it. Above all, these scholarly analyses attempt to discover both the authors' original intent and how that might be appropriated today. The text is seen as inexhaustible; it always has a surplus of meaning and new relevance for Christians. For example, Paul's letter to the Galatians was meant to quell controversy as to whether non-Jewish believers in Jesus had to adopt the Jewish Law in order to be Christians. Although this was a problem for an ancient group of communities in the early church, it does not trouble many believers today. Does this mean that Paul's letter can no longer be relevant or revelatory? A central purpose of Christian biblical scholarship is to reveal facets of the text that can bring it to life for modern readers.

THEMES OF THE BIBLE

One reason why the Bible is so foundational for Christianity is that it provides the enduring patterns, motifs, and core religious framings that structure Christian self-understanding. Certain themes in both the Old Testament and the New Testament dominated the religious horizons of ancient Jews and early Christians. Being a "biblical Christian" is fundamentally about exploring, appreciating, and applying these themes within the context of one's spiritual life and one's engagement with contemporary society. It is as though the Bible were telling believers to think *this* way, imagine God like *this*, relate to each other through *these* values, and understand their relationship to God like *this*. The Bible's central themes include creation, covenant, sin and redemption, monarchy, temple and priesthood, sacrifice, prophecy, wisdom, law and grace, kingdom of God, and prayer. We will investigate these themes in the next two chapters and later see how they play out in Christian history and theology.

SUMMARY QUESTIONS

- What are some reasons why the study of religion is important for society?
- What are the four interplaying sources of the Wesleyan Quadrilateral, and how do they mutually inform each other?
- What does it mean to say that the Bible has authority, and how extensive is it?
- What are some problems with biblicism?

DISCUSSION QUESTIONS

- The author believes that Americans are undereducated regarding religion. In addition to the reasons provided, are there other factors in American culture that might have contributed to such a lack of understanding?
- The author distinguishes between "insiders" and "outsiders" in scholarship. What are examples in your own life in which you are privy to information or experience unobtainable from the outside?
- What is your view of the biblicist position? Do you agree with the author's critique? Why or why not?

KEY TERMS

Biblicism   Wesleyan Quadrilateral

BIBLIOGRAPHY

- Brown, William, ed. 2007. *Engaging Biblical Authority: Perspectives on the Bible as Scripture*. Louisville: Westminster John Knox Press.
- Eliade, Mircea. 1958. *Patterns in Comparative Religion*. Trans. Rosemary Sheed. New York: Sheed and Ward.
- Grant, Robert, and David Tracy. 1984. *A Short History of the Interpretation of the Bible*, rev. ed. Minneapolis, MN: Fortress Press.
- Prothero, Stephen. 2007. *Religious Literacy: What Every American Needs to Know—and Doesn't*. New York: HarperOne.
- Putnam, Robert, and David Campbell. 2010. *American Grace: How Religion Divides and Unites Us*. New York: Simon & Schuster.
- Schneiders, Sandra. 1991. *The Revelatory Text: Interpreting the New Testament as Sacred Scripture*. New York: HarperSanFrancisco.

- Smith, Christian. 2011. *The Bible Made Impossible: Why Biblicism Is Not a Truly Evangelical Reading of Scripture.* Grand Rapids, MI: Brazos Press.
- Smith, Christian, with Melinda Lundquist Denton. 2005. *Soul Searching: The Religious and Spiritual Lives of American Teenagers.* Oxford: Oxford University Press.
- Sparks, Kenton. 2008. *God's Word in Human Words.* Grand Rapids, MI: Baker Academic.
- Whitehead, Alfred North. 1926. *Religion in the Making.* Cambridge: Cambridge University Press.

NOTES

1. Prothero, *Religious Literacy*, 38–39.
2. Ibid., 63.
3. Putnam and Campbell, *American Grace.*
4. Whitehead, *Religion in the Making*, 50.
5. Austin Flannery, ed., *Vatican Council II: The Conciliar and Post Conciliar Documents*, rev. ed., Vol. 1 (Northport, NY: Costello Publishing Company, 1975), 750–752.
6. Sparks, *God's Word in Human Words*, 230, 244.

2

The Old Testament

Timeline

3000–2000 BCE	Beginnings of civilization in the ancient Near East
c. 1850–1750 BCE	Abraham migrates to Canaan; beginning of the patriarchal period
c. 1250 BCE	Moses leads the Exodus from Egypt; the Israelites make a covenant at Sinai
c. 1220–1020 BCE	Joshua leads the invasion of Canaan; the period of the Judges (tribal confederacy)
c. 1020–1000 BCE	Saul reigns as first king of the Israelite people
c. 1000–961 BCE	David reigns as king, expanding and solidifying the nation
961–922 BCE	Solomon reigns as king and builds the Temple in Jerusalem
922 BCE	Kingdom divides into two kingdoms: Israel (north) and Judah (south)
721 BCE	The northern kingdom of Israel is defeated by the Assyrians
597 BCE	The southern kingdom of Judah is defeated by the Babylonians
587 BCE	Babylonian Exile
538 BCE	Return to Palestine (Temple rebuilt 520–515 BCE)
c. 500 BCE	Beginning of compilation of Hebrew Bible
334–326 BCE	Alexander the Great conquers the Near East, institutes the process of hellenization
c. 250 BCE	Beginning work on the Septuagint, translating the Hebrew Bible into Greek

167 BCE	Maccabean Revolt; Jewish control of Palestine
63 BCE	Romans conquer Palestine and capture Jerusalem
37–4 BCE	Rule of Herod the Great over Palestine; massive building projects including renovation of the Temple
27 BCE–14 CE	Reign of Caesar Augustus, first Roman emperor

WHAT TO EXPECT

This chapter introduces the Old Testament, or *Tanakh*. It investigates questions about the Bible and history and how biblical authors understood the nature of their narrative. It also outlines major events in Old Testament history that are central to both Judaism and Christianity. Finally, it addresses major themes in Old Testament theology that are crucial in understanding Judaism and were engaged by Jesus in his ministry.

INTRODUCTION

As we saw in the first chapter, the Bible is an extraordinarily authoritative book for Christianity. It offers the recurrent themes, images, teachings, and sacred history that dominate the Christian imagination. The word "Bible" comes from the Greek *ta biblia*, literally meaning "the books." These books collectively represent the canon for Christians and Jews. **Canon** originally referred to "rule" or "measuring stick," and today is the term for authoritative texts in a given religion or discipline. What makes up a religion's canon can be complicated, as there are typically competing schools of thought as to which texts are truly authoritative. In Jesus's day, the Jewish canon was widely debated. Most of the priestly class believed that it should be restricted to the first five books of the Bible, while most rabbis believed it should include the Prophets and other wisdom texts as well, though which of these latter texts were canonical was also hotly debated. By the first century BCE the most used canonical collection among Jews living outside of Palestine was a Greek translation called the **Septuagint**, which included some books that Judaism ultimately relegated to noncanonical status.

One of the problems for Christians today in discussing the Jewish canon is what to call it. Typically, it has been called the Old Testament, but in an age of greater sensitivity to the Jewish faith, this term can imply that this canon was superseded by the New Testament, with "old" implying "worn out." Some scholars have preferred other titles, such as Hebrew Bible, First Testament, Original Testament, or Shared Testament. We will be using the traditional term "Old Testament," because it has become standard and feels less imposed, though we ought to realize that "old" should mean what it did in the ancient world: venerable and grounding.

Jews refer to the canon as the *Tanakh*, a Hebrew acronym for the three parts of the Jewish scriptures: *Torah* (Law, or teaching), *Nevi'im* (Prophets), and *Khetuvim* (Writings). The **Torah** is composed of the first five books of the Bible, also called the Pentateuch (Greek for "five scrolls"). These are Genesis, Exodus, Leviticus, Numbers, and Deuteronomy and are sometimes also called the "Books of Moses," imagining that they came from Moses himself, though virtually no modern scholar thinks this is the case. While much of the material of the Torah has ancient sources, the collection of these texts occurred comparatively late.

The *Nevi'im* collection is divided into the Former Prophets and the Latter Prophets. The Former Prophets are the texts of Joshua, Judges, First and Second Samuel, and First and Second

Kings, which are actually historical books. Most scholars believe that this collection was edited sometime in the sixth to fifth centuries BCE. The Latter Prophets are texts drawn from the sayings of actual prophets and include the books of the major prophets—Isaiah, Jeremiah, and Ezekiel—and the books of the minor prophets—Hosea, Joel, Amos, Obadiah, Jonah, Micah, Nahum, Habakkuk, Zephaniah, Haggai, Zechariah, and Malachi.

The *Khetuvim* consists of miscellaneous texts, such as the Psalms, Proverbs, Ruth, Lamentations, Ecclesiastes, the Song of Solomon, Esther, Daniel, Ezra, Nehemiah, and First and

Second Chronicles. The Septuagint also included books that the Jewish canon would ultimately discard: Tobit, Judith, First and Second Maccabees, Wisdom, Sirach, Baruch, and additional parts of Esther and Daniel.

The Protestant Old Testament canon is the same as the Jewish canon, while the Roman Catholic and Eastern Orthodox canons also include those texts that were represented in the Septuagint. The Eastern Orthodox canon also includes the Prayer of Manasseh, an additional Psalm, Third and Fourth Maccabees, and First and Second Esdras. These latter texts are considered rather marginal, even for Orthodox Christians.

DOCUMENTARY HYPOTHESIS

Most modern biblical scholars subscribe to the **documentary hypothesis**, which argues for four main sources for the Old Testament: the *Yahwist* (ninth century BCE), the *Elohist* (eighth century BCE), the *Deuteronomist* (sixth century BCE), and the *Priestly* (sixth to fifth century BCE). The argument is that the Old Testament contains clearly different writing styles and theological interests that reveal different sources. The Yahwist style is eloquent, with graceful narratives that do not hesitate to depict God, always referred to as *Yahweh*, in human terms. The Elohist focuses on prophetic leadership, covenants, and fear of God. The Deuteronomist always refers to God

as *Yahweh Eloheinu* and focuses on interpreting Israel's experience—both its flourishing and its suffering—with regard to covenant loyalty. Finally, the Priestly source frames God as somewhat distant and foreboding. Here Temple worship dominates, as do lists, genealogies, and dates. Scholars who adhere to this hypothesis note that some biblical books reflect a synthesis of several sources that have been woven together. The documentary hypothesis has more recently been challenged by alternative explanations, such as the *supplementary* and *fragmentary hypotheses*, but these have yet to dethrone the documentary hypothesis.

THE BIBLE AND HISTORY

For the Christian, is the Bible true? Is it accurate? These are loaded questions and far more complicated than they appear. Truth need not be a relative term, but the way one applies it differs depending upon what is being looked for. For a man in love with a woman to say that he would go to the moon and back for her or that he would do anything for her does not mean that he has the capacity to go to the moon nor that he's willing to commit murder for her. He does mean, however, that he absolutely adores her and is decidedly committed to her well-being. So he's

speaking the truth, but truth need not be identified with his literal words in this case.

As we saw in Chapter One, we must recognize a text's genre as well as the history and culture from which it arose in order to understand the mind of its author. When critics of Christianity (and Judaism) challenge the creation stories, for example, they often imagine that the texts were supposed to both be scientifically accurate and represent history in the way that the modern mind understands history. This is an anachronism (*ana*, against; *chronos*, time). Anachronisms fail to recognize how language and culture worked in a different time and place, and instead try to impose a modern-day framing on an earlier period that thought very differently. Why, popular atheist author Richard Dawkins challenges, is there no mention of dinosaurs in the Book of Genesis, or, for that matter, no discussion of evolution and DNA? The answer is that such a discussion would have been incomprehensible to the ancient author and reader alike, and this kind of challenge mistakes the type of literature Genesis is and the mindset the biblical authors had.

When the Bible describes historical figures or events, these descriptions are laden with history, theology, themes of national identity, intercultural conflicts, and so on. Comparing the biblical narrative's descriptions of places and events to outside sources sometimes confirms and sometimes challenges the biblical text from a purely scientific or "objective" historical framework. Let us take two examples, one from the Old Testament and one from the New.

The first example comes from the second creation account found in chapters 2–11 of Genesis. Here we find the stories of Adam and Eve, Cain and Abel, the genealogy of many heroes, the flood and repopulation of the earth, and so on. To some biblical literalists, all of this is historically accurate from a modern point of view. One of the most famous defenders of this position was the Anglican archbishop James Ussher, who in 1650 calculated the creation of the world to have occurred on Sunday, October 23, 4004 BCE. This is obviously impossible in light of what scientists have learned in the past two centuries. Critics and biblical scholars alike have shown that many of the elements of the Genesis story also appear in creation-flood stories from Mesopotamia, Sumeria, and Egypt, such as the tales of Gilgamesh and Atrahasis. Is Genesis true? Apparently the biblical authors used the ancient Near East creation-flood story as a template to describe their own story, which is filled with revelatory insights into the nature of human beings, the nature of sin, and the challenging relationship humans have with God and each other. For Jews and Christians, the Genesis account certainly reveals truth, even though it is not a scientific or historical text.

A second example comes from the New Testament. In Luke 24:50–53 the risen Jesus ascends to heaven on the evening of Easter Sunday. But in Acts 1:1–12, written by the same author, he ascends forty days after his resurrection. Did Luke, the author of Acts, not remember what he had written in his Gospel? Which one is right? Which one is true? The reader steeped in a biblical imagination can discern two different theological aims. In the Gospel of Luke, Jesus's ascension recalls the image of Elijah ascending to heaven found in Second Kings (2:12). In that narrative, Elijah's disciple Elisha receives his master's prophetic spirit as he watches him ascend. So too Jesus's disciples receive the Holy Spirit that empowers their mission. Luke tells a different story in Acts. The number forty is highly symbolic: the Israelites spent forty years in the desert preparing to enter the Promised Land, and Jesus spent forty days in the desert preparing for his public ministry. These allusions, now associated with the ascension, tell us that Jesus prepared his disciples for their ministry over a forty-day period of time. In both cases, Luke uses various biblically laden insights to help his readers understand what the ascension ought to mean for them. He thought he was free to do so.

Biblical authors believed that their history was sacred, an expression of an overarching divine plan. They saw connections within their history and wrote in such a way as to highlight those connections. A biblical person or event often foreshadows future persons or events, and later persons and events echo or fulfill former ones. Joseph, one of the sons of the patriarch Jacob, has a history that looks very much like that of Moses. Both are shepherds who become rulers, both endure exile, both marry daughters of foreign priests and father two sons, both endure conspiracies and exile, and both have Egypt as the central place of their saving mission for the Israelites. The alignment between the two illustrates divine providence. Jesus himself is a type of Moses, with both surviving the slaughter of innocents, experiencing childhood in Egypt, and delivering God's law from a mountain.

These cross-references are very intentional. They give depth and additional meaning to biblical events and persons.

For Christians, the relationship between the Old Testament and the New Testament is intrinsic; the two collections rely on each other utterly for understanding. As noted in the first chapter, the Old Testament gives Christianity its foundational themes. The New Testament presumes acceptance of these themes, builds on them, and understands itself as fulfilling them. In presenting these themes and the sacred history around them in the following sections, I will particularly highlight those that are later taken up in the New Testament and Christian theology. I will present them as they are presented in the text itself. As with our previous examples, one may question: Did these things happen exactly in the way they are narrated in the Bible? The short response is, do not demand answers to questions that would have been meaningless to the biblical authors themselves.

 ## GENESIS AND THE CREATION OF THE WORLD

GENESIS 2:4b–11:9: ADAM AND EVE

The first eleven chapters of Genesis tell two stories of creation (1:1–24a and 2:4b–11:9). They are **cosmogonies**, that is, stories of how the world or universe was created. The oldest of these two stories is actually the second one. In this account, God creates a man from dust of the lifeless earth and God's own breath. God also creates a garden in Eden in which exist the tree of life and the tree of knowledge of good and evil, both of which he strictly forbids Adam to eat from. Adam is God's gardener. God creates animals as companions for Adam, but none of these are suitable, so from Adam's rib he forms Eve. A serpent encourages Eve to eat the fruit from the tree of knowledge so that she might become like God. She and Adam do eat and immediately become ashamed of their nakedness. When God sees that they have made clothes, he realizes they have eaten this fruit. God curses the serpent to now crawl on its

belly, and he curses **Adam and Eve** to a much more difficult life. Alarmed, God tells other gods, "See, the man has become like one of us, knowing good and evil; and now, he might reach out his hand and take also from the tree of life and eat, and live forever" (3:22). So God expels Adam and Eve from Eden.

Adam and Eve eventually have two children: Cain, a farmer, and Abel, a shepherd. Cain becomes jealous of Abel and the favor God gives him and slays his brother. God discovers the deed and curses Cain to be a wanderer for the rest of his life. Eventually Adam and Eve have another son, Seth, and Genesis gives us a genealogy of Seth's descendants. Now the story gets even more dramatic: "When people began to multiply on the face of the ground, and daughters were born to them, the sons of God saw that they were fair; and they took wives for themselves. . . . The Nephilim were on the earth in those days—and afterwards—when the sons of God went in to the daughters of humans, who bore children to them. These were the heroes that were of old, warriors of renown" (6:1–4).

At this point, human wickedness becomes so alarming to God, who regrets ever having created human beings, that he floods the earth. The only people spared are Noah and his family, who have remained devout. Under God's command, Noah builds an ark (or boat) 300 cubits long and 50 cubits wide (about 150 yards by 25 yards) and places in it seven pairs of clean animals and one pair of unclean animals along with every kind of food. After these preparations, God floods the world and destroys all the peoples and animals not in the ark. Genesis then goes on to give us the descendants of Noah and the nations or peoples they eventually create. Even then, the people are incorrigible. They start to build a city (Babel) and a tower so great and high that it alarms God, who disperses them and gives them different languages.

GENESIS 1:1–2:4a

The first chapter of Genesis tells a very different story of the creation of the heavens and the

FIGURE 2-1 The expulsion of Adam and Eve. According to Genesis, God did not trust that they would refrain from eating from the tree of life and thus become gods.

earth. Here the earth is created in six days: Day 1 sees the creation of light; Day 2, the creation of a dome separating the heavenly waters and the waters of the earth; Day 3, the creation of dry land and vegetation; Day 4, the creation of the sun and moon; Day 5, the creation of animals; and Day 6, the creation of humanity. This final capstone of creation is particularly important: "Then God said, 'Let us make humankind in our image, according to our likeness.' . . . So God created humankind in his image, in the image of God he created them; male and female he created them" (1:27). Afterward, "God . . . rested on the seventh day from all the work that he had done. So God blessed the seventh day and hallowed it" (2:3).

In this description, we find extraordinary order and a great deal of repetition. The description of each day begins with: "And God said, 'Let there be' [light, waters, creatures, etc.]." Immediately, these things appear. The description of each day ends with: "And there was evening and there was morning, the first [second, third, etc.] day."

MAKING SENSE OF THE TWO STORIES

It is widely believed that the second creation myth is the oldest in Jewish oral history. It is by far the messier of the two and, from a narrative point of view, the most fascinating. Cosmogonies frequently depict how things were originally intended and explain why things are the way they are today. Originally, God intended his creation to be harmonious, peaceful, flourishing, and even wholesome. Because of its disobedience, humanity unravels throughout the rest of the story. Soon we find jealousy and murder and ultimately a human race so wicked that God destroys all but Noah's family. Western theology will later call this "original sin," a distortion of the will that originally came from the first humans.

God's relationship with humanity in this account is highly complex. Adam and Eve are cast out of Eden not as a punishment for sin, but because God can't trust them. If they were to eat from the tree of life, they would live forever and indeed be gods. This is a breach that God cannot tolerate. A breach also comes from the divine realm when the "sons of God" copulate with human women, creating a race of giants. Even the city of Babel represents a threat. Human beings are spiritual and have great potential, but they are not gods.

The story also explains questions such as why it is so hard to make a living (Adam's curse), why society is patriarchal (Eve's curse), why snakes slither (serpent's curse), and why humans can't get along and speak different languages (curse at Babel). The story is also problematic in many ways. For example, it contains many **anthropomorphisms**. An anthropomorphism applies human qualities to nonhumans. In Genesis, the serpent talks, God walks through the garden, and sons of God have sex with humans! Here we find a God who wants to walk with and befriend humans. This is a key theme in Jewish and Christian theology: God is a personal God. On the other hand, God does not seem to be much in control here.

Genesis 1:1–2:4a represents a very different picture. God is above creation and orders it perfectly. The very order and regularity of each day highlight God's control over it all. Humans are created in the image and likeness of God, another fundamental theme in Jewish and Christian theology. What Genesis 1 teaches is that God is transcendent and perfect, and that humans have something of God's holiness in their very nature.

Collectively, the accounts depict God as both personal and transcendent, and humans with both profound dignity and yet a propensity to sin.

GENESIS AND THE PATRIARCHS (EIGHTEENTH CENTURY BCE)

The rest of the Book of Genesis tells the story of the great patriarchs of the Jewish people. The most important figure in ancient Judaism is the patriarch **Abraham**. The term **patriarch** comes from the Latin *patris* (father), and Abraham is considered the father of the Jewish, Christian, and Muslim religions. In Genesis, he comes originally from Ur, in modern-day Iraq. Abraham's father Terah takes him, his wife, and his grandson Lot to settle in the land of Canaan (modern-day Israel), but they settle in Haran (modern-day eastern Turkey) instead. It is in Haran that God calls Abraham to Canaan: "Go from your country and your kindred and your father's house to the land that I will show you. I will make of you a great nation, and I will bless you, and make your name great, so that you will be a blessing" (12:1–2). Consequently, Abraham and Lot migrate to Canaan. Once there, Abraham's wealth grows considerably. Genesis tells of a covenant Abraham makes with God. Abraham sacrifices to God and during the night a flaming torch representing God's presence passes between the parts of the animals he sacrificed.

The great problem for Abraham is that he and his wife Sarah are childless, making God's earlier promises a bit difficult to imagine for him. Sarah

FIGURE 2-2 This 1713 painting by Giambattista Pittoni depicts an angel stopping Abraham's sacrifice of Isaac, a possible ultimate test of Abraham's faith and obedience.

convinces Abraham that she can have children through her slave-girl Hagar, who bears him a son named Ishmael. Muslims trace their Arabian heritage through Ishmael and understand this story very differently. But in Genesis, Hagar begins to lord the fact that Abraham has a son through her over Sarah, and Sarah convinces Abraham to dismiss Hagar and Ishmael. When Abraham is ninety-nine years old and Sarah ninety, God appears to him and reiterates his covenant; later, he promises that by the next year Sarah will bear him a son. Finally, Sarah does have a son, as God promised, and names him **Isaac**. This at last is the fruit of the promise God made.

THE BINDING OF ISAAC

One of the strangest parts of the narrative of Abraham is when God demands that Abraham sacrifice Isaac to him. Abraham obeys and binds Isaac. At the last second before Abraham plunges the knife into Isaac, an angel of the Lord intervenes. What ought we to make of the attempted sacrifice of Isaac? It could be an expression of Abraham's absolute faith in God's commands. It could also suggest that Abraham is willing to offer anything to God, even his future hopes for Isaac. Still another interpretation of the "binding of Isaac" is that Isaac is symbolically bound to the covenant; his future life will be offered to advance the covenant. This turns out to be the case.

Abraham sends one of his servants to his kinfolk in Haran to find a suitable wife for Isaac; the servant finds Rebekah, Isaac's third cousin. Isaac and Rebekah have twin sons, Esau and **Jacob**. Esau, who is clearly Isaac's favorite, is born first, meaning that he will receive the lion's share of the twins' inheritance as well as his father's blessing. But one day when Esau is famished, he sells his birthright to Jacob for a mere bowl of stew Jacob has made. Later, Jacob convinces his aging and blind father that he is Esau and receives the coveted blessing.

Jacob goes to Haran to find a wife and discovers a suitable daughter of his uncle Laban, Rachel. On the wedding night, however, Laban switches women, and Jacob unwittingly marries Leah, Rachel's older sister. Eventually, by laboring for Laban for seven years, Jacob is able to marry Rachel as well. These two wives, along with their two servants, whom Jacob takes as concubines, give Jacob twelve sons. The families of these sons will come to make up the twelve tribes of the people of **Israel**, with "Israel" being the name God gives to Jacob during his strange wrestling encounter with God's angel. The term literally translates as "one who wrestles with God."

One of Jacob's sons, Joseph, has the gift of prophecy and can interpret dreams, which makes his brothers hotly jealous of him. The brothers plot to kill him, but eventually sell him as a slave to traders heading for Egypt instead. The traders in turn sell him to an officer of Pharaoh, but after Joseph rebuffs the officer's wife's advances, she falsely denounces him for attempted rape. He is sent to prison, where he gains the reputation for interpreting dreams. When Pharaoh has a dream of seven fat cows being eaten by seven thin cows that none of his sorcerers can interpret, he hears of Joseph's gift and calls for him. Joseph informs him that the cows represent seven years of great harvest and seven years of famine. Pharaoh recognizes this to be true and appoints Joseph to guide Egypt in a program of saving grain during the abundant years so as to sell it during the ensuing famine— a strategy that enriches Pharaoh and saves Egypt. He then makes Joseph second-in-command over all of Egypt.

When Jacob's family in Canaan feels the devastation of famine, he sends some of his sons to Egypt to buy grain. Joseph immediately recognizes them, though they do not recognize him.

Keeping one of the brothers as hostage, he demands that the whole clan come down. When they arrive, he reveals himself and forgives them. He convinces them to remain in Egypt, and the families of Jacob's children (the twelve tribes of Israel) remain in northeast Egypt (Goshen) for the next four hundred years.

MAKING SENSE OF THE PATRIARCHS

The story of the patriarchs found in the Bible is far more ribald and fascinating than this short synopsis. We find promises being made and broken, murders, incest, and much more. The narrative provided here focuses us on the most central issues. Here we find the beginnings of the family that will become the people of Israel. Out of sheer graciousness, God calls Abraham to become particularly his own. He promises Abraham will be the father of nations and of a particular people whom God will providentially guide. He brings Abraham to the promised land of Canaan and makes a covenant with him, binding him to unremitting faith. From Abraham to Isaac to Jacob we find the fathers of the twelve tribes of Israel. Genesis tells us finally how the Israelites leave the Promised Land and end up in Egypt. As we shall see, Exodus tells us how they fare there and how God brings them full circle back to Canaan.

EXODUS (THIRTEENTH CENTURY BCE)

Genesis ends the story with the twelve tribes prospering in Egypt, but in Exodus things change: "Now a new king arose over Egypt, who did not know Joseph. He said to his people, 'Look, the Israelite people are more numerous and more powerful than we. Come, let us deal shrewdly with them, or they will increase and, in the event of war, join our enemies and fight against us and escape from the land.' Therefore they set taskmasters over them to oppress them with forced labor" (1:8–11). In order to keep Israel in check, Pharaoh even demands their male children be killed, but one Israelite woman

puts her baby boy in a basket to save him. When Pharaoh's daughter discovers the child, she decides to raise him in her household. This is **Moses**. One day, when Moses sees one of his kinsmen being beaten by an Egyptian, he slays the Egyptian and flees from Egypt. In what is now the Sinai Peninsula, Moses encounters God in a burning bush at the base of Mount Sinai. God tells him that he has heard his people's cry and commands Moses to lead them from Egypt to freedom.

During the encounter, Moses asks God his name. This is important, as the Jewish people believed that one's name often revealed his or her character. God responds, "I AM WHO I AM. . . . This is my name forever" (3:14–15). The Hebrew word for God's name is *Yahweh*. God's name—I AM WHO I AM—could represent his refusal to be captured by an ordinary name; he is not like other gods, but something absolute. "Yahweh" could also be translated as "I WILL BE WHO I WILL BE," that is, I will show myself in my presence through your history. Jews, from the ancient period to today, hold so much reverence for God's revealed name that they do not pronounce it out loud, but substitute *Adonai* (Lord) for it.

Moses is hesitant to undertake the role of leader of his people, as he is "slow of speech and slow of tongue" (4:10), so God appoints his brother Aaron as his spokesperson. When Moses and Aaron approach Pharaoh, he refuses to listen. In fact, Exodus says that God himself hardens Pharaoh's heart *not* to listen. To persuade Pharaoh, God sends ten plagues to Egypt, ranging from turning the Nile into blood to plagues of frogs, gnats, flies, disease, boils, hail, locusts, and darkness. Finally, God strikes the Egyptians with the death of the firstborn of every household and all the livestock of Egypt. At this point, Pharaoh begs the Israelites to leave, and the Egyptian people give them their jewelry, clothing, and even food to hasten their departure. After the Israelites leave, Pharaoh regrets having allowed this nation of slaves to depart and takes his army to follow them. Moses lifts his staff, and God blows a wind strong enough to

FIGURE 2-3 Nineteenth-century picture of Moses descending from Mount Sinai with God's commandments.

part the Reed Sea (often rendered "Red Sea"). Once the Israelites have passed, God sends the waters back, and Pharaoh's army is drowned.

Moses leads the Israelites to Mount Sinai, where he first encountered the burning bush, and there he receives the Law of God, including the Ten Commandments. God makes a covenant with Moses and the people. At the base of Sinai, Moses sets up twelve pillars surrounding a large altar. He sacrifices oxen and splashes some of the blood of that sacrifice on the altar; the rest he sprinkles on the people.

Covenants among persons or groups bind them to each other with mutual loyalty. Unlike contracts, which are impersonal business deals, covenants are personal; they become part of one's identity. We recall that the first covenant God makes is with Abraham, to whom God promises the flourishing of his family and great lands. God has but one demand: "Walk with me, and be blameless" (Gen. 17:1). The covenant is ratified with sacrifices and the circumcision of the males.

While this is a dramatic covenant, it is also relatively vague. What "blameless" means is not discussed, nor is how Abraham and his children would "walk" with God. Like Abraham's covenant, the Sinai covenant is ratified with the sacrifice of animals. Unlike the first covenant, however, the Sinai covenant through Moses also includes a vast array of laws. These include a moral code, religious rites, and the foundations of the Jewish faith. What we find in the Sinai covenant is the beginning of a bona fide religion with all the marks that involves.

God's plan is to have the Israelites return to Canaan, the land of the patriarchs, "a land of milk and honey" (3:8), and to prosper there, and Moses guides them for forty years, until they approach the eastern side of the Jordan River. At the death of Moses, his commander Joshua leads the Israelites in battle across the Jordan and into Canaan.

MAKING SENSE OF THE EXODUS

The literary genre of the Exodus is something like a saga of national identity. We need not doubt historically that Israelites lived in Goshen and were an oppressed minority, or that Moses led them to freedom through the Sinai. The narrative as it reads, however, stretches the historical imagination and even creates moral problems. What do we make of the plagues, and why would God harden Pharaoh's heart to make matters worse? Finally, did God really kill every Egyptian firstborn human and piece of livestock? If we enter into the cultural ethos and embrace a biblical imagination, we might see the story as a narrative of increasing drama in which several important themes arise. God, by making Pharaoh resistant, creates a narrative tension that explodes in catastrophe for the Egyptians, who after all enslaved the Israelites. The story shows Yahweh as extremely powerful and daunting, far more so than Pharaoh or Egypt's gods, and as someone who ought to be revered with awe. God demands absolute fidelity, and both Moses and Joshua regularly remind Israel of the consequences of their covenant. God also cares about the Israelites' needs and desire for freedom. He hears the cries of the oppressed and comes to their aid. These two themes are particularly repeated throughout the Old Testament: God is loyal, and he is merciful. Above all, Exodus reveals part of God's providential plan. Canaan is a land he has prepared for his people, and Exodus tells about how God achieved this aim.

JUDGES (c. 1220–1020 BCE)

The Old Testament depicts Canaan not as a nation per se, but as a loose association of small city-states. In the Book of Joshua the Israelites conquer one city after another, frequently going to war against a collective army of cooperating Canaanites. Once Joshua has consolidated the center of Canaan, he concentrates his attention on upper Galilee, attaining victories over often substantially larger armies. Israel conquers most of the Canaanites, but cannot conquer the powerful Philistines who control the southwestern seaboard. Joshua assigns each of the family groups or tribes of Israel parts of what we now call the Holy Land. From the thirteenth to the eleventh centuries BCE, the Israelites dwell as a loosely confederated people in the Holy Land, with elders ruling each modestly self-sufficient tribe. At times of national crisis—typically in times of war—a charismatic leader arises to lead them. This individual is called a *shofet*, which we usually translate as "**judge**," and the first 200 years of Israel's existence in the Holy Land are known as the "time of the judges."

There is a pattern in the Book of Judges. When Israel is faithful to its covenant with Yahweh, the tribes prosper and are safe. But when they fail to uphold the covenant, particularly by worshipping other gods, they become oppressed by their warring neighbors. Yahweh goes from being their protector to withholding his protection and allowing them to become vulnerable. The Israelites then inevitably repent of their unfaithfulness and cry out to Yahweh, who appoints a judge to unite the people, call them to greater covenant fidelity, and lead them into victory over their enemies.

The Book of Judges ends ominously: "In those days there was no king in Israel; all the people did what was right in their own eyes" (21:25). This is to say that the system of a loose confederation of tribes with no central leadership or organization has degenerated. The book notes a further problem as well: the shrine in Shiloh, where the Israelites worship God, has also spiritually deteriorated because of corrupt priests. Eli, the high priest at the time, cannot trust his sons, who are easily bribed and who undermine authentic worship. So Eli transfers the priesthood to a young man named Samuel, who is both holy and prophetic: "And all Israel from

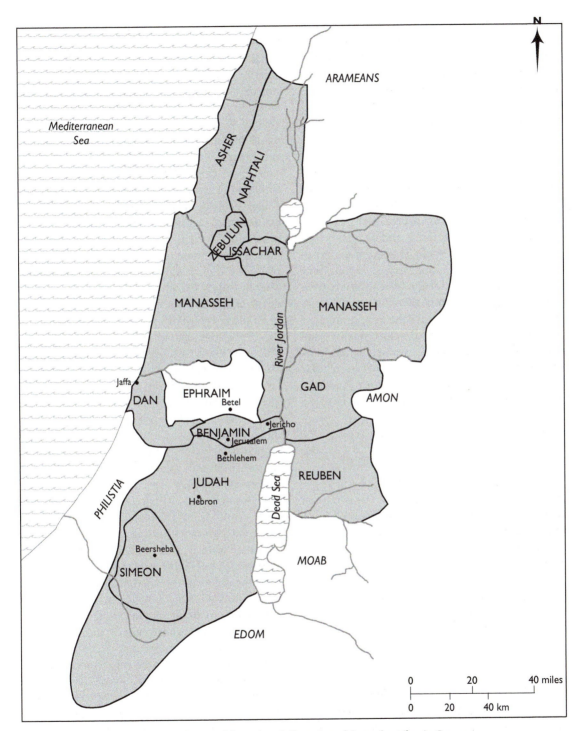

FIGURE 2-4 Twelve tribes of Israel: Map of the assigned dispersion of the twelve tribes in Canaan.

Dan to Beer-sheba knew that Samuel was a trustworthy prophet of the Lord" (1 Sam. 3:21). Samuel is not just the high priest at Shiloh, but also the judge of Israel. When he becomes old, he appoints his sons to be judges over Israel, "yet his sons did not follow in his ways, but turned aside after gain; they took bribes and perverted justice" (1 Sam. 8:3).

MAKING SENSE OF THE JUDGES

The period of the judges tells the story of the first 200 years of the people of Israel in the Promised Land. These people, who are principally agrarian and localized, lead a loose and relatively unstructured existence. While they have a kind of religious institution, it is not strong. The mode of social organization is local and egalitarian, with leadership in the hands of elders and judges whose authority discourages the development of a centralized power. While the Israelites are modestly successful, they are also regularly assaulted by their neighbors. One of the regular themes of Judges is how difficult it is to keep the people from worshipping other gods, an issue we will take up at the end of the chapter.

MONARCHY (c. 1020–586 BCE) AND OTHER DYNASTIES

After Samuel turns over power to his sons, the Israelites grow displeased with the condition of things: "Then all the elders of Israel gathered together and came to Samuel at Ramah, and said to him, 'You are old and your sons do not follow in your ways; appoint for us, then, a king to govern us like other nations'" (1 Sam. 8:4–5). Samuel is crestfallen, and God seems to be disappointed as well: "The Lord said to Samuel, 'Listen to the voice of the people in all that they say to you; for they have not rejected you, but they have rejected me from being king over them'" (1 Sam. 8:7). God hoped that the Israelites would exist in a kind of spiritual monarchy under him. But he acquiesces to the Israelites' demand and allows a human king to act as his regent.

God chooses **Saul**, a large, handsome, charismatic man, as their first king, and almost immediately the new ruler proves himself a great warrior against the Philistines, Israel's most powerful enemy. But Saul fails on two occasions to obey God's commands, so God instructs Samuel to anoint another king behind Saul's back; privately, Samuel anoints **David** of the town of Bethlehem, and "the spirit of the Lord came mightily upon David from that day forward" (1 Sam. 16:13). Here the narrative becomes decisive. The Israelites have a king, and yet secretly another has been anointed to replace him. Through the next several years we see how David comes to replace Saul. David, who plays the lyre, is sent to Saul to comfort him after he falls into a kind of divinely orchestrated depression; Saul becomes fond of David. Then, in a military standoff between the Israelites and the Philistines, David volunteers to battle the Philistine giant Goliath, with the winner taking all. David slays Goliath, and from that point on he becomes Saul's military general and subsequently his son-in-law.

But Saul is jealous of David's successes, even though they are good for his kingdom, and subsequently tries to have David killed. David eludes capture and flees to the south, where he creates a mercenary army that battles several of Israel's neighbors. By giving some of the booty of these conflicts to the elders of the southern tribes, he ingratiates himself to them. When Saul dies in a battle against the Philistines, the tribes of the south ask David to be their king. Two years later, the elders of the northern tribes ask David to become their king as well. He quickly creates the capital city of Jerusalem.

David's reign is portrayed on the one hand as glorious, a kind of golden age, and on the other hand as very complicated and compromising. Some texts tell of God's unequivocal favor toward David, his great piety, and even Israel's universal love for David: "So David reigned over all Israel; and David administered justice and equity to all his people" (2 Sam. 8:15). They also record the expansion of David's kingdom and its success in making neighbors vassal states. Other texts tell a different story. In these, David is an adulterer with Bathsheba, and even arranges for the death of her husband. He also has a dysfunctional royal household, with one of his sons raping his half-sister and another staging a coup that briefly takes the kingdom from his father. Toward the end of David's life, another rebel gets the northern tribes to virtually secede from the kingdom. Truly, all is not well in the monarchy of David.

One of the most momentous theological events of David's rule recorded in the Old Testament occurs when he asks his court prophet Nathan whether it would please God for him to make a temple in Jerusalem. God's response is that he should prepare for it, but that his son **Solomon** will build the temple. God also makes a promise that will be remembered as a covenant: "Your house and your kingdom shall be made sure forever before me; your throne shall be established forever" (2 Sam. 7:16).

David rules from 1000 to 961 BCE, and when he is quite old, he appoints his son Solomon to take over his throne. Solomon's rule (961–922 BCE), as recorded in the Old Testament, is even more complex than David's. A great builder, he enlarges Jerusalem and builds the great Temple there. He also is known for his wisdom, and under his rule Jerusalem becomes an impressive intellectual center. He dramatically expands the administrative apparatus of the monarchy and the religion. The cost of this expansion is great: "King Solomon conscripted forced labor out of all Israel; the levy numbered thirty thousand men" (1 Kings 5:13). He and his court live lavishly, while his people are impoverished. Solomon also enters into a number of marriages. While polygamy was not considered morally problematic in this era, his marriages to foreign women—some no doubt political unions—give him sympathy for their religions, and he builds shrines to and worships other gods along with Yahweh.

When Solomon dies, it is obvious that the kingdom is at the breaking point. The elders of the northern tribes come to Rehoboam,

Solomon's son and the new king, to ask him to be less demanding than his father. When he refuses, the north secedes. Now the tribes constitute two different monarchies: Israel, which eventually takes as its capital city Samaria, and Judah, with the capital city of Jerusalem.

Second Kings records the great catastrophe that came to the northern country in the eighth century BCE, when the Assyrian dynasty dramatically extended its borders under King Tiglath-Pileser III in 745 BCE. Israel fell in 721 BCE, with most of its population dispersed by the Assyrians and replaced by other conquered peoples. The southern country of Judah survived the Assyrian conquest and remained intact, although it was forced to pay a yearly tribute to the Assyrians. With only Judah remaining, it is probably from this era that the terms "Jew" and "Jewish" are derived, as representing the Israelite people and their religion.

Toward the end of the seventh century BCE, the balance of power shifted to the emerging Babylonian Empire. In 612 BCE, the Babylonians and the Medes, under the Babylonian ruler Nebuchadnezzar, destroyed the Assyrian capital of Nineveh and extended its reach to the eastern Mediterranean seaboard. In 598 BCE, they invaded Judah, and Jerusalem surrendered. Nebuchadnezzar appointed a puppet king, Zedekiah, but when he rebelled in 589 BCE the Babylonians devastated the city (586 BCE). All but the poorest of the land were either killed or taken into exile in Babylonia. Psalm 137:1 speaks of the Judeans' lament: "By the rivers of Babylon—there we sat down and there we wept." Perhaps the greatest shock to the Jewish religion was the fall of Jerusalem and the Davidic monarchy. Did not God promise it would be everlasting? Apparently, the Old Testament concludes, their sins undermined even this absolute promise. Furthermore, without the Temple and the sacrifices made there, what kind of religion could they have?

The loss of Judah and Temple sacrifice was not long-lived. In 550 BCE, Cyrus the Great of Persia became ruler, and in 539 he conquered Babylonia and began a policy of repatriation of

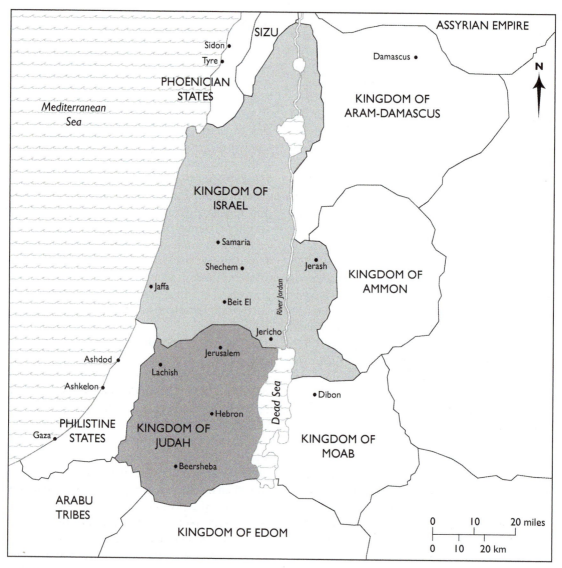

FIGURE 2-5 The kingdoms of Israel and Judah: From 922 BCE on, the united kingdom of tribes was divided into two kingdoms.

all the exiled peoples. Cyrus also financed some of the funds needed to rebuild Jerusalem and the Temple. It would be another hundred years before the city and Temple would be rebuilt and fully in operation, albeit under the authority of the Persian Empire. This era, from roughly 539 BCE to the year 70 CE, is known as the **Second Temple Period**.

In 334 BCE, Alexander the Great of Greece crossed into the Middle East, and by 326 he had conquered the Persian Empire, extending the Greek Empire all the way to the Indus River in India. When Alexander died suddenly in 323 BCE, his empire was broken up into three kingdoms. For Israel, the most important were the Ptolemy kingdom controlling Egypt and the

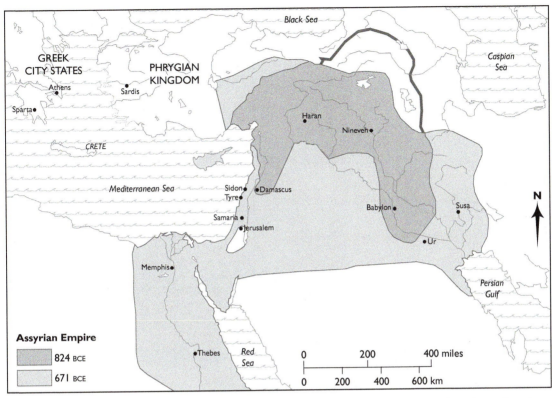

FIGURE 2-6   The Assyrian Empire: Map showing the massive expansion of the Assyrian Empire from the ninth to the seventh century BCE.

Seleucid kingdom controlling the Middle East. The Holy Land found itself between the two, first being controlled by the Ptolemy kingdom and then in 198 BCE by the Seleucid kingdom. By the 170s, Seleucid pressure on the Jews to renounce their religion and take up a fully Greek culture had become unrelenting. Up to this point, many Jews had welcomed modest **hellenization** ("Hellas" being another word for Greece). They learned the Greek language and culture, and even reluctantly tolerated the building of Greek gymnasiums in Jerusalem. But when Seleucid king Antiochus IV Epiphanes rededicated the Temple to Zeus and made it illegal to practice Judaism (punishable by death), he sparked a Jewish revolt in 167 BCE that led to full independence in 142 BCE. This revolt was led by Judas Maccabeus, and for the first time since the sixth century, Jews controlled the Holy Land. Judas's royal family line was known as the **Hasmoneans**.

In 63 BCE, the Roman general Pompey captured Jerusalem from the Hasmoneans, and thus began Roman occupation of the country for the next 700 years. The Romans eventually installed Herod the Great as a client king over all of the Holy Land. Herod ruled from 37 to 4 BCE. When he died, his realm was divided among three of his sons: Archelaus, who ruled Idumea, Judea, and Samaria until he was deposed and replaced by a Roman governor; Antipas, who ruled Galilee and Peraea; and Philip, who ruled the regions northeast of Galilee and southern Syria.

MAKING SENSE OF THE MONARCHY

First Samuel begins ominously. The people want to unite as a bona fide nation and demand a

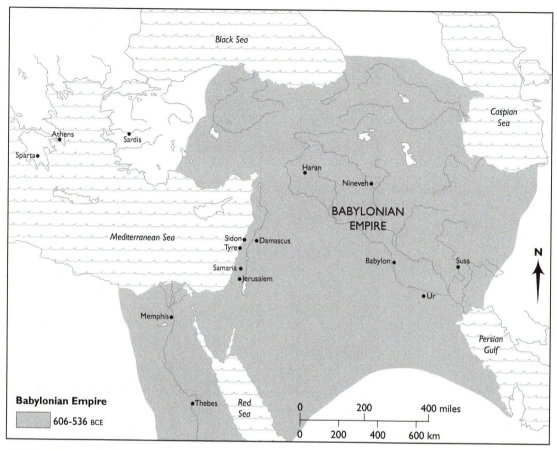

FIGURE 2-7 The Babylonian Empire: The Babylonian Empire at its height.

king. The decision to establish a monarchy is a good choice for the culture to advance. It is the condition that allows for cities to be built, a priestly institution to become sophisticated, education to expand, and military defense (and aggression) to be firmly established. God, it seems, is particularly invested in David and his dynasty, though this too will eventually fall.

In one sense, the development of a monarchy allowed the Israelites to become a regional force with a developed religion. In another sense, the monarchy is portrayed as disappointing. Solomon abuses his people, and many kings are only half-heartedly faithful to the covenant, if at all. According to First and Second Kings, the northern country of Israel was the least faithful and as a result was conquered in the eighth

century BCE. By the sixth century BCE, the southern country of Judah had also fallen. Although it was rebuilt and a new Temple put in place, the monarchy was no more. While the Jews would rule their own country under the Hasmoneans for 100 years, a good deal of Old Testament history shows them as being dominated by other dynasties. What is remarkable is that their faith remains intact through it all. By the time of Jesus, comparatively speaking, the Jewish religion was sound and thriving.

PROPHETS

Some of the most important figures in the Old Testament are **prophets**, God's spokespersons who act under his inspiration. The principal

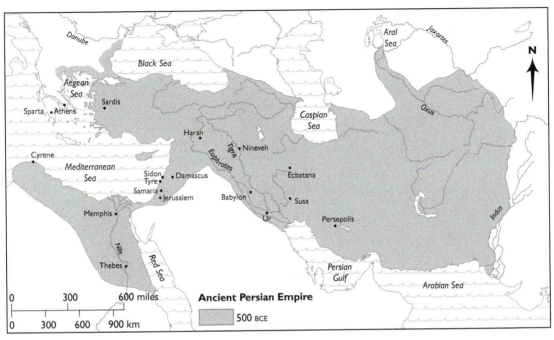

FIGURE 2-8 The Persian Empire: The Persian Empire at its height, after expanding into Greece.

term for "prophet" in Hebrew is *nabi* (one who announces). A prophet is also identified by *hozeh* (visionary) and *roeh* (seer). In Old Testament Israel, the prophet's role was to interpret the signs of the time in light of the tradition. Sometimes prophets predicted the future. More typically, they called the people and their leaders to greater fidelity to the covenant. Some of the greatest prophets worked for and advised the king. In fact, kings often had a guild of prophets working for them. One of the problems with court prophets was that they were supported by the most powerful man in Israel, and it could be all too easy to tell the king what he wanted to hear. Other prophets worked completely independently of the king and were often punished for opposing his agenda.

The Book of Isaiah records the work of the eighth-century BCE prophet Isaiah under both King Ahaz and his son Hezekiah. While Isaiah often speaks challenging words to them, he also assures them of God's ongoing support and deliverance during the attempted Assyrian invasion. In contrast, the prophet Jeremiah in the sixth century BCE opposes the king's prophets and tells Judah to surrender to the Babylonians. He is considered a traitor to the people, aiding and abetting the enemy, even though he proves to be right.

Two issues dominate the prophets' concerns. One is authentic worship. Throughout much of Israel's history, both kings and people regularly worship other gods in addition to Yahweh. And when they do worship Yahweh, that worship is often done poorly, adding insult to injury. A second concern is social justice. In a world where there were a few wealthy and powerful individuals and many who were poor and powerless, prophets spoke up for the weak. So important is concern for the common good and the welfare of the vulnerable that even authentic worship of Yahweh is undermined by a lack of social concern. Isaiah speaks for God: "I cannot endure solemn assemblies with iniquity. Your new moons and your appointed festivals my soul hates. . . . Even though you make many prayers, I will not listen. . . . Learn to do good, seek

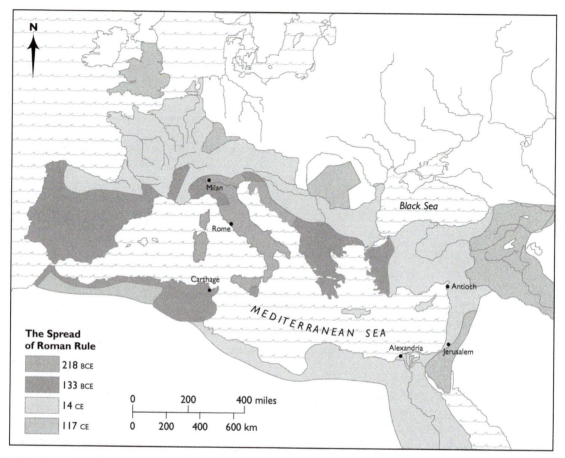

FIGURE 2-9   Israel under Roman rule: The Roman Empire at its height, of which Judea is but one small segment.

justice, rescue the oppressed, defend the orphan, plead for the widow" (1:13–17).

Christians look to the prophets in interpreting Jesus's message and ministry. Isaiah predicts a maiden with a child who will save the people (7:1–11) and celebrates the birth of a Davidic savior who will be designated "Wonderful Counselor, Mighty God, Everlasting Father, Prince of Peace" (9:6). This savior he associates with a light shining in Galilee (9:1–2); he will be a shoot sprouting from the stock of Jesse (David's father) who will bring justice and faithfulness (11:1–5). Jeremiah predicts a reconstitution of David's monarchy: "The days are surely coming, says the Lord, when I will raise up for David a righteous Branch, and he shall reign as king" (23:5).

Finally, the latter parts of the Book of Isaiah describe a servant of the Lord who will act as a vicarious sacrifice for the sins of the people: "But he was wounded for our transgressions, crushed for our iniquities; upon him was the punishment that made us whole, and by his bruises we are healed" (53:5).

Another important set of prophecies for Christians are those that announce a new covenant. Jeremiah prophesies: "The days are surely coming, says the Lord, when I will make a new covenant with the house of Israel and the house of Judah. . . . I will put my law within them, and I will write it on their hearts" (31:31–33). Ezekiel, a prophet during the exile, similarly announces for God, "I will make a new covenant of peace with them; it shall be an everlasting covenant" (37:26). One might ask: When did this new covenant take place? How was it ratified, and what were its conditions? The Christian tradition sees in the ministry of Jesus the fulfillment of these prophecies and the answers to these questions.

The Jewish tradition honors these prophecies as well, though it does not see Jesus as the fulfillment of them. Rather, this tradition takes Isaiah's messianic figure to be the historical Hezekiah, and the suffering servant to be a personification of Israel during the Babylonian Exile. The Christian tradition may also recognize these as legitimate interpretations but holds that the fullness of these prophecies unfolds with Jesus.

MAIN THEOLOGICAL THEMES AND DEVELOPMENTS IN ANCIENT ISRAEL

Early in this chapter we addressed the question about the relationship between the Old Testament and history. While it is generally agreed in scholarship that some of the Old Testament displays something of an enhanced history, what strikes many scholars is how accurately representative much of it probably is. It is a theological interpretation for sure, and one with competing lenses of different authors from different times. Not only do we see the good, the bad, and the ugly in the people and religion of ancient Israel, but we also see theological development that is representative of the time. The following sections highlight some Old Testament themes that are particularly important as we move into the New Testament, and some of which demonstrate dramatic theological development.

LAW

One of the most important themes of the Old Testament is that of the Law, or Torah. The word "Torah" is complicated. It can refer to the first five books of the Bible, but it can also mean "law," "way," or "teaching." Jews are people of the Torah. In our culture today, "law" can have harsh connotations, viewed as a necessary evil

for society to exist. Not so for Judaism, both ancient and modern. In the Jewish mind, Torah is God's expression of his favor. It allows Israel to "be holy, for I the Lord your God am holy" (Lev. 19:2). For devout Jews, the Torah is a delight and God's greatest gift. Torah marks them as different and as particularly God's own. In the ancient world religious law dominated Jewish sensibilities. It marked what was holy and what was profane, and how to properly live out a life of faith and justice. In short, the Law taught the Jews a life that was both socially and divinely ordered.

PRIESTHOOD AND SACRIFICE

We have not said much thus far about the priesthood, but it was crucially important in the Old Testament world. Priests, like prophets, gave oracles to the people from God. They also instructed the people about the Torah and were Israel's central religious leaders. Above all, they offered sacrifices. We have seen how sacrifices are used in the Old Testament to ratify the covenants of both Abraham and Sinai. Actually, however, they were offered daily. Sacrifice was understood as bridging the distance between God and humanity. In sacrifice, humans presented to God what was vital and dear to them, and in so doing they recognized that everything comes from God as a gift. Typically, in the ancient Israelite world, sacrifices were unblemished animals from their livestock or first fruits of their harvest.

Sacrifices also allowed humans to commune with God, who was recognized as utterly holy and transcendent. Take, for example, the sacrifice of an unblemished lamb. This animal would be set apart by the priest and consecrated for this holy purpose. In slaughtering it, some of the blood—symbolic of its life force—would be sprinkled on the altar. Then parts of the animal would be wholly burned, and other parts roasted. Presuming that God accepted the sacrifice, it would then be spiritually taken up into God's realm and made holy. Those who presented the sacrifice as well as the priest who offered it up would then eat the (now-cooked) animal and would in this way commune with God's holiness.

Sacrifices were made on many different occasions and for different purposes. They could be peace offerings after a victory, or free will offerings to give thanks to God. They could also be used as atonement for sin—one of the most important aspects of Temple sacrifice, which Leviticus identifies as especially holy (6:17–23, 7:15). For particularly serious sins Jews offered an unblemished male from their herd as a petition to God to forgive them. Once a year on the Great Day of Expiation, two goats were brought to the Temple, and then lots were thrown. The goat that *won* was sacrificed. The high priest took the other goat and confessed the sins of the people over it before sending it out into the wilderness, presumably to die. It is from this practice that we get the term "scapegoat."

POLYTHEISM TO MONOTHEISM

Judaism is a monotheistic religion, that is, it believes that there is just one God. Because of this, it is often assumed that this belief is reflected throughout the whole of the Bible, but this is not true. When exactly the religion became decidedly monotheistic is difficult to say, but it is clear that many of its oldest traditions reflect a much more complex imagined spiritual world. Ancient Jews were challenged to be faithful to Yahweh, who was either their particular god or the greatest god among the variety of gods. Ancient Israelites' belief that there were other gods explains why Israelites frequently worshipped them, even as priests and prophets alike condemned the practice. Perhaps we could consider the practice something like hedging one's bet. If one were a farmer or cattle herder, even though Yahweh was worshipped as the great god or the god of one's people, why not also offer sacrifice and prayer to Baal, the Canaanite fertility god who was said to secure good harvests, many healthy children, and an increase in one's flocks?

It is not merely that some ancient Israelites believed in other gods. Rather, much of the Old Testament itself holds this belief. In Genesis,

God speaks to other gods about Adam and Eve (3:22), and he has sons who copulate with human women, creating giants (6:1–4). Yahweh is regularly depicted as greater than the other gods (Exod. 15:11, 18:11; Ps. 82:1, 82:8–9, 89:6–7, 95:3, 135:5), and even the Philistine god bows to him (1 Sam. 5:3). Deuteronomy depicts sons of God as leading the other nations, while Yahweh himself chose Israel (32:8–9).

It was only relatively late that the very existence of these gods came into question. While worshipping the idols of other gods was condemned early on, it wasn't until the monarchy was long established that these gods were pronounced to be nonexistent. Jeremiah, in the sixth century BCE, felt the need to proclaim, "Everyone is stupid and without knowledge; goldsmiths are all put to shame by their idols; for their images are false, and there is no breath in them" (10:14). And the part of Isaiah that was written during the sixth century BCE exile declares, "They [idols] do not know, nor do they comprehend. . . . Shall I fall down before a block of wood? . . . Is not this thing in my hand a fraud?" (44:18–20).

Clearly, by the Second Temple Period after the exile, Israel and the scriptures that represent its faith had become monotheistic. Before this time, it seems clear from the Old Testament texts that both the Israelites of the time and the Bible itself imagined a world of gods, where the great challenge was to refrain from imploring them for aid.

SHEOL, HEAVEN, AND HELL

Another theological development in the Old Testament has to do with the state of one's existence after death. The vast majority of the Old Testament imagines no real life after death. There is no heaven and no hell. Rather, good and bad alike go to **Sheol**, a place of watery darkness where the soul rests. There is only one clear reference in the Old Testament to a person going to heaven; this is Elijah, who is taken up in a fiery chariot. It was not imagined that he attained some kind of eternal life there; rather, it was believed that he would return at the end of time (Mal. 4:4). With this exception, everyone—whether a devout soul like Jacob or Samuel (Gen. 37:35; 1 Sam. 28:14), a compromised soul like Saul or his sons (1 Sam. 28:19), or a great sinner (Num. 16:30)—was assumed to simply end up in Sheol.

After the exile, deutero-canonical writings—those Old Testament texts accepted by the Roman Catholic and Eastern Orthodox churches—began to provide a very different vision, one with a last judgment and a final destiny in heaven or hell: "In the eyes of the foolish they seemed to have died . . . but they are at peace . . . their hope is full of immortality" (Wisd. of Sol. 3:2–4). So late was this belief in a last judgment, as well as in heaven and hell, that in Jesus's day the noble and priestly class of Sadducees refused to accept this theological innovation, even as many rabbis among the Pharisees embraced it.

SATAN

Aligned with the emerging belief in heaven and hell is the belief in supernatural evil. This concept is virtually absent from the Old Testament, in which Satan appears briefly and lacks the features of the fallen angel Lucifer. *Ha Satan* is something of a title, meaning "the accuser," and Satan appears in the Jewish canon only in Job 1–2, First Chronicles 21:1, and Zechariah 3:1–2, all of them late texts. Even in these he lacks the nefarious characteristics of supernatural evil. To the ancient Jewish mind, God controlled everything, certainly all good, but even evil. God hardens Pharaoh's heart (Exod. 7:3), places an evil spirit in Saul (1 Sam. 16:14), sends a lying spirit to the prophets of the king of Israel (1 Kings 22:23), and even incites David to sin by ordering a census (2 Sam. 24:1).

Fallen angels only appear quite late and, again, only in deutero-canonical texts, such as Wisdom. Late noncanonical texts, such as Enoch, Jubilees, and the Testament of the Twelve Patriarchs, portray Satan as a fallen angel who led a rebellion against God and now, with his army of evil angels or demons, tempts and torments humans. By Jesus's day, the assumption of supernatural evil was taken for granted by most Jews, and certainly by Jesus himself. But it was a late development.

ISRAEL'S RELATIONSHIP WITH OTHERS

Much of the Old Testament imagines Yahweh as Israel's god, one who is either the greatest among the gods or their national god. The gods of other peoples were to be left alone and could even be considered rival gods. In a similar way, other peoples were competitors, those whose domination by Israel would reflect Yahweh's glory. Like other nations, the Israelites denigrated their neighbors. Yahweh was, among other things, a warrior God.

Israel goes through a transformation of consciousness throughout her ancient history, particularly after the exile. As Israel became far more strictly monotheistic, Yahweh came to be understood as the singular universal God, one who loved and cared for all creation and all peoples. In the Jerusalem Temple, priests yearly offered sacrifices for all the nations, that God might bless them too. What was Israel's role in God's plan for universal salvation? It was to be a spiritual guide for all peoples. Isaiah proclaims, "I will give you as light to the nations, that my salvation may reach to the ends of the earth" (49:6). And Zechariah predicts, "Many peoples and strong nations shall come to seek the Lord of hosts in Jerusalem, and to entreat the favor of the Lord" (Zech. 8:22).

ⓒ CONCLUSIONS

This chapter has been an all-too-brief foray into the history of ancient Israel. We've seen the extravagant history of a people whom God has chosen to work out his providential universal salvation. From the patriarchs to Moses, through the time of the judges and kings, and eventually through the many centuries of occupation, God has been drawing Israel to himself, both blessing the Israelites when they are faithful and punishing them when they are not. God has revealed himself to be steadfast and extraordinarily forgiving. He is merciful and fair, and he never seems to let his people go. God has struck his tent with Israel and remains with its people throughout.

We've also seen theological developments and might imagine them as a kind of theological or revelatory trajectory, a progressive learning about God and his plans throughout Israel's history. As we mentioned earlier, Yahweh, whose name means I AM WHO I AM, can also be translated I WILL BE AS I WILL BE, that is, you will come to understand me as I reveal myself through your history. For devout Jews and Christians, such developments reflect not a loss of continuity but a progressive understanding of a God whose providence leads them still.

It cannot be overstated how important knowing Old Testament theology and history is for understanding Christianity. The Old Testament witnesses to the religion of Jesus and his followers.

Abraham is their father in faith and the model of trust. The patriarchs represent the tribes of Israel, through whom the promises of God are played out. The Torah that Moses receives is the Torah that Jesus followed and interpreted according to his mission. The time of the judges was a time when theoretically God was king, and this came to influence the central theme of Jesus's preaching: the concept of the kingdom of God. From David on, God has promised fidelity to an eternal dynasty. Throughout the Israelites' history, prophets predicted its reconstitution, and thus many Jews in Jesus's day were awaiting a messiah, a new king. One simply cannot understand Jesus's ministry without knowing about David's dynasty, God's promise for it, and the expectation that it would be revived under God's providence. According to the New Testament, Jesus is the fulfillment of many sayings from the prophets. His preaching also clearly advances their interest in moral and spiritual purity. Little of anything in the New Testament makes sense without knowing the themes and history of the Old Testament.

SUMMARY QUESTIONS

- What are the similarities between the two versions of the creation story? What theological themes do they respectively highlight?
- Who were the patriarchs, and what are the major features of their lives?
- How was Israel organized after it conquered Canaan?

- How did Israel's monarchy arise, and what were its benefits and liabilities?
- What was the role of the prophets, and what were their central concerns?
- What are some of the central themes from ancient Israel that are especially important for understanding Christianity?

DISCUSSION QUESTIONS

- What do you make of the plagues in Exodus? What does this imply about God?
- What is most surprising to you in the history of ancient Israel and why?
- The author says that Christians look to the prophets in interpreting Jesus's message and ministry. He concedes that the Christian tradition recognizes the Jewish tradition's

interpretation that many "messianic" texts could have intended historical persons at the time of the prophecy, but that it is legitimate for Christians to see that the "fullness of these prophesies unfolds with Jesus." Do you think this is a position that is intellectually defensible? Why or why not?

KEY TERMS

Abraham	Hasmoneans	Prophet
Adam and Eve	Hellenization	Saul
Anthropomorphism	Isaac	Second Temple Period
Canon	Israel	Septuagint
Cosmogonies	Jacob	Sheol
Covenant	Judges	Solomon
David	Moses	Tanakh
Documentary hypothesis	Patriarch	Torah

BIBLIOGRAPHY

- Barton, John, and John Muddiman, eds. 2001. *The Oxford Bible Commentary.* Oxford: Oxford University Press.
- Clifford, Richard. 2006. "Did It Happen? Is It True?" *America*, January 2.
- Clifford, Richard. 2008. "The Original Testament: A Catholic Approach to the Hebrew Bible." *America*, September 29.
- Harpur, James, and Marcus Braybrook. 1999. *The Collegeville Atlas of the Bible.* Collegeville, MN: Liturgical Press.
- Levine, Amy-Jill. 2007. *The Misunderstood Jew: The Scandal of the Jewish Jesus.* New York: Harper.
- MacCullouch, Diarmaid. 2009. *Christianity: The First Three Thousand Years.* New York: Penguin.
- McGrath, Alister, ed. 1993. *The Blackwell Encyclopedia of Modern Christian Thought.* Oxford: Blackwell.
- Westermann, Clause. 1964. *The Genesis Accounts of Creation.* Philadelphia: Fortress Press.

3

Jesus and the New Testament

This chapter focuses on the person and ministry of Jesus in the New Testament. It begins by offering something of the lay of the land. Judaism in the first century was not a uniform whole, but consisted of various groups that understood their Jewish faith differently or at least with different emphases. We also find in this chapter an introduction to the eventual formation of the canon, or official texts, that make up the New Testament. Early

Christians had different interpretations of Jesus and his ministry, and it was not until the late fourth century CE that the canon was officially closed. Most of the chapter focuses on the portraits of Jesus found in the four canonical gospels. As will be evident, they each have their own understanding of Jesus. Collectively, these represent Christianity's understanding of who Jesus was and what he meant according to his life story.

THE SETTING

Recall from Chapter Two that Palestine during Jesus's day was controlled by the Roman Empire, with a regional governor and regional kings ruling on its behalf. Judaism during this period was far from monolithic. The Jewish historian Josephus (37–100 CE) divided the religious culture of first-century Palestine during Jesus's day into three *philosophical sects*, or religious parties. All three emerged as responses to the previous 100-year reign of the Jewish Hasmonean dynasty.

One religious party was the **Pharisee** party. At the time of Jesus, Josephus numbered this group at about 6,000. The term "Pharisee" literally

means "separated ones." They saw themselves as leading the charge for Jews to live particularly holy lives, to resist hellenization, and to distinguish Jewish culture and religion from foreign influences. They emerged clearly around 110 BCE and were initially respected by the Jewish Hasmonean rulers. Between 90 and 80 BCE, however, they became persecuted by the Hasmonean ruler Alexander Jannaeus, who killed many of them and tried to marginalize them within society. In spite of this, by the time of Jesus, the Pharisees were the most popular group of religious leaders among the common people. They were also, by this time, most open to the theological developments noted in Chapter Two. For them, the Jewish canon comprised all three parts of the Tanakh (Torah, Prophets, Writings) and thus included those prophets who anticipated a **messiah**, that is, an anointed king who would reestablish a righteous monarchy. They also embraced late writings that depicted a last judgment, heaven and hell, and resurrection from the dead. The Pharisees supported both the written Law of Moses and the oral Law, that is, authoritative commentaries on how to live out the Law. They were certainly no friend of Rome and opposed the Roman occupation, but they did not support open rebellion.

Another religious party was the **Sadducees**. As a religious group, they show up at about the same time as the Pharisees in the form of a protest party. The Hasmoneans had placed their own family members as high priests, in violation of the Jewish Law that demanded priests only come from the family line of Aaron of the Levite tribe. Sadducees, or *Sadakai*, took their name from King David's high priest Zadok, and they objected to the Hasmonean innovation, though historically the Law regarding the high priest had been violated regularly. When the Hasmoneans repressed the Pharisees, the Sadducees ironically became a favored party. By the time of Jesus, their members included many from the Jewish upper class, the priestly class, and the nobility. They also dominated the Jewish court (the Sanhedrin). While surely few Jews were happy about the Roman occupation, the Sadducees tried to collaborate with the Romans in order to ensure Jewish religious freedom. They might be considered the most theologically conservative Jews of the day. For example, while they respected the texts of the Prophets and the Writings, their canon only included the first five books of the Torah. Thus they rejected later innovations, such as a last judgment or the resurrection of the dead. They typically did not look for a future messiah, since this was not recorded in the first five books. If the Law was the most important aspect of Judaism for the Pharisees, the Temple, with its rites and sacrifices, dominated the Sadducees' emphasis.

Finally, Josephus describes the **Essenes**, whom he numbered to be around 4,000. Like the Sadducees, they believed the Hasmoneans had corrupted the priesthood and Temple. Unlike the Sadducees, however, they refused to engage the larger society, withdrawing to create their own isolated community at Qumran, on the shores of the Dead Sea. The famous Dead Sea Scrolls are texts from the Essenes. Josephus tells us that the Qumran community itself was celibate, while other members of the sect lived in nearby cities and villages with their families. This was an apocalyptic group. They waited in the desert for a time when God would intervene dramatically in history to restore the rightful priesthood and rid the country of the Romans. One famous text, the "War Scroll," anticipates a battle between the "sons of light" (the Essenes themselves) and the "sons of darkness" (Romans and corrupt Jews) in which God would vanquish all evildoers. Like the Pharisees, the Essenes embraced all three parts of the Tanakh and were very strict about living out the Torah, both written and oral. Also like the Pharisees, they anticipated a messianic age, a period of righteousness in which a God-given royal messiah would lead the charge against the Romans and reestablish a holy kingdom, and a messianic high priest would reconstitute the Temple for proper sacrifice.

In addition to these three parties mentioned by Josephus, a fourth group active in Jewish society at this time was the **Zealots**. This was a group that sought national independence by armed conflict against the Romans. Ordinary Jews would have considered them either freedom fighters or foolish insurrectionists. Insurrections did happen periodically, and never for the good of the people. In 4 BCE, a Zealot named Judas led a revolt in the town of Sepphoris, a few miles from Nazareth, Jesus's hometown, where the people proclaimed him king. The Romans responded by destroying the town and selling the insurrectionists into slavery. In 40 CE, a Jewish man named Theudas led a nonviolent tax protest against the Romans. Even in this case, the Romans reacted violently. Not long after, another Jew, known only as "The Egyptian," instigated a march around Jerusalem, imagining that if they circled the city seven times the walls would crumble, allowing an attack on the Romans. The Romans suppressed this uprising easily. More dramatically, in 66 and in 131 CE two Zealot wars broke out against the Romans. Both were overpowered by Rome, eventually leading Rome to destroy Jerusalem and rebuild it as a Gentile city that Jews were forbidden to enter.

Life for the ordinary Jew was typically hard. Perhaps 90 percent of the Jewish populace were "people of the land," or peasants. Without the knowledge or even ability to adhere to the Law as strictly as the Pharisees wanted, they were often looked down upon. Worse still, their lives were a day-to-day struggle. Jews of the first century were doubly taxed. In addition to facing a high Roman taxation burden, they were also taxed by Jewish authorities to keep their religious institution maintained. Roman tax collecting went like this: The Romans sought bids on the taxes of a given district, with the highest bidder becoming the tax collector. The Romans received the money upfront, and then the tax collector had the imperial power to later collect these taxes from the people, often with a strong arm and at a decent profit. It was a system in which the empire was assured its imagined proper due and in which the tax collector, if he wanted, could act as a legally protected extortionist. With such a system in place, villagers often lost their ancestral land by having to sell it to pay their taxes. These lands would be consolidated by the wealthy into large estates, which were often run by stewards on behalf of absentee landlords. Thus, many of the people existed under a system of wage labor, tenant farming, or even debt slavery, causing a profound crisis in Jewish village society.

The common Jew, the peasant, would have lived a difficult life, virtually hand-to-mouth, to survive. Many faithful Jews imagined that God would not allow such forces of injustice to continue forever. Many, like a number of the Pharisees, looked for a time when a messiah (anointed king) would reestablish a just kingdom. Some took solace in the many apocalyptic texts floating around the Jewish world. The semi-canonical Book of Daniel predicted a supernatural person

who would come from heaven (7:13). Other, noncanonical books, such as Enoch and Second Esdras, imagined a divinely appointed arbiter of the last judgment or a military leader, respectively. In all three texts, the protagonist is referred to as a "Son of Man," a term Jesus particularly used for himself in his preaching.

Another prominent religious and separate cultural group was the Samaritans, though Jews from Galilee and Judea did not consider them religiously legitimate. The Samaritan situation is interesting. In 721 BCE, the Assyrian Empire conquered the northern kingdom of Israel, with the city of Samaria as its capital. The Assyrians then dispersed many of the natives and repopulated the region with peoples from other conquered countries. Second Kings tells us that the Assyrians sent back one of the Jewish priests to teach the settlers "the law of the god of the land" (17:27). This disparate group created a temple, probably in the fourth century BCE, in which they worshipped Yahweh. Jews south and north of Samaria viewed Samaritan worship, theology, and rejection of the Temple in Jerusalem with disdain. Many Jews traveling between northern Galilee and southern Judea refused to even travel through Samaria, and arduously went around it. Others, including Jesus, hoped for a time when both orthodox and Samaritan Jews would reunite.

 ## THE NEW TESTAMENT AND HOW IT WAS FORMED

We saw in Chapter One that the Old Testament is a complex collection of oral and written traditions. This was compiled sometime around the fifth century BCE and then added to with later written texts. What made up the canon was widely disputed by Jews, even up to Jesus's day and beyond. All believed the first five books, the Torah, were legitimate, but for some the canon stopped there. For these Jews, the Prophets and Writings were valuable, but not canonical. Most Jews, including the Pharisees, believed these texts to be canonical. Yet even among them, what counted as canonical was hotly debated. Judaism would not definitively conclude its canon until the middle of the second century, when some of the later texts that had made it into the Greek translation of the Tanakh, the Septuagint, were removed.

Christianity likewise lived through controversies as to which of its writings were canonical. Archeological finds in the twentieth century, such as those at Nag Hammadi, Egypt, confirm the existence of numerous Gospels, various apocalypses, and many letters purportedly penned by apostles, prominent followers of Jesus. Which are authentic? Which represent the actual person of Jesus of Nazareth or were written by actual apostles? It is obvious that the movement Jesus spawned contained widely different interpretations of him, his ministry, and the nature of the church. Even if some were considered authentic to the tradition, should these necessarily be part of the canon? Christianity would not solve this problem for centuries.

To say that there were many interpretations of Jesus and his message does not suggest that everything was up for grabs. Some Gospels looked so out of place for first-century Palestine that they did not enjoy large acceptance. The church seems to have had criteria for what it believed represented authentic texts. The first was *apostolicity*: Was this text believed to have come from or represent the teachings of the apostles? The second, *antiquity*, followed: Did this text come from an early source? The third was *orthodoxy*: Did this text represent the modest consensus in mainstream Christianity? The final criterion was *broad acceptance*. Christian churches understood themselves to be in communion with each other and, by and large, knew which texts were recognized and which were not. No doubt, the decisions by major Christian centers such as Antioch, Rome, and Alexandria were also influential.

The least controversial texts that were disseminated were principally letters by St. Paul, a once-persecutor of the church who became its most public representative. Churches received his letters, copied them, and spread them to other churches. The Gospels of Matthew, Mark, and Luke were also widely copied and sent to other churches. John's Gospel had a good deal

of currency, though less than the first three. By 140 CE, Marcion, a Christian preacher in Rome, was arguing that the God of the Old Testament was morally complicit in violence and thus could not be the God of the New Testament. Furthermore, he argued, some Christian texts that were accepted by many churches ought to be rejected. Marcion provoked the need not only for other Christian leaders to insist on the continuity between the Old and the New Testament, but also for a consistent canon. The first official list of such a collection that we have today comes from Rome in the late second century. Here we find the Gospels of Matthew, Mark, Luke, and John; the Acts of the Apostles; thirteen letters from Paul; First and Second John; Revelation; and the Apocalypse of Peter. This last book would not survive the final canonical cut. Missing from the final canon were also Hebrews, First and Second Peter, James, and the Third Letter of John.

In the third century, First Peter, First and Second John, Jude, Hebrews, Revelation, and the Apocalypse of Peter were still disputed. Some earlier canonical lists had included First Clement, the Teaching of the Twelve Apostles (Didache), and the Shepherd of Hermas, but these were eventually dropped, even as they continued to be respected. James, Second Peter, and Third John were unknown to many churches even by then. By the fourth century, the great church historian Eusebius of Caesarea (260–339 CE) tells us that the standard list included the four Gospels, Acts, all the letters attributed to Paul, and First Peter, with churches disputing the inclusion of James, Jude, Second Peter, and Second and Third John. Revelation and Hebrews, he says, were acceptable at a given church's discretion. Finally, in 367, Athanasius, the great bishop of Alexandria, Egypt, realized that some churches were still not on the same canonical page, so he disseminated a universal letter to all the churches insisting on the twenty-seven books that are now standard as the New Testament in Christianity. In 397, a local synod of bishops at Carthage ratified the full canon. Universal acceptance of the New Testament's specific books, however, would take almost another 100 years to become the absolute rule.

FIGURE 3-1   Mosaic of Jesus from the Church of the Hagia Sophia in Istanbul, Turkey.

PROCLAMATION FROM THE SYNOD OF CARTHAGE, 397 CE

It was also determined that besides the Canonical Scriptures nothing be read in the Church under the title of divine Scriptures. The Canonical Scriptures are these: Genesis, Exodus, Leviticus, Numbers, Deuteronomy, Joshua the son of Nun, Judges, Ruth, four books of Kings [First and Second Samuel, First and Second Kings], Ezra, Nehemiah, two books of Paraleipomena [First and Second Chronicles], Job, the Psalter, five books of Solomon [Proverbs, Ecclesiastes, Song of Songs, Wisdom, Sirach], the books of the twelve prophets, Isaiah, Jeremiah, Ezekiel, Daniel, Tobit, Judith, Esther, two books of Esdras, two books of the Maccabees. Of the new Testament: four books of the Gospels, one book of the Acts of the Apostles, thirteen Epistles of the Apostle Paul, one epistle of the same to the Hebrews, two Epistles of the Apostle Peter, three of John, one of James, one of Jude, one book of the apocalypse of John. Let this be made known also to our brother and fellow-priest Boniface, or to other bishops of those parts, for the purpose of confirming that Canon. Because we have received from our fathers that those books must be read in the Church. Let it also be allowed that the Passions of Martyrs be read when their festivals are kept.[1]

THE GOSPELS OF JESUS

Gospel, or *euangelion* in Greek, is a word that means "good news." It was the title given to texts in the Roman world that were found at imperial temples and declared at public festivals. Typically, such texts lauded the Roman emperor, who was imagined as a semi-deity who ensured peace and justice in the world. Because Christians thought that Jesus was the true savior, they applied this term to the story of Jesus. Mark even begins his Gospel with: "The beginning of the good news (*euangelion*) of Jesus Christ, Son of God" (1:1).

The first three Gospels, Matthew, Mark, and Luke, are relatively similar to each other. They are called the **synoptic Gospels**, as *synoptic* (literally "same eye") means that they share the same viewpoint. John's Gospel reads quite differently and obviously comes from a very distinct perspective. The Gospels were not written by eyewitnesses, and there is internal evidence that they also reflect concerns of the church from later in the first century. That recorded accounts of Jesus's life come from a couple of generations after he lived shouldn't surprise us. The early Christians believed that Jesus would return in their lifetime. Thus, there would be no need to record an account of his life. Paul, for example, placed himself among those still living when Jesus would return (1 Thess. 4:15) and exhorted his listeners that "the appointed time has grown short" (1 Cor. 7:29). But Jesus did not return in the next generation, and the apostles eventually died. It became obvious to Christians that they needed an authentic witness to Jesus's life and message.

The relative consensus among scholars is that the first canonical Gospel is Mark, written somewhere around 65–70 CE. Matthew and Luke rely on him and sometimes quote him verbatim. Sometimes, however, we see that they have made changes, editing his source Gospel with their own slant. Matthew and Luke also cite another source, which we do not have but can be confident existed. This is called **Q**, short for the German word *quelle*, meaning "source." Finally, both Matthew and Luke have material that is all their own. Matthew and Luke are widely believed to have been written around the year 80 CE. John's Gospel, with far more developed theology and showing internal evidence of late first-century church experience, is believed to have been written sometime between 90 and 100 CE.

Q SAYINGS

Several of dozens of examples that come from Q:

Love your enemies, do good to those who hate you.

Be merciful just as your Father is merciful.

No good tree bears bad fruit, nor again does a bad tree bear good fruit; for each tree is known by its own fruit.

The harvest is plentiful, but the laborers are few; therefore ask the Lord of the harvest to send out laborers into his harvest.

Make purses for yourselves that do not wear out, an unfailing treasure in heaven, where no thief comes near and no moth destroys. For where your treasure is, there your heart will also be.

All who exalt themselves will be humbled, and those who humble themselves will be exalted.

Whoever does not carry the cross and follow me cannot be my disciple.

No slave can serve two masters; for a slave will either hate the one and love the other, or be devoted to the one and despise the other. You cannot serve God and wealth.

Are the Gospels historically reliable? Recall the discussion in Chapter Two on historicity and the Bible. Ancient writers enjoyed broad latitude to write narratives that they believed told the truth in ways that allowed for symbolism, typology, and so on to express that truth. Having said that, many secular historians use the Gospels, particularly the synoptic Gospels, as historical references for the life of Jesus of Nazareth. Secular historians may not believe the miracle stories in the Gospels, particularly if they reject the possibility of miracles in the first place. They may also reject the resurrection on the same ground. But they do generally rely on these narratives of Jesus's ministry. The quest for the historical Jesus is a fascinating endeavor that has continued from the mid-nineteenth century until today. It has gone from extracting all miracles stories to interpreting Jesus as an apocalyptic prophet to advancing the supposed chasm between the "Jesus of history" (about whom we know nothing) to the "Christ of faith" (proclaimed in the Bible).

The most responsible, up-to-date scholarship on the subject is John Maier's *A Marginal Jew*, a five-volume, 3,500-page inquiry into the historicity of Jesus in the Gospels. In working with the Gospels, Maier employs standard academic criteria to wrestle with the text's historical reliability. Questions he addresses include:

1. Does the section of the text (*pericope*) have multiple sources?
2. Does the section fit with exterior knowledge of people and events?
3. Does the text properly locate itself in the culture of the day?
4. Do odd parts of the text help explain what we do know, that is, are out-of-place parts strangely fitting?
5. Does the text reveal later events in church history placed into the narrative retrospectively?
6. Does the text reflect heavy symbolism or theologizing?

Maier then imagines how a Christian historian, Jewish historian, and generally secular historian might weigh in on that text's historical reliability. Fairness and intellectual honesty dominate Maier's work.

Readers could be modestly confident in assuming the Gospels, particularly the synoptic Gospels, to be *fundamentally* historical. In saying this, we need to provide several important caveats. The first is that these are faith documents. They were written by people of faith and intended for people of faith, with the aim of inculcating a deeper faith in Jesus. Second, the narratives come from decades-old oral history, and the subject matter is provocative. This is a particularly important consideration, as the longer the distance from the event described and the more ideological the material, the more the text is likely to be heavily molded. Scholars widely believe that the texts least likely to be historically accurate are those that represent things not publicly known, including the childhood of Jesus, his private prayers, and so on. Finally, as mentioned in Chapter Two, ancient authors believed they had license to frame their narratives according to symbolic and theological themes. So again, what we call "historical" today (as the term would be used

in an accurate newspaper story) would not register with the style and assumptions of the first-century world.

THE MINISTRY OF JESUS

With the factors outlined in the previous section in mind, let us proceed as we did with the Old Testament, telling the story of Jesus as it appears in the Gospels. First I will offer a brief synopsis of Jesus's life and ministry, and then I will glean from the specific Gospels themselves different portraits of Jesus and how collectively they highlight different aspects of a Christian understanding of Jesus as the Christ.

Jesus was raised in Nazareth, a small town in the territory of Galilee in northern Palestine. Herod Antipas, son of Herod the Great, ruled Galilee on behalf of Rome. Around 30 CE, a prophet named John, known as the "Baptizer," was preaching repentance and preparation for a coming new age and baptizing Jews as a sign of renewal and anticipation. Whether John expected a new Davidic king (messiah) or had a more radical apocalyptic vision is unclear.

Jesus presented himself for baptism and then went into the wilderness for forty days of intense prayer. Shortly thereafter, he began his own public ministry. Like John, he announced that a new era was upon the world, which he called the "kingdom of God." He became an itinerant preacher, going from town to town in Galilee. Before long he attracted many disciples, and among them chose twelve with whom he was particularly close and whom he instructed far more extensively than other followers. These individuals are called "**apostles**," which means "those sent out."

Jesus was a miracle worker, particularly a healer, and he associated his healing with the nature of the kingdom of God. Typically, he required faith in those he healed. He was also an exorcist and cast out many demons. While the ancient world did not clearly distinguish physical or mental illness from demon possession, it is clear that some of his actions were seen as directly countering supernatural evil. Because of his teaching and healing he was widely popular in Galilee. On at least one occasion, he sent out his disciples to various towns he intended to visit. They too experienced spiritual authority over evil and even received healing powers as his emissaries.

One of the hallmarks of Jesus's ministry was his breaking of several taboos. He touched lepers, had women followers, and consorted with some of the most disreputable people in society. He went to banquets offered by tax collectors and allowed women to touch him, even washing and anointing his feet. To many religious officials he seemed scandalous, even as the common people celebrated him. Jesus regularly flaunted the Pharisees' understanding of the oral Law. He seemed comfortable contradicting generally recognized interpretations of the Law regarding such things as scrupulous washing and work on the Sabbath. On the other hand, he demanded a great deal of inner purification for his followers to embrace the kingdom of God, as well as a wholehearted devotion to those in greatest need. Because of Jesus's demands, and given the fact that he seemed dismissive of strict interpretations of the Law, he made many enemies among religious and political leaders, including highly regarded Pharisees and members of Herod's court. Jesus exacerbated this tension by lambasting religious authorities in many of his sermons.

Interpretations of Jesus and his ministry were varied. Some imagined him a prophet of the last days, others a potential messiah or king who would rid them of the Roman occupation, still others a figure from heaven. Many people from his hometown were baffled, given that he had been a common laborer (a carpenter) throughout his young adulthood. Jesus himself contributed to the confusion through his preaching about the kingdom of God. Although he preached using common images and metaphors that would have been appropriate for his peasant listeners, figuring out just what the "kingdom" meant was difficult. At times the kingdom

seemed to be apocalyptic. At other times, Jesus seemed to be advancing a movement of inner holiness that had little to do with the current society. At still other times, he seemed to be challenging the status quo and the religious and cultural conventions of the powerful in ways that seemed revolutionary. Some people called him "**son of David**," a clear messianic reference. Some saw the choice of twelve apostles as symbolic of the twelve judges of the twelve tribes of Israel, harkening back to the time before the monarchy when judges ruled with God as the king. These images, however, do not cohere. Was the kingdom of God a pre-monarchy arrangement, the renewed Davidic monarchy that Jeremiah and Isaiah predicted, or an apocalyptic kingdom? It could not be all of these at once. A further challenge in understanding the kingdom of God is that at times Jesus proclaimed it to be something already upon the people, at other times something just about to come, and at still other times something in the unknown future, a time he said that even he did not know.

Jesus not only announced the emerging kingdom, he also advanced himself as the central player of that kingdom. He spoke with God's authority in striking, confusing, and even scandalous ways. He forgave sins, he proclaimed himself higher than the Law, he referred to God as his *abba* (dad), and he preached that he was the mediator of that kingdom. He also regularly referred to himself as the "**Son of Man**," who was probably an apocalyptic heavenly figure. His personal claim to authority seemed unbounded. Many followers, particularly the twelve, saw in him divine authority and even the working of the divine. They were convinced he was the messiah, even as he could not be a traditional messiah.

During the Passover week, Jesus and his disciples entered Jerusalem. His fame had already preceded him, and the people rejoiced by placing their cloaks and palm branches before him. They proclaimed him "son of David," that is, the messiah, a title he did not resist. During this Passover week Jesus regularly preached and healed in the Temple, which continued to disturb the Temple officials.

The great Passover supper, or Seder, was Thursday, and Jesus gathered his closest disciples for the Seder meal. During this supper he proclaimed a new covenant, perhaps as a fulfillment of the prophecies of Jeremiah and Ezekiel. He took unleavened bread and identified his own body with it. He broke it and had his disciples eat it. Likewise he took the cup, possibly the final toast of the Seder, which looked forward to the end time, and identified his blood with it. The disciples drank from this shared cup. In doing these things he was anticipating his death, both as a sacrificial atonement and as the sacrifice that would ratify the covenant. Eating and drinking this bread and wine—his body and blood—implicated his disciples; through them they entered the new covenant.

One of the twelve, Judas Iscariot, had agreed to hand Jesus over to the Sanhedrin, the Jewish court that convened at the Temple, and left the meal early to alert the authorities. After supper, Jesus and a few of his closest disciples went to the Mount of Olives, just east of Jerusalem, to pray. Judas led the Temple guards there, and they arrested Jesus, who was tried that night by the Sanhedrin and convicted of blasphemy. The next morning, he was led to the Roman governor

Pontius Pilate for another trial. Hoping that Pilate would execute him, the Sanhedrin advanced a different charge: Jesus was a revolutionary, a seditionist. Pilate flogged Jesus and, at the insistence of the religious leaders of Jerusalem, condemned him to death by crucifixion. Jesus died that Friday afternoon at three o'clock.

Because Jews could not work on the Sabbath (which ran from Friday night through Saturday night), an obscure disciple, Joseph of Arimathea, quickly buried Jesus in a nearby tomb. Sunday morning after the Sabbath, women disciples came to the tomb in order to anoint his body for a proper burial. They found that the boulder before the tomb had been moved and the tomb was empty. That Sunday and for many days after, the resurrected Jesus periodically appeared to the disciples. The Gospels tell that he was both the same Jesus and different, sometimes not being immediately recognized and with the ability to appear and vanish quickly. They were certain that he was not a mere ghost, but rather the resurrected and glorified messiah they had followed. These disciples became immediately transformed from fearful and rather clueless believers to bold proclaimers that Jesus of Nazareth was the Christ (messiah) who had been raised from the dead and was now savior of the world.

SYMBOLS OF THE GOSPELS

The Book of Revelation (4:7) describes four winged creatures around the throne of God. From Irenaeus (180 CE) on, these figures were used to symbolize each of the Gospel writers: "The first (Mark) was an animal like a lion, symbolizing his [Christ's] effectual working, his leadership and royal power; the second (Luke) was like an ox, signifying his sacrificial and priestly office; the third (Matthew) had, as it were, a human face—an obvious description of his advent as a human being; the fourth (John) was like a flying eagle, pointing out the gift of the Spirit hovering over the Church. And the Gospels, therefore, are in agreement with these things among which Christ dwells" (*Against Heresies* III.11.8).

THE GOSPEL OF MARK

Mark portrays Jesus as an urgent, even apocalyptic messenger of God. He is the "Son of God" (1:1), though we are not told what this means.

In this Gospel Jesus starts his ministry with the urgent exhortation: "The time is fulfilled, and the kingdom of God has come near; repent and believe in the good news" (1:15). The world is a

FIGURE 3-2 This page from the Book of Kells depicts the four Gospels under the images of a lion, an ox, a human, and an eagle.

dramatic stage where the powers of evil threaten the people and are threatened by Jesus. Almost immediately after Jesus begins preaching he encounters a possessed man in the synagogue. "What have you to do with us, Jesus of Nazareth?" it screams out. "Have you come to destroy us?" Evil spirits recognize him as the Son of God and the messiah, but he will not let them speak.

There is in Mark a regular theme known as the **messianic secret**. When evil spirits acknowledge Jesus's identity, he silences them, and when his disciples realize he is the messiah, he tells them to keep it to themselves. Jesus even tells those he has healed to keep the event quiet. Why? Could it be that he fears the crowds will imagine him a political messiah, which

he is not? Could it answer a later question about why too few Jews converted (they didn't know)? Perhaps it represents a narrative device for Mark to reflect the overwhelming power of Jesus; his message and ministry simply cannot be suppressed: "Jesus ordered them to tell no one; but the more he ordered them, the more zealously they proclaimed it" (7:36). Whatever the reason, it coincides with the darkness of the narrative and the drama between Jesus and evil forces. But it isn't only supernatural evil that opposes him. Even as he heals many, he finds quick resistance among the authorities: "The Pharisees went out and immediately conspired with the Herodians against him, how to destroy him" (3:6).

Jesus's messianic ministry is one of self-offering, something he demands of his disciples as well. When he predicts his sacrificial death, Peter challenges Jesus. Jesus then declares, "If anyone wants to become my followers, let them deny themselves and follow me. For those who want to save their life will lose it, and those who want to lose their life for my sake and for the sake of the gospel will save it" (8:34–35). Discipleship is daunting, and the powers against him and the kingdom are strong. But Jesus is stronger, and he assures his followers that they will have the strength of his Spirit: "They will hand you over to councils; and you will be beaten in synagogues. . . . When they bring you to trial and hand you over, do not worry beforehand about what you are to say; but say whatever is given to you at that time, for it is not you who speak, but the Holy Spirit. . . . You will be hated by all because of my name. But the one who endures to the end will be saved" (13:9–11). Endurance through all trials to the end marks this Gospel.

Mark depicts Jesus as particularly apocalyptic toward the end of his preaching ministry:

> For in those days there will be suffering, such as has not been from the beginning of creation. . . . And if the Lord had not cut short those days, no one would be saved. . . . But in those days, after that suffering, the sun will be darkened and the moon will not give its light, and the stars will be falling from heaven, and the powers in the heavens will be shaken. Then they will see the Son of Man coming in clouds with great power. Then he will send out the angels, and gather his elect from the four winds, from the ends of the earth to the ends of heaven. (13:19–27)

Mark's original Gospel ending describes three women disciples who go to the tomb early Sunday morning: Mary Magdalene, Mary the mother of James, and Salome. There they find the tomb empty and a young man inside who tells them that Jesus has been raised. He orders them to tell the disciples to go up to Galilee in order to meet the risen Lord. "So they went out and fled from the tomb, for terror and amazement had

seized them; and they said nothing to anyone, for they were afraid" (16:8).

THE GOSPEL OF MATTHEW

If Jesus is an apocalyptic hero in Mark, he is the personification of Israel and a new Moses in Matthew. Matthew begins by providing us with Jesus's genealogy through his adoptive father, Joseph, listing three sets of fourteen generations from Abraham to David, from David to Jechoniah and the exile, and from Jechoniah to Joseph. One sees God's extraordinary providence through Jewish salvation history; in Jesus, Israel's salvation is now coming to fruition.

In Matthew's Gospel, Jesus's family dwells in a house in Bethlehem, King David's city. Jesus's mother Mary is a virgin, engaged to Joseph, but before they live together she finds herself pregnant by the Holy Spirit. Joseph receives a vision in a dream of an angel who tells him to take Mary as his wife. Like a "light to the nations" (Isa. 49:6), Jesus's birth is preceded by a star that calls wise men from the east, who bring gifts. King Herod the Great is alarmed by the threat of a new king of the Jews, and kills all the babies in Bethlehem to destroy him. But, like Israel of old, Jesus and his parents escape to Egypt, the place of exile in Exodus. After Herod dies, Jesus's parents believe it safe to return, but decide to move up to the Galilee region to keep away from Herod's firstborn son, who now rules in Judea. They settle in Nazareth.

After the arrest of John the Baptist, Jesus begins his ministry, preaching the kingdom and healing all who come. Everyone streams to Galilee to see him. His first recorded sermon is lengthy. Climbing a mountain, as Moses did to receive the Law, he teaches about the kingdom of God:

> Blessed are the poor in spirit, for theirs is the kingdom of heaven. Blessed are those who mourn, for they will be comforted. Blessed are the meek, for they will inherit the earth. Blessed are those who hunger and thirst for righteousness, for they will be filled. Blessed are the merciful, for they will receive mercy. Blessed are the pure in heart, for they will see God. Blessed are the peacemakers,

for they will be called children of God. Blessed are those who are persecuted for righteousness sake, for theirs is the kingdom of heaven. Blessed are you when people revile you and persecute you and utter all kinds of evil against you falsely on my account. Rejoice and be glad, for your reward is great in heaven. (5:3–12)

As Jesus continues his great sermon, he demands that not only do the people have to abide by the Law, but they also have to be transformed. Instead of simply refraining from murder or adultery, they have to rid themselves of anger and lust. This is what the kingdom is like. Jesus has not come to abolish the Law and the prophets, but to fulfill them. Everything that smacks of self-righteousness or show has to be challenged. You have to become holy: "Be perfect, therefore, as your heavenly Father is perfect" (5:48).

Jesus's message is focused on works of righteousness. The kingdom is not principally about believing, but about doing: "Not everyone who says to me 'Lord, Lord,' will enter the kingdom of heaven, but only the one who does the will of my Father in heaven" (7:21); "Therefore I tell you, the kingdom of God will be taken away from you and given to a people that produces the fruits of the kingdom" (21:43). Jesus seems to even identify with those in need of care. In one of his final sermons he describes a last judgment scene, saying to those who will be saved that "I was hungry and you gave me food, I was thirsty and you gave me something to drink . . . I was naked and you gave me clothing, I was sick and you took care of me" (25:35–36). He goes on to assure them, "Just as you did for the least of these who are members of my family, you did it to me" (25:40). To those who will be damned, he assures, "Just as you did not do it for one of the least of these, you did not do it to me" (25:45).

THE GOSPEL OF LUKE

Luke portrays Jesus as a universal savior. Like Matthew, he also provides a genealogy of Jesus, though this time Luke takes us back to Adam and Eve, the ancestors of the whole human race. Luke tells us that Jesus's parents were from Nazareth

and provides a much more dramatic encounter between the Virgin Mary and the angel Gabriel, who proclaims to her that she will bear a son by the Holy Spirit who will be the Son of God. During her late pregnancy she and Joseph have to travel to Bethlehem to enroll in a census; this is why Jesus is born in Bethlehem. After Mary's time of purification, they proceed to the Temple before returning home to Nazareth. Luke's infancy narrative is filled with speeches from Mary and prophets in the Temple praising God for this time of redemption. Mary's praise of God is telling:

My soul magnifies the Lord, and my spirit rejoices in God my Savior, for he has looked with favor on the lowliness of his servant. . . . He has shown strength with his arm; he has scattered the proud in the thoughts of their hearts. He has brought down the powerful from their thrones, and lifted up the lowly; he has filled the hungry with good things, and sent the rich away empty. He has helped his servant Israel, in remembrance of his mercy, according to the promise he made to our ancestors, to Abraham and his descendants forever. (1:46–55)

Mary's praise encapsulates one of the great themes of Luke's Gospel: God's salvation is marked by a reversal of fortunes. The hungry are fed and the poor are raised up, while the satisfied and arrogant are cast down. Jesus's own beginnings reveal this theme. Instead of being born in a house in Bethlehem, he is delivered by his parents in a stable. Jesus is visited not by royal emissaries from the east, but by poor shepherds. His glory and majesty are hidden in his simplicity and poverty. Jesus clearly sees an important part of his ministry in these reversals. In his first act of public ministry he goes to the synagogue and cites Isaiah 61:1: "The Spirit of the Lord is upon me because he has anointed me to bring good news to the poor. He has sent me to proclaim liberty to the captives and recovery of sight to the blind, to let the oppressed go free, to proclaim a year of the Lord's favor" (Luke 4:18–19).

One sees this emphasis on poverty and its reversal in the kingdom of God in Jesus's great sermon in Luke, the counterpart to Matthew's

Sermon on the Mount. In Matthew, recall that Jesus proclaims, "Blessed are the poor in spirit, for theirs is the kingdom of heaven. . . . Blessed are those who hunger and thirst for righteousness, for they will be filled" (5:3, 6). In Luke, however, Jesus proclaims, "Blessed are you who are poor, for yours is the kingdom of God. Blessed are you who are hungry now, for you will be filled. Blessed are you who weep now, for you will laugh" (6:20–21). And then the reversal: "But woe to you who are rich, for you have received your consolation. Woe to you who are full now, for you will be hungry. Woe to you who are laughing now, for you will mourn and weep" (6:24–25). Clearly, as Matthew focuses on interior transformation, Luke focuses on those who are literally poor, hungry, and suffering.

Even as Mark and Matthew provide many parables of Jesus, Luke gives us far more, and we often see in them a different slant. In Luke's parables, God regularly takes up the cause of the poor, and the kingdom of God is about elevating such people. In these same parables, those who are wealthy and powerful are challenged to solidarity with the poor and powerless, and indeed, their acceptance into the kingdom of God has everything to do with whether or not they align their lives with the weak.

THE GOSPEL OF JOHN

Mark begins his Gospel with the public ministry of Jesus. Matthew and Luke begin theirs with Jesus's conception by the Virgin Mary through the power of the Holy Spirit. John begins his Gospel with the creation of the world. He identifies Jesus as something like the Old Testament figure of Wisdom, who exists with God before creation and through whom God creates all things (Wisd. of Sol. 7–8). John even identifies Jesus with God himself in some way:

> In the beginning was the Word, and the Word was with God and the Word was God. He was in the beginning with God. All things came into being through him, and without him nothing came into being. What has come into

being was the life, and the life was the light of all peoples. . . . And the Word became flesh and lived among us, and we have seen his glory, the glory of a father's only son, full of grace and truth. . . . No one has ever seen God. It is God the only Son, who is close to the Father's heart, who has made him known. (1:1–4, 14, 18)

The person of Jesus is most dominant in this Gospel. Recognizing him as the face of God, and thus believing in him, is imperative: "For God so loved the world that he gave his only Son, so that everyone who believes in him may not perish but may have eternal life. . . . Those who believe in him are not condemned; but those who do not believe are condemned already, because they have not believed in the name of the only Son of God" (3:16–18). In Jesus's preaching in John, it becomes clear that he mediates everything spiritual. He is "the bread of life" (6:48), "the light of the world" (8:12), the "resurrection and the life" (11:25), and "the way, and the truth, and the life" (14:6).

In one sense, Jesus appears not to be God, but to work for God: "My Father is still working, and I also am working" (5:17); "I have received this command [to lay down his life] from my Father" (10:18). Furthermore, the works he does are in his Father's name (10:25). In another sense, he seems to identify with God, including assuming the identity of the "I Am," or Yahweh (8:24, 28, 58; 13:19). Jesus is a presentation of the Father, an experience of God, even the presence of God before the people.

Paradoxically, he is most glorified and most revealing of the divine when he has emptied himself on the cross. In the synoptic Gospels, the cross is a place of horror, a moment of Satan's imagined victory, with the resurrection symbolizing God's reversal and ultimate victory over death. In these Gospels Jesus suffers at the thought of the cross and even prays before he is arrested, "My Father, if it is possible, let this cup pass from me; yet not what I want but what you want" (Matt. 26:39). Luke even reports that "his sweat became like great drops of blood" (22:44). Not so in John, where the cross becomes his place of glory (17:5, 22, 24) and exaltation, a moment where he "will draw all people to myself" (12:32). The cross and indeed Jesus's whole life are viewed as expressions of his and the Father's love for the world (3:16; 15:13).

Love is a second dominant theme in John's Gospel: "I give you a new commandment, that you love one another. Just as I have loved you, you also should love one another" (13:34). This self-offering in love is portrayed as a model for all believers: to embrace such a love, John promises, will bring profound intimacy with Jesus and his Father. Before his arrest Jesus prays that his believers "may all be one. As you, Father, are in me and I am in you, may they also be in us . . . so that they may be one, as we are one, I in them and you in me, that they may be completely one" (17:21–23).

Discipleship is twofold in John's Gospel. It represents a decision to believe in Jesus and embrace his way of self-offering love. These two interdependent dynamics dominate the Gospel. To John, following Jesus is a matter of life or death, of salvation or damnation. There are no half-measures here. Jesus's preaching is filled with metaphors of absolute distinction: Are you for light or darkness, truth or falsehood, spirit or flesh? Are you children of God or children of the devil? You must choose.

THINKING ABOUT THE PORTRAITS OF JESUS

In deciding to include all four Gospels in the canon, the church concluded that all are true, even as they are different. Many scholars believe that Mark's Gospel was written in Rome, where the church suffered great persecution and martyrdom and to be a Christian was difficult and dangerous. Looking at Jesus through Mark's lens reveals Jesus's message and ministry as an engagement against powers of evil, both social and supernatural. Mark reveals a messiah who is stronger than these powers. Even if one were to fall victim to them, Jesus has ultimately conquered them. And even in one's suffering, discipleship represents a confident walk with the victorious Lord through it all.

Matthew's Gospel, clearly written for a converted Jewish community, is a portrait of Jesus in the great continuity of God's providential salvation through Israel's history. Jesus is the fulfillment of the expectations of the Old Testament. His kingdom is a new covenant that completes the Torah through inner purification and exterior acts of compassion.

Luke's Gospel moves discipleship toward a search for God's presence among the poor and, like the prophets of old, a focus on those most in need. It is a Gospel in which lowliness and humility become the context for God's hidden glory to be encountered, and in which the kingdom of God is a place where full flourishing of all must be paramount. Here Jesus demands a daunting examination of one's values, priorities, and decisions. Taking the side of the weak and identifying with them is what the kingdom requires.

John's Gospel is a message of decisiveness. There is no room for lukewarm discipleship here, and one cannot be *sort of* Christian. It is all or nothing, and the "all" means offering oneself unreservedly. As daunting a message as this seems, its possibilities are extraordinary. One becomes "born from above" (3:3), a bona fide child of God (1:12) who may now know profound intimacy with God through Jesus.

◎ CONCLUSIONS

What does one make of these different versions of Jesus? Is any one of them more likely to be the *real* or *historical* Jesus? Did the infant Jesus go to his home in Nazareth shortly after his birth or flee to Egypt only to relocate to Nazareth sometime later? Was he unnerved at his impending crucifixion or pleased to anticipate its glory? The Gospel writers all intended to represent the *real* Jesus, even as they believed (as all ancient writers did) that they had narrative license in crafting their portrayal. The Gospels represent something more like impressionistic paintings than photographs. Claude Monet's panels of water lilies and Vincent van Gogh's wheat fields are not photographs, and thus could be charged with being "less accurate" than a snapshot. On the other hand, in very different ways, they draw the viewer into moving, even transforming visions of reality that are arguably truer than any photo could be. This "historical accuracy" question becomes a false start.

Another false start would be to blur the Gospels together, as if their details can be shuffled into a neat stack that collectively tells the history of Jesus. Christian culture has tended to do this at Christmastime, when the infancy stories of Jesus from Matthew and Luke get conflated. Each Gospel represents a very intentionally different framing of Jesus and his message. The best theological discourse today honors those different presentations and tries to respect each vision as a whole.

A final false start would be for Christian theology to focus on one or two Gospels to the neglect of the others. Christians see Christ's self-offering love on the cross in John's Gospel as containing a deep, profound truth—that it is in emptying oneself that one allows God to shine brightly in one's life. But to glamorize the cross without seeing it through the eyes of the synoptic Gospels is to neglect another Christian insight, which is that the cross can *also* reveal an image of the human condition ravaged by sin. Both understandings can be true, but they represent different access points to different truths. Discipleship, as witnessed in Matthew's Gospel, is a slow, progressive learning from Jesus. Christians see a truth here: one does not become holy in a day. Discipleship, as witnessed in John's Gospel, is a once-and-for-all decisive event in which one has to be fully committed and radically transformed here and now. Both insights can be true, but from very different vantage points. The first shows how people on spiritual paths mature, while the second challenges any mediocrity in discipleship. To the Christian who is suffering persecution, Mark's Gospel is particularly apropos. To the Christian who is all too comfortable in a middle-class cocoon, Luke's Gospel becomes a prophetic challenge.

SUMMARY QUESTIONS

- What were the four main religious parties during the late Second Temple Period? What were their main characteristics, and how did they differ from each other?
- What were the criteria for deciding which texts were accepted into the New Testament canon?
- What are the main criteria John Maier uses to assess the historicity of sections of the Gospels?

- Compare and contrast the four Gospels. In what ways are they similar? What are the distinctive features of each Gospel?
- What were Jesus's central teachings?
- What are some of the different ways Jesus framed the kingdom of God?

DISCUSSION QUESTIONS

- Do you think that the time and place in which he lived was conducive to Jesus's message? How so or why not?
- Does the plurality of interpretations of Jesus in the four Gospels bring confusion to his message or fill it out? Explain.

- Is there a particular Gospel that appeals more to you than others? What do you think this implies about your life?

KEY TERMS

Apostle	Messianic secret	Son of David
Essenes	Pharisees	Son of Man
Gospel	Q (*quelle*)	Synoptic Gospels
Messiah	Sadducees	Zealots

BIBLIOGRAPHY

- Bowe, Barbara. 2003. *Biblical Foundations of Spirituality: Touching a Finger to the Flame*. Oxford: Rowman & Littlefield.
- Brown, Raymond. 1997. *An Introduction to the New Testament*. New York: Doubleday.
- Donahue, John, and Daniel Harrington. 2002. *The Gospel of Mark*. Collegeville, MN: Michael Glazier.
- Eusebius of Caesarea. 1989. *The History of the Church*, rev. ed. Trans. G. A. Williamson. New York: Penguin Books.
- Johnson, Luke Timothy. 1991. *The Gospel of Luke*. Collegeville, MN: Michael Glazier.
- Johnson, Luke Timothy. 2011. *Prophetic Jesus, Prophetic Church: The Challenge of Luke-Acts to Contemporary Christians*. Grand Rapids, MI: Eerdmans.
- Josephus. 1988. *Josephus: The Essential Works*. Trans. and ed. Paul Maier. Grand Rapids, MI: Kregel Publications.
- Lohfink, Gerhard. 2012. *Jesus of Nazareth: What He Wanted, Who He Was*. Trans. Linda Mahony. Collegeville, MN: Michael Glazier.
- Maier, John. 1991–2016. *The Marginal Jew: Rethinking the Historical Jesus*. 5 vols. New York: Doubleday.
- Ratzinger, Joseph (Pope Benedict XVI). 2007. *Jesus of Nazareth: From the Baptism in the Jordan to the Transfiguration*. Trans. Adrian Walker. New York: Doubleday.
- Robinson, James, ed. 1988. *The Nag Hammadi Library in English*, 3rd ed. San Francisco: Harper & Row.
- Schneiders, Sandra. 1991. *The Revelatory Text: Interpreting the New Testament as Sacred Scripture*. New York: HarperSanFrancisco.

NOTE

1. The Latin text and English translation are from B. F. Westcott, *A General Survey of the History of the Canon of the New Testament*, 5th ed. (Edinburgh, 1881), 540–542, as cited in https://en.wikipedia.org/wiki/Councils_of_Carthage#Synod_of_397.

4

Christian Faith in the New Testament

Timeline

c. 27–30 CE	Ministry of Jesus
c. 33 CE	Conversion of Paul of Tarsus
c. 49 CE	Jerusalem Council decides Gentile converts are free from Torah requirements
50s CE	Paul's epistles are written
60–64 CE	Martyrdoms of Peter and Paul in Rome
65–70 CE	Gospel of Mark is written
66–70 CE	Jewish Revolt; Temple in Jerusalem is destroyed
80–110 CE	Remaining books of the New Testament are written

WHAT TO EXPECT

This chapter describes how the disciples of Jesus got their bearings as they began to preach that he was the messiah who had been raised from the dead and glorified, and that his kingdom had begun under the inspiration and power of the Holy Spirit. As Gentiles (non-Jews) underwent the experience of being empowered by the Spirit, the disciples were forced to wrestle with what to demand of them in terms of the Torah, or Law. Most of this chapter details the person and teachings of Paul, an initial persecutor of the church who became its most dynamic missionary. The theology in Paul's letters would determine a great deal of Christian beliefs both in the early church and throughout its history.

INTRODUCTION TO THE REST OF THE NEW TESTAMENT

The four Gospels we encountered in the last chapter constitute roughly the first half of the New Testament. The rest of the New Testament is made up of the Acts of the Apostles; thirteen letters attributed to Paul; the letter to the Hebrews; the letter of James; two letters attributed to **Peter**; three letters by John, sometimes imagined to be from the same author as the Gospel of John; and the Book of Revelation, an apocalyptic text written to Christian communities in western Asia Minor (modern Turkey).

These works address the newly formed church trying to make sense of what it means to be Christian. The church would have to decide what to believe, who had authority, how to structure the community, what constituted membership, and how Christians ought to live. Responses to these issues were not easy or obvious to the early church. None of the earliest believers thought that Jesus had started a new religion different from Judaism, and Jesus himself left no structure for a new community and few instructions. Certainly, the twelve apostles played a crucial role in providing early leadership and continuity. But this does not mean that they controlled the church or knew exactly what to do about its growth or development. As far as the early disciples knew, they were to preach faith in Jesus and his kingdom and await his imminent return in glory. As we saw in Chapter Three, Jesus himself preached a message that could have been interpreted as anything from a version of the return to the time of the judges to a reconstituted spiritual monarchy to an apocalyptic intervention from heaven.

There is no question that the apostles interpreted Jesus through their Jewish faith. Jesus was the fulfillment of Old Testament prophecy; he was the messiah. As Jews, the apostles were strict monotheists, believing in Yahweh, the one God who ruled heaven and earth. Jesus himself prayed to God, calling him *Abba*, and assured his listeners that he was devoted to following God's will. As we saw, however, the disciples also believed Jesus was something more than just an ordinary man or even an extraordinary prophet. Jesus's sense of his own personal authority was striking. He was not only the messiah; he was also the Son of God. What did it mean for him to be the ruler, and what could "Son of God" have meant to a strict monotheistic Jew?

The Acts of the Apostles depicts early preaching about Jesus, including an account of Peter's first extemporaneous sermon, addressed to Jews in Jerusalem who had witnessed the apostles' reception of the Holy Spirit. First he describes this event as evidence that the "last days" prophesied by Joel are upon them. Peter quotes Joel's prophecy at length, which ends with, "Anyone who calls on the name of the Lord shall be saved" (Acts 2:21). Then Peter continues:

> "You that are Israelites, listen to what I have to say: Jesus of Nazareth, a man attested to you by God with deeds of power, wonders, and signs that God did through him among you, as you yourselves know—this man handed over to you according to the definite plan and foreknowledge of God, you crucified and killed by the hands of those outside the law. But God raised him up. . . . This Jesus God raised up, and of that we are all witnesses. Being therefore exalted at the right hand of God, and having received from the Father the promise of the Holy Spirit, he has poured out this that you both see and hear. . . . Therefore let the entire house of Israel know with certainty that God has made him both Lord and Messiah, this Jesus whom you crucified." Now when they heard this, they were cut to the heart and said to Peter and to the other apostles, "Brothers, what should we do?" Peter said to them, "Repent, and be baptized everyone of you in the name of Jesus Christ so that your sins may be forgiven; and you will receive the Holy Spirit." (Acts 2:14–38)

In this sermon, Peter sees the current time as an apocalyptic one and Jesus as a man empowered by God, raised by God, and made Lord and messiah. The Greek word for messiah is "Christ," which from Peter's sermon forth becomes Jesus's

FIGURE 4-1   In the upper room, the Holy Spirit descends on the disciples in the form of "tongues of fire," empowering them to preach.

title. He is now seen as exalted at the right hand of God and as the giver of the Holy Spirit, that is, the giver of God's power and presence. It is also clear that salvation depends on Jesus: his followers need to be baptized in his name. The focus of the prophet Joel's exhortation to "call on the name of the Lord" is transferred from God to Jesus. Peter does not call Jesus God and distinguishes him from God, but he certainly blurs some lines.

The second sermon recorded in Acts comes from a young Christian leader, Stephen, who was seized for preaching about Jesus and taken to the Sanhedrin, the Jewish council. In Stephen's lengthy speech in Acts, he details the fundamentals of Jewish salvation history and how it has all been preparation for the "coming of the Righteous One" (7:52). The members of the council are enraged. "But filled with the Holy Spirit, [Stephen] gazed into heaven and saw the glory of God and Jesus standing at the right hand of God. 'Look,' he said, 'I see the heavens opened and the Son of Man standing at the right hand of God'" (7:56). Stephen

was subsequently stoned for his blasphemy, with Saul, later known as the convert and missionary **Paul**, serving as the official and approving witness. In Acts, Stephen understands Jesus as something of the Son of Man prophesied in Daniel and other apocalyptic texts of the day, a heavenly figure working for God's ultimate kingdom.

From this point on, the apostles set about preaching this fundamental message. Jesus was crucified, died, was raised by the power of God, and ascended to God's right hand. Salvation is to be found in faith in Jesus. He is the fulfillment of Jewish salvation history and the made ruler of the universe.

ACTS OF THE APOSTLES

Acts, much like the Gospels, intended to represent an authentic account of the events of the early church. Like the Gospels, it also represents a theology (Luke's), along with a certain narrative license in describing persons and events. Scholars, both secular and religious, use Acts to glean historical information about the early church, even while recognizing that Luke provides this information through a theological lens. It is clearly also important to Luke that the church be presented in an idealized manner. In his account relationships are quite smooth and controversies quickly solved: "Now the whole group of those who believed were of one heart and soul" (4:32). We find out in Paul's letters, however, that all was not smooth and controversies were far from quickly solved.

Acts begins with the apostles in Jerusalem, where they have remained after having experienced the risen Christ on various occasions. Realizing the symbolic nature of the "twelve," they choose by lots Matthias to replace Judas, who betrayed Jesus and then killed himself. Soon they experience a rush of the Holy Spirit that fills them with power. After Peter's first speech, many come to believe in Jesus:

So those who welcomed his message were baptized, and that day about three thousand persons were added. They devoted themselves to the apostles' teaching and fellowship, to the breaking of the bread and the prayers. Awe came upon everyone, because many wonders and signs were being done by the apostles. All who believed were together and had all things in common; they would sell their possessions and goods and distribute the proceeds to all, as any had need. (2:41–45)

Centered in Jerusalem, the apostles and other believers continue the ministry of Jesus and are described in many of the same ways that Jesus himself was described. Stephen, the first martyr, forgives his persecutors by uttering virtually the same words that Jesus said on the cross. Peter heals by command. Everything is done in the name of Jesus. As Peter, who with John is soon arrested, testifies to the Sanhedrin, "There is salvation in no one else, for there is no other name under heaven given to mortals by which we must be saved" (4:12). Peter and John are eventually released but ordered not to preach about Jesus, an order they refuse to obey. Soon, all the apostles are arrested and flogged for continuing to preach, but "as they left the council, they rejoiced that they were considered worthy to suffer dishonor for the sake of the name" (5:41).

Before long, many of the apostles and other Christian leaders spread out to preach the gospel. According to Acts, Philip went to Samaria and Peter traveled throughout Judea and western Galilee. Fourth-century church historian Eusebius says that Thomas and John went to Persia. Tradition also has Thomas traveling as far as southern India, where he was martyred. Eusebius says that Andrew preached in Scythia (central Eurasia), and Peter went to Asia Minor (Turkey) and then to Rome. Historically, we know that Alexandria, Egypt, had an early church. Christian communities in Damascus and Antioch in Syria also quickly emerged. Reliable information about the exact spread of the faith is sketchy, but it is certain that it spread in large cultural and trade centers.

Because all the early disciples were Jewish and indeed saw Jesus as the Jewish messiah, early missionary energy was devoted to converting Jews to what Acts calls "the Way" (9:2; 19:23; 24:22). One of the most striking innovations in the early church was the experience of some non-Jews of being filled with the Holy Spirit. These were part of a group whom Jews at the time called **God-fearers**, that is, Gentiles who admired and even followed much of the Jewish religion without being formal members of the community. The term *yirei Hashem* ("Fearers of the Name") had been part of Judaism for centuries before Christ. One reason many God-fearers had not fully converted was that taking on the full weight of the Torah, including the dietary restrictions it imposed, would have been very difficult. Another reason was that the males would have to be circumcised, something far more daunting in adulthood than in infancy.

FIGURE 4-2 Paul, the most influential early missionary of Christianity, whose letters determine much of Christian theology.

Acts tells us that Peter was led to the Roman centurion Cornelius, "a devout man who feared God" (10:2). On the way to Cornelius's house, Peter has a vision instructing him that nothing created by God is unclean to eat. Given Jewish kosher eating laws, this would have been a shocking revelation. Upon meeting Cornelius, Peter comes to the realization, "I truly understand that God shows no partiality, but in every nation anyone who fears him and does what is right is acceptable to him" (10:34–35). As Peter continues talking, the Holy Spirit fills everyone in the house, and Peter baptizes all the members of the household. This practice of baptizing and admitting Gentiles who were not formally Jewish was new for the newly forming community. Adjustments for Gentiles proved to be very controversial.

THE APOSTLE PAUL (c. 5–64 CE)

One of the most important events in the life of the early church was the conversion of a Pharisee named Saul to the Jesus movement. Saul is a Hebrew name, and he is better known by its Greek equivalent, **Paul**. Paul was born in Tarsus, Asia Minor (Turkey), to devout Jewish parents. They must have been prominent, because at least one of them was a Roman citizen with special rights and privileges. This made Paul a Roman citizen as well. After Paul's birth the family immigrated to Jerusalem, where Paul was raised. At some point he trained under Gamaliel, the most famous rabbi of the time. Paul was a zealous Jew and, along with most members of the Sanhedrin, believed the Jesus movement to be heretical, that is, religiously false.

With the authority to interrogate and arrest members of the movement, Paul received permission to travel to Damascus, where many Jews believed in Jesus. According to Acts, on the way to Damascus Paul encounters the risen Lord: "Now as he was going along and approaching Damascus, suddenly a light from heaven flashed around him. He fell to the ground and heard a voice saying to him, 'Saul, Saul, why do you persecute me?' He asked, 'Who are you, Lord.' The reply

came, 'I am Jesus, whom you are persecuting. But get up and enter the city, and you will be told what you are to do'" (9:3). At that moment, Paul becomes blind and has to be led into the city. In Damascus, the risen Jesus instructs a disciple named Ananias to seek Paul out and baptize him. Ananias is alarmed, given that Paul has persecuted members of the church in Jerusalem and has come to Damascus to arrest believers there, but Jesus tells him, "Go, for he is an instrument whom I have chosen to bring my name before Gentiles and kings and before the people of Israel" (9:15). Upon meeting Ananias, Paul is baptized and his blindness leaves him. Afterward, he begins "to proclaim Jesus in the synagogues, saying, 'He is the Son of God'" (9:19–20).

According to Acts, Paul is so bold in his proclamations that fellow believers fear for his life. He returns to Jerusalem and is introduced to the believing community there. As in Damascus, Paul speaks publicly about Jesus as the messiah and Son of God. Soon, he is taken to the coast and goes to Tarsus. Clearly one of the most important missionaries to the early movement, Paul produced many letters to which scholars look, along with Acts, to understand his missionary agenda. Typically, they assign him with three missionary journeys, all of which concentrated on modern-day Turkey and Greece.

Upon arriving in a new city, Paul's strategy was to go to the synagogues there to proclaim Jesus as the messiah. Paul's success in converting Jews was mixed. On a few occasions Acts tells us that many Jews came to the faith, yet on most occasions he was decidedly opposed by the majority of Jews in the cities where he preached. He tended to be most successful with God-fearers. Like Peter and other apostles, he not only was a bold proclaimer of Jesus but also had the power to heal. This power represented evidence of the Holy Spirit and a sign of the kingdom of God.

PAUL, THE EARLY CHURCH, AND THE JUDAIZERS

Soon most Christian communities had both Jewish and Gentile believers. Given that Jesus

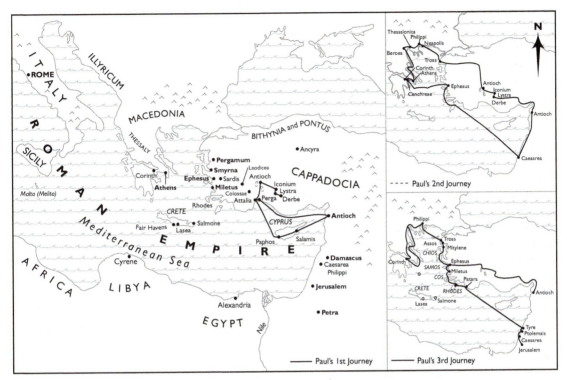

FIGURE 4-3 Paul's missionary journeys: Paul's four missionary journeys, the last of which was taken as a prisoner heading to his trial in Rome.

was a Jew and was viewed as the Jewish messiah; that no one imagined he had started a new, separate religion; and that all of his early believers were Jews, the question of Gentiles became more imperative: What should the movement demand of Gentile believers? Did they have to become Jewish like Jesus and his disciples? The problem came to a head when members of the Jerusalem community went to Antioch, where a large number of both Gentile and Jewish believers had met, and demanded that all Gentiles take on the whole of the Law of Moses (Torah) and, if male, be circumcised. Scholars have named this Christian contingent the **Judaizers**, that is, those who demanded Gentiles become Jews in order to join the faith. Paul and his fellow missionary Barnabas went to Jerusalem to settle the matter. The subsequent meeting that took place there is known as the **Council of Jerusalem**.

Acts describes this meeting as relatively quickly resolved. Paul and Barnabas testify to the dramatic conversions of Gentiles and how they have been welcomed by Jewish believers throughout many communities without requiring that they take up the Law. The missionaries are countered by Pharisee believers, who insist that every member has to take on the whole of the Law. Then Peter speaks about how God does not seem to make distinctions among Jews and Gentiles in giving the Holy Spirit. James, the head of the Jerusalem church who was not an original apostle but is called "the brother of the Lord" (Gal. 1:19), then pronounces his definitive decision: "We should not trouble those Gentiles who are turning to God, but we should write them to abstain only from things polluted by idols and from fornication and from whatever has been strangled and from blood" (15:19–20).

"BROTHERS OF THE LORD"

Mark records that Jesus had brothers and sisters (3:32), and Paul says that other missionaries were "brothers of the Lord" (1 Cor. 9:5). Further, James, the head of the Jerusalem church, is said to have been one of Jesus's brothers (Gal. 1:19). Most Protestant and Evangelical Christians take this identification at face value, while Roman Catholic and Eastern Orthodox Christians insist that Mary gave birth only to Jesus. Either position is possible, as "brother" or "sister" could mean many things, from blood sibling to step-sibling, imagining Mary's husband Joseph could have been a widower with previous children. The term could even refer to close relatives who were integrated into the family.

What does such a decision mean? In Roman cultural practice, some butchers sacrificed animals to gods and then sold this meat in the marketplace. This would surely have been religiously tainted meat from a Jewish point of view. Additionally, the basic **kosher** laws proscribed the consumption of strangled animals and, because it was considered the life force of an animal, their blood. Thus, Jewish kosher laws required that animals be bled in their slaughter. The demand for sexual purity seems obvious and even unnecessary. What the Jerusalem Council decided, then, was that Gentiles did not have to become Jews, but they did have to avoid basic immorality and meat preparation that was particularly odious to Jews.

Acts describes the controversy about Gentiles and the Law as settled by the Council, and never mentions it again. But other texts show that the dispute was not settled nearly as cleanly as, or at least with the clarity that, Acts portrays. Paul wrote one of his most important letters, the Letter to the Galatians, to deal with the controversy that later reemerged on this issue. Some Jewish believers among the communities of Galatia were again demanding that Gentiles take on the whole of the Law. In this epistle Paul reminds them that the Jerusalem Council has already decided this question. He then recounts that he met Peter after the Council in Antioch and "opposed him to his face, because he stood self-condemned. For until certain people came from James, he used to eat with Gentiles. But after they came, he drew back and kept himself separate for fear of the circumcision faction. And the other Jews joined him in this hypocrisy" (Gal. 2:11–13). Paul then said to him publicly, "If you,

though a Jew, live like a Gentile, and not like a Jew, how can you compel the Gentiles to live like Jews?" (Gal. 2:14).

Peter apparently believed that he could violate the kosher laws for the sake of table fellowship with Gentile believers. This itself was controversial for a Jew. What is most striking is that Paul mentions representatives from James, the Jerusalem leader who in Acts decides Gentiles do not have to adopt the Law. Of course, the ostensible problem here is Peter's violating kosher. But Paul sees the James faction as influencing Peter to "compel the Gentiles to live like Jews." They are part of the "circumcision faction," that is, Judaizers who are insisting that Gentiles take on the Law. Apparently the controversy was not fully cleared up or the decision universally embraced.

We cannot underestimate the importance of this issue. If Gentiles had been forced to adopt the Law, many of them would probably not have done so, as they hadn't before. They would have remained a Christian version of God-fearers and not fully part of the community. This would apparently have undermined the work of the Holy Spirit, who empowered these Gentiles without resort to the Law. It would also have made the movement little more than a small sect of Judaism. If Christianity was to really represent a movement of universal salvation, then the Law would be an extraordinary liability among Gentiles. The decision, when fully embraced by the whole church, allowed Christianity to become truly universal.

PAUL'S LETTERS

About a quarter of the New Testament is made up of Paul's letters, either to communities he had spent time with or knew or to individuals he knew well. All of them were *occasional* letters, that is, they were occasioned by a controversy Paul wanted to address or questions the community members had that he wanted to answer. This makes trying to understand Paul's theology rather difficult. None of these texts is a doctrinal treatise in which Paul lays out a clear, complete understanding of the Christian faith. An understanding of Paul would have to be ferreted out by looking at some of Paul's repeated themes and the theological commitments that underlie them. Of the thirteen letters attributed to Paul, many are disputed today as not being directly from Paul himself. Letters attributed to him include Romans, First and Second Corinthians, Galatians, Ephesians, Philippians, Colossians, First and Second Thessalonians, First and Second Timothy, Titus, and Philemon; they are ordered this way in the New Testament not according to when they were written or to whom, but merely according to their size, with Romans being the longest letter and Philemon the shortest. Among these, the disputed letters are Ephesians, Colossians, Second Thessalonians, First and Second Timothy, and Titus.

In the ancient world, writing under someone else's name was not necessarily considered bad form. A disciple might consider it appropriate to write in the name of his master. It might even be seen as presumptuous to write under one's own name when one was continuing the legacy of the master. On the other hand, it was a controversial practice, and Paul himself recognized that others might be writing in his name and not with his permission. While he used a secretary to actually pen his dictated letters, he often made sure to authenticate many letters by personally signing off on them (see Gal. 6:11; 1 Cor. 16:21; Col. 4:18; 2 Thess. 3:17; Philem. 19). Ironically, two of these five, Colossians and Second Thessalonians are disputed, meaning that some scholars think someone other than Paul signed Paul's name!

There are different reasons for challenging the authorship of some of these letters. Ephesians and Colossians appear to reflect a theology close to that found in Paul's undisputed letters, but that theology is more advanced and seems to represent a second layer of reflection after Paul. First and Second Timothy and Titus seem to reflect a more settled church, one concerned with church order and structure that backtracks some of the earliest church's practices. For example, the early church had deaconesses and women missionaries whom Paul commends, and he even refers to Junia as "prominent among the apostles" (Rom 16:1-7). Further, Paul recognizes women who pray and prophesy in the assembly (1 Cor. 11:5). But in First Timothy we find that women are required to be silent, that the role of deacon is now reserved for men (2:11-12; 3:8-13), and that the role of bishop or overseer in a community is now a bona fide church "office" (3:1). Finally, in Paul's undisputed letters he uses the term "faith" to represent entrusting oneself to God, while in First and Second Timothy and Titus the term is also used as an expression of doctrine or even to represent the whole of one's religion. In short, these texts seem to reflect a more established church with some settled doctrine.

PAUL'S THEOLOGY

As mentioned in the previous section, Paul's theology is never laid out clearly in some kind of doctrinal treatise. Rather, one discovers it through letters occasioned by questions or controversies. Paul does, however, have a theology. The earliest central Christian message, or **kerygma**, had just a few articles of belief: (1) Jesus came in fulfillment of the Old Testament promises; (2) Jesus performed mighty deeds and preached the emergent kingdom of God; (3) according to God's plan, he was crucified on the cross and died; (4) God raised him from the dead and made him Lord and Christ; (5) these events call for the repentance of sins, being baptized in the name of Jesus, and receiving his gift of the Holy Spirit. There is no question that Paul believed all of these tenets; he also, however, believed in much more.

While the Gospels were concerned with the specific teachings of Jesus, Paul shows little concern for such matters in his letters. Perhaps in part this is because his audience already knew many of these stories, but mostly it is because Paul's interest is focused on who Jesus is, how Jesus saves, and how Christians should live the faith.

Regarding Jesus's identity, Paul principally draws on two streams of Jewish thought. The first is that of Wisdom, a preexistent creative power of God through which the universe was created. Paul writes, "There is one God, the Father, from whom are all things and for whom we exist, and one Lord, Jesus Christ, through whom are all things and through whom we exist" (1 Cor. 8:6). To Paul, Jesus "is the image of the invisible God, the firstborn of all creation; for in him all things in heaven and on earth were created . . . all things have been created through him and for him" (Col. 1:15–16). While he is not the Father (God), still "in him the whole fullness of deity dwells bodily" (Col. 2:9).

The second stream of Jewish thought in Paul's theology is that of an anticipated preexistent messiah who will come to redeem God's chosen ones: "But when the fullness of time had come, God sent his Son, born of a woman, born under the law, in order to redeem those who were under the law" (Gal. 4:4–5). As redeemer, God sent Christ (the messiah) "to gather up all things in him, things in heaven and on earth" (Eph. 1:10). Paul's vision of Christ is utterly cosmic: "When all things are subjected to him, then the Son himself will also be subjected to the one who put all things in subjection under him, so that God may be all in all" (1 Cor. 15:28). It seems that the "Father," whom Paul also simply calls God, has the ultimate priority, while Christ works to carry out God's cosmic plan of salvation. But as we saw previously, Christ is not merely a human worker; he is an expression of God himself, or at least of God's presence.

Central to Paul's message is the activity of the Holy Spirit. Paul distinguishes the Holy Spirit from the Father and the Son, but also blurs their distinctions. For Paul, the Holy Spirit is something like the sanctifying presence of Christ. In some cases, he describes the Spirit as a gift from the risen Lord. The Holy Spirit is the vehicle for receiving the love of God (Rom. 5:5). It makes Christians holy (Rom. 15:16), reveals God (1 Cor. 2:10, 13), and guides Christian souls (Gal. 5:18). While the fullness of Christian life is union with God in heaven, the gift of the Holy Spirit in believers' hearts is the "first installment" of that existence (1 Cor. 1:22; 2 Cor. 5:5), already transforming believers (2 Cor. 3:18; Gal. 5:22).

In other cases Paul seems to even identify Christ himself with the Holy Spirit: "Now the Lord is the Spirit" (2 Cor. 3:17). Consider this fascinating passage: "But you are not in the flesh; you are in the Spirit, since the Spirit of God dwells in you. Anyone who does not have the Spirit of Christ does not belong to him. But if Christ is in you, though the body is dead because of sin, the Spirit is life because of righteousness. If the Spirit of him who raised Jesus from the dead dwells in you, he who raised Christ from the dead will give life to your mortal bodies also through his Spirit that dwells in you" (Rom. 8:9–11). Here we see a complete blurring of Father, Son, and Holy Spirit. Initially, the Spirit is the Spirit of God (Father). In the next sentence, the Spirit is identified with Christ. Then, this same Spirit is identified either with the Father who raised Jesus or as separate from the Father who apparently raised Jesus. This same Spirit is finally said to reside in believers and again is identified as Christ within.

Does Paul have a clear Trinitarian theology: one God—Father, Son, and Holy Spirit—in three persons (or relations)? This Christian doctrine would be centuries in the making. In one sense, Paul's metaphysics seem confused. Are Christ, the Father, and the Holy Spirit the same reality? Seemingly not, but their identities are conflated.

PAUL'S SOTERIOLOGY: HOW CHRISTIANS ARE SAVED

Soteriology is the reflection on salvation: how are humans saved, and from what? For a devout Jew who believed in the last judgment, as many first-century Jews did, salvation came from God and was given to those who were just. Jews were to "be holy, for I [God] am holy" (Lev. 11:45). The way to be holy was to follow the Law. When one sinned and fell from holiness, one could atone for those sins by sacrifice and be assured of God's forgiveness. The commandments of God were understood not as an odious burden, but as an opportunity to live God's holiness. Perhaps the greatest witness to the Law is Psalm 119, in which the Law is celebrated as a delight for Jews and a way to be intimate with God. "I love your law!" (vs. 97) the Psalmist proclaims, "I long for your commandments" (vs. 131), which have been "established . . . forever" (vs. 152). Recalling Jesus's Sermon on the Mount, introduced in Chapter Three, Jesus appears to reflect this view:

> Do not think that I have come to abolish the law or the prophets. I have come not to abolish but to fulfill. For truly I tell you, until heaven and earth pass away, not one letter, not one stroke of the letter, will pass from the law until all is accomplished. Therefore, whoever breaks one of the least of these commandments, and teaches others to do the same, will be called least in the kingdom of heaven; but whoever does them and teaches them will be called great in the kingdom of heaven. (Matt. 5:17–19)

In this sermon, Jesus reflects on some broad commandments, such as the prohibitions on murder and adultery, only to demand that one's heart be free from anger and lust. In this way he does not abrogate or nullify the commandments, but rather demands utter interior purity of heart so as to expand their requirements.

Of central importance for Paul is how humans are saved, and his most important consideration is what it means to be justified before God. **Justification** (*dikaioun*) means many things, such as being aligned (a justified margin), being acquitted in a court of law, or being made upright or righteous (just). Paul believed that to be saved, one has to be justified before God. Further, one's salvation requires that one understand justification correctly. Paul sometimes even uses "justification" as synonymous with salvation itself. In one classic

line from Romans, he teaches that righteousness will be reckoned to Christians "who believe in him who raised Jesus our Lord from the dead, who was handed over to death for our trespasses and was raised for our justification" (Rom. 3:24–25). In this one passage we see two important aspects of justification. The first is that Jesus died for our trespasses, or sins. Recall from Chapter Two that a central component of Judaism at this time was sacrifice to God. These sacrifices were offered for several reasons, including to ratify covenants, to atone for sins, and to obtain communion with God. Early Christians saw Jesus's death on the cross as involving all of these. The new covenant that he proclaimed at the Last Supper was ratified by his sacrifice on the cross. This sacrifice was also a **sacrificial atonement** for sins: Jesus died for our sins. We see this belief not only in Paul but also in the Gospels. Mark, the earliest Gospel, records Jesus as saying, "For the Son of Man came not to be served but to serve, and to give his life a ransom for many" (10:45). In John's Gospel, John the Baptist identifies Jesus as "the Lamb of God who takes away the sin of the world!" (2:29). Finally, Christians have traditionally thought of Jesus's death on the cross as a communion sacrifice, one that brings intimacy with God.

While Paul addresses all three understandings of sacrifice in his letters, in the Romans passage cited previously he emphasizes atonement. Here the resurrection becomes crucial. The cross effects God's forgiveness and the atonement for sin, and the resurrection breaks the bonds of death, allowing salvation. In First Corinthians Paul says that "if Christ has not been raised, then our proclamation has been in vain and your faith has been in vain. . . . Christ has been raised from the dead, the first fruits of those who have died. . . . [F]or as all die in Adam, so all will be made alive in Christ" (13:14–22). In short, it is the death and resurrection of Jesus that condition freedom from sin and justification, which for Paul includes salvation in heaven.

We might consider here that we have something of a clash of theologies. On the one hand, Jews believed that following the Mosaic Law justified them before God, and Jesus himself seemed to preach the Law's necessity, even as its fullness required a complete spiritual renewal on an interior level. On the other hand, Paul says that Jesus's death on the cross and resurrection offered justification and salvation. Compounding this problem is the experience of the early church regarding Gentiles who converted without reference to the Law, and its decision that these Gentiles need not adopt the Mosaic Law. In light of this, what does one make of the Law? If the Law actually justified followers, then what was the point of Jesus?

THE LETTER TO THE GALATIANS

Paul wrote his letter to the Galatians as a response to the controversy over Gentiles and the Law, which he thought was settled. Some Jewish believers among the churches in Galatia (Asia Minor) were demanding that Gentiles adopt the Law. In this text Paul reminds them of the decision of the Jerusalem Council and recalls that Titus, a fellow missionary and Gentile, was never required to take on the Law by the leaders in Jerusalem. Paul could have ended his letter here, insisting that everyone in Galatia accept the decision of the Jerusalem Council. But he goes on to interpret Jewish salvation history.

This is Paul's basic argument: God gave Israel two covenants, one to Abraham and one to Moses on Mount Sinai. In the first covenant, God made promises to Abraham and his offspring, the offspring being singular. Some 430 years later God made a covenant with Moses and the people of Israel, represented by the Law. But this second covenant did not annul the first one. Rather, it was an intermediary covenant for the period before the fulfillment of the first covenant. Christ is that offspring anticipated in God's first covenant. Now that Christ has come, the first covenant has been fulfilled and enters back in force, while the second one is annulled.

What, then, was the purpose of the second covenant with Moses, the one that established the Law? Paul argues that it was a provisional covenant, comparing it to a "disciplinarian" waiting for the time of faith. The Greek word for disciplinarian is *paedagogos*, which could refer to a teacher or even a servant who raises children on behalf of wealthy owners. In short, the Law trained Jews in holiness and kept Judaism in line until it came of age. Now that it is of age, it no longer needs a *paedagogos*. Now, Paul says, we who are co-heirs with Christ have received the gift—Christ—promised to Abraham and his offspring: "My point is this: heirs as long as they are minors, are not better than slaves, though they are owners of all the property; but they remain under guardians and trustees until the date set by the father. So with us. . . . But when the fullness of time had come, God sent his Son, born of a woman, born under the law, in order to redeem those who were under the law, so that we might receive adoption as children" (4:1–5). Positively, the Law taught and trained Jews for holiness and kept them in order, much like a *paedagogos* would an underage child. Negatively, the Law was something of an enslavement, a condition in which one was not truly free to receive one's inheritance. To continue to embrace the Law not only would keep one essentially enslaved, but would also renounce one's true inheritance. Embracing the Law for Paul becomes tantamount to rejecting the actual justification of Christ now available.

Paul then uses an allegory to bring home the difference between being a slave and being a free person. He contrasts Abraham's two sons, Ishmael, born of the slave Hagar, and Isaac, born of the free woman Sarah. He associates the Law with Ishmael, who did not receive the covenantal promises, and the life of Christ with Isaac, who did. In short, the Law is slavery, while Christ is freedom. This is less an argument than an image to convey two choices for the Galatians, and indeed for all Christians: Are you choosing slavery and rejecting Christ, or are you choosing freedom and accepting Christ's justification? "For freedom Christ has set us free," Paul argues. "Stand firm, therefore, and do not submit again to a yoke of slavery. . . . You who want to be justified by the law have cut yourselves off from Christ; you have fallen from grace" (5:1–4).

Paul understands God's **grace** as God's favor, God's saving gift of himself, and God's life within the individual. God gives humans salvation as a free gift. The condition for receiving that gift is faith, that is, entrusting oneself fully to God. While Paul does not use the terms "grace," "faith," or "justification" perfectly consistently, this is his fundamental message. Trying to justify oneself by works of the Law is in his view a rejection of God's grace, a faith in one's own works and not in God's free gift; it is a pseudo-justification. In contrast, *justification by grace through faith* allows one to receive God's salvation and places one in a position of dependence on God; this is how one is justified.

Paul ends his letter by telling the Galatians that freedom consists in the life of the Spirit; otherwise one would be enslaved to one's sins: "For you were called to freedom brothers and sisters; only do not use your freedom as an opportunity for self-indulgence" (5:13). Paul's rhetorical devices include the regular alignment of terms: law–slavery–flesh–passions and grace–freedom–spirit–service in love. The former group promises nothing but sin, while the second offers life in the Spirit: "Now the fruit of the spirit is love, joy, peace, patience, kindness, generosity, faithfulness, gentleness, and self-control. There is no law against such things. And those who belong to Christ Jesus have crucified the flesh with its passions and desires. If we live by the Spirit, let us also be guided by the Spirit" (5:22–25).

Was Paul then challenging Jesus's teaching, particularly his Sermon on the Mount? Possibly, and there is no evidence that Jesus interpreted the covenants in the way Paul did. On the other hand, Paul could respond that he extended the message of Jesus's sermon to its final implication, that is, to an inner renewal and life in the Spirit in which the essence of the commandments was now embraced robustly through the life of the Spirit: "Circumcision [taking on the Law] is nothing, and uncircumcision [letting go of the Law] is nothing; but obeying the commandments of God is everything" (1 Cor. 7:19); "For it is we who are the circumcision, who

worship in the Spirit of God and boast in Christ Jesus" (Phil. 3:3); "Owe no one anything, except to love one another; for the one who loves another has fulfilled the law" (Rom. 13:8).

In short order, Paul nullified the Law not just for Gentiles—the outcome of the Jerusalem Council—but for Jews too. The Law was now declared obsolete. What is interesting is that there is no evidence that other contemporary Christian leaders taught Paul's interpretation of the two covenants. In fact, it appears obvious that the Jerusalem Council assumed that Jewish Christians would continue to follow the Law of Moses, while Gentile Christians did not have to. Paul himself appears to have lived out his life according to standard Jewish practices—which we may call the Law—as did his contemporary Jewish apostles. His fundamental point was that the Law simply did not justify individuals, and that those using it *in order* to be justified not only failed to be justified but ultimately rejected Christ's free gift of saving grace. Paul's interpretation of the nullification of the Law—that its provisional time had ended—sowed the seeds for the Jesus movement's separation from its Jewish roots. It was the theological start of a new religion.

THE END OF PAUL'S LIFE

We learn of the last days of Paul through the Acts of the Apostles. Paul's last journey to Jerusalem was fateful. He and several companions had sailed from Cyprus to Syria and intended to go on to Jerusalem, where they planned to bring donations from many other churches throughout Greece and Asia Minor in order to provide help during a famine then occurring in Palestine. In the port cities of Tyre and Caesarea, many of Paul's friends cautioned him against going to Jerusalem, but he was determined. Once in Jerusalem, he met with James and other elders of the Jerusalem church. There was a great deal of anguish among many believers upon hearing that Paul had told Jewish believers to no longer follow the Law. Paul went through a rite of purification that included sacrifice in the Temple, and the leaders of the Jerusalem church insisted that the rule was for Jews to continue following the Law, even while Gentiles did not have to. Indeed, they insisted that this was Paul's position too.

Reading Galatians alone, one would get the impression that the rumors about Paul were true, that he did teach that the Law had been displaced, even for Jewish believers. Paul might have thought that the Law was still the way Jewish believers ought to live in the sense that it was a religiously skillful way of being a Jewish believer; however, his principal point was that the Law was not connected to justification. In response, some Jews who were not believers in Jesus seized him in the Temple precincts and accused him of teaching against the Law. While they were beating Paul, Roman soldiers intervened and arrested him. Taken before the Roman tribune, Paul defended himself, saying that he was a Jew in good standing, had been educated by the great rabbi Gamaliel, and was an adherent of the Law. He then offered an account of his conversion experience. About to be flogged by the tribune, he insisted that he was a Roman citizen and therefore had a right to formal Roman legal proceedings.

The next day, the tribune had Paul stand before the Jewish Sanhedrin, and Paul began his defense by saying that he was a Pharisee and merely on trial for professing the resurrection of the dead. Recall that such a belief was controversial: many Jews of the first century, especially within the Pharisee party, did hope for the resurrection of the dead, but many Jewish leaders among the Sadducees rejected this idea. What Paul did was instigate an intra-Jewish debate. The tribune, thinking Paul would be ambushed by the mob, took him away to the barracks as a kind of safety arrest. Fearing for Paul's life, he then sent him to Felix, the governor of Judea, who resided in Caesarea. While Paul was in Caesarea, the Jewish high priest Ananias, along with some Temple elders, went to Felix and accused Paul of agitating Jews "and a ringleader of the sect of the Nazarenes" (24:5). Felix wanted Paul to return to Jerusalem for trial; believing that such an event would seal his fate, Paul appealed as a Roman citizen to the emperor's tribunal in Rome.

Felix ultimately passed Paul on to Festus, who would become the next governor. Soon King Agrippa, ruler of Galilee and grandson of Herod the Great, involved himself in Paul's trial. In Acts, Agrippa makes an interesting aside to Festus: "This man could have been set free if he had not appealed to the emperor" (26:32). Ultimately Paul went to Rome for trial, where he stayed with some freedom of movement for the next two years. Unchallenged tradition has it that Paul lost this final trial and was martyred in Rome. At the end of the first century, Clement of Rome offered the following witness:

> Because of jealousy and strife Paul showed the way to the prize for patient endurance. After he had been seven times in chains, had been driven into exile, had been stoned, and had preached in the east and in the west, he won the genuine glory for his faith, having taught righteousness to the whole world and having reached the farthest limits of the west. Finally, when he had given his testimony before the rulers, he thus departed from the world and went to the holy place, having become an outstanding example of patient endurance.[1]

CONCLUSIONS

The early church believed to the point of martyrdom that Jesus of Nazareth was not only the messiah, but also the Son of God who had been raised and glorified. It continued to proclaim the kingdom of God as Jesus had, but with an emphasis on Jesus as the inaugurator of that kingdom and the sender of the Holy Spirit as a means of empowering his followers to live out that kingdom. While seemingly distinguishing Jesus from God, the church applied divine authority to him that was striking. Paul was the most decisive and important member of this early church in terms of church history and theology. Not only was Paul a successful evangelist, he was also the first Christian theologian, and Christian theology follows Paul's understanding of justification, grace, and the figure of Christ as cosmic Lord. Despite the confusion in the early church about the requirements for Jews and Gentiles for membership, Paul's theology of Jesus's covenant as a fulfillment of God's promises to Abraham and his position that the Law was no longer in effect became consolidated doctrine for Christianity. If Paul was a controversial figure in his day among the members of the early church, he became the standard bearer of what Christianity ought to look like. Paul's influence on Christian thought and practice simply cannot be overstated.

SUMMARY QUESTIONS

- What were the major doctrinal issues early Christian believers faced, and what were some of their most impending social pressures?
- Which Pauline letters are disputed regarding authorship, and what are the reasons for disputing them?
- What was the significance of the issue regarding whether Gentile converts had to uphold the Jewish Law?
- What are the main doctrines in Paul's theology?
- How did Paul argue that Christ's covenant supervened the Mosaic Law?

DISCUSSION QUESTIONS

- Some of Jesus's ministry was apocalyptic and seemed to understand the end of the world was imminent. The preaching of the apostles seems to support this. Given that the end of the world did not happen in the first century, what ought one to make of this kind of preaching? How does your reasoning then address the fact that some Christians today think that the end of the world is imminent?
- The council of Jerusalem decided that Gentiles did not have to take on the Jewish law (Torah), but certainly presumed that fellow Jewish believers would continue. Does then Paul's argument that the time of the law for everyone is over contradict this? How might Paul defend himself against this claim?
- The author sees Paul as both distinguishing and blurring distinctions among God, the Holy Spirit, and Jesus Christ, even that "Paul's metaphysics seems confused." If this is correct, what does this say about biblical inspiration? What does it imply about using the Bible to derive secure Christian doctrines?

KEY TERMS

Council of Jerusalem	Justification	Peter
God-fearers	Kerygma	Sacrificial atonement
Grace	Kosher	Soteriology
Judaizers	Paul	

BIBLIOGRAPHY

- Di Berarndino, Angelo, ed. 1992. *Encyclopedia of Early Christianity.* Trans. Adrian Walford. New York: Oxford University Press.
- Ellis, Peter. 1982. *Seven Pauline Letters.* Collegeville, MN: Liturgical Press.
- Holmes, Michael W., trans. and ed. 2006. *The Apostolic Fathers,* 3rd ed. Grand Rapids, MI: Baker Academic.

- Johnson, Luke Timothy. 2011. *Prophetic Jesus, Prophetic Church: The Challenge of Luke-Acts to Contemporary Christians*. Grand Rapids, MI: Eerdmans.
- Metzger, Bruce, and Roland Murphy, eds. 1991. *The New Oxford Annotated Bible with Apocrypha*. New York: Oxford University Press.
- Nolan, Albert. 1992. *Jesus Before Christianity*. Maryknoll, NY: Orbis Books.
- Perrin, Norman, and Dennis Duling. 1982. *The New Testament: An Introduction*, 2nd ed. San Diego: Harcourt Brace Jovanovich.
- Stowers, Stanley. 1996. *Rereading of Romans: Justice, Jews, and Gentiles*. New Haven, CT: Yale University Press.
- Tobin, Thomas. 1987. *The Spirituality of Paul*. Collegeville, MN: Michael Glazier.
- White, Michael. 2004. *From Jesus to Christianity*. San Francisco: HarperSanFrancisco.

NOTE

1. Holmes, *Apostolic Fathers*, 45.

5

Christianity Becomes a Religion

Timeline

c. 90 CE	Expulsion of Christian Jews from synagogues
94–96 CE	Persecution of Christians under Emperor Domitian
115 CE	Ignatius, bishop of Antioch, martyred
165 CE	Martyrdom of Justin in Rome
c. 180 CE	Irenaeus, bishop of Lyons, writes a treatise against gnostics
249–251 CE	Persecution of Christians under Emperor Decius
257–260 CE	Persecution of Christians under Emperor Valerian
258 CE	Martyrdom of Cyprian, bishop of Carthage
260–340 CE	Life of Eusebius, father of church history
303–305 CE	Persecution of Christians under Emperor Diocletian
311 CE	Emperor Galerius issues the Edict of Toleration, which allows freedom of religion throughout the Roman Empire

WHAT TO EXPECT

This chapter discusses the historical circumstances that led to the belief in Jesus becoming a separate religion from Judaism, the religion of Jesus and his early followers. As Judaism became less pluralistic and Christians became more sociologically distinct from Jews, the separation of these strands of thought into two different religions happened relatively quickly. What, then, *is* Christianity? In its early years, there were competing interpretations, those that inclined to interpreting Jesus's ministry along lines similar to Greek mystery religions and those that eventually consolidated into an early version of what has become standard Christianity. As a unique religion, Christianity also had to deal with persecutions from the Roman Empire and formulate strategies to defend itself as an intellectually legitimate faith.

FROM JUDAISM TO CHRISTIANITY

The primitive church understood itself as thoroughly Jewish. Jesus was Jewish and proclaimed a kingdom of God that drew entirely on various Old Testament themes. He was proclaimed the messiah, an exclusively Jewish term that represented being anointed by God, typically as a Jewish monarch. All of Jesus's disciples were Jewish, as were those to whom he principally preached. Thus, when we think of Saint Paul's conversion, we should imagine not so much a conversion from Judaism into a new religion called "Christianity," as a transition from the rejection of Jesus as the messiah to the conviction that Jesus was indeed both the messiah and the savior, and even the cosmic Christ. As Paul argues in Galatians, Jesus is the fulfillment of the promises God made to Abraham, the Jewish patriarch. Paul makes this clear in his letter to the Romans: "I ask then, has God rejected his people? By no means! I myself am an Israelite, a descendant of Abraham" (11:1). Later in this passage Paul provides the image of Israel as the tree of salvation onto which Gentiles are grafted (11:17–24). At this time Gentiles were seen as being able to gain salvation, but this was still viewed as an entirely Jewish salvation. Between Paul's martyrdom (c. 64 CE) and the beginning of the second century, however, Christianity did indeed become a new religion. How did this happen, and why?

One of the most decisive events in the history of Judaism became one of the most crucial in the emergence of Christianity as a separate religion: the Jewish Revolt and the fall of the Temple. In 66 CE, Palestinian Jews revolted against Roman rule and retook Jerusalem and Galilee. While the rebellion was initially successful, ultimately the Roman general Vespasian invaded Judea with four legions and, with his son Titus, quashed the rebellion. In doing so, the Romans destroyed the Temple. Recall the four Jewish groups discussed in Chapter Three: Sadducees, Zealots, Essenes, and Pharisees. Three of these four leading groups did not survive the counterattack. The Sadducees

were aligned with the noble class and priesthood, which were destroyed in the war. The Essenes did not participate in the revolt, but this did not stop the Romans from destroying them as well. The Zealots, as the principal revolutionary group in Israel, certainly lost their members in the war. The only religious group that did survive was the Pharisee party, as it was not formally part of the religious institution or Temple. It is the Pharisees who reconstituted the Jewish faith exclusively around the Torah. Though the Jews no longer had the Temple, they still had the *temple of the Torah*. Modern Judaism finds its roots in the Pharisees' revision of Judaism into what is now called **Rabbinic Judaism.**

The vast majority of Pharisees, along with the majority of Jews, did not believe Jesus was the messiah, much less savior of the world. Under Pharisee leadership, Judaism became a religion of the synagogue, and by the late first century it was policy in Palestine, if not more widely, that proclaiming Jesus as the messiah was heresy, a false belief that kept believers in Jesus from participating in synagogue worship. The separation between this now-orthodox Jewish position and the stance of Jews who believed in Jesus is reflected in the Gospels. Jesus was ultimately tried and convicted of insurrection by the Roman authorities, but the Gospel narratives emphasize the Jewish responsibility: "His blood be on us and our children," the crowds announce in Matthew (27:25). In John's Gospel the crowds even threaten the governor Pilate in a way that seems exaggerated: "If you release this man, you are no friend of the emperor" (19:12). We also see something odd in John's Gospel that surely represents the experience of the Jewish believers in Jesus in the late first century. In this account Jesus heals a blind man in the Temple and the Pharisees question his parents, who do not cooperate, because they are "afraid of the Jews, for the Jews had already agreed that anyone who confessed Jesus to be the Messiah would be put out of the synagogue" (9:22). This decision would not have been made until after the Jewish Revolt. We also see here the composite term "the Jews." Throughout John's Gospel Jesus and the narrator use language that distinguishes his followers from "the Jews," as though they are not themselves Jewish, which of course they all were.

Even where this policy of eliminating believers in Jesus from the synagogue was not in force, we might also imagine a natural shifting of loyalties and communities. Imagine being Jewish and believing in Jesus as the messiah. Not only would there have been antipathy to such beliefs in the synagogue, which must have been painful for Jewish believers in Jesus, one would also have met with Jesus believers on Sunday to share fellowship and celebrate the Eucharist, or Lord's Supper. This new community had its own leadership, its own framework of mutual support in belief in Jesus, its own rituals, and, increasingly, its own scripture. It simply drew Jewish believers to a new community of faith.

Another important factor in the divergence was that faith in Jesus tended to undermine the prominence of the Torah, or Law. Recall that the Jerusalem Council decided that Gentiles did not have to follow the Torah, but were acceptable without it. Implicitly, then, the Law was seen as having nothing to do with salvation. The Law represented Jewish identity and piety, and it constituted the covenant that allowed Jews to "be holy as I [God] am holy" (Lev. 11:45). As time passed holiness was divorced from the Law. As noted in the last chapter, Paul even taught that the time of the Law was over now that Jesus had come. Consider this provocative statement: "For through the law I died to the law, so that I might live to God. . . . If justification comes through the law, then Christ died for nothing" (Gal. 2:19–21).

An additional factor in the creation of Christianity as a separate religion was simply sociological. In terms of sheer numbers Christianity was becoming a Gentile religion. Initially it was a Jewish reform movement that allowed Gentiles (mostly God-fearers) into its midst. By the end of the first century, however, the percentage of believers had been reversed. Now there was a minority of Jewish believers and a majority of Gentile believers. It looked like and was experienced as a different religious group. The Romans came to see it this way as well, and they did so in a short time frame. The Roman emperor Claudius (r. 41–54 CE) expelled many Jews from Rome for causing disturbances "at the instigation of Chrestus" (Christ). We see here an initial complete association between Jews and Christians. In the rule of Nero (54–68 CE), however, Christians (not Jews) were falsely blamed for a large fire in Rome and were persecuted. In this short time we see the Roman Empire coming to distinguish Christians from Jews.

It may have initially even been advantageous to Christians to be imagined differently. After the Jewish Revolt, the Romans placed on Jews a punitive tax in place of the voluntary contributions Jews had previously made to the Temple. For Roman bureaucrats and citizens alike it was important to know who was Jewish. In separating their identity from Judaism, Christians would not have been forced to pay this tax. On the other hand, Judaism enjoyed the status of an officially recognized religion, one free from any pagan worship. This was an enviable exception, one that Christians would not enjoy for centuries. The separation from Judaism into a bona fide religion on its own shifted the status of Christianity from a *religio licita* (legal religion) to a persecuted one. As we will see in the following section, the Roman law was clear: *Non licet esse Christianos*—it is against the law to be a Christian.

WHAT IS CHRISTIANITY?

GNOSTICISM

We saw in Chapter One that there is an inherent relationship between scripture and tradition, and that the scriptures chosen by Christianity to make up its canon reflected what was believed to be the authentic tradition of the apostles. In early Christianity, it was less clear what the *apostolic tradition* exactly was, including who Jesus was or what his salvation meant. Interpretations of this tradition and of Jesus himself varied wildly. We also saw in Chapter Two that the formation of the canon was a long process and not without some controversy. The term **orthodox** means "right teaching," and **heresy** (literally "choice") refers to false teaching. But who got to decide which beliefs were orthodox and which were heretical? We noted in Chapter Two that there were many Gospels and letters purported to have been written by apostles. In the Nag Hammadi collection we find texts such as *The Gospel of Truth*, *The Gospel of Thomas*, *The Gospel of Philip*, and *The Gospel of Mary*, as well as apocalypses supposedly written by Paul, Peter, and James. Recently, scholars have even uncovered the ancient *Gospel of Judas*. These were just some of the competing texts that existed in the first two centuries of Christianity, and they represent versions of Jesus's ministry and message at odds with the Gospels and other texts that did make it into the canon.

Scholars often call these texts **gnostic**. *Gnosis* is a Greek term that means "knowledge," and an underlying theme in some of these texts is that Jesus came to bring secret divine knowledge to his followers. Even in the canonical literature, we find expressions that point to parts of the gospel that were secret. In Mark Jesus tells his disciples, "To you has been given the secret of the kingdom of God, but for those outside, everything comes in parables" (4:11). Paul also reminds his Christian readers that they have received the mysteries of God that have not been revealed to unbelievers (Eph. 3:9; Col. 2:2; 1 Tim. 3:16), and even that believers have to prove mature enough to receive the fullness of the mysteries of the faith (1 Cor. 3:1-2).

Christian gnosticism ran with this mystery theme. Principally its secret gnosis was twofold: the truth of how the universe was constructed and operated and the realization of one's own spiritual dignity and truth. In such texts Jesus makes the following declarations:

- "If those who lead you say to you, 'See the kingdom is in the sky,' then the birds of the sky will precede you. If they say to you, 'It is in the sea,' then the fish will precede you.

Rather, the kingdom is inside of you, and it is outside of you. When you come to know yourselves, then you will become known, and you will realize that it is you who are the sons of the living father. But if you will not know yourselves you dwell in poverty and it is you who are that poverty." (*Gospel of Thomas*, 3)[1]

- "If one has knowledge, he receives what is his own, and draws it to himself. . . . Whoever is to have knowledge in this way knows where he comes from, and where he is going." (*Gospel of Truth*, 21.11–22.15)[2]

- "Say then from the heart that you are the perfect day, and in you dwells the light that does not fail. . . . For you are the understanding that is drawn forth. . . . Be concerned with yourselves; do not be concerned with other things which you have rejected from yourselves." (*Gospel of Truth*, 32.31–33.14)[3]

- "You saw the spirit, you became the spirit. You saw the Christ, you became the Christ. You saw [the Father, you] shall become Father. . . . You see yourself, and what you see you shall become." (*Gospel of Philip*, 61.29–35)[4]

Both Irenaeus of Lyons (130–202 CE) in his *Against Heresies* and Hippolytus of Rome (170–235 CE) in his *Refutation of All Heresies* identified and attacked no less than thirty-three Christian groups that expressed different versions of Christianity at odds with what they believed was the authentic tradition. Most, if not all, of them were forms of gnosticism. Perhaps the most famous gnostic Christian was Valentinus. Valentinus was classically trained in Alexandria, Egypt, a great intellectual center of the Roman Empire. He came to Rome about 140 CE as a professional teacher and attracted many students. For a while he was a member of the proto-orthodox Christian congregation in Rome, though his theology eventually put him at odds with most of the church at large.

Valentinus's **cosmology**, or understanding of the structure of the universe, was extraordinarily complex and, from a modern sensibility, bizarre.

Yet at the time he had quite a large following. In brief, this is what he taught: The unknowable and transcendent God has a companion called *thought* and fourteen pairs of male–female beings called *aeons* (eternities), which emanated out of that unknown God. Collectively, they make up the spiritual cosmos called the *pleroma* (fullness). This *pleroma* existed before time and represents the spiritual universe. A disruption in the *pleroma* led to the escape of a spiritual substance called *pneuma* (spirit) that was stabilized by being encased in physical bodies. The Jewish God Yahweh is not the true God, but the creator of the material universe, one who created the physical world to trap the escaped *pneuma*. In the fullness of time, the heavenly Christ, one of the *aeons*, sent another being, Jesus, to save the spirits in the trapped bodies by teaching them their true spiritual nature. Realizing their true spiritual nature allowed these beings to return to the *pleroma* and thus be saved. Valentinus believed there were three types of persons. Some were simply physical human beings for whom there would be no salvation, since there was nothing spiritual about them to be saved. Others, presumably ordinary Christians, had a kind of spirit but not a full spirit. These could enjoy a modest version of heaven. Finally, there were the complete spirits, who would return to their greatness in the *pleroma*. These were the gnostics. One reason ordinary Christians did not accept the true teaching, according to Valentinus, was because they were not fully escaped spirits. Thus, the message did not correspond to their spiritual possibilities.

While Valentinus's understanding is only one of the several theories posited in gnosticism, it reveals recurrent themes in the wider movement. One is that the physical world is a tragic entrapment, even something evil. Second, the God of the Old Testament is not the absolute God, but something else, either a creator god who set up the conditions for salvation or a menacing god who created the evil physical world. Third, the way out of the predicament is by Christ through secret knowledge, knowledge that can only be obtained with spiritual practice and secrets shared by gnostic leaders with those who are spiritually mature enough to receive them. Typically, in gnostic literature, Jesus is not really a human being, but only appears to be human in order to share his secret salvation to true believers. This position is called **docetism**, from the Greek *dokein*, meaning "to appear." Jesus *appeared* to be human and have a physical body, but he certainly could not have actually been human with a physical body.

SELECTIONS FROM THE *GOSPEL OF PHILIP*

[Jesus said]: Light and Darkness, life and death, right and left, are brothers of one another. They are inseparable. Because of this neither are the good good, nor evil evil, nor is life life, nor death death. For this reason each one will dissolve into its earliest origin. But those who are exalted above the world are indissoluble, eternal. Names given to the worldly are very deceptive, for they divert our thoughts from what is correct to what is incorrect. Thus one who hears the word *God* does not perceive what is correct, but perceives what is incorrect. So also with *the Father* and *the Son* and *the Holy Spirit* and *life* and *light* and *resurrection* and *the Church* and all the rest—people do not perceive what is correct but they perceive what is incorrect, unless they have come to know what is correct. The names which are heard are in the world. . . deceive. If they were in the Aeon, they would at no time be used as names in the world. Nor were they set among worldly things. They have an end in the Aeon. . . .

Great is the mystery of marriage! For without it, the world would not exist. Now the existence of the world . . . , and the existence of . . . marriage. Think of the . . . relationship, for it possesses . . . power. Its image consists of a defilement. The forms of evil spirit include male ones and female ones. The males are they which unite with the souls which inhabit a female form, but the females are they which are mingled with those in a male form, through one who

(Continued)

was disobedient. And none shall be able to escape them, since they detain him if he does not receive a male power or a female power, the bridegroom and the bride. One receives them from the mirrored bridal chamber. . . .

And so he dwells either in this world or in the resurrection or in the middle place. God forbid that I be found in there! In this world, there is good and evil. Its good things are not good, and its evil things not evil. But there is evil after this world which is truly evil—what is called *the middle*. It is death. While we are in this world, it is fitting for us to acquire the resurrection, so that when we strip off the flesh, we may be found in rest and not walk in the middle. For many go astray on the way. For it is good to come forth from the world before one has sinned.[5]

Some gnostic Christians were part of the larger Christian community, or proto-orthodox community, with whom they shared fellowship. They also thought of themselves as part of an elite expression, one that also met privately to learn the fullness of the gospel. Generic Christianity was fine for the spiritually immature, but these gnostics had transcended this limited appropriation of the gospel. Surely, a bishop's authority was generally acceptable and even necessary for the average, unenlightened Christian, but in the end gnostics were their own authority. Such an association could not last, and many gnostics were eventually expelled from the proto-orthodox community. We see evidence of this tension in some of the gnostic literature. The *Apocalypse of Peter*, for example, states, "And there shall be others of those who are outside our number who name themselves bishop and also deacons, as if they have received their authority from God. They bend themselves under the judgment of the leaders. Those people are dry canals."[6]

PROTO-ORTHODOX CHRISTIANITY

In one sense, we might dismiss gnostic Christianity as a variant fluke. It certainly did not last. It also seems outrageous to modern ears: *aeons*, escaped spirits, trapped souls? Who would believe that? On the other hand, some of the material in John's Gospel looks gnostic in style, and this text was eventually accepted. Further, some of the ancient world's greatest philosophical voices, including Plato, believed that souls were trapped in bodies, and that escape came from transcending this entrapment through higher knowledge. The concept of knowledge of one's true self or condition as necessary for escape from the physical world is also a cornerstone of venerable Eastern traditions such as Hinduism and Buddhism.

Elaine Pagels, one of the foremost scholars of gnostic Christianity, reminds us that early Christianity was far from the seamless and unified expression most modern Christians have been taught. "It is the winners who write history—their way," she writes. "No wonder, then, that the viewpoint of the successful majority has dominated all traditional accounts of the origin of Christianity."[7] Furthermore, she argues, "Had Christianity remained multiform, it might well have disappeared from history, along with dozens of rival religious cults of antiquity. I believe that we owe the survival of Christian tradition to the organizational and theological structure that the emerging church developed."[8]

Still, it is superficial to say that what became standard Christianity is merely a historical fluke or merely the variant with the most successful organizational structure. When one reads gnostic texts such as the *Gospel of Philip* (see the box on "Selections from the *Gospel of Philip*"), one cannot help but see a fusion of Greek mystery religions, wild cosmologies, an inscrutable and incomprehensible narrative, and a complete removal of Jesus of Nazareth from his Jewish roots. Further, in terms of the criteria for historical accuracy, which we encountered in Chapter Three (alignment with exterior historical knowledge, cultural placement, etc.), these texts seem to fail where the Gospels and letters that make up the accepted Christian canon do not.

What became *orthodox* Christianity shows a great deal of continuity with what the historical

Jesus of Nazareth likely would have looked and acted like and with what became overwhelmingly typical in the burgeoning new religion. There were developments, for sure, and, as we have seen, Christianity's ultimate divorce from its Jewish roots might have shocked Jesus. These developments, however, did not replace Jesus's message with a Greek mystery religion. The new Christian religion set up structures, developed creeds, formed rituals, created a canon, and expressed itself throughout the Roman Empire with a good deal of institutional stability and what appears to be continuity with the primitive church.

The Threefold Ministry
The term "the twelve" appears twenty-five times in the Gospels and is used by Paul to designate the first group of apostles. *Apostle*, from *apostolein*, means "to send out," and these twelve apostles in the New Testament are commissioned by Jesus to preach, heal, and cast out demons. In Matthew Jesus tells the twelve, "Truly I tell you, whatever you bind on earth will be bound in heaven, and whatever you loose on earth will be loosed in heaven" (18:18). Binding and loosening in contemporary rabbinic literature expressed the idea of making authoritative decisions about the Law. Clearly, the apostles were both symbolic, as judges of the twelve tribes of Israel (Matt. 19:28; Luke 22:30), and very real extensions of Jesus's ministry and authority.

The term "apostle" was also a bit of a floating concept that could refer to those other than the twelve. Paul speaks of two kinds of apostles: "apostles of Jesus Christ," who were sent out by the risen Lord (1 Cor. 9:1–2), and "apostles of the churches" (2 Cor. 8:23; Phil. 2:25), who were missionaries sent out by a local church. Paul identifies himself with the former (1 Cor. 15:8–10) but also recognizes a wide variety of others (1 Thess. 2:7; 1 Cor. 9:5–6).

Beyond apostles, we find in the New Testament groups of leaders who are often called *presbyters* (elders). Leadership at this time was typically a collective venture. Sometimes the New Testament also identifies bishops or

overseers (*espiskopoi*), but this designation seems to be equivalent with that of presbyters (Titus 1:5–6; 1 Tim. 5:17). In his first epistle, Peter himself exhorts the presbyters as a fellow presbyter (5:1–5), and the author of Second and Third John identifies himself as a presbyter. The early apostolic church also recognized deacons (servants), who took on some kind of leadership role. Stephen, the first martyr, was one of the initial deacons of the Jerusalem church and was already preaching publicly when he was martyred, presumably with the apostles' approval.

By the late first century or early second century, a pattern for church leadership had emerged. Each Christian congregation had a single leader, a bishop or overseer (*episkopos*), who was directly supported by a group of elders (*presbyteroi*) and a group of deacons (*diakonoi*). This development took place sooner in Syria and western Asia Minor than it did in Greece or Italy. These offices were also imagined to be essentially permanent positions, barring scandal.

In an interesting case of the late first century (c. 96 CE), **Clement**, the leading presbyter of Rome, was asked to settle a dispute for the church at Corinth. Many of the congregation wanted to oust their leaders and replace them, and they wanted to know what Clement thought. In Clement's response letter he identifies the role of leadership in the following way:

> The apostles received the gospel for us from the Lord Jesus Christ; Jesus the Christ was sent forth from God. So then Christ is from God, and the apostles are from Christ. . . . [T]hey appointed their first fruits, when they had tested them by the Spirit to be bishops and deacons for the future believers. . . . Our apostles likewise knew, through our Lord Jesus Christ, that there would be strife over the bishop's office. For this reason, therefore, having received complete foreknowledge, they appointed the leaders mentioned earlier and afterwards they gave the offices a permanent character; that is, if they should die, other approved men should succeed to their ministry.[9]

At this time, the Corinthian church (and the Roman church) probably had no single bishop, but a group of leaders referred to as both bishops and presbyters. Nonetheless, what is fascinating is that their ministry is identified with the ministry and authority of the apostles, and that this position was considered permanent. The problem with the Corinthians, according to Clement, is that they do not understand the nature of this office.

Less than two decades later, Bishop **Ignatius of Antioch** wrote to a number of churches while he was in chains and en route to Rome to be martyred for the faith. In these letters we get a glimpse of what was going on in early first-century Christianity, including the persistence of some Christians in following the Jewish Law. What is first and foremost on Ignatius's mind, however, is church structure. In all seven letters, church harmony dominates as his chief concern. Intimately related to this issue is his insistence that such harmony can only come from observing the threefold structure of ministerial leadership:

- "Thus it is proper for you to run together in harmony with the mind of the bishop, as in fact you are doing. For your council of presbyters . . . is attuned to the bishop as strings to a lyre. Therefore in your unanimity and harmonious love Jesus Christ is sung."[10]
- "Be eager to do everything in a godly harmony, the bishop presiding in the place of God and the presbyters in the place of the council of the apostles, and the deacons, who are especially dear to me, since they have been entrusted with the ministry of Jesus Christ . . . [Y]ou must not do anything without the bishop and the presbyters."[11]
- "There is one altar, just as there is one bishop, together with the council of presbyters and the deacons."[12]

We ought not to understand Ignatius as exactly saying that the bishop stands for God, the presbyters stand for apostles, and the deacons stand for Jesus. Rather, there is one absolute leader (bishop) just as there is one God, there is a council of authoritative representatives (presbyters) just as Jesus was surrounded by a council of apostles,

and there is authoritative service (deacons) just as Jesus was a trustworthy servant. This threefold ministry of permanent clergy increasingly became the model for orthodox Christianity.

THE CATHOLIC CHURCH

Ignatius of Antioch was the first to use a common term for Christianity: *he katholike ekklesia*, the catholic church. *Katholikos*, from *katholou*, means "of the whole" or "universal." *Ekklesia* is typically translated as "church," though it literally means "assembly." Each Christian community, whether it was a modest group in a small town or a large group in a city like Ignatius's Antioch, understood itself as a church, an assembly, where the body of Christ met, baptized new members, and celebrated the Eucharist. It was, however, a church that belonged to the universal church. The whole church was expressed both locally in churches and universally as a large collective of churches, a church of churches. By the mid-second century, churches were relatively secured in the threefold ministry.

These ministers, particularly the bishops, also represented the church. Ignatius wrote in his letter to the Christian community of Tralles that when he saw their bishop Polybius, he experienced the whole of the church: "In him I saw your entire congregation." And to the Christians of Magnesia he wrote: "I was found worthy to see you [the whole congregation] in the persons of Damas, and your worthy presbyters Bassus and Apollonius, and my fellow servant, the deacon Zotion."[13] The communion of local churches with the larger *katholikos* was carried out by the bishop, who represented his local church. Agreement among bishops and their representative communities collectively created this communion.

Eventually, bishops would identify not strictly with a singular assembly, but with a region, representing administrative districts of the Roman Empire, called a diocese. A given diocese might have a number of small towns, each of which worshipped separately, with the bishop presiding over the largest congregation, but he was responsible to them all and often delegated his responsibility to some of his presbyters. Still, the Christians in each diocese considered themselves a single church under one bishop, while his communion with other bishops secured the catholicity of Christianity and indeed an orthodox faith.

 ## PERSECUTIONS

There were many religious traditions throughout the Roman Empire. Some of these were merely specific devotions to a given god, even as belief extended to the whole collection of gods. Others, such as the Egyptian religion, were quite different from traditional Roman practice. All of these were tolerated, with the caveat that their adherents had to concede that the emperor was also a god (or some manifestation of the divine). Thus, making offerings to the emperor showed one's loyalty and patriotism. Judaism was the only religion exempt from this requirement. The exemption was framed as respect for an ancient and venerable religion, but more likely it was due to the fact that Jews simply would not worship the emperor. Recall that in the second century BCE, the Seleucid king Antiochus IV Ephiphanes demanded Jews renounce their faith. The result was a revolution. Until the Temple was destroyed in 70 CE, the Jewish high priest did make a daily sacrifice for the emperor, but this was understood not as worship of him but rather as a prayer to Yahweh on his behalf. This practice seemed acceptable to Jews, and, indeed, they offered sacrifices on behalf of all the nations.

Christians did not enjoy this exemption. The Romans saw them as fools for worshipping a man who had been killed and as unpatriotic for resisting making any offerings to the emperor or joining the army (though a few did). For the most part, they were simply disliked. As mentioned previously, Emperor Nero persecuted Christians in Rome in 64 CE on the pretext that they had started a fire there, which was actually probably started by Nero himself. The Roman historian Tacitus (d. 117 CE) wrote that it was the Christians' unpopularity that made them easy targets:

Nero substituted as culprits, and punished with the utmost refinements of cruelty, a class of men, loathed for their vices, whom the crowd styled Christian. Chrestus, the founder of the name, had undergone the death penalty in the reign of Tiberius . . . and the pernicious superstition was checked for a moment, only to break out once more, not merely in Judea, the home of the disease, but in the capital itself. . . . First, then, the confessed members of the sect were arrested; next, on their disclosures, vast numbers were convicted, not so much on the count of arson as for hatred of the human beasts. And derision accompanied their end: they were covered with wild beasts' skins and torn to death by dogs; or they were fastened on crosses, and, when daylight failed, were burned to serve as lamps by night.[14]

According to Tacitus, Christians were simply widely disliked and distrusted. Still, the persecution of Christians in Rome was short and local. Decades later Pliny (the Younger), a Roman intellectual, was sent to govern Bithynia-Pontus, a province along the Black Sea, and there arrested a number of Christians who had been denounced by other local citizens. If they refused to renounce their faith, he had them executed, "for," he recorded, "I was in no doubt that, whatever it was to which they were confessing, they had merited some punishment by their stubbornness and unbending obstinacy." When Pliny received an anonymous notebook with the names of Christians in it, he was unsure how to respond and wrote Emperor Trajan (r. 98–117 CE) for advice. Trajan responded that any anonymous accusations should not be followed up on, nor should Pliny hunt down the individuals listed. However, he directed, "if they are brought before you and the charge against them is proved, they must be punished, but in the case of anyone who denies that he is a Christian, and makes it clear that he is not by offering prayers to our gods, he is to be pardoned as a result of his repentance however suspicious his past conduct may be."[15]

It was against the law to be a Christian. Still, Roman authorities were mostly concerned about public order and gathering taxes. Christians were by and large left alone, and they kept a low profile to ensure this. Periodically, in a given province or local municipality, Christians were harassed, persecuted, and even killed. Those severely persecuted but not killed were called by the church **confessors**, for heroically witnessing to the faith. Those killed were called **martyrs**, a term that literally means "witness" but was typically reserved for those who witnessed by dying for the faith. One of the most dramatic persecutions happened in the region of Lyons and Vienne in Gaul (modern France), where mob violence against Christians came to a head. Roman authorities intervened to restore order, but not without arresting and torturing a great number of Christians. Like Pliny, these authorities consulted the emperor, who was then Marcus Aurelius (r. 161–180 CE). Like Trajan, Marcus Aurelius commanded that the Christians be put to death unless they renounced their faith. Those who were Roman citizens were only beheaded, while those who were not formal citizens were used for sport in public games, including facing wild beasts or undergoing public torture.

MARTYRDOM OF PERPETUA AND FELICITAS

The day of their victory shone forth, and they proceeded from the prison into the amphitheatre, as if to an assembly, joyous and of brilliant countenances; if perchance shrinking, it was with joy, and not with fear. Perpetua followed with placid look, and with step and gait as a matron of Christ, beloved of God; casting down the luster of her eyes from the gaze of all. Moreover, Felicitas, rejoicing that she had [been] safely brought forth, so that she might fight with the wild beasts; from the blood and from the midwife to the gladiator, to wash after childbirth with a second baptism. . . . When they came within sight of Hilarianus, by gesture and nod, they began to say to Hilarianus, "Thou judgest us," say they, "but God will judge thee." At this the people, exasperated, demanded that they should be tormented with scourges as they passed along the rank of the venatores. And they indeed rejoiced that they should have incurred any one of their Lord's passions.

And when the populace called for them into the midst, that as the sword penetrated into their body they might make their eyes partners in the murder, they rose up of their own accord, and transferred themselves whither the people wished; but they first kissed one another, that they might consummate their martyrdom with the kiss of peace. . . . But Perpetua, that she might taste some pain, being pierced between the ribs, cried out loudly, and she herself placed the wavering right hand of the youthful gladiator to her throat. Possibly such a woman could not have been slain unless she herself had willed it, because she was feared by the impure spirit.

O most brave and blessed martyrs! O truly called and chosen unto the glory of our Lord Jesus Christ! whom whoever magnifies, and honours, and adores, assuredly ought to read these examples for the edification of the Church, not less than the ancient ones, so that new virtues also may testify that one and the same Holy Spirit is always operating even until now, and God the Father Omnipotent, and His Son Jesus Christ our Lord, whose is the glory and infinite power for ever and ever. Amen.[16]

Roman policy changed toward Christians over the period from 249 to 260 CE. At this time, the empire was losing prosperity and stability, as was the office of emperor—between 235 and 284 CE, some twenty-six emperors reigned, all but one of whom died a violent death. In 248 CE, the 1,000-year anniversary of the founding of the city of Rome was celebrated. The mounting problems of the empire made many conclude that the gods were angry. Emperor Decius (r. 249–251 CE) ordered a general sacrifice to the gods, which Christians refused to participate in. Anti-Christian riots erupted in response throughout the empire. In 257 CE, Emperor Valerian (r. 253–260 CE) became convinced that the gods were offended by the Christians because of their disloyalty to the empire. Unlike Decius's general sacrifice,

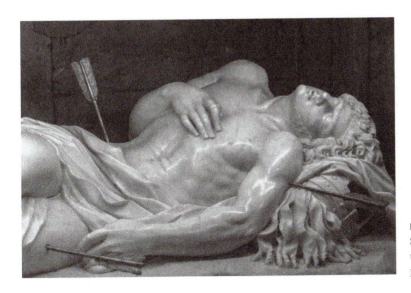

FIGURE 5-1 Statue of Saint Sebastian, who was martyred under Emperor Diocletian's persecution.

the sacrifice ordered by Valerian was directed explicitly toward Christians. Since many local magistrates knew who the bishops, presbyters, and deacons were, these people were particularly rounded up and ordered to sacrifice. In the authorities' attempts to break them, many were mutilated during their torture. Some broke down and did renounce their faith, others withstood the torture and were released as broken men, and still many others were executed. Before Valerian could fully implement his empire-wide persecution, he died in captivity in Persia. Gruesomely, he was skinned, stuffed, and used as the Persian king's footstool. Valerian's son Gallienus (r. 260–268 CE) halted the persecution and restored confiscated property to the churches.

Perhaps the greatest persecution was instigated by Diocletian (r. 284–305 CE). It began oddly. In 303 CE, Diocletian was participating in an official ceremony that included Roman priests who practiced divination (reading the future) using the entrails of animals. By now, the Christians had experienced fifty years of relative peace and prosperity. Some among their numbers were wealthy and prominent citizens and even members of the government. During the ceremony, those Christian government officials made the

sign of the cross. The priests complained that they could not proceed because of this. Diocletian went into a rage and ordered that all church buildings be destroyed and Christian assemblies forbidden. Within weeks, Christians were stripped of all legal rights. Syrian Christians rebelled, which only confirmed Diocletian's conviction that Christians were dangerous. He ordered that all clergy be arrested and imprisoned. Initially he refrained from imposing torture and the death penalty, but this was to change. The church witnessed its greatest number of martyrs during this persecution.

When Diocletian retired in 305 CE, he appointed in his place his general Galerius (r. 305–311 CE), who in 311 CE issued the Edict of Toleration, which allowed freedom of religion across the empire. It was clearly intended for Christians. In 313 CE, the co-emperors Constantine and Licinius issued the Edict of Milan, which specifically legalized Christianity across the empire.

APOLOGISTS

The word "apology" comes from the Latin *apologia*, which means "defense" or "explanation," and one way that Christians responded to the persecutions they experienced was to defend or explain their religion, particularly to government officials and intellectuals. Christianity seemed to many a superstition born from lower-class uneducated people. Some Romans considered Christians atheists, because they did not believe in the gods. Others, with little knowledge of what Christians understood the Eucharist to be, imagined that they even practiced cannibalism by consuming the body and blood of Christ.

We know of about ten formal defenses of Christianity in the second and third centuries, though some of these writings are only alluded to in other sources. Origen (185–254 CE), perhaps the most famous Christian theologian of the early church, wrote a response to the Greek philosopher Celsus, who had attacked Christianity. Tertullian (160–220 CE) wrote at least three apologies countering negative views about Christianity. And Justin (100–165 CE) also wrote three apologies, which are considered the most famous of such writings. One of Justin's apologies was written to the emperor Antoninus Pius (r. 138–161 CE) and the Roman Senate.

Justin had been raised in Samaria and classically trained. After his conversion to Christianity, he went to Rome and opened a school of philosophy, believing that Christianity was the highest philosophy. In his apology to Antoninus Pius and the Senate he challenges the misinformation that Roman intellectuals had about the faith. Christians had been considered immoral, even being accused of practicing incest. Justin responds that Christians are of the highest morality. They pay their taxes, and are loyal, disciplined, honest, generous, and peaceful. Why, he asks, would immoral people be willing to endure torture and death if they could avoid such punishment by mere superficial sacrifice to the emperor or one of the gods? With regard to emperor worship and the charge that Christians were disloyal, he wrote, "Whence to God alone we render worship, but in other things we gladly serve you, acknowledging you as kings and rulers of men, and praying that with your kingly power you be found to possess also sound judgment."[17] Citing Matthew's Gospel, he argues that far from being disloyal and unpatriotic, Christians' very faith commands that they ought to "render therefore to Caesar the things that are Caesar's and to God the things that are God's" (Matt. 22:21).[18] Justin also challenges traditional Roman religiosity by showing that many celebrated myths betray that the gods themselves were often immoral. It was also the case, he points out, that many educated Romans and Greco-Roman philosophers were, in fact, monotheists and did not believe in the gods.

One of the charges against Christianity was that it condemned anyone who was not a Christian to eternal hell; particularly vexing was its apparent condemnation of those who lived before Christ and thus had no chance to be

FIGURE 5-2 Saint Justin the Martyr, one of the great apologists, or defenders, of Christianity to Roman intellectuals and leaders.

saved. Justin responds that this perception is simply not the case. Citing Paul's letter to the Philippians, in which Paul tells them to think about "whatever is true, whatever is honorable, whatever is just" (4:8), Justin argues that much of Greek philosophy was indeed true, honorable, and just. Thus it had to be inspired by God, the source of all that is true and good. Justin also looks to the prologue of John's Gospel, where we find that the world was created by the Word, or *Logos*: "In the beginning was the Word, and the Word was with God, and the Word was God. He was in the beginning with God. All things came into being through him" (John 1:1). Justin argues that Plato, who thought that God created the universe through the *Logos*, had reflected this very insight. Jesus, Justin says, was the incarnation of this very divine activity that Plato had witnessed to. Further, anyone who had been ruled by reason (*Logos*) before the incarnation was actually Christian without even knowing it:

> But lest some should, without reason, and for the perversion of what we teach, maintain that we say that Christ was born one hundred and fifty years ago . . . taught what we say He taught; and should cry out against us as though all men who were born before Him were irresponsible—let us anticipate and solve the difficulty. We have been taught that Christ is the first-born of God, and we have declared above that He is the Word [*Logos*] of whom every race of men were partakers; and those who lived reasonably are Christian, even though they have been thought atheists; as, among the Greeks, Socrates, and Heraclitus, and men like them.[19]

Justin's argumentation and Christian witness did not sway the emperor or Senate; he was executed in 165 CE and by this gained the name "Justin Martyr." Still, he and other **apologists** not only demonstrated that Christianity was intellectually coherent and moral, they also formed early expressions of Christian theology. To the Romans, Christianity could at least be imagined as reasonable. As to fellow Christians, these apologies helped them understand their faith better.

CONCLUSIONS

It is virtually impossible to imagine that Jesus or his earliest disciples considered that they were forming a new religion. As we have seen, the reasons Christianity eventually separated from Judaism were as sociological as they were theological. For Christianity, the separation turned out to be providential. Without it, the Jesus movement would have remained something like a small sect of Judaism instead of becoming the world's largest religion. After the separation, the church was forced to address various interpretations of the gospel and how to assess them. While one might argue that Christianity became what it was by simple historical luck, it would be more accurate to say that the seeds of many of these decisions had already been planted by the apostolic church. The church became quite different from its Jewish parents for sure, but it also retained many of its Jewish sensibilities. The gnostic interpretation eventually lost the battle for influence over the church, largely because it did not look enough like Jesus of Nazareth or the message the apostles left behind.

SUMMARY QUESTIONS

- What were some of the societal factors that contributed to the process of Christianity becoming a religion distinct from Judaism?
- What were the distinctive features of gnostic texts?

- What is the threefold ministry, and who were some important contributors to its formulation?
- What were some of the ways that the early church was persecuted, and why was this the case?

DISCUSSION QUESTIONS

- We have seen that the gnostic Christian Valentinus thought that the God of the Old Testament was different from the true God of the Christians. What do you think of this view? Is it completely far-fetched, or is there some plausibility to it?
- Given that early church apologists confronted complaints against Christianity with reasoned argument, what are some issues that the church faces today that are most in need of apologetic answers?
- Do you think Christianity is now a religion under persecution? If so, in what ways?

KEY TERMS

Apologist
Clement of Rome
Confessor
Cosmology
Docetism
Gnostic
Heresy
Ignatius of Antioch
Justin
Martyr
Orthodox
Rabbinic Judaism

BIBLIOGRAPHY

- Ehrman, Bart. 2003a. *Lost Christianities: The Battles for Scripture and the Faiths We Never Knew.* New York: Oxford University Press.
- Ehrman, Bart. 2003b. *Lost Scriptures: Books That Did Not Make It into the New Testament.* New York: Oxford University Press.
- Holmes, Michael, trans. and ed. 2006. *The Apostolic Fathers*, 3rd ed. Grand Rapids, MI: Baker Academic.
- Jurgens, William, trans. and ed. 1970. *The Faith of the Early Fathers*, Vol. 1. Collegeville, MN: Liturgical Press.
- Lynch, Joseph H. 2010. *Early Christianity: A Brief History.* New York: Oxford University Press.
- Pagels, Elaine. 1979. *The Gnostic Gospels.* New York: Vintage Books.
- Roberts, Alexander, and James Donaldson, eds. 1996. *The Ante-Nicene Fathers*, Vol. 1, rev. ed. Edinburgh: T & T Clark.
- Robinson, James, ed. 1988. *The Nag Hammadi Library in English*, 3rd ed. San Francisco: Harper & Row.
- Schaff, Philip, and Henry Wace, eds. 1894. *Nicene and Post-Nicene Fathers*, Vol. 7. Trans. Edwin Hamilton Gifford. Buffalo, NY: Christian Literature Publishing Co.
- Sullivan, Francis. 2001. *From Apostles to Bishops: The Development of the Episcopacy in the Early Church.* New York: Newman Press.

NOTES

1. Robinson, *Nag Hammadi Library*, 126.
2. Ibid., 42.
3. Ibid., 47.
4. Ibid., 147.
5. Ibid., 142–143.
6. Ibid., 376.
7. Pagels, *Gnostic Gospels*, 142.
8. Ibid.
9. 1 Clement, nos. 42–44, in Holmes, *Apostolic Fathers*, 61–63
10. Ephesians, no. 4, in ibid., 97.
11. Magnesians, no. 6-7, in ibid., 104–105.
12. Philadelphians, no. 4, in ibid., 118.
13. Trallians, no. 1 in ibid., 108; Magnesians, no. 2, in ibid., 103.

14. Tacitus, *Annales* 15:44, cited in Lynch, *Early Christianity*, 83.

15. Pliny, *Letters*, 10.96, cited in ibid., 84.

16. Tertullian, "The Passion of the Holy Martyrs Perpetua and Felicitas," *Early Christian Writings*, accessed at http://www.earlychristianwritings.com/text/tertullian24.html.

17. *The First Apology of Justin*, ch. 17, in Roberts and Donaldson, *Ante-Nicene Fathers*, 168.

18. Ibid.

19. *The First Apology of Justin*, ch. 46, in ibid., 178.

6

The Life of the Early Church

The first and second generations of the church are often referred to collectively as the **apostolic church**, that is, the church dominated by the earliest witnesses to Jesus, and one that was still developing an understanding of itself. This period is distinguished from that of the **patristic church**, a lengthy period of time roughly spanning the second through sixth centuries. "Patristic" refers to "father," and this period is marked by the "fathers" of the church—almost exclusively

bishops—who progressively formed the theological and spiritual foundations of Christianity. The apostolic and early patristic churches saw themselves in contrast to the people and culture of the Roman Empire and as increasingly different from Judaism. Over time they formed their own kind of culture. This chapter investigates several fundamental characteristics and practices of the late apostolic and early patristic churches.

 ## FROM APOCALYPTIC TO ESCHATOLOGICAL

From the beginning, the church saw Jesus's ministry, death, and resurrection as part of the **eschaton**, the final period of human history. Jesus's covenant was considered the final and eternal one, inaugurating the kingdom of God. One particular framing of the church's eschatology in the first and early second centuries was **apocalyptic**. Apocalyptic literature in Judaism emerged during the late Second Temple Period, and its context was always persecution. The Book of Daniel, for example, is widely believed by scholars to have been produced during the Seleucid

persecution of Jews prior to the Maccabean Revolt, and Enoch, a noncanonical text, references both the Seleucid oppression in its early chapters and the Roman occupation in its later chapters. One fascinating aspect of apocalyptic literature is that it frames the current oppression of the righteous as an expression of a larger cosmic war between good and evil, between God and the devil. It was during the time of apocalyptic writings that the story of Satan and his followers revolting against God and being cast out of heaven appeared in Jewish literature. Apocalyptic texts depict the earthly struggle as something of a microcosm of the heavenly battle between

FIGURE 6-1   1913 depiction of the horsemen of the apocalypse. The Book of Revelation (6:1–8) describes horsemen sent from heaven to destroy sinful humanity.

God and supernatural evil. The texts promise God's victory and urge the faithful victims of persecution to hold tightly to the faith. Both Daniel and Enoch speak of a "Son of Man" who will ultimately come from heaven to overthrow the wicked, both human and supernatural.

Some of Jesus's own teachings reflect such an apocalyptic worldview, even as Jesus also drew on many other parts of the Jewish tradition that were not at all apocalyptic. In Mark, for example, Jesus tells his followers, "But in those days, after that suffering, the sun will be darkened, and the moon will not give its light, and the stars will be falling from heaven, and the powers in the heavens will be shaken. Then they will see *the Son of Man coming in clouds* with great power and glory. Then he will send out the angels, and gather his elect from the four winds, from the ends of the earth to the ends of heaven" (13:24–26). In this text, Jesus himself quotes Daniel, and many of the early disciples believed they were living in the end times. Peter's first sermon declares the present "the last days" (Acts 2:17), and Paul himself assumed that he would be among those still alive when Jesus returned in glory (1 Thess. 4:17).

The Book of Revelation reflects a persecuted church and one that expected the imminent return of Jesus. Revelation attributes the persecution of Christians to both natural and supernatural agents, working together and even overlapping. For example, the famous "beast" who works for Satan has a mark: "This calls for wisdom: let anyone with understanding calculate the number of the beast, for it is a number of a person. Its number is six hundred and sixty-six" (12:18). The number is code, reflecting a kind of numerology that assigns numbers to letters. The Hebrew letters that make up the name of the Christian persecutor Caesar Nero are: resh, 200; samekh, 60; qoph, 100; nun, 50; vav, 6; resh, 200; and nun, 50, for a total of 666.

Despite the fact that some Christians approach the Book of Revelation as a literal depiction of the historical end of the world, it is better understood as a depiction of what was taking place during early Christian history. The Book of Revelation offers assurance to a persecuted church: know that in the midst of your plight God is on your side fighting for you. While horrors come from all sides, they will not prevail, as the Lord is coming soon. This immanent victory is even now being celebrated in heaven (chs. 4–5), and the final victory will conclude with a heavenly wedding between Christ the groom and the church his bride (ch. 19). After this, there will be a new heaven and a new earth, a paradise for the just to live in peace, love, and union with God (ch. 21).

The early church embraced a spirituality of suffering with the "Crucified One" and clinging to him in trust. As noted in Chapter Five, Christians referred to those persecuted for the faith as confessors and those who died for the faith as martyrs (literally, "witnesses"). While those tortured and martyred appeared to be victims from the world's perspective, the church argued that they were really heroes and role models. In one apocalyptic text, *The Shepherd of Hermas*, the Christian Hermas experiences a vision of the heavenly banquet table to which he is invited, but at which he is not allowed to sit on the right (favored) side. This side is reserved for martyrs "who have already pleased God and have suffered for the sake of the Name."[1]

Although the church remained a persecuted community throughout the second and early third centuries, it gradually lost much of its

apocalypticism. After all, Jesus did not quickly return as anticipated. Nevertheless, the church remained eschatological in its outlook. Christians saw themselves as part of a grand design, a plan God had to bring the world to its fullest or truest end. The Bible is neither clear nor consistent about what this end might look like. It could be the fiery destruction of the current universe and its subsequent replacement with another (2 Pet. 3:10–13), a spiritualization of the current world and all the living within it (Rom. 8:21), a new universe descending from heaven (Rev. 21:1–2), or something else entirely. Church fathers did not focus on the specific form of this renewed world, but they were highly invested in two beliefs: first, that God's providence was drawing the world toward an end or final goal, and second, that Christianity was a religion of living *in* the world but not *of* the world. The world as they experienced it was not their true home.

 ## CHURCH AS CENTER

BAPTISM

From the start Christians practiced two rituals that would ground their identity: **baptism** and the **Eucharist**. The risen Jesus commissions his disciples: "All authority in heaven and on earth has been given to me. Go therefore and make disciples of all nations, baptizing them in the name of the Father and of the Son and of the Holy Spirit, and teaching them to obey everything that I have commanded you" (Matt. 28:18–20). After Peter's first sermon he likewise says to the crowd, "Repent and be baptized every one of you in the name of Jesus Christ so that your sins may be forgiven; and you will receive the gift of the Holy Spirit" (Acts 2:38).

Baptism in the early church represented a wholly new life. Being plunged into the water represented entering into the tomb with Christ, and rising from it was rising to new life. Paul describes this concept as follows: "Did you not know that all of us who have been baptized into Christ Jesus were baptized into his death? Therefore we have been buried with him by baptism into death, so that, just as Christ was raised from the dead by the glory of the father, so we too might walk in newness of life. . . . We know that our old self was crucified with him. . . . So you also must consider yourselves dead to sin and alive to God in Christ Jesus" (Rom. 6:3–11).

DIDACHE ON BAPTISM

Now concerning baptism, baptize as follows: after you have reviewed all these things, baptize in the name of the Father and of the Son and of the Holy Spirit in running water. But if you have no running water, then baptize in some other water; and if you are not able to baptize in cold water, then do so in warm. But if you have neither, then pour water on the head three times in the name of the Father and Son and Holy Spirit. And before the baptism let the one baptizing and the one who is to be baptized fast, as well as any others who are able. Also, you must instruct the one who is baptized to fast for one or two days beforehand.[2]

The *Didache*, a late first-century text, reiterates Paul's sense of baptism as a radically new life. It begins, "There are two ways, one of life and one of death, and there is great difference between these two ways."[3] The text goes on, in the voice of Jesus to his apostles, demanding the love of enemies and laying down prohibitions against murder, adultery, corruption of others, promiscuity, stealing, magic, sorcery, abortion, being angry, being jealous, being lustful, being an astrologer or a magician, or even being interested in seeing such people. The *Letter of Barnabas* (c. 100) reiterates the same imperative to be upright both inwardly and outwardly: "This, therefore, is the way of light."[4]

In baptism, converts were proclaimed washed of their sins. They were "illuminated" and admitted to the ranks of the faithful. In his *Apostolic Tradition*, **Hippolytus of Rome** (170–235) says that initiates had to undergo a training period of three years, during which they learned about the faith and were tested morally. This was the time of the catechumenate, from the word **catechumen**, meaning "hearer" or "learner." These catechumens would come to the Christian assembly to hear the scriptures proclaimed along with a sermon. They were then excused, being considered unready for even witnessing the Eucharist. Hippolytus explains that when the catechumens

were judged ready, they would bathe on Thursday, fast (along with their supporters) on Friday and Saturday, spend Saturday night in prayerful vigil, and then be baptized at dawn.

According to Hippolytus, the catechumen would present him or herself, strip, renounce Satan, be anointed with the "oil of exorcism," and plunge into the water three times for the Father, Son, and Holy Spirit. The presbyter would then anoint each candidate again with the "oil of thanksgiving." They would then dry off and put on white garments. After being led to the assembly, the bishop would lay his hands on their heads and pray over them. Finally, he would anoint them yet a third time, so that they might be "sealed by the Holy Spirit." The ceremony would mark the first time these initiates observed and participated in the Eucharist. They also drank from a cup of water and milk mixed with honey, symbolizing their entrance into the "land flowing with milk and honey" (Exod. 3:8).

More symbols were added to the ceremony during subsequent centuries, and surely there was some variation in the ritual throughout the Christian world. Yet the core symbolism remained: baptism signified an entirely new life, a transformation from darkness to light, from an immoral world to a moral one, from being lost to being saved. It was dramatic.

FIGURE 6-2   The Last Supper, when Jesus inaugurated the Eucharist as a rite to celebrate his final covenant.

THE EUCHARIST

The Eucharist, or Lord's Supper, was also essential to Christian identity. Christians gathered on Sunday evening, the day commemorating the resurrection, and celebrated a rite of "thanksgiving," the translation of *eucharistia*. The Lord's Supper was understood as a shared meal of thanksgiving for Jesus's salvation. Each of the synoptic Gospels describes the Last Supper as a Seder or Passover meal during which Jesus inaugurated his new covenant and anticipated his sacrificial death. As mentioned in Chapter Three, Jesus identified himself with the bread and wine. The disciples, in eating and drinking this bread and wine, now identified as his body and blood, thus entered into his new covenant. In Luke, Jesus commands them to continue the ritual: "Do this in remembrance of me" (22:19). Thus, the earliest disciples regularly engaged in the Eucharist: "They devoted themselves to the apostles' teaching and fellowship, to the breaking of the bread and the prayers" (Acts 2:42). Later, Paul criticizes the community at Corinth for discriminating against the poorer Christians who come to the Sunday gathering late, as presumably they had to work the full day:

For I received from the Lord what I also handed on to you, that the Lord Jesus on the night when he was betrayed took a loaf of bread, and when he had given thanks, he broke it and said, "This is my body that is for you. Do this in remembrance of me." In the same way he took the cup also, after supper, saying, "This cup is the new covenant in my blood. Do this, as often as you drink it, in remembrance of me." For as often as you eat this bread and drink the cup, you proclaim the Lord's death until he comes. Whoever therefore eats the bread or drinks the cup of the Lord in an unworthy manner will be answerable for the body and blood of the Lord. (1 Cor. 11:23–27)

So important was the Eucharist that we see in Paul's description a virtual verbatim retelling of the Gospel accounts. This is extraordinary, since Paul rarely ever references specific things Jesus taught during his ministry. We also see that Paul identifies the Eucharistic action as a proclamation of or engagement in the sacrificial death of Jesus.

From the writings of the early church fathers, we can glean additional insight into what Christians thought they were doing in celebrating the Eucharist. Two themes become prominent: sacrifice and communion with God through the body and blood of Jesus in the form of bread and wine. These two themes were intertwined in the minds of the church fathers. Consider this witness from **Irenaeus of Lyons** in his book *Against Heresies*:

> Again, giving direction to His disciples to offer to God the first-fruits of His own created things. . . . He took that created thing, bread, and gave thanks, and said, "This is My body." And the cup likewise, which is part of that creation to which we belong, He confessed to be his blood, and taught the new oblation of the new covenant; which the Church receiving from the apostles, offers to God throughout all the world. . . . The oblation of the Church . . . [is] a pure sacrifice, and is acceptable to Him. . . . Inasmuch, then, as the Church offers with single-mindedness, her gift is justly reckoned a pure sacrifice with God. . . . Then again, how can they say that the flesh, which is nourished with the body of the Lord and with His blood, goes into corruption and does not partake of life? . . . But our opinion is in accordance with the Eucharist, and the Eucharist in turn establishes our opinion. For we offer to Him [the Father] His own [the Son], announcing consistently the fellowship and union of the flesh and Spirit. For as the bread, which is produced from the earth, when it receives the invocation of God, is no longer common bread, but the Eucharist, consisting of two realities, earthly and heavenly; so also our bodies, when they receive the Eucharist, are no longer corruptible, having the hope of the resurrection to eternity.[5]

In this text, Irenaeus is arguing against certain gnostic Christians who believed that the created world was evil or inconsequential and who denied the resurrection of the body. Irenaeus uses the Eucharist as his counterargument. If the physical bread and wine can become the actual body and blood of Jesus—something now heavenly and incorruptible—so too can the human body become spiritualized. And so it does through participation in the Eucharist, the very ritual that conditions immortality. Further, we see that the Eucharist is regularly referred to as both the original sacrifice of Christ on the cross and a sacrifice made by the church.

Typically, the sacred rites within a given religious tradition facilitate transformative experiences through that tradition's deep, archetypal (core) symbols. The rituals become *presentations* of the reality symbolized, that is, they become realizations of their very truth. They are meant to transform believers by allowing them to experience the reality of salvation through the mediation of the symbols that engage it. The Eucharist as a sacred rite possesses these characteristics. However, according to Irenaeus, it must be enacted with "single-mindedness" or a pure heart in order to effect such transformation. Irenaeus regards Christians celebrating the Eucharist as reentering the original sacrifice of Christ, offering themselves to God through it, and communing with the actual body and blood of Jesus, now risen and glorified.

The conviction that the Eucharist was a sacrifice and literal communion with the body and blood of the risen Lord—and, indeed, that it created the conditions for transforming Christians—was widely shared. Ignatius of Antioch reminds his readers that there is just one altar of sacrifice in the church and criticizes heretics who do not "acknowledge that the Eucharist is the flesh of our Savior Jesus Christ." In his view, the Eucharistic food is the "medicine of immortality."[6] Early Christian theologian Tertullian (160–225) describes Jesus at the Last Supper as "He made it His own Body."[7] And the Christian apologist Justin (100–165) describes it thus in the *First Apology*:

> And this food is called among us *Eukaristia*, of which no one is allowed to partake but the man who believes that these things we teach are true, and who has been washed with the washing that is for the remission of sins, and unto regeneration, and who is so living as Christ has enjoined. For not as common bread and common drink do we receive these; but in like manner as Jesus Christ, having been made flesh by the Word of God, had both flesh and blood for our salvation, so likewise have we been taught that the food which is blessed by the prayer of his word, and from which our blood and flesh by transmutation are nourished, is the flesh and blood of that Jesus who was made flesh.[8]

DAILY GATHERINGS

The Eucharist united early Christians. For them, the church constituted the body of Christ, a holy community. The great patristic theologian Augustine once wrote that "a man possesses the Holy Spirit in the measure that he loves the church."[9] Many Christians not only met on Sundays for Eucharist; they also met daily to pray before and after the workday, a prayer that today is called the Liturgy of the Hours, or the Divine Office. They sang hymns, chanted psalms, and offered prayers. Because many were illiterate, they memorized particular hymns and psalms that reflected the time of day. Morning prayer often included psalms that expressed trust in God, specific canticles, such as Zechariah's prayer (Luke 1:68–79), a Gloria, intercessions of the community, and a concluding blessing and dismissal by the bishop. Evening prayer consisted of a ritual lighting of lamps, symbolizing Christ as the light of the community; psalms that sought God's protection through the night; the burning of incense, representing prayers rising to God; hymns; intercessions; and a blessing and dismissal. Gathering in community structured the day for many Christians.

MORAL RIGOR

Christians assumed that those living a new life in Christ ought to uphold high moral standards in manifesting that life. As mentioned previously, Paul taught that baptism meant "our old self was crucified with him. . . . So you must consider yourselves dead to sin and alive to God in Christ Jesus" (Rom. 6:3–11). Christians perceived a radical distinction between the way of life offered by Christianity and the way of death represented by standard Roman culture. Of course, as we saw in Chapter Five, Christians recognized good in many of the values of pagan philosophy, particularly Platonism and Stoicism. Still, the outside culture was often characterized as the place of yielding to passions such as greed, anger, and lust. As we saw, one of the

three anointings in baptism was that of the "oil of exorcism." It is not that Christians viewed the unbaptized as possessed by the devil; rather, they believed that sin and the influence of temptations, whether from one's unreformed habits or from supernatural evil, had to be exorcised from one's soul.

As noted previously, the period of the catechumenate was a time of moral testing, and some catechumens were not deemed acceptable. Obviously, even after baptism Christians continued to engage in sins, such as outbursts of anger, gossip, or gluttony. These relatively minor sins were seen as part and parcel of the long journey of sanctification, that is, the process of becoming increasingly holy. The church, however, saw some sins as particularly egregious, such as apostasy (renunciation of the faith), idolatry, and adultery. Christians debated whether such sins warranted permanent excommunication. The general consensus was that Christians guilty of serious wrongdoing but repentant could return to the faith, but not easily. They were required to enter into a process that came to be known as the **Order of Penitents**. During this period of penance, they continued to go to church but were barred from receiving communion. At the Eucharistic assembly, they stood apart while the rest of the community continued to pray for them on this journey of spiritual recovery. When the local bishop decided that their period of repentance was complete, he received them back into full communion. Cyprian (d. 258), the great bishop of Carthage, detailed how the church received Christians who had lapsed during the Decian and Valerian persecutions. These individuals remained in the Order of Penitents for five years. In the first year, they were "hearers" who stood in the back of the church. For the next three years, they were "prostrators" who joined the congregation but knelt or lay flat on the ground during the service. In the final year, they were "standers" who stood with the congregation but were denied communion. They wore sackcloth and ashes, and regularly fasted during this lengthy time. Finally, they were re-admitted to good standing on Holy Thursday before Easter. Christianity was clearly not for the faint of heart.

ASCETICISM

A number of Christians lived a highly ascetic life. **Asceticism** means "discipline," and in this context it means more than simply an ordered life. Some Christians used certain types of deprivation, such as fasting, as a way to increase their moral purity and interior openness to God. One theme that comes up regularly in early church texts is a suspicion of the body. Early Christians did not view the body as bad or evil or a prison for the soul, as did the gnostics and Plato, but they did see it as quite vulnerable to the passions, a word derived from the Latin *passio*, meaning "suffering." We suffer when our desires are inordinate. If one is hungry, then one ought to eat. Gluttony, however, is an inordinate passion for food. It is perfectly fine to desire material goods in order to live a modest life. Avarice, however, is the inordinate passion for money or things.

The remedy that Christians, along with Greek philosophers and their followers, strived to attain was *apatheia*, or "no-suffering." This state involved an unattached, nongrasping mind and heart. The English cognate for *apatheia* is apathy, but for the ancient world *apatheia* did not connote a lack of care. Rather, when one achieved *apatheia*, one was no longer controlled by the passions; it freed one from being a slave or prisoner of attachments to sensible comforts. With *apatheia* one could now live under the law of reason and could care for others without being conditioned or controlled by what was pleasant or unpleasant. Synthesizing such aspirations much later, the spiritual giant Maximus the Confessor (580–662) saw four steps to full *apatheia*: (1) abstain from sin; (2) train the thoughts not to consent to sin; (3) make all affections subject to reason; and (4) purify the mind to be a mirror of divinity.

CONSECRATED VIRGINITY

As mentioned, Christians, along with certain highly conscientious non-Christians, viewed the body as morally fragile. Many Christians particularly distrusted sex and thus highly commended celibacy for the sake of the kingdom. A celibate Christian life was imagined to be wholly dedicated to the service and knowledge of God. Paul reflects this value in First Corinthians when he writes, "To the unmarried and widows I say that it is well for them to remain unmarried as I am. But if they are not practicing self-control, they should marry, for it is better to marry than to be aflame with passion" (7:8–9). In that same chapter Paul lays out a fuller argument, stating that an unmarried person is anxious about the Lord rather than a spouse or the "things of the world." Paul allows for marriage, but it is as though marriage is a concession for those who cannot be celibate (7:32–38). Of course, Paul also believed that Christ would soon return; this was the context of his advice. Still, in his writings he associates virginity with freedom from sexual passions and reserves legitimate marriage for those who appear still enslaved by such passions.

The fathers of the church, as well as most Greek philosophers, saw sexual desire not only as the prime example of the passions, but also as the most egregious way to lose self-control and spiritual energy. They even believed that human physiology worked to that end. Having intercourse was thought to make one's blood boil, turning it into a foam of semen. In *De anima* Tertullian asks, referring to sex, "Do we not feel something of our very soul go out from us?"[10] In contrast, he portrays abstinence from sex as an excellent way to purify and free the soul: "Let us look at our own inner world. Think of how a man feels in himself when he abstains from a woman. He thinks spiritual thoughts . . . it fills his whole being with enjoyment; if he exorcises a demon, he does so confident in his own strength."[11]

The church's concern with sexual passion and physical pleasure shows a decided shift from its Jewish heritage. The rabbis did not idealize the ascetic who shunned the world and its pleasures, but extolled those who knew how to live in moderation and to take pleasure in the fullness and richness of creation. They taught that on judgment day one would be held accountable for the good things God provided that one *did not* partake of. As the Talmud, Judaism's authoritative commentary, says, "he who indulges in fasting is called a sinner."[12] Regarding marriage, Judaism understood it as a prerequisite for a mature spiritual existence: "The unmarried person lives without joy, without blessing, and without good. He is not a man in the full sense of the term."[13] This stands in stark contrast to a typical reflection by Pope Gregory I:

> The custom of the Romans [the church in Rome] from antiquity has always been, after sexual intercourse with one's spouse, both to cleanse oneself by washing and to abstain reverently from entering the church for a time. In saying this we do not intend to say that sexual intercourse is sinful. But because every lawful sexual intercourse between spouses cannot take place without bodily pleasure, they are to refrain from entering the holy place. For such pleasure cannot be without sin.[14]

Consecrated virginity afforded Christian women an additional bonus: it freed them from the oppressive control of a patriarchal married culture and opened a way for greater participation and informal leadership in the Christian community. The Greco-Roman culture considered a wife subordinate to her husband in all things, and it expected women to marry and play this submissive role. Surely, many women, Christian or otherwise, wanted to marry. They loved and were loved by their husbands, and were grateful for their children. Still, it was a culturally restrictive life. In contrast, virginity for the sake of the kingdom challenged the social structure of the day and opted for a different cultural and ecclesial arrangement. It was a sign of the kingdom, where "in the resurrection they neither marry nor are given in marriage, but are like angels in heaven" (Matt. 22:30).

VENERATION OF SAINTS

One of the most fascinating characteristics of early church spirituality is the reverence Christians gave to their saints, particularly those who died for the faith. In his *Confessions*, Augustine makes a curious reference to a practice his saintly mother Monica had: "In accordance with my mother's custom in Africa, she had taken to the memorial shrines cakes and bread and wine."[15] Apparently it was a practice in North Africa for Christians to celebrate a memorial meal with others at a saint's grave. Ambrose, the bishop in Milan, where Augustine and Monica later lived, forbade the practice, as it looked superstitious to him. Monica readily accepted his decision, but we see from this account that the practice was widespread in North Africa.

Christians believed—and still do—that every member of the church is part of the mystical body of Christ. That is, Christians are not merely individuals who believe in Jesus, but together have a corporate identity. The early church thought that Christians who had died remained an active part of that body. Further, saints—particularly martyrs—represented heroes of the faith. They manifested the presence and transforming possibilities of God's grace in their lives. Given their extraordinary holiness and their continued presence in the mystical body, they were thought to intercede for those still on earth. We might consider it this way: if a Christian living today needed intercessory prayers, he or she would not hesitate to ask other Christians to pray on his or her behalf. The whole of the Christian tradition has consistently believed in the efficacy of intercessory prayer. How it works is another matter, for few Christians believe that God needs advice on how to act. Still, Christianity has always practiced such prayer. Further, it wouldn't be unusual to ask particularly holy Christians to pray for one, rather than lapsed or mediocre Christians. If we grant this, how much more powerful would the prayers of the saints be, given their special relationship with God?

Saints were seen as somehow uniting heaven and earth, and their tombs were particularly hallowed; they were like poles where heaven and earth met. The fourth-century Greek historian Eunapius of Sardis mocked Christians for this practice: "For they collected bones and skulls of criminals . . . [and] made them out to be gods, and thought that they became better by defiling themselves at their graves. *Martyrs* the dead men were called, and ministers of a sort, and ambassadors with the gods to carry men's prayers."[16] Obviously, this view represents a pagan outsider looking in with a bit of confusion. Still, it conveys something of the extraordinary veneration Christians had for the saints. Christians went so far as to hold vigils and services at their saints' graves, and felt certain that the saints would intercede on their behalf. The great biblical scholar Jerome (347–420) remarked, "When I am angry or have some bad thought . . . I do not dare to enter the shrines of the martyrs. I quake with body and soul."[17] These shrines were considered particularly holy because the remains were believed to be relics that represented the saints on earth in a special, powerful way. Gregory of Nyssa (335–395) taught that such relics were still heavy with the presence of the beloved saints, and in defending the resurrection of the dead, Augustine cited as evidence miracles performed by saints at the local shrines he personally knew.[18]

In many respects a saint became a spiritual version of a Roman patron, that is, a wealthy benefactor who took others under his wing and financed their worthy undertakings. Historian Peter Brown has remarked, "The saint was a good *patronus*: he was the *patronus* whose intercessions were successful, whose wealth was at the disposal of all, whose *potential* [power] was exercised without violence and to whom loyalty could be shown without restraint."[19]

Veneration of the saints was an important aspect of early Christianity, a spiritual practice that continues in the Roman Catholic, Anglican, and Eastern Orthodox traditions. In addition to relying on the saints' intercessions, early Christians honored them on feast days (typically the day they were martyred), celebrating their heroism and spiritual transformation. Such practices also highlighted the possibilities of God's grace. As the fifth-century *Decretum Gelasianum* declared, "We must include also [for public reading] the deeds of the saints in which their triumph blazed forth through the many forms of torture that they underwent and their marvelous confession of faith. For what Catholic can doubt that they suffered more than is possible for human beings to bear, and did not endure this by their own strength, but by the grace and help of God?"[20]

CONCLUSIONS

The late apostolic and early patristic churches were both serious and impressive. Of course, not all Christians were highly ascetic, and only a decided minority became consecrated virgins. Still, by any measure, to embrace the Christian faith was to take on a religious ethos that demanded real differences, some from its Judaic past and a great deal from the Greco-Roman culture in which it otherwise existed. As noted in Chapter Five, to be a Christian was to risk one's very life. Such a risk demonstrates the dedication Christian practice required. A clearly virtuous life was expected, and serious sin was not tolerated. Baptism represented a wholly new existence, and the Eucharist the ongoing ritual expression of that

existence. Christian heroes were martyrs who helped bridge the distance between heaven and earth, and Christians saw themselves and history as progressing to a glorious future. Their glory was not that of the empire, but that of God's providence and Christian participation in that providence. Above all, Christianity was filled with joy and love. The great apologist Tertullian in his *Apology* describes the generosity and mutual care Christians have for each other, writing, "But it is mainly the practice of such a love which leads some to put a brand upon us. 'See,' they say, 'how they love one another.'" And in describing the Eucharist, he writes, "The purpose of our meal is shown by its name: it is called by a work which to the Greeks means *love* [agape]."[21] The communion and spiritual joy Christians shared with each other marked not only their inner existence, but also their witness to the Greco-Roman world.

SUMMARY QUESTIONS

- What were the distinctive features of the early church?
- In what ways was the early church apocalyptic?
- Why did the early church value lifelong virginity? What were some of the important cultural phenomena that resulted from this practice?

DISCUSSION QUESTIONS

- The early church thought that Jesus's return was imminent and ultimately discovered that it was not. Do you think there are implications to be gleaned from this when reading the Bible today, particularly those texts that assume an imminent second coming?
- What is the significance of the Eucharist according to Paul and the church fathers?
- The author thinks that the best way to read apocalyptic texts is to see them as expressions of the faith at the time they were written and not as predictions of the future. Evaluate his reasons for this and offer your own position with reasons of your own.

KEY TERMS

Apatheia	Baptism	Hippolytus of Rome
Apocalyptic	Catechumen	Irenaeus of Lyons
Apostolic church	Eschaton	Order of Penitents
Asceticism	Eucharist	Patristic church

BIBLIOGRAPHY

- Brown, Peter. 1981. *The Cult of the Saints: Its Rise and Function in Latin Christianity*. Chicago: University of Chicago Press.
- Brown, Peter. 1988a. *The Body and Society: Men, Women, and Sexual Renunciation in Early Christianity*. New York: Columbia University Press.
- Brown, Peter. 1988b. "The Notion of Virginity in the Early Church." In *Christian Spirituality*, ed. Bernard McGinn, John Meyendorff, and Jean Leclercq, 1:427–443. New York: Continuum.
- Chadwich, Henry. 1967. *The Early Church*. New York: Penguin.
- Holmes, Michael, trans. and ed. 2006. *The Apostolic Fathers*, 3rd ed. Grand Rapids, MI: Baker Academic.
- Jurgens, William, trans. and ed. 1970. *The Faith of the Early Fathers*, vol 1. Collegeville, MN: Liturgical Press.
- Neuner, J., and J. Dupuis, eds. 1982. *The Christian Faith*, rev. ed. New York: Alba House.
- Roberts, Alexander, and James Donaldson, eds. 1996. *The Ante-Nicene Fathers*, Vol. 1, rev. ed. Edinburgh: T & T Clark.
- Sullivan, Francis. 2001. *From Apostles to Bishops: The Development of the Episcopacy in the Early Church*. New York: Newman Press.

- Taft, Robert. 1986. *The Liturgy of the Hours in East and West: The Origins of the Divine Office and Its Meaning for Today.* Collegeville, MN: Liturgical Press.
- Tugwell, Simon. 1986. "The Apostolic Fathers." In *The Study of Spirituality*, ed. Cheslyn Jones, Geoffrey Wainwright, and Edward Yarnold, 102–108. New York: Oxford University Press.
- Zizioulas, John. 1988. "The Early Christian Community." In *Christian Spirituality*, ed. Bernard McGinn, John Meyendorff, and Jean Leclercq, 1:23–43. New York: Continuum.

NOTES

1. *Shepherd of Hermas*, no. 9 in Holmes, *Apostolic Fathers*, 212.
2. *Didache*, no. 7 in ibid., 166–167.
3. *Didache*, no. 1 in Ibid., 163
4. Barnabas, no. 19, in ibid., 179.
5. Irenaeus of Lyons, *Against Heresies*, IV.17.5–18.5 in *The Ante-Nicene Fathers*, 484–486.
6. Philadelphians, no. 4, 118; Smyrnaeans, no. 6, 123; Ephesians, no. 20, 102, in Holmes, *Apostolic Fathers*.
7. Tertullian, *Against Marcion*, 4.40.3, in *The Faith of the Early Fathers*, Vol. 1, ed. and trans. William Jurgens (Collegeville, MN: Liturgical Press, 1970), 141.
8. Justin Martyr, *First Apology*, ch. 66, in Roberts and Donaldson, *Ante-Nicene Fathers*, 185.
9. *Patria Latina*, 35.1646.
10. Tertullian, *De anima*, 27.5, in Brown, *Body and Society*, 18.
11. Tertullian, *De ieiunio*, 5.1, in ibid., 78.
12. *Taanit* 11a, in Ben Zion Bokser and Baruch Bokser, *The Talmud: Selected Writings*, trans. Ben Zion Bokser (New York: Paulist Press, 1989), 46.
13. *Yebamot* 63a, in Ibid., 34.
14. *Epistolarum liber*, IX.64.
15. Augustine, *Confessions*, 6.2, in Augustine of Hippo, *Confessions*, trans. Henry Chadwick (Oxford: Oxford University Press, 1991), 91.
16. Brown, *Cult of the Saints*, 7.
17. Ibid., 11.
18. Augustine, *City of God*, 22.8, in *City of God*, trans. Henry Bettenson (New York: Penguin, 1984), 1033–1047.
19. Brown, *Cult of the Saints*, 41.
20. *Decretum Gelasianum*, P.L. 59.171, in ibid., 79.
21. Tertullian, *Apology*, 39.7, 17, in Jurgens, *Faith of the Early Fathers*, 1:116.

The Imperial Church

Timeline

313 CE	Co-emperors Constantine and Licinius issue the Edict of Milan, specifically allowing freedom for Christians to follow their faith in the Roman Empire
319 CE	Beginnings of the Arian controversy
325 CE	Council of Nicaea defines the full divine nature of Jesus and condemns teachings of Arius
328 CE	Athanasius becomes bishop of Alexandria and strongly attacks Arianism
380 CE	Co-emperors Theodosius I and Gratian issue the edict *Cunctos Populos*, which mandates the Nicene Creed, makes the bishops of Rome and Alexandria judges of orthodox doctrine, and makes Christianity the sole religion of the empire
381 CE	Council of Constantinople; Nicene Creed is confirmed and expanded
391 CE	Emperor Theodosius declares Christianity the official religion of the Roman Empire
412–444 CE	Cyril serves as bishop of Alexandria
431 CE	Council of Ephesus condemns the teachings of Nestorius; Church of the East separates
451 CE	Council of Chalcedon adopts the statement that Christ is "one person with two natures"; dissent leads to breakup of the church and establishment of Eastern Christian churches in Armenia, Syria, Egypt, Ethiopia, Eritrea, and India

This chapter discusses the impact of the progressive union between church and state in the Roman Empire. In the fourth century, emperors went from persecuting the church to embracing it, and by the end of that century Christianity had become the state religion. Further, emperors went from seeing themselves as responsible for the Christian faith to being in some sense head of both church and state. This shift had enormous consequences. With imperial support, bishops met for the first time in church-wide councils to discuss and even debate Christian teaching. This led to the unification of teachings, but also

the eventual breakup of the church for those Christian communities that could not accept the councils' decisions. From these councils also developed centers of Christianity over which bishops, called patriarchs, held particular clout and territorial responsibility. The growth of such power structures led to conflicts between East and West, as the bishop and patriarch of Rome claimed preeminence over all the other patriarchates as the inheritor of the authority of the apostle Peter. This claim represented the greatest, most divisive issue between the Eastern and Western churches.

CONSTANTINE

Emperor Diocletian had divided the empire into sections ruled by an imperial board and co-emperors as a way to restore stability to a weakening empire. **Constantine's** father had been one of three co-emperors with Diocletian, and when he died in 306, Constantine succeeded him. For the next several years, Constantine battled for control of the western half of the empire against Maxentius. In 312, a decisive battle was waged at the Milvian Bridge, just outside of Rome. According to two slightly different traditions Constantine was given a promise in a dream that he would win that battle if he fought under the sign of the Christian God. In this dream he was instructed to place the cross of Christ on the shields of his soldiers. Therefore, he ordered that the first two letters of the Greek spelling of "Christ"—a chi (χ) and a rho (ρ)—be placed on his men's shields; it would have looked like this: ☧. Constantine triumphed in battle, and the following year he and his co-emperor in the East, Licinius, promulgated the Edict of Milan (313), which mandated universal religious toleration, and specifically toleration of Christianity. Constantine later battled Licinius for sole rule of the empire and defeated him in 324. He ruled as the sole emperor until 337.

FIGURE 7-1   A bronze statue of Constantine, the first emperor to support Christianity.

Was the new emperor Christian? Probably, but it is not certain. On the one hand, some of the coins he issued under his rule contained pagan religious symbolism, and he waited until his deathbed to be baptized. On the other hand, his mother, Helena, was a devout Christian, and Constantine spent his rule sponsoring and supporting the Christian religion. One reason for his not being baptized sooner could have been that Christians at this time were expected to live a strictly moral life. As we saw in Chapter Six, serious sin placed one in the Order of Penitents for a lengthy period. Further, after this second chance there would typically be no third chances. Because of this, it would not have been unusual for some would-be Christians to wait until late in life to be baptized. The weightiest evidence that Constantine was indeed Christian (at least in sympathy) is that favoring Christianity was not a politically savvy move. A sizeable portion of the populace was not Christian, especially among the army and the upper class. If Constantine merely wanted to unite the empire under a religious banner, Christianity would not have been a likely vehicle.

Loyalty to Christianity was, for Constantine, a way of placing the empire under the Christian Godhead and thereby ensuring God's favor. Constantine devoted government funds to Christian charitable work and built impressive churches in Rome, including the Basilica of John Lateran and another on the traditional grave of Saint Peter. Through his mother Helena's initiative, he also built a great church in Jerusalem where Christ was said to have been buried and raised; today it is called the Church of the Holy Sepulchre. He also gave Christian clergy tax exemptions and the authority to act as judges in civil cases. He even made Sunday an official day of rest in Constantinople.

Constantine's understanding of Christianity and his role in it reflect a dramatic change in the Christian ethos. Christians under his rule were favored in the Roman Empire, a stark contrast to the last 300 years. Further, Constantine created the conditions for a *Christian nation*, and he saw himself as ruler over this newly formed alliance. He and his succeeding emperors called church councils to decide on controversial issues and forcibly exiled those church leaders who would not submit to the decisions of this larger church. While Jesus and the faithful who had followed him were persecuted outsiders, Christians in Constantine's empire would increasingly be numbered among the favored. Jesus taught non-violence and acceptance of hatred by many, exhorting his followers: "Blessed are the poor in spirit. . . . Blessed are the meek. . . . Blessed are the peacemakers. . . . Blessed are those persecuted for righteousness' sake" (Matt. 5:3–10). Contrast this to Constantine's vision before his victory at the Milvian Bridge, in which he saw "a cross of light in the heavens, above the sun, and an inscription, CONQUER BY THIS."[1] His newly formed love of Christianity also did not keep him from invading the eastern part of the empire and conquering Licinius, making himself sole emperor. As a Christian nation, Christianity was fused, at least in Constantine's mind, with the fortunes and agenda of the Roman Empire.

One of the most interesting decisions Constantine made under his new rule was to move the empire's capital. He had little attachment to Rome, and before his victory at the Milvian Bridge he may not have ever entered Rome. Further, the ruling class in Rome was most unsympathetic to Christianity and still clung to the ancient Roman religion, with its many temples in the city. Constantine instead chose as his capital city Byzantion, a city at the entrance to the Black Sea that commanded some of the trade routes east and west. He renamed it Constantinople after himself, although the old name also persisted, eventually being Latinized to Byzantium. While the Western Roman Empire would eventually collapse over the next century, the Eastern Roman Empire, the Byzantine Empire, would remain for the next 1,000 years.

Centered in Constantinople, Christianity became transformed from the faith of a persecuted minority to a dominant and favored religion, one that received a massive influx of funds for grand church structures. Instead of being ambivalent (at best) about the Roman Empire, Christians were now expected to be vigorous supporters of it. The empire came to be seen as having been instituted by God, with the emperor acting as his regent. From this point on, Christians tended to equate Christianity with the Roman Empire, something that was bound to compromise consciences all around. The institutional church would eventually use its new power to persecute heretics and unbelievers. Further, Jews progressively lost many of their legal protections, and even Persian Christians were suspected of being traitors.

COUNCILS AND DOGMAS

It may come as a surprise to readers, Christian and non-Christian alike, that the creation of the New Testament canon was relatively late. Of course, most of the texts that made it into the canon were widely used far earlier, and there was a modest consensus about many of the texts early on. Still, it would not be until the late fourth century that Christianity definitively concluded its New Testament canon. One of the reasons for canonical plurality, even among the most influential centers of Christianity, is that communication among bishops was difficult, and large gatherings of bishops were unheard of.

A parallel can be seen with regard to the development of doctrine, particularly the dogmas of Christianity. A **doctrine** is a religious teaching of importance. A **dogma** represents a core teaching, and one that is presumably unalterable. Christians were of relative agreement on many issues from early on. They widely thought that Jesus was the messiah and Lord, and that he died as a sacrificial atonement for sin and was raised up to provide believers with a future life in heaven. They believed that the Holy Spirit was infused in their lives and conditioned ongoing sanctification or growth in holiness. They baptized in the name of the Father, the Son, and the Holy Spirit. But despite this general agreement, there was still a great deal of plurality in exact beliefs about the nature of Jesus; the relationships among the Father, Son, and Holy Spirit; and other important theological issues.

Periodically, emperors called bishops together to decide on these issues, believing that the communion of orthodox Christianity was at

FIGURE 7-2 Seventeenth-century fresco depicting the 325 Council of Nicaea, the first ecumenical council of the church.

risk. The fullest expressions of these bishops' councils are called **ecumenical councils**, with "ecumenical" meaning "worldwide." The reasons Christianity later accepted the decisions of a given council were complicated, and were influenced by whether there was political pressure on the bishops and whether the council was seen as truly representing the whole church. Those councils held in the fourth and fifth centuries—Nicaea (325), Constantinople (381), Ephesus (431), and Chalcedon (451)—proved to be decisive in establishing Christian dogma for the Eastern Orthodox, Roman Catholic, and later Protestant communities. At them, Christians faced some of the weightiest of issues.

NICAEA (325 CE)

Following their Jewish heritage, Christians believed themselves to be decidedly monotheistic. Given this, what ought they to think about Jesus? Was Jesus God? If the Father was God and Jesus was not the Father, then how could Jesus be God? Was Jesus merely human, someone God raised to a glorified status? Was he fully human? What about the Holy Spirit? Was the Holy Spirit distinct from God, part of God, or another God? Although Christians believed in just one God, the language they used in speaking about Jesus and the Holy Spirit seemed to assign divinity to them. Were Christians then really tri-theists (believers in three Gods)? Appealing to emerging canonical texts (the New Testament) alone would prove to be challenging. As we saw in Chapter Four, Peter's first sermon frames Jesus as a man whom God worked through, raised up, and exalted at his right hand (Acts 2:14–38). Paul also regularly distinguishes Jesus from God: "There is one God, the Father from whom all things and for whom we exist, and one Lord, Jesus Christ, through whom are all things and through whom we exist" (1 Cor. 8:6). Here Paul claims we come *from* God, but live *through* Jesus. Or consider his statement that "when all things are subjected to him [God], then the Son himself will also be subjected to the one [God] who put all things in subjection under him, so that God will be all in all" (1 Cor. 15:28). Jesus certainly appears subordinate to God in

this passage. Even the high Christology in John's Gospel seems to distinguish Jesus from God in some manner: "In the beginning was the Word and the Word was with God and the Word was God. He was in the beginning with God" (John 1:1–2). Here Jesus is both identified as God and distinguished from God.

Arius (256–336) was a priest and influential theologian from Alexandria, Egypt, a theological center for Christianity. He taught that in order to preserve monotheism, the Son could not be God proper, but somehow must be subordinate to the Father. The Son emanated from the Father and became the necessary link between God and his created world. For Arius, Jesus protected God's transcendence and allowed the divine life to be experienced through the Son, God's first emanation. As evidence, Arius could point to the texts mentioned in the previous passage, as well as such texts as "The Son can do nothing on his own, but only what he sees the Father doing" (John 5:19), "What I speak, therefore, I speak just as the Father has told me" (John 1:50), and even "The Father is greater than I" (John 14:28). Arius in no way thought that Jesus Christ was simply a human being elevated to divine glory. He saw the Son as quasi-divine and the bridge for humans to God.

Initially, Arius's bishop, Alexander, called a local council of bishops in 318 to discuss the issue. Surely he intended to get this body of bishops to condemn Arius. He and his supporters argued that Jesus was fully divine and as proof drew on scriptures such as "The Father and I are one" (John 10:30), "Whoever has seen me has seen the Father" (John 14:9), and "Through him [Jesus] all the fullness of God was pleased to dwell" (Col. 1:19). But they did not rest on scripture alone: they also drew on the fact that the church from its earliest days had *worshipped* Jesus Christ, which would be idolatry if the Son was not fully divine. This argument represents an explicit use of what has become known as the principle of *lex orandi, lex credendi*, that is, the law of worship is the law of belief. Further, Alexander and his supporters pointed to the universally held belief that Jesus Christ had redeemed them from sin and was the savior. These were prerogatives of God, not of another created being. In the end, the majority of this relatively small local council of bishops agreed that the Son had a fully divine nature. However, the condemnation of Arius's position highlighted a problem: the church was not in one accord on this issue. In fact, a number of other bishops in the eastern part of the empire were sympathetic to Arius's position.

In 325, Emperor Constantine called the first ecumenical council at Nicaea, a large city close to Constantinople, to decide on this issue. At this council the majority of the bishops did not side with Arius, but argued that the Son's divine nature was eternal and of the "same substance" as the Father (*homoousios*), rather than a "similar substance" (*homoiousios*). Further, the bishops created a **creed**, a short statement of decisive beliefs that ensured this decision would be asserted throughout Christianity. Creeds were not new and were often drawn from baptismal formulas. What makes this creed important was its specificity about the divine nature of Jesus and the fact that it was now supposed to be a universal statement of belief.

CONSTANTINOPLE (381 CE)

Nicaea did not solve all controversies. What did it mean to say that the Son had the same nature as the Father? If he was not the Father, then ought believers to imagine two Gods with the same nature? Despite the establishment of the creed at Nicaea, many Christians in the eastern part of the empire remained Arians. Constantine's son and successor in the East, Constantius II, was sympathetic to the Arian position and exiled many "Nicene" bishops, including Athanasius, who had become the bishop of Alexandria in 328. Constantius II was succeeded by Emperor Constans, who supported Nicaea and reinstated Athanasius. Julian followed Constans and during his two-year reign tried to reinstate the ancient Roman religion. Jovian, the next emperor, died on his way to take the throne in Constantinople and was followed by Valentinian who also died within months, and then by Jovian, who only

reigned for eight months. Valens, the next emperor in the East, was also sympathetic to the Arian position. Gratian followed Valens, but died five months into his rule. In 379, the Eastern Empire, and later the whole empire was under the rule of **Theodosius**, a decidedly Nicene Christian. In 380, he published the edict *Cunctos Populos*, which mandated acceptance of the creed established at Nicaea, seemed to have made the bishops of Rome and Alexandria the judges of orthodox doctrine, and made Christianity the sole religion of the empire:

> It is our desire that all the various nations which are subject to our Clemency and Moderation, should continue to profess that religion which was delivered to the Romans by the divine Apostle Peter, as it has been preserved by faithful tradition, and which is now professed by the Pontiff Damasus, and by Peter, Bishop of Alexandria, a man of apostolic holiness. According to the apostolic teaching and the doctrine of the Gospel, let us believe in the one deity of the Father, the Son and the Holy Spirit, in equal majesty and in the holy Trinity. We authorize the followers of this law to assume the title of Catholic Christians; but as for the others, since in our judgment they are foolish madmen, we decree that they shall be branded with the ignominious name of heretics, and shall not presume to give to their conventicles the name of churches. They will suffer in the first place the chastisement of the divine condemnation and in the second the punishment of our authority which in accordance with the will of Heaven we shall decide to inflict. (*Codex Theodosianus*, xvi.1.2)

Theodosius convened an ecumenical council of bishops in the Eastern Empire's capital of Constantinople in 381. At this gathering the creed introduced at Nicaea was both confirmed and expanded to include a reference to the Holy Spirit. The additions asserted that the Father was the source of the Spirit, and that the Spirit also had the same divine dignity as the Father and Son. This creed has become the universal stance for Christian faith, and today Christians typically call it the Nicene Creed, although technically it is the Nicene-Constantinopolitan Creed.

THE NICENE-CONSTANTINOPOLITAN CREED

We believe in one God, the Father almighty, maker of heaven and earth, of all things visible and invisible. And in one Lord Jesus Christ, the only-begotten Son of God, generated from the Father before all ages, Light from Light, true God from true God, begotten, not made, one in being [*homoousios*] with the Father, through whom all things were made. For us men and for our salvation He came down from the heavens, and became flesh from the Holy Spirit and the Virgin Mary and was made man. For our sake too He was crucified under Pontius Pilate, suffered and was buried. On the third day He rose again according to the Scriptures, He ascended to the heavens and is seated at the right hand of the Father. He shall come again in glory to judge the living and the dead; to His Kingdom there will be no end. And in the Holy Spirit, the Lord and Giver of life, who proceeds from the Father, who together with the Father and the Son is worshipped and glorified, who has spoken through the prophets. [And] in one Holy Catholic and Apostolic Church. We acknowledge one baptism for the forgiveness of sins. We expect the resurrection of the dead and the life of the world to come. Amen.[2]

The theological underpinnings of the **Council of Constantinople** as well as the next council in Ephesus (431) relied in great measure on three theologians of the fourth century: Basil of Caesarea (330–379), his brother Gregory of Nyssa (335–395), and Gregory of Nazianzus (329–390), who are often referred to as the **Cappadocian Fathers**, as they came from the province of Cappadocia (modern Turkey). In their theological writings, they advanced concepts and principles that helped negotiate the otherwise strange claims of Christianity. First, they insisted that all conceptualizations of God are only analogous. Human language simply cannot address the mystery of what is spiritual and not physical, and is all the more problematic when talking about God. Second, they argued that the *members* of the **Trinity** should be considered distinct, but that they were not separate beings. Rather, the *persons* of the Trinity represented different *relations* within God. The Father, Son, and Holy Spirit were not different faces of God, but they referenced real differences within the triune Godhead. Finally, the Cappadocian Fathers clarified what *substance* or being (*ousia*) could mean regarding God. In this context, substance was not a *thing*, but a nature—in this case, the divine nature. So, while God was seen as having one substance (divine nature), he was also understood as having three inner relations (persons).

EPHESUS (431 CE)

Following Constantinople, Christians continued to debate core teachings about Jesus. While there was broad acceptance that Jesus had a divine nature, Christians did not agree as to the nature of his humanity. Even though the gnostic idea that Jesus had only appeared to be human was no longer viable, whether he was *fully* human remained an open question. If he was, how could he be both human and divine? Was he two beings in one? Did God die on the cross? Certainly, no philosophically minded bishop would want to concede that God had died. They were sure that divinity was *impassible*, that is, God could not suffer or change. They were all the more sure that God could not die.

One school of thought—the Antioch school—emphasized the full humanity of Christ, but risked imagining Jesus as two separate beings. Nestorius, the bishop of Constantinople, argued that Mary was merely the mother of the human nature of Jesus, and not mother of the incarnate Son. In short: God cannot be born. Another school of thought—the Alexandrian school—focused on the singularity of Jesus, whereby from the moment of his inception he was both God and human as a single reality. This position risked making problematic proclamations about God, particularly those related to his suffering and dying. It also risked imagining the human nature of Jesus as something overwhelmed or even taken over by the divine.

At the **Council of Ephesus**, the bishops tried to settle these controversies. Broadly, historians and theologians have interpreted Ephesus as siding with the Alexandrian school. After all, its conclusions led to Nestorius being formally condemned and deposed from office. However, it seems much more likely that the council worked out a way to honor both positions. Ephesus decided that Jesus had two full natures—human and divine—and that these natures were never blurred or confused. Jesus was not a hybrid of divinity and humanity, but represented both fully. This union was called the *hypostatic union*, with *hypostasis* referring to subsistence, and both subsistences—human and divine—being united into a singular being: Jesus Christ. Thus, Mary was deemed *theotokos*, or "God bearer." Further, the council argued that Jesus simply had to have everything that a human had: body, soul, mind, and will. Gregory of Nazianzus earlier had persuasively argued: "That which was not assumed has not been healed; but that which is united to God, the same is saved. If only half of Adam fell, then what is assumed and saved may also be only half; but if the whole of Adam fell, it must be united as a whole to Him that is born, in order to be wholly saved."[3] This is to say that Jesus saved everything human, and in order to do this he must have *assumed* or taken up everything human.

CHALCEDON (451 CE)

The Council of Ephesus did not end the controversy, and twenty years later Emperor Marcian convened yet another ecumenical council. The **Council of Chalcedon** represented the culmination of the first three councils, and being a *Chalcedonian* Christian is something of a code word today for Christians who have affirmed these first four councils. The bishop of Rome, Pope Leo I,

sent to this gathering a letter, now known as *The Tome of Leo*, that he believed articulated authentic belief; it stands as an example of the bishop of Rome's assumption that his position was the correct position and that he had the authority to articulate the universal faith of the church. Indeed, the teaching of Chalcedon followed Leo's position and logic. But the fathers of Chalcedon also read out loud Cyril of Alexandria's (378–444) Second and Third Letters to Nestorius, as well as a document called *The Formula of Reunion* from the church of Antioch. Positions from all three found their way into the council's formal declarations. Briefly, Chalcedon taught that Jesus was totally divine and totally human, with the same natures of God and humanity. As the eternal, divine Son, he was begotten from the Father from all eternity, and there was never a Father without the Son (or, implicitly, without the Holy Spirit). While his divine nature was eternal, as a hypostatic union, Jesus was born in time from the Virgin Mary. At the moment of his inception, he was fully human and fully divine. He had two natures, which were never mixed with each other, but he was a singular being: one person, two natures.

 CHRISTOLOGICAL AND TRINITARIAN DOGMAS IN BRIEF

Even though the Trinitarian and Christological dogmas of the church developed quite late, one ought not to assume that they were formulated in a haphazard way or created on the fly. The decisions reflect core commitments that the church embraced from early on. The dogmas were the fruit of church experience, spirituality, and reflections from worship, and they were deemed philosophically necessary to protect long-standing values. What is clear is that they did not come directly from the Bible itself, even as the Bible provided some of the raw material for them. The Bible never details these dogmas, and it contains both evidence and counterevidence for all of them.

JESUS THE CHRIST

The church came to believe that Jesus had to be fully divine. Why? Because he was from the beginning proclaimed savior, and only God can save. We also see in the Gospels that Jesus took on prerogatives that Jews could only imagine God taking, such as forgiving sins or announcing covenants on the basis of his own authority. From the beginning, Christians worshipped Jesus, which would have been idolatry if they did not believe Jesus was (somehow) legitimately divine. Parts of the Bible do identify Jesus as divine in some way, even as they distinguish him from the Father.

The church also argued for a robust understanding of the incarnation, which was tied to its understanding of salvation. Christians came to believe rather early on that salvation involved a full union with God, that is, fully living God's life with God. This came later to be called *theosis*, which literally means "becoming God" and is sometimes referred to as *divinization*. Christians did not think that their natures would change from human to divine, but that they would experience the divine life radically. The Bible hints at this idea, but only later did theological reflection provide a deeper understanding of it. In the First Letter of John we find the statement, "Beloved, we are God's children now; what we will be has not yet been revealed. What we do know is this: when he [God] is revealed, we will be like him, for we will see him as he is" (3:2). In Second Peter we read that believers were given everything for godliness so that they "may become participants in the divine nature" (1:4). In John, Jesus prays to the Father about his disciples "that they may all be one. As you, Father, are in me and I am in you, may they also be in us" (17:21). Finally, in Paul's vision of heaven, "God will be all in all" (1 Cor. 15:28). Consider too some of the early witnesses predating the councils, a list that could go on for dozens of pages:

- Justin Martyr (100–165): "And we have learned that those only are deified who have lived near to God in holiness and virtue" (*First Apology*, XXI).

- Irenaeus of Lyons (130–202): "That faith of men to be placed in God has increased . . . that man might too become a partaker of God." (*Against Heresies*, 5.28.2).
- Clement of Alexandria (150–215): "Logos, the Word of God, became man in order that you can learn through the intercession of Man how many can become God by grace" (*Protreptikos*, 1.8).
- Hippolytus of Rome (170–235): "Friends of God and coheirs with Christ . . . we shall have become divine" (*Refutation of All Heresies*).
- Origen (185–254): "Let us pray unceasingly with that disposition of soul which the word may make us divine" (*Notebook on Prayer*).

The full humanity of Jesus is implied widely in the Bible. Jesus got tired, hungry, and thirsty, and he exhibited the full range of human emotions. It is also clear from these accounts that Jesus suffered and died as a human being. Jesus had a God and prayed to God. His full humanity was deemed necessary if he was to be savior of everything that makes up a human being. As we saw earlier from Gregory of Nazianzus, "whatever is not assumed is not saved."

Why, then, the controversies? First, it should not surprise one that the Bible is hesitant to identify Jesus as divine. Jewish theology would have been utterly unprepared for an actual divine messiah. The fact that Peter's first sermon identifies Jesus as a man glorified by God makes complete sense when we view this apostle as a Jew testifying to salvation in Jesus. What might be seen as astounding is that biblical evidence aligns him with divinity at all and applies to him prerogatives that were seen as only belonging to God. One could, on the other hand, also imagine how difficult it would have been to imagine Jesus as really human. This is certainly part of why gnostic Christianity appealed to some Christians. For the gnostics, if Jesus was the savior and humans cannot save, then he could not have been human. Further, Christians worshipped him, and this would have been blasphemous if he were a human being. The council fathers responded that his humanity was aligned to his divinity, conditioning the possibility of our humanity being united to his divinity. While one does not worship creatures but only the creator, one could worship Jesus because in doing so he or she worshipped the singular identity of the God-man.

The council fathers were actually quite philosophically savvy. We must remember that they did not think divinity was a *thing*, an object like other objects one could point to. They did not think that one *thing*, divinity, was fused with another *thing*, humanity, as if these necessarily had to be either side-by-side or welded into a kind of hybrid. Their understanding was different. Abstract as this may sound, they came to believe that the second person of the Trinity (with the Trinity collectively being the infinite, transcendental, supernatural ground and horizon of all reality) became intrinsically one with and personally identified with the human nature of Jesus of Nazareth from the moment of his conception. From that point on, the identity of the eternal second person of the Trinity could not be extricated from the identity or person of Jesus, nor he from it.

THE TRINITY

The patristic church argued among four positions regarding the Trinity. One of these positions has been called **dynamic monarchianism** and was represented by Arius and others. In this view, the Father is properly God, while the Son and Holy Spirit are believed to be emanations from God—a sort of second tier of divinity—and dependent on God. While God is utterly transcendent and eternal, the Son and Holy Spirit were created before the physical world and represent God's presence or grace to the created world. A second framing was **modalistic monarchianism**, whereby God is singular but is experienced in different modes or faces. God in the mode of creator is the face of God as the Father, God in the mode of redeemer is the face of God as the Son, and God in the mode of sanctifier is the face of God as the Holy Spirit. A third possibility was

FIGURE 7-3 A modern rendition of Andrei Rublev's icon of the Trinity, with associations to the Eucharist.

simply that there are three separate beings—Father, Son, and Holy Spirit—who all share the same divine substance. We might consider this **tri-theism**. None of these positions ultimately survived. The first two protect monotheism, but the first subordinates the Son and Spirit to something less than God, while the second does not distinguish the persons of the Trinity in any way beyond human experiences of God. There is no actual Trinity in either of them—or at least this is what the council fathers believed. The problem the church fathers had with the third was that it seemed philosophically impossible for there to be three distinct divine individuals. Philosophically, God was considered *simple*, that is, without parts. So, the third option seemed to violate the idea of divine simplicity as well as the fundamental commitment to monotheism.

The fourth possibility became the decision of the council fathers: the Trinity references the inner life of God, and this one God consists of a community of *relations*. Thus, the Father, Son, and Holy Spirit are persons only insofar as they can be distinguished by divine inner relations. The Father has a kind of priority in that the Father *begets* the Son and the Holy Spirit *proceeds* from the Father. But this framing was believed to represent the eternal life of God. There was never a Father without the Son and Holy Spirit. Eternally, God was always Father, Son, and Holy Spirit. In his monumental treatise *The Trinity*, Augustine of Hippo (354–430) offers two analogies for understanding the Trinity. One is Mind–Thinking–Thought. An active mind, Augustine states, must think, and it must think thoughts. There is never an active mind that is not engaged in these acts simultaneously. Even though mind, thinking, and thought can be distinguished from each other, they form a necessary collective. Augustine's second analogy is Love–Beloved–Love Shared. For one to love, he argues, there has to be a beloved, and the communion in love they have necessarily becomes part of the relationship. There is never one without the other two. These, Augustine believed, were only human analogies. Still, he thought it was possible to distinguish three relations, and even have an originating relation, without violating the necessity of all three happening at once and necessitating each other.

Most Christians probably think of God either in terms of dynamic monarchianism or tri-theism. The biblical language divides the persons of the Trinity all the time and certainly never expresses the theological idea the council fathers decided on. The council fathers were reasoning philosophically and quite abstractly in order to preserve Trinitarian monotheism. Most people think of God less in terms of philosophical purity and more in terms of how a *person* is imagined in the created world. After all, our minds and our language are built to negotiate a world of subjects and objects. Consequently the human mind naturally separates the Trinity into three objects or distinct persons of reflection. Christians regularly pray to the Son, as if he were separate from the Father and Holy Spirit, and

they invoke the Holy Spirit as if it were distinct from the Father and the Son. The council fathers never imagined such practices to be improper, and, indeed, church rituals and formal prayer follow such patterns all the time. That is how language works. Technically, in terms of Christian dogma, however, God cannot be separated into distinct persons or beings, as we use these terms in regular parlance. Whenever God works, it is as the triune God. God can only be separated in the sense of distinct relations *within* the Trinity itself. Nevertheless, for Christians to observe this philosophical caveat in the context of a robust prayer life would be most difficult, or even unhelpful.

COUNCILS AND THE BREAKUP OF THE PATRISTIC CHURCH

While the ecumenical councils solidified the teachings that became core dogmas for what eventually became the Eastern Orthodox, Roman Catholic, and mainstream Protestant churches, their decisions were not accepted by all—a disagreement that led to the first clear breakup of the *katholikos ekklesia*, the catholic (universal) church. Ephesus argued that Jesus Christ was a singular person with two natures from the very beginning of his conception. It even called Mary the *theotokos*, "the Mother of God" or "God-bearer." Recall that Nestorius, the bishop of Constantinople, adhered to a severe version of the Antioch school, one that insisted that the divine Logos *indwelled* in the human, and was unwilling to see Jesus Christ as a whole, integral person with both natures. For him, Mary was certainly not the *theotokos*, but only the *christotokos*. After Ephesus condemned Nestorius and those in his camp, the Assyrian Church of the East (located in modern Iraq) split with the rest of the church over this issue.

The unity of the church was further weakened when representatives of the Armenian, Syrian, Ethiopian, and Egyptian churches refused to accept the decisions of Chalcedon. For them, is seemed, Jesus could only have one nature, which was typically understood as a union of the divine and human in a single synthesis. The champions of Chalcedon called these believers **monophysites** (*mono*, one; *physis*, nature), a term they found pejorative. To outsiders looking in, these churches look extraordinarily like other Eastern Orthodox churches, with the same threefold ministry and the same rites, but to Christians of the day, these philosophical questions about Jesus were considered so crucial that the universal church was willing to divide over them.

Was the breakup of the church necessary? Addressing this question might follow two different tracks. It could mean, Were these dogmatic differences so decisive for church identity that staking a claim required rejecting alternative claims and breaking communion with those who held them? From that point of view, the patristic church surely thought the breakup was necessary. But another way to address the question is to ask, Did these Christian communities really differ in their dogmatic beliefs enough to actually be at real odds with each other? Possibly not. Since the early twentieth century, scholars have questioned whether these theological camps actually understood each other. In 1897, an unknown text (now published as *Liber Heraclidis*) partially written by Nestorius was discovered. In it, we find that Nestorius believed the *Tome of Leo* and the Council of Chalcedon actually *vindicated* his position. Further, modern dialogues between churches have revealed that the Church of the East never believed Jesus Christ was not an integral single being, both human and divine, and that the technical term used by Cyril of Alexandria and the Coptic Church to describe Jesus, *miaphysis* (literally "one nature"), refers to the whole of the person and does not deny the distinct human and divine natures. In a historic statement called the Vienna Christological Formula, signed by Pope John Paul II and representatives of the Coptic Church and the Church of the East, all three ancient Christian communions declared themselves of fundamental accord. At the center of the formula is the affirmation:

We believe that our Lord and Savior, Jesus Christ, is God the Son Incarnate, perfect in his divinity and perfect in his humanity. His divinity was not separated from his humanity for a single moment, not for the twinkling of an eye. His humanity is one with his divinity without commixture, without confusion, without division, without separation. . . . We both recognize the legitimacy and rightness of these expressions of the same faith and we both respect the preference of each church in her liturgical life and piety. . . . The controversies of the past led to anathemas, bearing upon persons and on formulas. The Lord's Spirit permits us to understand better today that the divisions brought about in this way were due in large part to misunderstandings. Whatever our Christological divergences have been, we experience ourselves united today in the confession of the same faith in the Son of God who became man that we might become children of God by his grace.[4]

CHURCH AND STATE

From Constantine onward, there was a symbiotic relationship between church and state. With the exception of Julian's two-year rule (361–363), the emperors were all Christian and understood themselves as important to the life of the church. It was the emperor, not the bishops, who called councils, and emperors did not hesitate to exile bishops who did not accept the councils' decisions—that is, unless an emperor himself had not accepted a given council's decision. Emperor Valens (r. 364–378), for example, exiled Athanasius of Alexandria for *not* being an Arian, a view the emperor believed should have triumphed at Nicaea. Other emperors, namely Constantine and his son Constantius, had exiled Athanasius earlier for other reasons.

As noted earlier, Theodosius made Christianity the sole supported religion of the empire. This did not mean, however, that every citizen had to become a Christian, but rather that Christianity was understood as the empire's official religion. Later, Emperor Justinian (r. 527–565) revised Roman law so that it would better integrate

Christian values. Justinian's Code (*Codex Juris Civilis*) was foundational for many European systems of civil law over the centuries. While Constantine had surely seen himself as the head of state, and thus responsible for its religion, Justinian and other emperors saw themselves as head of both church and state, an arrangement sometimes referred to as *Caesaro-papism*. In Constantinople, Justinian built what would remain for centuries the largest church in Christianity, the Hagia Sophia (Holy Wisdom). Imperial processions to the Hagia Sophia would typically include standard bearers leading the way, high-ranking civil and military leaders following, and then the emperor, surrounded by his imperial guard. When the procession reached the Hagia Sophia, the emperor would be received by the bishop of Constantinople—himself appointed by the emperor—along with other bishops, and would join them behind the wall of icons where the presiding bishop would consecrate the Eucharist. This space was supposedly reserved only for clergy.

This political and religious interdependence probably served both parties quite well in some ways. The church legitimated the political hierarchy as a God-given order, and the state protected and supported the church. The church was not, however, the state's lackey. Bishops believed themselves successors to the apostles, charged with spiritual authority. Often bishops allowed themselves to be deposed by the emperor rather than give way to what they believed was wrongly considered doctrine. They even openly challenged imperial power. Consider, for example, Ambrose (340–397), the bishop of Milan, a decidedly Christian city (unlike Rome) with five churches and, at this time, the Western Empire's imperial court. In 385, Ambrose was summoned to the imperial palace and ordered to give up one of the city's churches to Christians who were Arians. He refused. A few weeks later, Justinia, the mother of both the Eastern and the Western emperors, specifically demanded that he give up the Basilica of Portius, a church outside the city walls, to the Arians. Again, he

refused. The next Sunday, which was Palm Sunday, Ambrose went to the Basilica of Portius to celebrate the Eucharist and found it surrounded by soldiers. Defying them, he and his clergymen passed through the gauntlet of armed men and remained inside the basilica throughout the night. The emperor relented. Ambrose declared, "In the matter of faith it is the practice for bishops to judge Christian emperors, not emperors bishops."[5] Ambrose would later face down Emperor Valentinian for supporting a pagan procession in Rome and Theodosius for killing thousands of citizens of Thessalonica.

A second example of the limits of the church–state relationship is John Chrysostom (347–407), bishop of Constantinople. Chrysostom alienated the upper class by challenging ostentatious wealth. Some of his sermons seemed to address the emperor's family itself, particularly the extravagant Aelia Eudoxia, the wife of Emperor Arcadius. The emperor ultimately deposed and replaced him, sparking public objection by the bishops of Rome and Milan. That the emperors meddled in church affairs, particularly through the power of the state, shows something of their influence and control. That bishops were willing to challenge the emperors, even at the risk of their own demise, shows something of the bishops' backbone and assertion of their own spiritual authority.

The supposed fusion of the identities of the church and state ironically led to some fragmentation of the church. As noted previously, some Christian churches did not accept the conclusions of the Council of Chalcedon and operated independently. The church in the Persian Empire, a competitor and enemy of the Byzantine Empire, began to assert its own independence and identity as well. Additionally, the rejection of Chalcedon by "monophysite" Christians was theological, but also had political implications. In rejecting Chalcedon, Christians from diverse regions, such as Syria, Egypt, Ethiopia, and Armenia, asserted independence from the Byzantine Empire. Armenia was the first nation to officially identify itself as Christian in the fourth century, with Ethiopia following in the sixth century. Ethiopia's national epic, the *Kebra Nagast* (Glory of Kings), reflects this identity: here we find the virtuous Christian King Kaleb meeting with the Byzantine emperor in Jerusalem and agreeing to partition the world between the two kingdoms. Saint Gregory the Illuminator, who led the conversion of Armenia, then declares that Byzantium will be taken over by the Persians, while Ethiopia will remain strong, the last true holdout of the Christian faith.

The rejection of Chalcedon by Christians in Persia worked to their favor. Zoroastrianism was the official state religion of the time, but Persia was religiously tolerant. Under threat, however, Christians could be marginalized, and they were sometimes persecuted. Rejection of Chalcedon highlighted the perception that their religion was not the Christianity of the Byzantines, the enemy empire. Perhaps for this reason more than any other, Christianity was allowed to spread in the Persian Empire and beyond. Christians followed the Silk Road and eventually entered India, Sri Lanka, and finally China. In fact, we find evidence that as early as 635 Christians had a secure, albeit modest, presence in China, which lasted until the ninth century and was later revived under Mongol support in the thirteenth and fourteenth centuries. It ultimately did not survive, probably because it competed with religions that were more ethnically entrenched, such as Confucianism and Buddhism.

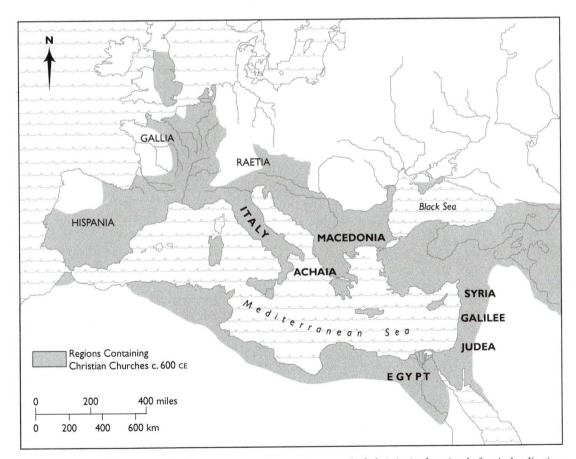

FIGURE 7-4 Early Christianity: In this map, one sees the massive spread of Christianity from just before its legalization to the early medieval period.

PATRIARCHAL SEES

Bishops represented the authority of the apostles and the symbolic unity of the church. Not only were they the overseers of a local church, but their communion with each other represented the *katholikos ekklesia*, the catholic or universal church. As Christianity developed, these bishops became overseers of dioceses or municipal areas, typically centered on cities. A diocese might have had several church buildings, with the presbyters acting as the bishop's representatives in each. Here we see the word "church" meaning a number of things. It could refer to a church building and the people who gathered there regularly, a diocese with a presiding bishop who usually presided at the cathedral, or the universal church. The reason the principal church building in a diocese is called a cathedral is that it held the bishop's *cathedra*, or "chair" of authority.

In theory, all churches (dioceses) and their bishops were equal, but of course the largest cities and the bishops who oversaw the church in those cities held greater authority than those in more rural dioceses. Further, local churches were grouped together in ecclesiastical provinces that had the same boundaries as civil provinces. Bishops met regularly in provincial synods, or councils, to discuss church order, doctrine, ministry, and so on. These provinces were presided over by the bishop of the capital of the province, called the **metropolitan**. Typically the metropolitan chose or had great influence over who would become bishops in his province.

The **Council of Nicaea** (325) allowed for an exception to this general rule through the establishment of **patriarchal sees**. "Patriarch" refers to an authoritative father figure, and "see" refers to seat, as in "seat of authority." Nicaea created three patriarchal sees: Antioch (Syria), Alexandria (Egypt), and Rome (Italy). These three cities were the largest in the empire, and they had the advantage of containing long-standing authoritative Christian communities. To these three, the Council of Constantinople (381) added Jerusalem and Constantinople, the latter because it was understood to be the "new Rome." Chalcedon (451) divided up the Roman world into these five patriarchates, in which the patriarch had the privilege of presiding over metropolitan elections, even as the metropolitans themselves oversaw the bishops in their immediate jurisdictions.

The relationship of the five patriarchal sees is complicated, particularly regarding claims about the Roman See. As noted earlier, Theodosius's *Cunctos Populos* (380) made the bishops of Rome and Alexandria the ultimate arbiters of church doctrine. The Council of Constantinople also declared that the See of Constantinople itself was subject to Rome in terms of honor. The bishop of Rome, however, saw his place as more authoritative than what was implied by mere honor, and, indeed, so did many of the bishops in the East. Since the second century the bishop of Rome had been seen in some ways as responsible for the church at large. As noted in Chapter Four, for example, the Corinthian church sought advice from Clement of Rome on how to handle its schism. Clement responded pastorally, but also authoritatively. Through the third, fourth, and fifth centuries Eastern bishops regularly looked to Rome for refuge, for support, and as a kind of court of appeal. Eventually this bishop took on the title of **pope**, meaning "father."

Roman Catholics who see the bishop of Rome as having universal authority also point to other evidence. For example, Irenaeus of Lyons, in his treatise *Against Heresies*, marks Rome as the surest place of authentic teaching, as it has a direct line of apostolic succession that goes back to Peter and Paul, who were martyred there. Further, the Roman church was so decisive in the West that a legate of the bishop of Rome often spoke for the whole of Latin Christianity. In every case, the position of the bishop of Rome was the position that the councils adopted. The Eastern patriarchs themselves regularly affirmed the bishop of Rome as the successor to the apostle Peter. When Pope Leo sent his famous *Tome of Leo*, outlining what he believed was the orthodox tradition, to the Council of Chalcedon, the Eastern bishops replied, "Peter has spoken through Leo."

A final piece of evidence that seems to support a kind of universal authority of the Roman bishop comes from the Bible. The apostle Peter's original name was Simon. After Simon asserts that Jesus is "the Messiah, the Son of Living God," Jesus responds:

> Blessed are you Simon son of Jonah! For flesh and blood has not revealed this to you, but my Father in heaven. And I tell you, you are Peter [Rock], and on this rock I will build my church, and the gates of Hades will not prevail against it. I will give you the keys of the kingdom of heaven, and whatever you bind on earth will be bound in heaven, and whatever you loose on earth will be loosed in heaven. (Matt. 16:15–19)

What ought one to make of this evidence? On the surface, it seems quite persuasive. In truth, it is less so. There is little question that the Roman church and its representative bishop were held in high esteem throughout the church, both East and West. Eastern bishops afforded it a high position in the hierarchy of honor. But whether it held actual authority or hierarchical supremacy is far less clear. When the Council of Chalcedon listed the patriarchal sees, in listing Rome it did not frame its reason in terms of the chair of Peter or Peter's successors, but rather stated that it was the city that held the historical emperor and senate. Further, when the Eastern bishops declared that "Peter has spoken through Leo," they also reflected other great patriarchal voices, such as that of Cyril of Alexandria.

The proof text from Matthew's Gospel might also be problematic. The citation seems quite clearly to recognize Peter as leader of the disciples, and the "keys of the kingdom" are given to him personally. On the other hand, in the very same Gospel, we find all the apostles given authority to bind and loose (18:18), and it is said that they will all "sit on twelve thrones to judge the twelve tribes of Israel" (19:28). As noted in Chapter Four, while Peter was clearly a leader in the early church, he was not the head of the Jerusalem church, nor apparently the head of any of the churches. Irenaeus places assurance of authentic teaching on Rome, but does not say that Peter was the first bishop of Rome. Rather, he notes that both Peter and Paul were martyred there. Clearly, there was an active church in Rome before Peter's arrival and eventual martyrdom. We also saw earlier that the single-bishop model came later to the West than to the East. Irenaeus identifies a line of bishops in Rome going back to the time of Peter and Paul, but some scholars question its accuracy, arguing that Rome probably had several Christian communities and, even as a singular Roman collective, seems to have worked on the group-presbyter model until the second century. Those figures Irenaeus identifies as bishops could very well have been the leading presbyters of the church, but there probably would not have been a clear, singular office of bishop in the first century.

Was Peter the first pope or bishop of Rome? It would be fairer to say that his authority was assigned to the bishop of Rome and that the church, both East and West, widely believed the bishop of Rome was his successor. What does this mean? To the bishops of the East, it meant that the bishop of Rome ought to be assigned the position of honor, as first among equals. For the church in the West, it increasingly meant that the bishop of Rome ought to have juridical authority over the whole church, that is, the power to legislate church life everywhere. This difference came to mark a dividing line between the Western (Latin) church and the Eastern (Greek) church. For political and cultural reasons, East and West would split and ultimately go their own ways. From a theological view, the differing interpretations of the role of the chair of Peter became a wall of separation that has never been successfully removed.

CONCLUSIONS

By any standard the early patristic church was an impressive religious witness. To be a Christian was to risk death, often preceded by torture. Christians had high expectations of each other and focused themselves on life in the church. In its early years the church clearly distinguished itself from the Roman Empire. When the empire began to sponsor the church, things changed. The empire's alignment with the church afforded church leaders the opportunity to meet and debate publicly and to become public players in the life of the empire. There is little evidence that Christianity was corrupted by this process, but it could not help being compromised in some way. Christians were increasingly expected to identify themselves with this newly Christian empire. Emperors thought themselves responsible for, or even leaders in, the church and did not hesitate to periodically immerse themselves in church decisions and personnel. Councils, called by emperors, succeeded in creating doctrines, practices, and dogmas that would permanently mark the church. Such decisions also created permanent divisions among Christians. By the end of this period, the *katholikos ekklesia* was no more.

SUMMARY QUESTIONS

- Describe the relationship and power dynamics between bishops and the Roman emperors during the first few centuries after Christianity was adopted by the Roman Empire.
- What are some of the different conceptions of the Trinity that were discussed in the early years of Christianity, and what is the orthodox position?
- What were the central issues that each of the main councils addressed? What did they decide, and why?
- Rome claimed a special status among the five sees. What are the arguments supporting and challenging this special status?

DISCUSSION QUESTIONS

- Christianity became part of the Roman Empire with a complicated power dynamic. Compare and contrast this situation to that of today. How does separation of church and state affect how the church carries out its mission? How would society be different if the church and state were still aligned?
- The claim for the primacy of Rome is controversial. Where do you stand on this issue, and why?
- Constantine was a complicated and highly influential figure in church history. What do you think about his motivations and ambitions?

KEY TERMS

Arius
Cappadocian Fathers
Constantine
Council of Chalcedon
Council of Constantinople
Council of Ephesus
Council of Nicaea
Creed

Doctrine
Dogma
Dynamic monarchianism
Ecumenical council
Metropolitan
Miaphysis
Modalistic monarchianism
Monophysite

Patriarchal sees
Pope
Theodosius
Theosis
Trinity
Tri-theism

BIBLIOGRAPHY

- Bellitto, Christopher. 2002. *The General Councils: A History of the Twenty-One Church Councils from Nicaea to Vatican II.* New York: Paulist Press.
- Jurgens, William, ed. 1970. *The Faith of the Early Fathers*, Vol. 1. Collegeville, MN: Liturgical Press.
- Lefebure, Leo. 1999. "Christology in Ecumenical Dialogue: Expressing the Identity of Jesus Christ." *Chicago Studies* 39:154–164.
- Norris, Richard A., Jr., ed. and trans. 1980. *The Christological Controversy.* Philadelphia: Fortress Press.
- Rusch, William, ed. and trans. 1980. *The Trinitarian Controversy.* Philadelphia: Fortress Press.
- Schaff, Philip, and Henry Wace, eds. 1894. *Nicene and Post-Nicene Fathers*, Vol. 7. Trans. Edwin Hamilton Gifford. Buffalo, NY: Christian Literature Publishing Co.
- Stevenson, J., ed. 1989. *Creeds, Councils and Controversies: Documents Illustrating the History of the Church AD 337–461.* London: SPCK.
- Sullivan, Francis. 2001. *From Apostles to Bishops: The Development of the Episcopacy in the Early Church.* New York: Newman Press.

NOTES

1. Stevenson, *Creeds, Councils and Controversies*, 283–84.
2. J. Neuner and J. Dupuis, eds., *The Christian Faith*, rev. ed. (New York: Alba House, 1982), 9.
3. Gregory of Nazianzus, *Letter to Cledonius the Priest* in *Faith of our Fathers*, vol. 2, p. 41.
4. Cited in Lefebure, "Christology in Ecumenical Dialogue," 159–161.
5. Robert Louis Wilken, *The First Thousand Years: A Global History of Christianity* (New Haven, CT: Yale University Press, 2012), 123.

8

The Great Fathers and the Quest for Union with God

WHAT TO EXPECT

This chapter introduces some of the greatest, most influential theologians of the patristic church, all of them bishops. As we saw in Chapter Seven, many of these theologians either directly or indirectly affected the outcomes of the ecumenical councils. As intellectuals, they drew on the philosophical assumptions of the day, a relatively sophisticated understanding of scripture, the

worship life of the church, and their experience as pastors. Most of them had a mystical bent, that is, they saw the Christian faith as providing the possibility of coming into direct union with God. This chapter discusses their theological principles as well as how these principles worked in the living out of a holy life, as they understood such an idea.

 BACKGROUND

Many of the most influential theologians of the church were intellectuals. Widely educated in Greco-Roman culture, political theory, history, philosophy, and rhetoric, they not surprisingly shared many of the same assumptions as other well-educated non-Christian intellectuals of the day. As noted earlier, Christian apologists were well versed in and highly respectful of many Greco-Roman philosophers. The philosophy of Stoicism is a good example. Christians saw in Stoic philosophers shared values, such as performing one's duty without attachments and cultivating *apatheia*. The Stoic emperor Marcus Aurelius (r. 161–180), for example, provides a

commendable example in his personal notebook *Meditations*: "Perceive at last that you have within yourself something stronger and more divine than the things which create your passions and make a downright puppet of you. What is my consciousness at this instant? Fright, suspicion, appetite? Some similar evil? First, do nothing aimlessly nor without relation to an end. Secondly, relate your action to no other end except the good of human fellowship."[1]

It was not as though Christians encountered such texts and "Christianized" them. Rather, such wisdom was simply part of the intellectual air they breathed alongside other well-read Romans. Plato was another admired source, although he was much more directly appropriated. As noted in Chapter Five, Justin thought that Plato and others were influenced by the eternal *Logos* (Christ) before the incarnation. Other Christians were just as impressed. Clement of Alexandria remarked, "For what is Plato but Moses speaking in Attic Greek?"[2] And Augustine asserted, "So if these men [Platonic philosophers] could live their lives again today . . . with the change of a few words and sentiments, they would become Christians, as many Platonists of recent times have done."[3]

Plato believed that the world emanated from God, who represented pure goodness, truth, and beauty. The soul can only experience these *transcendentals* as they are manifested in the created world. From God, there emanated a *Logos*, an archetype of God's reason, through which the universe was created. Out of the *Logos* came eternal forms and ideas, and these were made concrete in the created world. The soul, Plato thought, is eternal and spiritual, but trapped in the created world. Still, it has the ability to transcend creation and enter the existence of the eternal forms and ideas. Such a transcendence makes one wise, for one sees truth in its purity. If you really want to understand justice, he argued, you must look not just at instances of justice in this world, but the eternal idea of justice. For Plato, the created world was a weak mediator of these pure forms and ideas. He likened humans' situation to that of prisoners trapped in a cave, seeing only shadows of puppets. The true philosopher learns to leave the cave and see everything in the true light of day. The real world is the spiritual world.

Plato's philosophy was influential among intellectuals and became all the more so with its resurgence in the third century CE. The most important voice of this resurgence, called *Middle Platonism*, was Plotinus (205–270). Plotinus believed that everything emanated from God, whom he called ONE, and is destined to return to God. Through moral purification and deep introspection, one can even encounter the ONE. "Many times it happened," he recounts in *The Enneads*, "lifted out of the body into myself; becoming external to all other things and self-encentered; beholding a marvelous beauty . . . acquiring identity with the divine."[4] This account might strike one as strangely paradoxical. Plotinus is "lifted out of the body" and "self-encentered." What he seems to mean is that he is able to leave consciousness of his body and the physical world by becoming utterly attentive to the center of his soul. It is in the center of his very being that he discovers God.

Plotinus's spiritual program consisted of several stages. First, one had to be truly convinced that the physical world is a poor mediator of the divine—an essentially useless place. Second, one had to endure extensive moral purification, which would have included significant asceticism and the acquisition of virtue. These were preliminaries. Third, one began practicing contemplation, thinking not of things but of the spiritual life of the soul within. With enough practice, he thought that one could actually experience God in this stage directly. To him, contemplation was the very essence of the soul's authentic activity: "All things come from contemplation and are contemplation."[5]

Christianity took these insights and developed an understanding of spiritual progress known as the **purgative way**, the **illuminative way**, and the **unitive way**. Initially, one worked to strip oneself from sin and pursue the virtues. "Purgative" here represented purging the soul of sin. Once free from the tyranny of sin, one's prayer life could deepen to more intimate experiences of God within—the illuminative way. With greater availability and a great deal of contemplative practice, the Christian was believed to be able to know God quite directly—the unitive way.

Christianity did not accept everything taught by Greek philosophers. The patristic fathers, with few exceptions, did not believe that the soul was eternal from the past, and none believed it was imprisoned in the body. Indeed, they proclaimed the resurrection of the body and that creation was a gift from God. On the other hand, many did see the universe as emanating from God, and many also believed that the created world, while good, could not mediate the divine directly. The physical world was something that one had to transcend if one desired direct union with God. The patristic fathers also shared the belief that God dwelt most profoundly in the center of the soul, and that one could attain experiences of union with God through contemplation.

FATHERS OF THE EAST

ORIGEN (185–254 CE)

We know about **Origen** mostly through the fourth-century church historian Eusebius. According to Eusebius, Origen was born of a Christian family in Alexandria. When he was seventeen, his father was martyred under the persecution of Septimius Severus in 202. As an adolescent, Origen embraced a highly ascetic life of fasting, extended prayer, and moderate sleep on the floor. After the death of his father, he supported his family by teaching, and within two years Bishop Demetrius of Alexandria had appointed him head of the Catechetical School in Alexandria, a leading center of learning in the Christian world.

Origen became famous in the church and traveled extensively throughout the empire. At the invitation of the emperor's mother, he even expounded the Christian faith at the imperial court. In 230, he went to Caesarea in Palestine and was persuaded by the bishop there to become ordained a priest. Upon Origen's return to Alexandria, Demetrius was so offended that he had been ordained in another diocese that he sent Origen back to Caesarea, where he lived out the rest of his life. During the persecution of Decius in 250, Origen was arrested and tortured. He was not martyred, but he ultimately died of the injuries from that torture.

According to Eusebius, Origen wrote over 2,000 books, though today we would see most of these as chapters of books. A clear Christian Platonist, he believed that the fundamental truths articulated by Platonism were the same truths revealed in the scriptures, even though

FIGURE 8-1 Origen became controversial centuries after his lifetime, but during it he was the most influential theologian in Christianity.

sometimes the Platonists needed to be corrected by revelation. In short, he found Platonic thought capable of expressing the truth of the gospel. Long after his life, some of Origen's thought, such as the belief that souls were eternal and that salvation would ultimately include all souls, was condemned, most notably by the Second Council of Constantinople (553), though not before he influenced most of the Greek-speaking Christian world.

Some of the Christian Trinitarian thought that was decided on in the ecumenical councils came from Origen. He was the first to describe the nature of the Trinity in terms of relations and to argue that the Father, Son, and Holy Spirit in relation to each other represent a unified divinity. The Son, for example, in relation to himself can be understood as distinct, allowing the Son to be both divine and a mediator to divinity.

Plotinus had understood the *Logos* as an initial emanation of God in the creation of the universe, providing the pattern or archetype for the universe. Origen agreed: this emanation, he believed, is the Son. Thus, Origen believed that Christianity solves how the Son could be both creation's archetype and divine mediator and divine at the same time. As mediator, the Son binds God and creation in unity; as divine, the Son is wholly an expression of God's inner life.

Origen thought that originally God created purely spiritual beings after the pattern of the true image of the *Logos*, or Son. These spiritual beings lived a joyous life of contemplating God, "a pure and perfect reception of God into itself."[6] One of the most important qualities of these spiritual beings was freedom, and this freedom allowed for the fall. What led to the fall? According to Origen, "sloth and weariness of taking trouble to preserve the good, coupled with disregard and neglect for better things, began the process of withdrawal from the good."[7] Angels represent those spiritual beings who retained a good deal of their contemplative focus, while those who would become human beings fell much further because of neglect. The spiritual beings who fell the furthest were those who were not only slothful, but contentious to the good; these became demons. Creation, for Origen, represented the possibility of human recovery. The physical world allowed for a kind of re-education of the soul, and having bodies allowed for souls to develop.

Much of Origen's writing concerns the soul's journey back to God in its original state of contemplation. Jesus, he says, who never lost perfect contemplation of God, becomes the model and way back. The incarnate *Logos* entered into our fallen state as a model and teacher of all in order to rescue us. As a Christian, and in contrast to Plato, Origen believed in the resurrection of the body, but he saw the body as a spiritual entity, having little to no resemblance to our own. This view may in fact align him with Paul, who wrote, "There are both heavenly bodies and earthly bodies, but the glory of the heavenly is one thing, and that of the earthly is another. . . . So it

is with the resurrection of the dead. What is sown is perishable, what is raised is imperishable. . . . It is sown a physical body, it is raised a spiritual body" (1 Cor. 15:40–44).

How does one attain such a union on earth? Union presumes a rigorously moral and ascetic life. Like many in the early church, Origen was suspicious of the passions, particularly the sexual passions. Eusebius wrote that Origen castrated himself in order to be free from sexual desire, though no one knows if this was actually the case. Like many other patristics, Origen believed that *apatheia* frees one from ego and selfish desires, allowing for service and care of others. Contemplation and action complement and purify each other. The more deeply one prays, the more the soul is charged with divine love and thus is able to love others. And the more loving one is to others, the easier it is to enter into contemplation. Ultimately, he argues, union with God comes only from contemplation, which is the soul's most authentic activity and indeed the reason for its existence. Like Plotinus, he believed that one must center on the soul's presence within to discover God at the core.

One thing that distinguished Christian contemplation from that of the Platonists was the dynamic of love. Metaphorically, Origen wrote about love of God as the relation of a bride to a groom. He taught that the soul should be "wounded in love" (smitten by God), share with God the kiss of lovers (ecstatic encounters with God), and seek the full embrace of the groom (union with God). We should consider this *deep metaphor*. That is to say, Origen's language is obviously symbolic, but it represents a real dynamic of the soul.

ATHANASIUS (c. 300–373 CE)

The historian Rufinus describes **Athanasius's** career as starting from boyhood. Alexander, the bishop of Alexandria, saw adolescents playing by imitating the baptismal ritual. He interviewed the boy who had taken the part of the bishop and discussed the seriousness of baptism. Impressed by Athanasius's part in the conversation, the bishop invited him to prepare for a clerical career. Athanasius enrolled in the Catechetical School and immersed himself in classical and theological study. After Alexander ordained him, he accompanied the bishop to the Council of Nicaea as his secretary. Within three years of Nicaea, Athanasius himself became bishop of Alexandria. Even though Arianism had been decided against at Nicaea, some bishops and emperors remained Arian. His opposition to Arianism led Athanasius to be exiled several times.

While Athanasius was clearly trained in Origen's theology, one sees a real divergence between their two views. Origen believed that the gospel revelation was aligned to the common human aspiration for union with God. In this sense, Christianity becomes the flowing of what everyone's heart already knows on its deepest level. For Athanasius, everything starts with the historical revelation of God found in the scriptures, particularly regarding the incarnation. Further, for him the fact of the incarnation means that God can be accessed profoundly here and now. His is no elitist theology of withdrawal and contemplation. Rather, given the insights of the incarnation—in which God is fully manifested in the human condition—the life of the church provides radical possibilities for divine encounter:

> He took to Himself a body, a human body even as our own. . . . For the solidarity of humankind is such that, by virtue of the Word's indwelling in a single human body, the corruption which goes with death has lost its power over all. . . . When, then, the minds of men had fallen finally to the level of sensible things, the Word submitted to appear in a human body, in order that He, as Man, might center their senses on Himself.[8]

Athanasius saw the saving actions of the incarnate Lord as overwhelmingly perceptible through the senses of the sacraments, other Christians, and the scriptures themselves. In his famous *Festal Letters*, disseminated to the whole church to announce Lent, Easter, and Pentecost, one sees the same focus repeatedly: our physical experience of faith draws us into direct encounter with the incarnate Lord.

THE CAPPADOCIANS

As noted in Chapter Seven, three important bishops, collectively known as the "Cappadocian Fathers," were particularly influential in the ecumenical councils of the church. They devised some of the language, concepts, and philosophical categories that helped the church come to terms with how God ought to be understood as a Trinity that is still monotheistic. They also produced theological treatises that came to influence the Eastern church (and, to a lesser degree, the Western church) not only at the time but also throughout the history of Christianity.

Basil of Caesarea (330–379 CE)

Basil was born into a family of saints. His father's side of the family belonged to a wealthy, politically influential, and devout family, and his grandmother played a key role in his Christian education. Between 304 and 311, her whole fortune was confiscated under persecution, though it would subsequently be regained. His mother's side included several generations of Christians, including bishops and priests. Basil's sister Macrina formed a monastery (an institution addressed in the next chapter). Two of Basil's brothers became bishops, including Gregory, who is discussed later in this chapter. Basil and Gregory of Nazianzus ultimately founded a monastic community and were instrumental in producing and disseminating a collection of Origen's writings.

Basil, like many great Christian voices, represented a kind of noble class of Christians, that is, individuals who were wealthy, sophisticated, highly intelligent, and well educated. These were men who could have had it all according to social standards, but who embraced voluntary poverty and assumed the role of patrons in helping the poor, the sick, and refugees. In fact, during a severe drought and after an earthquake that destroyed Nicaea in 368, Basil's sermons against the rich who held their wealth tightly were accompanied by his own personal financing of the building of a hospital and hospice.

Basil is best known for his teaching on the Holy Spirit and for influencing the ecumenical councils regarding the inner Trinitarian relations, and particularly regarding the Holy Spirit. Recall that Arianism would still be afoot in the church for another century. This doctrine taught that neither Jesus Christ nor the Holy Spirit had a fully divine nature. For Basil, one could prove the Spirit's divine nature by looking at the Spirit's work in the dynamics of salvation. The Spirit sanctifies and thus must be divine, as only God can sanctify. Further, the Spirit is the fundamental driving force in the liturgy and the inspiration of scripture. If these are divine mysteries leading to divine union, and if the scriptures are the word of God, then, he argued, the Spirit must be divine.

Gregory of Nazianzus (c. 325–390 CE)

Like Basil, **Gregory of Nazianzus** was born into a devout patrician family. As a child and adolescent, he was classically trained, particularly at a famous school in Caesarea, the capital of Cappadocia. He was even tutored by the same teacher who would train John Chrysostom, the later great patriarch of Constantinople. It was in Caesarea that Gregory and Basil became fast friends. During the time Athanasius was bishop-in-exile, Gregory continued to study both in Palestine and in Alexandria. Only as an adult was he baptized, probably in Athens or back home in Nazianzus. He initially wanted to become a lawyer or possibly a professor of rhetoric, but he also had a desire for the contemplative life. In 361, his father, the bishop of Nazianzus, pressed him into becoming a priest, and subsequently Basil, who had become the metropolitan of Cappadocia, urged him to become a bishop in the small town of Sasima. Gregory agreed but never physically made it there, as he remained in his hometown to assist his aged father.

In 380, Emperor Theodosius summoned him to become patriarch of Constantinople, and Gregory eventually oversaw the Council of Constantinople in 381. Like all the councils, this one was heated. Some bishops even refused to recognize Gregory as the patriarch of Constantinople, arguing that his transfer from Sasima was illegitimate.

Exhausted, Gregory saw his position as polarizing at a time when he had hoped for unity, and so he resigned and returned to Nazianzus, where he became the bishop.

Gregory's theological works remained important, however, particularly those regarding an orthodox understanding of the Trinity. Gregory was the first theologian to explicitly use the title "God" for the Spirit, and it was he who used the concept of *procession* to understand the relation of the Holy Spirit to the Father. While the Son was *begotten* by the Father, the Spirit *proceeded* from the Father, he argued, making the Spirit's relationship to the Father distinct from the Son's relationship to the Father: "Scripture speaks of 'the Holy Spirit, who proceeds from the Father': who, since He proceeds from there, is not a creature; who, since He is not begotten, is not a Son; who, since He is between the Unbegotten and the Begotten, is God."[9]

Gregory spent the last five years of his life dedicated to prayer and writing, principally in poetic form, and his addresses and sermons are considered some of the most classically eloquent of the patristic period.

Gregory of Nyssa (c. 335–394 CE)

The last of the Cappadocian Fathers is **Gregory of Nyssa**, Basil's younger brother. Like Basil and Gregory of Nazianzus, Gregory was sent off to school in Caesarea for classical training. He married and had a son, and between 365 and 372 he followed the profession of rhetorician, or public orator. In 372, Basil appointed him bishop of Nyssa. After Basil's death, Gregory increased his doctrinal contribution and would participate in the Council of Constantinople.

Gregory was the most systematic of the Cappadocian Fathers. He was clearly influenced by Origen, and Christian Platonism dominated his outlook. For him, the created world was an expression of the divine order and harmony. Unlike Origen, who believed souls were created before the physical world, Gregory saw the physical world as a reflection of God. Humans were supreme in this creation, having been created in the divine likeness with free will, rationality, and virtue, but he thought of the human condition as bordering on the two worlds, the physical and the spiritual. Being "positioned on the frontier," fallen humanity inclined toward sin but kept the principles of the spiritual world. Like Athanasius, the incarnation was for Gregory the remedy that overcame sin and united man to God's very self, allowing him the divine friendship for which he was created. The resemblance between God and humanity rested on the incarnate Christ, by whose grace man was led to the perfection of such a resemblance. Gregory was very optimistic about the human condition, which he saw as now redeemed in Christ:

> If a man's heart has been purified from every creature and unruly affection, he will see the Image of the Divine Nature in his own beauty. I think that in this short saying the Word expresses some such counsel as this: There is in you, human beings, a desire to contemplate the true good; but when you hear that the Divine Majesty is exalted above the heavens, that Its glory is inexpressible, Its beauty ineffable, and Its Nature inaccessible, do not despair of ever beholding what you desire. It is indeed within your reach; you have within yourselves the standard by which you apprehend the Divine. For He Who made you did at the same time endow your nature with this wonderful quality. For God imprinted on it the likeness of the glories of His own Nature, as if molding the form of a carving into wax. But the evil that has been poured all around the nature bearing the Divine Image has rendered useless to you this wonderful thing that lies hidden under vile coverings. If, therefore, you wash off by a good life the filth that has been stuck on your heart like plaster, the Divine beauty will again shine forth in you.[10]

Beyond his theological work on Christian dogma, Gregory elaborated perhaps the richest doctrine of Christian mysticism in the ancient Greek-speaking world—the unitive way. Origen had developed a method of biblical interpretation whereby the text was understood to represent various levels of meaning. It could be read literally, typically as a historical text. It also could be read at the level of morality. A given text might not appear at first blush to be about morality, but a deeper reading often revealed truths about the purgation of the soul. Finally, the text could be read as a mystical document, with persons and narratives representing allegorical types or symbols of spiritual realities. This threefold understanding later became a **fourfold method of interpretation**: the *literal* teaches what to know, the *moral* teaches what to do, the *allegorical* teaches what to believe, and the *anagogical* reveals what to hope for, that is, ultimate things. Not all texts, in this view, are meant to be taken literally, as some have symbolic meaning that has to be culled from the narrative. Some rare texts can involve all four interpretations, while others may include combinations of these four. Gregory's *Life of Moses*, for example, interprets the Exodus event, in which Moses led the Israelites out of Egypt. For him, this narrative involves all four levels of interpretation, ultimately depicting how the soul is to achieve union with God.

Consider the narrative at face value: God calls Moses from the burning bush at Sinai to lead the Israelites to the Promised Land. Moses seeks freedom for his people from Pharaoh, but God hardens Pharaoh's heart, so God sends ten plagues upon Egypt to break Pharaoh's resolve. In one plague God makes the waters of the Nile red like blood, and in another he sends a plague of frogs that sickens the Egyptians. The final plague leads to the destruction of all of Egypt's firstborn males, and on this night the Israelites celebrate the first Passover. After this last plague, Pharaoh releases the Israelites, and, in the so-called *despoiling of the Egyptians*, the Egyptians are so anxious to see them leave that they give them many of their jewels. Pharaoh soon regrets his decision and sends his army to attack the Israelites and take them back into slavery. God allows the Israelites to cross the Red Sea and then drowns the Egyptian army. Even after their escape into freedom, the Israelites rebel against God and Moses. Still, God feeds them and protects them in their subsequent battles. The high point of the Exodus event occurs when Moses ascends Mount Sinai to receive the Law. There he encounters God profoundly while being covered by a dense cloud.

What could this story ultimately mean? Gregory believed that most (although not all) of the Exodus event happened literally and historically, but the deeper meaning of the text reveals the dynamics of the Christian life. Allegorically, Moses is a *type* or symbol of a baptized Christian. For example, Gregory sees God's command that Moses remove his sandals at the burning bush as referring to the "animal skin of sense perception." God, as a transcendent being, can only be directly encountered by withdrawing vision from the perceptible world. One first experiences God as light, as in the burning bush. Thus, God offers initial enlightenment to the intellect and can be known in some fashion by the natural workings of the mind. Pharaoh is a symbol of the human will. Gregory is sure that God could not have literally hardened Pharaoh's heart, since this would be contrary to God's nature and would violate the human freedom of the will. Rather, the narrative here really represents human nature's failure to acknowledge God and its inclination toward evil. Thus, one must train the will to always recognize God and seek the good. The plagues are symbols of how the passions work. Evil corrupts the clear waters of life, and the frogs are symbols of evil in the heart, bringing illness to the soul. Finally, the Israelites' departure from Egypt represents the transience of life itself, and Moses's commandment that the Israelites eat the Passover meal with sandals on their feet and with their cloaks tightly drawn by a belt represent the journey of life, with the belt signifying the virtue of prudence. The Passover food itself represents faith, and the fire that heats it is the life of the Holy Spirit within the soul.

The despoiling of the Egyptians is particularly interesting. For Gregory, this represents pagan learning, something to which he himself had been widely exposed in his classical education. Pagan learning is not Christian per se, but it can be of help when it is beautified by the riches of reason and true Christian doctrine. The crossing of the Red Sea represents baptism, in which one escapes from the slavery of unbelief to the freedom of the Christian faith. And, just as the Egyptian army is drowned in the Red Sea, so everything contrary to Christian truth must be drowned in the waters of baptism. Gregory writes: "Those who pass through the mystical water in baptism must put to death in the water the whole phalanx [mass] of evil—such as covetousness, unbridled desire, rapacious thinking, the passion of conceit and arrogance, wild impulse, wrath, anger, malice, envy, and all such things."[11] The manna (food sent by God) the Israelites eat in the desert is the word of God that nourishes the soul, and the strength Israel receives in its several battles in the Sinai desert references the spiritual strength given to the soul by the Holy Spirit.

The most important part of Gregory's narrative has to do with Moses ascending Mount Sinai. Moses experiences God as directly as one can in this life, in the midst of a dense cloud. For Gregory, as well as all the patristics, God cannot directly be known conceptually or by any natural means of perception. The human brain is created to negotiate the material world, and God transcends creation. Of course, God can be known in a mediated way through the created world, and certainly through true doctrine, but to encounter God directly, one has to bypass this natural way of knowing to embrace a supernatural way. To the created intellect, God is incomprehensible. There is a faculty of the soul, which Gregory calls *spiritual senses*, that can know God directly, but only when one withdraws from one's natural ways of knowing and perceiving and enters the dark cloud of contemplation.

AUGUSTINE (354–430 CE) AND THE WEST

All the ecumenical councils took place in the East, within the Greek-speaking church. The Western Latin-speaking church barely participated, sending only a handful of bishops and a formal representative of Rome. Further, most of the greatest theologians of the patristic era were from the East. As noted earlier, the first four great councils were dominated by the theological insights of Athanasius of Alexandria, Basil of Caesarea, Gregory of Nyssa, and Gregory of Nazianzus. They themselves stood on the shoulders of such greats as Origen, Cyril of Alexandria, and Cyril of Jerusalem. Even some of the earliest Western apologists and champions of orthodoxy, such as Justin and Irenaeus, were themselves originally from the East. Still, the West could boast of a few luminaries of its own. Tertullian was an important theological voice in the early church, as was Cyprian of Carthage. The most impressive theological voice by the end of the fourth century was **Ambrose of Milan**.

Ambrose's rise to Christian notoriety is an interesting story. He had been the governor of a northern Roman province that included Milan, where the imperial court had relocated. In 373, a new bishop needed to be named for Milan, but there was tension between Arian Christians, who had not accepted the conclusions of Nicaea, and Catholics, who had. While trying to keep the peace, Ambrose was popularly proclaimed the next bishop. Like many upper-class citizens in Milan, he had been a Christian catechumen since his youth, but had not yet been baptized. Even though the Council of Nicaea banned the rapid promotion of a catechumen to the office of bishop, he was quickly baptized and then ordained. He literally had to learn theology on the job. Fortunately, he was brilliant and philosophically well read, and knew Greek. He quickly absorbed all the best theological works from the East and gained the reputation of being a superb bishop, teacher, and preacher. He wrote theological texts, works of guidance on Christian virtue, and even hymns for religious services. One of his legacies was the influence he had on the conversion of **Augustine**, who had come to Milan to take on an imperial post as a teacher of rhetoric and chief orator of the Western Roman Empire. Augustine became by far the most important theologian in Western Christianity.

FIGURE 8-2 Nineteenth-century painting of Saint Augustine, the most influential theologian in the western church.

THE LIFE OF AUGUSTINE

Because of Augustine's importance, we know a great deal about him and his impact. We also know a good deal about him from two biographies, one written eight years after his death by Possidius, bishop of Calama, *The Life of Augustine*, and the other his own autobiography of his early life and conversion, *Confessions*. Augustine was born in the small North African city of Thagaste, about sixty miles from the Mediterranean. His father, Patrick, held a minor local office and had some land; his household was thriving but modest. Though Augustine's father was not a Christian, his mother, Monica, was an utterly devout believer.

As a child, Augustine was clearly a prodigy, and through his family's financial aid along with the help of a benefactor he was schooled in Latin and Greek grammar, rhetoric, and classical studies. At seventeen, he went to Carthage, the third-largest city in the Western Roman Empire, to continue his education. With the exception of Greek, which he never learned well, Augustine seemed to absorb everything. In his monumental book *City of God*, he displays a command of Latin politics, drama, mythology, history, and philosophy, often quoting large sections of seminal Latin works, presumably from memory. One of the most striking events in Augustine's three years in Carthage as a student was his encounter with Cicero's *Hortensius* (now lost). In this exhortation, Cicero challenges readers to devote their lives to the pursuit of wisdom at all costs and renounce any other ambition. From this time on, Augustine became devoted to pursuing the truth.

After a short two-year return to Thagaste, he went back to Carthage to take up the profession of teacher. He took on a concubine, something of a common-law wife, with whom he had a son, Adeodatus (meaning "gift of God"). He also became interested in the Manichean religion developed by Mani (216–276), a Persian prophet and religious innovator, who combined parts of Christian gnosticism, Zoroastrianism, and personal prophecies. Mani taught that the cosmos was a place of constant battle between two eternal beings: a God of light, truth, and goodness and a God of darkness, error, and evil. Augustine, who was highly sensitive to his own conscience, recognized the power of sin in his life and his seeming inability to conquer it. He also recognized the problem of the passions, as had many Christians and Greek philosophers over the centuries. What were they? How did they work? Where did they come from? Such questions occupied him for much of his life.

Manichean teachings initially answered these questions: evil came from the supernatural forces of the God of darkness. Sin represented these forces working on the soul, particularly through the passions. The material world was part of the problem, and it had to be overcome. Manicheanism was a religion of two different types of members: the *elect* and the *hearers*. The elect represented those who counteracted the power of evil and the trappings of the material world by celibacy, vegetarianism, and renunciation of all physical delights. Upon death, they would escape the imprisonment of the material world and join the God of light. The hearers represented Manicheans who were less devout. Members of this group would begin to purify themselves of their passions and could hope to be reincarnated as elect in the next life.

Augustine became a hearer, yet even during this time he continued to ask hard questions of representatives of his new religion. He found them simply incapable of providing a satisfying intellectual response. This was particularly disturbing, since the religion claimed to be based on knowledge of the actual order of the universe. The Manichean leaders Augustine challenged responded that all would be well when he met Faustus, the most impressive Manichean intellectual in the West. Upon meeting Faustus, whom he found likeable and charming, Augustine was disillusioned: "What could the most presentable waiter do for my thirst by offering precious cups? My ears were already satiated with this kind of talk, which did not seem better to me because they were more elegantly expressed."[12] While Augustine continued in a passing way to be associated with Manicheanism, he continued his search for truth elsewhere.

In 383, Augustine moved from Carthage to Rome, partially to teach what he hoped would be a better class of students and partially to escape from his mother, whom he may have found too smothering and who had already followed him to Carthage. Neither strategy worked, as his students often failed to pay him and his mother quickly found him out in Rome. Augustine soon joined a circle of intellectuals organized by Quintus Aurelius Symmachus, prefect of the city of Rome. Symmachus had the responsibility of choosing the court orator for the emperor Valentinian, who resided in Milan. He chose Augustine.

In 384, Augustine moved to Milan with his concubine, son, mother, brother, two cousins, and a body of students, slaves, stenographers, and copyists. He became instantly wealthy and famous. Milan was a thoroughly Christian city, and Augustine, who had been made a catechumen by his mother during his early childhood, paid a visit to Ambrose, the bishop, and, because it was the culturally expected practice, attended Eucharist, though without participating. Nevertheless, Augustine had little interest in Christianity. It seemed to him a vulgar religion of the masses, something unworthy of being taken with intellectual seriousness. The idea that God would become human seemed absurd, and the Bible appeared to promote a God who looked little better than the gods of Latin mythology. Further, when he compared the quality of literature of the Bible to that of Cicero or Virgil, it simply could not match up.

When he met Ambrose, however, Augustine became fascinated. Here was a man of masterful intellect, morality, and piety. Ambrose's sermons showed how the biblical text could be understood in intellectually satisfying ways. Ambrose's use of the fourfold method of interpretation, particularly the allegorical method, could stay Augustine's objections against a God who seemed vain, jealous, and all too human. Augustine became very interested in this system of belief. Since Ambrose did not have time to directly mentor Augustine, he assigned his head priest, Simplicianus, to teach Augustine the Christian faith. The first thing Simplicianus did was assign him Platonic philosophy books to read. From this more grounded philosophical starting point, Simplicianus guided Augustine through Christian doctrine, which now for the first time made sense to him.

Augustine was intellectually converted to Christianity within two years, but then he faced the question of what to do next. Could he be a Christian and still pursue a life of at least modest wealth and fame? At Monica's insistence, he had separated from his concubine, who returned to Africa, and he became engaged to a girl from an aristocratic family. Could he be a married man? Of course, Christianity did not forbid a comfortable life, marriage, or even fame, if it happened to

come. The issue for Augustine was twofold. First, he was convinced that if he were to be a Christian, there would be no halfway measures. Within Christianity, a life of celibate, prayerful austerity was widely praised by many, including Ambrose. Second, and even more importantly, the issue was with what to align his soul. If he were to pursue wealth for wealth's sake or sexual pleasure solely for gratification, then he would not be pursuing God as the true good. It was not a matter of putting God first and then seeking the rest second. For Augustine, it was a matter of seeking God singly, so that all other values or experiences were then referenced through God. This was Augustine's version of *apatheia*, being freed from the passions so as to be free for God and others, and, indeed, for his truest self, known only in God.

In 387, Augustine was baptized along with his son. He had already resigned from his imperial post, and decided to return to Africa with his son and mother. Monica died before they made it home, and his son died shortly after arriving back in Thagaste. On a trip to Hippo Regius, a coastal city in North Africa, Augustine was forcibly ordained a priest by the bishop of Hippo. At the time, it would not have been unusual for church members and leaders to insist on ordaining highly learned and pious Christians. He wept during the ceremony, as he initially had sought a contemplative life but was now thrust into active ministry. Still, the church had called him, and he committed himself to his newfound role. He became a celebrated preacher and was soon ordained a coadjutor bishop in 395. In 397, he became the singular bishop of Hippo.

Augustine wrote ninety-three books and 400 letters, and 400 of the 8,000 sermons he preached have been preserved. But he was not a mere intellectual with a church position. He pastorally oversaw a large church, acted as the city judge, and trained priests, many of whom became bishops throughout the North African church.

THE DONATIST CONTROVERSY

One of the most challenging problems in the North African church at this time was that it was in schism. During Diocletian's persecution of 303–305, some bishops were tortured and others martyred. Some of those tortured capitulated and either renounced their faith outright or handed over their scriptures to the Roman authorities. This latter group was known as the *traditores*, literally "those who hand over [books]," from which we get the English word "traitor."

When the persecution subsided, the question emerged as to what to do with repentant bishops who had succumbed to the torture and become *traditores*. Many believed that, at best, they could return to the church after a lengthy penance, but they certainly had lost their authority to be bishops. In 311, Caecilian was appointed bishop of Carthage. One of the ordaining bishops was Felix, bishop of Aptunga, who was accused of having been a *traditore*. Thus, the ordination itself was believed by some to be invalid. Their argument was simply that if a bishop no longer had the Holy Spirit, he could no longer convey the Holy Spirit at ordination. An investigation found that Felix was not guilty and that the evidence against him had been forged. This did not satisfy some bishops or lay people, who still suspected him. Hard-line bishops elected Majorinus to displace Caecilian, and this led to a schism. Majorinus soon died and was replaced by Donatus, who acted as bishop for the separatists from 313 to 355. Now there were two churches in Africa: the Donatist Church, named after Donatus, and the Catholic Church. Of course, the Donatists believed they were the real Catholics and that their opponents represented a tainted or even false church.

In 313, the bishop of Rome, Miltiades, presided over a council to decide the matter. Its conclusion was that Caecilian's ordination was valid. The Donatists then appealed to the emperor Constantine, who in 314 ordered a second council to take up the issue. Once again, the council sided with Caecilian and rejected Donatus's claim to be the true bishop of Carthage. By now many towns and cities in the region had rival churches, those aligned with the Donatists and those aligned with the Catholics. In 405, an imperial edict was posted in Carthage that declared the Donatists heretics and decreed that their churches should be confiscated. This task proved difficult, as the Donatists had the support of many lay people and the emperor was hesitant to use force.

In 411, a conference between the Donatists and Catholics was held in Carthage under the presidency of an imperial commissioner. Fascinatingly, there were more bishops in attendance at this gathering than at either of the ecumenical councils of Nicaea or Constantinople. One can see the even split in the makeup of the bishops: 286 Catholic bishops and 284 Donatist bishops. The Donatists had no real strategy and acted fundamentally as dissemblers. They refused to sit down with the Catholic bishops and often heckled and interrupted them. The star of the Catholic side was Augustine. In short, these were Augustine's arguments: First, he claimed that the Donatists' facts were bad. Some of the Donatist bishops had been ordained by *traditores* themselves, while neither Caecilian nor the bishops who ordained him were *traditores*. Second, he argued that even if the Donatists had some kind of pure line of transmission, they could not represent the pure church because they had violated catholicity (unity) by their schism. While the Donatists imagined they were the sinless bride of Christ, their very dissension from the unity of the church betrayed that they themselves were sinners. His third line of argument is even more important, for it was a theological argument about the nature of the church itself. The institution of the church includes both sinners and saints, he maintained, and God would distinguish them only on the last day. The church was holy, for sure, but that holiness came from Christ, not from the supposed guarantee that everyone or even every bishop was holy. As evidence, Augustine drew on one of Jesus's parables about a field filled with wheat and weeds (Matt. 13:24–31). The point of the parable is that if one tries to pull the weeds out before the harvest, the wheat may be pulled out prematurely. The separation between the two ought to happen only at harvest time (i.e., last judgment).

Augustine's final line of argument was that the Donatists simply did not understand how sacraments work. Sacraments were the work of Christ's grace. It is Christ who baptizes through the mediation of the priest or bishop, Christ who takes on the form of bread and wine at the Eucharist, Christ who seals bishops with the Holy Spirit during ordination. The issue was not that the church could not guarantee that its ministers were holy, though of course some were more so and others less so. The real issue was that sacraments are made effective by God's faithfulness, God's holiness, God's grace. The minister, if duly ordained, had the authority and thus power of holy orders to perform the ordination, but was not conveying something he personally possessed. These latter three arguments—the importance of church unity, the nature of the church, and how sacraments are valid—became core theological principles in Western medieval theology.

Augustine tried to take the high road with the Donatists. Even though they had lost their property and been declared heretics, he invited them back to the Catholic communion, promising each would keep his post as bishop in his own church until the next generation would unify under one bishop. He even suggested that the Donatist bishop of Hippo share his own pulpit until both died and could be replaced by a single bishop. The Donatists accepted none of this. Donatism was never completely eviscerated in Augustine's day, despite imperial punishments and persecutions, and the North African church remained somewhat divided until the whole of North Africa was overtaken by Muslim invaders in the eighth century.

THE PELAGIAN CONTROVERSY

The Western church underwent another controversy around this time, this one surrounding a person named Pelagius who came to Rome in the 380s. A leader in the burgeoning ascetic movement that would have pleased the likes of Ambrose and Augustine, Pelagius was shocked at the undisciplined lives and moral laxity of many Christians in Rome. He was well received by

some members of the church leadership and became the spiritual advisor to many highly placed Christian families there.

But Pelagius was no fan of Augustine. When he encountered Augustine's *Confessions*, for example, he was disturbed by the celebrated prayer "Grant what you command and command what you will."[13] It looked to Pelagius like Augustine believed God had to give the grace needed for obedience in order for the Christian to be able to follow God's will. It was as though God controlled one's moral life, and without it failure was inevitable—tantamount to denying free will. Pelagius once wrote, "Whenever I have to speak on the subject of moral instruction and the conduct of a holy life, it is my practice first to demonstrate the power and quality of human nature and to show what it is capable of achieving."[14] He defended his position most clearly in his *Letter to Demetrias*, in which he argued for the goodness of human nature, man's creation in the image and likeness of God, and the naturally endowed conscience. He also argued that God could not punish sin or reward virtue if we had no free choice in the matter. Further, he believed that Augustine's position implicitly abdicates one's responsibility to follow God's law. For Pelagius, God doesn't *make* us faithful and control our moral actions, as if we have no choice. Rather, God *calls* us to be faithful, and we are accountable for our actions.

Augustine's position can be characterized by his own conversion, detailed in his *Confessions*. He had found himself trapped in his passions for pleasure, money, and fame.[15] Then he experienced the liberating word of God. He fell to his knees weeping, claimed a life of faith, and experienced the dramatic healing of all that had heretofore imprisoned him. Was it his independent will that made him decide to live for Christ? After all, he did claim, "You are my choice."[16] Or was it God's compelling grace that *caused* his will to be moved toward Christ? He wrote, too, "The effect of *your converting me* to yourself was that I did not now seek a wife and had no ambition for success in this world."[17]

After the sacking of Rome in 410, Pelagius fled to North Africa. His utter confidence in the goodness of an independent will raised the ire of the North African bishops, and he was condemned. He then relocated in Palestine, only to be subjected to two ecclesiastical trials orchestrated by the great biblical scholar and theologian Jerome. He was exonerated at the first, and the second collapsed without a verdict. Pelagius died on his way to a third trial in Rome, this one arranged by Augustine.

It is not as though Pelagius believed we had free will and Augustine did not. Rather, Pelagius seemed to think that free will operates independently of God's grace, while Augustine believed that without grace the will simply cannot function well. For Augustine, sin isn't simply a poor moral choice; it is more an expression of a diseased soul that needs to be healed. Augustine believed that people are compelled to follow their desires, their loves. Without grace, the soul is bound to follow lesser goods of the world rather than God, who is their source. Above all, people have an inherent tendency to "self-love," that is, to relate to oneself as though one were the highest good rather than God. Augustine believed that we inherited this fundamental narcissism from the sin of Adam, and that this **original sin** cannot be removed without conversion to God and baptism. Baptism was certainly initiation into the church, but to Augustine it was also the sacrament that removed original sin. Does this mean that, once baptized, one would no longer sin? No, Augustine thought that wrestling with one's sinful dispositions was a lifelong struggle. But baptism did mean that one had the grace to be free from sin's tyranny. Following Augustine, the Western church came to distinguish between the bondage of original sin and the ongoing effects of original sin still to be purged from the soul.

The Eastern church never warmed up to Augustine, particularly on this point. It tended to emphasize human freedom, much like Pelagius did. But the Western church embraced Augustine's position completely. In 529, the Second Council of Orange tried to negotiate the roles of free will and grace in salvation. Fundamentally, it decided that God's grace alone justifies and saves, and that humans need grace to be faithful. The council also decided that humans are free to co-operate with that grace or reject it. Still, even this desire to consent is itself under the influence of grace. The consensus of the Council of Orange became the Western church's official position. One might think of its conclusions in Platonic terms. If God is the source of all goodness and truth, then God's presence is the condition for the soul to participate in the good and true. God's grace does not compel the soul so much as it creates the possibility for the soul to operate well.

CITY OF GOD

The Western Roman Empire was weak in Augustine's day. The emperor did not feel safe in Rome and moved his imperial headquarters first to Milan in 286 and later in 402 to Ravenna, which was easier to defend. In 387, a Gallic tribal army overwhelmed Rome's defenses and briefly took over the city. In 408, a Germanic tribe, the Visigoths, led by Alaric (an Arian Christian) laid siege to Rome and in 410 looted it. Alaric led his armies south with the intention of occupying Sicily and North Africa, but his fleet was destroyed during a storm at sea, and he died shortly afterward. Augustine would die not long before the Vandals, yet another Germanic tribe, sacked Rome again.

After Alaric's invasion of Rome, tensions rose between Roman Christians and those who followed the traditional Roman religion. Roman pagans argued that Christianity was to blame for the empire's troubles because Rome was neglecting to worship the Roman gods, who had now abandoned their people. Augustine set to work to write a tour de force defending Christianity from this claim and explaining his views on the relationship between the political world and the ecclesiastical world. He called it the *City of God*.

To challenge the claim that Christianity was to blame for Rome's woes, he marshaled mountains of historical evidence to show that the empire had experienced many invasions, military defeats, famines, and even plagues, all well before Christianity. He also drew on Roman political theory, morality, and religious mythology to show that they were comparatively deficient when compared to Christianity. Above all, he described the difference between the "city of man" and the "city of God." In his depiction, there is an earthly city and a heavenly city, and each has a different agenda and different ends. The earthly city, especially Rome itself, is built on the lust for power, wealth, and worldly pleasure, while the city of God is built on obedience and is itself on pilgrimage to the heavenly Jerusalem. Of course, believers live in the earthly city and contribute to its natural flourishing. Christians, Augustine argued, do this much better than pagans. But the earthly city is not their true home, and the logics of both cities are opposite. The successes or failures of the Roman Empire were not due to the gods' favor or disfavor, or even that of the Christian God. Rather, they evidenced the transiency of all human endeavors.

Church historian Eusebius of Caesarea had envisioned a unified whole: one emperor, one empire, one church, one God. Collectively these elements represent a unified worldview, a nation under God. Augustine, living a century later in a falling Western Roman Empire, had a different worldview and indeed conceived two different worlds. The life of the empire, whether Christian or not, was not to be identified with the life of the gospel. No institution could be, not even the church. As a political theory, this view incorporated the hope that Christians would be responsible citizens and that the laws of the nation would reflect Christian values. Still, in Augustine's framework, there is a city of man and a city of God, and these have different agendas and different destinies.

AUGUSTINE AND UNION WITH GOD

Like other patristic fathers and Greek philosophers, Augustine believed that God transcended all conceptualizations of the mind. His famous dictum was *si comprehendis non est Deus* (if you

understand, it is not God). In his *Homily on Psalm 99* he writes, "Before you had the experience, you used to think you could speak of God. You begin to have the experience, and there you experience that you cannot say what you experience."[18] Two famous passages from his *Confessions* particularly reveal his experience of mystical union with God. The first passage tells of a shared moment with his devout mother Monica just before she died, and the second passage fascinatingly records an experience he had before he was even baptized. In this first passage, Augustine and Monica are sitting on a ledge, overlooking a garden:

> We asked what quality of life the eternal life of the saints will have. . . . The conversation led us towards the conclusion that the pleasure of the bodily senses, however delightful in the radiant light of this physical world, is seen by comparison with the life of eternity to be not even worth considering. Our minds were lifted up by an ardent affection towards eternal being itself. Step by step we climbed beyond all corporeal objects and the heaven itself, where sun, moon, and stars shed light on the earth. We ascended even further by internal reflection and dialogue and wonder at your works, and we entered into our own minds. We moved beyond them so as to attain to the region of inexhaustible abundance where you feed Israel eternally with truth for food. . . . And while we talked and panted after it, we touched it in some small degree by a moment of concentration of the heart. And we sighed and left behind us the first fruits of the Spirit.[19]

Here both Augustine and Monica yearn for knowledge of God and eternity. They begin with the experience of the beauty of the created world, which makes them desire the absolute beauty beyond physical things, that is, God. They move from outward sensory perceptions to the inner imagination, and from there to their minds, or souls, where they believe God is most profoundly present. Finally, with a degree of concentration, they "touch it," with "it" being either God or God's inexhaustible abundance.

The second passage records something even more extraordinary:

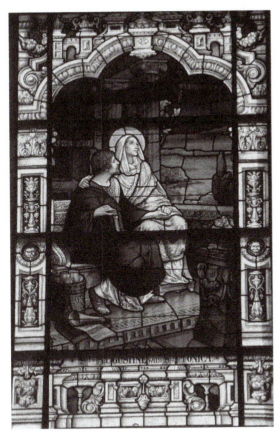

FIGURE 8-3   Stained glass depicting Augustine and Monica meditating on the union with God.

By the Platonic books I was admonished to return into myself. . . . I entered and with my soul's eye, such as it was, saw above that same eye of my soul the immutable light higher than my mind—not the light of every day, obvious to everyone, nor a larger version of the same light. . . . It was not that light, but a different thing, utterly different from all our kinds of light. It transcended my mind. . . . It was superior because it made me, and I was inferior because I was made by it. The person who knows the truth knows it, and he who knows it knows eternity. Love knows it. Eternal truth and true love and beloved eternity: you are my God. . . . What I saw is Being. . . . I trembled with love and awe . . . and heard as if it were a voice from on high: "I am the food of the fully grown; grow and you will feed on me. And you will not

change me into you like the food your flesh eats, but you will be changed into me."[20]

In Augustine's soul he meets God. He hears God tell him to feed on God's very self so as to become transformed into the divine, an expression of divinization noted in Chapter Seven. In his ascent to God, he clearly follows the pattern of withdrawal from the sense world, interior contemplation into the depths of his soul, and elevation to the vision of God: "I passed beyond myself that I might touch him."[21] Unlike Platonic union with God, Augustine identifies God as love, which is typical for Christianity. He even goes a step further by saying, "Love knows it," that is, one knows God and has a vision of God in the context of love. For Augustine, union with God is love meeting Love: "When as someone who is like him, you begin to draw near to him and to become fully conscious of God, you will experience what to say and what not to say insofar as love grows in you, because *God is love* [1 John 4:8]."[22]

AUGUSTINE'S LEGACY

In many ways Augustine's theology aligns with much of what we have seen broadly in the early and patristic churches. His work resonates with the greats of both East and West who preceded him. Still, it would not be an understatement to say that much of Western theology rides on his shoulders. His grasp of the various ways to know and serve God, his understanding of the church, his views of how sacraments work and why, his presentation of grace and its relationship to both an unreformed and a spiritually renewed soul, his political philosophy, his incisive and deep understanding of the human condition, and simply the ethos of his writings have influenced countless theologians through the centuries. The Eastern church, however, was not much affected by Augustine. By his time East and West were becoming culturally and politically divided, and theologically, many Eastern bishops and theologians thought that Augustine overemphasized the degradation of the human soul. The Western church, however, was in constant dialogue with his works. For the West, he is simply and clearly the most influential thinker in Christianity since Saint Paul. It would eventually be Augustine's theology that, over 1,000 years after he died, came to dominate the theological discourse of the Protestant Reformation. His importance cannot be overestimated.

 ## CONCLUSIONS

Theologically and spiritually, the patristic church continues to dominate Christian consciousness. As will be discussed in later chapters, the Eastern church continues to rely on the church fathers' contributions as utterly decisive. These contributions not only came to create the foundations for the East, but constitute virtually all of Eastern theology. For the West, the patristics set the stage and have continued to influence the theological agenda, though not as completely. Of course, there have been other voices and contributions than the five discussed here. Still, the brief snapshots of these individuals give us a sense of their importance in their day and their lasting power in terms of both Christian imagination and doctrines that would remain throughout the medieval and modern periods.

SUMMARY QUESTIONS

- What were the central Platonic philosophical ideas that most shaped conceptualizations of Christians' search for union with God?
- What were the central theological disputes in the Donatist controversy, and how did Augustine argue against the Donatists?
- What was the Pelagian controversy? What was the central issue of this dispute, and what were the opposing views of Pelagius and Augustine?

DISCUSSION QUESTIONS

- What aspects of Platonic philosophy do you think are beneficial to Christianity? Which ones do you think are particularly harmful?
- The Donatist controversy began with the problem of the authority of bishops who had renounced the faith under persecution, but were now restored. Augustine's position was that the sacramental power which they administrated had nothing to do with their personal holiness but only God's grace. Is this coherent to you? How is it defensible or not defensible to have sinful ministers who still have sacramental authority?
- The Pelagian controversy proved to be an important debate in the history of Christianity. What are your views on free will? Did the Council of Orange succeed in your mind in settling the issue? Explain.

KEY TERMS

Ambrose of Milan
Athanasius
Augustine of Hippo
Basil of Caesarea

Fourfold method of interpretation
Gregory of Nazianzus
Gregory of Nyssa

Origen
Original sin
Purgative way/illuminative way/unitive way

BIBLIOGRAPHY

- Augustine of Hippo. 1953. *Augustine: Earlier Writings*. Trans. John Burleigh. Philadelphia: Westminster Press.
- Augustine of Hippo. 1984. *City of God*. Trans. Henry Bettenson. New York: Penguin.
- Augustine of Hippo. 1991. *Confessions*. Trans. Henry Chadwick. Oxford: Oxford University Press.
- Augustine of Hippo. 2003. *The Trinity*. Trans. Edmund Hill. Hyde Park: New City Press.
- Aurelius, Marcus. 1946. *Meditations*. Trans. and ed. S. S. L. Farquharson. New York: Alfred A. Knopf.
- Brown, Peter. 1967. *Augustine of Hippo*. Berkeley: University of California Press.
- Fransen, Piet. 1987. "Augustine, Pelagius and the Controversy on the Doctrine of Grace." *Louvain Studies* 12:172–181.
- Gregory of Nazianzus, *Fifth Theological Oration* in *The Faith of the Early Fathers*, vol. 2, 32–33.
- Gregory of Nyssa. 1978. *The Life of Moses*. Trans. Abraham Malherbe and Everett Ferguson. New York: Paulist Press.
- Kannengiesser, Charles. 1984. "The Spiritual Message of the Great Fathers." In *Christian Spirituality: Origins to the Twelfth Century*. Bernard McGinn, John Meyendorff, and Jean Leclercq, eds. New York: Crossroad.
- McGinn, Bernard. 1992. *The Foundations of Mysticism: Origins to the Fifth Century*. New York: Crossroad.
- McGinn, Bernard. 1994. *The Growth of Mysticism: Gregory the Great Through the 12th Century*. New York: Crossroad.
- McGinn, Bernard, John Meyendorff, and Jean Leclercq, eds. 1988. *Christian Spirituality I: Origins to the Twelfth Century*. New York: Crossroad.
- Origen. 1979. *Origen: An Exhortation to Martyrdom, Prayer and Selected Works*. Trans. Rowan Greer. New York: Paulist Press.
- Plotinus. 1991. *The Enneads*. Trans. Stephen Mackenna. New York: Penguin.
- Pseudo-Dionysius. 1987. *Pseudo-Dionysius: The Complete Works*. Trans. Colm Luibheid. New York: Paulist Press.

NOTES

1. Marcus Aurelius, *Meditations*, XII.19–20, in *Meditations*, trans. and ed. S. S. L. Farquharson (New York: Alfred A. Knopf, 1946), 90.
2. Clement of Alexandria, *Stromata* 1.22, accessed at http://www.earlychristianwritings.com/text/clement-stromata-book1.html.
3. Augustine, *On True Religion*, no. 7, in Augustine of Hippo, *Augustine: Earlier Writings*, 229.
4. Plotinus, *Enneads*, IV.8.i, in Plotinus, *Enneads*, 334.
5. Plotinus, *Enneads*, III.8.7, in ibid., 249.
6. Origen, *De Principiis*, 1.6.1, in McGinn, *Foundations of Mysticism*, 115.
7. Origen, *De Principiis*, 4.4.9, in ibid., 113.
8. Athanasius, *On the Incarnation* 8, 9, 16, in Kannengiesser, "Spiritual Message of the Great Fathers," 64.
9. Gregory of Nazianzus, *Fifth Theological Oration*, in *The Faith of the Early Fathers*, vol. 2, 32–33.
10. Gregory of Nyssa, *Homily 6 on the Beatitudes*, in Kannengiesser, "Spiritual Message of the Great Fathers," 73–74.
11. Gregory of Nyssa, *Life of Moses*, II.129, in *Life of Moses*, trans. Abraham Malherbe and Everett Ferguson (New York: Paulist Press, 1978), 84.
12. Augustine, *Confessions*, 5.6, in Augustine of Hippo, *Confessions*, 77–78.
13. Augustine, *Confessions*, 10.29, in Augustine of Hippo, *Confessions*, 202–203. See Chadwick's footnote here: "This passage was quoted in the ears of Pelagius. . . . The incident marked the start of the Pelagian controversy, Pelagius being the unqualified advocate of an ethical perfectionism as a requirement of the gospel and the opponent of the passivity in Augustine's understanding of grace."
14. Robert Louis Wilken, *The First Thousand Years: A Global History of Christianity* (New Haven, CT: Yale University Press, 2012), 190.
15. Augustine, *Confessions*, 6.6, 97.
16. Augustine, *Confessions*, 10.2, 179.

17. Augustine, *Confessions*, 8.12 (emphasis added), 153–154.

18. Augustine, *Homily on Psalm 99*, in McGinn, *Foundations of Mysticism*, 241.

19. Augustine, *Confessions*, 9.10, 171.

20. Augustine, *Confessions*, 7.10, 123–124.

21. Augustine, *Homily on John*, 20.11, in McGinn, *Foundations of Mysticism*, 241.

22. Augustine, *Homily on Psalm 99*, in ibid.

Christianity's Spiritual Life

Timeline

251–356 CE	Life of Antony, model hermit of early monasticism
318 CE	Pachomius founds his first monastery
330–379 CE	Life of Basil the Great; establishment of monastic rule for Eastern church
340 CE	Monasticism moves to the West
c. 529 CE	Benedict creates a monastery at Monte Cassino and legislates his Rule, which becomes the Western norm
787 CE	Council of Nicaea II defends veneration of icons

WHAT TO EXPECT

This chapter discusses the spiritual life of the patristic church, with a particular focus on its expressions in the East, where they were either more pronounced or elaborate. Given that the early church praised consecrated virginity, asceticism, and a life of prayer, it was natural for some Christians to live out these ideals in dramatic ways in monastic forms. Initially, the monastic movement was noninstitutional, perhaps even representing a critique of the status quo of the institutional church, particularly as it became a regularized part of the empire. Soon, however, monasticism became an indispensable model for Christian holiness and its own institution, one that the church at large incorporated. Alongside monasticism, Christianity developed a certain style of piety and liturgical practice. This chapter will investigate those practices, particularly as they are expressed in the Eastern church.

MONASTICISM

EASTERN MONASTICISM

As we have seen, in its most committed forms early Christianity inclined toward a life of prayer and asceticism, and a preference for celibacy. These ways of life were thought to enrich each other. Celibacy allowed for an undistracted life of prayer and service. Asceticism freed one from inordinate desires or passions, and facilitated deeper prayer. Syrian and Egyptian Christians embraced these values with particular rigor and quite independently from each other developed the tradition of monasticism. *Monachos*, Greek for "solitary," is the word from which we get "monk" and "monasticism." The terms *monachos* and *apotaktikos* (one who denies himself) appear in early fourth-century Egyptian writings to reference devout men and women who were considered particularly holy. These individuals prayed, fasted, kept long nighttime vigils, and were regarded as models of the spiritual life. Because of their reputed holiness, they were believed to be potent intercessors to God on behalf of individual persons or the community at large.

Expressions of early monasticism varied. In Syria, there were often fraternities of monks who lived in their own huts close to each other, prayed together daily, and placed themselves at the service of the local bishop for ministry among the people. In Palestine, they lived in clusters of huts or caves, arrangements that facilitated prayer in a common central space. Early Egyptian monastics tended to live alone, though sufficiently close to each other to allow for mentor relationships by monks at more advanced stages of the interior life.

Monasticism was considered a kind of martyrdom. When Christianity was illegal, martyrs for the faith were considered heroic figures and models. Theirs was a "baptism in blood," an imitation of Christ's own self-offering on the cross. During the patristic era, this "red" martyrdom was replaced by a "white" martyrdom, not a single combat against the beasts of the Coliseum, but a lifelong battle against the beasts of internal sinfulness. These individuals were spiritual athletes, praying constantly while eating and sleeping little. One of the strangest expressions of monastic asceticism is the figure of Symeon the Stylite (pillar-dweller), who died in 459. After living in a monastic community outside of Antioch for ten years, Symeon went to live as a hermit. He placed himself on a pillar at the edge of a hill's cliff and continued to build up the pillar for the next several decades. Eventually it became sixty feet tall. There he sat almost perpetually in prayer, while provisions were hoisted up to him periodically. People came from neighboring cities and villages to seek his advice and appeal to his reported ability to heal. While Symeon was a rare and even eccentric figure in monasticism, he stands out as an example of someone utterly committed to a life of asceticism and prayer and a model of the belief that the fruit of such prayer was wisdom and even special spiritual powers.

FIGURE 9-1 Russian fresco of Saint Antony, the most famous figure of the early monastic movement.

The greatest representative of early monasticism is **Antony of Egypt** (251–356), whom we know about from Athanasius's *Life of Antony*. This book became a literary sensation; it was translated into Latin and Syriac, and widely read in Syria, Asia Minor, Palestine, Italy, Northern Africa, and Gaul (France). Antony's life became a kind of paradigm for **anchoritic monasticism**. The term "anchoritic" comes from the Greek *anachoresis*, meaning "retiring" or "retreating," and is used to refer to a solitary hermit. When Antony was around eighteen, his wealthy parents died, leaving him a large estate and a sister to care for. While considering how to make his life more radically Christian, he heard this Gospel verse in church: "If you wish to be perfect, go, sell your possessions, and give the money to the poor, and you will have treasure in heaven" (Matt. 19:21). Since he had been meditating earlier that day on this very verse, and because it struck him at church with overwhelming vigor, he believed that God was calling him to literally do just this. He quickly made provisions for his sister's care and sold the rest of his family's belongings, giving the proceeds to the poor. Antony then sought out a solitary wisdom figure, a mentor (*abba*), who lived a life of prayer just outside the village, and gave himself over to manual labor and constant prayer. Athanasius tells us that Antony was often tempted by the devil to abandon his way of life: "First he [the devil] attempted to lead him away from the discipline, suggesting memories of his possessions, the guardianship of his sister, the bonds of kinship, love of money and of glory, the manifold pleasure of food, the relaxations of life, and finally, the rigor of virtue, and how great the labor that earns it."[1]

Antony's life became one of progressive withdrawal. After being sufficiently mentored, he completely removed himself from town life, dwelling among the tombs of a cemetery. Athanasius tells us that the devil became so alarmed by Antony that demons came one night and beat him. Later, Antony relocated to live farther from civilization, in an abandoned fort. His friends from Alexandria came periodically and left him food, but did not see him. After twenty years as a spiritual recluse he finally reappeared; his friends found him physically robust and reported that he had barely aged. Finally, he went to live on a mountain near the Red Sea. Despite his secluded habitat, many came to visit him seeking spiritual direction and physical healing, which he reportedly had the power to perform. Even though he lived a solitary life, he was a gracious host, who fed guests from a garden he planted just for visitors and housed them in a hut he had built specially for them.

We see in Antony a model of an anchorite. He did not brazenly go into the wilderness unprepared, but only after being mentored by one who knew the way of prayer and asceticism. He progressively moved to more remote places as he gained the spiritual strength to do so. We also see that the rigors of the monastic life paid off spiritually. He reportedly became deeply holy and attained spiritual gifts for the service of others. Further, we see that the monastic life was imagined to provide something of a state of harmony, both interiorly and bodily. He lived to be 105 years old, aging very slowly. Finally, we see in Athanasius's biography that Antony was repeatedly assaulted by the devil, exemplifying the nature of monastic life as one of spiritual combat. Athanasius frequently tells us that Antony's own strength was not enough; he had to rely on God's grace through it all. The monastic life required great strength and resilience, both physically and spiritually, but it also required great humility, as monks had to consistently rely on God's grace.

One of the most intriguing aspects of monastic life during the patristic era is that it seemed to challenge the institutional church in many ways. The church was an urban phenomenon, one centered in towns and cities and focused on community, the sacraments, and the clergy. Monasticism, particularly anchoritic monasticism, was decidedly individualistic, expressed its own kind of prayer, and had its own self-authorization. It was an alternative Christianity; we might call it a *silent revolution*. Paradoxically, representatives of the institutional church praised and commended it. Many church leaders recognized the monastics' extraordinary lives and revered their holiness. There was no rush to rein these monks in. Like Athanasius, many bishops viewed monks as heroic figures.

Some of the heroic models of the desert were women. These were the **ammas**, or mothers, of the monastic movement, and they also acted with great spiritual authority. As noted in Chapter Six, the choice of virginity for the sake of the kingdom of God afforded women possibilities of spiritual leadership. Nowhere was such leadership more clearly expressed than in monasticism. Women served as spiritual guides for other women ascetics, and even for some men. In the early fifth century, Palladius of Galatia archived the lives of early Christian monks and noted almost 3,000 women living in the desert, including many *ammas*. We also know of women saints in the desert from the *Lives of the Desert Fathers*, a patristic text detailing the history of Egyptian monasticism. What we find is an array of women leaders whose authority, like that of male monastic leaders, rested not on church office but on their reputation for holiness and wisdom. Two of the most well known of these figures are Amma Sarah and Amma Syncletica, whose sayings were authoritative enough to be included in the *Sayings of the Desert Fathers*, an ancient collection of classic sayings from the monks of Egypt.

SAYINGS OF THE *AMMAS*

Amma Sarah:

- "Then the spirit of fornication appeared corporeally to her and said, 'Sarah, you have overcome me.' But she said, 'It is not I who have overcome you, but my master, Christ'" (no. 2).
- "If I prayed God that all men should approve of my conduct, I should find myself a penitent at the door of each one, but I shall rather pray that my heart may be pure towards all" (no. 5).
- "I put out my foot to ascend the ladder, and I place death before my eyes going up it" (no. 6).

Amma Syncletica:

- "In the beginning there are a great many battles and a good deal of suffering for those who are advancing towards God and afterwards, ineffable joy. It is like those who wish to light a fire; at first they are choked by the smoke and cry, and by this means obtain what they seek . . . so we also must kindle the divine fire in ourselves through tears and hard work" (no. 1).
- "Just as the most bitter medicine drives out poisonous creatures so prayer joined to fasting drives evil thoughts away" (no. 3).
- "Imitate the publican, and you will not be condemned with the Pharisee. Choose the meekness of Moses and you will find your heart which is a rock changed into a spring of water" (no. 11).

Even though the hermit's life was initially the preferred style of monasticism in Egypt, it did not last as the dominant expression there but was increasingly replaced by **coenobitic monasticism**, from *koinos*, meaning "communal," and *bios*, meaning "life." Over time the communal monastic life became the norm. One of the great innovators of communal monasticism was **Pachomius** (290–346). Before he became a Christian, Pachomius entered the military as a young man. Later as a seasoned soldier he was profoundly moved by a group of Christians he witnessed at Thebes. His troop had just returned from battle and was transporting prisoners. Christians came out to care for the wounded, including both Pachomius's fellow soldiers and enemy prisoners. The universal love and tenderness they expressed overwhelmed him, and after his release from the army he was baptized. Initially following the anchoritic model, he was mentored for six years by a famous monk named Palemon. Even though he saw the value of the solitary life, he also believed it to be potentially dangerous: in anchoritic monasticism there was little to keep bizarre personalities in check, and while there were many famous and holy spiritual masters, there were also poor or even unbalanced monastics. Two dangers dominated Pachomius's concern: spiritual pride and lack of discretion. Without accountability to a community one could easily fall into vainglory, a deluded sense of one's own importance, and without discretion, one could lead a life of exaggerated asceticism. Fasting is good, but can also destroy the body. Long vigils are necessary, but an unbalanced lack of sleep can undermine one's prayer. The monastery provided a lifestyle that brought competent training, mutual support, and accountability.

Pachomius was wildly successful. He founded nine monasteries and by 330 had roughly 9,000 monks living under his rule. He built monasteries much like the army forts he knew from his military days. Sturdy walls offered protection from marauders, and each complex included a kitchen, bakery, dining hall, infirmary, assembly hall, and church. The community was divided into houses, each holding forty monks, who had their own rooms (cells) where they slept and prayed privately.

In Cappadocia, Basil, one of the great architects of Christian orthodoxy, founded a number of monasteries. Like Pachomius, he viewed the communal life as far superior to the anchoritic ideal. Unlike Pachomius's monasteries, however, his institutions were far more likely to be urban centered, either near towns or even within them. For Basil, monasteries functioned not merely for mutual support of monks, but also as resources for the community at large. His monasteries often included schools, orphanages, and places of hospitality for the sick and needy. If one were to read Basil's monastic Rule, it would appear strict and dauntingly demanding, even world-denying: a monk is to give up "ties of physical relationship, human friendships and . . . repudiated all worldly affections. . . . He will deem all possessions foreign

FIGURE 9-2 Monastery of Saint Catherine at the base of Mount Sinai in Egypt. Built in the seventh century, it is one of the oldest working monasteries in Christianity.

to him [and be] crucified to the world; Leanness of body and pallor produced by the exercise of continency [celibacy] mark the Christian . . . making a sparing and frugal use of necessities, ministering to nature [by eating] as if this were a burdensome duty, and begrudging the time spent on it."[2] At the time of its writing, however, Basil's Rule was considered to be quite balanced. It eventually became the standard for the Eastern church.

WESTERN MONASTICISM

Monasticism was quickly adopted in the West. In Italy and Africa, some bishops, including Ambrose and Augustine, required their priests to live a semi-monastic existence of communal living and prayer, as well as take vows of poverty and celibacy. Augustine's prominent quasi-monastery produced many African bishops. In Gaul, Hilary of Poitiers (300–368) left the life of a soldier to take up the monastic life, as did Martin of Tours (317–397), another leading figure. After he was named bishop of Tours, Martin established many monasteries in France. Often housing some of the most educated, upper-class Christians of the day, these monasteries became centers of culture and learning, and many bishops were chosen from among their ranks.

One of the most influential figures in Western monasticism is **John Cassian** (360–435). Cassian came from a Latin-speaking province in the East, now Romania. For about a decade he visited monasteries in Palestine and Egypt. With his friend Germanus he was ordained in Constantinople under John Chrysostom, and when Chrysostom was deposed by the emperor, they traveled to Rome to appeal to the pope. Cassian stayed in Rome for ten years and then traveled to Gaul, where he founded two monasteries in Marseilles, one for men and one for women. There he wrote his *Institutes*, which outlines the monastic way of life he had witnessed in Egypt and influenced how monasteries were subsequently run. His most influential book was the massive *Conferences*, a collection of dialogues he had with Egyptian monks. This book constituted, for the West, a compendium of wisdom concerning the monastic way. Another famous document of the time was the *Regula Magistri* (Rule of the Master), an early anonymously written expression of monastic life in the West. In both the writings of Cassian and the *Regula Magistri*, the monk's sole accountability to God lies in his or her obedience to the **abbot** (or **abbess**), while the abbot is accountable for the good of the souls of the monks under his care. Obviously, monks were not imagined to be so blindly obedient that they would follow an order that led to sin, but still, their obedience was virtually identified with God's will for them.

Cassian makes it clear that contemplation is the central aim of monastic life. In reflecting on the biblical story of the working Martha's complaint about her sister Mary, who only wants to sit by the Lord's feet (Luke 10:38–42), Cassian

wrote, "You see that the Lord considered the chief good to reside in theoria alone—that is, in divine contemplation. Hence we take the view that the other virtues, although we consider them necessary and useful and good, are to be accounted secondary because they are all practiced for the purpose of obtaining this one thing."[3]

The most famous, and ultimately most influential, legislator of monasticism in the West is **Benedict of Nursia** (480–543). Benedict was born to a prosperous family northeast of Rome. As a young man he abandoned his life of privilege and embraced an anchoritic life on Mount Subiaco. There he gained a reputation as a particularly holy figure, and the monks of the monastery in Vicovaro asked him to be their abbot, though this turned out to be a disastrous choice. Benedict was, at the time, very strict, and the Vicovaro monks were decidedly not so. Soon they rebelled and actually tried to poison him. Benedict returned to Mount Subiaco and started over with a number of other monks who had sought his mentorship. Soon he had established a dozen monasteries, each with its own abbot. Two of these monasteries were particularly important. One was a monastery for men on the hills above Cassino, about eighty miles south of Rome. The second was a nearby monastery for women headed by his sister Scholastica. The monastery at Cassino would become the most famous in the West, and it was there that Benedict wrote his rule. The *Rule of Benedict* became the standard for the Latin church and by the year 800 was the required Rule for all monasteries.

As the saying goes, the medium is the message, and this was certainly true in the case of Benedict's Rule, a short, highly adaptable Rule that allowed monastics from different areas and eras to adapt it to their particular circumstances. It is filled with metaphor: physical objects, human activities, and people are portrayed as mediations of God's grace. Think of the monastery, the Rule teaches, as a school to learn the Lord's service (Prologue), a workshop to build holiness (no. 4), and the very altar of worship

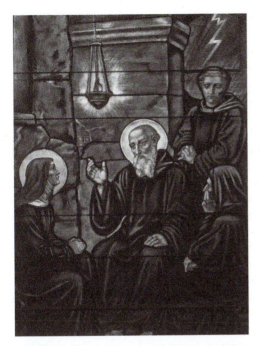

FIGURE 9-3 Stained glass of Saint Benedict and his sister Saint Scholastica. Benedict's Rule became the norm for the West in the ninth century.

(no. 31). Regard the goods of the monastery as though they are vessels of the altar (no. 31). Who is Christ, and where is he to be found? The Rule instructs monks to consider Christ as embodied by the community (no. 4), in the abbot (no. 53), and in any visitor to the monastery (no. 53). Benedictine hospitality is famous even today and is grounded in a spiritual perspective that considers visitors not as obstructions to prayer, but as manifestations of Christ among the hosts. Monastic life for Benedictines was, and continues to be, a vision of a sacramental world in which everything is alive with spiritual possibilities.

Benedictine life is often depicted through the phrase *ora et labora* (prayer and work). The monks rose before dawn for *matins*, which consisted of a lengthy biblical reading. They then returned to their rooms (cells) to pray before entering chapel for morning prayer, or *prime*, at which they chanted the psalms. Then, after breakfast, they worked, whether at manual labor,

manuscript reproduction, or other tasks assigned to them. At mid-morning they returned to chapel for more biblical prayer (*terse*) before resuming work again, only to return to chapel at noon (*sext*). This was followed by lunch and work, chapel (*none*), and yet more work, from which the monks were called back to chapel for evening prayer (*vespers*). The day ended with a light meal, private reading, and then another short communal prayer (*compline*).

Unlike Cassain's writings, Benedict's Rule has nothing to say about contemplation. Rather, the day was something like an ongoing absorption in the word of God. While many Benedictines may have experienced the kind of mystical prayer that we saw expressed in the writings of Origen, Gregory of Nyssa, or Augustine, this subject is not discussed in Benedict's Rule. Benedictine life was one infused with *lectio divina* (divine reading); monks engaged the word of God throughout the day.

Interestingly, such divine reading was eventually aligned to the kind of contemplation Cassian envisioned. *Lectio divina* became a fourfold method of prayer, a method still used today. It begins by reading or hearing a biblical text (*lectio*). Then one probes the text and mulls it over, focusing on how one might encounter God through the text (*meditatio*). Third, one responds to God's inspiration in prayer (*oratio*). Finally, in communing with God through the word, one can be drawn to simply sitting before God (*contemplatio*). The twelfth-century abbot Guigo II (d. 1189) describes this process as follows:

> Reading comes first and it is as it were a foundation; it provides the subject matter which we must use for meditation. Meditation considers more carefully what is to be sought after; it digs as it were for the treasures which it finds and reveals, but since it is not in meditation's power to seize upon the treasure, it directs us to prayer. Prayer lifts up to God with all its strength and begs for the treasure which it longs for, which is the sweetness of contemplation. Contemplation, when it comes, rewards the labors of the other three; it inebriates the thirsting soul with the

dew of heavenly sweetness. Reading is an exercise of the outward senses, meditation is concerned with the inward understanding, prayer is concerned with desire, contemplation outstrips every faculty.[4]

SPIRITUAL PRACTICES AND THE PUBLIC CHURCH

Once Christianity became the favored religion of the Roman Empire, its public presence was undeniable. Constantine and his successors directed state funds toward the construction of great churches, and Christianity gained prominence in society. During Christianity's first three centuries, Christians typically met in private homes for worship and fellowship. Because Christianity was often tolerated, even if illegal, there were some small churches of a sort: large houses with an assembly hall and a smaller room for baptism. In the Christian imperial period, by contrast, many churches arose as large, ornate structures. The most common form of church building was a **basilica**, which replicated the model of large public buildings in Roman cities. These were long, rectangular buildings with high ceilings supported by columns. In Christian basilicas the main part of the building was called a "nave," and one end of the church had a semi-circular ceiling called the "apse." The portion below the apse was separated from the nave by a railing that distinguished between the place of the people and the place of the clergy. The part of the building containing the apse was called the "sanctuary" and included an altar and a raised pulpit where the scriptures were read and sermons delivered. If this was the bishop's church, the cathedral, the sanctuary also contained the bishop's chair (*cathedra*).

Churches in the East sometimes differed in that they had a dome in the center, often with a representation of Christ as Lord over the community and world. In such churches, the sanctuary was much smaller and architecturally less grand. These sanctuaries were separated from the rest of the building by screens containing **icons**, or images of Christ and the saints. Lay people could see above and around the icons to where the clergy consecrated the bread and wine into the body and blood of Christ.

SACRAMENTS: WHERE HEAVEN AND EARTH MEET

Chapter Five noted some of the fundamental dynamics of baptism and the Eucharist, but to get a fuller picture, it's important to consider how rituals have historically been understood in Christianity. Until the early modern period, with the advance of some forms of Protestant and Evangelical Christianity, the most important activity Christians performed was **liturgy**, from the Greek term *leitourgia*, referring to a work or action that people performed in public. The ancient Greek version of the Old Testament (Septuagint) uses the term *leitourgia* to refer to various services led by priests in the Temple. In the church, today as in the past, liturgical rites are called **sacraments**. Sacraments are understood as symbolic actions that mediate divine realities. In this case, sacramental symbols are not merely signs that point to something else, but ways to make *present* other realities; they participate in the reality they symbolize. Sacraments do not merely disclose sacred truths, but also enable participants to engage with them directly and encounter God's grace through them.

Sacraments work with archetypal forms. They involve a series of symbols and actions that connect an individual to central salvific historical events so that he or she may experience, in the present, the grace inherent in those key events. The technical term for engaging these past events is *anamnesis*, which literally means "remembering." When worshippers receive sacraments, they are not merely recalling, but becoming radically united with (re-membered) the reality being celebrated. Christians believe that through a given sacrament, they ritually enter into the original event and experience its transformative power. In response to the Protestant Reformation, which challenged many of the sacramental practices of the time, both Roman Catholics and Eastern

Orthodox numbered the sacraments at seven. As mentioned in Chapter Six, baptism and the Eucharist are the most important of this number. In addition to these two, there are five others: confirmation (chrismation), which completes initiation and seeks the gifts of the Holy Spirit; marriage, which both expresses the holy union between couples and symbolizes the covenantal relationship between Christ and his church; holy orders, which grant the hierarchical leadership positions of deacon, presbyter (priest), and bishop; penance, which engages repentance from sin; and anointing of the sick, which seeks both physical and spiritual healing in times of serious illness.

THE CENTRALITY OF THE EUCHARIST

From the time of the early church, the Eucharist dominated church life. As noted in Chapter Six, from its apostolic origins, the Eucharist was understood as a sacrificial meal during which the consecrated bread and wine become Christ's actual body and blood. Beyond that, the apostolic church apparently allowed for a good deal of variety in how the Eucharist was celebrated. In some contexts, it may have been a relatively simple ritual. For example, the *Didache* (c. 100) offers instructions for prayers before and after communion allowing "prophets" in the church to continue to pray extemporaneously (see box), but no further instructions are provided.

DIDACHE ON THE EUCHARIST

Now concerning the Thanksgiving meal, give thanks in this manner. First, concerning the cup: "We thank You, our Father, for the Holy Vine of David Your servant, whom You made known to us through Your Servant; May the glory be Yours Forever." Concerning the broken bread: "We thank You, our Father, for the life and knowledge which You made known to us through Your Servant; May the glory be Yours forever. As this broken bread was scattered over the mountains, and was gathered together to become one, so let Your Body of Faithful be gathered together from the ends of the earth into Your kingdom; for the glory and power are Yours forever. But let no one eat or drink of your Thanksgiving, unless they have been baptized; for concerning this is taught, 'Do not give what is holy to dogs.'"

After the meal, give thanks in this manner: "We offer thanks, Holy Father, for Your Holy Name which fills our hearts, and for the knowledge, faith and eternal life, You made known to us through Your Servant; Yours is the glory forever. Almighty Master, You created all things for Your own purpose; You gave men food and drink to enjoy, that they might give You thanks; but to us You freely give spiritual food and drink, and eternal life through Your Servant. Foremost, we thank You because You are mighty; Yours is the glory forever. Remember Your Body of Servants, to deliver it from everything evil and perfect it according to Your love, and gather it from the four winds, sanctified for Your kingdom which You have prepared for it; for the power and glory are Yours forever. Let Your grace come, and let this world pass away. Hosanna to the God of David! May all who are holy, come; let those who are not, repent. Maranatha [Come, Lord]. Amen." But permit the prophets to make Thanksgiving as they wish.[5]

As the church continued to organize in both East and West, the Eucharist became a particularly complex sacrament with many layers. On one level, it involves an anamnesis of the Last Supper. Jesus drew his disciples together during the Passover (Seder) supper, the Jewish celebration of God's liberation of the Jewish people from slavery in Egypt. The Passover is intrinsically connected to God's covenant with Moses on Sinai.

During this highly symbolic meal, instead of focusing on God's liberation of the Jewish people from slavery and the Sinai covenant, Jesus initiated a new covenant, one that would liberate believers from sin and death and formally inaugurate the kingdom of God. He took bread and identified it with his body, and then he took wine and identified it with his own blood. In doing so, he anticipated his sacrifice on the cross the very next day.

On another level, the Last Supper involved the disciples entering into this new covenant themselves. Just as Moses had offered sacrifices and sprinkled blood on the people to ratify the covenant at Sinai, Jesus had his disciples consume the sacrificial offering—symbolizing his own offering on the cross—in the form of bread and wine. They communed with him and his covenant. In doing so, he implicated them in that very self-offering; they too were offering themselves to God and the kingdom. The Eucharist thus involves Christians confirming their participation in Christ's new covenant and offering themselves to God alongside Christ's original self-offering on the cross.

On yet another level, the community of Christians celebrating the Eucharist participates in Jesus's victory over death and his elevation to Lordship over heaven and earth. The Eucharist thus engages the very dynamics of heaven. The Book of Revelation imagines heaven to be a wedding banquet that celebrates the union of bride (church) and groom (Jesus). In this manner, communing with Jesus during the Eucharist dramatizes a nuptial union with God in Christ and invites the presence of the angels. Finally, the church understands itself as the body of Christ. Thus, in celebrating the Eucharist the church expresses most fully its own nature, or spiritual essence.

When one examines the prayers and ritual gestures of the Eucharist, one sees all these levels working with one another and even blurring into each other. This is, of course, intentional, as each level implicates and gives deeper meaning to the other levels. Until the sixteenth century, when the Reformation challenged the traditional understanding of the Eucharist, Christians believed that the Eucharist engaged the dynamics and spiritual reality of the Last Supper: like the disciples present during that pivotal gathering, worshippers would enter into the new covenant, honor the sacrifice of Christ on the cross, make their own self-offering to God in union with Christ, commune with one another as the body of Christ, and experience a foretaste

of the heavenly wedding banquet at which church and Christ will be united forever.

Eastern Orthodox Christians developed a particularly stunning way of celebrating the Eucharist. In their version of the sacrament, they bring to life the conviction that in the Eucharist heaven and earth have merged, and that in taking part in the Eucharist, they engage in a type of heavenly liturgy with the angels. The church buildings themselves have traditionally been beautifully designed to highlight this. One story, whether embellished or not, highlights the close connection between Eastern Orthodoxy and beauty. In 988, Prince Vladimir of Kiev sent ambassadors to Constantinople. At one point, they entered the great cathedral of the Hagia Sophia built by Emperor Justinian in 537. Upon entering, the ambassadors reported that they did not know whether they were still on earth or had entered heaven. According to the *Russian Primary Chronicle*, it was this event that led the Russians to embrace the Orthodox faith.

From the patristic period until today, entering an Orthodox church has made for a dazzling experience. The central dome usually contains an enormous painting of Jesus as *pantocrator* (ruler of all), surrounded by angels and saints. Icons of saints are everywhere, as though one were joining them in heaven. The sanctuary is separated from the rest of the church by a series of icons called the **iconostasis**. One can see

FIGURE 9-4 Sicilian mosaic of Christ the Pantocrator, or universal ruler.

FIGURE 9-5 An iconostasis, or wall of icons, separates the sanctuary and altar from the church at large.

something of the priest, deacons, and servers within the sanctuary as they attend to the altar, but their activities are partially blocked by the iconostasis. Orthodox Christians might say that one has to look *through* the icons to see the altar, that is, to penetrate through the spiritual space created by the saints surrounding the sanctuary. The sanctuary itself functions like the Holy of Holies of the ancient Jewish Temple, where only the high priest was permitted, and where he potentially could encounter God directly.

The liturgy derived from John Chrysostom is the most common Eucharistic celebration,[6] and we here provide an overview of it; this is but a small snapshot of a highly complex and lengthy liturgy that intends to be literally otherworldly. The liturgy opens with a series of prayers, hymns, and responses, each led by a deacon, with the congregation chanting memorized responses. This exchange between deacon and congregation is highly rhythmic and intended to be meditative. The introductory portion of the liturgy ends with a prayer offered by the presiding priest.

In the next part of the liturgy, the priests and servers carry the book of the Gospels in procession. The priest then prays the following:

> Holy God, You dwell among Your saints. You are praised by the Seraphim with the thrice holy hymn and glorified by the Cherubim and worshiped by all the heavenly powers. You have brought all things out of nothing into being. You have created man and woman in Your image and likeness and adorned them with all the gifts of Your grace. You give wisdom and understanding to the supplicant and do not overlook the sinner but have established repentance as the way of salvation. You have enabled us, Your lowly and unworthy servants, to stand at this hour before the glory of Your holy altar and to offer to You due worship and praise. Master, accept the thrice holy hymn also from the lips of us sinners and visit us in Your goodness. Forgive our voluntary and involuntary transgressions, sanctify our souls and bodies, and grant that we may worship and serve You in holiness all the days of our lives, by the intercessions of the holy Theotokos [Mary] and of all the saints who have pleased You throughout the ages.

This prayer highlights that just as God is eternally glorified by heavenly angels, so Christians now glorify him before the altar. The difference between the altar on earth and a kind of heavenly altar (and heavenly liturgy) begins to blur, and heaven and earth are imagined to merge. Although the priest recognizes that all are sinners, he also notes that they have been redeemed. Even so, he asks God to forgive their sins so that they might worship him with purity of heart. Following this prayer, the deacon reads passages from the Bible before the priest offers a sermon. More litanies and prayers follow.

The initial procession of the priest with the book of the Gospels is called the *Little Entrance*. The next procession after the sermon is known as the *Great Procession*, which consists of a much more elaborate procession of the priest, deacons, and servers throughout the church. They carry with them the bread and wine to be consecrated, as well as incense and fans, with the latter representing the wings of the angels attending before God. The prayers are lengthy and designed to prepare the congregation for the Eucharist proper. One prayer is particularly striking: "We who mystically represent the Cherubim sing the thrice holy hymn to the life-giving Trinity. Let us set aside all the cares of life that we may receive the King of all invisibly escorted by the Angelic Hosts. Alleluia!"

The Eucharistic prayer principally consists of thanking God for all the ways in which God saved humanity through Jesus Christ. It moves to the consecration of the bread and wine with the words of Jesus himself:

> He took bread in His holy, pure, and blameless hands, gave thanks, blessed, sanctified, broke and gave it to His holy disciples and apostles, saying: Take, eat, this is my Body which is broken for you for the forgiveness of sins. Likewise, after supper, He took the cup, saying: Drink of it all of you; this is my Blood of the new Covenant which is shed for you and for many for the forgiveness of sins. Remembering, therefore, this command of the Savior, and all that came to pass for our sake, the cross, the tomb, the resurrection on the third day, the ascension into heaven, the enthronement at the right hand of the Father, and the second, glorious coming, we offer to You these gifts from Your own gifts in all and for all. Once again we offer to You this spiritual worship without the shedding of blood, and we ask, pray, and entreat You: send down Your Holy Spirit upon us and upon these gifts here presented. And make this bread the precious Body of Your Christ. And that which is in this cup the precious Blood of Your Christ, changing them by Your Holy Spirit, so that they may be to those who partake of them for vigilance of soul, forgiveness of sins, communion of Your Holy Spirit, fulfillment of the kingdom of heaven, confidence before You, and not in judgment or condemnation. Again, we offer this spiritual worship for those who repose in the faith, forefathers, fathers, patriarchs, prophets, apostles, preachers, evangelists, martyrs, confessors, ascetics, and for every righteous spirit made perfect in faith.

The Eucharistic prayer continues by honoring Mary and the rest of the saints, and commemorating all who have died. It also asks that such worship advance the salvation of all the world. Throughout the prayer, the congregation chants (or sometimes recites) responses to the priest's prayer. Then the community collectively prays the Lord's Prayer and lines up to receive communion, while the choir sings: "We have seen the true Light; we have received the heavenly Spirit;

we have found the true faith, worshipping the undivided Trinity; for this has saved us."

Additional prayers and blessings conclude the service, and congregants leave after further receiving blessed (but not consecrated) bread to be eaten for the journey back into the world. This practice expresses the idea that they are leaving heaven and returning to the world.

THE ROLE OF MARY

As noted in Chapter Six, Christianity developed a strong tradition of venerating saints. Exemplars of authentic and usually heroic faith, saints constituted concrete expressions of the extraordinary ways in which God's grace could work. They were also imagined to be much more: intermediaries between heaven and earth, God and his

FIGURE 9-6 Mosaic of Mary holding Jesus in the Church of the Hagia Sophia in Istanbul, Turkey.

people. They were patrons who intercede before God on Christians' behalf.

The quintessential saint is Mary, whom the Council of Ephesus (431) declared *Theotokos* (God-bearer). Ephesus made this claim to support its view that Jesus not only had both divine and human natures, but also had a singular identity from the time of his conception. Thus, Mary from the beginning bore the God-Man. While Ephesus's primary intention was to make a claim about Christ, still, the title "God-bearer" is extraordinary and reveals a profound devotion to Mary. Both West and East developed a particular devotion to Mary, though this devotion was initially more pronounced in the East.

During the time of the imperial church, Mary was understood by Christians to be intrinsically related to Christ's redemptive work. She acted as the archetypal recipient of the *Word-made-flesh*, the model for everyone's reception of Christ into their own lives. She was also an image of the church itself. Many ancient liturgical hymns even depict Mary as the "Bride of God," as she exemplifies the church in being the "bride." One striking prayer for the feast of the Entry of the Theotokos into the Temple reads, "O Virgin, fed in faith by heavenly bread in the temple of the Lord, thou hast brought forth unto the world the Bread of Life, that is, the Word; and as his chosen temple without spot thou was betrothed mystically through the Spirit, to be the Bride of God the Father."[7] Another theological theme from the patristic era draws parallels between Mary and Eve. In one sense, Mary is another Eve: as Eve was the mother of humanity, Mary is the mother of the new humanity in Christ. In another sense, Mary is a contrast to Eve: as Eve's disobedience brought death to the world, Mary's obedience brought the life (Jesus) that brings salvation.

As Eastern Orthodoxy continued to develop, virtually all Orthodox rituals and many prayers came to repeatedly appeal to Mary. Orthodox Christians consider her utterly integral to the ways in which God blesses the world in general and Christians in particular. Orthodox iconography depicts Mary far more frequently than any of the other saints. Defenders of Orthodoxy would insist that in no way does Mary replace the Trinity or have any intrinsic spiritual power of her own; she is a saint like all the saints. Still, they would argue that God wills Mary's presence and intercessions; God blesses the church through her presence in the mystical body of Christ. For the Orthodox, both ancient and modern, one does not properly love God without also venerating Mary, and those who skillfully venerate Mary are led to her Son. Many liturgical texts refer to her as "Light-Bearer"; that is, she lights the way to God.

ICONS

Central to the Christian message is the belief that Jesus is the incarnation of God, the view that God took on flesh in Christ. Platonic philosophy, otherwise so influential in the patristic church, found this idea preposterous. In Platonism, the created world could mediate the divine qualities of truth, goodness, and beauty, but only modestly. In contrast, Christianity proclaimed that the uncreated God united himself intrinsically to the created world by becoming a human being. Of course, direct encounters with God had to transcend the limits of the physical world as well as any conceptions the human mind might hold. Still, created reality was understood as a gift of God, and through it one could encounter God's grace. Jesus was, for the church, the supreme exemplar of God's presence in the created world. John of Damascus wrote, "I do not worship matter. I worship the Creator of matter who became matter for my sake, who willed to take his abode in matter, and through matter wrought my salvation."[8]

One of the great articulators of mysticism in the patristic church was Dionysius the Areopagite (known today as Pseudo-Dionysius), who argued that one can experience God by engaging with the created world and progressively transcending it. For Dionysius, the sacraments in general, the levels of holy orders, and the types of church membership all expressed God's revelation and presence. One experienced the sacraments through the senses and then transcended the senses to engage their conceptual truths. From there, one transcended these conceptualizations to experience God, who is beyond our human concepts. Dionysius taught that these expressions, which could be known perceptually and conceptually, revealed key truths about God and participated in God. His was a broad Christian understanding. By uniting these insights with the Christian conviction of God made human in Jesus, the church was able to countenance wide possibilities of divine mediation. One of the most important expressions of this understanding can be found in iconography. The word *icon* means "image," and Christians from the patristic time on have used icons to depict Jesus, the saints, and even the Eucharist.

The use of icons generated controversy, and an **iconoclastic** (literally, "image breaking") movement emerged in full force during two periods (730–787 and 813–843). Some Christians objected that icons were idols. The Second Commandment states, "You shall not make for yourself an idol, whether in the form of anything that is in heaven above, or that is on the earth beneath, or that is in the water under the earth. You shall not bow down to them or worship them" (Exod. 20:4–5). Indeed, Christians were bending down to venerate icons, even kissing them and using them in processions. As noted previously, the interior of a typical church was filled with them.

Iconodules (literally, "image venerating"), those Christians who supported icons, argued that the incarnation overrode this prohibition. God had become visible in the Son and thus could be represented in graphic form. In 787, the Second Council of Nicaea decided on the side of the iconodules, distinguishing between worship (*latreia*), which may only be given to God, and veneration (*doulia*), which can be offered to persons or objects associated with God, including images of Christ and the saints. Nicaea II made three main arguments: First, it argued that icons

had been part of Christianity from the start. Thus, iconography was a decided part of the apostolic tradition: "The tradition of making painted images . . . existed already in the time of apostolic preaching. . . . The holy fathers witness to it, and these historians whose writings have been preserved until our times, confirm it."[9] (In fact, the historicity of this claim may be exaggerated.) Second, Nicaea II focused on the Christian belief that God is known through Jesus, that is, God is experienced in the physical body of Jesus. The incarnation thus becomes the key: "[Icons] guarantee that the incarnation of God the Word is true and not illusory."[10] Finally, the council argued that icons were helpful in facilitating true veneration toward what they represent:

> The more frequently they are seen in representational art, the more are those who see them drawn to remember and long for those who serve as models, and to apply these images the tribute of salutation and respectful veneration. Certainly this is not the full adoration in accordance with our faith, which is properly paid only to the divine nature, but it resembles that given to the figure of the honored and life-giving cross, and also to the holy books of the gospel. . . . Further, people are drawn to honor these images with the offering of incense and lights, as was piously established by ancient custom. Indeed, the honor paid to an image traverses it, reaching the model and he who venerates the image, venerates the person represented in that image.[11]

Ultimately, what Nicaea II was addressing was the Christian doctrine of creation. The materiality of the human being is spiritually potent. In short, humans are not saved *from* the material world, but *with* the material world and *in* the material world. Theodore the Studite, one of the great supporters of iconography, insisted, "The fact that the human person is made in the image and likeness of God means that the making of icons is in some way a divine work."[12]

The style of iconography partially reflected the Greco-Roman art prominent in the patristic era. For example, saints and Jesus were depicted with halos, which Greco-Roman art also used in depicting its gods. And in both types of art, images look flat, lacking the three-dimensional feel or perspective typical during later periods. On the other hand, Christians forged a new style. Their use of colors was highly symbolic, and instead of the sophisticated use of light typical in pagan art, they used a unique style of shading that allowed the light to appear to come from within the figures depicted. Most importantly, their images were created to seem essentially without emotion. Unlike Greco-Roman art, which could be dramatic and was sometimes intended to provoke an emotional response in viewers, icons were crafted to cultivate inner stillness. One reflects on the icon, in a sense going through it, in order to enter into a contemplative experience that the icon facilitates. Icons are intended to work like sacramental channels, fostering encounters with the divine and helping viewers commune with the mysteries depicted.

HESYCHASM: UNCEASING PRAYER AND STILLNESS

At this point, we have seen how the celebration of the Eucharist, veneration of Mary, and iconography represent central spiritual trends in the church, both East and West. This chapter has emphasized these themes as they have been manifested in the Greek-speaking church. This final portion of our chapter on Christian spirituality focuses on another phenomenon associated with Eastern Orthodoxy: the hesychast movement. **Hesychasm** means "inner stillness" and was a principal practice in Eastern monasticism. While Western monks were practicing *lectio divina*, Eastern monks (and some lay people)

were practicing inner stillness. The great spiritual master **John Climacus** (525–606) offers a number of insights on inner stillness in his classic *The Ladder of Divine Ascent*: "The first task of stillness is disengagement from every affair good and bad. . . . Second is urgent prayer. Third is inviolable activity of the heart. . . . Stillness is worshipping God unceasingly and waiting on Him. . . . Let the remembrance of Jesus be present with every breath."[13]

In these instructions, Climacus gets to the core of the movement. He describes the cultivation of a life in which one perpetually focuses on being solicitous to God and to God's movements within the heart. As the hesychast movement developed during the medieval period, Climacus's injunction to "let the remembrance of Jesus be with every breath" became codified in the practice of the **Jesus Prayer**. The prayer works like this: First, one sits with head and shoulders bowed and the gaze of one's eyes directed toward the heart. The idea is that one attempts to physically symbolize what the Greek monks called the "descending of the mind into the heart," a state in which intellect, emotions, and soul unite. Second, one slows one's breathing and coordinates the Jesus Prayer to one's inhalations and exhalations. The inhalation of the breath is imagined as a physical expression of the descent of the mind into the heart. On the inhalation of the breath, one meditates on the words "Lord Jesus Christ," and on the exhalation, "Have mercy on me." This repetitive mantra is said to eventually become part of one's psyche, a perpetual silent prayer from one's center.

◎ CONCLUSIONS

In medieval Christianity, both East and West, monasticism as an institution and a style of spirituality became a dominant force that was both versatile and resilient. It also became a source of missionary work. As Christianity began to expand beyond the Roman Empire, monks

spearheaded missionary efforts, and monasteries often became thriving centers of Christian worship and other activities. Monasteries ministered to surrounding populations, establishing schools, hospitals, and other places of hospitality. The monastery was imagined to be the place where God could be known and served most profoundly.

Paradoxically, the movement that began as an alternative to normal church life ultimately became a model for Christian holiness within the larger church institution. While lay Christians still gathered for morning and evening prayer in cathedral churches, clergy took monks as their models and embraced the monastic liturgy of the hours, praying psalms and other scriptures throughout the day. Even today, while Eastern Orthodox priests can be married, bishops are chosen only from the ranks of celibate monks. Celibacy became the norm for priests in the West, and some patristic and early medieval bishops even demanded a quasi-monastic life for all their priests.

The patristic church was rich in mediations, symbols, and metaphors. Mary became a larger-than-life patron for Christians, and icons become avenues for veneration and perceptual doors to the sacred. And the sacraments, particularly the Eucharist, became symbolic ways to access the graces they celebrated. All of these elements became core Christian means to encounter the sacred.

SUMMARY QUESTIONS

- Who were the major figures who shaped monasticism, both East and West, and what were their contributions?
- How are sacraments believed to work?
- What are the various theological or spiritual roles Mary has played in the history of Christianity?

- What roles have icons played in Christianity? What were the central concerns of those who opposed them, and how did those who supported them respond?

DISCUSSION QUESTIONS

- In the early church, there were deeply rooted disagreements concerning the use of icons. Even today, there is a diversity of approaches to their use. From a Christian theological view, do you think the church decided rightly or wrongly on the issue in the eighth century? What are your reasons for your views?
- One of the most exotic expressions of monastic asceticism is that of Symeon the Stylite, who dwelt for years on a pillar. As the author notes, Christians from neighboring cities and villages hoisted food for him and sought his spiritual advice as well as intercessions for healing. What do you make of such a Christian witness?
- The Orthodox use of the *Jesus Prayer* claims that ultimately one could worship God in a kind of utter stillness. What is your reaction to this claim? Do you think it is possible or even commendable for having a "perpetual silent prayer" ongoing in one's psyche? Explain your answer.

KEY TERMS

Abba	Benedict of Nursia	Iconodule
Abbess	Cassian, John	Iconostasis
Abbot	Climacus, John	Jesus Prayer
Amma	Coenobitic monasticism	Liturgy
Anchoritic monasticism	Hesychasm	Pachomius
Antony of Egypt	Icon	Sacraments
Basilica	Iconoclast	

BIBLIOGRAPHY

- Athanasius. 1980. *Athanasius: The Life of Antony and the Letter to Marcellinus.* Trans. Robert Gregg. New York: Paulist Press.
- Basil of Caesarea. 1950. *St. Basil: Ascetical Works.* Trans. Monica Wagner. New York: Fathers of the Church.
- Benedict of Nursia. 1982. *The Rule of St. Benedict.* Trans. Timothy Fry. Collegeville, MN: Liturgical Press.
- Bilaniuk, Petro. 1993. "Eastern Spirituality." In *The New Dictionary of Catholic Encyclopedia,* ed. Michael Downey. Collegeville, MN: Michael Glazier.
- Cassian, John. 1997. *The Conferences.* Trans. Boniface Ramsey. New York: Newman Press.
- Cassian, John. 2000. *The Institutes.* Trans. Boniface Ramsey. New York: Newman Press.
- Chariton, Igumen, ed. 1997. *The Art of Prayer: An Orthodox Anthology.* Trans. E. Kadloubovsky and E. M. Palmer. London: Faber and Faber.
- Chryssavgis, John. 2008. *In the Heart of the Desert: Spirituality of the Desert Fathers and Mothers.* Bloomington, IN: World Wisdom.
- Climacus, John. 1982. *The Ladder of Divine Ascent.* Trans. Colm Luibheid and Norman Russell. New York: Paulist Press.
- Earle, Mary. 2007. *The Desert Mothers: Spiritual Practices from the Women of the Wilderness.* New York: Morehouse.
- Gribomont, Jean. 1988. "Monasticism and Asceticism: Eastern Christianity." In *Christian Spirituality,* ed. Bernard McGinn, John Meyendorff, and Jean Leclercq, 1:89–112. New York: Crossroad.
- Guigo II. 1978. *The Ladder of Monks: A Letter on the Contemplative Life and Twelve Meditations.* Trans. Edmund College and James Walsh. Garden City, NY: Doubleday Image Books.
- Hausherr, Irenee. 1982. *Penthos: The Doctrine of Compunction in the Christian East.* Kalamazoo, MI: Cistercian Publications.
- Healey, Charles. 1999. *Christian Spirituality: An Introduction to the Heritage.* New York: St. Pauls.
- John of Damascus. 1980. *On the Divine Images.* Trans. David Anderson. Crestwood, NY: St. Vladimir's Seminary Press.
- Joncas, Jan Michael. 2009. "Eastern Christianity." In *The Christian Theological Tradition,* 3rd ed., ed. Catherine Cory and Michael Hollerich, 194–210. Upper Saddle River, NJ: Pearson.
- Jones, Cheslyn, Geoffrey Wainwright, and Edward Yarnold, eds. 1986. *The Study of Spirituality.* New York: Oxford University Press.
- Leclercq, Jean. 1961. *The Love of Learning and the Desire for God: A Study of Monastic Culture.* Trans. Catharine Misrahi. New York: Fordham University Press.
- Leclercq, Jean. 1988. "Monasticism and Asceticism: Western Christianity." In *Christian Spirituality,* ed. Bernard McGinn, John Meyendorff, and Jean Leclercq, 1:113–131. New York: Crossroad.
- Lossky, Vladimir. 1976. *The Mystical Theology of the Eastern Church.* Trans. Fellowship of St. Alban and St. Sergius. Crestwood, NY: St. Vladimir's Seminary Press.
- Louth, Andrew. 2007. *The Origins of the Christian Mystical Tradition: From Plato to Denys,* 2nd ed. Oxford: Oxford University Press.
- McGinn, Bernard. 1992. *The Foundations of Mysticism: Origins to the Fifth Century.* New York: Crossroad.
- McGinn, Bernard. 1994. *The Growth of Mysticism: Gregory the Great through the 12th Century.* New York: Crossroad.
- McGinn, Bernard, John Meyendorff, and Jean Leclercq, eds. 1988. *Christian Spirituality I: Origins to the Twelfth Century.* New York: Crossroad.
- Palamas, Gregory. 1983. *The Triads.* Trans. Nicholas Gendle. Mahwah, NJ: Paulist Press.
- Palmer, G. E. H., Philip Sherrard, and Kallistos Ware, trans. and eds. 1979–1995. *The Philokalia,* 4 vols. London: Faber and Faber.
- Regnault, Lucien. 1999. *The Day-to-Day Life of the Desert Fathers in Fourth-Century Egypt.* Petersham, MA: St. Bede's Publications.

- Swan, Laura. 2001. *The Forgotten Desert Mothers: Sayings, Lives, and Stories of Early Christian Women*. Mahwah, NJ: Paulist Press.
- Tugwell, Simon. 1985. *Ways of Imperfection: An Exploration of Christian Spirituality*. Springfield, IL: Templegate.
- Ward, Benedicta, trans. and ed. 1975. *The Sayings of the Desert Fathers: The Alphabetical Collection*. Kalamazoo, MI: Cistercian Publications.
- Ware, Kallistos. 1986a. *The Power of the Name: The Jesus Prayer in Orthodox Spirituality*. Oxford: SLG Press.
- Ware, Kallistos. 1986b. "The Spirituality of the Icon." In *The Study of Spirituality*, ed. Cheslyn Jones, Geoffrey Wainwright, and Edward Yarnold. New York: Oxford University Press.
- Ware, Kallistos. 1995. *The Orthodox Way*, rev. ed. Crestwood, MI: St. Vladimir's Seminary Press.
- Wybrew, Hugh. 1978. "The Byzantine Liturgy from the *Apostolic Constitutions* to Present Day." In *The Study of Liturgy*, ed. Cheslyn Jones, Geoffrey Wainwright, and Edward Yarnold, 209–219. New York: Oxford University Press.

NOTES

1. Athanasius, *Life of Antony*, no. 5, 33..
2. Basil of Caesarea, *St. Basil: Ascetical Works*, 253, 273.
3. Cassian, *Conferences*, 1.8, 47.
4. Guigo II, *Ladder of Monks*, 92–93.
5. Accessed at http://web.archive.org/web/20101009033540/http://ivanlewis.com/Didache/didache.html.
6. The modern version of the Liturgy of St. John Chrysostom can be found at http://www.ocf.org/OrthodoxPage/liturgy/liturgy.html. All subsequent references come from this source.
7. See http://www.provoslave.ru/english/66118.htm.
8. John of Damascus, *On the Divine Images*, 1.16 as accessed in https://www.christianhistoryinstitute.org/study/module/john-of-damascus/.
9. Cited in Oupensky, "Icon and Art," 382–383.
10. Cited in Ware, "Spirituality of the Icon," 196.
11. Cited in Bellitto, *General Councils*, 32.
12. Ware, "Spirituality of the Icon," 197.
13. Climacus, *Ladder of Divine Ascent*, 268–270.

Expansion and Change in the East and North

WHAT TO EXPECT

It would not be unusual for readers in the West to be unaware of Christianity's substantial and even dominant ancient presence in lands that today have only a small minority of Christians, such as Syria, Iraq, or parts of northeast Africa. This chapter describes development and changes in the church in those lands. It also recounts the expansion of the Byzantine church into Slavic territories, where Christian missions were massively successful as a result of wholesale baptisms of the peoples there. Finally, we see how the surging of Islam in the seventh and eighth centuries rewrote the religious and political map of the Middle East and North Africa.

 EGYPT, NUBIA, AND ETHIOPIA

EGYPT AND COPTIC CHRISTIANITY

As noted in Chapter Seven, the Council of Nicaea's decision that Christ had a fully divine nature was not accepted by all Christians, some of whom followed Arius's theology instead. Controversy would continue in both East and West for the next century. Progressively, Arianism died out, though it would linger in the West for more than two centuries. The divisions stemming from the Council of Chalcedon's decision that Christ had two distinct and unmixed natures in a single person or identity proved to be lasting. After Chalcedon, the Alexandrian patriarch Dioscorus was deposed, and the emperor Marcian ordered that a new election be held to replace him. Christians in Alexandria resisted this, as they considered Dioscorus their legitimate patriarch. Although they ultimately elected Proterius, a presbyter under Dioscorus, who was sympathetic to Chalcedon, many of the faithful felt betrayed. Emperor Marcian died in 457, and a group of bishops quickly consecrated Timothy as the new patriarch, even though Proterius was still in office. In essence, they were creating a parallel church, much like we saw with the Donatist controversy in North Africa. So intense were the divisions and animosity that a violent mob seized Proterius and ran a sword through him—in church, no less.

Egypt is an interesting case study of culture. Its great city was Alexandria, one of the leading centers of learning and sophistication in the empire. Alexandria stood on the Mediterranean as Egypt's northernmost city, and its language and culture were thoroughly Greek. The heart of the country, however, never identified with the Greek culture. The people's language was Coptic, and by the early third century Coptic-speaking Christians began to form their own separate Christian identity. The Bible was translated into Coptic, as were Egyptian liturgical rites. Most of Egypt's Christian literature south of Alexandria was also in Coptic, including homilies, monastic Rules, and theological treatises. Even the great saints of the monastic movement, Antony and Pachomius, spoke Coptic rather than Greek. Indeed, Coptic monasticism dominated the Egyptian Christian landscape. One of the most important early monastic figures was Shenoute, who in the late fourth century presided over a double monastery with as many as 2,200 men and 1,800 women. Shenoute was the first influential writer in Coptic, and one finds in his letters and sermons a version of Christianity that was simple, disciplined, and highly ascetic. It was as a result of the monastic movement that regular churches were built throughout the country south of Alexandria.

The Egyptian church's rejection of Chalcedon, along with its cultural distinctiveness from the rest of the empire, set the stage for a church that was independent from the imperial church. Interestingly, it is exactly because most of Christianity in Egypt was independent and separated from Constantinople that Coptic Christianity survived the Muslim invasion of the seventh century, as Muslims did not perceive it to be a political threat.

NUBIA

South of Egypt was Nubia, a country stretching from the Nile's first cataract at Aswan to Ethiopia. Even in the time of the pharaohs, Nubia represented a cultural and linguistic divide from Egypt. Christianity had modestly penetrated Nubia in the fifth century, but it was not until the sixth that it became truly Christian when the emperor **Justinian** (r. 527–565) was persuaded by his wife Theodora to send a mission to Nubia. Theodora was a monophysite, while the emperor was a staunch supporter of Chalcedon. Theodora chose a monophysite presbyter from Alexandria named Julian to lead the mission. Justinian tried to check this move by sending a Chalcedonian bishop to precede Julian with ambassadors bringing gifts for Silko, the king of the Nubians. Theodora, however, had these ambassadors delayed so as to give Julian time to convert the Nubians to monophysite Christianity. By the time the Chalcedonian ambassadors arrived, the king was already aligned with the Coptic monophysite version of Christianity, though he probably would not have appreciated the theological disagreement. With lightning speed Nubia became a Christian nation, displacing the traditional religion of the Nubian people. Although the Nubians were monophysite, they continued to maintain strong ties to Constantinople, and their liturgies and architecture reflected the Byzantine style. Churches were built throughout the land in the eighth and ninth centuries, and Christian culture flourished into the tenth century, even as Muslim advances were taking over Arabia and North Africa. Eventually, Islam came to dominate the northern part of Nubia, and by the twelfth century Christianity was in serious decline. By the fifteenth century the Nubian language had been replaced by Arabic and virtually disappeared, while its populace drifted to Islam.

 ETHIOPIA

The ancient Greeks thought of Ethiopia as utterly exotic. The Greek playwright Aeschylus described it as a "land far off, a nation of black men." Indeed, it was far off, approximately 1,500 miles south of Alexandria. In the ancient period, Ethiopia and southern Arabia were part of a Red Sea Semitic culture, and Ethiopians spoke a Semitic language known as Geez. It was an extraordinarily advanced culture, prosperous and well organized. It was also the home of an ancient Christian tradition dating back to the second or third century.

According to Rufinus's fourth-century *Ecclesiastical History*, Meropius, a Christian intellectual from Tyre, was journeying to India with two young companions, Frumentius and Aedesius. The customary route was the Red Sea, and they stopped at the port of Adulis, Ethiopia. Some hostile inhabitants killed Meropius and took the young men as slaves for the king. Through the years, they became high-placed officials in the king's administration. At the king's death, they were given leave to return to Tyre, but the queen mother asked them to remain as administrators until her son came of age to rule the country. Frumentius encouraged Christian merchants to settle in Askum, and they formed a fledgling Christian community. Soon, the young king himself became a convert and provided royal support for the building of churches.

When the king was of sufficient age and training to administer his own country, he gave both Aedisius and Frumentius leave to return home. Frumentius traveled to Alexandria and reported to Athanasius that the new church needed leadership. Athanasius consecrated Frumentius the first bishop of Ethiopia sometime in the late 340s.

Rufinus's chronicle aligns with what we know from elsewhere. The name of Frumentius, for example, is mentioned in a letter from Emperor Constantius II (r. 337–361) to the Ethiopian king Ezana (r. 320–356). Additionally, in an Ethiopian inscription of the same period, the

Christian God is praised for delivering Ezana's military victories. The link between Alexandria and Ethiopia was strong, and the Alexandrian patriarch would appoint its leading bishop well into the modern period.

In its infancy, Ethiopian Christianity concentrated itself in the port city of Adulis and its capital at Aksum. By the late fifth century, it had expanded through the efforts of monks, who brought the faith to an increasingly wider circle of villages. Like those in southern Egypt and Nubia, the church of Ethiopia quickly translated the Bible, liturgy, and Christian literature into its native language. Unlike Egypt, Ethiopia would not be conquered by Islamic armies, in part because it was allowed its own autonomy. This may have been because the Ethiopian king gave some of Muhammad's family and early followers safe haven when they were initially persecuted in Mecca.

Ethiopia had a Semitic language and was influenced by Judaism, which had a presence in Yemen, just across the Red Sea. In fact, Ethiopia politically controlled Yemen for centuries in the Common Era. This may explain the distinctively Judaic qualities of Ethiopian Christianity. For example, their Sabbath day is not Sunday, but Saturday, following Judaism. They also follow some of the Jewish dietary laws and circumcise their males on the eighth day, as Jews do.

Ethiopian Christianity saw itself as something of a renewed Israel. In Ethiopia's national Epic, *Kebra Nagast* (Glory of the Kings), the biblical story of the queen of Sheba's visit to King Solomon (1 Kings 10:1–13) is given a twist. This queen is identified as Makeda, the queen of Askum. She is so impressed with Solomon's wisdom that she converts to Judaism. She also leaves Jerusalem pregnant with Solomon's son, whom she names Menelik. As a young man, Menelik travels to Jerusalem, and Solomon anoints him king and sends him back with a number of Jewish families. During their journey, Menelik finds that some of these Israelite immigrants have taken the Ark of the Covenant with them. So Ethiopia understood itself as the new Israel, not only in the spiritual sense but also in

the political and even biological sense; its kings were descendants of Solomon.

 THE CHURCH OF THE EAST

While many bishops from Egypt returned home from the Council of Chalcedon disappointed (or perhaps aghast!), the bishops from Syria returned home delighted by the "two natures" decision about Christ. Ultimately, however, most of them would also reject Chalcedon. How this came about is something of a strange story. The theological battle waged initially at the Council of Ephesus and later at Chalcedon could be simplified to the fight between those who followed Cyril of Alexandria and those who followed Nestorius, the archbishop of Constantinople who was deposed at Ephesus. Cyril had emphasized the unity of Christ to such a degree that he could be interpreted as having blurred Jesus's distinct natures, or at least as having reduced his human nature as inconsequential (the monophysite view). Nestorius, on the other hand, had emphasized the distinctions between Jesus's natures so strongly that he was interpreted as denying the unity of the person of Christ. Cyril represented the Alexandrian school of thought, while Nestorius represented the Antiochene. The two sides—Alexandrian and Antiochene—could not have been further apart on this issue. Ephesus and Chalcedon affirmed Cyril's Christology, but only insofar as it could be interpreted along Chalcedon's line (two separate natures in one single person). Many of Cyril's interpreters understood Chalcedon as rejecting Cyril.

One of the great articulators of the Antiochene school was Theodore of Mopsuestia. So revered was Theodore that he became known in Syrian Christianity as "the Interpreter," that is, the great articulator of scripture and authentic Christian faith. Theodore died widely respected, but his reputation suffered greatly as his writings were increasingly appealed to by Nestorians. This trend created a rift between representatives of the imperial church and many Syrian and Persian Christians who considered Theodore one of the great theologians of the church.

The eventual separation between the Syriac-speaking church and the imperial church became even more oddly strained when the patriarch of Antioch, Severus (r. 512–518), defended a monophysite interpretation of Cyril's teaching and tried to sway those under his leadership to the Coptic monophysite position—a position the imperial church was sure he had never really held. Now there were Christians of various theological commitments in the Middle East: those who followed Chalcedon came to be called Melkites (from the Syriac word for emperor) and Marionites (after the influential monk Maro); monophysites were called Jacobites (following Jacob Baradeus, the great sixth century bishop of Edessa); and those who followed Nestorius became the Church of the East.

In 489, the emperor Zeno tried to end all divisions and insist that all Christians embrace Chalcedon's decisions. He drove out all the teachers and public supporters of Theodore of Mopsuestia from Edessa, a theological center at the edge of the Roman Empire. They settled in Nisibis in the Persian Empire. This school became perhaps the key theological resource for the Church of the East. The Jacobites, like the Copts of Egypt, created their own separate church and lines of authority. The Syrian church, however, continued to see itself as part of the larger church.

Initially, the Christians of the Persian Empire were under the jurisdiction of the patriarch of Antioch. In 424, however, Persian bishops declared

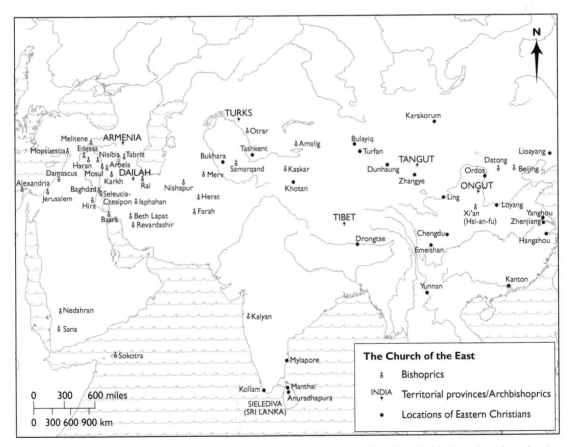

FIGURE 10-1 The Church of the East: One sees here the enormous reach of the Church of the East, though modest in numbers outside of Persia.

that they had their own jurisdiction. They would be in communion with Constantinople, but insisted on their own patriarch, whom they called the *"catholicos* of the East." The Roman emperor agreed and recognized their independent authority. Their communion with the imperial church would not last. By embracing Nestorianism, and due to their political separation from the Roman Empire, they ultimately became a separate Christian community.

One ought not to downplay the importance of these Christians, who sometimes fall off the map of Western Christian consciousness. The Church of the East spread across the Middle East and today reflects the principal form of Christianity in southeastern Turkey, Azerbaijan, Iraq, Kuwait, Saudi Arabia, Bahrain, the United Arab Emirates, Oman, Iran, Turkmenistan, Uzbekistan, and Afghanistan.

The Church of the East is also responsible for the development of Christianity in India, Sri Lanka, and China. Tradition has it that the apostle Thomas brought Christianity to India in the first century. The story of Thomas's missionary journey is found in the *Acts of Thomas*, a Syriac text from the third or fourth century. As the story goes, the risen Jesus appeared to Thomas in a dream and told him to evangelize the peoples of India. Shortly afterward, Thomas met a merchant from India with orders from King Gundaphar of Punjab to bring back architects to build his royal palace. Thomas agreed to the job and traveled to India. When Thomas saw the severe poverty of the people, however, he took the king's money and used it to alleviate their suffering. When the king discovered this, he was outraged and unswayed by Thomas's defense. The king then received a vision in which he saw his royal palace in heaven. This led to his conversion to Christianity. Thomas continued to evangelize the Indian population until he was martyred in what is now the city of Chennai.

That the apostle Thomas would have impressed this agent of the Indian king as a magnificent architect stretches the imagination. Other accounts have the first evangelization of India beginning with the apostle Bartholomew.

Whatever the case, there seems to have been some Christian presence in the region early. In Eusebius's *Ecclesiastical History* he says that a Christian philosopher traveled to India in the late second century and discovered Christians already living there. They even possessed the Gospel of Matthew in Aramaic.

Roman trade with India had already been established in the ancient period; of particular interest was the Roman delight of pepper. Trade routes were established along the Silk Road, as well as by sea around the Horn of Africa. By the

FIGURE 10-2 Created in eighth-century China, the Nestorian Stele details a Chinese form of the Christian message.

late third century Christians had a network of churches throughout Persia and around the Indian Ocean. David, the third metropolitan of Basra, made a journey to India around the year 300 and visited Christian communities in both the north and south.

Thanks to the Church of the East, Christianity also arrived in China in the sixth century and enjoyed a well-established presence by the eighth. At the time, the T'ang dynasty had diplomatic and trade relations with the Persian Empire and politically controlled Manchuria, northern Korea, Mongolia, and Tibet. Christians appeared in the capital city (modern Xi'an) sometime in the early to mid-seventh century. In an imperial decree we find the following:

> The Persian monk A-lo-pen has come from afar bringing scriptures and teaching. . . . The meaning of the teaching has been carefully examined; it is mysterious, wonderful, calm; it fixes the essentials of life and perfection; it is the salvation of living beings; it is the wealth of man. It is right

that it should spread through the empire. Therefore let the local officials build a monastery in the I-ning quarter with twenty-one regular monks.[1]

The most impressive documentation of Christianity in China is an enormous black limestone monument discovered in the seventeenth century on the precincts of a temple close to Xi'an. Erected in 781, it contains 1,700 Chinese characters interspersed with Syriac words. This monument offers a short account of Christian missions to China, including those of the Christian monk A-lo-pen from Persia. It mentions a number of texts of the Christian canon, liturgical rites, and even Rules for monks. Another fascinating discovery detailing the presence of Christianity in China comes from a set of documents discovered in the nineteenth century in a walled-up chapel. These writings came from Chinese Christian monks, and many were Chinese translations of Syrian texts, including a text called *Jesus Messiah Sutra* that contains the basic teachings of Christianity.

PORTION OF THE TEXT OF THE NESTORIAN STELE

Behold the unchangeably true and invisible, who existed through all eternity without origin; the far-seeing perfect intelligence, whose mysterious existence is everlasting; operating on primordial substance he created the universe, being more excellent than all holy intelligences, inasmuch as he is the source of all that is honorable. This is our eternal true lord God, triune and mysterious in substance. He appointed the cross as the means for determining the four cardinal points, he moved the original spirit, and produced the two principles of nature; the somber void was changed, and heaven and earth were opened out; the sun and moon revolved, and day and night commenced; having perfected all inferior objects, he then made the first man; upon him he bestowed an excellent disposition, giving him in charge the government of all created beings; man, acting out the original principles of his nature, was pure and unostentatious; his unsullied and expansive mind was free from the least inordinate desire; until Satan introduced the seeds of falsehood, to deteriorate his purity of principle. . . .

Thereupon, our Trinity being divided in nature, the illustrious and honorable Messiah, veiling his true dignity,

appeared in the world as a man; angelic powers promulgated the glad tidings, a virgin gave birth to the Holy One in Syria; a bright star announced the felicitous event, and Persians observing the splendor came to present tribute; the ancient dispensation, as declared by the twenty-four holy men [the writers of the Old Testament], was then fulfilled, and he laid down great principles for the government of families and kingdoms; he established the new religion of the silent operation of the pure spirit of the Triune; he rendered virtue subservient to direct faith; he fixed the extent of the eight boundaries, thus completing the truth and freeing it from dross; he opened the gate of the three constant principles, introducing life and destroying death; he suspended the bright sun to invade the chambers of darkness, and the falsehoods of the devil were thereupon defeated; he set in motion the vessel of mercy by which to ascend to the bright mansions, whereupon rational beings were then released, having thus completed the manifestation of his power, in clear day he ascended to his true station.[2]

Christianity was not to last in China. Monasteries were dependent on the favor of Chinese rulers, and by the ninth century this favor was removed. Monasteries and churches were suppressed, and by the end of the tenth century the church was for all intents and purposes extinct.

 ## EXPANSION OF THE BYZANTINE CHURCH

ARMENIA AND GEORGIA (IBERIA)

Armenia is a territory that borders the western part of the Caspian Sea, the northern part of Iraq, and the border of Turkey. In the Christian era it was divided into three geographical areas. The west was part of the Roman Empire, the east was part of the Persian Empire, and the south was bandied between the two for several centuries. Eusebius's *Ecclesiastical History* has Christianity reaching Armenia by the beginning of the fourth century, though it is unclear how. Traditionally, the conversion of the Armenian people at large to Christianity is credited to Gregory "the Illuminator," who came from an Armenian noble family. Gregory's father had been executed for assassinating the king, and Gregory had been banished to Caesarea in Asia Minor. There he was brought up in the Christian faith. Upon returning to Armenia, he worked his way up to becoming secretary to King Tiridates III (d. 330), but he refused to worship Anahit, the goddess venerated by the Armenians. The king imprisoned him for ten years, and upon his release he miraculously healed the ailing king, who subsequently had his court convert to Christianity. Gregory returned to Caesarea and was consecrated bishop. He then baptized the king and masses of his subjects in the Euphrates River. After Tiridates's baptism, he destroyed all pagan shrines and built churches throughout his kingdom.

In the early decades, the language of the scriptures and liturgy used in Armenia was either Syriac or Greek, because the native Armenian language had no formal script. Later, the Armenian

monk Mashtots created a script and had the scriptures translated into what was the first Armenian text ever produced. Tradition has it that Mashtots was received by the Armenians like Moses descending from Mount Sinai with the Law. Within a hundred years Armenian monasticism was so developed that many monks migrated to the Holy Land east of Jerusalem, where Armenian Christianity still has a presence.

When the controversy of Chalcedon broke out in the Armenian church, some of which was located in the Persian Empire, Armenian Christians readily aligned with the theology of Theodore of Mopsuestia and, by extension, Nestorius. Sahak, the great-grandson of Gregory the Illuminator, was the *catholicos* (premier bishop) of Armenia from 387 to 438 and was responsible for establishing an Armenian liturgy. His episcopal see was in Dvin, a city ruled by the Persians. Ultimately, Sahak aligned himself with Chalcedon's decision and its denunciation of Nestorius. This brought down the wrath of the Persian authorities, who saw it as nothing short of aligning with the Roman Empire. The Persians tried to limit contacts and influence between the Armenians and Greek-speaking Christians of the Roman Empire and to undermine the church in Armenia, ultimately demanding that all its citizens become Zoroastrian, the official religion of the Persian Empire. Sahak was executed. The persecution would not last, and Armenian Christianity survived. In the sixth century the Armenian bishops ultimately rejected both the Council of Chalcedon and Nestorianism, the latter of which had by then been implanted in the Church of the East.

The conversion of Georgia is strikingly like that of Armenia, both in its history of a saintly healer and in Christianity's creation of a literate culture. Georgia sits south of the Caucasus Mountains, east of the Black Sea, and west of the Caspian Sea. The western part of Georgia had been under the influence of the Roman Empire since the first century, and the emperor Nero annexed this region in the first century, making it part of the province of Cappadocia in Asia Minor. Late in the third century, Christianity made inroads into the territory, and the Council of Nicaea even included two bishops from the region. The conversion of the eastern part of the country, at this time an independent kingdom of Iberia, came about because of a Christian woman, Nino, who had been taken captive as a slave.

Nino had a great reputation among the people as a saintly woman with a strange religion. She lived a life of asceticism and constant prayer. She also had the reputation of being able to heal. When Queen Nana became ill, Nino was brought to her and healed her in the name of Christ. The delighted King Mirian was grateful and wanted to offer her gifts, but the now-healed queen told him that Nino would have nothing to do with material wealth; Nino only wished that the royal household would worship Christ. Days later, the king became lost in the forest and called on Christ to rescue him. When he found his way back to the city, he insisted that Nino instruct him and the queen in the Christian faith. He then sent an embassy to Emperor Constantine asking for Christian officials to build a church and convert the people. Soon a bishopric was created in the capital city of Mtskheta. Like Armenia, Georgia did not have its own alphabet, so Christian leaders created one in order to pass along the scriptures and liturgy. This became the foundation for independent literature to develop in the Georgian culture.

While the Armenians at large rejected the Council of Chalcedon, the Georgians fully embraced it, thus creating an alliance with the imperial church. This alliance was formalized by the Georgian king Vakhtang I (d. 522) and the emperor Zeno. Zeno recognized the Georgian church as independent, though under the jurisdiction of the patriarch of Antioch. By the seventh century, however, the Georgians had become completely independent juridically, even as they remained in communion with the church at large.

SLAVIC LANDS

From the fifth century onward, various groups of Indo-European Slavic peoples began to migrate into southern Russia, Hungary, Moravia, and the Balkans. In 862, Rastislav, the king of Moravia, asked Emperor Michael III to send missionaries to his kingdom, and Michael chose two brothers from Thessalonica, Greece: **Cyril** and **Methodius**. Some Slavs had migrated as far as southern Greece, and Cyril and Methodius were fluent in their tongue. Methodius also might have spent time in the Balkans. Both men were classically educated and known to be pious. As in Armenia and Georgia, the first task for these brothers was to translate Christian teaching and scriptures into the Slavic tongue. They had to actually create an alphabet to write it down. This alphabet, based on Greek letters, developed into what is called the Cyrillic script, and was adopted by the Slavic peoples living among the Rus, Serbians, and Bulgarians.

Actually, Christianity was already being practiced in Moravia (Slovakia) as a result of the influence of the Germanic Franks, many of whom were Christian. But King Rastislav wanted a Christian faith in the Slavic tongue, and the Frankish priests did not adapt well to the Slavic language. Rastislav's principal concern was to train his own Slavic clergy and to create a Slavic church.

The issue was also political. By now, the West was creating a competing Christianity, one centered on Rome, and a Western Empire that competed with the Byzantine Empire. Becoming Christian involved not merely embracing the faith, but also deciding which community to align with, the Latin West or the Greek East. Rastislav very well may have initially wanted to create an alliance with Constantinople, creating a political bond that would provide powerful supporters against the German kingdom. On the other hand, choosing to embrace a Latin Christianity rather than a Greek one could also allow for Western alliances. From the middle of the ninth century on, the Franks began to claim territory to their east, particularly Moravia and Bohemia (today's eastern half of the Czech Republic and western half of the Slovak Republic). Both the Moravians and Bohemians saw that there was more to be gained by political ties with their neighboring German kingdom than with Constantinople, which was far to the east. Thus they both accepted ties to the Latin church.

Subsequent to Bohemia's conversion to Christianity, the faith entered Poland. Mieszko, a Polish prince, became king in 960, and in 964 he entered into a marriage with Dobrawa, the daughter of the Bohemian king Boleslav. Clearly, this was a dynastic marriage intended to cement ties between these two countries as a way of checking the expansionistic designs of the Germans. Dobrawa came to Poland accompanied by Western priests and a Latin Christian faith. In 968, Pope John XIII commissioned Jordan, the first bishop of Poland.

RUSSIAN FAITH

In the early ninth century Rus merchants journeyed to Constantinople to open up trade. They were overwhelmed by the wealth of the city and returned with tales of its opulence. In 860, a fleet of 200 Rus ships attacked the city, which had been left defenseless as the empire's fleets fought the Arabs. Ultimately the siege ended quickly and unsuccessfully, and ambassadors from Constantinople went to Kiev and arranged a peace treaty.

In the middle of the tenth century, Olga, the widow of the Rus prince Oleg, journeyed to Constantinople. Like the traders a century before, Olga was taken by the city, its art, architecture, and culture. Further, the emperor treated her visit with great pomp and ceremony. He urged her to be baptized. She consented and returned to Kiev a Christian. While her son Svyatoslav had no interest in Christianity, her grandson **Vladimir**, who became ruler in 980, did embrace the faith. But Vladimir's conversion was not religiously tidy. He attacked Cherson, a Byzantine city in Crimea on the northern shore of the Black Sea, and cut off the city's water supply. He then demanded of Emperor Basil II that he give his

sister to Vladimir in marriage. Basil objected on the grounds that a Christian should not marry a pagan, but he assured Vladimir that he would arrange the marriage if Vladimir consented to be baptized. Vladimir agreed, and, upon baptism and his marriage, he had the people of Kiev baptized in the Dnieper River. The Rus became part of Constantinople's commonwealth, which brought not only a solidification of a common faith, but also higher culture and developing trade relationships with Constantinople.

While Vladimir's decision to become Christian was initially tied to political and economic factors, his subsequent Christian faith appears neither fraudulent nor superficial. Once baptized, he worked energetically for decades to bring the Christian faith to his people. He built

FIGURE 10-3 While Prince Vladimir may have become Christian for political reasons, he robustly advanced the Christian faith in Russia.

churches, set up bishoprics, and promoted the Slavic language and Christian literary culture. His kingdom inaugurated a new era in the history of Christianity and ultimately would become larger than the Byzantine Empire itself.

The Russian church was centered in Kiev, Ukraine, whose archbishop was the metropolitan for all the Rus people, but this would not last. Mongol armies under Genghis Khan (c. 1162–1227) fought the Rus in numerous battles, two of which (1223 and 1238) subjected them to Mongol rule. The metropolitan center of Russian Orthodoxy moved to Moscow, and in 1448 a council of Russian bishops declared itself independent of Constantinople. By 1589, Moscow had become a patriarchal see.

Despite the fact that the Rus people were controlled by the Mongolian Empire, religious toleration was typical, and monasteries flourished as centers of mission work, scholarship, and spirituality. Christianity continued to spread, even among the Mongol upper class. When Constantinople fell to the Ottoman Turks in 1453, the Russian Orthodox Church imagined itself the "Third Rome." Just as Rome had been the initial center of the empire, and Constantinople its successor, now the Russian people began to believe that they were destined to take on the ancient mantle. Initially this was more of a religious proclamation of authority and independence, and something of a conceit, but it would soon take on political significance. During the reign of Ivan III of Russia (1440–1505), the Mongols were defeated at the Battle of the Ugra River in 1408, and Russia emerged as a dominant power. Ivan had married Sophia Paleologue, the niece of Constantine XI, the last Byzantine emperor. This link allowed Ivan to consider himself the successor to Constantinople. Soon Russians regularly referred to their leader as *czar*, a Russian term for caesar, or emperor.

CONVERSIONS FROM THE TOP DOWN

Today, we tend to think of religious faith as highly personal and individualistic. Indeed, in early Christianity it was certainly that. The faith was technically outlawed, and seekers had to enter the church in a modestly clandestine manner. They were personally instructed and tested even before becoming catechumens. They then went through a rather rigorous process of initiation, culminating in baptism. Expectations were high, and embracing the faith was a morally costly venture. The logic of the Roman Empire was that embracing, at least minimally, the religion of the empire, with its gods and emperor worship, constituted loyalty to the empire; it was a sign of patriotism. Since Christians did not participate, they were outliers.

As Christianity became identified as the religion of the Roman Empire, increasingly persons wanted to join the church for social and economic reasons. Still, membership was imagined to be an individual decision, though now one with possibly mixed motives. The conversions of peoples outside the natural boundaries of the empire, however, changed the church's course. Many of these peoples, be they various Germanic tribes or Slavic countries, shared the same initial values of the Roman Empire: to be of one religion showed patriotism and loyalty. Thus, with the conversion of the rulers, whole swaths of their citizens were expected to take on the new faith. No longer were individuals discretely initiated over a long period of scrutiny and training. Now, once the monarch became Christian, it was expected that others would follow suit in short order. Further, because there was simply no sense of separation of church and state, government funding for the faith facilitated its quick expansion. Bishops or their representative priests baptized people en masse, often thousands at a time. Instead of preparing them for baptism, it was assumed that they would take on the faith more deeply as they attended Eucharist, heard sermons, and were affected by the laws and values of the church. This change from individual conversions to mass baptisms cannot be overestimated. The degree to which most citizens became authentically Christian would have to happen throughout their lifetime or over the next several generations.

THE SURGING OF ISLAM

Muhammad (570–632) was born into a leading tribe of Mecca, the Quraysh. His father died about the time he was born, and his mother when he was six. After two years of being cared for by his grandfather, he was adopted by his uncle and worked minding the family's flocks. In early adulthood he took up the caravan business and entered the service of Khadijah, a wealthy widow, whom he eventually married. From 610 on, Muhammad began to receive revelations from God that led to his creation of a new religion, Islam, one grounded in Jewish and Christian theological impulses. Muhammad and his followers were persecuted in Mecca and immigrated to Medina, where he became the civil and religious leader. Ultimately, after several battles with the Meccans, he established a unified religious and political order in the Arabian Peninsula.

Following Muhammad's death, Abu Bakr was controversially designated as the new *caliph*, or successor to Muhammad. Bakr only ruled for two years, but in that brief time he launched a series of military campaigns into both the Byzantine and Persian empires. The Byzantine army was weak at the time and was made up of Arab auxiliaries who regularly defected. After Damascus was taken, Emperor Heraclius gathered a huge force to confront the Muslim invaders. The decisive battle was at the Yarmuk River, just north of the Sea of Galilee. The Byzantine army was crushed even though they vastly outnumbered the Muslims. Jerusalem resisted on its own, but after a long siege the patriarch, Sophronius, negotiated terms for surrender.

This conquest was particularly shocking to the Christian imagination. Since the fourth century, when its population reached 50,000, Jerusalem had been a great place of pilgrimage and veneration. It was the center of the Holy Land, the place where Christ had been crucified and rose from the dead. Christians saw themselves as supersessionists, that is, their religion superseded Judaism, with Christ the fulfillment of all its promises. While Paul did not imagine

his faith as a separate religion from Judaism, he did teach that the Jewish Law was merely a disciplinarian waiting for Christ's fulfillment. In short, the Christian dispensation eclipsed the foundations of the Jewish faith. The New Testament's Letter to the Hebrews speaks to Christians on this score: Jesus, it says, brought a new covenant, making "the first one obsolete" (8:13). Jerusalem symbolized the superseding of Judaism by Christianity.

In a like manner, Islam saw itself as superseding Christianity. Muhammad and his followers thought his revelations *corrected* what was wrong with Christianity and portrayed Jesus as a prophet anticipating Muhammad. Islam saw itself as the fulfillment of the religion of the patriarchs and the inheritor of God's promises to Abraham. Further, Muhammad had experienced a supernatural flight into heaven (*al-mirage*) from Jerusalem's Temple Mount. In short, Jerusalem was their holy city, third only to Mecca and Medina.

The spread of Islam, both east and west, was unimaginably rapid. By 640, the Caliphate had extended into Mesopotamia, Syria, and Palestine. By 642, it had taken Egypt, and by 643 much of the Persian Empire. From this point on, three of the ancient patriarchal sees—Jerusalem, Antioch, and Alexandria—were in Muslim hands and no longer held theological prominence in the larger Christian world. The Umayyad Caliphate (661–750), based in Damascus, moved westward along the North African coast and into Spain. It was not until Charles Martel led the Franks in a counterattack at the Battle of Tours in 732 that Muslim expansion in Europe subsided. Before the end of the seventh century, however, Muslims had conquered Armenia, Persia, Syria, Palestine, Iraq, North Africa, and Spain. With lightning speed, Islam rewrote the map of the Roman Empire and came to dominate areas that had been part of the Christian civilization for centuries.

By and large, the Muslim takeover of Christian cities left their religious life relatively intact. Mosques were built, of course, and non-Muslims

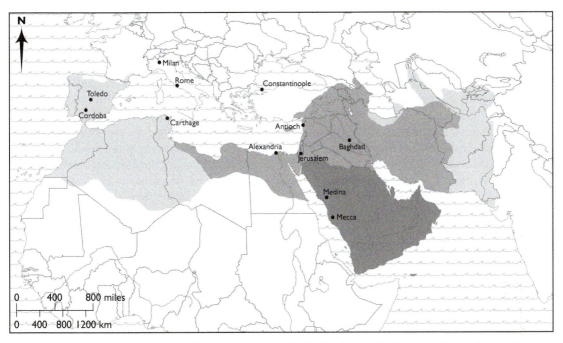

FIGURE 10-4 The spread of Islam: Within 120 years of the death of Muhammad, Islam spread throughout Arabia, Persia, North Africa, and the Iberian Peninsula.

were forced to pay additional taxes and obey the new civil laws, but Christian worship remained the same. Christians (and others) carried out their affairs relatively independently. This freedom, however, would not last entirely. Christians were often restricted and even controlled by their new Arab overlords. The Muslim governor in Alexandria, for example, insisted on playing a role in the election of bishops, and even the patriarch. Coptic was soon replaced with Arabic, except in church liturgies. As the press of Islamic invaders turned to North Africa, many leading Christian civil leaders and intellectuals fled to Europe. The North African church, once led by the likes of Cyprian of Carthage and Augustine of Hippo, would soon find itself losing its Latin language and intellectual heritage. By the twelfth century, North Africa was almost completely Muslim. Even in the most tolerant and progressive Muslim kingdom of Cordoba, Spain, Christians were not allowed to build churches or make any public display of their faith. Further, if a

Christian woman married a Muslim man, she was forced by civil law to become Muslim, as were their children. It would not be until the twelfth century that Muslims would constitute a majority in Spain, but this certainly did not mean that Christians had much political or cultural power.

Islam's political and religious developments were fraught with internal strife. When Muhammad died, his followers disagreed as to who ought to replace him as leader. Some believed that what singularly mattered was a respected leader of pious faith. Others argued for one from Muhammad's own family line. While Abu Bakr was chosen by the majority of Muslim leaders, he was not of Muhammad's bloodline. Those who insisted on a blood relative of Muhammad chose Ali, Muhammad's cousin and son-in-law, to succeed him. Conflict followed, with both of Bakr's next two successors as caliph, Umar (r. 634–644) and Uthman (r. 644–656), being murdered. Upon Uthman's murder, Ali was chosen as the fourth caliph, though this was over the objections of militant members of the Umayyad clan, to which Uthman belonged. With the support of Mu'awiyya, the governor of Syria, the Umayyads, particularly because they believed that Ali was implicated in Uthman's death, fought Ali's forces. During a battle in 657 a truce was called between Ali's forces and Uthman's supporters. They agreed to arbitration on the question of an authentic caliph.

While one might consider the question of who had the right to take on Muhammad's mantle to be purely religious, it was also sociological. Those who supported the Umayyad clan were members of the Meccan elite, many of whom were relatively late converts. Their choice of caliph was driven by pragmatic beliefs about who would be the most effective leader. Those who insisted on a caliph from Muhammad's family were early believers who had suffered from Meccan persecutions that had forced them to flee to Medina for their lives.

The settlement did not last long, and many believed that Ali had capitulated, compromising the very faith of Islam. Some initial supporters of Ali, the *Kharijites* (literally, "those who withdraw"), assassinated Ali in 661. Those who aligned with the Umayyad dynasty became known as Sunni ("right path") Muslims, while those who aligned with Ali became known as Shi'a ("partisans" of Ali) Muslims. Sunni leaders placed their capital in Damascus, Syria. Shi'ite leaders elected as caliph Ali's son Hussein, who led a revolt against the Umayyads in 680. In 750, with Shi'ite support, a branch headed by members of Muhammad's family created its own dynasty in Iraq, and its caliphate came to be known as the Abbasid dynasty.

Both dynasties flourished. The Umayyads spread their power to Spain, creating a great center of learning in its capital of Cordoba. The Abbasid dynasty survived for 500 years until it collapsed in 1258 from the impact of Mongol invaders. For both dynasties, these centuries would constitute the Golden Age for Islam. Islamic art, architecture, science, medicine, and learning flourished from Baghdad to Cordoba. Baghdad was perhaps the greatest center of scholarship in the world, and Cordoba was a particular center of interreligious learning among Muslims, Jews, and Christians. Much of the West's understanding of geography, mathematics, and astronomy has its foundation in Islamic scholarship. Even Christian medieval theology was influenced by philosophical and theological discussions advanced by Muslim scholars. Of particular importance was the rediscovery of Aristotle. Recall that early Christian intellectuals used Plato's philosophy to make their own theological projects intellectually rigorous. Aristotle, Plato's favorite student, and his works were seemingly uninteresting to early Christian thinkers. Apart from Aristotle's texts on logic, he was simply forgotten. The Islamic world, however, took a great interest in Aristotle, and many of his works were preserved in Arabic. Islamic writers such as **Ibn Sina**, Latinized to **Avicenna**, developed a philosophically robust approach to Islamic theology using Aristotle's thought. This combination of Greek philosophy and Islamic scholarship was further advanced by **Ibn Rushd**, known among the Latins as **Averroes**. Christians in Spain began to translate Aristotle's works into Latin, making them available to medieval thinkers. Ironically, the relative collapse of much of the Christian Roman Empire provided the conditions for the possibility of a great surge and advancement in Western scholarship.

 ## CONCLUSIONS

Between the fifth and tenth centuries Christianity expanded massively. Due to the reaction of the decisions of Chalcedon, however, it was not a unified faith. But this seeming liability also allowed for it to exist peacefully in lands that were in conflict with the Byzantine Empire. From Syria to Persia to Ethiopia, Christianity not only held its own, but grew and generated missions to the Far East. In Eastern European and Slavic territories, the Christian faith became the dominant religion. Christianity would not fare all that well against the spread of Islam. The northern coasts of Africa, the home of great leaders such as Cyril and Athanasius of Alexandria, Cyprian of Carthage, and Augustine of Hippo, would lose their Christian faith. The Middle Eastern church did better, but it nonetheless became a marginalized religion. In the early twenty-first century, with the disruption of Egypt, Iraq, and Syria, Christians would suffer even more.

SUMMARY QUESTIONS

- The Council of Chalcedon proved to be a watershed council for the church. List where each church fell regarding its decisions. What was the political fallout over its conclusions?
- What are the similarities and differences between the conversions of the Armenians and the Georgians?
- What is the main division in early Islam, and what was its cause?

- What was the impact of the rise of Islam on previously Christian-dominated civilizations?
- The Slavic King Vladimir's conversion was intertwined with political issues. What were they? Are there any other figures who bear resemblance to him in combining religious and political concerns?

DISCUSSION QUESTIONS

- What is your reaction to the story of Thomas's journey to convert India? Which parts do you think are historically factual, and which parts mythic? Does it matter, and why?
- Read the box with some of the text of the Nestorian Stele. Christianity is depicted in a way that looks foreign to its usual expression.

Do you think it represented the authentic Christian tradition or deviated from it? Explain.

- This chapter discussed the practice of mass conversions. Do you think these were, at the time, legitimate or illegitimate? Why or why not?

KEY TERMS

Cyril	Justinian	Muhammad
Ibn Rushd (Averroes)	Methodius	Vladimir
Ibn Sina (Avicenna)		

BIBLIOGRAPHY

- Browning, Robert. 1987. *Justinian and Theodora*. London: Thames and Hudson.
- Colish, Marcia. 1997. *Medieval Foundations of the Western Intellectual Tradition, 400–1400*. New Haven, CT: Yale University Press.
- Collins, Roger. 1995. *Early Medieval Spain*. New York: St. Martin's Press.
- Crone, Patricia. 2004. *God's Rule: Government and Islam: Six Centuries of Medieval Islamic Political Thought*. New York: Columbia University Press.
- Esposito, John. 1998. *Islam: The Straight Path*, 3rd ed. New York: Oxford University Press.
- Gregory, Timothy. 2010. *A History of Byzantium*. Oxford: Wiley-Blackwell.
- Griffith, Sidney. 2008. *The Church in the Shadow of the Mosque: Christians and Muslims in the World of Islam*. Princeton, NJ: Princeton University Press.
- MacCulloch, Diarmaid. 2009. *Christianity: The First Three Thousand Years*. New York: Penguin.

- Rahman, Fuzlur. 1979. *Islam*, 2nd ed. Chicago: University of Chicago Press.
- Roltz, Richard. 1999. *Religions of the Silk Road: Overland Trade and Cultural Exchange from Antiquity to the Fifteenth Century.* New York: St. Marin's Press.
- Wilken, Robert. 1992. *The Land Called Holy: Palestine in Christian History and Thought.* New Haven, CT: Yale University Press.
- Wilken, Robert. 2012. *The First Thousand Years: A Global History of Christians.* New Haven, CT: Yale University Press.

NOTES

1. Cited in Wilken, *First Thousand Years*, 241–242.

2. Accessed at http://en.wikisource.org/wiki/Nestorian_Stele.

11

The Church and the Western Empire

Timeline

399 CE	Ulfilas brings Christianity to the Germanic Goths
430s CE	Patrick evangelizes Ireland
455 CE	Vandals sack Rome
481–511 CE	Clovis unites Gaul (France) and adopts Christianity
597 CE	Augustine sent to England as a missionary
723 CE	Boniface sent as a missionary to Germanic tribes
756 CE	Rise of the Papal States
800 CE	Charlemagne crowned emperor by Pope Leo III; beginning of Holy Roman Empire
c. 850 CE	Evangelization of Sweden and Denmark begins
910 CE	Monastery founded at Cluny as base for monastic reform in the West
936–973	Emperor Otto the Great revives royal authority over the papacy
1033–1109 CE	Life of Anselm, theologian responsible for theory of substitutionary atonement
1054 CE	Schism between Eastern Orthodox and Roman Catholic churches
1073–1085 CE	Reign of Pope Gregory VII, who reforms the church and advances claims of papal jurisdiction
1096–1099 CE	First Crusade
1198–1216 CE	Rule of Pope Innocent III and the height of papal power

1202–1204 CE   Fourth Crusade; Western soldiers pillage Constantinople and set up Latin kingdom

1294–1303 CE   Reign of Pope Boniface VIII humiliated by French king Philip; issuance of *Unam Sanctam*

WHAT TO EXPECT

As Christianity expanded well into the Middle East, parts of Africa, and even pockets in Asia, as we saw in the last chapter, it also dramatically spread throughout modern-day Western Europe, even as the old Roman Empire in the West had broken down. This chapter details some of the major shifts that occurred during this period. Of particular importance was the Frankish kingdom, located in today's France. Under Charlemagne, this kingdom conquered much of central Europe, and the pope anointed Charlemagne "Emperor of the Romans," thus creating the Holy Roman Empire. This chapter also investigates the development of the papacy and its increasingly dominant role in the West. Finally, it discusses the problem of Christianity and violence, particularly the issues of what makes for a "just war," and how these criteria were (or were not) applied to the Crusades.

 ## RECONSTITUTION OF THE WEST

Historians typically use one of two dates to mark the fall of the Western Roman Empire and the beginning of the Middle Ages: 410, when Alaric the Goth sacked Rome, or 476, when the Roman general Flavius Odoacer deposed the last Western emperor and declared himself king of Italy. These were indeed decisive landmark events, but the transformation of the Western Roman Empire—and, indeed, its collapse—was far more complex, with advancements and regressions among various European peoples and their armies.

North of the Roman Empire's borders were peoples who spoke a semi-common language different from the Indo-European languages of Greek and Latin. This Germanic language base was shared among different tribes of the Goths, Vandals, Lombards, and Burgundians, all of whom the Romans lumped together as "barbarians." From around 100 to 400 CE, the Romans and various Germanic peoples faced each other along loosely controlled borders, such as the Rhine and Danube rivers. These groups were not united, and they fought each other constantly.

The imperial authorities practiced a "divide and conquer" strategy, often bribing Germanic chiefs to attack each other. It was a successful policy as long as the empire had the money to bribe them, but these funds dwindled in the fourth and fifth centuries. This was also a time when the Roman Empire's army was particularly weak and unable to prevent Germanic raiders from settling permanently within the empire's borders.

Pressure was also put on the Germanic Visigoths when the Asian conqueror Attila the Hun advanced across their borders. In 376, Eastern Emperor Valens (r. 364–378) allowed many Visigoths to cross the Danube into Roman territory to escape the Hun incursion. They entered peacefully, but had no intention of leaving or merely being absorbed into the empire. In 378, Valens met the Visigoths in battle at Adrianople, in modern-day Turkey. The imperial forces were decimated, and Valens died in the battle. In 410, the Visigothic king Alaric looted the city of Rome. He had intended to take southern Italy, but died shortly after sacking Rome. His army migrated to the Iberian

Peninsula (Spain and Portugal), where it defeated other tribes in the region and created a kingdom that lasted until the Muslim invasion in the early eighth century.

Another Germanic tribe, the Vandals, sacked Hippo in North Africa in 430, just days after Augustine's death, and then Rome in 455. They dominated these regions until Emperor Justinian reconquered North Africa and most of Italy in 535. The last significant Germanic invaders during late antiquity were the Lombards, who took most of Italy beginning in 568. By this time the Byzantine Empire held just a few enclaves, centered on Rome, Ravenna, and Naples.

What may be surprising is that most of these Germanic invaders were Christians. In 399,

Bishop Eusebius of Nicomedia, just west of Constantinople, ordained a Goth, **Ulfilas**, and commissioned him to bring Christianity to his people. Ulfilas is known as the "apostle of the Goths," and he had phenomenal success. Soon, the gospel spread to the Visigoths, Ostrogoths, Vandals, and Burgundians. Within a decade, many of the Germanic peoples and seemingly all of their leaders had become Christians. So, when Alaric stormed Rome in 410, he was a Christian attacking Christians. He forbade his army to loot churches or shrines, even as it destroyed much of the city. Of interesting note, Ulfilas and his mentor, Bishop Eusebius, had not accepted the decisions of the Council of Nicaea on the fully divine nature of Christ. Both were Arian Christians, and thus the

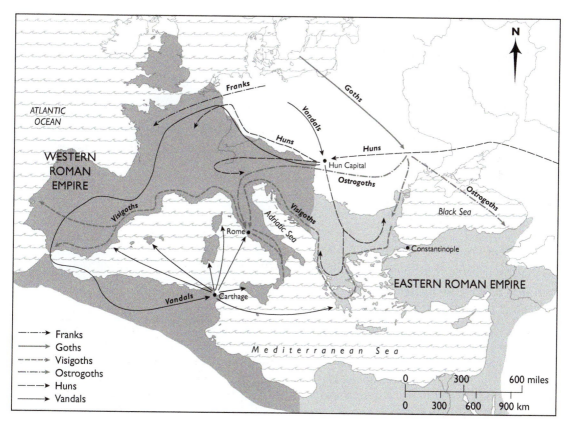

FIGURE 11-1 The Western Empire: Map of the various Germanic and Slavic tribes that made incursions into the Roman Empire.

Goths were Arians as well. For the most part this mattered little, and both Catholic and Arian Christians tolerated each other peacefully. The great exception was the Vandals, who were Arian Christians and thought that the Catholic Christians in North Africa were heretics and deserved to have their churches (and cities) burned; thus our modern-day term "vandalism."

Arian Christianity would not last. The Lombards in Italy transferred their allegiance to Catholic Christianity around the end of the sixth century, and the Visigoths in Spain officially abandoned Arianism after the Visigothic king Reccared accepted the bishops' insistence on a Catholic Christianity at the Council of Toledo in 589. The defection of these Germanic leaders, their armies, and their peoples from Arian Christianity to Catholic Christianity is hardly surprising. They had learned about and accepted Christianity from an Arian perspective, but they were ruling among a sea of Catholic Christians, who shared virtually the same faith as their overlords. Abandoning Arianism was part of the larger *Romanization* of these peoples, which had been going on for centuries. The Germanic tribes, through trade, diplomacy, and controlled migration, were becoming culturally imperial citizens, progressively taking on Roman values, laws, and cultural norms. They did not so much want to destroy the Roman Empire as to enjoy its benefits. Ultimately, Arianism simply faded away within about fifty years, largely disappearing by 589.

IRELAND, ENGLAND, AND SCANDINAVIA

Although the Irish were never subjects of the Roman Empire, by the fourth century, there was some semblance of Christianity in Ireland as a result of the influence of Christian merchants and slaves from England. Rome did control parts of England, and Christian communities flourished only a few miles from Ireland across the Irish Sea. **Patrick** (c. 390–460) is identified with the conversion of the Irish, or at least with the first large

change in the Irish religious course. Patrick was born in Wales to a devout Christian family. His grandfather had been a priest, and his father a deacon. When Patrick was sixteen years old and not personally very religious, he was captured and sold as a slave by Irish pirates who had crossed into Wales for booty and slaves to sell back in Ireland. After spending six years as a shepherd, Patrick eventually escaped and made his way back home. He credited his survival during those harsh years and his escape to Christ. Instead of bearing hatred or resentment toward the people of his captivity, he burned with zeal to bring the gospel to them. He was ordained in Gaul and returned to Ireland. While often treated harshly by the populace, Patrick states in his *Confessions* that he personally baptized thousands in Ireland. He introduced the typical bishop-centered version of Christianity, but this assumed a culture that was foreign to the Irish, who lived in kin groups.

FIGURE 11-2   Stained glass of Saint Patrick, the apostle of Ireland.

Ireland had no experience of Roman institutions, no cities, and no written language. What worked in the Roman Empire, with its already-demarcated cities and dioceses, would not work among the Irish clans. More successful was a monastic version of Christianity. Monasteries, as institutions of learning, culture, prayer, and asceticism, were impressive to the Irish and became the backbone of Christian Ireland, becoming affiliated with various kin groups. It was the monks, not diocesan priests, who were principally responsible for the pastoral care and education of the peoples in their realm. The bishops of Ireland were, in fact, often monks of a local monastery and subject to its abbot.

Irish Christianity developed its own organization, customs, and even liturgy, all in the Irish Gaelic tongue and different from those of the Latinized Christianity the Western Roman Empire knew. This monastic-centered form of Christianity put Irish Christianity somewhat at odds with the standard bishop-centered structure and threatened to undermine the traditional episcopal governance of the church. Irish monks also took on the task of missionary activity, even traveling as far as Iceland. Saints Brendan (d. 580) and Columba (d. 597) went to the coast of Scotland. Columba established the Scottish abbey of Iona as a missionary outpost, and from there Christianity spread southward and eastward. Aidan (d. 651), at the request of the king of Northumbria, established a missionary monastery off the east coast of England. Soon Celtic Christianity also entered France and had an influence in that region as well.

Because southern England was part of the Roman Empire's commonwealth, Christians had been in England for some time, but they were a decided minority. In 597, Pope Gregory I sent a Roman monk named Augustine (d. 604) to Britain at the request of Ethelbert, King of Kent, in southern England. Ethelbert's wife was a Christian, and he was well disposed toward the faith. Augustine settled in Canterbury and soon was ordained a bishop. His ministry, while brief, was wildly successful, drawing numerous converts, including Ethelbert. Churches and a diocesan structure soon developed. Given that Celtic Christianity had been developing along different institutional lines, one of the more decisive events in the growth of English Christianity was the Synod of Whitby, held in 664. Whitby was a northeastern town that had become famous when an Anglo-Saxon noblewoman, Hild (614–680), established a monastery

FIGURE 11-3 Ruins from Kilmacduagh Monastery, originally built in the seventh century.

and convent there in 657. This synod was principally aimed at deciding on when Easter should be celebrated, which was a point of dispute between the Celts and the mainstream church. In deciding to adhere to the Roman tradition, the bishops signaled their loyalty to the archbishop of Canterbury, who himself was aligned with the Roman Catholic Church and the pope, in contrast to what was becoming something of an independent Celtic (Irish) version of the faith. Throughout the medieval period, Ireland would progressively take on a more robust episcopal model typical of the church at large and align its religious practices to those of the universal church.

The advancement of Christianity into Scandinavia took somewhat of a different route. Scandinavian Norsemen had earned a reputation as fierce warriors and raiders, and they terrorized the inhabitants of what is today France, northern Germany, the British Isles, and Ireland. By the eighth century, they began leaving Scandinavia, sometimes as part of raiding parties (the Vikings), but other times for the purpose of peaceful settlement in places such as Russia, England, Normandy (northern France), Iceland, Greenland, and even Newfoundland in North America. Those who settled in Russia and Normandy converted quickly. The first Scandinavian Christian king was Harald Bluetooth of Denmark, who converted sometime around 950; however, Denmark would not become decidedly Christian until the early eleventh century, during the reign of Canute, who ruled both Denmark and England. In 955, the warrior Olaf Tryggvason, who had become enamored with Christianity in an earlier raid on England, became king of Norway and began advancing Christianity in his realm. His successor, Olaf Haraldsson II, became king in 1015 and continued to Christianize Norway. In Sweden, Christianity emerged in the ninth century, with bishops in place by the tenth. Overall, the spread of Christianity in Scandinavia was a movement of gradual conversions, and by the twelfth century the faith was decidedly in place, with a large number of adherents.

CHARLEMAGNE AND THE HOLY ROMAN EMPIRE

FROM THE MEROVINGIANS TO THE CAROLINGIANS

The list of famous emperors of the Roman Empire linked with Christianity is long and significant. As noted in earlier chapters, Constantine is the most important, since he allowed Christianity to flourish and provided imperial funds for its advancement. The list would also include Theodosius, who in the late fourth century made Christianity the sole religion of the empire, and Justinian, who in the sixth century advanced Christian culture and provided massive funds for the building of churches. **Charlemagne** ranks up among these figures, proving as important as any for the growth of the Western church. By the early medieval period the center of gravity for the Christian West had shifted. Although the West still maintained modest fraternal relations with the political and ecclesiastical powers of the East, from this point on it looked over the Alps to modern France and Germany. Gaul (France) had consisted of two Roman provinces since the time of Julius Caesar and subsequently solidified a Roman culture. In 481, Childeric I, son of Merovech and leader of the Franks, established himself as ruler of what is modern-day France. His son Clovis I (r. 481–511) united all of Gaul under Merovingian (named after Merovech) rule. Clovis had adopted Christianity, and his successors had a good relationship with the pope.

For almost three centuries the Merovingian dynasty flourished, but by the eighth century, it had been virtually reduced to ceremonial authority. "Nothing was left to the king," wrote Charlemagne's biographer Einhard, "except to be happy with the royal title and to sit on his throne with his flowing hair and long beard and to behave as if he had authority."[1] While Einhard's description is assuredly an exaggeration, it was the case that the "mayor of the palace" ran the administration of the kingdom, controlled the appointments for offices, and even controlled funds that came from royal lands on behalf of the king.

Charles Martel (d. 741), the mayor of the palace and the figure from whom the Carolingians received their name, was a powerful member of the Merovingian court. It was under Martel's leadership that the Muslim expansion from Spain into southern France was quelled with a spectacular victory. Charles's son Pippin III succeeded his father in office, and in 750 he sent a trusted abbot from the monastery of St. Denis in Paris to Pope Zacharias to inquire as to who should be the rightful leader of the Franks. The time was ripe on both sides. Pippin was functionally the ruler of the Franks, and Pope Zacharias was being threatened by the Lombards, who were encroaching on both Ravenna and Rome. Zacharias's predecessor, Boniface, had strived to reform the Frankish clergy, a mission with which Pippin was in full support. Pippin was considered a friend of Rome and a trusted ally in supporting a healthy church.

Pippin's emissaries asked the pope whether it was right that the king of the Franks continued to bear the title when the kingdom was actually being governed by the mayor of the palace. Zacharias gave him the response he was looking for, saying it was "better that he who had the power should bear the royal name than he who remained without power."[2] Pippin, now with the pope's blessing and moral authority, assembled the nobles of the realm, and they declared him king. He was then anointed by the bishops of Francia, thus inaugurating the Carolingian rule. This was in 751, the same year that the Lombards conquered Ravenna, the only remaining stronghold of the Byzantine Empire in northern Italy.

Zacharias died in 752, and his successor, Pope Stephen II, traveled to Francia in 753 to meet with the new king. They met in Ponthion, 100 miles east of Paris. In this meeting Pippin promised to defend Rome and its territories, and gave the pope temporal rule over other areas in central Italy. Pope Stephen personally anointed Pippin and conferred on him the title "patrician of the Romans." In 755, Pippin gathered his army and marched into Italy, where he quickly subdued the Lombard forces. He regained Ravenna

and handed over much of the territories of Italy to the control of the pope, creating what became known as the "Patrimony of Peter," a territory over which the pope exercised political jurisdiction. Sometime around 755 the papacy produced a document purportedly written by Emperor Constantine in the fourth century known as the *Donation of Constantine*. In this document, Constantine gave Pope Sylvester (d. 335) temporal rule over all of Italy and primacy over all the patriarchates in the church. The text became the legal basis in the medieval era for the pope's universal jurisdiction over the whole church. The Eastern church never believed it was authentic, but it served the papacy well in the Latin church for the next seven centuries, until it was exposed as a forgery in the fifteenth century.

What ought one to make of all this? On the one hand, it looks like nothing other than power relations, whereby the bishop of Rome became a monarch. Deals were made, political alliances were sealed, documents were forged, and the head of the Latin church seems to have lost his moral compass. As described later, there is a great deal of evidence for such an assessment. But it is a superficial, or at least insufficient, interpretation as well. These events unfolded during the Middle Ages, and to interpret them through a modern lens is to miss the assumptions of the time. Even Augustine's assertion that the "city of God" and the "city of man" were on different tracks did not mean for him or anyone else that it would be bad to consider society holistically. Until the modern period, few if any people ever considered a separation between church and state. Why would it be beneficial for a state to be run by pagans, those without Christian values or sensibilities? Why not use state laws, policies, and funds for the advancement of Christianity in a Christian state?

The papacy did get mired in conflicting interests and political machinations, and this history cannot be seen as anything but a scandal to the church. On the other hand, popes from the late patristic period throughout the Middle Ages used their families' wealth and the income from their landholdings to support churches, advance learning, and perform massive pastoral undertakings. Being responsible for both the temporal and spiritual well-being of the citizens in their realm would have seemed in the medieval period somewhat legitimate. It is also historically the case that citizens under the temporal rule of the papacy fared better than those under other rulers, Christian or otherwise.

CHARLEMAGNE

When Pippin died in 768, his kingdom was divided between his two sons, Carlomen and Charles. Carlomen, however, died early, at the age of twenty, and Charles proclaimed himself the king of all the Franks and ruled as such until 814. He was called Charles the Great (Carolus Magnus), or Charlemagne. In 772, Charlemagne waged war against the Saxons in northern Germany. By 784, his armies had conquered the Saxons, and he demanded that the Saxon leader be baptized. This

FIGURE 11-4   Charlemagne became the first emperor of the Holy Roman Empire when he was crowned in 800 by Pope Leo III.

forced baptism alarmed many Christian leaders, and one of Charlemagne's later advisors, Alcuin of York, challenged Charlemagne on this score. Subsequently, when Charlemagne conquered the Avars of the Balkans, Alcuin wrote him not to demand baptism, but rather to provide missionaries to the Avars, that they might convert freely if they wished. Charlemagne not only agreed to this, but even allowed the Saxons to revert to their original faith if they so desired. In 773, Charlemagne captured the Lombard capital of Pavia in Italy and added "King of the Lombards" to his long list of titles.

Charlemagne's forces were juggernauts, and his conquests were quick and many. Before he reached fifty years old he ruled over modern-day Belgium, Holland, France, Germany, Austria, Switzerland, northern Italy, Spain, Hungary, and part of Bohemia. The term "Europe" began to be used in writings of this period. Pope Hadrian hailed him as the new Constantine. Charlemagne built his capital in Aachen, on the border of present-day Germany and Holland.

In 799, Pope Leo III, who was experiencing a revolt in Rome, fled to Charlemagne, asking him to intervene and secure his position. Charlemagne entered Rome in November 800 and held a council, at which he declared Leo's rightful place as pope. At Mass in St. Peter's Basilica on Christmas Day of that year, the returned Pope Leo crowned him *Imperator Romanorum* (Emperor of the Romans). This was an extraordinary political move. When Odoacer had invaded Ravenna in 476, he had compelled Western Emperor Romulus Augustulus to abdicate. From that moment on, there had only been one emperor, the one in Constantinople. In 800, Constantinople was controlled by Empress Irene (r. 797–802), who ruled as regent of the empire until her son Leo came of age to succeed to the throne. Early on, Irene had sought ties to the papacy and the Carolingian dynasty, even arranging for a marriage between Charlemagne's daughter and her son Constantine, although she later broke off this engagement in 787. What Pope Leo was doing in anointing Charlemagne as Emperor of the Romans (what would later be called the *Holy Roman Empire*) was not merely acclaiming Charlemagne emperor over his specific rule, inaugurating something of a second empire, but deposing Irene and proclaiming Charlemagne the new emperor over the Roman Empire itself and the legitimate successor to the throne in Constantinople. Einhard, Charlemagne's biographer, says that Charlemagne was unaware of the pope's intent and even opposed to it, but ultimately accepted the crown as a new duty and burden. Given Charlemagne's ambitions, this assertion is difficult to take at face value.

The coronation of Charlemagne and the West's proclamation of him as the Roman emperor obviously did not sit well with Constantinople or the Eastern church, but they had to come to terms with it in some manner. Within a decade of Charlemagne's anointing and coronation, a Byzantine embassy traveled to Aachen and acclaimed Charlemagne *basileus* (king or emperor), but did not add "Roman" to the title, which they reserved to the emperor in Constantinople.

When Charlemagne died in 814, his empire was taken over by his son, Louis the Pious. But when Louis died in 840, civil war broke out. In the Treaty of Verdun (843), the Carolingian Empire was split into three parts, the kingdom of Charles, the kingdom of Lothar (which retained the title "Holy Roman Empire"), and the kingdom of Louis. The Carolingian dynasty would not last. Under the leadership of Henry I (r. 919–936) and Otto I (r. 936–973), the Holy Roman Empire came under the family rule known as the Ottonian dynasty, and the empire was reduced to what is now modern-day Germany.

The importance of the Carolingian dynasty cannot be overstated. The Europe of what is

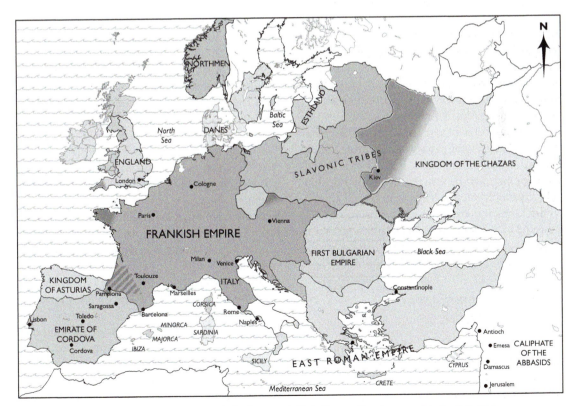

FIGURE 11-5 Europe in 814: The extent of Charlemagne's Holy Roman Empire upon his death in 814.

sometimes called the "Dark Ages" of the early medieval period during this time became a unified Europe with a unified faith. Charlemagne, along with the pope, strove to create a universal church in Europe, one of learning and revival. Charlemagne oversaw the unification of church laws and sacraments, and he carried out church reform. He also made Aachen a center of scholarship, recruiting talent throughout the empire. Under his leadership, workshops, or *scriptoria*, were established to produce texts for higher learning, and Charlemagne supported the development of schools at monasteries and cathedrals. So productive (and efficient) were these efforts to produce texts that a new script was developed using small letters along with capital ones, and for the first time punctuation was used, including commas, periods, and question marks, a system called the "Caroline miniscule script." While monastic and cathedral schools certainly preceded Charlemagne, they advanced significantly during his reign.

The Ottonian dynasty followed in Charlemagne's footsteps, advancing religious reform where needed, supporting missionary initiatives, and creating a partnership with the papacy. Grateful to Otto I for his service, Pope John XII in 962 crowned and anointed him emperor, a formal title not given to a ruler for a hundred years. This happy marriage between the papacy and the Holy Roman Emperor would not retain its nuptial bliss. Just as the pope believed he was responsible for and juridically empowered to lead the universal church, so did kings and emperors see themselves as empowered in the political realm. In subsequent centuries, as shown in the next section, popes would clash with emperors and kings alike.

 ## CONSIDERING PAPAL DEVELOPMENTS

POPES LEO I (r. 440–461)
AND GELASIUS I (r. 492–496)

As noted in Chapter Seven, the bishop of Rome, or the papacy, has long asserted itself as the center of the universal church, the place of juridical power as well as of honor. To the first ecumenical council, the Council of Nicaea (325), the bishop of Rome sent an emissary who intended to speak for the whole Latin church, and presumably the bishop of Rome imagined that his position would be embraced *because* he was the bishop of Rome. Pope **Leo I** also probably believed that his *Tome* sent to the Council of Chalcedon (451) would be followed for the same reason. It was indeed the case that all the ecumenical councils ended up embracing the positions that the bishop of Rome held. But it is also clear that the Eastern bishops did not consider Rome's declaration as absolutely decisive.

In the West, the centrality of the bishop of Rome became even more important during the early Middle Ages. Rome, and eventually the Western Empire, were virtually abandoned by the East. Earlier, the Western emperor, realizing his vulnerability in Rome, moved the imperial court to Milan and then to Ravenna, where the last emperor was deposed in 476. The bishop of Rome was then de facto the only legitimate authority in the city of Rome at large. When Rome was besieged for the second time, it was Pope **Gelasius I** who negotiated with the Ostrogoth king Theodoric and convinced him not to ravage the people of the city and even to donate food for its poor.

These were great popes and courageous leaders. They also had a large sense of their office. Leo was the first to use the term *Pontifex Maximus* (literally, "greatest bridge-builder"), a sacred term once used by the Roman emperors in times past. Gelasius was the first to use the term "vicar of Christ," that is, representative of Christ on earth, as a title for the papacy. This title was not widely used in his day, but it marks a crucial development in understandings of the papacy. It was also Gelasius who created the "two swords" theory of authority. In this view the temporal sword belonged to the state, and its authority was used to create laws and support social harmony. The spiritual sword belonged to the church, particularly its vicar of Christ, and was used to assert religious authority. Not

FIGURE 11-6 Statue of Pope Gregory I ("the Great"), one of the model popes of the late patristic period.

surprisingly, Gelasius saw the spiritual sword as greater, since it concerned the soul rather than the body.

POPE GREGORY I (r. 590–604)

Gregory I was one of the most outstanding popes of the late patristic age. Born to a prominent Christian family and classically trained, in his early career Gregory was the prefect—civil governor—of Rome. At thirty-four he abandoned his career and became a monk. He founded several monasteries, including one on his family property and another in the city of Rome. The rest of his family's fortune that was under his control he gave to the poor. In 579, Pope Pelagius II recruited Gregory to be his official representative in Constantinople, where he lived seven years with other Latin-speaking monks. When Pelagius died, Gregory found himself elected pope.

Gregory was a prolific writer. His archives include over 850 letters, numerous sermons, biblical commentaries, and pastoral texts. His *Book of Pastoral Care*, written to instruct bishops on how to lead their flocks, shows theological depth, pastoral sensitivity, and a psychological sophistication that was far before his time. This book was given to bishops during their consecration ceremony throughout much of the Middle Ages.

Gregory never gave up the ascetic life of extreme physical and spiritual discipline, and was believed to be extraordinarily holy. By this time Constantinople had virtually given up on the West, as it was embroiled in its own struggle with the Persians to the east. Rome was hemmed in by the Lombards, who in 568 came to control territory north, east, and south of Rome, and had designs on Rome itself. When thousands of refugees from these areas fled to Rome, Gregory took matters into his own hands. He drew on his family's money and papal income to feed and house the poor of the city and to organize troops to defend it. It was Gregory and not the Roman prefect who negotiated with the Lombards. Further, throughout this time of strife, he continued to commission missionaries to both the Lombard and the English peoples. Other popes followed suit, including Pope Gregory II (r. 715–731), who sent missions to the Saxons, particularly through the monk Boniface (672–754), who is known as the "apostle of Germany."

It is clear from his writings that Gregory I thought his place was as part of the Roman Empire, centered in Constantinople. He was solicitous to the emperor and supportive of his other fellow patriarchs. Like Leo and Gelasius, he also thought his authority was that of the Chair of Peter, the universal pastor. To depict the papacy Gregory coined the term *servus servorum Dei*: servant of the servants of God. While this appears humble, and probably was a personal expression of solicitude to the care of others, it was also a declaration of superiority. Bishops should serve those they lead, and the bishop of

Rome was the servant (leader) of all the other servants (bishops).

PAPAL QUAGMIRE, REFORM, AND THE SEPARATION OF EAST AND WEST

The time between the end of the ninth and the middle of the eleventh century was a particularly low point for the papacy, with a total of thirty-nine popes. The papacy was stuck in quicksand, as many of Rome's wealthy families jockeyed to put one of their members into the office. Easily a third of them died in suspicious circumstances. At eighteen, John XII (r. 955–964) was the youngest pope ever and, according to legend, died of a stroke while in bed with a married woman. Popes themselves did not even stick together. Stephen VI, for example, infamously led the *synodus horrenda*, or "cadaver trial," at which he tried the rotting corpse of his predecessor, Formosus, for perjury and seizing the papacy illegally. The jury found Formosus guilty. They dug up his body, stripped it of his papal regalia, cut off his right (blessing) hand, and threw his corpse into the Tiber River. Stephen himself was eventually deposed and ended up strangled in jail.

Because of the numerous scandals and irregularities, many in the church called for a reform of the papacy. This call was answered by Leo IX (r. 1049–1054), who was appointed by Holy Roman Emperor Henry III to the papacy. Leo insisted that the people and clergy of Rome approve his election, which they quickly did. He went on to institute a number of church reforms, particularly of the clergy in the West. He insisted on clerical celibacy and tried to end the practice of **simony**, whereby church offices were bought. Leo also transformed the cardinal clergy around Rome into an international body of reformers throughout Europe.

Leo is most known for his contribution to the most decisive break between the Western and Eastern churches, which became the Roman Catholic Church and the Eastern Orthodox Church. Leo had received numerous reports that the Normans in southern Italy were persecuting

and murdering Christians and destroying churches. In 1053, he led a military campaign against them that failed, leading to his capture. During his time of captivity, he sought the support of the emperor in Constantinople and decided to settle a long-overdue dispute. After Emperor Justinian had reconquered Italy in the sixth century, the southern part of the country had been placed under the control of the patriarch of Constantinople. This had annoyed the papacy for centuries, as Eastern Christianity had several customs, particularly liturgical practices, that differed from those in the West. In 1053, while Leo was in captivity, the metropolitan of Bulgaria sent a letter to the bishop of Trani in Apulia (in southeastern Italy) challenging Western practices as illicit and accusing the West of having broken church unity.

In 1054, the pope sent his legate, Cardinal Humbert, to Constantinople with letters he had written in captivity. His letter to the emperor was gracious and conciliatory. His letter to the patriarch, however, was nothing of the kind. In it, he set forth an argument for the superiority of the Roman patriarchate, calling on evidence ranging from the Chair of Peter to the *Donation of Constantine*. Constantinople was, in his view, a disobedient subject of the papacy, "sitting at home in delicate security, in pleasure and lasciviousness, in the dissipation of long leisure, refusing to take part in the fight waged on her behalf by the pious Mother . . . and with girlish levity offering to feed the Mother with the daughter's milk."[3] According to Leo, the very idea that Rome, the mother church, would be challenged for her liturgical practices showed Constantinople to be nothing but a "confabulation of heretics, a conventicle of schismatics, [and] a synagogue of Satan."[4]

Leo may have wanted to distance the emperor from the patriarch of Constantinople, but this did not happen. When the patriarch of Constantinople and his council received this letter—in the Hagia Sophia, no less—they were appalled and assured Humbert that under no circumstance were they subject to Rome. Humbert, then, in the name of Leo, excommunicated the archbishop of Constantinople, who then excommunicated Leo. These excommunications were not lifted until December 7, 1965.

The separation of the Eastern church and the Western church is widely dated to 1054. This is not entirely correct. For centuries the East and West had been drifting apart, with relations sometimes cordial and sometimes tense. Claims to the "primacy of Peter" had been asserted by the West regularly, and just as regularly had been ignored. Another decisive division occurred when the West changed the Nicene-Constantinople Creed. As early as the sixth century some Western churches added a clause—"and the Son"—to the statement: "We believe in the Holy Spirit, who proceeds from the Father." Thus, now it became ". . . who proceeds from the Father and the Son." This came to be known as the *filioque* controversy, with *filioque* being the Latin term "from the Son." For some Western minds, this extra clause reflected how salvation worked: the Father sent the Son, who gave the Spirit. It also pointed to the Holy Spirit as an expression of the Father and Son's relationship within the Trinity. This belief is reflected in Augustine's theology. Rome formally adopted a revision to the creed in the eleventh century. To the Eastern mind, however, there were two problems. First, the change seemed to take from the Father what was distinctive about the Father, namely, that the Father was the source of both Son and Spirit. Second, this innovation happened without the consent of the East and was an example of breaking a canon (legal decision) from the Council of Constantinople that forbade changing the creed. It was, in short, another example of the West's attempted bullying.

There were also moments later when both sides tried to reunite, such as the West's Fourth Lateran Council in 1215. Given the mutual excommunications noted here and the Western sacking of Constantinople, noted later in this chapter, reunion never happened. The year 1054 is only one marker of a larger story of separation, but it is a crucial marker.

GREGORY VII (r. 1073–1085)

The reforming interests of the Roman church continued with **Gregory VII**. Gregory was from one of the patrician families of Rome and classically educated. At the time of his election, he was not even a cleric, but a monk. Quickly after his election he was ordained a priest and then consecrated a bishop. Like Leo, he led the way of church reform among the clergy. And, like Leo and many other popes before him, Gregory considered the papacy to be the height of authority. He did not claim political authority explicitly, of course, but when the political sphere interfered with the ecclesiastical one, he maintained that it was the church's authority that reigned supreme. In 1075, Gregory issued his *Dictatus Papae*, a twenty-seven-point document regarding the papacy's right to universal sovereignty over the church. In it he asserted his right to name all bishops, to remove or transfer bishops from one diocese to another, and even to depose princes.

To appreciate the implications of these latter claims, one must enter into the medieval feudal mindset. In brief, feudalistic society was structured around large landowners. It involved reciprocal obligations among lords, the warrior nobility who were vassals to their lords, and the fiefs or peasants who worked the land. The feudal lord was responsible to those in his realm, and they in turn were supposed to be loyal to their lord. A feudal king, prince, duke, or any other local lord considered the welfare of the people within his realm to be his personal responsibility. This responsibility was not restricted to such things as keeping up roads, creating legislation, and ensuring civic protection, but also included overseeing the fundamentals of religion. Lords endowed monasteries and often built churches, and it seemed natural to them that they would be responsible for choosing clergy for these churches and abbots for these monasteries. Further, it was not unusual for them to choose members of their own families for such positions. This practice of **nepotism** probably solidified their realm and assured loyalty—but it was bound to be problematic for the church, in which an abbot might not be suitable at all for a monastery given to his control simply because he was the brother of a prince. Two additional problems arose. The first, mentioned briefly earlier, was that these positions were often bought and sold, enriching the monarch to the impoverishment of the people's spiritual lives. This practice was called simony, after the New Testament figure who tried to buy spiritual power from Peter and John (Acts 8:18). Even when nepotism or simony was not practiced, the very idea of a lay person having the authority to name bishops, priests, and abbots—a practice called **lay investiture**—was theologically problematic. Of course, only bishops could ordain other bishops (or priests), but candidates for these positions were controlled by the feudal lord, who himself was part of a ceremony "investing" or giving the symbols of office to the candidate being ordained. Such a practice subordinated the bishop to the lord, and was seen by the papacy as utterly unacceptable. Pope Gregory wanted to halt lay investiture, a privilege the Holy Roman emperor and many other feudal lords were unwilling to relinquish.

In challenging not only nepotism and simony, but also lay investiture, Gregory was challenging a feudal assumption that he believed needed reform. Angered, Holy Roman Emperor Henry IV convoked a synod of German bishops, who deposed Gregory. In response, Gregory excommunicated Henry and released his subjects from allegiance to him, thus allowing them to revolt. Henry's position was untenable. In 1077, he traveled over the Alps and met Gregory at the castle of Canossa in northern Italy. According to legend, for three days he knelt as a penitent in the snow outside the castle wearing sackcloth. Gregory finally lifted the excommunication. However, their reconciliation was broken in 1080, and Gregory again excommunicated Henry. In response, in 1084 Henry marched into Rome, deposed Gregory by force, and installed his own pope, Clement III.

FIGURE 11-7 Emperor Henry IV comes to Pope Gregory VII as a penitent in sackcloth. Gregory would restore him, only to later be exiled by him.

Gregory would be briefly freed from his imprisonment, but he died a short time later. The investiture contest would not be settled until 1122, at the Concordat of Worms, at which the emperor agreed to allow the clergy to elect bishops if, in turn, he was allowed to be present at—and thus influence—the elections. Further, he would receive feudal homage from the bishop as a vassal for any lands the bishop had received as part of his income.

The immediate end to Gregory's fight with the emperor was that he lost, was deposed, and exiled. The long-term end was the opposite. What Gregory had started was a process of reversing the church's loss of control over its clergy and institutions. While kings and emperors were anointed by the church, they were no longer imagined to have the kind of sacred power they once enjoyed. The papacy now controlled the Western church.

INNOCENT III (r. 1198–1216)

Gregory VII was certainly not the only pope to become embroiled in church–state matters. The strongest medieval pope, and the one most engaged in political affairs, was **Innocent III**. Until Innocent, Rome did not have a large bureaucracy, and claims of universal church control were more theoretical than practiced. This changed under Innocent, who expanded Rome's ability to oversee European Christendom by establishing a large papal court staffed by a college of cardinals. Because Innocent held feudal rights in Sicily, Aragon (part of Spain), Hungary, and Poland, he weighed in on the political machinations in all those realms. He also meddled in France, Bulgaria, Cyprus, and Armenia. In fact, he argued that he could intervene in any part of Christendom when faith or morals were at stake.

The greatest example of Innocent's power can be seen in his response to King John of England's objection to the election of the archbishop of Canterbury and advancement of his own candidate. Innocent excommunicated John and put all of England under **interdict** for five years. This meant that no sacraments could be performed throughout England—a true test of power and authority. Ultimately John capitulated and even agreed to give royal land over to Innocent as a feudal holding.

Innocent never claimed that he had political jurisdiction over Christendom, and he recognized Gelasius's two-swords theory of power, but he did have an extraordinary sense of his own office:

> To me is said in the person of the prophet [Jeremiah], "I have set thee over nations and over kingdoms, to root up and to pull down, and to waste and destroy, and to build and to plant" [Jer. 1:10] . . . thus the others were called to a part of the care but Peter alone assumed the plentitude of power. You see then who is the

servant set over the household, truly the vicar of Jesus Christ, successor of Peter, anointed of the Lord, a god of Pharaoh, set between God and man, lower than God but higher than man, who judges all, and is judged by no one.[5]

BONIFACE VIII (r. 1294–1303)

Popes could claim what they believed to be true, but this did not mean that all parties in the Christian West necessarily agreed or conceded. Popes' ability to successfully assert control depended on political factors that were often beyond their control. During the High Middle Ages (roughly the twelfth to fourteenth centuries), emerging centralized monarchies, such as England and France, were growing in power, and an international Christian empire was on the decline. The church at large, and not just the pope, found itself subjected to the political demands of these "nation-states."

When King Philip IV of France, for example, taxed clergy to finance his war with England, Pope **Boniface VIII** challenged the move to no success. Philip then declared his right to jurisdiction over French bishops and sought to establish a church independent from Roman control, something of a national church. He had, in fact, the majority of the French clergy on his side. Boniface responded in 1302 with the **papal bull** *Unam Sanctam*, which declared that salvation depended on being subject to the pope:

> [T]here is only one holy, catholic and apostolic Church we are compelled by faith to believe and hold, and we firmly believe in her and simply confess her, outside whom there is neither salvation nor remission of sins. . . . She represents one mystical body, the head of which is Christ. . . . This one and unique Church, therefore has not two heads, like a monster, but one body and one head, viz., Christ and his vicar Peter's successor . . . there shall be one fold and one shepherd. Furthermore we declare, state and define that it is absolutely necessary for the salvation of all men that they submit to the Roman Pontiff.[6]

The bold claims of both Innocent and Boniface were not as reckless or dictatorial as they may seem. They represented the broad teaching of the church, at least in the West. In 1215, the Fourth Lateran Council declared, "There is only one universal Church of the faithful, outside which none shall be saved." This teaching would be revised, and seemingly contradicted, by the late modern Catholic Church, but it did represent a widely held medieval belief. The context of Innocent and Boniface's declarations, as well as of the Fourth Lateran Council, was a perceived attack on the unity of the church. In the medieval worldview, such an attack constituted a break in the love, communion, and authority that Christ had invested in bishops as successors of the apostles, particularly the pope. The church conceived of itself as the body of Christ, with Christ as its head.[7] For the church, Christ could never be known distinct from his body. To separate from the body of Christ, especially from the vicar of Christ, was tantamount to separating from Christ himself. Regardless of this theological principle, King Philip refused to give way. Within months he sent agents to Rome and had Boniface arrested. The pope died shortly after, most likely from the brutal treatment he received from those who captured him.

CHRISTIANITY AND WAR

JUST WAR

As we have seen, one of the great transformations in Christianity is that it went from a religion based on individual conversions at great personal cost to the religion of the state. The vast majority of Christians celebrated this shift. As noted earlier, the church historian Eusebius of Caesarea imagined a social whole whereby the Roman Empire had one religion, one state, and one emperor who protected and oversaw a Christian society. In contrast, as noted in Chapter Eight, Augustine's book *City of God* challenged whether the state or any other human institution could be anything other than part of the "city of man." Time and time again, history has assuredly

validated Augustine's intuitions. States and their leaders have shown far greater interest in advancing wealth, power, and glory than in anything sincerely religious. Still, most Christians prior to the modern age embraced Eusebius's ideal of complete social integration.

At the time Augustine was writing *City of God*, he was concerned with two things. The first was the Donatist controversy, discussed in Chapter Eight. If it was illegal to be a Christian prior to Constantine, should it now be illegal to be a Donatist Christian? Could or should the state compel Christians to end their schism by force? The second controversy concerned the sacking of Rome by the Visigoths and the threats on North Africa by the Vandals. When should the state act violently, and could this be justified by Christian theology? On the surface, it seems that Christianity would be opposed to any violence by definition. Consider one of Jesus's exhortations to his disciples:

> Blessed are the peacemakers, for they will be called children of God. Blessed are those who are persecuted for righteousness' sake, for theirs is the kingdom of heaven. . . . You have heard it said, "An eye for an eye and a tooth for a tooth." But I say to you, do not resist an evildoer. But if anyone strikes you on the right cheek, turn the other also. . . . You have heard that it was said, "You shall love your neighbor and hate your enemy." But I say to you, love your enemies and pray for those who persecute you, so that you may be children of your Father in heaven. (Matt. 5:9–10, 38–39, 43–44).

Such teaching dominated Christian consciousness for the first 300 years of the faith. Christians saw themselves as peaceful, long-suffering, and willing to endure persecution for the sake of the gospel.

Positions of power, however, led to changes in Christianity. Augustine, for example, did think the state should repress the Donatists by arms. Even as he has been taken to task for this conclusion by modern interpreters, it is not obvious that **pacifism** is the greatest moral choice, much less a necessary Christian one. Most morally minded people think that it is often necessary to use force to prevent leaders, foreign or otherwise, from brutalizing and enslaving whole peoples. Do innocent sufferers not have justice claims? While Augustine had little confidence in a state's ability to institute a truly Christian society, he was also aware of the dangers of a state not acting with force when necessary. Augustine himself was the first great articulator of the Christian conditions for war. Briefly, his conditions for a **just war** are as follows: (1) the war has to have a just cause, principally one of self-defense or in response to a despotic ruler; (2) the war has to be motivated only by justice, rather than by vengeance or the pursuit of power or wealth; (3) the war has to be waged by a legitimate political authority; (4) the war has to be conducted justly; and (5) the war has to be the last resort. Augustine believed that all of these criteria have to be met for a war to ever be morally justified. Later Christian theorists would add other considerations, including never intentionally targeting noncombatants, confidence that a postwar society will be better than the prewar injustice, and having a plan for the recovery of the war-torn country that will institute a just society.

Most wars in the history of Christian nations, that is, nations with Christian rulers and predominantly Christian citizens, have failed to satisfy all of the just war criteria in advancing war, and sometimes they have met none of them. The Christian Alaric, for example, invaded Italy, sacked Rome, and ultimately took over the Iberian Peninsula by force. Christian Vandals attacked North Africa and destroyed many cities there. And Christian Lombards invaded and took over much of Italy. In all three cases Christians attacked other Christians for no reason except conquest.

Christians are not alone, however, either in having a just war tradition or in violating it. Islam, for example, has a just war tradition that is virtually identical to Christianity's. But this did not stop Muslims from invading and taking over the Persian Empire, much of Byzantium, North Africa, and Spain. It is not as though

Christian or Muslim states are more violent than other states. All of the twentieth century's great wars were secular, at the cost of over half a billion lives. Perhaps the only real difference between religious and secular warfare is that Christians and Muslims claim to be different. In the end, Augustine's distinction between the "city of God" and the "city of man," with their different agendas and values, holds true. The state, Christian or otherwise, acts like a state.

THE CRUSADES

The most notorious expression of medieval Christian violence was the **Crusades**, in which Western kings, knights, and volunteer soldiers violently attacked enemies, political or religious, of church or state. One could argue that there were hundreds of crusades, from Spain to the Baltics to Palestine, all of which involved the same vows, privileges, and responsibilities. The most famous ones were those that invaded parts of Byzantium and the Middle East.

In 1071, the Byzantine army suffered a horrendous loss to the Muslim Seljuk Turks, who were in the process of establishing a great empire east of Byzantium. Within a decade the Byzantine Empire was a shadow of what it once was, controlling only the western part of Asia Minor and the Balkan Peninsula. In 1095, Emperor Alexius I Comnenus pleaded with the West for help in defending the Byzantine Empire from the Muslims. This was the initial reason for the Crusades. Ultimately, there were nine Crusades sponsored by the Western church regarding the Holy Land between 1096 and 1272, but the first four were by far the most important.

What initially dominated Western consciousness was the Muslims' occupation of the Holy Land. Of course, the Holy Land had been under Muslim rule for well over four centuries by the time of the Crusades. Pope Urban II had heard stories of atrocities against Christians in Jerusalem, including torture, murder, and the burning of churches. These stories were true, but dated. Christians had suffered great persecution under the Arab ruler Al-Hakim bi-Amr Allah, who even burned down the Church of the Holy Sepulchre, but his successor, with some financial support from the Byzantine emperor, rebuilt the structure. By the time of Urban's rule, the actual persecution of Christians was a decades-old story, and Jerusalem was no longer even controlled by an Arab ruler, but by the Seljuk Turks, who had taken it in 1077. Nonetheless, Christians believed that the retaking of Jerusalem constituted the grounds for a just war, even a holy one.

Pope Urban responded enthusiastically to the emperor's plea and quickly convened the Council of Piacenza, which was attended by Italian, Burgundian, and French bishops in such great numbers that it had to be held in the open air. In late 1095, he also convened the Council of Clermont, summoning the European nobility to take up this holy cause. There are a number of versions of his most celebrated speech in Clermont, but probably the most accurate is that recorded by Fulcher of Chartres, who was present. In this version, Urban is quoted as having said, "I, or rather the Lord, beseech you as Christ's heralds to publish this everywhere and to persuade all people of whatever rank, foot-soldiers, Knights, poor and rich, to carry aid promptly to those Christians and to destroy that vile race from the lands of our friends. I say this to those who are present, it is meant also for those who are absent. Moreover, Christ commands it."[8]

Pope Urban was not alone in his religious enthusiasm for the Crusades. Consider **Bernard of Clairvaux**, one of Europe's greatest theologians and religious reformers of the time. Bernard went throughout France and Germany proclaiming the righteousness of the cause in language that makes modern Christians blush. In one of his letters to the Knights Templar, a religious order of knights created for the Crusades, for example, he states: "The Christian who slays the unbeliever in the Holy War is sure of his reward, the more sure if he himself is slain. The Christian glories in the death of the pagan, because Christ is glorified."[9]

FIGURE 11-8 Nineteenth-century illustration of Peter the Hermit, preaching in support of the First Crusade. Peter was one of many spiritual authorities who supported the Crusades.

BERNARD OF CLAIRVAUX'S SERMON (1145) ON THE SECOND CRUSADE

You cannot but know that we live in a period of chastisement and ruin; the enemy of mankind has caused the breath of corruption to fly over all regions; we behold nothing but unpunished wickedness. The laws of men or the laws of religion have no longer sufficient power to check depravity of manners and the triumph of the wicked. The demon of heresy has taken possession of the chair of truth, and God has sent forth His malediction upon His sanctuary.

Oh ye listen to me, hasten then to appease the anger of Heaven, but no longer implore His goodness by vain complaints; clothe not yourselves in sackcloth, but cover yourselves with your impenetrable bucklers; the din of arms, the dangers, the labors, the fatigues of war are the penances that God now imposes upon you. Hasten then to expiate your sins by victories over the infidels, and let the deliverance of holy places be the reward of your repentance.

If I were announced to you that the enemy had invaded your cities, your castles, your lands; had ravished your wives and your daughters, and profaned your temples—which among you would not fly to arms? Well, then, all these calamities, and calamities still greater, have fallen upon your brethren, upon the family of Jesus Christ, which is yours. Why do you hesitate to repair so many evils—to revenge so many outrages? Will you allow the infidels to contemplate in peace the ravages they have committed on Christian people? Remember that their triumph will be a subject for grief to all ages and an eternal opprobrium upon the generation that has endured it. Yes, the living God has charged me to announce to you that He will punish them who shall not have defended Him against His enemies.

Fly then to arms; let a holy rage animate you in the fight, and let the Christian world resound with these words of the prophet, "Cursed be he who does not stain his sword with blood!" If the Lord calls you to the defense of His heritage think not that His hand has lost its power. Could He not send twelve legions of angels or breathe one word and all His enemies would crumble away into dust? But God has considered the sons of men, to open for them the road to His mercy. His goodness has caused to dawn for you a day of safety by calling on you to avenge His glory and His name.

Christian warriors, He who gave His life for you, today demands yours in return. These are combats worthy of you, combats in which it is glorious to conquer and advantageous to die. Illustrious knights, generous defenders of the Cross, remember the example of your fathers who conquered Jerusalem, and whose names are inscribed in Heaven; abandon then the things that perish, to gather unfading palms, and conquer a Kingdom which has no end.[10]

The First Crusade (1096–1099) was the most militarily successful. Crusaders captured Edessa and Antioch in 1098 and Jerusalem in 1099. They did not, however, restore these lands to the Byzantines, but established the first Crusader States: the country of Edessa, with its capital in Antioch, and the Latin Kingdom of Jerusalem. The Crusaders would hold Jerusalem for the next ninety years, until the sultan of Egypt, Saladin, retook it in 1187. The Latin Kingdom would continue for another hundred years, but without Jerusalem. The Crusaders' behavior in conquering these lands was abysmal. In both Antioch and Jerusalem, once they conquered the city they systematically slaughtered virtually every inhabitant.

When Edessa fell back under Muslim rule in 1144, Pope Eugene III called for the Second Crusade (1145–1149), which was led by the kings of two Frankish states, Louis VII of France and Conrad III of the Holy Roman Empire. It was this particular crusade for which Bernard of Clairvaux preached. When the crusaders were defeated by the Turks, Bernard blamed their failure on their moral behavior, which included looting cities along the way, even in the Byzantine Empire. The Egyptian sultan Saladin's capture of Jerusalem in 1187 sparked the Third Crusade (1189–1192), which was led by Frederick of the Holy Roman Empire, Richard the Lionheart of England, and Philip Augustus of France. It was a fiasco from the start. Frederick died on the way, Philip got into a rift with Richard and left with his army, and Richard himself was eventually captured and held for ransom. If anything was achieved by the Third Crusade it was the negotiation by Richard of a treaty with Saladin whereby unarmed Christian pilgrims could enter Jerusalem.

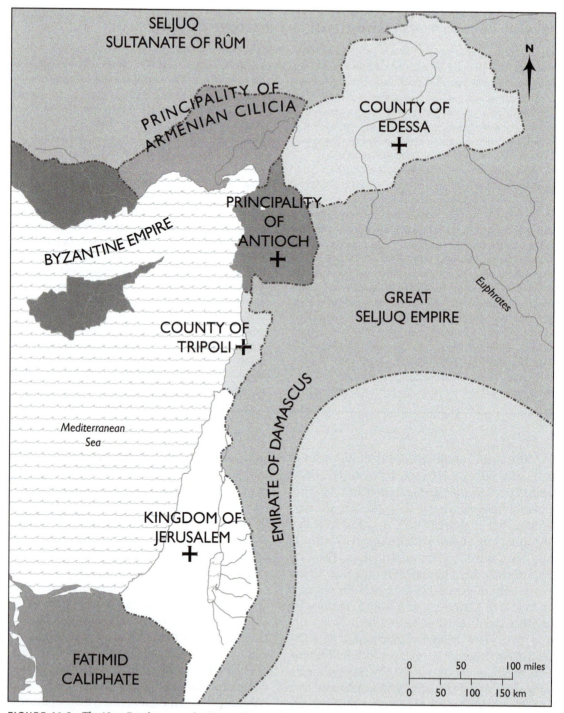

FIGURE 11-9 The Near East between the First and Second Crusades: Map of the Near East after the First Crusade. The Crusaders did not give their conquered territories back to the Byzantine Empire, but created their own independent states.

The Fourth Crusade (1201–1204) was the oddest and most disastrous for relations between East and West. Pope Innocent III called for this crusade, but the crusaders never made it to the Holy Land. Rather, the soldiers found themselves short on money and personnel, and decided to sack Constantinople instead and set up the Latin Empire based there. Innocent railed against the crusaders for abandoning their holy cause and fighting fellow Christians, but to no avail. The Latin Empire continued for the next five decades, but fell when Byzantine emperor Michael VIII Palaeologus recaptured Constantinople. Ultimately, the Byzantine Empire endured until 1453, when it was taken by the Turkish Ottoman Empire, but by the thirteenth century it was an empire only in name.

The other five crusades were smaller affairs, and succeeded in accomplishing virtually nothing besides exacerbating Muslim animosity toward the Christian West. The sacking of Constantinople is still a sensitive historical subject among Eastern Christians, who continue to resent the West for it. If there is a positive note to this most dark period in Western Christendom, it is that contact with both Byzantines and Muslims expanded Western consciousness in scholarship and the arts, which helped lead to the Renaissance. It also opened doors of trade, supporting a developing merchant class in Europe. Still, it is hard to imagine the Crusades were "worth it" on any level, nor can they be seen as legitimate by the Christian just war tradition.

CONCLUSIONS

With the expansion of Christianity in the British Isles and Scandinavia and the development of the Holy Roman Empire, the map of Western Europe dramatically changed. Regarding Christianity in the West, it was almost all for the good. Creating a Western emperor added strain to East–West church relations, but truth be told, the West had essentially been abandoned by Byzantium, as Constantinople simply did not have the resources to protect it. Unlike the patriarch in Constantinople, who had no political power, the patriarch of Rome (the pope) wielded a great deal. Some of the reason for this was theological, as Rome claimed juridical authority over all the church as the Chair of Peter. Some of the reason was that

the papacy found itself virtually holding the West together after the fall of the Western Roman Empire. And some of the reason was simply a coincidence of history. Even today, the Christian understanding of just war strikes many as a reasonable and defensible position. Most see a need to protect peoples against grave injustice, even if it involves violence. However, the concept of just war was applied by countries and the church itself in ways that never would have satisfied the strict criteria for war established by this tradition. Of particular historical tragedy were the Crusades, which sealed any hope of reconciliation between East and West and created animosity between Christians and Muslims that is still felt today.

SUMMARY QUESTIONS

- What were some of the factors that contributed to the transformation of the Western Roman Empire? In what ways did Romanism spread and continue to influence Europe and the church after the formal end of the Western Roman Empire?
- What were the major developments in the papacy according to this chapter?

- What criteria did just war theory set out for acceptable Christian warfare?
- What was the rationale for the involvement of the church in the West in state affairs?
- What reasons and events led to the separation between the Western and Eastern areas of the church?

DISCUSSION QUESTIONS

- Do you think the papacy's progressive authority and control in the West was wise at the time? Why or why not?
- Can the Crusades as a whole or any one of them be justified morally?

- While the author says that the papacy got mired in conflicting interests and political machinations, he also seems to defend, at least in some way, the papacy acting as a monarch in the Papal States. What are his reasons, and do you think his position is defensible?

KEY TERMS

Bernard of Clairvaux
Boniface VIII
Charlemagne
Crusades
Gelasius I
Gregory I

Gregory VII
Innocent III
Interdict
Just war theory
Lay investiture
Leo I

Nepotism
Pacifism
Papal bull
Patrick
Simony
Ulfilas

BIBLIOGRAPHY

- Adair, James. 2008. *Introducing Christianity.* New York: Routledge.
- Bede. 1990. *Ecclesiastical History of the English People*, rev. ed. Trans. Leo Sherley-Price. New York: Penguin.
- Brown, Peter. 1996. *The Rise of Western Christendom: Triumph and Diversity A.D. 200–1000.* Oxford: Oxford University Press, 1996.
- Canon Law Society of America, trans. 1983. *Code of Canon Law.* Washington, D.C: Canon Law Society of America.
- Evans, G. R. 2001. *The Medieval Theologians.* Oxford: Blackwell.
- Flannery, Austin, ed. 1975. *Vatican Council II*, Vol. 1, rev. ed. Newport, NY: Costello Publishing.
- Hillgarth, J. N. 1986. *Christianity and Paganism, 350–750: The Conversion of Western Europe*, rev. ed. Philadelphia: University of Pennsylvania Press.
- Kasper, Walter, ed. 2006. *The Petrine Ministry: Catholics and Orthodox in Dialogue.* Trans. Pontifical Council for Promoting Christian Unity. New York: Newman Press.
- Logan, Donald. 2012. *A History of the Church in the Middle Ages.* London: Routledge.
- McKitterick, Rosamund. 1977. *The Frankish Church and the Carolingian Reform, 789–895.* London: Longman.

- Neuner, J., and J. Dupuis, eds. 1981. *The Christian Faith in Doctrinal Documents of the Catholic Church*, rev. ed. New York: Alba House.
- Noble, Thomas. 1984. *The Republic of Saint Peter: The Birth of the Papal State, 680–825.* Philadelphia: University of Pennsylvania Press.
- Riley-Smith, Jonathan. 2008. *The First Crusaders, 1095–1131.* Lanham, MD: Rowman & Littlefield.
- Southern, R. W. 1970. *Western Society and the Church in the Middle Ages.* New York: Penguin.
- Tellenbach, Gerd. 1970. *Church, State and Society at the Time of the Investiture Contest.* Trans. R. F. Bennett. Toronto: University of Toronto Press.
- Tierney, Brian, ed. 1964. *The Crisis of Church and State, 1050–1300.* Upper Saddle River, NJ: Prentice Hall.
- Ullmann, Walter. 1972. *A Short History of the Papacy in the Middle Ages.* London: Methuen.
- Wallace-Hadreill, John Michael. 1983. *The Frankish Church.* Oxford: Clarendon.
- Wilken, Robert. 2012. *The First Thousand Years: A Global History of Christianity.* New Haven, CT: Yale University Press.

NOTES

1. Cited in Wilken, *First Thousand Years*, 333–334.
2. Ibid., 334.
3. Cited in Southern, *Western Society and the Church*, 71.
4. Ibid.
5. Cited in Tierney, *Crisis of Church and State*, 131–132.
6. Cited in Neuner and Dupuis, *Christian Faith in the Doctrinal Documents*, 218.
7. See Romans 12:4–5; 1 Corinthians 10:16, 12:27; Ephesians 4:4, 12; and Colossians 1:18.
8. Oliver J. Thatcher and Edgar Holmes McNeal, trans. and eds., *A Source Book for Medieval History* (New York: Scribners, 1905), 513–517, accessed at Internet Medieval Sourcebook, http://www.fordham.edu/Halsall/source/urban2-5vers.asp#Fulcher.
9. Cited in Adair, *Introducing Christianity*, 195
10. William Jennings Bryan, *The World's Famous Orations* (New York: Funk and Wagnalls Company, 1906), accessed at http://bartleby.com/268/7/4.html#txt1.

12

Medieval Piety and the Rise of the Universities

Timeline

1100–1160 CE	Life of Peter Lombard and the beginnings of scholastic theology
1184 CE	Beginning of the Roman Inquisition
1209 CE	Francis of Assisi founds Franciscan order
1216 CE	Dominic Guzmán founds Dominican order
1225–1274 CE	Life of Thomas Aquinas, the most influential scholastic thinker
c. 1250 CE	Beginning of the Beguine movement
1347–1351 CE	Bubonic plague (Black Death) decimates much of Europe
1347–1380 CE	Life of Catherine of Siena, mystic and authoritative presence in the Italian church
1414–1418 CE	Council of Constance ends rival papal claims and pronounces conciliarism

WHAT TO EXPECT

During the Middle Ages Europe was principally a feudal world with particular expectations governing relations between rulers and peasants and a different set of assumptions about the role of wealth. This chapter explores the early shifts in that culture related to capitalism and its subsequent social, economic, and religious changes during the massive expansion of cities that occurred in what we would call the High Middle Ages (roughly the twelfth and thirteenth centuries) and the Late Middle Ages (roughly the fourteenth to the early fifteenth century). This period saw the formation of new religious groups, some of which were persecuted and others that led the way toward spiritual reform. Of particular note was a shift toward "feminine" forms of piety that included both men and women. With the expansion of wealth and urban life, medieval Europe also expanded in terms of learning.

Universities and a new class of theologians emerged, theologians who, unlike the patristics, sought to systematize theology.

CULTURAL SHIFTS IN EUROPE

FROM A GIFT ECONOMY TO A PROFIT ECONOMY

As noted in Chapter Eleven, the culture of early medieval Europe was a blending of Roman law and culture with the feudal assumptions of the Germanic peoples. **Feudalism** was premised on noble leaders—kings, princes, dukes—taking responsibility for their realms. These leaders were large landowners who oversaw the lives of villagers and townspeople; peasants owed part of their produce to the lord, and the lord in return was responsible for their safety and well-being. In addition, lords built churches and monasteries and believed they had the right to control them. Within this system bishops and abbots functioned more as vassals than as independent leaders. It was a culture of concentrated wealth, and economic assumptions differed markedly from our society's capitalist convictions. Of course, people traded goods with the aim of profit, but often goods and services were exchanged without specific value assigned to them. This has been characterized as a **gift economy**. Power, prestige, and honor were expressed in gifts that obliged recipients to respond in kind.

The shift from a gift economy to a full-fledged **profit economy** would take centuries, but it was surely under way by the eleventh century. With the exception of the Crusades, Europe experienced almost two centuries of relative peace. Improved farming techniques dramatically increased crop production, and the balance of trade between East and West came to clearly favor the West. Industry also began to flourish, creating a network of new towns and structures that facilitated cultural development. At this point, money began to have a more calculated

value. Further, the West saw the formation of banks and other institutions that allowed merchants to trade more freely. Prior to this period, large trading deals were hazardous affairs: one risked getting robbed while journeying home with a chest full of coins. Now, a letter of credit from a bank could suffice. Banks also allowed for the development of capitalist ventures that were previously virtually impossible.

The development of a profit economy went hand in hand with the establishment of larger cities with organized markets. Many peasants and tradespeople flocked to cities in search of opportunity after being dislodged from landowners' property, a shift in population that expanded cities dramatically. Towering Gothic cathedrals and great municipal buildings were erected, and urban schools began to replace monasteries as centers of education. It was during this period that the great universities of Europe emerged.

All major cultural and economic shifts involve winners and losers, and certainly not everyone benefited from these developments. While some individuals migrated to cities in order to establish trade there, others were forced into the cities because a lord no longer wanted them on his land. Increasingly for many lords, taking responsibility for peasants' welfare no longer made financial sense. Lords also needed fewer knights and vassals than in the past, as they now could pay mercenaries to defend their property. So the flood into the cities included both would-be entrepreneurs and dislocated peasants. Consequently, cities contained both great wealth and extreme poverty.

As medieval culture took on an increasingly capitalistic character, morality itself began to be reconsidered. Before, when life was simple and unchanging, morality was also understood as relatively simple and unchanging. The vast majority of peasants had a place in the world and knew what it was and what was expected of them. In the anonymous city, they could reinvent themselves. Further, morality had to be considered in the context of making money. How could one morally make money merely through investment, that is, without producing a good or service?

EARLY RESPONSES TO THE SHIFT

Religious responses to the cultural shifts that marked the eleventh and twelfth centuries were many. Some Christians seemed to simply opt out, and we see during this period the beginnings of full-fledged anchoritic monasticism (hermits) in the West. Monasticism had become one of the cultural cornerstones of the feudal world. Education revolved around monasteries, with their massive libraries and educated monks. Monasteries also exemplified the gift economy: their wealth was displayed in their buildings and sanctuaries and was also given to the poor as an expression of Christian charity and feudal responsibility. As the economic landscape developed, these institutions began to participate in trade more robustly. In short, they became players in the profit economy.

Peter Damian (1007–1072) is a classic example of reaction against the new cultural shifts. Born into a wealthy family, he decided to abandon his life of luxury and become a monk. But he did not enter a Benedictine monastery, which he considered just another bastion of wealth. Rather, he chose a hermitage, from which he advocated a monastic life of radical poverty and flight from society. Others followed his lead, and many monastic communities developed along the lines of some form of seclusion and disengagement with culture. The **Carthusians**, started by Bruno of Cologne in 1084, created a new monastic Rule according to which monks lived as semi-hermits far from urban centers. The **Premonstratensians**, founded by Norbert in 1120

in France, represented a community of priests who continued to perform pastoral care but lived together without personal property and embraced an austere life. Common to all the new orders was the conviction that they represented a prophetic contrast to a church and society succumbing to the clutches of wealth.

Lay religious groups also sprung up as resistance initiatives challenging the greed endemic within church and society. One collective of priests and laymen who traveled throughout Italy preaching radical simplicity called itself the **Humiliati**. In addition to acting as a kind of protest group against church and culture, they also served the needs of many people who found themselves impoverished as a result of the shifts in society. Some of these groups were supported by the church itself, though always with the proviso that they subject themselves to the authority of the local bishop. The Third Lateran Council (1179) granted the movement official Roman support.

Another movement, the **Waldensians**, began in Lyons in 1175 when a successful merchant named Valdes gave up all his goods and preached radical poverty as *the* authentic Christian message. Valdes quickly attracted a following of both men and women. The earliest Waldensian preaching was directed at both the worldliness of the clergy and the heresy of the Cathars (see next paragraph). In 1179, Valdes and his followers sought ecclesiastical recognition, which Pope Alexander III approved, but with the requirement that they only preach publicly at the invitation of the clergy. Valdes soon refused to obey this restriction, and his movement organized itself apart from the institutional church, ignoring its sanctions and appointing their own ministers. They grew rapidly, spreading first into southern France and Spain, and then into Germany and Italy.

A particularly fascinating religious protest group was collectively known as the **Cathars** (or the Albigensians). Like the Waldensians, they saw themselves as the true church and claimed their own authority. Their opponents likened their views to the kind of Manicheanism that Augustine dabbled with in his day before becoming a Christian. Here the body was considered an evil that needed to be divorced from the spirit. The Cathars practiced rigid asceticism, rejected marriage and property, and renounced all animal products. Pope Innocent III called for the suppression of the group, which led to their widespread repression at the hands of a crusade in France.

THE INQUISITION

One of the more infamous, but also misunderstood, episodes of the medieval church is the **Inquisition**. In the twelfth century, Rome charged councils composed of bishops with establishing inquisitions, principally with concern for the Cathars. The first inquisition was established in Languedoc, France, in 1184. In 1232, Emperor Frederick II issued an edict ordering the hunting out of heretics. Pope Gregory IX, concerned with Frederick's political ambitions, claimed the responsibility for carrying out the task for the church and appointed papal inquisitors. These inquisitors traveled throughout Europe admonishing those guilty of heresy to confess their sins voluntarily. If they did confess, a penance such as fasting would be imposed. If

they did not confess, a trial was conducted, with a group composed of both clerics and laymen normally assisting as a kind of jury. Testimony required at least two witnesses, and the accused was offered counsel. This would not have been a modern version of a defense attorney, but rather someone who ensured the trial was conducted fairly. If it was evident that the accused was guilty, and if he or she remained obstinate, then he or she would typically be imprisoned under severe conditions. In 1252, Pope Innocent IV allowed the use of torture to break the accused's resistance. The Inquisition also had the power to impose daunting penalties in grave cases, including the confiscation of goods, imprisonment, and even surrender to the civil authority for the imposition of the death penalty.

One can only understand the mindset of the Inquisition if one brackets the modern values of religious freedom and the authority of conscience. Today in the West, so-called "heresy" is simply allowed in the marketplace of ideas. If one has a compelling message, then one draws followers, who feel free to break from their religious past. Everyone is free to believe and preach what he or she wants. But life was much different prior to the modern period. What was at risk in

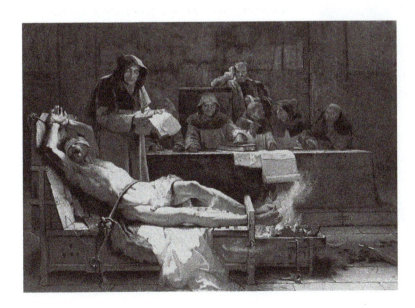

FIGURE 12-1 Established in 1478 by the Spanish Crown, the Spanish Inquisition regularly tortured religious and political suspects.

the medieval mind was not only the soul of the alleged heretic, but also the disruption of a religious society. Obviously, there were institutional control issues at play, but the church feared above all the loss of Christian souls. How could the church imagine itself as responsible for the salvation of souls and then allow renegades to poison these souls and consign them to hell for eternity?

In the main, the Inquisition was not as brutal as it is now imagined. According to one scholarly study of the Inquisition's suppression of Catharism in France, only about 1 percent of those found guilty were sentenced to death, while around 10 percent were imprisoned. Given the numbers of secular trials that involved confessions under torture and sentences often leading to the death penalty, the Inquisition was a

comparatively modest affair. The great exception was the Spanish Inquisition in the fifteenth century, which quickly came under secular control. Here, the Inquisition was used as a political instrument. Heretics, often those whose religious enthusiasm had led them beyond the bounds of customary religion or those believed to be politically suspicious, were subjected to imprisonment, confiscation of property, and sometimes death. Spanish and Portuguese inquisitors engaged in the infamous *auto-da-fe* (act of faith), which involved the public penance of condemned heretics, some of whom were burned at the stake in the public square. Obviously, the Spanish Inquisition involved great injustice, horror, and tragedy.

THE DOMINICAN RESPONSE

One response to the new cultural shifts and their concomitant heretical movements was the founding of the Order of Preachers, also known as the **Dominicans**, by **Dominic Guzmán** in 1216. Dominic was a highly educated and deeply pious priest of the Toulouse diocese who, along with his bishop, saw the need to address these various movements by responding in kind, that is, by preaching. The problem as he saw it was twofold. First, he wholeheartedly agreed that church authorities often represented wealth and power, and that such status interfered with authentic witness to the gospel. Second, he believed that many people were swayed by these movements, in large part because they simply did not understand the gospel. Most priests were modestly educated at best and were simply not up to the task of responding to these movements. What the people needed, they thought, was an authentic, intellectually compelling voice that spoke to them directly, one that also represented a disavowal of wealth.

Dominic and those who joined his newly founded order adopted a life known as *evangelical poverty*, in which they lived simply and austerely, and depended daily upon the support of others. These priests had no salary and carried

FIGURE 12-2 This Renaissance painting of Saint Dominic shows him holding up the church with the apostle Peter. It is as though Dominic is preserving the church Peter was charged with.

no money. As they went from town to town preaching, they also begged for food and lodging. They, like the Franciscans discussed in the next section, were called *mendicant friars*, literally, "begging brothers." Through their compelling preaching and inspiring lifestyle, the Dominicans were extremely successful in countering many of the heretical movements. Dominic created houses of study and recruited members from universities. Among those who would adopt the order's simple lifestyle were some of the best and the brightest of the Christian intellectual world, including Albert the Great (c. 1200–1270) and Thomas Aquinas (1225–1274). From the outset, study was an essential element of Dominican life. Every friary had a resident theologian, and many were themselves centers of theological study. Dominic's successor, Jordan of Saxony (d. 1237), circulated a letter to all the friaries emphasizing the brothers' responsibility to engage in serious study in order to save souls.

Given the order's focus on education and preaching, the original mendicancy or begging that marked its earliest years could not be sustained. Begging simply took too much time and energy. Dominican life became highly flexible, and this flexibility set Dominicans apart from other orders that had more stringent rules for community discipline and specific spiritual practices. Dominicans were also less austere than members of other religious orders, as their busy preaching and academic life made such austerity virtually impossible.

Religious orders are often marked by their spirituality, a certain concrete expression of discipleship, or way to God. The Dominican tradition differed in that it did not strongly emphasize a particular style of spirituality. As Dominican scholar Simon Tugwell has written, "Dominicans were generally unoriginal."[1] Preaching was central to their mission. The fifth superior of the order, Humbert (1200–1277), insisted that the brothers consider preaching as preferable to all other spiritual exercises, including prayer, sacraments, and spiritual reading. Dominican

spirituality, then as now, includes nothing about how to address the purgative, illuminative, and unitive stages or about particular ways of imagining Christ or living out a Christian lifestyle. This lack of content is actually viewed by the order as a strength. The Dominican tradition by and large rejects ideas of "grades" of prayer. "Perfection," for Thomas Aquinas, consists of perfect love, and this love should be expressed in all activities, with or without vivid experiences of God's presence. Performing one's tasks with dedication is de facto spiritual. Compared to other definitions of petitionary prayer, Aquinas's seems somewhat tepid: "Petition is a rational response to our total dependence on God and an expression of our readiness to subject

FIGURE 12-3 Because of Saint Francis's reputation for gentleness and love, a legend formed that he befriended a wolf that was terrorizing the town, ultimately making it the town's pet.

our will to his."[2] Such a definition fits well with the Dominican worldview. The focus is twofold: on one's heart's readiness to do God's will and on actually *doing* it. This emphasis follows Dominic's prime directive: "Do whatever is useful to souls."

THE FRANCISCAN RESPONSE

If understanding the cultural shifts in medieval Europe is important for understanding the Dominican response, it is all the more so for comprehending the **Franciscan** response, which resembles those of the Waldensians and the Humiliati in important respects.

Francis of Assisi (1181–1226) was the son of a wealthy cloth merchant who took advantage of the emerging profit economy. Francis was raised in comfort and received a fair education. He often gathered with other wealthy sons of merchants and loved to drink and sing the songs of the troubadours about courtly love. Although he had the reputation for being a lover of pleasure, he also had a generous spirit. In 1201, at the age of twenty, he participated in a military expedition against a neighboring city-state at war with Assisi and was captured, spending the next year as a prisoner. It was a decisive year, as he returned early in 1203 a different, much more serious person. In 1204, Francis experienced a serious illness that fostered a deepening disillusionment with his life of luxury, and in 1205 he had a decisive conversion experience: "The Lord granted to me, Brother Francis, to begin to do penance in this way: While I was in sin, it seemed very bitter to me to see lepers. And the Lord Himself led me among them and I had mercy upon them. And when I left them that which seemed bitter to me was changed into sweetness of soul and body; and afterward I lingered a little and left the world."[3] This experience led Francis to give away all his possessions and commit himself to charitable work for lepers and beggars around Assisi. From that point on, Francis lived a life of radical poverty, owning only "a miserable tunic and cord."

One day, while praying in the broken-down chapel of San Damiano, Francis heard Jesus speak from the crucifix: "Francis, rebuild my church." Initially, he believed this divine voice was commanding him to rebuild the chapel, a project he undertook. Only later did he realize that the "church" was not San Damiano, but the church itself. Soon Francis attracted other zealous companions who were interested in living his life of poverty and service. Deciding to create a brotherhood under God's directive, they entered the Church of St. Nicholas in Assisi and engaged in a practice called the *sortes apostolicae*, which involved opening the Bible three times and randomly pointing to a verse. God would, they believed, in this way reveal his will to them. These are the verses they arbitrarily fell upon: "If you wish to be perfect, go, sell your possessions, and give the money to the poor, and you will have treasure in heaven; then come, follow me" (Matt. 19:21); "Take nothing for your journey, no staff, nor bag, nor bread, nor money—not even an extra tunic" (Luke 9:3); and "If any want to become my followers, let them deny themselves and take up their cross and follow me" (Matt. 16:24). Collectively, these verses solidified their intuitions and guided their lifestyle of absolute poverty, total dependence on God, and self-denial.

The most dramatic part of Francis's life story occurred during the last year of his life. It began with a vivid experience he had during a forty-day retreat on Mount Alverna:

> While he was praying on the mountainside, Francis saw a Seraph [angel] with six fiery wings coming down from the highest point in the heavens. The vision descended swiftly and came to rest in the air near him. Then he saw the image of a man crucified in the midst of the wings, with his hands and feet stretched out and nailed to a cross. . . . Eventually he realized by divine inspiration that God had shown him this vision in his providence, in order to let him see that, as Christ's lover, he would resemble the fervor of his spirit. As the vision disappeared, it left his heart ablaze with eagerness and impressed upon

FIGURE 12-4   Saint Francis receives the stigmata, or wounds of Christ, from a vision of Christ in the form of an angel.

his body the miraculous likeness. There and then the marks of nails began to appear in his hands and feet. . . . His right side seemed as if it had been pierced with a lance and was marked with a livid scar which often bled, so that his habit and trousers were stained.[4]

This passage describes Francis's experience of receiving the **stigmata**, the wounds of Christ. The stigmata represent the pinnacle of his spiritual life: the experience *christified* him. For Francis, humility, obedience, servitude, and self-emptiness represented Christ, and the ultimate expression of these qualities was Christ's passion and death on the cross. Francis understood that becoming like Christ meant internalizing the same character traits. By means of his experience of the seraph, he came to the insight that in order to fully become Christ's beloved and imitator, he must resemble Christ perfectly. The wounds he acquired were therefore sweet to him, much like the experience of associating with lepers had been years before. Francis retained the stigmata for the rest of his short life. Fascinatingly, though the wounds bled daily, they never showed signs

of infection, nor did the flesh around them deteriorate.

By 1209, the followers of Francis had become a new religious order with the verbal approval of Pope Innocent III. They had two principal missions: to preach and to serve the poor and sick. By 1217, Franciscans were sending missions beyond Italy and throughout Europe. The first formal Rule of the order was sent to Rome in 1221, but it was rejected as unworkable: it was simply too idealistic. The second Rule was approved in 1223, much to Francis's sadness. There was a painful tension between Francis's original vision of apostolic spontaneity and radical simplicity and the institutional demands of an official religious order. Francis's vision really was too demanding, and his own asceticism was daunting. Further, the idea of wandering troubadours for Christ worked well for a small group of companions but conflicted with the reality of institutional demands, such as centers for the brothers' religious formation or houses for them to live in. The Franciscans initially imagined, much like the Waldensians, that they could freely preach the gospel without much training. As Dominic had learned, however, preaching without comprehensive theological training was problematic. Thus, schooling was soon deemed necessary.

Understanding the Franciscan movement is essential for understanding medieval piety, a piety that stood in great contrast to the Renaissance ideal, which will be discussed in the next chapter. Francis is one of the most beloved saints in the Western church, Catholic and Protestant alike. He is imagined by many to be one of the greatest imitators of Christ, one who embraced the gospel in all its fullness and radical demands. Of course, some in the modern age who love Francis see only an unthreatening version of him without his insistence on asceticism and obedience. Still, there was something powerful about his utter simplicity, humility, poverty, and even stigmata that spoke to the medieval world dramatically and still inspires followers today. Francis is not only revered by Christians of many denominations, but is also admired by members of other religions, such as Islam, Buddhism, and Hinduism.

MEDIEVAL FEMININE AFFECTIVE PIETY

As noted in Chapter Eight, the patristic theological and spiritual worldview was Platonic in many respects. Monastic spirituality, particularly in the East, found its highest expression in *apophatic mysticism*, that is, encounters with God that went beyond the sensible world. This type of spirituality deemphasized the human body and prized experiences that transcended the physical. Many of the spiritual masters of the patristic era drew on Platonic ideas directly. In their view, the created world was infused with God's presence, but union with God had to go beyond this.

The Western medieval world embraced many of these ideas and values, but it also saw the created world as filled with sacramental possibilities. In Benedictine monasticism, the community, the abbot (or abbess), and visitors were all believed to be sacramental manifestations of

Christ. Even the tools of the monastery were imagined to be potentially holy. The spiritual mediation of the created world was particularly highlighted in the medieval period. Perhaps the most well-known illustration of this worldview is Francis's poem the "Canticle of the Creatures," in which he sees the created world as both expressing God's grace and praising God in its own way. One stanza reads:

> All praise be yours, my Lord, through all
> that you have made.
> And first my lord Brother Sun, who brings
> the day;
> and the light you give to us through him.
> How beautiful is he, how radiant in all his
> splendor!
> Of you, Most High, he bears the likeness.[5]

Although many medieval saints, Francis included, abused their bodies by their asceticism, the reason they did so ironically lay in their belief that the body could act as a potent spiritual metaphor. If one had asked a patristic, such as Augustine or Gregory of Nyssa, if fasting was a good spiritual practice, he would have said that it was good insofar as it aided one in purifying any inordinate desires (passions) so that one's soul could be freer for God. Medieval saints would surely have agreed, but they might also have added that fasting was the body's expression of the soul's hunger and thirst for holiness, or that fasting helped the soul participate in the passion of Christ. Here, experience of the body became not only the context for spiritual expression, but the content of it, a locus for revelation of profound religious truth.

SEXUAL STEREOTYPES

Typical modern gender stereotypes characterize men as less emotional, less relational, and more rational, and women as more emotional, more relational, and more nurturing. These same stereotypes existed in the patristic and medieval worlds as well. What is fascinating is the difference in value attributed to those characteristics. While the patristic world saw these feminine qualities as obstacles to deep prayer and union with God, the medieval world saw them as important. Gregory of Nyssa offered one typical patristic assessment of the feminine: "For the material and passionate disposition to which human nature is carried when it falls is the female form, whose birth is favored by the tyrant [devil]. The austerity and intensity of virtue is the male birth."[6] To Gregory, women's supposed emotionality was a liability. Emotions got in the way of holiness; they showed that one was attached and lacked proper *apatheia*. Augustine, for example, lightly reproached himself for weeping at his mother's death: "I slipped towards weeping. . . . I was reproaching the softness of my feelings."[7]

Contrast these patristic notions to the beliefs expressed by the medieval great **Catherine of Siena** (1347–1380), for whom suffering and sorrow increased in proportion to her love of Christ and the church. In one of the mystical encounters recorded in her *Dialogues*, Christ tells her, "Bring, then, your tears and your sweat, you and my other servants. Draw them from the fountain of my divine love and use them to wash the face of my bride. I promise you that thus her beauty will be restored . . . through peace and through constant and humble prayers and sweat and tears poured out by my servants with eager desire."[8] For Catherine and so many other medievals, emotions were not obstacles to deep prayer or spiritual insight, but the foundations for authentic prayer and the restoration of the church. In her writings Catherine even relates a mystical experience in which different kinds of tears represent stages of spiritual growth: tears of fear regarding one's sins, tears of gladness for arising out of sin, tears of those who love others purely, and tears of perfect union with God. The medieval stereotype of women stressed emotions and weakness, which is how Christians of the time saw Christ. To imitate Christ was to be poor, exposed, empathic, and vulnerable.

JESUS AS MOTHER

The relational, nurturing, compassionate, and emotional components of femininity were for the medieval world key access points for knowing God and expressing authentic spirituality. Many of the great spiritual leaders of the day imagined God as mother, and even the male Jesus as a mother as well. We see these representations in the works of such greats as Bernard of Clairvaux (d. 1153), Aelred of Rievaulx (d. 1167), Guerric of Igny (d. 1157), Isaac of Stella (d. 1169), William of St-Thierry (d. 1148), and Anselm of Canterbury (d. 1109). Anselm wrote:

> But you, Jesus, good lord, are you not also a mother? Are you not that other who, like a hen, collects her chickens under her wings? Truly, master, you are a mother. For what others have conceived and given birth to, they have received from you. . . . It is then you above all, Lord, God, who are mother. . . . Christ, mother . . . your warmth resuscitates the dead, your touch justifies sinners. . . . May your injured one be consoled by you; may he who of himself despairs be comforted by you.[9]

One of the celebrated mystics of the medieval period is **Julian of Norwich** (1342–1416), who wrote, "And so I saw that God rejoices that he is our Father, and God rejoices that he is our Mother. . . . For the almighty truth of the Trinity is our Father, for he made us and keeps us in him. And the deep wisdom of the Trinity is our Mother, in whom we are enclosed. . . . How we are brought back by the motherhood of mercy and grace into our natural place in which we were created by the motherhood of love, a mother's love which never leaves us."[10]

Much of the feminine imagery of God aligned with understandings of divine nurturance and care. The relation between a woman's breasts and her child, for example, was an illuminating metaphor for the relation between Christ and his people. Bernard of Clairvaux wrote, "Suck not so much the wounds of as the breasts of Christ. He will be your mother, and you will be his son."[11] Bernard regarded this image as also apt for spiritual leaders, particularly abbots in monasteries, whom he saw as feeding and nurturing those in their charge as a woman's breasts provide nourishment for her children. One need not imagine a particular male fascination with breasts in this example. The medieval world was much freer with their religious and sexual metaphors than we are today, and their feminine language and imagery neither surprised nor scandalized people of the time.

FEMININE EROTIC MYSTICISM

Medievals also reversed these metaphors in such a way that God took on the masculine role to the believer's feminine role. This was nothing original. In the Old Testament, Israel is sometimes imagined as the bride of Yahweh (Isa. 62; Ezek. 16; Hosea 1–3). The New Testament picks up the image when Paul refers to Christ as the husband of the church (1 Cor. 11:2; Eph. 5:32). From the patristic period on, the Old Testament Song of Songs was seen as an allegory for a kind of nuptial relationship between the church and God, or, alternatively, between the soul and Christ.

The medieval mind began to use this metaphor more intensely. A classic example can be seen in Bernard of Clairvaux's collection of sermons on the biblical Song of Solomon. The Song of Solomon begins, "Let him kiss me with the kisses of his mouth." Bernard devotes many sermons to just this one verse, which he uses as a springboard to theologize on the nature of the Trinity, the incarnation of Christ, the state of the soul, mystical experiences, and even stages of spiritual growth—all associated with kissing. In his first sermon Bernard argues, "This sort of song only the touch of the Holy Spirit teaches, and it is learned by experience alone. Let those who have experienced it enjoy it; let those who have not burn with desire. . . . It is a wedding song indeed, expressing the embrace of chaste and joyful souls, the concord of their lives and the mutual exchange of love."[12]

A particularly dramatic example of this kind of nuptial spirituality and, indeed, mysticism is found in the writings of the thirteenth-century Hadewijch of Antwerp: "The beloved and lover penetrate each other in such a way that neither of the two can distinguish oneself from the other. . . .

They abide in one another in fruition, mouth in mouth, and soul in soul, while one sweet divine nature flows through them both, and they are both one thing through each other."[13]

What does one make of such language? Surely, these medievals understood that they were speaking metaphorically: God was not their literal lover, and they were not sexually aroused during their spiritual experiences. They understood, of course, that God was pure spirit and transcended all physicality. Still, we ought to consider the romantic love expressed in these writings to be something of a *deep metaphor* for an experience that drew up all the energies and emotions (including those that were sexual) so as to fully engage God's love. Sexual language was not merely used as an analogy, but as a way of engaging God. God could be feminine, and the medieval often related to God as mother. God could also be masculine, while the souls of both men and women could take on the feminine expression of a beloved bride. In both cases, medieval piety was deeply absorbed in a world filled with passion and emotion.

The feminine imagination was located not only in metaphor, but in the spiritual presence of women themselves, some of whom served as religious authorities. Many women from noble or otherwise wealthy families saw the vowed religious life as an attractive alternative to marriage. Such a life gave them opportunities for independence and spiritual leadership from which they otherwise would have been exempt. Women leaders of religious communities even exercised political influence. Sophia I, as abbess of Gandersheim (975–1039), played a decisive role in the elections of Henry II and Conrad II as Holy Roman emperors. Petronilla de Chemillé (d. 1149) became the first abbess of the "double monastery," including separate living for both men (monks) and women (nuns), financed by William IX, duke of Aquitaine; she was followed by Matilda of Anjou, the aunt of Henry II, king of England. This abbey was a center for wealthy and powerful women for years and enjoyed an important role in western France.

While most women who entered the vowed religious life were cloistered, others took different routes. Catherine of Siena, for example, was a member of the Third Order Dominicans, a lay organization aligned with the Dominican order. Her mystical experiences and perceived holiness gave her enough clout to write popes and civic leaders urging them to reform. Along with those mentioned previously, such as Julian of Norwich and Hadewijch of Antwerp, there were great mystics and saints who were regarded as spiritual authorities, such as Mechthild of Magdeburg (c. 1207–1282), Angela of Foligno (c. 1248–1309), and Catherine of Genoa (1447–1510). The most outstanding was Hildegard of Bingen (1098–1179), who produced works on philosophy, theology, science, drama, music, and mysticism.

Other women attracted to the apostolic life joined independent communities known as **Beguines**. Such women, including Hadewijch and Mechthild, were not officially part of a religious order but lived together in a common life focused on prayer and ministerial service. Because of their fierce independence and some (typically unwarranted) charges of heresy, most of these communities ended up being suppressed and ordered to take on a monastic Rule. The Beguine movement did persist, however, in several forms until the last century. Its development fit the medieval mindset, one marked by cultural shifts and new ways of life.

◎ SHRINES, MIRACLES, AND THE MEDIEVAL MIND

In the medieval world the supernatural was taken for granted. The spiritual world that interpenetrated the physical one was filled with angels, ghosts, saints, and demons. That supernatural activity happened regularly was unquestioned; the focus was on the origins of such activity. For example, demons and black magic could effect miracles, as could God, either alone or through saintly interventions. Various types of prayers (or incantations) were deemed orthodox or heterodox only when it was determined whether a saint or demon caused something supernatural to occur in response. Still, miracles, remedies, and magic blurred in the minds of the laity and clergy alike.

The tenth-century Anglo-Saxon *Leehbook* lists remedies for affliction caused by elves; these treatments are part medicine and part magic. One German antidote for infertile fields includes mixing holy water with dirt, oil, honey, milk, tree bark, and herbs into clods. The priest would then pray, "Grow and multiply and replenish the earth," and would perform four Masses (Eucharists) over the clods and plows. Burchard of Worms wrote a pastoral manual called *The Corrector* in 1010, which prescribes fixed penances for specific sins. In it we find that Christians who confessed to having consulted with magicians to find a lost item had to observe fast days more rigorously for two years. Other sins included dancing or drinking on graves, consulting a woman for love brews, and marking the stars to determine the right day to marry. Priests were expected to bless weapons and offer the right kinds of prayers against illness, hail, storms, and demons. Practicing the faith principally meant attending Mass, offering tithes, fasting, and abstaining from sex during penitential seasons. The laity did not participate much in the liturgy. The Mass was delivered in Latin, which few knew, and for many it looked something like "good magic." By this time the church had demanded that people take communion on the tongue, as church leaders feared that otherwise some would use the consecrated host to make spiritual concoctions or place it in a locket around their necks as an amulet.

As noted in Chapter Six, Christians have venerated saints since the time of the early church. As early as the patristic era, they saw saints not only as heroic examples of faith, but as loci of spiritual power. Above all, through their intercessions, saints were understood to function like Roman patrons: they had access to spiritual wealth and desired to share such wealth. The Western medieval world expanded the role

FIGURE 12-5 Altar at Bamberg, one of the most famous pilgrimage sites in Germany in the eleventh century.

of the saint by constructing great shrines to which pilgrims journeyed to venerate and pray to them for their intercession with God. Towns often were dedicated to a given saint and boasted of that saint's power for miracles. There was a kind of interdependence between piety and economics. As exemplars of the life of faith, saints really were venerated and loved, and they were really believed to intercede fruitfully on the faithful's behalf. At the same time, townspeople boasting of miracles attributed to their patron saint made for good business, fostering something of a pilgrimage trade. Pilgrimages were themselves expressions of devotion. Many pilgrims did not seek a healing miracle per se, but rather went on pilgrimage as an extended spiritual exercise.

The most popular, elaborate sites of pilgrimage were those associated with Mary, the Blessed Mother. Journeys to such sites tended to be pure acts of devotion. Other saints' shrines were local affairs: a given saint's popularity, shrine, and town of patronage were intertwined. But Mary was the universal saint. There was no need for a particular shrine to establish her sanctity or spiritual power via a list of miracles attributed to her intercession. No one doubted that her mediation was infinitely powerful or that she loved humanity as a mother

loves her children. The medieval popularity of Mary, pilgrimages to Marian sites, and devotional practices associated with Mary can scarcely be exaggerated. During this period, Saturdays even become dedicated to her. In regard to Mary, the Western and Eastern churches were of one accord: both expressed deep love for and devotion to her. She was the patron of the whole church. Whereas God was often associated with judgment, particularly during harsh periods such as times of plague, Mary was associated with maternal care. Under her love and through her intercession, even God's just anger at a sinner could be mollified.

THE RISE OF THE UNIVERSITIES

The rise of universities was the happy result of a number of developments in Western Europe. As noted previously, Europe during the Late Middle Ages enjoyed a period of relative peace, good harvests, flourishing trade, and the emergence of cities with wealth. Further, with the development of paper, texts became far more easily available. Finally, literate Western Christians were exposed in this era to a wealth of classical works that had been lost to the West during the early Middle Ages. Contact with Eastern Christians as well as Muslim and Jewish scholars through the Crusades and the Islamic rule in Spain resulted in a revitalization of Western scholarship. Muslims had discovered Aristotle and found his works helpful for understanding the relationship between faith and reason. Works that had been lost to the West, such as Aristotle's *Prior Analytics*, *Posterior Analytics*, *Physics*, and *Metaphysics*, thus came to circulate throughout the intellectual world of medieval Europe.

Education during the Early Middle Ages was principally a monastic affair. Monasteries housed great libraries and educated monks, who established schools that attracted the sons of those with financial means. The primacy of monastic schools was progressively replaced with that of cathedral schools, which were supported by bishops and priests on or near the cathedral property. Cathedral schools were principally training grounds for clergy, but served as centers of learning for lay students as well. Soon, they expanded into universities. *Universitas* means "totality," and today's universities are so named because they encompass the whole scope of education. During the Middle Ages, the word "university" initially referred to *universitas scholarum* or *universitas magistorum*, designating a self-governing community of scholars who were recognized and sanctioned by church or civil authority, respectively. A university was an academic guild.

In Italy, cities financed their own schools, copying the institutions of higher education that Muslims had created in great cultural centers such as Baghdad and Toledo. These Italian universities retained their lay domination for centuries. Bologna was the earliest, formally recognized in 1158, but there were others as well, such as Oxford (1167), Modena (1175), Cambridge (1209), Salamanca (1218), Toulouse (1218), Orleans (1235), Siena (1240), Prague (1348), Krakow (1370), Heidelberg (1386), and Cologne (1388). Within these institutions, education had three tiers. First, one studied logic, grammar, and rhetoric. These were known as the *trivium* (three ways), from which we derive the English word *trivial*, which originally meant "elementary." After this basic education came the *quadrivium*, or

FIGURE 12-6 Oxford University was founded in 1167 and was one of dozens of prestigious new universities of the High Middle Ages. It continues to be one of the greatest universities in the world.

four disciplines of arithmetic, astronomy, geometry, and music. Finally, those who mastered these areas could go on to specialize in theology, law, or medicine. Bologna became famous for law and Paris for theology.

CHRISTIAN SCHOLASTICISM

Early Christian scholarship was scholarship of occasion, that is, great Christian thinkers typically wrote to weigh in on theological disputes or provide instruction on core Christian ideas or practices. By the High Middle Ages, scholarship had been reconfigured in a scholastic system. The agenda now was to understand all of the Christian faith in a reasoned and systematic way. For this, scholars needed philosophy, the *ancilla theologiae* (literally, "handmaid of theology"). They were particularly impressed by Aristotle, whom the medievals simply called "The Philosopher," and whose account of reality struck them as coherent and sophisticated. Muslims and Jews were likewise impressed with Aristotle. Of particular importance in understanding his work were the writings of the Muslim scholars Avicenna (980–1037) and Averroes (1126–1198), whom Christians called "The Commentator" (of Aristotle's works). Medieval scholars were also influenced by **Moses Maimonides** (1135–1204), whose *Guide to the Perplexed* synthesized Judaic theology with Aristotelian philosophy. Finally, Plato's philosophy resurged as well and would be influential for both Thomas Aquinas (discussed in the next section) and Franciscan greats such as Bonaventure.

One of the most important forerunners of scholasticism was **Peter Abelard** (1079–1142), who became a famous teacher at the cathedral school in Paris. Wealthy families throughout Europe sent their gifted sons to Paris to study under him. One of his students was, however, a young woman from a powerful family named Heloise. While Abelard was tutoring Heloise, they fell in love, secretly married, and even had a son together. When her family found out, they kidnapped and castrated him. Ultimately Abelard ended his career in a monastery, and Heloise became a nun. While they were determined to be devout monastics, they also continued corresponding throughout their lives. Abelard's greatest contribution to scholasticism was his book *Sic et Non* (*Yes and No*), which takes on 150 theological questions and shows how the Bible and commentaries by church fathers differ in addressing them. Abelard's aim was to challenge his students to resolve apparent contradictions and devise some kind of higher synthesis. This model of inquiry was used widely by later scholastics.

The second great voice in forming the scholastic method was **Peter Lombard** (1100–1160), whose *Four Books of the Sentences* weave together biblical and patristic texts thematically. His first book addresses the Trinity, his second creation and sin, his third the incarnation and Christian life, and the fourth the sacraments and eschatology (last things). Lombard not only provided a core collection of texts—a valuable contribution in itself—but also provided commentary and strove to resolve differences to reach a higher synthesis, much like Abelard. Many towering medieval theologians wrote commentaries on Lombard's *Sentences*, including Aquinas, Bonaventure, and Duns Scotus.

THOMAS AQUINAS (1225–1274)

By far the most important scholastic theologian of the medieval period was **Thomas Aquinas**.

FIGURE 12-7   Saint Thomas Aquinas was the most influential scholastic theologian of his day. His theology continues to be important to Roman Catholics in the modern era.

Aquinas was born in Roccasecca, Italy, the son of a nobleman. A prodigy from his youth, his family sent him to be educated at the most famous monastery of the day, Monte Cassino, and his father had designs for Thomas to eventually become abbot there. When Aquinas came of age, however, he announced that he wanted to become a Dominican, a move his family saw as a decided step down. As noted earlier, Dominicans embraced strict poverty and were still known at this time for begging on the streets. To this aristocratic family, such a life was unimaginable. Compared to the Benedictines, the Dominicans were seen as a poor, ragtag group of preachers who smelled bad and made little of themselves. Actually, by Aquinas's day, the Dominicans were teaching at some of the most prestigious universities of the period, but this did not assuage his family's rejection of his choice. When Aquinas insisted on becoming a Dominican, his brothers locked him up in a tower of the family's castle, hoping he would relent. Eventually, he wore them down and joined the Dominican order. Among his teachers was Albert the Great (1200–1280), the finest scholar among the Dominicans, who recognized the power of his pupil's mind. Aquinas's fellow students had nicknamed him the "Dumb Ox" for his reticence to speak up in class as well as his large size. Albert once remarked, "Gentlemen, you call Thomas the 'dumb ox,' but some day that ox will let out such a bellow that his noise will fill the earth."

Aquinas began his teaching career at the University of Paris and taught there from 1245 to 1259. He later returned for a second stint from 1269 to 1272, and also taught at several Dominican schools during his career. He became one of the most famous teachers in Western history. One of the academic practices at the time was the *quodlibetal debate*: a public event in which one professor would enter a debate with other professors without his having any prior knowledge of its topic. During the debate, this vulnerable scholar would be subject to questions and comments from a group of other professors who had prepared ahead of time and could draw on their expertise. This was a risky venture; if one lost the debate—which was set up on an incredibly uneven playing field from the start—one could also lose public face as well as pupils, with the latter being a huge financial risk. Aquinas engaged in numerous *quodlibetal debates* and simply dominated his challengers.

Aquinas's theological output was massive. He wrote commentaries on the scriptures and other theological works, such as the *Sentences*, religious poetry, and mammoth works of systematic theology. His most famous was the *Summa Theologiae* (*Summary of Theology*), intended for philosophically trained Dominicans who lacked the opportunity to engage in advanced theological study. He imagined it as a text for beginners, but the work is so dense that

it continues to be the fodder for numerous doctoral dissertations to this day.

Aquinas and other scholastics sought to provide a unified, systematic, consistent Christian worldview, one that drew on the wisdom and philosophical categories they thought most compelling. Faith, they believed, was based on revelation and thus could not be proven by natural reason. But they were also convinced that faith was aligned with reason and could be shown to be grounded in it. They assumed there were harmonious relations between the natural and supernatural, reason and faith, the created world and the spiritual world. Grace does not abolish nature, Aquinas argued; it perfects it and takes it to its supernatural end.

NOMINALISM

One of the great debates of the time focused on whether universals exist as something real (apart from and independent of human minds) or as useful ideas but nothing more. Aquinas, for example, thought that goodness exists in God as an absolute value and in humans as a relative value. Further, God is good *as* God, while humans are good *as* humans. While God's goodness can only be known by analogy to human goodness, the two types of goodness correspond to each other. Others taught that universals such as goodness, beauty, unity, and humanity are merely concepts. Such scholars were called **nominalists**, because that maintained that universals exist in *name* only. While this debate sounds like a polite disagreement among scholars in the ivory towers of academia, the implications of these positions were profound. Arguably, nominalism implies that there is a categorical difference between our knowledge of the natural world and the reality of the supernatural world, and this implication separates heaven and earth, faith and reason.

While those who believed in the reality of universals saw a unity between the supernatural and natural worlds, the nominalists saw no intrinsic relationship. Nominalists argued that God is not constrained by human ideas of goodness or justice, but is completely free and unlimited. In this view, what we know about God is what we know from revelation, and God is certainly not captive to human concepts. Given nominalism, human ideas of morality are, from God's point of view, just as flawed as any human creation. The same could be said of church structure or even teachings, at least those not based exclusively on revelation. Nominalism also implied that forms of government are not fixed in heaven, but can be changed. As we will see, nominalism eventually supported the possibilities for reconfiguring church life and doctrine and rethinking political arrangements. Such transformations were later emphasized in the sixteenth century with the Protestant Reformation and the emergence of democracies in the West.

Within less than a century, the influence of Aquinas's great synthesis began to wane. The views of nominalist theologians, such as John Duns

Scotus (c. 1265–1308) and William of Ockham (1285–1347), became legitimate competitors. Certainly, these thinkers saw themselves as part of the same scholastic movement, and they too utilized scholastic philosophical categories in their theological projects. Nevertheless, they set the theological stage for separating faith and reason, revelation and philosophy. Prior to the Reformation, the intrinsic unity of faith and reason and assumptions about the divine mandate for church order, particularly the papacy, were central to Roman Catholic self-understanding. One might consider this the "Aquinas effect." In contrast, challenging the church's authority and divorcing natural reason from revelation became hallmarks of the Reformation. Ultimately, as the effects of the Reformation show, the debate concerning the status of universals was pivotal to this shift.

 ## CONCLUSIONS

Medieval life during the High and Late Middle Ages represented a great change from the Early Middle Ages. European culture was shifting dramatically, as was Christian piety. The growth of cities called for new political, economic, and social conventions, and academic learning became far more professional and intricate. None of this happened in a day or even a century, but the gradual shifts were unambiguous and ultimately dramatic. The patristic world of Basil and Augustine did not

have the cultural or perhaps imaginative resources to support the explosion of the kind of feminine piety that became standard during the High Middle Ages. And the world of Charlemagne would have scarcely recognized the culture of Paris or Cologne, or the widespread wealth that existed in those cities. Modern culture owes a great deal to the High and Late Middle Ages, a period that set the foundations for the key cultural structures and practices that characterize our world today.

SUMMARY QUESTIONS

- What were some of the ways that the transition toward a capitalist economy prompted religious and societal changes?
- What were some of the common characteristics of the religious institutions that formed as a reaction against capitalism?
- Why were some of the religious institutions that formed during this time viewed as a threat by the church? How did the church respond to them, and how did it justify its responses?
- Describe the evolution of education in medieval society up to scholasticism and mention

the factors and aims that directed this development.
- What characteristics have traditionally been considered feminine? How did attitudes toward these characteristics change during the Middle Ages? What impact did these shifts have on the religious language that was used at the time, especially the metaphors used in mystical descriptions?
- Describe in your own words the debate between nominalists and realists concerning universals. What implications did this debate have for larger societal structures?

DISCUSSION QUESTIONS

- How would you distinguish Dominican spirituality from Franciscan spirituality? Which of the two looks more attractive, and why?
- The author describes groups like the Waldensians and Cathars rising up in the Middle Ages. This ignited the Inquisition and suppression of heresy. Today we have a separation of church and state and widely believe in the primacy of the conscience where anyone can believe and speak out whatever theology one wants. How did the author defend the ideology of the medieval period as a contrast to today? Do you think that Christianity is better off with anyone representing Christianity in any way he or she sees fit?
- What assets do you find in using feminine imagery for God and Jesus? Is there anything disturbing about such imagery for you?

KEY TERMS

Abelard, Peter
Aquinas, Thomas
Beguines
Carthusians
Cathars
Catherine of Siena
Damian, Peter
Dominicans

Feudalism
Francis of Assisi
Franciscans
Gift economy
Guzmán, Dominic
Humiliati
Inquisition
Julian of Norwich

Lombard, Peter
Moses Maimonides
Nominalism
Premonstratensians
Profit economy
Stigmata
Waldensians

BIBLIOGRAPHY

- Augustine of Hippo. 1991. *Confessions*. Trans. Henry Chadwick. Oxford: Oxford University Press.
- Bernard of Clairvaux. 1987. *Bernard of Clairvaux: Selected Works*. Trans. G. R. Evans. New York: Paulist Press.
- Bynum, Caroline Walker. 1982. *Jesus as Mother: Studies in the Spirituality of the High Middle Ages*. Berkeley: University of California Press.
- Bynum, Caroline Walker. 1987. *Holy Feast and Holy Fast: The Religious Significance of Food to Medieval Women*. Berkeley: University of California Press.
- Catherine of Siena. 1980. *Catherine of Siena: The Dialogue*. Trans. Suzanne Noffke. New York: Paulist Press.
- Cook, William R., and Ronald Herzman. 2012. *The Medieval World View: An Introduction*. New York: Oxford University Press.
- Davies, Brian. 1992. *The Thought of Thomas Aquinas*. Oxford: Oxford University Press.
- Fatula, Mary Ann. 1987. *Catherine of Siena's Way*. Collegeville, MN: Michael Glazier.
- Francis and Clare of Assisi. 1982. *Francis and Clare: The Complete Works*. Trans. Regis Armstrong. New York: Paulist Press.
- Gregory of Nyssa. 1991. *The Life of Moses*. Trans. Everett Ferguson and Abraham Malberbe. New York: Paulist Press.
- Habig, Marion, ed. 1983. *St. Francis of Assisi: Omnibus of Sources*, 4th ed. Trans. Raphael Brown, Benen Fahy, Placid Hermann, Paul Oligny, Nesta de Robeck, and Leo Sherley-Price. Chicago: Franciscan Herald Press.
- Hadewijch. 1980. *Hadewijch: The Complete Works*. Trans. Columba Hart. New York: Paulist Press.
- Julian of Norwich. 1978. *Showings*. Trans. Edmund Colledge and James Walsh. New York: Paulist Press.
- Lambert, Malcolm. 2002. *Medieval Heresy: Popular Movements from the Gregorian Reform to the Reformation*. Malden, UK: Blackwell.

- McGrath, Alister. 2013. *Christian History: An Introduction*. Malden, UK: Wiley-Blackwell.
- Pieper, Josef. 2001. *Scholasticism: Personalities and Problems of Medieval Philosophy*. South Bend, IN: St. Augustine's Press.
- Southern, R. W. 1970. *Western Society and the Church in the Middle Ages*. New York: Penguin.
- Tyerman, Christopher. 2006. *God's War: A New History of the Crusades*. Cambridge: Harvard University Press.
- Ward, Benedicta. 1987. *Miracles and the Medieval Mind: Theory, Record and Event, 1000–1215*, rev. ed. Philadelphia: University of Pennsylvania Press.

NOTES

1. Simon Tugwell, "The Mendicants: The Spirituality of the Dominicans," in *Christian Spirituality: High Middle Ages and Reformation*, ed. Jill Raitt (New York: Crossroad, 1989), 23.
2. *Summa Theologiae* 2a.2ae.q.83.
3. Francis and Clare of Assisi, *Francis and Clare*, 154.
4. Habig, *St. Francis of Assisi*, 730–731.
5. Ibid., 130–131.
6. Gregory of Nyssa, *Life of Moses*, 55.
7. Augustine of Hippo, *Confessions*, 174.
8. Catherine of Siena, *Catherine of Siena*, 54.
9. Cited in Bynum, *Jesus as Mother*, 114.
10. Julian of Norwich, *Showings*, 52, 54, 60.
11. Cited in Bynum, *Jesus as Mother*, 117.
12. Bernard of Clairvaux, *Bernard of Clairvaux*, 214–215.
13. Hadewijch, *Hadewijch*, 66.

The Renaissance

Timeline

1265–1321 CE	Life of Dante Alighieri, whose poetry anticipates the Renaissance
1309–1377 CE	Avignon papacy in France
1320–1384 CE	Life of John Wycliffe, English church reformer
c. 1350 CE	Beginnings of the Renaissance
1372–1415 CE	Life of Jan Hus, reformer burned at the stake by order of the Council of Constance
1440 CE	Invention of the printing press
1466–1536 CE	Life of Erasmus of Rotterdam, Renaissance leader

WHAT TO EXPECT

While the High and Late Middle Ages represent dramatic shifts in culture and religion, nothing comes close to the dramatic change that occurred during the Renaissance period. It is as though these medieval periods formed the roots that ultimately came to fruition in Renaissance life. This chapter details some of the most important shifts of the Renaissance. Of particular note is the celebration of classical culture that during this period was appropriated into a new kind of humanism, one that celebrated the glory of God through human achievement. Art and language came to have power in ways that they hadn't before. The papacy played an influential role in the Renaissance but also showed itself particularly morally vulnerable, as popes regularly looked like wealthy power players rather than spiritual leaders. This chapter also describes early reform voices whose legacy would only reveal itself during the time of the Reformation, when the Western church broke up.

FROM THE LATE MIDDLE AGES TO THE RENAISSANCE

Dante Alighieri (1265–1321) so profoundly impressed the Italian world with his poetry, particularly with his *Divine Comedy*, a three-book meditation on hell (*Inferno*), purgatory (*Purgatorio*), and heaven (*Paradiso*), that the Italian poet Petrarch (1304–1374) proclaimed it represented a *renascita* (rebirth) of poetry. Later nineteenth-century scholars used this word in its French form, *Renaissance*, to describe the new cultural phenomenon. By the fourteenth century Europe was beginning to undergo a massive cultural shift, leaving behind the Late Middle Ages and entering into the **Renaissance**. Large cultural shifts never have exact dates that denote the clear change from one form of society to another, from one set of assumptions to a wholly different set, and these periods were no exception. When the Middle Ages end and the Renaissance begins involve a series of gradual shifts. Dante was not a Renaissance poet, but he was an early voice of change, one that drew on both classical and medieval insights to produce a new perspective.

While this shift was gradual and marked with a great deal of continuity, there are markers that illustrate and condition the move from a medieval worldview to a Renaissance one. One such marker was the West's increased experience of Byzantine and Muslim scholarship and the rediscovery of Greek philosophy, which led to an exponential growth in scholarship in the West. Another marker was the burgeoning middle class of merchants, whose demand for an education inspired initiatives to make learning accessible and books available. Both of these developments were noted in Chapters Eleven and Twelve. There were assuredly other factors as well that prepared the way for the Renaissance and allowed for it to happen. Wealthy families in Europe, particularly in Italy, believed that it was their duty to use some of their fortune to support education and the arts. In many ways, they financed the Renaissance. Further, the Byzantine

Empire at this time was fading and rapidly losing territory to the Ottoman Turks. As a result, scholars from the East regularly emigrated to the West. Eventually, by the time of the fall of Constantinople in 1453, the West enjoyed many riches of the Byzantine brain trust.

Two centuries of encounters with Byzantine and Islamic scholarship introduced the West to the great classical thinkers of the ancient age. The rallying cry of the Renaissance was *Ad Fontes* (To the sources!). These sources were Greek and Roman classics that had long been lost to the West. To the degree that medieval scholars read ancient texts, they had little sense that there was much of a cultural difference between that period and their own. Of course, they realized that these works came from another time, but they did not imagine that time as a radically different culture. It was in the Renaissance that scholars recognized the classical world as very dissimilar from their own, with unique cultural assumptions. They were able to compare their cultural perspective with that of another and in so doing absorb these alternative values. In short, the classics allowed them to forge a different view of humanity and the world.

The medieval world emphasized the community much more than the individual, and the next life much more than this one. As noted in the previous chapter, one of the great heroes of the medieval period was Francis of Assisi, a poor, simple saint who fasted assiduously, placed great importance on submission and humility, and understood the gospel as the joy of being little. He identified with the figure of Christ who lowered himself in the incarnation, and named his order *Friars Minor* (Little Brothers). In contrast, the Renaissance world celebrated learned men, explorers, artists, poets, and architects. In this view, God was glorified by the full development of the human person, and the exaltation of the individual hero reflected great possibilities God had intended for man. Francis preached a simple message in simple terms. The Renaissance exemplar spoke with the eloquence of Cicero, the ancient Roman master of rhetoric.

A TRANSFORMATION OF CULTURE

One of the great shifts that corresponded with the transition from the Middle Ages to the Renaissance was political. The medieval world was, in part, a feudal one, in which Europe was a patchwork of small principalities (ruled by princes) and duchies (ruled by dukes), with little central power. In theory, much of the continent was unified by the political authority of the Holy Roman emperor, but in practice there was little centralized power. Chapter Twelve noted that as trade and agriculture advanced, cities became much larger, and many feudal assumptions concerning rights and responsibilities began to fade. Rulers ejected many peasants from their lands and no longer needed the coterie of knights and vassals they had once required.

During the Renaissance, powerful monarchs began to control larger regions, particularly in Spain, France, and England. The feudal territories of France, originally ruled by relatively independent nobles, were united into a single kingdom between the mid-fifteenth and the mid-sixteenth century. English monarchical power was strengthened by the Tudor kings Henry VII (r. 1485–1509) and Henry VIII (r. 1509–1547). In Spain, Ferdinand of Castile married Isabella of Aragon in 1469, ultimately uniting two kingdoms into one with considerable power. In 1492, after centuries of conflict between Spanish Christians and Spanish Muslims (Moors), Spain succeeded in capturing the last Muslim Spanish city of Granada, completing the reconquest (*reconquista*) of Spain from the Moors. Tragically, and in contrast with the more tolerant Muslim rule, Spanish Jews and Muslims were forced to either convert or emigrate. While unjust, even perhaps by that day's own standard, this move allowed the fully Catholic Spain to become a center of absolute unity and even religious revival.

In contrast to a regenerating Europe and powerful Catholic Church, the Byzantines were on a spiral downward. The Byzantine Empire had been eroding for centuries as a result of Islamic conquests. Most Christians there lived in areas controlled or threatened by Muslim rule. The Orthodox Church continued to operate, and did so on the ancient model of bishops and patriarchs with spiritual authority over their realms. But the imagined perfect union of one empire and one faith would no longer fit.

Consequently, the Eastern church began to look inward and backward, stressing the soul's relationship to God, rather than the culture's participation in the kingdom of God. Perhaps the greatest proponent of this emphasis was Symeon the New Theologian (949–1022), who emphasized mystical contemplation as the virtually exclusive concern of the soul. Among other writings, he composed many hymns (collected as the *Hymns of Divine Love*) for Christians to sing, almost all of which focused on the inner life. Byzantine Christians continued to look to the patristics for their inspiration. The East's stagnation and reversion to the patristics became a tremendous boon for the West. Eastern intellectuals emigrated to the West in droves, and they brought with them ancient texts long ignored or forgotten in the West.

In 1397, Manuel Chrysoloras came to Florence from Constantinople and began teaching Greek at the university in Florence. He, along with other Byzantine scholars, infused Italians with enthusiasm for the language and other elements of classical Greek knowledge. When Plato's *Dialogues* were translated into Latin in the fifteenth century, they became the basis for the recovery of Christian Neoplatonism, which had been neglected for centuries.

No innovation spurred on the Renaissance more than the invention of the printing press by **Johannes Gutenberg** in 1440. The Middle Ages, with its rapidly developing universities and burgeoning literate middle class, saw a soaring demand for books. Books at that time were rare and expensive. Europe had already developed paper, but texts had to either be copied by hand or produced from wooden block print. The latter was more efficient, but not by much. In this method, publishers engraved pages on a wooden block with knife and gouge. They then put ink on the blocks and pressed these down on paper. Each block represented a single sheet and was both time-consuming and costly to produce, as it could only be used for that page. Multiple editions were made, of course, but making a 100-page book involved the painstaking carving of 100 different blocks. Gutenberg's innovation was the development of moveable type, in which letters were made from metal and placed in a stamp. The stamp was then inked and pressed on a piece of paper. Again, multiple editions could be made from these stamps, but the advantage—and it was great—was that these metal letters could then be reused for future pages. It is estimated that 6 million books were printed between 1450 and 1500, more than were produced over the previous 1,000 years, and at far less cost. Europe was, comparatively speaking, flooded with books.

HUMANISM AND THE DISCOVERY OF THE INDIVIDUAL

Historian Jacob Burckhardt (1818–1897) argued that the Renaissance created *individuals*, that is, people began to see themselves less as a part of a static medieval world where community dominated and more as those who could excel on their own merits. His thesis has been widely accepted. Something of this shift was noted in Chapter Twelve in the discussion of the mass movement of people to cities and their reinvention of themselves as tradesmen, merchants, and even religious virtuosos. A corollary to this new emphasis on the individual was the advance of **humanism**. Today, humanism tends to be equated with secularism or even atheism. It was nothing of the kind in the Renaissance period. Rather, the term represented two things. The first was the particular enthusiasm for the liberal arts, or the *humanae litterae*, particularly philosophy, literature, and rhetoric, with the latter being the art of speaking and persuasion. The scholar who was particularly enthusiastic about these subjects was called a *humanista*. Second, and more importantly, humanism was

the celebration of the human subject. The Renaissance is known for its **anthropocentricism**, or focus on the human. People at the time did not view this focus as an insult to God, but a celebration of God's glory in his greatest creation.

In 1486, Giovanni Pico della Mirandola, one of the great voices of the Italian Renaissance, gave a famous lecture called the "Oration on the Dignity of Humanity." It was a manifesto for humanism. In contrast to the rather stilted and flat Latin of the Middle Ages, his lecture was given in highly polished, elegant, classical Latin. His main theme was that humans have the capacity to determine their own destiny. God has not only infused human beings with great possibilities, but mandated humans to excel. Mirandola's oration was received with great acclaim, and his lecture's text was disseminated widely. It fit the times, which contrasted mightily with the medieval assumption of a fixed world where traditional authorities and class structure could not be challenged.

Humanist Renaissance thinkers, artists, poets, and musicians drew widely on the classical world. Mirandola brought ancient works to the University of Paris and lectured widely on the newly translated texts of the famous ancient Egyptian thinker Hermes Trismegistus (*Corpus Hermeticum*), as well as the ancient *Chaldean*

FIGURE 13-1   Botticelli's fifteenth-century *Birth of Venus* shows the goddess Venus emerging from the sea. Renaissance artists and intellectuals drew on ancient themes to highlight new cultural possibilities.

Oracles and *Orphic Hymns*. No longer was it unacceptable to draw on classical imagery, pagan religion, and even pagan deities. Consider, for example, one of Sandro Botticelli's (1445–1510) most famous paintings, *The Birth of Venus*.

Botticelli, along with other artists, worked under the patronage of Lorenzo de Medici, a member of one of the wealthiest families of Florence. Botticelli and others took pagan themes from the classical world and reinvented them along humanist lines. The priest and scholar Marsilio Ficino (1433–1499) celebrated Venus as a reflection of the Christian life. In his view, the goddess had all the virtues of *humanitas*, such as love, dignity, and modesty. Ficino interpreted the myth of the birth of Venus as a description of the birth of the spiritual faculty of the soul. Mediating the intellect and material world, this spiritual faculty was able to unite heaven and earth. He wrote: "For Humanity herself is a nymph of excellent comeliness born of heaven and more than others beloved by God all highest. Her soul and mind are Love and Charity, her eyes Dignity and Magnanimity, the hands Liberality and Magnificence, the feet Comeliness and Modesty. The whole, then, is Temperance and Honesty, Charm and Splendor. Oh, what exquisite beauty!"[1]

SOUTHERN RENAISSANCE

TEXTS AND THE POWER OF WORDS

Much has been written distinguishing the northern and southern Renaissance. The reality is that they differed only in emphasis and were characterized by a great deal of convergence. Still, there is something valuable in distinguishing these emphases. The Renaissance began in the northern Italian cities of Florence, Rome, and Venice. It was primarily concerned with the recovery of Latin and Greek literature, art, sculpture, and architecture. With regard to politics and literature, the first-century BCE politician and philosopher Cicero was perhaps the most important figure. In 1421, Cicero's

treatise on rhetoric was rediscovered in the cathedral library at Lodi in northern Italy. Civic humanists in Florence, a city-state modestly based on a republican model, saw his vision of political order as their guide. More broadly, humanists saw him as the ideal model for persuasive Latin prose. Humanists loved words. For them, words did not simply relate information. Rather, they had intrinsic power when elegantly expressed. They literally moved people to wisdom. Renaissance Europe embraced this new emphasis on rhetoric with enthusiasm. In 1488, a visiting Italian humanist came to the University of Salamanca to lecture on the Roman poet Juvenal's *Second Satire*. The throng of students who came to hear him was so dense that, after his two-and-a-half-hour lecture, he had to be passed bodily over their heads just to leave the auditorium.

Renaissance literary studies also produced the earliest versions of **literary criticism**, a method of scrutinizing texts. Renaissance scholars had three advantages over their medieval peers. First, they had advanced knowledge of classical Latin and Greek. Second, they simply had access to a far greater number of texts and were beginning to search for the best manuscript traditions. By comparing a number of different manuscripts, they could see where copyists had added glosses to the text, or where marginal notes had found their way into subsequent manuscripts. Finally, as noted, they had a greater sense of the difference between the classical world and the medieval one. Words, phrases, political themes, and ideas came to be understood as having a history, and Renaissance scholars eagerly learned when and where these came from. The most famous example of this new literary criticism was the exposure of the *Donation of Constantine*, noted in Chapter Eleven, as a fraud. Lorenzo Valla (1407–1457) used his extensive knowledge of classical Latin to show that the document, which for centuries popes had used to buttress their claims to temporal rule and religious primacy, simply could not have been written by Constantine in the fourth century.

The language and political assumptions of the text, Valla found, were medieval and not in use until the eighth century.

ART AND ARCHITECTURE

The glory of the Middle Ages was the Gothic cathedral. These churches boasted grand spires that stressed the greatness and transcendence of God. Worshippers entering a Gothic cathedral were caught up in the worship that went heavenward. The Renaissance period, in contrast, drew on ancient Roman and Greek thought that emphasized symmetry, proportion, and geometry. Instead of great spires, Renaissance churches used semi-circular arches and hemispherical domes. Architects, particularly those from Italy, created forms that expressed their purpose.

Very few medieval artists or architects are known. Because the world was directed toward eternity and not personal honor, their names and fame were not considered important. In contrast, Renaissance artists and architects are clearly known, as the Renaissance valued individuality and emphasized accomplishment and glory—ancient values, not medieval ones. Consider such greats as Michelangelo, Raphael, and Leonardo da Vinci. Under the patronage of wealthy families, Renaissance artists decorated city squares with the statues of great men. Renaissance art also produced something otherwise rare: the individual portrait.

New interest in the natural world as revealed through art and science characterized the Renaissance spirit. The discovery of perspective denotes the importance Renaissance artists placed on the ability to depict the world and persons with accuracy. Leonardo da Vinci dissected over thirty corpses in order to better understand human anatomy for his paintings and sculptures. Landscape painting had virtually disappeared in the Middle Ages, but now it became the rage.

The Renaissance period was also the age of the great explorers. Portuguese sailors explored the east coast of Africa in the mid-fifteenth century, and by 1498 they had sailed around the Cape of Good Hope to reach India. Columbus discovered the Americas in 1492, opening up commercial, colonizing, and missionary possibilities. Not surprisingly, cartography (mapmaking) developed dramatically. In contrast to

FIGURE 13-3   Leonardo da Vinci's *Mona Lisa.*

FIGURE 13-2   Begun in 1506 and completed in 1626, St. Peter's Basilica reflects Renaissance architecture and values.

the Middle Ages, during which accuracy often gave way to theological themes, even in maps, accuracy now assumed the highest value.

THE AVIGNON PAPACY, CONCILIARISM, AND RENAISSANCE POPES

One cannot get a complete understanding of the times or the Protestant Reformation that followed without recognizing a curious development in the papacy in the fourteenth century and the response of Roman Catholic bishops to it. In 1305, a large faction of French cardinals elected Clement V as pope. Rome was at the time a dangerous place for the pope, and Clement, surely with the support of King Philip of France, moved the papal court to Avignon in 1309. This move, which was supposed to be temporary, lasted through the reigns of six more popes, until 1377. Given that the feudal assumptions of the Middle Ages were waning and nation-states were emerging, it looked to all of Christendom that the papacy was in the pocket of the French and their national interests. To make the situation even worse, these Avignon popes lived lavishly, and the funds they used to do so were derived from the very practices popes Leo IX and

Gregory VII had tried to reform: nepotism and simony. The popes were giving church offices to their family members, friends, and often the highest bidder.

By the middle of the fourteenth century, European Christendom was pressuring the pope to return to Rome. Pope Gregory XI did move the papal court back to Rome in 1377, but he died quickly after. Pope Urban XI succeeded Gregory and began to reform the papal curia (the College of Cardinals). Many of the French cardinals balked: claiming that they had been pressured to elect Urban, they withdrew their vote and elected a competing pope, Clement VII, who quickly reconstituted the Avignon papacy. Urban did not back down and remained in Rome, meaning that the church effectively had two claimed popes, Urban in Rome and Clement in Avignon. For almost forty years there would be two competing papacies. The decision as to which pope to support fell along political lines. France and its allies of Scotland, Navarre, Castile, and Naples supported the Avignon pope, while England and its allies of Scandinavia, northern Italy, Flanders, Ireland, Portugal, Hungary, and Poland supported the papacy in Rome.

In 1409, a group of bishops met in Pisa, Italy, to settle the matter, electing Pope Alexander V to

FIGURE 13-4 When Rome became unsafe, Pope Clement V moved the papacy to Avignon, France. Living lavishly there, the papacy would not return to Rome for seventy-two years.

replace both the Avignon pope and the Roman pope; the existing popes, however, refused to abdicate. Now the church had three claimants to the papacy. The bishops then met yet again in the **Council of Constance** (1414–1418). At this gathering, they declared that councils themselves had authority directly from Christ and that everyone, including the bishop of Rome, was subject to it. This doctrine became known as **conciliarism**, that is, the belief that councils hold the ultimate authority. On the basis of conciliarism, the council deposed all three popes and elected Martin V (r. 1417–1431) to replace them all.

Conciliarism would not last in the Roman Catholic Church. During the Council of Basel (1431–1449), bishops appealed to the principle of conciliarism in order to reform the church. Pope Eugene IV balked and removed his support from the council. In 1460, Pope Pius II condemned conciliarism insofar as it taught that councils have superior authority to that of the papacy. The problem was never really solved well. The Catholic Church did reject the position that councils could trump the pope, but it also has taught as recently as the Second Vatican Council (1962–1965) that, together with the pope, bishops as a collective exercise "supreme and full power over the universal Church."[2] Does this mean that something of conciliarism prevailed? This is hard to say, as the Second Vatican Council also asserted (in the same paragraph!) that "the Roman Pontiff, by reason of his office as Vicar of Christ, namely, and as pastor of the entire Church, has full, supreme and universal power over the whole church, a power which he can always exercise unhindered."[3] Catholic theologians have widely questioned how both the college of bishops *and* the pope personally can have supreme power and authority. The problem has really never been solved theologically, although canon law did solve it juridically: "The bishop of the Church of Rome . . . is head of the college of bishops, the Vicar of Christ and the Pastor of the Universal Church on earth; therefore in virtue of his office

he enjoys supreme, full, immediate and universal ordinary power in the Church, which he can always freely exercise" (Canon 331). For all practical purposes, any spirit of conciliarism has died in the Catholic Church.

As has been noted, popes were often members of wealthy, powerful Italian families, particularly those from Florence and Rome. Politics, power, and influence were certainly reasons for this, but one need not be completely cynical about the choices of church leaders during this time. The papacy was a massively important cultural phenomenon, and it only made sense to both medieval and Renaissance cultures to choose popes from among the most talented, educated, and elite sources. It was also the case that popes were temporal rulers, that is, they were monarchs of central Italy, the Papal States. Popes at the time were enthusiastic supporters of the Renaissance. Like members of other wealthy families, they spent their own personal wealth to support humanist learning, art, and the building of magnificent churches. They also spent church monies to fund these projects. Pope Nicholas V (r. 1447–1455) collected over 5,000 books to begin the Vatican Library, the largest collection of texts in Europe, and still one of the greatest repositories of learning in the world. Pope Julius II (r. 1503–1513) commissioned works from Michelangelo and Raphael, and began the rebuilding of St. Peter's Basilica, using designs from such Renaissance greats as Donatello, Michelangelo, Maderno, and Bernini. This masterpiece is the most renowned work of Renaissance architecture and remained the largest church in the world until the construction of Notre-Dame de la Paix, built in the Ivory Coast's capital of Yamoussoukro between 1985 and 1989. The rebuilding of St. Peter's Basilica would continue under successive popes, only to open fully in 1626. Popes literally rebuilt the city of Rome, making it the center of the Italian Renaissance, and the Vatican Museum one of the greatest museums of the West.

Renaissance popes in fact looked more like princes and wealthy patrons than universal pastors. They were far more concerned with high culture and its development than with addressing any needed reform of the church. Further, their lifestyle corresponded to that of other wealthy patrons and power players. Pope Paul III (r. 1534–1549) was an exception to this rule. Certainly he was a Renaissance pope who enjoyed his wealth, but he was also concerned with church life and attempted to carry out reform. He appointed a number of reform-minded churchmen to the College of Cardinals and created a commission to recommend reforms for the church. At the time, simony, absentee bishops, a lack of celibacy, and lax faith were rampant within the church. The cardinals' report revealed many serious problems that needed to be addressed. Pope Paul did institute a few of the recommendations but neglected to follow through on a full-fledged program of reform of the church.

NORTHERN RENAISSANCE

As noted earlier, the difference between the southern and northern Renaissance can be exaggerated. Renaissance art flourished not only in Italy, but also in France and Flanders. Further, the focus on classical texts was a pan-European phenomenon. The decisive difference between the two movements was in their emphasis. Renaissance thinkers in northern Europe focused their knowledge of Greek and Latin on study of the Bible and church fathers, with a particular emphasis on reforming the church based on biblical and patristic ideals.

The greatest exemplar of the northern Renaissance is **Erasmus of Rotterdam** (1466–1536), who was born in modern-day Holland. His parents were not legally married, as his father was a priest. At the time, priestly celibacy was church law in the West, but it was often disregarded, as a number of priests had common-law wives. Erasmus was given the highest education available, being schooled in monastic or semi-monastic schools. In 1492, he was ordained a priest. Shortly after his ordination, he was offered the post of

FIGURE 13-5 Erasmus of Rotterdam (1466–1536) was one of the great Renaissance intellectuals, advocating reform via lay piety.

secretary to the bishop of Cambrai in France. With the support of his bishop, he continued his studies at the University of Paris, which was by now well under the influence of Renaissance humanism. Erasmus's career took him from Paris to Leuven (Belgium), Cambridge (England), and Basel (Switzerland). His stay in Cambridge infused him with the desire to master Greek, which he had studied earlier in his education, for the purpose of advanced study in the New Testament. Finally, he received a doctor of divinity degree from Turin University in Italy.

While Erasmus wrote a number of books, his most influential were *Handbook for the Christian Soldier* (1503), *In Praise of Folly* (1509), and a critical Latin translation of the Bible from the best Greek manuscript sources of the day (1516). In his *In Praise of Folly*, Erasmus ridicules the pretentiousness and worldliness of the church and society. It was a lampoon that won him wide respect. His *Handbook for the Christian Soldier* was initially published in 1503 and then reprinted in 1509, but it wasn't until its third printing in 1515 that it made a tremendous impact on Christendom. In this classic, Erasmus develops the thesis that the church can only be reformed by the laity, and only if they return to the wisdom of the patristics and scripture. Daily reading and meditating on scripture, he argues, are the keys to a new lay piety. The Christian soldier he has in mind is the average lay person, who would fight for inner purification and outer reform. The Renaissance's insistence on the power of words is nowhere more evident than in Erasmus's contention that the Bible itself has the power to move the soul to greater love of God and neighbor. What is fascinating about this book is that it makes little reference to the traditional medieval piety addressed in Chapter Twelve. There is no mention of shrines or pilgrimages, and little about saints. In fact, his book challenges many medieval practices as little more than superstitions. Also fascinatingly, his book's version of Christian piety fails to even mention the sacraments or church institution. Faith, for him, is a matter of the individual's heart and mind—an interior piety.

Erasmus's critical edition of the Bible was also challenging to the church institution. The official language of the Western church was Latin, which also served as the language for all academic study throughout Europe. The church used the Latin translation of the Bible produced by Jerome (347–420). Jerome was a great intellectual of his day, and when he emigrated from Rome to Palestine, he took to learning Hebrew along with deepening his understanding of ancient Greek. The Latin version of the Bible he produced was known as the **Vulgate**, and for the Western church the Vulgate *was* the Bible.

Returning to the best available Greek manuscripts of the Bible, Renaissance scholars encountered errors or problems in the Vulgate translation. Of particular importance were translation decisions that the church used to defend some of its theology. For example, in the Vulgate's First Letter of John one reads, "For there are three that

bear record in heaven, the Father, the Word, and the Holy Spirit" (5:7). Traditionally, this was used as a proof text for the doctrine of the Trinity. Of course, other Trinitarian texts might be drawn on for support, but this was believed to be the clearest. Erasmus found that these words did not exist in the Greek, and, further, that they had been added to the Vulgate at least 400 years after Jerome. Another problem was that some of Jerome's translation decisions involved word choices that had changed meaning in Latin as the language progressed. In Mark's Gospel, Jesus's first words are: "The time is fulfilled, and the kingdom of God has come near; repent, and believe in the Good news" (1:15). The Greek word for "repent" is *metanoeite*, which means "reverse one's mind." The connotation here is a moral

FIGURE 13-6 Sculpture of Moses, depicted with horns. The Latin Vulgate mistranslated Exodus 34; instead of reading that Moses's face was shining, Jerome thought the passage stated that he had horns.

reversal, so "repent" is a good translation. The Vulgate, however, reads *paenitenimi*, "do penance," which the church understood as mandating the use of the sacrament of penance. Further, when the Greek New Testament uses the term *mysterion*, Jerome translated this as *sacramentum*. While potentially accurate in Jerome's time, this translation was assumed by the later church to refer directly to the sacraments or rites of the church, which it could not have been originally intended to mean.

One of the most amusing parts of the Vulgate is an episode in Exodus 34, which describes Moses coming down from Mount Sinai with the Ten Commandments. Exodus says that Moses's face was shining. Jerome, however, mistook two Hebrew particles and turned the description into Moses wearing horns. Medieval (and even Renaissance) art regularly depicted this important biblical event with Moses having horns coming out from the sides of his head.

⊚ VOICES OF REFORM

Some late medieval and Renaissance churchmen were also intent on reform. One great early reformer was **John Wycliffe** (1320–1384), a priest and Oxford scholar. Wycliffe challenged clergy to live in common and under the auspices of the kind of evangelical poverty, noted in Chapter Twelve as the Premonstratensians. For Wycliffe, this lifestyle should not be restricted to *some* expressions of the clerical state, but should be embraced by all priests and bishops. Wycliffe also believed that the Bible should be available to all literate Christians. He consequently translated the Bible into Middle English and disseminated copies among those sympathetic to his cause.

Wycliffe imagined the true church as represented by an invisible body of believers and not every baptized member of the church. In itself, this was nothing new. Augustine also had argued in the Donatist controversy that the field of the church had both weeds and wheat, which God would separate on the last day (Matt. 13:24–30). Wycliffe's innovation was the belief that the true church was represented *only* in this invisible body, not in priests, bishops, or the pope. In fact, he claimed, those churchmen who were not part of the invisible body had no authority over real Christians. This was seen as nothing short of a renunciation of the institution of the church and its authority. Wycliffe's theological positions on some articles of faith were equally controversial. For example, he argued against **transubstantiation** of the Eucharistic elements of bread and wine. On this, the church taught that while the physical matter of the bread and wine remained just bread and wine, their essence (which Aristotle called "substance") was changed into the body and blood of Christ. Wycliffe argued that Christ was *mystically* present in the bread and wine, but that they themselves did not change. Although Wycliffe died thirty years before the Council of Constance, the council condemned him and his teachings. His body was then dug up, burned, and dumped into the River Swift.

Another reforming figure was **Jan Hus** (1369–1415), the rector of the University of Prague in Bohemia. Hus was more interested in reforming the clergy than in any particular theological issue. One sees in his sermons, however, some themes aligned to Wycliffe, including challenging the authority of the church. Like Wycliffe, Hus believed the church was under the authority of scripture and could be criticized to the degree that it failed to correspond with the scriptural witness. He publicly railed against the pope. Although he did not embrace Wycliffe's notion of the Eucharist, he did challenge transubstantiation. For him, Christ dwelled literally in the bread and wine, but along with the bread and wine. Like Wycliffe, Hus also translated the Bible into the vernacular—in this case, Czech—in order to make it more accessible to the people. Finally, he railed against the practice of indulgences, whereby the church believed it had the authority to remit the temporal punishment associated with sins, an idea that will be further discussed in Chapter Fourteen.

One unfortunate part of Hus's controversial public life is that he, along with most Bohemian

(Czech) Catholics, supported Alexander V, who was elected pope at the Council of Pisa during the Avignon papacy crisis. Alexander was ultimately deposed and his supporters placed under suspicion. Hus was summoned to the Council of Constance in 1414. He had been promised safe passage there and back, but the bishops reneged on that promise, and he was arrested. Ultimately, when he refused to recant his positions, he was tried as a heretic, found guilty, and burned at the stake. The Bohemian church was outraged and rebelled. The West fought crusades against the "Hussites," but to no avail. By the mid-1430s radical and moderate Hussites were fighting among themselves. Eventually the moderate Hussites suppressed the more radical wing and won a concession from Rome that allowed them to worship in the vernacular. Now Bohemian Catholics would have two different "rites," one in Czech and another in Latin, both under the same bishop.

A further reforming voice of note was Girolamo Savonarola (1452–1498), a Dominican priest who came to Florence in 1490 and initiated an intense preaching program that challenged the worldliness of society and church, and, indeed, some of the values of the Renaissance. Ironically, he had come to Florence at the invitation and with the support of Lorenzo de Medici, a great supporter of the Renaissance and member of a family that would eventually produce four popes: Leo X (1513–1521), Clement XII (1523–1534), Pius IV (1559–1565), and Leo XI (1605). The Renaissance was premised on wealthy patrons and the celebration of the human person. Savonarola would have none of this. He attacked what he perceived as the evils of his time, especially excessive wealth and power, thus offending clergy, secular authorities, and the wealthy patrons of cultural renewal. Savonarola's church, however, was packed. In 1495, King Charles VIII of France invaded Florence and made Savonarola ruler of the city. Almost immediately Savonarola called for a "Bonfire of the Vanities," to which Florentine citizens voluntarily brought items he identified

as associated with immorality, particularly vanity. They threw their mirrors, jewelry, books, and works of art into a pile at the center of the city square, where they were burned in a great bonfire.

The state of religious fervor in Florence would quickly wane and within just three years of Savonarola's leadership and perpetual ranting against extravagance, the people of Florence rebelled. Pope Alexander VI, a member of the powerful Borgia family and a patron of the arts, condemned Savonarola as a heretic. The people of Florence were delighted. They arrested him and two of his associates and had them burned at the stake at the very site where the bonfire had earlier stood.

Spain was another site of reform. After Ferdinand and Isabella united Spain, they instituted a rigorous program of reform of all religious monastic and ministerial orders, such as the Franciscans and Dominicans. The penalty for opposing reform was high: those who resisted had their property confiscated and sold, with the proceeds going to the building of hospitals and schools, and to address the needs of the poor. One of the great figures of reform was Cardinal **Ximenes de Cisneros** (1436–1517). Ximenes founded the University of Alcalá and made it one of the great universities of Europe, particularly in the study of scripture. Under his guidance, scholars there produced the first polyglot Bible, in which Hebrew, Greek, Latin, and, in some cases, Aramaic were set side by side in columns. Ximenes carried out a strict reform of monasteries and clergy, especially the Franciscans, an order he himself had joined while a high-ranking priest in his diocese. He eventually served as regent of the Castilian state when Ferdinand died and until Ferdinand's son Charles was of age to rule.

Another reform movement among the clergy was advanced in southern Europe. This was the formation of the **oratory**, an association of priests who committed themselves to common prayer and mutual support while they discussed and tried to institute reform. The most famous of these groups was the Oratory of Divine Love (*Divino Amore*), founded in Rome around 1517. A new religious order emerged out of this oratory, the Theatines, founded by four priests. One of these, Cajetan, would be canonized as a saint, and another, Giovanni Pietro Carafa, would become Pope Paul IV. The mission of the Theatines was to reform the clergy and reinfuse

piety among the faithful. As noted previously, Pope Paul III (r. 1534–1549) was enthusiastic about reform. He appointed a number of reformers to be part of the College of Cardinals, all of whom were members of the Oratory of Divine Love. In the end, however, his reform efforts were modest. A Renaissance agenda was, for him, more imperative.

CONCLUSIONS

The Renaissance represents one of the greatest cultural shifts in European history. It was a wildly fascinating time, when society and even the human person were envisioned anew. In some sense, it represents a rejection of the past. Old sureties were no longer so secure. The Latin Bible came to be seen as a problem, and the temporal claims of the papacy did not hold up. The ancient past was viewed as different from the present, and these differences mattered, as they allowed medieval cultural assumptions to be challenged. Even views about humanity were reconsidered. The heroes of the Renaissance were scholars and explorers, not mendicants. In

another sense, however, this period represents the crown of the Middle Ages. The medieval development of a profit economy came to full fruition in the Renaissance, allowing wealthy merchants to finance massive projects in art and architecture. The burgeoning middle class of the medieval period became the cornerstone for widespread education and learning in the Renaissance. And the medieval expressions of such greats as Dante became a consistent aspect of Renaissance culture. As will be clear in the next chapter, the Renaissance also provided the conditions for far-reaching reform that would ultimately overwhelm the Western church.

SUMMARY QUESTIONS

- The start of the Renaissance is not marked by a single event. List and briefly explain several markers and causes of the Renaissance that are described in this chapter.
- A feature of the Renaissance is its shift away from the values that were held by medieval society. Briefly explain individualism, humanism, and anthropocentrism, and what these meant for the Renaissance worldview.
- One marker of the Renaissance is the beginning of literary criticism. What developments made

criticism possible, and what were the methods that were used to conduct literary criticism? Of particular importance in this project was the Bible. How was the Vulgate challenged by literary criticism?
- The Renaissance included some reforming voices in the church that were important forerunners for the Reformation. What criticisms of institutionalized Christianity were made by Wycliffe, Hus, and Savonarola?

DISCUSSION QUESTIONS

- As noted in this chapter, the Middle Ages can be distinguished from the Renaissance by the shift in focus from the community to the

individual. What are some of the assets and liabilities of such a shift?

- Renaissance popes were responsible for much of the architectural glory of Rome, some of which was achieved at their own expense. Given that they also lived lavishly, do you think that their witness of Christianity was basically admirable or basically scandalous?

- The pope moved the papacy to Avignon, France, because Rome was a dangerous place to live for the pope, and he risked assassination. Eventually, this move proved disastrous for the papacy and its spiritual legitimacy. But do you think that the pope *initially* acted wisely to move? Why or why not?

KEY TERMS

Alighieri, Dante
Anthropocentrism
Conciliarism
Council of Constance
Erasmus of Rotterdam

Gutenberg, Johannes
Humanism
Hus, Jan
Literary criticism
Oratory

Renaissance
Transubstantiation
Vulgate
Wycliffe, John
Ximenes de Cisneros

BIBLIOGRAPHY

- Bossy, John. 1985. *Christianity in the West: 1400–1700*. Oxford: Oxford University Press.
- Colish, Marcia. 1997. *Medieval Foundations of the Western Intellectual Tradition: 400–1000*. New Haven, CT: Yale University Press.
- Kraye, Jill, ed. 1996. *The Cambridge Companion to Renaissance Humanism*. Cambridge: Cambridge University Press.
- Nauert, Charles. 2006. *Humanism and the Culture of Renaissance Europe*. Cambridge: Cambridge University Press.

- Tanner, Norman. 2008. *The Church in the Later Middle Ages*. London: I. B. Tauris.
- Weiss, Roberto. 1988. *The Renaissance Discovery of Classical Antiquity*. Oxford: Blackwell.
- Welsh, Evelyn. 2001. *Art in Renaissance Italy, 1350–1500*. Oxford: Oxford University Press.

NOTES

1. Cited in David Chideser, *Christianity: A Global History* (New York: HarperOne, 2000), 294.
2. "Dogmatic Constitution of the Church (Lumen Gentiun, #22)," in *Vatican Council II*, Vol. 1, rev. ed., ed. Austin Flannery (Northport, NY: Costello Publishing, 1975), 375.
3. Ibid.

The Reformation

Timeline

1517 CE	Martin Luther writes his Ninety-Five Theses challenging indulgences
1521 CE	Luther is excommunicated at the Diet of Worms
1523 CE	Ulrich Zwingli leads reform movement in Zurich
1527 CE	Reformation begins in Sweden and Denmark
1534 CE	King Henry VIII creates separate Church of England
1536 CE	Calvin leads reform movement in Geneva; Tyndale's English Bible is printed
1555 CE	Peace of Augsburg signed, allowing German princes to establish Lutheranism or Catholicism in their realms

WHAT TO EXPECT

Every enduring human organization, whether believed to be divinely established or not, experiences the need for reform and renewal. Forms and structures that functioned well during one era prove inadequate in another. Cultures change, and institutions that do not adapt find themselves increasingly out of step or even irrelevant. "Adapt or die" is a popular expression of this truth. Further, every institution is filled with morally fallible members and contains leaders who scandalize those they seek to lead. This reality is endemic to the human condition. Christianity is no exception; it has never been immune to the need to alter its structures or renew its expressions. A common early modern articulation of this inescapable fact is *ecclesia reformata semper reformanda*: the church is reformed and always reforming.

Throughout the history of Christianity we find the ongoing need for reform, as Chapters Eleven and Twelve made particularly clear. During the eleventh century

(*Continued*)

WHAT TO EXPECT (*Continued*)

Pope Gregory VII strove to wrest control of the church from lay rulers and reform the spiritual lives of bishops and priests. During the thirteenth century the Franciscans and Dominicans arose to revitalize the faithful. During the fifteenth century the Council of Constance had to reconstitute the papacy itself. Other examples abound. All of these reforms happened within the church, though not without resistance. The

sixteenth century witnessed dramatic reform that broke Western Christianity institutionally apart and forever changed the face of Christianity. This chapter details those efforts and their results. As we shall see, the Reformation acted like a breached floodgate. Once broken, the waters of reform flooded Europe, beginning in Germany and Switzerland and then sweeping to the British Isles, to Scandinavia, and to other parts of Europe.

 BACKGROUND

The Renaissance formed the Reformation's cultural backdrop. As discussed in the last chapter, rigorous study of classical texts was a fundamental theme of the Renaissance. Further, Renaissance expressions of a full-fledged humanism in art, science, and exploration were reaching their zenith in the early sixteenth century. Humanism gave voice to a conviction that virtue was not learned through dry scholastic logic moving from one deduction to another. Rather, one read and absorbed the wisdom of classical giants, attended carefully to the moral models they provided, and thereby developed a noble character. During the Renaissance many literate Christians were drawn to the writings of patristic masters, such as John Chrysostom and Augustine, rather than to the abstract presentations of theology developed by scholastic figures such as Aquinas. Though these more classical expressions of the faith were less systematic, many Christians viewed them as possessing much greater rhetorical power and biblical imagination. To them, the power of the word in these texts highlighted transformative religious possibilities.

There was also a kind of democratic quality to the Renaissance period. During the High and Late Middle Ages, a literate middle class had slowly but progressively developed. With the invention of the printing press in 1440, books were no longer the privilege of the nobility alone, and access to ideas became much broader. This was a time of personal empowerment, of opportunity

to think and speak with personal authority. As we shall see, when the great reformer Martin Luther focused on the **priesthood of the baptized**, he was not only making a crucial theological point, but also giving voice to the aspirations of an increasingly confident middle class. Consider the most popular Renaissance voice of the early sixteenth century, Erasmus of Rotterdam, discussed in Chapter Thirteen. He sought to replace a dry and professionally oriented theology with a much more accessible spirit-filled approach. Further, he invited the faithful to consider themselves and their day-to-day lives as potentially holy.

One sees this confidence in the substantial **grievance literature** that circulated throughout this time, most of which challenged church leadership and policies. There was much to grieve. Though the laity respected some members of the clergy, they had reservations or outright disdain for many others. And, with the exception of the clergy in more high-profile churches, many parish priests were virtually illiterate. The magical terms *hocus pocus* actually come from a botched Latin expression for the consecration at the Eucharist: *hoc est enim corpus meum* (this is my very body). Indeed, many priests recited mangled versions of the Latin Mass (Eucharist), as well as of the other sacraments. Latin was a language some priests did not know, in the language of texts they could hardly read.

The hierarchy had its own problems in Christian witness. Bishops often purchased their offices and practiced their ministry as feudal lords. Frequently, they were not even residents of the dioceses they ran. In France, for example, Antoine Duprat (1463–1535), the archbishop of Sens, entered his cathedral church only once, and that was as a corpse during his own funeral. In 1451, Duke Amadeus VIII of Savoy secured the appointment of his son as archbishop of Geneva when his son was only eight years old. The papacy was a particular problem. As noted in Chapter Thirteen, the papacy during the Renaissance moved from Rome to Avignon, lived lavishly, and was widely regarded as a puppet of the French government. Perhaps the most extravagant pope was Alexander VI (r. 1492–1503), a member of the politically powerful Borgia family. He was infamous for having bribed his way to the papacy despite having a number of mistresses and at least seven known illegitimate children.

In addition to such problems in the church, general political conditions helped pave the way for the Reformation. As noted in Chapter Thirteen, Europe was developing into a collective of nation-states that were both powerful and independent. For example, Ferdinand and Isabella's marriage in 1469 eventually united a powerful Spain. England's sense of independence and greatness was also noteworthy, and France, with its daunting consolidation of feudal territories, was another power to be reckoned with. As early as the late fourteen and early fifteenth centuries, the French king Philip IV sought autonomy from Rome. Even Germany, the center of the Holy Roman Empire, saw itself as more German than "Holy Roman." And the smaller magistrates that made up what is now Germany did not hesitate to flex their sense of moderate autonomy.

Further upheavals were under way in the early sixteenth century as well. Rome was politically weak, and its ability to lean on secular powers in Europe was ebbing. In 1515, the French king Francis I conquered both the Swiss and the papal armies. In the ensuing treaty he established a military force in the Papal States and acquired the right to appoint all senior

FIGURE 14-1 Martin Luther (1483–1546). Luther was the first great Reformation figure. His movement eventually severed the German church.

clergy in France. Just twelve years later Holy Roman Emperor Charles V sacked Rome, put the pope under house arrest, and installed an army of 20,000 soldiers in the city. In Switzerland, which was made up of fiercely independent city-states called cantons, independence allowed each canton to decide for itself if and how reform should take place.

 LUTHERAN REFORMATION

Martin Luther (1483–1546) was born in Eisleben of Saxony, a territorial state of the Holy Roman Empire in today's northeast Germany. His father was a successful miner who eventually came to own mine shafts and copper smelters. Luther began his university education in Erfurt in 1501 and initially sought a law degree in response to his father's urging. In 1505, while returning to the university after a family visit, he got caught in a thunderstorm. He was terrified and cried out to Saint Anne, the patron saint of miners, "Help me, Saint Anne! I will become a monk!" According to tradition, shortly after making that vow he regretted it, and his friends tried to talk him out of it. But renouncing a sacred vow was a mortal sin, and within weeks he had entered the Augustinian order and become a monk. It could be that Luther was more enthusiastic about entering the monastic life than a legal one. He was on leave of absence from his studies at the time, and when his father tried to discourage him from entering the monastic life, he assured his father that he could do more for the family through his prayers than he ever could as a lawyer. As it turned out, he embraced religious life enthusiastically. "I was a good monk," he later affirmed, "and I kept the rule of my order so strictly that I may say that if ever a monk got to heaven by his monkery, it was I. All my brothers in the monastery who know me will bear me out."[1]

In 1507, Luther was ordained a priest, and in 1512 he attained a doctor of divinity degree. At that point he began his career as a professor of biblical studies at the University of Wittenberg. During his first several years as a professor Luther was troubled. He exceeded his contemporaries in religious practice and even went to confession daily, but this activity did not bring him any lasting peace or assurance of his salvation. Recall the Augustine–Pelagius controversy discussed in Chapter Eight. Pelagius and his followers argued that human beings have the free will to follow God's commands, while Augustine argued that man is so damaged by original sin that he needs grace at every turn. Augustine did not deny the existence of free will, but he rendered it virtually powerless in relation to humanity's salvation or ability to follow God without the aid of grace. The Second Council of Orange (529) supported Augustine's view that grace is necessary for salvation and, indeed, that grace alone justifies. This council even affirmed the view that humans need a kind of predisposing grace to facilitate their acceptance of justifying grace. But Orange also taught that humans have the free will to

accept that grace or reject it, to participate with grace in one's life or neglect its movements.

These ideas were not challenged in Luther's day. The prevailing consensus was that humans are saved by grace. One's responsibility lies in co-operating with God's transformative action by disposing oneself to God's justifying grace and, once justified, leading a fully engaged Christian life. Without actively living a Christian life, one can fall from grace and lose one's justification. Can a Christian have utter confidence in his or her salvation? The Catholic answer was that one can have good confidence, but not absolute certainty. The dictum of the day was: "God will not refuse grace to those who do what is within them" (*facere quod in se est*). Salvation is effected by grace, but it also requires man's cooperation. Thus, one can always ask: Is my cooperation with grace adequate?

Luther's response to this set of issues was not simply that Christians are *justified by grace through faith*—everyone believed that. Rather, he saw God's justification and subsequent salvation as being disconnected from man's free will. There is no cooperation and humans play no part in God's justification. Luther believed that humans exercise free will in their day-to-day lives, and of course urged Christians to exercise this will through virtue and service. But in his view there is no free will regarding salvation. Even faith itself is not an act of the will; it is the soul's compelled response to having been saved. Luther would later debate Erasmus on this issue through their competing texts, *On the Freedom of the Will* (Erasmus) and *On the Bondage of the Will* (Luther). Three key concepts regarding justification came into play for him. First, man is justified *passively*, without any cooperation with grace. Second, man is justified *irresistibly*. God's grace literally takes over and transforms the soul without the soul's ability to resist. Does this make God a bully? Hardly, for Luther. Rather, God frees man from his slavery to sin and gives him the freedom enjoyed as God's children. Finally, man's righteousness is that of *alien righteousness*, that is, it is God's righteousness humans claim, which has nothing to do with their own righteousness. For Luther, Christians are *justus et peccator simul*—simultaneously just and sinners. In his writings Luther describes coming to this final key insight:

> I greatly longed to understand Paul's Epistle to the Romans and nothing stood in the way but that one expression, "the justice of God," because I took it to mean that justice whereby God is just and deals justly in punishing the unjust. My situation was that, although an impeccable monk, I stood before God as a sinner troubled in conscience, and I had no confidence that my merit would assuage him. Therefore I did not love a just and angry God, but rather hated and murmured against him. . . . I pondered until I saw the connection between the justice of God and the statement that "the just shall live by faith" [Rom. 1:17]. Then I grasped that the justice of God is that righteousness by which through grace and sheer mercy God justifies us through faith. Thereupon I felt myself to be reborn and to have gone through open doors into paradise.[2]

THE INDULGENCE ISSUE

The Roman Catholic Church taught that God's justification and subsequent salvation of souls required some kind of initial consent of the will and ongoing practice in the faith. Luther, in contrast, viewed justification and salvation as literally forced on the soul. Still, this was not yet a point of public contention with the institutional church. Luther's first public challenge concerned the practice of **indulgences**.

From its beginnings the church practiced what later came to be known as the sacrament of **penance**, otherwise known as confession. The church held that once Christians were baptized, their moral lives would reflect a new life in Christ. While no one imagined Christians to be perfect, small sins were to be addressed through one's ongoing process of sanctification. But what about grave sins such as adultery? The patristic church dealt with these sins through the Order of Penitents, described in Chapter Six. Christian repentance was taken quite seriously. Those

under the Order of Penitents were separated from the rest of the faithful at the Eucharist and were not permitted to take communion. The faithful prayed for them and supported them during their often-lengthy periods of penance. The local bishop, when satisfied with their efforts, then proclaimed them absolved and allowed them to rejoin the full life of the church.

As Christianity spread, this practice continued but underwent various changes. During the Middle Ages the church taught that Christians needed to account for every sin and to do so in private with their local priest. Priests regularly used manuals that prescribed specific penances for particular sins. One example, noted earlier, is Burchard of Worms's eleventh-century manual *The Corrector*.

The sacrament of penance thus became a way of addressing both modest and serious sins. There were four constitutive parts to the sacrament: *contrition*—one had to be utterly sorry for one's sins; *confession*—one had to confess these sins to the priest; *absolution*—the priest had the authority to express the forgiveness of God and the removal of any penalties associated with sin; and *satisfaction*—one had to undergo the temporal punishment associated with sin.

The concept of **purgatory** arose naturally with the practice of penance. Unless and until a Christian had fully purged the blight of sin from his or her soul, some post-death experience of purgation was necessary. The Bible offers scant evidence for this view. In Second Maccabees, Judas Maccabeus offers a sacrifice for those soldiers who have died in battle wearing pagan amulets. The text records, "In doing this he acted very well, taking account of the resurrection. For if he were not expecting that those who had fallen would rise again, it would have been superfluous and foolish to pray for the dead" (12:39–45). In this text, the church saw evidence of the purging effect of meritorious works on behalf of the souls of the dead. First Corinthians also introduces the conception of salvation of some "only as through fire" (3:11–15), perhaps suggesting some kind of purgation.

Despite the paucity of scriptural warrant, the patristic church fully embraced the concept of purgatory. In the East, figures such as Clement of Alexandria, Cyril of Jerusalem, Origen, and John Chrysostom taught that purgatory existed. In the West, giants such as Ambrose, Augustine, Caesarius of Arles, and Gregory the Great taught the same. The idea of purgatory is simply this: Christians die in an imperfect state, and full union with God represents a life of utter purity. Thus, any and all imperfections remaining in the soul must be purged. Augustine's writings depict purgatory variously, from a place of purifying pains to a kind of hospital for healing. Purgatory only became formal doctrine in the Council of Lyons (1274) and reaffirmed in the Council of Florence (1439). The teaching was modest: purgatory or some post-death purgation exists, and pious prayers and works are useful for the departed. Even this latter belief that prayers and works can affect another's purgation had a patristic history. As early as the third century, bishops allowed the intercession of *confessors* and those awaiting martyrdom to shorten the disciplinary period of penitents. Given this teaching, it became easy to believe that the prayers and merits of Christ and the saints could be used to shorten such punishment itself. The medieval church taught that such merits were at the pope's disposal and that he could provide an *indulgence* that reduced (partial indulgence) or eliminated (full indulgence) the satisfaction due in purgatory. Full indulgences were offered to warriors who died in the Crusades.

Typically, penances involved some form of prayer, fasting, or almsgiving, three traditional means of renewal. Alms could be given either to the poor or to the church. The potential for corruption and abuse is immediately apparent: indulgences became a fundraising tool. Many challenged the practice. As noted in Chapter Thirteen, the Bohemian reformer Jan Hus (1369–1415) publicly railed against them and their abuse. While the church never taught that indulgences freed one from sin—only God's forgiveness could do that—paying money for indulgences to be freed from temporal punishment resulting from sin looked to the faithful like a way of avoiding the consequences of sin. To the reform-minded, it also looked like a way of enriching Rome.

In 1517, Pope Leo X authorized Archbishop Albrecht of Mainz to sell indulgences throughout northern Germany. This was good for Albrecht, as some of the proceeds would help him pay off the debt he had accumulated in acquiring the office of archbishop. The lion's share would go to Rome to finance the rebuilding of St. Peter's Basilica. This special indulgence, however, constituted a financial strain for the German princes, as disposable income was no longer supporting the local economy, and it constituted a theological problem for Martin Luther.

THE NINETY-FIVE THESES AND THE LEIPZIG DEBATE

According to tradition, on October 31, 1517, Luther nailed his **Ninety-Five Theses** (statements) challenging indulgences to the door of the chapel of Wittenberg Castle. This action constituted a challenge for public debate, and popularly marks the beginning of the Reformation.

SOME OF LUTHER'S NINETY-FIVE THESES CHALLENGING PENANCE AND INDULGENCES

Thesis 8: The penitential canons are imposed only on the living, and, according to them, nothing should be imposed on the dying.

Thesis 12: In former times the canonical penalties were imposed not after, but before absolution, as tests of true contrition.

Thesis 13: The dying are freed by death from all penalties; they are already dead to canonical rules, and have a right to be released from them.

Thesis 27: They preach . . . that so soon as the penny jingles into the money-box, the soul flies out [of purgatory].

Thesis 28: It is certain that when the penny jingles into the money-box, gain and avarice can be increased. . . .

Thesis 36: Every truly repentant Christian has a right to full remission of penalty and guilt, even without letters of pardon [indulgences].

Thesis 82: Why does not the pope empty purgatory, for the sake of holy love and of the dire need of the souls that are there, if he redeems an infinite number of souls for the sake of miserable money with which to build a Church? The former reasons would be most just; the latter is most trivial.

Thesis 86: Why does not the pope, whose wealth is today greater than the riches of the richest, build just this one church of St. Peter with his own money, rather than with the money of poor believers?[3]

In the summer of 1519, Luther and his colleague Andreas Karlstadt met Johann Eck in Leipzig to debate Luther's theses. Initially, Luther was only to be Karlstadt's advisor, as he had been silenced by Rome the previous year. He did, however, have permission to participate if he was personally attacked, which he assuredly was. Soon the debate was between Eck and Luther. Both men drew extensively on scripture and church teaching. As the debate progressed, it shifted in focus from indulgences to the nature of church authority, including the papacy and church councils, and Luther ended up arguing that both the pope and councils could err. He even gave modest support to some of the teachings of Jan Hus, whom the Council of Constance had earlier declared a heretic.

Theological faculties were supposed to determine a winner based on the transcripts of the debate. Among those present, the audience was divided; Luther himself believed that the majority cheered Eck as the winner. Eck traveled to Rome with transcripts of the debate, and these were subsequently sent to university faculties. The universities of Louvain and Cologne condemned Luther. In June 1520, a papal bull was issued from Rome demanding that Luther recant or be excommunicated. He had sixty days to decide. He didn't need them. In short order he publicly burned the papal bull. Further, because the bull also instructed that his books be burned, the students of Wittenberg staged their own book burning of texts on canon law and scholastic theology.

That year, 1520, was intellectually fruitful for Luther; during it, he wrote and published three great works. In his *Address to the Christian Nobility of the German Nation*, he calls on German princes to reform the church if the hierarchy

FIGURE 14-2 The Diet of Worms, at which Luther was excommunicated.

refuses to do so. In his *On the Babylonian Captivity of the Church*, he argues that the gospel has become captive and twisted by the institutional church. In this book he also claims that there should only be two sacraments, baptism and the Eucharist, and he rejects the teaching on transubstantiation of the bread and wine of Eucharist into the body and blood of Christ. Luther emphasizes that he believes in the real and full presence of Christ in the consecrated bread and wine, but he rejects the use of philosophical categories to explain the mystery. Finally, he published *On Christian Liberty*, a book in which he describes the dynamics of a life of faith.

THE DIET OF WORMS

Frederick the Wise, Luther's immediate ruler and benefactor, thought it only just that Luther receive a full public hearing before Germany's rulers, and maintained that he should not be condemned without one. Holy Roman Emperor Charles V agreed and summoned Luther to Worms, Germany, for the rulers' next formal meeting, referred to as a diet. The emperor and the German princes had weightier matters on their minds, particularly the Ottoman Turks, who had conquered Constantinople the century before and were already pressing toward Austria. Luther's part in the **Diet of Worms** was small but decisive. A representative of the archbishop of Trier pointed to Luther's published books on a table. Luther was asked whether he had written them and whether they contained anything he would now want to recant. Luther's response after a day of deliberation is famous. Tradition has him saying, "Here I stand, I can do no other." What he actually said was more substantive, even if less pithy:

> Unless I am convinced by the testimony of the Scriptures or by clear reason (for I do not trust either in the pope or in councils alone, since it is well known that they have often erred and contradicted themselves), I am bound by the Scriptures I have quoted and my conscience is captive to the Word of God. I cannot and will not retract anything, since it is neither safe nor right to go against conscience. May God help me! Amen![4]

There is much to unpack here. The first point is that Luther did not regard church authority as absolute. He had shown himself over the past few years to be respectful of the institution, its history and traditions, but not slavishly. He recognized reason as important and was open to a convincing theological argument, but it would have to be made explicitly. The Bible for him stood above any human authority; indeed, he would declare it his sole authority. In his words, he was *captive* to the word of God and its power to transform souls. In fact, he believed that God's irresistible grace came through the medium of the word preached. Finally, Luther embraced the primacy of conscience. Faith was, in the end, intensely personal, stemming from a direct connection between the believer and God.

When Luther left Leipzig, Charles V declared him an outlaw and subject to capital punishment. Frederick had prearranged with Luther that Frederick's men would "kidnap" him on the way back to Wittenberg, and Luther stayed with Frederick incognito for the next year, growing a beard, wearing a knight's garment, and adopting the name Junker Jörg (Sir George). During a period of ten months at Frederick's castle, he translated the New Testament into German for wide use among the people.

LUTHERAN SEPARATION

Those who wanted to follow Luther's path of reform, and thus declare independence from the Catholic Church, traveled a rocky road. In 1526, the First Diet of Speyer decided that until a council could be held to definitively determine whether and how reform might be brought about, each German prince could choose to implement Luther's reform and thus separate from the Roman Catholic Church or choose to remain loyal to Rome. The Second Diet of Speyer (1529) declared that the Lutheran reform would be tolerated only where it could not be suppressed without violence. Further, in an area where the local prince favored reform, Catholics must have freedom of worship. However, in an area where the local prince remained faithful to Catholicism,

Lutherans would have no religious rights. Six Lutheran princes protested this arrangement and thus gained the name **Protestant**, a term that would eventually refer to any Western Christian who was not Roman Catholic. In 1530, Charles V presided over the Diet of Augsburg. Luther was not permitted to attend, and his friend and colleague Philip Melanchthon presented the formal Lutheran position, the **Augsburg Confession**. Many reform-minded Christians embraced the Confession, and it became the foundational document of the Lutheran Church. Other reformers, particularly those from Switzerland, rejected it and eventually submitted their own statements. The **Peace of Augsburg** (1555) made it law that each prince was to choose between the Lutheran or Catholic alignment, and that all citizens within a prince's given lands would have to either embrace their prince's faith or emigrate to other lands following their conscience. Southern Germany remained widely Catholic, while northern Germany adopted Lutheranism.

Frederick the Wise opted for Luther's reform, and Luther became a pastor in Wittenberg. His years in this role were both highly fruitful and increasingly difficult. He discovered that many Christians in Lutheran lands had little knowledge of the faith, and thus he produced two catechisms, the *Small Catechism* for children and the *Large Catechism* for adults. He also revised the liturgy and produced a German hymnbook. Perhaps his greatest disappointment, though, was in the moral and spiritual lives of his flock. People took seriously his insistence that works were entirely disconnected from salvation and that only one's conscience (as opposed to the laws of the church) needed to be obeyed. In Wittenberg, church attendance fell off markedly. In a sermon on November 8, 1528, an exasperated Luther preached:

> What shall I do with you, people of Wittenberg! I shall not preach to you the kingdom of Christ, because you don't take it up. . . . To you I must preach the law! . . . By the grace of God, you ingrates, who although you thirst so greedily for money, you do not give anything. . . . You have been freed from tyrants and papists. You ungrateful beasts are not worthy of this treasure of the gospel. If you don't do otherwise, repenting of your sins, I'm going to cease preaching to you, lest I cast pearls before swine or give holy things to dogs.[5]

Ironically, over the next couple of centuries Lutheran pastors increasingly preached vehement sermons about hell to urge their members to obey the disciplines of the Lutheran Church.

LUTHER'S VISION

While Luther may be imagined to have been a radical, he never intended to be. He embraced much of the church's historical tradition and theology. While demoting in importance a number of the traditional sacraments, he still incorporated all the rites of the traditional church, including penance. His vision was one of absolute faith and the freedom that comes from it. For Luther, when man looks at himself to see if he is acceptable, he is already failing. The Christian life is all about looking at Christ, at what he did to secure salvation and at what he is now doing in one's life. If security comes only

FIGURE 14-3 Ulrich Zwingli (1484–1531) led the Swiss Reformation in Zurich.

from God and a Christian life is wholly focused on Christ, then Christians find themselves free from any other kind of servitude. One is free from any law, save only the law of love. Being a servant of God then makes one a free servant of humanity. Luther elegantly frames this paradox in *On Christian Liberty*: "A Christian is a perfectly free lord of all, subject to none. A Christian is a perfectly dutiful servant of all, subject to all."[6] For Luther, the gospel was centered on the message of Saint Paul, a message that undermined both pride and insecurity by teaching Christians to focus only on God, in complete dependence to him. Luther believed in ordination and institutional leadership, but challenged the idea that holy orders made one a different kind of Christian. He argued for the *priesthood of the baptized*, that is, the idea that all Christians are priests by virtue of their baptism. His message, from start to finish, was freedom and empowerment.

 ### SWISS REFORMED CHRISTIANITY

ULRICH ZWINGLI (1484–1531)

As mentioned previously, Switzerland (the Confederation Helvetica) was an association of small, largely independent states called cantons. **Ulrich Zwingli** was born just months after Luther in the canton of St. Gallen in eastern Switzerland.[7] Zwingli attended the University of Vienna (1498–1502) and then moved to the University of Basel (1502–1506). Both of these universities were deeply absorbed in Renaissance learning and Erasmus's desire for reform, and Zwingli initially desired a reform in keeping with Erasmus's agenda. In 1506, he was ordained a priest and served in Glarus, a town close to his hometown. Later, he also took on duties in nearby Einsiedeln, which had a shrine to the Virgin Mary. Zwingli regarded the shrine as an expression of superstition and idolatry. In 1519, he moved to Zurich to be the main preacher at the largest church in the city. By this time he had become convinced that Christian belief and practice ought to be based on scripture alone,

rather than conditioned by church tradition. In Zurich he actively preached against many aspects of traditional Catholicism. This alarmed the city council, and in 1523 it arranged a debate between Zwingli and supporters of traditional Catholicism, with the city council members as judges. Zwingli won the debate decisively.

Zwingli's victory led the city council to institute as official policy a program of reform based on scripture. In 1524, Zurich ruled that all religious imagery was to be removed from churches. Iconoclastic riots spread throughout the Swiss confederation, including Bern (1528), Basel (1529), and Geneva (1535). The city of Bern's adoption of the reform was especially significant, since Bern was a military and political power within the confederation. By 1525, the city council had replaced the Eucharist with a liturgy largely created by Zwingli himself. The Eucharist, which he believed constituted a memorial meal, ultimately became marginalized in worship. Like Luther and Erasmus, Zwingli believed that the church needed to realign itself to the teachings and practices of the New Testament. For him, such realignment meant that if a given claim or practice was not in the text, then it was either optional (e.g., Lenten fasting), suspicious (e.g., tithing), or heretical (e.g., intercession of saints). Further, he was convinced that the Bible could be interpreted clearly and unambiguously on all important matters.

Could the Bible be so clearly interpreted? Luther's reform centered on slogans such as *Sola scriptura* (scripture alone), and other reformers embraced this idea as well. Yet Luther was aghast by the Swiss reform movement. His reform more or less honored the Catholic tradition. For example, he thought devotion to Mary as the Mother of the Lord both proper and important; saw no need to remove icons of saints as long as the faithful focused on Jesus; and was certain that while the Eucharist was not a sacrifice (something on which both Catholicism and Orthodoxy insisted), the consecrated bread and wine genuinely embodied Christ's real presence. Zwingli denounced all of these views.

FIGURE 14-4 John Calvin (1509–1564) oversaw the Reformation in Geneva. His *Institutes of the Christian Religion* became fundamental to the Reformed Church.

In 1529, Luther met Zwingli and others at Marburg Castle at the behest of Philipp I of Hesse. Philipp wanted to unite Protestant states in a political alliance and saw the need for religious harmony. The meeting, known as the Marburg Colloquy, spanned four days and attracted many major reform leaders. But they could not agree on exactly what scripture taught. Take, for example, Luther's core principle of justification by faith alone. Catholics were not the only Christians to question this doctrine, given that the New Testament does not use the word "alone" and the Epistle of James explicitly teaches justification by faith and works (2:24). Zwingli saw Luther's doctrine as undermining the Christian obligation to do good works. Further, according to Zwingli, the Bible clearly teaches that the Eucharist is merely a memorial meal, while Luther was certain it teaches that the Eucharist is the real presence of Christ. Whose interpretation of

such central issues was authoritative? For Lutherans, the answer was decided pastor by pastor in accordance with the Augsburg Confession. For the Swiss reform movement, authoritative interpretation ultimately became the province of the city council.

JOHN CALVIN (1509–1564)

John Calvin was born in 1509 in the town of Noyon, France, about seventy miles northeast of Paris. He wanted to follow his brothers into the priesthood, but his father insisted that he study law at the University of Orleans. After attaining his law degree, however, he came to Paris to study theology in 1531. Paris at this time was a hotbed of controversy and decidedly hostile to Luther's ideas, even as Calvin himself was utterly sympathetic. As a result, he left Paris for Basel, Switzerland, and set out to publish something akin to Luther's *Small Catechism*, a text he entitled *Institutes of the Christian Religion*. Calvin worked on the *Institutes* for the next two decades, honing, refining, and dramatically expanding it from its initial six chapters to eighty. Although he intended to settle down in Strasbourg, France, to a life of study and writing, he found the route impassible because of war and went instead to Geneva, Switzerland, a city that had just evicted its bishop. The leaders there asked him to stay and support the cause of the Reformation.

Not all went well. Calvin's attempts at reform of both doctrine and practice were controversial and widely resisted, so much so that he was evicted from Geneva, only to be replaced by weak and ineffective ministers. Could Geneva return to Roman Catholicism? Hoping it could, the French cardinal Jacopo Sadoleto wrote to appeal to the Genevans. In his appeal, he clearly recognized the corruption pointed out by reformers, but argued that the Catholic Church was still the authentic church. Geneva's city council asked Calvin to return and respond, which he did with his famous *Reply to Sadoleto*. In it he argued that it was not the reformers who had drifted from the authentic tradition of the church, but the Catholics, by not giving adequate solicitude to the Bible.

> You teach that all that has been approved for fifteen hundred years or more by the uniform consent of the faithful is, by our rashness torn up and destroyed. . . . [But] our agreement with antiquity is far closer than yours; all we have attempted has been to renew the ancient form of the Church which, at first distorted and stained by illiterate men of indifferent character, was afterwards criminally mangled and almost destroyed by the Roman pontiff and his faction.[8]

For Calvin there were only two essential functions of the Christian church: preaching the biblical word and administering the sacraments. He recognized the problem of the plurality of interpretations of the Bible, but argued that an authentic interpretation was possible. Indeed, a large part of his revisions to the *Institutes* consisted of adding rigorously reasoned and defended biblical interpretations as well as critiques of alternative interpretations.

In certain ways Calvin was a moderating voice between Luther and Zwingli. For example, he believed in the real presence in the Eucharist but focused less on spelling out what exactly this presence constitutes and more on examining its transformative effects: "Our souls are fed by the flesh and blood of Christ in the same way that bread and wine keep and sustain physical life. . . . [This] cannot happen unless Christ truly grows into one with us, and refreshes us by the eating of his flesh and drinking of this blood."[9] In his *Book of Confessions* he answers the question of what it means to eat Christ's crucified body and to drink his shed blood as follows: "It is not only to embrace with a trusting heart the whole passion and death of Christ, and by it to receive the forgiveness of sins and eternal life. In addition, it is to be so united more and more to his blessed body by the Holy Spirit dwelling both in us and in Christ."[10]

Calvin also prescribed a more democratic church structure. His system of church government involved presbyteries and synods made up of lay people rather than bishops. The city of Geneva itself represented a church/state democracy: it was run by twelve members, four of whom were elected city officials, four of whom were pastors, and four of whom were lay elders of the congregation.

In other ways the Geneva reform was quite extreme. It instituted laws that severely restricted public speech, social prohibitions such as dancing, and even restrictions on names that could be given to children. Most severe was Calvin's understanding of the nature of the person before God and the dynamics of God's salvation, including his doctrine known as **double predestination**. Recall Luther's belief that souls have no free will regarding their election, and that God's grace works on them without their consent in an irresistible way. In this understanding even faith is not an act of the will, but the compelled response of a soul moved by God. Humans have no choice, one way or the other. If one embraces Luther's views and assumes that God does not save everyone, then Calvin's reasoning is an easy logical step from Luther's: from eternity, God creates some persons for heaven and some for hell, and there is nothing anyone can do about it. Like Luther, Calvin regarded this idea as freeing: stop thinking about yourself and get on with serving the kingdom of God. In light of Calvin's concept of double predestination, Luther would eventually alter his view of free will to argue that we are not free to say yes to God, but we are free to reject God. Thus, we are not predestined to hell, but are responsible for our rejection of God. For many scholars, this caveat amounts to a distinction without a difference. If the only way one can be saved is through the irresistible grace of God, and if one does not receive such grace, then *freely* rejecting God seems the only option and hardly an expression of free will.

Calvin's position raises three questions: Is God then unjust in damning persons who have no ability to be saved? What is the source of one's motivation for being good if salvation is already out of one's hands? Can one know whether one is among the saved, and if so, how? Regarding the first question, it does seem on the surface that God would be positively evil in creating a human person necessarily doomed to eternal hellfire. Calvin's answer was that all people are sinners, and thus all deserve damnation. In this sense, double predestination allows God to exercise his justice and mercy. To those damned, he evidences his right justice. To those saved, he evidences his unbounded mercy. Since salvation is a gift anyway, who can demand what can never be merited and only given freely? With respect to the second question, Calvin believed that one should never have any motivation beyond the desire to glorify God. The truly elect understand that this is the soul's only authentic interest. Regarding the question of how one might know one has been eternally elected, Calvin taught that one can obtain confidence that one is among the elect through the evidence of one's new life in the Spirit. Further, Calvin's writings frequently describe a saved Christian's palpable knowledge of God's indwelling in the soul, that is, a dramatically felt experience of God's presence.

ARMINIANISM AND T.U.L.I.P.

Jacob Arminius (1560–1609) was a Reformed Dutch pastor and theologian who had been taught by Calvin's successor, Theodore Beza, at the University of Geneva. Arminius and others were troubled by some of Calvin's theology, particularly the views that Christ does not redeem all (only those predestined), and that human will is uninvolved in justification or in retaining one's justification. For them, the weight of scripture seemed to attest to human free will and the universal atonement of Christ. Holland's States General requested that Arminius outline his views, but he died before preparing them. In 1610, his followers prepared a "remonstrance," or presentation of opposition, that was signed by forty-five ministers and submitted to the States General. The remonstrance had five fundamental articles: (1) salvation or condemnation is conditioned by the graciously enabled human faith or rejection; (2) Christ's atonement is universal, though only those who are saved benefit from it; (3) humans require grace to respond to God's will; (4) grace is the beginning,

continuance, and accomplishment of good, yet it can be resisted; and (5) believers can be assured of God's grace, but whether they can fall from grace still needs to be scripturally determined. Arminius's followers called themselves the "Remonstrants," though the movement historically took on the title of **Arminianism**.

Following the five articles of remonstrance, Dutch Calvinists convened a national synod in Dordrecht, The Netherlands (1618–1619), to settle the matter. Representatives of eight foreign Calvinist churches also attended the meeting as voting members. They renounced all five articles of the remonstrance. In rejecting the Arminian position, they articulated what are sometimes referred to as the five points of Calvinism and collectively given the acronym **T.U.L.I.P.**, for **t**otal depravity of the soul, **u**nconditional election, **l**imited atonement, **i**rresistible grace, and **p**erseverance of the saints. In short, souls are utterly sinful and spiritually dead; God's election of a soul (to heaven or hell) is from eternity; Christ died only for the elect; grace effects election without the will's engagement; and if one is elected, then one will persevere in faith—that is, once saved, always saved. These became Calvinist dogma.

Across Holland, Arminians suffered at the hands of the state. Some were removed from office, and others were imprisoned or banished. Within twelve years Arminians were allowed to worship freely in Holland, though the animosity between the group and traditional Calvinists would continue for centuries. Calvinists could boast of biblical passages supporting their view, such as Paul's famous reflection on the Exodus event as a parallel to Christian justification:

> Is there injustice on God's part? By no means! For he says to Moses, "I will have mercy on whom I have mercy, and I will have compassion on whom I have compassion." So it depends not on human will or exertion, but on God who shows mercy. For the scripture says to Pharaoh, "I have raised you up for the very purpose of showing my power in you, so that my name may be proclaimed in all the earth." So then he has mercy on whomsoever he chooses, and he

hardens the heart of whomsoever he chooses. (Rom. 9:14–18)

Or consider Jesus's words, "And this is the will of him who sent me, that I should lose nothing of all that he has given me, but raise it up on the last day" (John 6:39). However, Arminians too could offer biblical texts that conflict with these points. For example, Jesus proclaims that he came to save the world (John 3:16; 12:46). Or further, Paul proclaims elsewhere that God wishes to have mercy on all (Rom. 11:32). Additionally, God wills that all be saved (1 Tim. 2:4; 2 Peter 3:9). And last, Jesus promised that he would not reject any who would come to him (John 6:37). These texts had to be ignored or at least given strained interpretation by those who posited T.U.L.I.P.

One might appreciate the Arminians' critique and the implications of T.U.L.I.P. by reflecting on a striking scene in John Updike's novel *In the Beauty of the Lilies*. In this story a conversation takes place between two members of an early twentieth-century Calvinist Presbyterian congregation. A dying man, Mr. Orr, asks his pastor, Clarence Wilmot, what Wilmot thinks of his chances of being one of the elect. Orr is a salt-of-the-earth faithful member of the church and utterly religiously serious. But he hasn't exactly enjoyed a "palpable experience of the living Christ," something Calvin viewed as a sign of one's election to heaven. Wilmot assures him of God's election, but Orr demands to know on what basis Wilmot offers such an assurance. God's election, Orr reminds him, is not just inscrutable; it is arbitrary. Maybe God chose him for heaven, or maybe God chose him for hell, and there is no question of participating in, co-operating with, or in any way addressing that decision made from eternity. "There is nothing a poor body can do," Orr declares as he dies, somewhat resigned and perfectly unnerved.[11]

Arminian theology did not die in the seventeenth century. Today, many Baptists and Methodists, otherwise highly Calvinistic in their theology, have embraced the five articles of remonstrance in their own theological tradition.

THE RADICAL REFORMATION

As contentious as these early reformers were with one another, nothing shocked them more than what has been called the Radical Reformation, a name scholars have given to the loosely associated reform movements in Germany and Switzerland that rejected both the Augsburg Confession and Zwingli and Calvin's reform agendas. Zwingli called these people **anabaptists** (re-baptizers) because of their insistence that only freely consenting adults could authentically be baptized, and thus their infant baptism did not count. They seem to have first emerged within Zurich following Zwingli's reforms in the 1520s. Conrad Grebel, a member of the Zurich council, argued that although Zwingli believed that he abided by the *sola scriptura* principle, in fact he retained a number of practices that were not sanctioned in scripture, including infant baptism and engagement in warfare. Grebel further argued that every individual is free to interpret the Bible as God leads him or her, without constraints provided by tradition. Both Calvin and Zwingli believed that the church had existed continuously since apostolic times, even though it had swerved off course. Grebel and his sympathizers believed that it had simply ceased to exist during the medieval period. Four basic principles characterize the relatively disparate Radical Reform movement: (1) believer's baptism, in which only adults who willingly embrace Christianity can be baptized; (2) restorationalism, in which true Christians must embrace a return to the faith and life of the primitive church; (3) separatism, according to which these Christians are the righteous remnant; and (4) pessimism, the belief that the world cannot be trusted.

One of the early voices associated with the Radical Reform movement was **Thomas Müntzer** (1489–1525). In 1520, Muntzer became a pastor in Zwickau, Saxony, though his appointment there or anywhere else never lasted long. Initially Müntzer seemed to embrace the Lutheran reform movement, but he quickly became radicalized. In the Peasants' War in Germany, he was something of an apocalyptic preacher and leader, ultimately leading 8,000 peasants at the 1525 Battle of Krankensausen, in which his forces were crushed.

While modern denominations flowing from the historical Radical Reformation, such as the Amish and the Mennonites, are renowned for their peaceable qualities, sixteenth-century Anabaptists were not. In 1530, for example, **Melchior Hoffman** preached that God chose Strasbourg as the New Jerusalem and demanded the overthrow of the city's authorities. Regarding reformers such as Luther, Calvin, and Zwingli, Hoffman proclaimed, "Woe, woe to all such blind leaders who willfully publish lies for the truth; their inheritance and portion is eternal damnation."[12] In 1534, Hoffman's followers took over the city of Munster and demanded that everyone remaining in the city either be rebaptized or face execution. In response, Zurich made it a law that whoever did get rebaptized would also face execution.

FIGURE 14-5 Henry VIII (r. 1509–1547) declared himself the head of the Church of England, making loyalty to Roman Catholicism treason.

No one in the leadership of the Lutheran or Reformed traditions imagined that the dogmas declared by the decisive early ecumenical councils ought to be challenged. But why not, if councils were fallible, and particularly if their decisions could not be decisively proven by scripture? The Italian Radical Reform movement held a council in Venice in 1550, led by Lelio Sozzini, over such issues as whether the Trinity or the preexistence of the Son were scriptural. After Sozzini's death, his nephew, Fausto Sozzini, published his uncle's theology. He eventually moved to Poland and joined a Reformed church there, but the congregation split in 1565 over issues such as whether God is Trinitarian, whether it is proper to pray to Christ, and whether one should believe in the virgin birth, all of which Sozzini denied.

THE ENGLISH REFORMATION

Henry VIII (r. 1509–1547) was not a religious reformer, and at the beginning of the Reformation he wrote against the movement's rejection of the seven sacraments. For this, Pope Leo X even awarded him the title "Defender of the Faith." Henry's problem was more political. With a dispensation from Rome, Henry married Catherine of Aragon, the widowed wife of his brother. Catherine was the daughter of Spain's Ferdinand and Isabella, and the marriage was certainly intended to help seal political bonds. The problem for Henry was that Catherine failed to produce a male heir to the throne. Actually, she did have a son, also named Henry, but he did not survive past infancy. Their only surviving child was their daughter, Mary Tudor. Henry decided to divorce Catherine and sought an annulment of the marriage from Rome. Not only would granting an annulment be a reversal for Rome, given its earlier dispensation for the pair to marry, but it would have created great tension between the papacy and Spain. Rome refused.

In response, Henry declared the church in England a national church, the Church of England, and himself the head of it, thus separating England from the Roman Catholic communion. There was some historical precedent for Henry's move. As noted in Chapter Thirteen, John Wycliffe had argued for a national church and challenged the papacy's authority. Further, throughout the medieval period France periodically acted as a virtual national church, with the monarchy, for example, controlling all high appointments. Finally, Henry could look to the ancient Byzantine model whereby emperors regarded themselves as heads of the universal church. Almost immediately Henry received an annulment from the Church of England and soon married Anne Boleyn, the second of what would eventually be six wives.

Once Henry declared the Church of England juridically separate from Rome, he dissolved all monasteries in England and took hold of their possessions. This was a savvy move, as it personally enriched him as well as ensured there would be no independent Christian centers that might stay loyal to Rome. Not everyone was pleased. Some refused to accept Henry's newly proclaimed authority as head of the Church of England. The most famous objector was Thomas More, Henry's chancellor and friend. More and other leaders loyal to Rome were tried and executed as traitors.

Henry installed **Thomas Cranmer** as archbishop of Canterbury and charged him with presiding over the English Reformation. Both Henry and Cranmer sought modest reform. Cranmer marshaled the wide distribution of an English version of the Bible and created the **Book of Common Prayer**, a new guide for liturgy. He also worked on a document that was later finalized as the **Thirty-Nine Articles**, a list of doctrines that set out both similarities and differences between the Church of England and the Roman Catholic Church.

When Henry died in 1547, his son Edward took over the throne at the age of nine. His regents, the dukes of Somerset and Northumberland, were strong advocates of the Reformation, and they instituted a number of changes. When Edward died in 1553, his half-sister, Mary Tudor, took over the throne. Mary was a staunch supporter of Catholicism and restored it as the official religion of the realm. After a 1554 plot to overthrow her failed, she reacted by reinstating heresy laws and oversaw the trial and execution of many Protestant clergy and scholars, for which her enemies dubbed her "Bloody Mary." Mary's five-year reign was tumultuous, and after she died she was succeeded by Elizabeth I. Like Henry VIII, Elizabeth advocated a modest reform. Protestants were restored to power, and practicing Catholics were often imprisoned and executed. Still, Christianity in England was quite similar to the Roman Catholicism of the time.

During the sixteenth century, Scotland had an independent monarchy, though it was often tied by blood and marriage to the English throne. At the time, the Scottish king, James V (1512–1542), opposed both the Protestant Reformation and the Church of England. His successor, Mary Stuart (Mary, Queen of Scots), remained Catholic, but had Protestant sympathies. Mary coveted the throne of England and conspired to take it from Elizabeth. Upon thwarting the plot, Elizabeth had her executed, leaving Scotland briefly adrift. After her execution, John Knox, a former Catholic priest who had traveled the continent and worked with both John Calvin and Heinrich Bullinger, Zwingli's successor in Zurich, returned to Scotland and organized the Church of Scotland, a national church that adopted both Calvin's theology and Geneva's governing structure.

CONCLUSIONS

What does one make of the Reformation? It unfolded during a politically complex time, a period of great cultural shifts, and a religiously earnest era. The church in the West fragmented

dramatically, and this fragmentation subsequently deepened. Lutheranism would successfully spread north to replace Scandinavian Catholicism, but would also break into various expressions with decidedly different doctrines and policies. Those most aligned to Zwingli's understanding of reform today include the Disciples of Christ, the United Church of Christ, and many Baptist churches. Those mostly aligned to Calvin's understanding include the Christian Reformed Church, as well as the Presbyterian Church, though these churches represent dramatically different theologies and practices. The Radical Reform movement gave rise to Quakers, Amish, Mennonites, and the Church of the Brethren. Very few contemporary theologians from these communities embrace all the historical doctrines from the early Reformation period, though clearly they are influenced by them. Indeed, few theologians believe that the Bible alone can resolve all theological controversies.

The Reformation was also a religiously glorious time of critical examination of Christianity's assumptions, and it strived to renew the church with a wholly biblical imagination. Figures such as Luther, Zwingli, and Calvin stand among the giants of the Christian theological tradition. They inspired the Reformation, and their powerful voices transformed Christianity in the West.

SUMMARY QUESTIONS

- Briefly describe the social and political trends in Europe at the time of the Reformation and list some of the factors that caused the Reformation.
- Why did Luther think that indulgences were theologically and institutionally problematic?
- Differing degrees of reform can be seen in each of the five movements discussed in this chapter. In terms of the level of reform, the English Reformation was the most moderate, and the Radical Reformation was the most severe. Starting with the English Reformation, chart some of the ways that each movement further distinguished itself politically and theologically from the Catholic Church.
- What were the theological difficulties that Calvin encountered as a result of his double predestination doctrine, and what were his answers to them?
- Later disputes in Calvinism were settled with the emergence of T.U.L.I.P. List and briefly explain T.U.L.I.P. in your own words.

DISCUSSION QUESTIONS

- Indulgences came as part of a theology of the sacrament of penance and the belief in purgatory. The author notes that the biblical evidence for purgatory is meager at best, but also that many important church fathers taught it. Given the importance of both theological resources, do you think the medieval world's belief in purgatory was legitimate?
- What challenges does Calivinism's T.U.L.I.P. face biblically or logically? Does it strike you as theologically satisfying? Defend your answer.
- Zwingli's iconoclasm is reminiscent of the church's controversy over icons in the eighth century. Do you think his renewal of this issue was justified? Why or why not?

KEY TERMS

Anabaptists	Augsburg Confession	Cranmer, Thomas
Arminianism	Book of Common Prayer	Diet of Worms
Arminius, Jacob	Calvin, John	Double predestination

Grievance literature
Henry VIII
Hoffman, Melchior
Indulgences
Luther, Martin
Müntzer, Thomas

Ninety-Five Theses
Peace of Augsburg
Penance
Priesthood of the baptized
Protestant
Purgatory

Sola scriptura
T.U.L.I.P.
Thirty-Nine Articles
Zwingli, Ulrich

BIBLIOGRAPHY

- Bainton, Ronald. 1950. *Here I Stand: The Life of Martin Luther.* New York: Abington.
- Calvin, John. 1960. *Institutes of Christian Religion.* Ed. John McNeill, trans. Ford Lewis Battles. Philadelphia: Westminster Press.
- Coffey, Euan. 2012. *The European Reformation.* Oxford: Clarendon Press.
- Dodds, Gregory. 2009. *Exploiting Erasmus: The Erasmian Legacy and Religious Change in Early Modern England.* Toronto: University of Toronto Press.
- Ford, Gerhard. 1997. *On Being a Theologian of the Cross: Reflections on Luther's Heidelberg Disputation, 1518.* Grand Rapids, MI: Eerdmans.
- Hendrix, Scott, ed. and trans. 2009. *Early Protestant Spirituality.* New York: Paulist Press.
- Hoffman, Bengt, trans. 1980. *The Theologia Germanica of Martin Luther.* Mahwah, NJ: Paulist Press.
- Luther, Martin. 1955–1986. *Luther's Works,* 55 vols. St. Louis: Concordia Publishing.
- Luther, Martin. 2003. *On Christian Liberty.* Trans. W. A. Lambert. Minneapolis: Fortress Press.
- MacCulloch, Diarmaid. 2003a. *The Reformation: A History.* New York: Viking.
- MacCulloch, Diarmiad. 2003b. *Reformation: Europe's House Divided: 1490–1700.* London: Allen Lane.
- Marius, Richard. 1999. *Martin Luther: The Christian Between God and Death.* Cambridge: Harvard University Press.
- Ozment, Steven. 1980. *The Age of Reform.* New Haven, CT: Yale University Press.
- Rex, Richard. 2006. *Henry VIII and the English Reformation.* New York: Macmillan.
- Rice, Howard. 1991. *Reformed Spirituality: An Introduction for Believers.* Louisville, KY: Westminster/John Knox Press.
- Rupp, E. Gordon, and Philip Watson, eds. 1969. *Luther and Erasmus: Free Will and Salvation.* Philadelphia: Westminster Press.
- Senn, Frank, ed. 2000. *Protestant Spiritual Traditions.* Eugene, OR: Wipf and Stock.
- Wicks, Jared. 1983. *Luther and His Spiritual Legacy.* Wilmington, DE: Michael Glazier.
- Williams, George H., and Angel Mergle, eds. 1957. *Spiritual and Anabaptist Writers.* Library of Christian Classics, Vol. 25. Philadelphia: Westminster.

NOTES

1. See Bainton, *Here I Stand,* 45. See also Luther 1955–86, 38:143.
2. Ibid., 38:65.
3. Ibid., 21:25–33.
4. Ibid., 32:112–113.
5. Cited in Marius, *Martin Luther,* 475.
6. Luther, *On Christian Liberty,* 2.
7. Technically St. Gallen was not part of the confederation, but a treaty in 1451 allied the canton to the confederation, and Zwingli certainly regarded himself as Swiss.
8. "Calvin's 'Reply to Sadoleto,'" accessed at http://rels365fa10.pbworks.com/w/page/33320860/Calvin%27s%20%E2%80%9CReply%20to%20Sadoleto%E2%80%9D.
9. Calvin, *Institutes of Christian Religion,* IV.XVIII, 7.
10. Cited in Rice, *Reformed Spirituality,* 191–192.
11. John Updike, *In the Beauty of the Lilies* (New York: Alfred A. Knopf, 1996), 43–48.
12. Williams and Mergal, *Spiritual and Anabaptist Writers,* 192.

The Catholic Reformation

Timeline

1515–1582 CE	Life of Teresa of Avila, Carmelite reformer and spiritual master
1540 CE	Jesuits founded by Ignatius of Loyola and companions
1542–1591 CE	Life of John of the Cross, Carmelite reformer and spiritual master
1545–1563 CE	Council of Trent reforms the Roman Catholic Church
1547–1584 CE	Czar Ivan IV dramatically expands Russia and the Orthodox Church
1764 CE	Russian empress Catherine II issues decree of religious toleration

WHAT TO EXPECT

Luther, Zwingli, Calvin, and others were not the only voices calling for reform. Within the Catholic Church, lay people, priests, bishops, and even some popes believed the church was in need of reform but had no intention of breaking from it. This chapter details initiatives within the church before, during, and after the Protestant Reformation. Some individuals formed new religious reforming orders and produced spiritual literature that would highly influence how the interior life is imagined in Catholic spirituality. Most importantly, the bishops of the Catholic Church held the Council of Trent, a council that would reform and remake Catholic practice up to the late twentieth century.

COUNTER-REFORMATION OR
CATHOLIC REFORMATION?

The Catholic Church's direct response to the
Protestant Reformation is often called the
Counter-Reformation, as Catholicism strove to
distinguish itself from Protestantism and try as
best it could to neutralize or even reverse the
Protestant threat. Its hallmark was the Council
of Trent (1545–1563), a gathering known for its
many *anathemas. Anathema sit* literally means
"let them be set aside," and many of Trent's declarations ended with that phrase, declaring that
anyone who would reject that given teaching be
considered outside the Catholic Church.

The term "Counter-Reformation" is something of a misnomer. Initiatives for reform in the
Catholic Church preceded Martin Luther, and
many continued in the midst of the Protestant
Reformation. While Trent's decisions were certainly interested in defining the Catholic faith in
light of the Reformation, many of them addressed reform issues that had been brewing
within the Catholic Church for some time. Further, one ought not to take the decrees of Trent or
its anathemas out of context. This was an era for
all Western Christians—Lutheran, Reformed,
Anabaptist, and Catholic—to differentiate themselves from each other, and it was punctuated by
a wealth of dismissals and condemnations. The
more accurate term for what was going on in Catholicism, before, during, and after the Protestant Reformation, is the **Catholic Reformation**.

As mentioned in Chapter Thirteen, the
Catholic Reformation began well before Luther.
John Wycliffe challenged the church in the fourteenth century, and Jan Hus in the fifteenth. The
conciliarism movement that sought to elevate
church councils over the papacy continued into
the sixteenth century. Humanists such as Erasmus widely challenged the church to reform
itself, and Catholic clergy united in groups of
oratories in order to support reform. During the
heat of the Reformation, Pope Paul III (r. 1534–
1549) even reconstituted the College of Cardinals from members of one of the most dynamic
oratories, the Oratory of Divine Love.

New religious orders were also formed
before, during, and after the Protestant Reformation as part of the Catholic reform movement. As
noted in Chapter Thirteen, in 1524 the Theatines, an order of clergy under the Augustinian
Rule, emerged for the purpose of training and
reforming the clergy. In 1528, Matteo da Bascio
received permission from Pope Clement VII to
organize a new vision of the Franciscans, which
soon became the Capuchin order. This order also
helped revitalize faith within the church. A century later, other religious orders dedicated to
reform of the church emerged, such as the
Congregation of the Mission (the Vincentians)
started by Vincent de Paul, and the Ursuline
Sisters, started by Angela Merici. Both orders
devoted themselves to education and care of
the sick and needy.

In the late fifteenth and throughout the sixteenth centuries, Spain experienced great religious revival. Ferdinand and Isabella demanded
that monasteries, religious orders, and clergy
reform, with Isabella and Cardinal Ximenes personally visiting many monasteries to ensure that
they engaged in authentic practice. Isabella also
took steps to see that priests receiving a high office
in the church did so because of their piety and
competence rather than their family connections.

 CARMELITES AND FURTHER
DEVELOPMENTS OF MYSTICISM

One of the more interesting developments in
Spain was a new order of Carmelite nuns and
monks: Discalced (shoeless) **Carmelites**. The Carmelite order began in Palestine in the early thirteenth century and initially consisted of a group
of monks who lived in hermitages on or around
Mount Carmel. Some migrated to Europe by the
middle of the century, and the rest were expelled
by their Muslim rulers by 1291. In Europe, many
of these monks were ordained as priests, and the
order experienced a tension between its original
contemplative mission and the pastoral care of
others outside the monastery. In 1452, the
church approved the reception into the order of

women, who then formed their own monasteries. The Carmelite nun **Teresa of Avila** (1515–1582) became convinced that the order was lax and had lost its contemplative agenda, and began advancing reform. She started sixteen monasteries and eventually received permission in 1580 for her movement to be considered a separate Carmelite order. The women's order was in fact negligent, and Teresa's initiatives constituted a significant reform. The men's order, however, was not lax at all, although it did reflect the conflict between a strictly contemplative life and one of pastoral service. One of Teresa's friends and a supporter of reform to the men's order was **John of the Cross** (1542–1591), a profoundly prayerful and scholarly monk who also sought to reform the order to one of greater contemplative withdrawal. John had more trouble than Teresa. While he had the support of the Spanish church authorities, he lacked the support of Rome. Thus, on the charge of disobedience, Carmelites kidnapped him from his monastery, took him to another, and locked him in what amounted to little more than a closet for six months. He eventually escaped and continued the Discalced men's movement. Both Teresa and John are

FIGURE 15-1 Teresa of Avila, a Carmelite reformer and mystic.

FIGURE 15-2 John of the Cross became one of the greatest theological articulators of the dynamics of the mystical life.

considered spiritual heroes and guides in both the original Carmelite and Discalced Carmelite orders.

What makes Teresa and John particularly important is not their reform of the Carmelite order, though the women's reform was successful. Rather, their value lies in their articulation of the life of prayer and how it proceeds to union with God. Both Teresa and John were mystics who enjoyed many experiences of profound union with God. Their writings detail the stages of prayer, interior transformation, and how progress in the interior life ought to be accomplished. Such detailed discussion of the mystical life was highly unusual for this period. Historically, a great deal of spiritual writing in the Christian tradition had focused on prayer that was mediated through scripture, liturgy, and the normal use of the mind

in response to images. Far less writing was devoted to more direct interior knowledge of God within one's soul, and less still was devoted to the subject of full-fledged union. There were exceptions, such as Gregory of Nyssa's *Life of Moses*, noted in Chapter Eight. In this text Gregory describes how a soul moves from a life of sin to a life of virtue through God's grace, and then from mediated prayer to unmediated knowledge of God. Gregory's book, however, pales in comparison to the works of Teresa and John, which excel in detail and display a profound sense of psychological and spiritual savvy. John's university training made his works particularly important, as he grounded them in philosophy and theology. John was also a poet, and his poetry is considered among some of the best in the Spanish language, even by secular assessments.

JOHN OF THE CROSS'S "THE DARK NIGHT"

"The Dark Night: Songs of the soul that rejoices in having reached the high state of perfection, which is union with God, by the path of spiritual negation."

En una noche obscura,
con ansias en amores inflamada,
¡oh dichosa ventura!
salí sin ser notada,
estando ya mi casa sosegada.

A oscuras y segura,
por la secreta escala disfrazada,
¡oh dichosa ventura!
a oscuras y en celada,
estando ya mi casa sosegada.

En la noche dichosa,
en secreto, que nadie me veía,
ni yo miraba cosa,
sin otra luz y guía
sino la que en el corazón ardía.

Aquésta me guiaba
más cierto que la luz del mediodía,
adónde me esperaba
quien yo bien me sabía,
en parte donde nadie parecía.

One dark night,
fired with love's urgent longings
—ah, the sheer grace!—
I went out unseen,
My house being now all stilled.

In darkness, and secure,
by the secret ladder, disguised,
—ah, the sheer grace!—
in darkness and concealment
My house being now all stilled.

On that glad night
in secret, for no one saw me,
nor did I look at anything
with no other light or guide
than the one that burned in my heart.

This guided me
more surely than the light of noon
to where he was awaiting me
—him I knew so well—
There in a place where no one appeared.

¡Oh noche que me guiaste!   O guiding night!
¡Oh noche amable más que el alborada!   O night more lovely than the dawn!
¡oh noche que juntaste   O night that has united
Amado con amada,   the Lover with his beloved,
amada en el Amado transformada!   Transforming the beloved in her Lover.

En mi pecho florido,   Upon my flowering breast,
que entero para él solo se guardaba,   which I kept wholly for him alone,
allí quedó dormido,   there he lay sleeping
y yo le regalaba,   and I caressing him
y el ventalle de cedros aire daba.   There in a breeze from fanning cedars.

El aire de la almena,   When the breeze blew from the turret,
cuando ya sus cabellos esparcía,   as I parted his hair,
con su mano serena   it wounded my neck
en mi cuello hería,   with its gentle hand,
y todos mis sentidos suspendía.   suspending all my senses.

Quedéme y olvidéme,   I abandoned and forgot myself,
el rostro recliné sobre el Amado,   laying my face on my Beloved;
cesó todo, y dejéme,   all things ceased; I went out from myself,
dejando mi cuidado   leaving my cares
entre las azucenas olvidado.   forgotten among the lilies.[1]

IGNATIUS OF LOYOLA AND THE SOCIETY OF JESUS

Ignatius of Loyola (1491–1556) was born to a noble family in the Basque village of Loyola in what is today northern Spain. He spent much of his early adulthood as a soldier, striving to promote himself in the royal court. For ten years he was successful, but in 1521 a cannonball shattered his leg. He returned to his family's property in Loyola to convalesce. Prior to his injury he had absorbed many stories of chivalrous glory, which had inspired him. During his recovery he only had religious literature to read, such as the scriptures and lives of the saints, and he realized that they kindled within him the same kind of enthusiasm. But he also realized something else: while tales of chivalry had inspired him at the time he had read them, they ultimately left him restless and dry. In contrast, when he read the heroic lives of the saints, he found he retained this inspiration long after. Ignatius discovered that he experienced a profound satisfaction and inner joy in considering giving his life to God

that worldly glory could not provide. Ludolph of Saxony's *The Life of Christ*, a commentary on the Gospels, proved particularly important to Ignatius's spiritual development. Through this text Ignatius found within himself a burning desire to be like Christ and to emulate the heroic lives of the saints. In his autobiography, *A Pilgrim's Journey*, Ignatius describes the change he experienced from "having a vain and overpowering desire to gain renown" to demanding of himself: "Saint Dominic did this, so I have to do it too. Saint Francis did this, so I have to do it too."[2]

In 1522, Ignatius, now recovered, made a pilgrimage to the Benedictine abbey in Montserrat, Spain. There he dropped "his sword and dagger at our Lady's altar in the church."[3] He left the abbey as a poor pilgrim and went to live in a cave in Manresa, where he prayed for many hours a day. It was in Manresa that he began formulating the **spiritual exercises**, the framework for the extended retreat that stood at the heart of his spiritual path. Eventually, Ignatius decided that if he were to help souls he would need a theological

FIGURE 15-3 Ignatius of Loyola began the order of the Society of Jesus (Jesuits). The Jesuits were foundational for the Catholic Reformation, as well as for missions.

education, which he began at the University of Alcala and ended at the University of Paris. It was in Paris that he formed a group of fellow students who desired to live exclusively for the service of God and the church. They would ultimately migrate to Rome and form the religious order called the Society of Jesus, commonly known as the **Jesuits**. The mission of the order was utterly open-ended; they wanted to do whatever the church needed, anywhere and at any time. Ignatius and other Jesuits guided many men and even a number of women in the spiritual exercises, which led to a rapid expansion of the order. By the time Ignatius died in 1556, over 800 Jesuits lived throughout Europe, with a few even engaging in missionary work as far away as India and Japan.

Most religious orders have a certain spirituality or apostolic mission. To be a Dominican was to be a learned preacher; to be a Franciscan was to

witness to the simplicity of the Christian life through poverty; to be a Carmelite was to live a deeply contemplative life. But what did it mean to be a Jesuit? In 1552, two of Ignatius's closest associates, Juan de Polanco and Jeronimo Nadal, asked Ignatius to dictate his autobiography. Nadal then traveled to every Jesuit house in Europe to propagate both the order's revised constitution and Ignatius's story, which Nadal thought was paradigmatic for what it meant to be a Jesuit. It was Nadal who coined the famous phrase *contemplation in action*, that is, to be a Jesuit was to learn how to experience God's movements in one's soul in the context of active service. Above all, the Ignatian spirit was one of *indifference*, that is, being completely open and without preference to whatever God moved the soul to do.

The spiritual exercises represent a silent month-long retreat designed for two aims: first, to ingrain in the retreatant an identification with Christ and his mission, and second, to help the retreatant make a decision, called an election, toward a vocation of service or to confirm on a deep level a decision he or she has already made. It serves as a systematic way to come to a deep spiritual conversion and embrace the will of God. Ignatius wrote: "By the term *spiritual exercises* is meant every method of examination of conscience, of meditation, of contemplation, of vocal and mental prayer, and of other spiritual activities . . . every way of preparing and disposing the soul to rid itself of all inordinate attachments, and, after their removal, of seeking and finding the will of God in the disposition of our life for the salvation of our soul."[4]

The spiritual exercises became an enormously valuable tool for the Catholic Reformation. Those who could afford to leave their families for this month-long retreat—generally members of the nobility and the wealthy middle classes—returned with greater zeal for their Christian faith and its mission. The banner of the Jesuits and those under their influence was *Ad Majorem Dei Gloriam*: For the greater glory of God. Ignatian spirituality also taught Christians how to discover the presence of God in their day-to-day lives and how to distinguish between movements from God and movements that were disordered in their souls.

Jesuits soon became some of the best and brightest Christians in the Catholic Church. Ignatius and his companions had no sense that their ministry would be academic; rather, they imagined themselves as more associated with missionary work and ministry to the needy. But early on, and at the request of Pope Paul III, they started a college in Rome. Soon, academic excellence became a hallmark of the ministry of the Society of Jesus, and its members acted as intellectual responders to Protestant theologians and doctrine.

THE COUNCIL OF TRENT (1545–1563)

The **Council of Trent** was decidedly the biggest event in the Catholic Reformation. Through it Catholicism cleaned up many abuses, created a uniform liturgy, and articulated its theology, particularly as a contrast to Lutheran, Reformed, and Anabaptist doctrine. It also set up a kind of wall separating Catholicism and Protestant traditions.

ATTEMPTED REFORMS PRIOR TO TRENT

One of the little-known facts about the Catholic Church is that the Council of Trent was actually the second council in the sixteenth century. In 1512, Pope Julius II (r. 1503–1513) assembled the council known as Lateran V (1512–1517). The backstory to Lateran V is itself fascinating. The Council of Constance had demanded that regular councils be held, mostly to keep the papacy in check. One such council was the Council of Basel, which initially met in 1431 and would eventually migrate to Ferrara and then to Florence. Basel reiterated conciliarism, the principle that councils had greater authority than the pope. When Pope Eugene IV moved subsequent meetings of the council to Ferrara, some bishops refused to relocate and remained in Basel. There, they deposed Pope Eugene and elected a new pope, Felix V. Eugene commanded Felix to

abandon his claim and acknowledge Eugene as the true pope. With little backing for Felix in the larger church, the remnant at Basel remained in place for years. Eugene died in 1447 and was replaced by Pope Nicholas V. In 1449, the bishops who had remained in Basel, seeing that their cause was lost, then "elected" Nicholas, who had already been pope for two years. It was Nicholas who formally accepted Felix's abdication. In short, Basel was a mess. In 1460, Pope Pius II formally condemned conciliarism.

In 1511, several dissatisfied cardinals gathered for a council in Pisa, initially with the support of the French king and the Holy Roman emperor. The bishops—only a small contingency of whom actually went—met in late 1511 to early 1512. At this gathering, they reasserted conciliarism and, like Basel, deposed the pope. Pope Julius II then called Lateran V in an effort to undermine Pisa and once again denounce conciliarism. He also took the opportunity to formally condemn a French legal document known as the *Pragmatic Sanction of Bourges*, which restricted the pope's authority to naming bishops, abbots, and other church officials in France.

One of the most impressive voices of Lateran V was that of Giles of Viterbo, the head of the Augustinian order, to which Martin Luther had also belonged. At the opening of the council Viterbo announced the importance of such gatherings: "[T]he church cannot perform well without the attention of the councils. . . . With the light of councils and the Holy Spirit, the winds blow and the dead eyes of the church come to life again and receive the light. . . . Without councils, faith cannot stand firm. Without councils, therefore, we cannot be saved."[5] He then challenged the council to look deeply into a church that was seriously flawed and in need of reform:

> When has ambition been more unrestrained, greed more burning? When has the license to sin been more shameless? When has the temerity in speaking, in arguing, in writing against piety been more common or more unafraid? When has there been among the people not only a greater neglect, but a greater contempt for the

FIGURE 15-4 Council of Trent, reforming Roman Catholicism after the Protestant Reformation.

sacred, for the sacraments, for the keys [penance], and for the holy commandments? When have our religion and faith been more open to the derision even of the lowest classes?[6]

Lateran V did legislate reform, particularly against simony, priestly concubinage, and the lay control of church rights. But the rules it wrote had so many loopholes that it later proved easy to avoid the restrictions. Fundamentally, the papacy, cardinals, and bishops simply had little interest at the time in legitimate, hard-hitting reforms. These would have to wait until the Council of Trent, which would not come until after the Protestant Reformation.

TRENT (1545–1563)

In 1535, Pope Paul III announced his intention to call another council, but it would not be until a decade later that the first session met. One problem was where to hold such a gathering. The Holy Roman emperor, Charles V, wanted it to be held in Germany, believing it might have the psychological power to directly contest the growing Lutheran threat. The French, often at odds with the Holy Roman Empire, balked at the idea, while Italian cardinals argued that the council should be held in Rome, their power base. Trent was ultimately chosen as a compromise site. It was technically within the boundaries of the Holy Roman Empire, but essentially sat on Italian soil, and today is part of northern Italy. The council consisted of three different convocations that spanned eighteen years and the reigns of four different popes. The first meeting (1545–1547) primarily dealt with doctrinal matters, the second (1551–1552) focused on some doctrinal and practical issues, and the third (1562–1563) focused on other reform and disciplinary issues.

One reason that Trent has been imagined as the Counter-Reformation council is that it addressed many doctrines that were directly challenged by Protestant reformers. Take, for example, the Lutheran and Reformed position on justification. Recall that for Luther and Calvin justification happened passively and irresistibly. Further, at least for Luther, one's righteousness was an *alien* righteousness, that is, it was imputed to the soul without necessarily changing the condition of the soul. The following, which is only a small part of Trent's decrees on justification, is an example of the lengths to which Trent went to clarify Catholic doctrine both for itself and in light of the Protestant challenge.

> The causes of this justification are: The final cause is the glory of God and of Christ and life everlasting; the efficient cause is the merciful God who washes and sanctifies (1 Cor 6:11) gratuitously, signing and anointing with the Holy Spirit of promise, who is the pledge of our inheritance (Eph 1:13ff.). The meritorious cause is His most beloved only begotten, our Lord Jesus Christ, who, when we were enemies (Rom 5:10), for the exceeding charity wherewith he loved us (Eph 2:4), merited for us justification by His most holy passion on the wood of the cross and made satisfaction for us to God the Father. The instrumental cause is the sacrament of baptism, which is the sacrament of faith, without which no man was ever justified finally. The single formal cause is the justice of God, not that by which He Himself is just, but that by which He makes us just, that, namely, with which we being endowed by Him, are renewed in the spirit of our mind (Eph 4:23), and not only are we reputed but we are truly called and are just, receiving justice within us, each one according to his own measure, which the Holy Spirit distributes to everyone as He wills (1 Cor 12:11) and according to each one's disposition and cooperation.[7]

This seemingly long description is only a portion of the text, but it reveals a great deal. In this view justification comes entirely from God as a gift and is conditioned on the merits of Christ and his saving work. Thus, the council argued that there was no conflict with the Reformers on this point. Nevertheless, it challenged the Reformers' position by insisting that one who is justified is *actually* justified by God, that is, one does not merely have imputed justice but is changed by God's grace. Later in the decree one finds the statement: "[W]hence man through Jesus Christ, in whom he is ingrafted, receives in that justification, together with the remission of sins, all these infused at the same time, namely, faith, hope and charity."[8] Further, the quality of the state of one's soul is understood as being marked in part by one's "disposition and cooperation." As for Luther and Calvin's insistence that one is passively and irresistibly justified, Trent countered that justification is a *voluntary reception*. "Man himself," the decree declares, "neither does absolutely nothing while receiving that inspiration [grace], since he can reject it."[9] There is no question here of "works righteousness," but there is the necessity of the soul's free activity in cooperating and participating in that justification.

Trent argued two further things. First, it is possible that through sin one can lose one's justification. Thus, Trent rejected Calvin's "once saved, always saved" understanding of justification. Second, Trent argued that, given the nature of free will, a Christian must continue to cooperate with God's grace and pursue an authentic Christian life. Failure to do so will result in the loss of one's justification. To the Protestant position that justified Christians simply do good works because these reflect the state of the saved soul, Trent argued that one must also do good works because these reflect the ongoing cooperation with grace. This is not a mere distinction without a difference. For the Protestants, good works were disconnected from salvation in any way, a position they viewed as relieving the Christian from worrying about whether he or she had done enough. For the Catholics, Trent clarified that the salvation project is not simply wrapped up in a one-time justification event. One truly is responsible for living out the Christian life, and one's salvation depends on it.

This lengthy discussion about justification provides a good example of how Trent tried to distinguish Catholic from Protestant theology. The texts of the council address other controversial issues as well. Luther argued that there were only two sacraments, baptism and the Eucharist, and other Protestants seemed to see baptism as the sole sacrament. Trent reiterated, described, and defended seven. The Reformed and Anabaptist traditions were thoroughly iconoclastic, seeing images of Jesus or the saints as nothing more than idolatry. Trent responded that they are valuable tools for authentic devotion. The Anabaptists argued against infant baptism, so Trent described why it is valid.

One of the most defining issues of the Reformation was the role of scripture. The Reformers argued that scripture was the sole authority for doctrine, and most believed it the only authoritative source for Christian life. Further, following Renaissance biblical scholarship, the Reformers argued both for the primacy of the Hebrew (Old Testament) and Greek (New Testament) texts and for the right to translate these texts into the common language, or vernacular. Trent responded by insisting on the Latin text, a cleaned-up version of Jerome's Vulgate, as the church's Bible. Further, it argued that revelation comes not only from scripture, but also from tradition, and that these are intrinsically united. And finally, it stated that the church's interpretation of the text, through the magisterium of bishops, councils, and popes, would be determinative. From a modern perspective, it appears as though Trent had a point. As noted in earlier chapters, there is a necessarily intrinsic relationship between scripture and tradition, and few modern theologians today herald *sola scriptura* as a workable theological principle. Further, the Reformers had discovered that interpreting scripture was complicated and controversial. For those following Zwingli or the Anabaptist tradition, the Bible could mean virtually anything to anyone who picked up the book. For Calvin, authentic biblical interpretation came from scholarly argument, although ultimately it was decided by a given city council. And for Lutherans, biblical interpretation was decided ad hoc by pastors through the lens of the Augsburg Confession, itself not a biblical text. Most scholars today agree that these interpreting sources acted as an authoritative magisterium, much like the Catholic magisterium.

The oddest insistence of Trent was that the Vulgate, a translation of the original languages in which the Old and New Testaments were written, be preferred over the actual original text, or at least the best available manuscript. Why privilege a translation over the original? Ultimately, it took Catholicism 400 years to formally wean itself off of the Vulgate. From the beginning of the modern period on, few if any Catholic biblical scholars worked with the Vulgate at all, and surely none gave it greater authority than the original texts. Trent would be unable to show how the Latin translation was necessarily preferable to a vernacular translation. The consequence of this insistence on the Vulgate was centuries during which Catholic lay people simply did not read the Bible. There is a myth that Catholicism forbade Catholics from reading the Bible privately. It never did. The problem was the Vulgate.

A final biblical question resolved at Trent concerned the very texts that made up the Bible. Since the patristic church, there had been no controversy about which texts made up the New Testament. Until the Protestant Reformation, there was virtually no controversy about the Old Testament either. But Luther and the Reformers who followed him challenged a number of Old Testament texts as noncanonical. These texts were part of the Septuagint, the Greek translation of the Old Testament that Jews used during the late Greek and early Roman dynasties. The Septuagint included books that were not originally written in Hebrew: Tobit, Judith, First and Second Maccabees, Wisdom, Sirach, Baruch, and parts of Esther and Daniel. Until the Protestant Reformation, their inclusion was never challenged. They were even insisted upon by the Synod of Carthage (397) as noted in Chapter Three.

Luther could argue that eventually Jews themselves did not include them in their canon, the Tanakh. But Luther surely had another concern: Second Maccabees 12:39–45 presented a Catholic proof text for the doctrine of purgatory and the practice of praying for the souls in purgatory. As noted in Chapter Fourteen, the doctrines surrounding purgatory were denounced by Luther. The Reformers' Bible did not include these texts, while Trent insisted on them. The result was that Protestants, Catholics, and Orthodox have since the sixteenth century used differing Old Testaments. The difference between the Catholic and Orthodox canons is marginal,[10] and both Catholic and Orthodox churches think that their agreed-on books are important. For the Protestants, these books remain part of the **apocrypha**, a word that can mean "hidden" as well as "false." Such texts remain interesting for Protestant scholars but are simply not considered canonical.

Trent also addressed areas in need of reform. Bishops had to become residents of their dioceses and could not have multiple "benefices," or outside sources of income. Simony and nepotism were abolished with hard and fast rules. Trent also required that bishops ensure the formal training of their priest candidates. From then on, priests had to be either classically trained at a university or educated through a seminary designed for priesthood training. The church's liturgical rites were revised and standardized. Other abuses were also addressed, such as the sale of indulgences. While indulgences were maintained as a practice, they could no longer be bought or sold. Trent also both commended and reformed religious devotions. Icons, relics, and other devotions were supported, but were challenged to be free of any superstitions or exaggerations. Finally, Trent pronounced the need for a catechism, which was eventually compiled by Charles Borromeo, the reforming archbishop of Milan.

 ## EASTERN ORTHODOXY AT THE TIME OF THE REFORMATION

The Protestant Reformation had little impact on the Eastern Orthodox Church. Western representatives from Protestant and Catholic countries kept Orthodox leaders regularly aware of the debates and controversies within their church, but the Orthodox showed little interest in them. Perhaps the most telling encounter was a dialogue in 1573 between a group of leading Lutheran theologians and Jeremias II, the patriarch of Constantinople. They gave him a copy of the Augsburg Confession translated into Greek. Jeremias studied the texts and returned with three sets of *Answers*, wherein he addressed their positions. In every set of his *Answers*, he explained the Orthodox understanding of theology and how it differed from Lutheran theology. He conceded essentially nothing outlined in the Augsburg Confession. After he gave the theologians his third set of *Answers*, he ended the dialogue. In his mind, there was nothing more to say.

The Catholic Reformation had more of an impact on the Orthodox Church, though not without controversy. Catholics had for some time strived to reunite with the Orthodox Church. This had almost happened in the late thirteenth century after the Council of Lyons II (1272–1274), and then again at the Council of Basel in 1439. At the latter gathering, the two churches agreed to reunite, but the emperor refused to promulgate the agreement of unity, *Laetentur Coeli*. During the time of the Catholic Reformation, Catholics and Orthodox clashed in the Ukraine. When the Mongols captured Kiev, Russia lost the Ukraine, which came under the domination of modern-day Poland and Lithuania, producing a Catholic majority ruling over an Orthodox minority. Jesuit priests negotiated with Orthodox leaders to reunify Orthodoxy and Catholicism, but when a council was called in 1596 at Brest-Litovsk, the Orthodox hierarchy was ambivalent and ultimately backed out. Some Eastern communions did unite with Rome and ultimately formed the Eastern Rites of the Roman Catholic Church.

By this time the church in Russia had become the dominant presence within Orthodoxy. While Mediterranean Orthodox Christians were floundering under the weight of Muslim advances, Russia was expanding its empire. As it did so, the Orthodox Church grew. Czar Ivan IV (r. 1547–1584), also known as "Ivan the Terrible," was responsible for much of this expansion. He also saw himself as protector of the church and expected support from the church in return. One possible reason that Russian church leaders stayed aloof from attempts at unification is that the Russian Orthodox Church was a deeply monastic one. Of course, Russia had a patriarchate and was based on the ancient episcopal model of church leadership. But the real power was with the monasteries, which dominated landholdings in Russia and were responsible for a great deal of pastoral ministry. Monasteries, by their nature, tend to be parochial in their view rather than universal. In Russia, their leaders saw far less need for grand church unity than for the practice of the faith right in front of them.

As noted earlier, many Orthodox, and certainly the vast majority of Russian Orthodox, considered Moscow the Third Rome when it became a patriarchate in 1589, with its emperor as czar and guardian of the Orthodox faith. During the 1650s Czar Alexis gathered scholars, linguists, and theologians together to review the ritual, morality, and spirituality of the Russian church. Patriarch Nikon (r. 1652–1658) took on a prominent role in this reform. Though it was modest and based on the Greek model, many ultra-traditionalists, known as "Old Believers," balked and started a schism. At stake for the Russian czar and the

patriarch was the special status of the Third Rome as guardian of the Orthodox tradition. A shockingly large number of Old Believers took their lives rather than submit to the innovations. During the reign of Peter the Great (1682–1725), the persecution of Old Believers and their subsequent mass suicides reached their peak. For Czar Peter, the religion of the Old Believers was tantamount to treason. By the end of his reign as czar, he had enacted a number of laws that mandated church attendance for Christians and imposed fines on anyone who did not attend communion or make confession at least once a year.

Ultimately, Empress Catherine II (r. 1762–1796) issued a decree of religious toleration in 1764, which was particularly important for Slavic pagans, Jews, and Muslims, as well as for the Old Believers. For Catherine, any state coercion violated not only religious freedom—a French Enlightenment idea that had migrated to Russia—but also the very integrity of the Christian faith.

CONCLUSIONS

When one compares the Catholic Church at the beginning of the sixteenth century to that of the century's end, one sees a dramatic change. Many of the abuses in the church from the Late Middle Ages and Renaissance periods were rectified. There was renewed spiritual vigor and greater institutional competence. Bishops were far more likely to receive their posts because of their piety and competence, and priests were required to be broadly educated and better trained to guide their flocks. Catholic doctrine was clarified and devotional practices purified to some degree of their exaggerated or superstitious layers. Until recently, many scholars, Catholic and Protestant alike, had derided much of the Council of Trent, characterizing it as a tragic reactionary council that set the church back. Now, the scholarly consensus is that Trent was a robust council that reset the Catholic Church in many important ways.

There were, however, two downsides to the Catholic Reformation. The first is that it simply came too late. Early in the century, Lateran V was convoked with at least a modest reform agenda, but in the end it achieved virtually nothing. One can only wonder whether the Protestant Reformation would have been necessary if Lateran V had had the energy and commitment that Trent would have decades later. Second, the Catholic Reformation created such a clear distinction between Catholicism and Protestantism that it effectively kept both camps from dialogue. The Catholics became known as "papists" or "Romanists" by Protestants, and they in turn became known as "schismatics" and "heretics" by Catholics. Catholicism entrenched itself behind high walls, much to its future harm. It would be 300 years before another council, Vatican I (1869–1870), convened, and an additional 100 years before Catholicism, in Vatican

II (1962–1965), opened its gates to dialogue with Protestants. The Catholic world cleaned much of its house in the sixteenth century, but with regard to other Christians, it continued to carry Trent's well-worn phrase in its heart: *anathema sit.*

SUMMARY QUESTIONS

- Why is the term "Counter-Reformation" a misnomer?
- What were some of the reforming actions taken by the Catholic Church prior to the Reformation?
- In what ways was the Jesuit order beneficial for the Catholic Church during the Reformation?

- What were some ways in which the Council of Trent differentiated Catholicism from Protestant groups doctrinally? What institutional reforms did the council make?

DISCUSSION QUESTIONS

- Why does the author believe that the term *Counter-Reformation* is a misnomer? Given that much of it did in fact counter Protestantism, do you think his reasoning is sound? Explain.
- According to the author, the Society of Jesus (Jesuits) did not start as a religious order interested in education, but quickly became its hallmark. Do you think that this move was a corruption from the vision of Ignatius or aligned with it? Explain.
- Review the lengthy quote on justification from the Council of Trent. Do you think that it principally aligns or departs from that of the Protestants? Regarding any divergences from the Protestants, do you think Trent's position more intellectually cogent than that of Luther or Calvin? Why or why not?

KEY TERMS

Apocrypha
Carmelites
Catholic Reformation
Council of Trent

Counter-Reformation
Ignatius of Loyola
Jesuits
John of the Cross

Spiritual exercises
Teresa of Avila

BIBLIOGRAPHY

- Bellitto, Christopher. 2002. *The General Councils: A History of the Twenty-One Church Councils from Nicaea to Vatican II.* New York: Paulist Press.
- Burrows, Ruth. 1987. *Ascent to Love: The Spiritual Teachings of St. John of the Cross.* Denville, NJ: Dimension Books.
- Chadwick, Owen. 1965. *The Reformation.* Baltimore: Penguin.
- Egan, Harvey. 1976. *The Spiritual Exercises and the Ignatian Mystical Horizon.* St. Louis: Institute of Jesuit Sources.

- Fleming, David. 1978. *The Spiritual Exercises of St. Ignatius: A Literal Translation and a Contemporary Reading.* Trans. Elder Mullan. St. Louis: Institute of Jesuit Sources.
- Ignatius of Loyola. 1991a. *A Pilgrim's Journey: The Autobiography of Ignatius of Loyola.* Trans. and comm. Joseph Tylenda. Collegeville, MN: Michael Glazier.
- Ignatius of Loyola. 1991b. *Ignatius of Loyola: Spiritual Exercises and Selected Works.* Ed. George Ganss. Mahwah, NJ: Paulist Press.

- John of the Cross. 1991. *The Collected Works of John of the Cross*, rev. ed. Trans. Kieran Kavanaugh and Otilio Rodriguez. Washington, D.C.: Institute of Carmelite Studies.
- Mullett, Michael. 1999. *The Catholic Reformation*. London: Routledge.
- Olin, John. 1990. *The Catholic Reform: From Cardinal Ximenes to the Council of Trent, 1495–1563*. New York: Fordham University Press.
- O'Malley, John. 1993. *The First Jesuits*. Cambridge: Harvard University Press.
- O'Malley, John. 2000. *Trent and All That: Renaming Catholicism in the Early Modern Era*. Cambridge: Harvard University Press.
- O'Malley, John. 2013. *Trent: What Happened at the Council*. Cambridge: Harvard University Press.
- Puhl, Louis, trans. 1951. *The Spiritual Exercises of St. Ignatius*. Chicago: University of Loyola Press.
- Teresa of Avila. 1976–1985. *The Collected Works of St. Teresa of Avila*, 3 vols. Trans. Kieran Kavanaugh and Otilio Rodriguez. Washington, D.C.: ICS Publications.
- Toner, Jules. 1991. *Discerning God's Will: Ignatius of Loyola's Teaching on Christian Decision Making*. St. Louis: Institute of Jesuit Sources.

NOTES

1. John of the Cross, *Collected Works*, 50–52.
2. Ignatius of Loyola, *A Pilgrim's Journey*, 7, 14.
3. Ibid., 26.
4. Puhl, *Spiritual Exercise*, no. 1, 1.
5. Bellitto, *General Councils*, 98.
6. Ibid.
7. "The Council of Trent: Session VI: Celebrated on the thirteenth day of January, 1547 under Pope Paul III," accessed at http://www.ewtn.com/library/COUNCILS/TRENT6.HTM. This text was modestly edited in punctuation.
8. Ibid.
9. Ibid.
10. The Orthodox canon also includes the Prayer of Manasseh, an additional Psalm, Third and Fourth Maccabees, and First and Second Esdras.

The Enlightenment

FROM CONFLICT TO TOLERANCE

Timeline

1533 CE	Copernicus publishes *On the Revolutions of the Heavenly Spheres*, advancing heliocentrism (planets revolving around the sun)
1598 CE	Edict of Nantes guarantees freedom to French Calvinists (Huguenots)
1611 CE	King James Bible completed
1618–1648 CE	Thirty Years' War, ended by the Peace of Westphalia (1648)
1620 CE	Puritans arrive in North America on the *Mayflower* and establish a colony at Plymouth
1633 CE	Trial and condemnation of Galileo

WHAT TO EXPECT

The Protestant Reformation was a tumultuous time in European Christianity, but nothing compares to subsequent events. The first development that this chapter investigates has to do with the various "Wars of Religion" that followed the Reformation. The breakup of the Western church was part of a larger current of social and political upheaval, in which religion as well as many other factors played a large part. Between the mid-sixteenth and the mid-seventeenth century, some or even most of the European nations fought each other. This chapter will also discuss just how religious the so-called Wars of Religion really were. The next century was just as tumultuous to Christianity, but for another reason. As the scientific method developed and philosophers attempted to answer the question of how knowledge was secured, Europe entered into the period of the Enlightenment. During this time, religious faith itself was questioned. The Enlightenment produced few nonbelievers, but it did set the stage for the modern world, in which atheism became a bona fide contender for the hearts and minds of European intellectuals.

THE WARS OF RELIGION

From the beginning of the Protestant Reformation until the middle of the seventeenth century, Europe was engaged in a series of wars, sometimes dubbed the **Wars of Religion**. In many ways, this framing of these European conflicts is accurate. Before the Peace of Augsburg in 1555, the Holy Roman Empire was engaged in war with much of its Lutheran German nobility. The Low Countries of the modern-day Netherlands, Belgium, and Luxembourg were also involved in conflicts between various Catholics and Protestants seeking to secure their religious faith. France also experienced great interior conflict based on religion, and, the British Isles underwent over a decade of civil wars, some of which were religiously motivated. Nevertheless, the truth of the matter is more complex, in that many of these wars were also highly political and economic. Take, for example, the German Peasants' War of 1524–1525. This was mostly a war waged by German commoners against the feudal nobility. Martin Luther was on the side of the nobility in this case, and saw the war as an unjustified civil war. A decade later, a second uprising in Westphalia had religious overtones, but again it was predominantly an economic and political challenge. Yet another decade later, the Schmalkaldic War in the 1540s sought to replace the Holy Roman Empire itself. This conflict was partly religious, as it responded to the emperor's attempt to privilege Catholicism, but it also had a great deal to do with overall resentment against the Holy Roman emperor and the imperial state. These three wars were the beginnings of the Wars of Religion, and as is clear from these overviews, much of the conflict was really about German politics.

THE THIRTY YEARS' WAR

The **Thirty Years' War** was more decidedly religious than its predecessors, though power politics played a large role in it too. Recall from Chapter Thirteen that Bohemia had many citizens who were drifting from the Latin rite of the Catholic Church, with an uneasy truce between them and Rome. Recall also that Bohemia held a number of much more radical separatists who had been repressed, the Bohemian and Moravian Brethren. By the mid-sixteenth century their ranks had swelled as a result of German Calvinists fleeing Germany after the Peace of Augsburg in 1555. The Peace of Augsburg decided that each German principality would be either Catholic or Lutheran, depending on the faith of the prince. It made no provisions for Calvinists, who either had to submit to the Catholic or Lutheran tradition or leave. Many went to Bohemia. In 1617, Ferdinand II, a staunch Catholic, became king of Bohemia and alienated his Protestant subjects by doing away with religious freedom. In 1618, a group of Protestant nobles went to the Royal Council in Prague to demand the restoration of their religious rights. When the council refused to hear their case, the nobles threw two of the king's representatives out of a high window. They only survived because they fell into a pile of dung. This event marked the beginning of the Thirty Years' War.

Bohemian Protestants and Catholics both sought outside European support. German Lutherans refused to support the Protestant cause because the Moravian Brethren were Calvinists and not Lutherans. But others did support the Protestants, including England, the Netherlands, Denmark, and Sweden. The Holy Roman Empire sent troops to support the Catholic side, but not all Catholic countries were so eager. At the time, Spain, the Holy Roman Empire, Austria, and Bohemia were all ruled by members of the **Hapsburg** family. In an attempt to weaken Hapsburg control, Catholic France aided the Protestant cause.

Initially, the Bohemian Calvinists seemed to succeed. They dethroned Ferdinand and installed as their king Frederick V, who happened to be the son-in-law of the English king, James I. Soon, however, Ferdinand was named Holy Roman emperor and invaded Bohemia, deposing Frederick. In 1625, Denmark invaded Germany; although its forces were ultimately conquered, the Danes served to weaken the

Holy Roman Empire. Still, Ferdinand was now determined to take advantage of the war and restore large sections of Lutheran Germany to Catholicism. In 1630, the king of Sweden, Gustavus Adolphus, launched another attack on Germany, turning the tide of the war. In 1635, the French, who had already financed some of the war, openly joined the fight on behalf of the Swedes. Ultimately, there was no clear victor, and in 1648 all of the combatant nations signed the Peace of Westphalia, which returned all parties to the decisions of the Peace of Augsburg—that is, the ruler's faith was to be the faith of the land, although the list of acceptable faiths now included Calvinism. Those who belonged to Anabaptist traditions did not enjoy this liberty and continued to be persecuted.

Given the fact that the Peace of Westphalia fundamentally restored the decisions made a century earlier, the Thirty Years' War was nothing but a debacle that resulted in horrendous losses. Many of the powers involved virtually bankrupted themselves. Germany experienced massive famine and disease; ultimately, Germany and Bohemia's population was reduced by 30 percent. Swedish armies destroyed over 2,000 German castles and one-third of its towns. And finally, while the Holy Roman Empire technically survived the conflict, it was divided into hundreds of relatively independent states.

THE LOW COUNTRIES

In the sixteenth century, the Low Countries were ruled by Catholic Spain, and Catholicism was the enforced Christian tradition, with punitive actions regularly taken against Protestant Christians. Calvinist preaching in the southern Netherlands organized anti-Catholic protests that grew in frequency and violence. In 1566, several hundred members of the nobility petitioned the governor, Margaret of Parma, to suspend actions against the Calvinists, but she refused. Soon Catholic churches were being stormed and desecrated throughout the Netherlands. In 1568, Holland's Prince William supported the Protestant attempt to take over the Netherlands, with his brothers' forces invading from Germany and northern France. After two particularly bloody battles, the first won by the Spanish and the second by the rebel army, the campaign ended when William ran out of money to pay his troops.

By 1570, the Spanish believed they had successfully suppressed the rebellion, but in 1572 Dutch Calvinists who had taken refuge in England invaded the northern Netherlands. Immediately, many cities in Holland and the western Netherlands sided with the rebels. Over the next seven years, battles were waged, cities were looted by mutinous mercenary armies, and loyalties switched sides and switched back again. Ultimately, the northern part of the Netherlands became firmly Calvinist, and the southern Netherlands as well as modern-day Belgium remained Catholic. War would reignite in 1622, only to be finally ended in 1648 with the Treaty of Munster, a part of the overall Peace of Westphalia.

While the contest in the Thirty Years' War advanced little, the Peace of Westphalia does mark the beginning of the modern era in Europe. Among other things, it established the sovereignty of nation-states and the principle of legal equality among states. In principle, weaker or smaller states no longer had to fear the possibility of stronger neighbors invading them at will. Finally, the Peace established the practice of binding treaties among states. In the past, treaties were made between ruling families; now they were forged between sovereign states.

FRANCE

Protestantism had a slow start in France. The first Protestant congregation was not established until 1555, though Calvinism grew rapidly thereafter. French kings vacillated between tolerance and persecution. Soon, Protestant Christians, called **Huguenots** in France, had appeared among the French nobility. The highest-ranking Huguenot was Henry Bourbon, king of Navarre (modern-day northern Spain), who had French royal blood. In 1571, Bourbon married the French king's sister, Margaret of Valois.

On the day of the wedding, nobleman Henry of Guise tried to assassinate Admiral Coligny, the leader of the Huguenots, although the attempt failed. In 1572, Henry of Guise tried again, leading the massacre of 2,000 Huguenots in Paris in what became known as the St. Bartholomew's Day Massacre. Admiral Coligny was killed, and Henry Bourbon was imprisoned and compelled to renounce his Protestantism. Quickly, persecutions of Huguenots spread throughout France, with tens of thousands killed. In 1576, Bourbon escaped prison and returned to Navarre, again identifying as a Protestant. The French king, Henry III, had no heirs, and, after some untimely royal deaths, Bourbon was in line to take the French throne. Henry of Guise then declared himself the legitimate heir of the throne based on a forged document, and for several years France became engaged in a war known as the War of Three Henrys. Eventually, Henry Bourbon proclaimed his allegiance to Catholicism—the fifth conversion of his life—and took the throne as the legitimate king. In 1598, he issued the Edict of Nantes, which gave Protestants the right to worship throughout France, with the exception of in Paris. France became a religiously divided country, albeit one now at peace.

Armand Jean du Plessis (1585–1642), typically known as Cardinal Richelieu, became a bishop in 1608, was named King Louis XIII's secretary of state in 1616, and became a cardinal in 1622. In 1624, King Louis made him chief minister, and he fundamentally became the power behind the throne. While Richelieu supported the Protestant cause in the Thirty Years' War, which he saw as weakening the Holy Roman Empire, he quickly suppressed any political power among the Calvinists in France, though he supported the toleration of worship. His successor, Cardinal Mazarin, continued the policy of toleration.

After Mazarin's death, however, King Louis XIV refused to appoint a successor to the secretary of state, and in 1685 he issued the Edict of Fontainebleau, reversing the toleration of the Edict of Nantes, which had given Calvinists civil rights and religious protection. Hundreds of thousands of Huguenots left France for more religiously hospitable countries. This may have strengthened Catholicism, but it was devastating for the French economy, as many who emigrated were among the country's educated class. After Louis XIV's long seventy-two-year reign (he technically took the throne at the age of five), he was succeeded by his great-grandson, Louis XV. Louis XV also had an extraordinarily long reign, and it was also marked by persecution of the Huguenots. Despite this, French Calvinism continued to grow as an outlaw faith. In 1787, Louis XVI reinstated religious toleration in France, thus ending 100 years of Huguenot persecution.

THE PURITAN REVOLUTION

As noted in Chapter Fourteen, Queen Elizabeth's reforms in England were not far-reaching. The Church of England retained the ancient episcopal system of governance, and it left the sacraments intact. While they were not free to worship, both Catholics and more radical Protestants were tolerated, even if they were fined for not attending the Church of England's liturgies. The situation changed under King James I (r. 1603–1625), who had previously been the king of Scotland. During his reign, some English and Scottish Christians advocated for more radical reforms. These individuals were known as the **Puritans**, with their name derived from their attempt to *purify* English and Scottish Christianity from any semblance of Catholicism. Puritanism was actually a quite diverse movement that included those who wanted to institute a **presbyterian** model of church governance, that is, a church ruled by a council of elders. Others sought the absolute independence of each individual church or faith community. The Puritans had strong support in the British Parliament, as many members distrusted the king, whose mother, Mary, Queen of Scots, had been a staunch Catholic. Further, while James had supported the Protestant cause in the Thirty Years' War, he refused to lend any financial help to it. Thus, many English leaders wondered if he really was sympathetic to the cause.

To counteract the power of Parliament, James threw his support to the Church of England's bishops, who themselves were among the strongest supporters of the king. The tension was really between the emerging understanding of a representative government and an ancient belief that both king and bishops ruled their respective realms by divine right. In 1604, the archbishop of Canterbury declared this very principle: bishops ruled by divine ordinance. The House of Commons, which included many Puritans, rejected the claim.

If Protestants were concerned that James might really have Catholic sympathies, their concerns were allayed when in 1605 some Catholic opponents of the king planned to blow up the Parliament building while the king was addressing the assembly, an event that came to be known as the Gunpowder Plot. The plot to kill both king and high-ranking Puritan leaders was foiled, and many leading English Catholics were tried and executed.

Perhaps the greatest religious achievement of James's tenure as king was the production of the **King James Bible**. Other English translations of the Bible had previously been in use, such as the Great Bible, the Bishop's Bible, and the Geneva Bible—the latter of which Shakespeare used in his plays—but none had been definitively authorized. James assembled leading biblical scholars, theologians, and linguists to produce perhaps the finest translation of the Bible in the vernacular to date. It remained a favorite among Protestants for over 300 years.

Over time, the Puritans began to split, with some favoring reforming the Church of England and others preferring to create congregations that were separate from the Anglican Church. Such an action was at the time illegal, and some separatist Puritans left England to find religious freedom, particularly in the Netherlands. One separatist group, led by John Smyth, settled in Amsterdam and created the first Baptist church in 1609. Some separatists, such as Thomas Helwys, returned to England to establish Baptist churches, which were characterized by clearly Anabaptist leanings. Helwys was eventually imprisoned and executed. Other Baptist churches developed in the 1630s with strong Calvinistic theologies; these congregations came to be called *Particular Baptists*. Still another separatist Puritan group returned to England and departed from Plymouth on September 20, 1620, on the *Mayflower* with the dream of establishing a pure church and model society on the frontiers of the American wilderness. After separating from them, Roger Williams, who founded Rhode Island, established the first Baptist church in the Americas. Fascinatingly for the time, he argued in his book *The Bloody Tenent of Persecution* for the separation of church and state and for universal toleration of religion.

Between 1625 and 1640, the Puritan movement grew stronger, as did the king's opposition to it. James I was succeeded by Charles I. Charles rarely convened Parliament, which was difficult, since only Parliament could enact new taxes. In 1640, Parliament enacted a law that prevented the king from dissolving it without its approval. This was a time of great unrest in England, particularly among the poor and middle classes, from which the Puritans had their greatest support. When Charles tried to arrest leaders of the House of Commons, Parliament assembled its own militia, and civil war broke out in England. **Oliver Cromwell**, a wealthy Puritan and member of Parliament, led the militia and, with the support of the Scots, captured the king. Cromwell took control of political power in England as Lord Protector and oversaw the execution of Charles I in 1649 for treason. Quickly, Parliament passed a number of laws that supported the Puritan vision, including abolishing the episcopacy and instituting a presbyterian form of church government. It also instituted a number of laws that enforced Puritan beliefs, such as the mandated observance of Sunday services, the banning of Christmas on the grounds that it was originally a pagan holiday, and the outlawing of immodest dress and "frivolities," such as sports and the theater.

Cromwell died in 1658, and by then England had had enough of Puritan extremism.

Parliament invited Charles I's eldest son, Charles II, to retake the English throne, though they also feared his Catholic leanings. In fact, at his deathbed he converted to Catholicism. Charles II's brother, James II, tried to revert England to Catholicism, but England was by this time far too Protestant, and another revolt, the Glorious Revolution, ended his reign. Parliament then invited William of Orange and his wife, Mary, the daughter of James II, to take the thrones of England and Scotland in 1688. The Scottish church retained its presbyterian structure, while England regained its historical episcopal structure. Under William and Mary, all Christians were accepted as long as they would swear allegiance to the Thirty-Nine Articles, which Thomas Cranmer had helped devise a century earlier.

HOW RELIGIOUS WERE THE WARS OF RELIGION?

The 100 years of the Wars of Religion were certainly charged with religious conflict; of that, there can be no doubt. But they were also a time of class struggle; conflicts over economics, politics, and the balance of power; and early shifts from monarchies to representative governments. Further, religious loyalties were regularly blurred in order to advance some of these other social and political values. In William Cavanaugh's *The Myth of Religious Violence: Secular Ideology and the Roots of Modern Conflict*, he details over fifty substantive examples of events in which religious interests were trumped by other concerns, and in which Catholics, Lutherans, Calvinists, and others often worked together.

In the early decades of the Reformation, most of the minor wars were between Catholic France and the Catholic emperor. In these conflicts, the Protestant princes of the Holy Roman Empire generally supported the Catholic emperor against France. Emperor Charles V granted wide control to Protestant princes in exchange for military support. Sometimes, however, Lutheran princes supported Catholic France over the emperor, perhaps most notably in 1552, a move that led to the Peace of Augsburg in 1555. In the French Wars of Religion (1562–1598),

Huguenot and Catholic nobles often openly helped each other in quelling commoners' revolts. Collaboration among Catholic and Protestant peasants was also widespread in efforts to resist power abuses by nobles or the monarchy. Dutch Calvinists frequently supported the Catholic French Crown and fought with the French against other Calvinists, while Catholic Spain supported Protestants against the French monarchy. And, as noted previously, Sweden's King Gustavus Adolphus was subsidized by France, and the latter half of the Thirty Years' War was fundamentally a proxy war between Catholic France and the Catholic Hapsburgs.

Many of these battles were fought with private mercenaries—some of whom were of the noble class—who sold themselves to the highest bidder, regardless of religious or political interests. For example, the German military commander Ernst von Mansfeld worked first for Catholic Spain in the Thirty Years' War, then for the Lutheran Frederick V, and subsequently switched sides three more times. Protestant Scots and Englishmen also served in Catholic armies in France, sometimes switching sides depending on circumstances.

There was massive upheaval in the sixteenth and seventeenth centuries, and a great deal of violence. Some of it was religious, but much of it was also, and perhaps even predominantly, political, social, and economic. In this sense, the label "Wars of Religion" is a misnomer. These were European wars, and religion was just one important factor.

SECURED STATEMENTS OF FAITH

After the Protestant Reformation, all four mainstream Christian bodies—Catholic, Church of England, Lutheran, and Calvinist—strove to secure their doctrines. Catholicism did this with the Council of Trent, and the Church of England satisfied itself ultimately with the Thirty-Nine Articles and the Book of Common Prayer. The Lutheran and Reformed traditions were more complicated. The primary document of the Lutheran Church is the Augsburg Confession

(1530), presented by Luther's university colleague and friend Philip Melanchthon after Luther was deemed an outlaw. While Luther was still alive, he remained the primary interpreter of Lutheranism, and upon his death Melanchthon became the unofficial authority. Melanchthon, however, did not always agree with Luther. He remained friends with Erasmus and other Catholic humanists, and held out hope for reconciliation. Melanchthon disagreed with Luther that the human will is utterly enslaved and plays no part in justification. In this, he was more Catholic than Lutheran. Other notable Lutherans would follow in this line of thought later. Georg Calixtus, for example, proposed that any doctrine that had not been decided by the early church councils was inessential to the faith, and that Catholics and Calvinists, while erring in many areas, were still legitimately Christian. This position was, however, a minority one in Lutheranism.

In 1576, Elector August of Saxony gathered a number of German Lutheran scholars to create a definitive text that consolidated the Lutheran faith. They produced the Formula of Concord (1577), which provided a Lutheran creedal statement of faith, and the *Book of Concord* (1580), a detailed exposition of Lutheran positions to be accepted. Unlike the Augsburg Confession, which intended to distinguish the Lutheran faith from the Catholic, the Formula of Concord intended to distinguish it from the Reformed tradition. These texts were signed by three electors, twenty princes and dukes, twenty-four counts, four barons, the leaders of thirty-five free cities, and over 8,000 pastors. Not all would accept them, however. The leaders of some German Lutheran cities objected, as did the Lutheran communions in Denmark and Sweden.

The seventeenth century saw the earliest large, multivolume works on Lutheran systematic theology and the beginning of Lutheran scholasticism. The idea was to provide an intellectually compelling, all-encompassing understanding of the Christian faith according to Lutheran doctrine. Ironically, these works tended to employ the very Aristotelian methods to which Luther had so clearly objected.

Reformed theology was based primarily on Calvin's *Institutes*, but this was not without controversy. As noted in Chapter Fourteen, the Dutch Reformed Church split over Arminianism. While the five articles distinguished Arminians and continued to influence Reform theology, by and large Calvinism secured its faith through the decisions of the synod in Dordrecht, the Netherlands. It was at this time that T.U.L.I.P. became Calvinist dogma.

THE ENLIGHTENMENT

The **Enlightenment** is a useful term to describe the transition from the Renaissance to the modern period. The Enlightenment emerged from various fronts, most prominently from philosophical discourse and the development of the scientific method. Scientific discoveries and an increasingly rigorous and independent-minded scientific community paved the way for this shift. The Enlightenment's cultural ethos presented a core set of values that eventually challenged traditional institutions while vesting extraordinary faith in rationality, science, and progress. Hierarchies, rationally unsupported authority, and beliefs without evidential warrant all became suspect. This was the *age of reason*.

THE SCIENTIFIC REVOLUTION

As noted previously, scientific advancements initially preceded the Enlightenment and in many ways conditioned it. One of the greatest challenges perceived by people today to Christianity as it entered the beginnings of what is known as the modern period was the **scientific revolution**. A great pioneer in the scientific revolution was **Nicholas Copernicus** (1473–1543), a typical Renaissance man whom everyone could admire. He was a Catholic priest, a mathematician, classicist, jurist, diplomat, and artist. Among his many interests was astronomy. By 1532, he had completed his famous work on planets orbiting the sun, *On the Revolutions of the Heavenly Spheres*.

Copernicus hesitated, however, to publish his theory of **heliocentrism**, the view that the sun is the center of the solar system. His fear was not the scorn of the church, but rather the scorn of other scientists, because he challenged basic principles of Aristotle's physics and the working models of the second-century astronomer and mathematician Ptolemy. Copernicus was challenging the science of the day, not the church of the day. In 1533, Copernicus's theory was sent to Rome and presented to Pope Clement VII and several cardinals.

CARDINAL NIKOLAUS'S LETTER TO COPERNICUS

Cardinal Nikolaus von Schönberg wrote to Copernicus from Rome:

Some years ago word reached me concerning your proficiency, of which everybody constantly spoke. At that time I began to have a very high regard for you, and also to congratulate our contemporaries among whom you enjoyed such great prestige. For I had learned that you had not merely mastered the discoveries of the ancient astronomers uncommonly well but had also formulated a new cosmology. In it you maintain that the earth moves; that the sun occupies the lowest, and thus the central, place in the universe; that the eighth heaven remains perpetually motionless and fixed; and that, together with the elements included in its sphere, the moon, situated between the heavens of Mars and Venus, revolves around the sun in the period of a year. I have also learned that you have written an exposition of this whole system of astronomy, and have computed the planetary motions and set them down in tables, to the greatest admiration of all. Therefore with the utmost earnestness I entreat you, most learned sir, unless I inconvenience you, to communicate this discovery of yours to scholars, and at the earliest possible moment to send me your writings on the sphere of the universe together with the tables and whatever else you have that is relevant to this subject. Moreover, I have instructed Theodoric of Reden to have everything copied in your quarters at my expense and dispatched to me. If you gratify my desire in this matter, you will see that you are dealing with a man who is zealous for your reputation and eager to do justice to so fine a talent. Farewell. (Rome, 1 November 1536)[1]

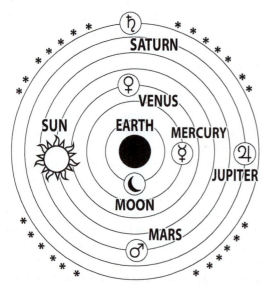

FIGURE 16-1 At the time of Copernicus, Ptolemy's model of the universe, derived in the first century CE, was widely accepted as fact.

When Copernicus did publish his book, he dedicated it to the current pope, Paul III, who was one of his many admirers. Why didn't his findings upset the church? Weren't scientific claims in opposition to those of the Bible? Some surely thought so, but many did not have this concern. It was now 1,200 years since Augustine had taught in one of his commentaries on Genesis, *De Genesi ad literam*, that the language of scripture was aligned to the preconceptions and understandings of the culture in which it was written, and consequently, the limitations and distortions of that given culture are not to be taken as fact, much less revelation. Copernicus was buried with honors inside the Frombork Cathedral in his homeland of Poland.

Copernicus was followed by **Galileo Galilei** (1564–1642). Galileo brought his substantial intellect to Copernicus's theory, along with his own improvements to the telescope, and provided

FIGURE 16-2 Galileo Galilei, an Italian astronomer, physicist, and mathematician, uncovered greater evidence for a sun-centered solar system.

more evidence for Copernicus's hypothesis. In 1610, Galileo published *The Sidereal Messenger,* which won immediate acclaim. He went to Rome the next year, and a whole coterie of Jesuit intellectuals publicly confirmed his discoveries. Pope Urban VIII rather liked him, became one of his benefactors, and even arranged for a pension for Galileo's son. In 1623, the pope feted Galileo and encouraged him to publish whatever he wanted about the heliocentric theory. The only condition was that Galileo publish it as hypothesis and not as fact. This angered Galileo, since he insisted that he had proven heliocentrism. Actually, he hadn't. Galileo's theories would not be considered conclusive for another 200 years, until Foucault's pendulum in the mid-nineteenth century. His observations on sunspots, the moon, the phases of Venus, the tides, and so on provided additional support for the theory, but not conclusive evidence.

In 1633, Galileo published a book called *Dialogues on the Two World Systems* in which the designated fool of the dialogues said things that Urban himself had earlier said in public. Thus, it was widely received as a direct mockery of the pope. Pope Urban had Galileo tried for the heresy of publishing as fact what he had yet to prove. Galileo's sentence was that he be restricted to his villa in Florence, though he was given

permission to leave on occasion. He was also allowed to continue his scientific work freely, although not on heliocentrism.

One of the main insights we might derive from the Galileo affair concerns Galileo's understanding of the relationship between science and religion. Basically, he saw none. He believed that all physical phenomena were about math and mechanics, and that these fields were not the place for theology. Many others agreed. As his contemporary Cardinal Baronius declared, "The intention of the Holy Spirit is to teach us how one goes to heaven not how the heavens go."[2] All this is not to say that Copernicus and Galileo were not controversial to some in the church. The claim that the Earth moved did seem biblically and theologically problematic, and Galileo's trial certainly included these objections. Given the Protestant Reformation, the church's long-friendly attitude toward science was at the time somewhat strained.

Johannes Kepler (1571–1630), a contemporary of Galileo, grounded his science in mathematics. What is interesting about Kepler is that he drew theological associations with mathematical and astronomical observations. In today's scientific world such links seem quite strange. Kepler thought, for example, that there were five other spheres revolving around the sun, for a total of six planets in the solar system. This is what everyone believed, but for him it pointed to the glory of God: God, he thought, was represented by the sun, with six spheres revolving around it, just like the perfect number seven. Together, it all reflected the perfection of the Creator. He also saw the Trinity reflected in the sun (Father), fixed stars (Son), and intermediate space (Holy Spirit).

Isaac Newton (1642–1727) framed science as the universal scope of knowledge and then argued for God as the foundation of the mechanical universe. For him, God drew up nature's laws and eternally grounds the universe in intelligence and power. Like Thomas Aquinas, he advocated deducing causes from effects. That is, he recognized the lawfulness of the universe, its unity, predictability, and intelligibility—and, indeed, its very existence—and concluded that it implied God and reflected God's glory.

The eighteenth-century thinkers Denis Diderot and Paul d'Holbach both accepted Newton's assumption that the physical world worked according to universal laws that could be explained through mathematical principles. They also embraced the widely held belief that matter and the laws of motion worked mechanically. To these assumptions, they added the arguments that the universe was dynamic and that movement was intrinsically part of matter. Newton, René Descartes, and other scientists and philosophers believed that God was necessary to provide matter its initial motion, but that the rest happened necessarily. In contrast, Diderot and d'Holbach argued that a divine first cause was unnecessary: "No one needed a god to give the first impetus to matter. It is there already and had been there forever; motion and matter are inseparable."[3]

PONTIFICAL ACADEMY OF SCIENCE MISSION STATEMENT

The Pontifical Academy of Sciences is distinctive in its kind because it is the only supranational academy of sciences in the world. Founded as the Linceorum Academia in Rome on 17 August 1603 as the first exclusively scientific academy in the world, Galileo was one of its early presidents. It was given its current name and statutes by Pius XI in 1936. Its mission is to honor pure science wherever it may be found, ensure its freedom, and encourage research for the progress of science.

The Academy is governed by a President with the assistance of the Council. Its 80 Pontifical Academicians are appointed for life by the pope following proposals by the Academic body and chosen without any form of ethnic or religious discrimination from the most eminent scientists and scholars of the mathematical and experimental sciences of every country of the world. Scientists from thirty-six countries are currently represented. They participate in study groups and meetings organized by the Academy to examine specific issues. Their deliberations and scientific papers are published by the Academy or jointly with other publishers.

One should not think that Christianity was opposed to science, as it never was. The Catholic Church, with its history of benefactors, particularly supported scientific discovery, and some of this support was, in fact, quite theological. Christianity widely believed that the universe was created by God as both good and rational. It was worthy of study, and church-sponsored universities gave scholars the space and freedom to investigate it. Consider some of the scientific giants of the West, past and present, all of whom were priests: Roger Bacon (1214–1294), forerunner of the scientific method; Nicolas Steno (1638–1686), father of geology; Gregor Mendel (1822–1884), father of genetics; Pierre Teilhard de Chardin (1881–1955), the paleontologist and geologist who discovered Peking Man; and Georges Lemaître (1894-1966), physicist and father of the big bang theory. The great challenge Christianity faced from the scientific revolution was the philosophical implication that some drew from the Enlightenment: God is not needed to explain anything. As Ernst Cassirer argued, "The basic idea underlying all the tendencies of the Enlightenment was the conviction that all human understanding is capable, by its own power and without any recourse to supernatural assistance, of comprehending the system of the world and that this new way of understanding the world will lead to a new way of mastering it."[4]

RATIONALISM

Each branch of Christianity, particularly Catholicism and Lutheranism, developed answers to many, if not all, imagined theological problems. And they responded to these problems with surety. However, they were not the only voices in the intellectual world. Others challenged the very foundations on which they built their theological edifices, arguing that reason, rather than revelation, ought to secure knowledge. This position is known as **rationalism**.

The seventeenth-century French philosophers Leonard Lessius and Marin Mersenne believed that a secure knowledge of God could be had, but that it would only be credible to the modern mind if it appealed to *rationes philosophicae*, or philosophical reason.

Another crucial figure of the day was René Descartes (1596–1650), who looked for the basis of sure knowledge. He started with doubting all that could be doubted in order to arrive at some first principle that would ensure the foundations of knowledge. He concluded that he could not doubt his own existence by his famous statement, *cogito ergo sum*: I think, therefore I am. From this starting point, Descartes sought to examine how the thinking person could come to rational knowledge of other things, the world at large, and even God. Descartes was a devout Catholic and in no way considered his approach to knowledge a stumbling block to authentic faith. Still, his deconstruction of how knowledge was imagined to be secured was picked up by other philosophers, who came to challenge Christian claims as unreliable sources of knowledge.

One of the greatest minds of the era was German philosopher Immanuel Kant (1724–1804). Kant believed that God was necessary as the condition for both morality and free will to exist, and indeed that Christian revelation far exceeded his philosophy. Given that, however, his work overwhelmingly was concerned with how one knows things and what kinds of demands religion ought to make. In his *Critique of Pure Reason*, he outlines structures for knowing in the human mind and the difference between what can be known directly but only partially (*phenomenal*) and what cannot be known directly (*noumenal*). He also outlines his moral framework, which is based on reason. Kant's contribution to philosophy was monumental in many ways. Above all, he challenged his readers to rely on reason: *sapere aude* (dare to know); this, he claimed, ultimately is what God demands.

EMPIRICISM

The search for how one comes to know something took a turn with the development of **empiricism**, that is, knowledge by experience. English philosopher John Locke (1632–1704) argued that human minds were a kind of blank slate (*tabula rasa*) at birth and subsequently came to know things by experience. Humans, he thought, have experience of themselves, of the world through the senses, and of God directly through self-experience, and these were avenues of a kind of secured knowledge. Revelation that was not based on direct experience, however, was not certain. Locke was a Christian, and he believed that Christianity could be successfully argued as the most reasonable religion, but he also believed that revelatory claims were at best probable and not certain. From this, he advocated religious tolerance, since certitude on matters of religion was impossible. Just as important, he argued that data from revelation, if not justified by experience, added little to religion. His was a faith based on reason and experience alone.

Scottish philosopher David Hume (1711–1776) carried empiricism further and also drew attention to its limitations. While empiricist philosophers claimed that knowledge was most sure when based on the experience of the senses, Hume argued that much of what we believe to be true in that regard is really based on patterns the mind creates rather than actual direct experience. While the universe runs on causation, we cannot observe this. Rather, we extrapolate cause and effect from experience. Our knowledge, he thought, is quite limited.

Locke and other Christian empiricists, such as Irish Anglican bishop George Berkeley, believed that their philosophical positions supported Christianity in various ways. Locke thought the Christian religion was rational and that human experience of God was a compelling source of secured knowledge. Berkeley believed that God's eternal perception of all created reality was necessary to advance confidence that anything actually exists and continues over time. Hume and others, however, advanced the empiricist approach to philosophy as one that undermined revelation. While Hume was a theist, he thought little of religious creeds. One of his most devastating essays, "Of Miracles," in his book

FIGURE 16-3 Lord Edward Herbert, who in the seventeenth century formulated the philosophy of deism.

An Inquiry Concerning Human Understanding, fundamentally challenges miracles as representing a prescientific imagination, violations of nature, and assertions without sufficient evidence.

DEISM

A particularly interesting religious movement that grew from the Enlightenment is **Deism**, founded by Lord Herbert of Cherbury (1583–1648). Lord Herbert argued that belief in God ought to be determined only by reason, and not by revelation. Strongly influenced by Newtonian mechanics, Deists believed that God could not possibly be engaged in the created world, as that would both violate God's nature and compromise God's perfection. Deists believed that God created the universe, set it in motion, and then let it run on its own accord according to naturalistic principles. Anything contrary to scientific

reason, such as miracles, was to be rejected. Lord Herbert believed that there were only five religious truths: God exists; God should be worshipped; virtue is the core principle of one's life; people should repent of their sins; and God will reward or punish one after death according to the conduct of one's life. While this is indeed a religious posture, it is clearly divorced from any creeds or specific faith.

Deists believed that religious institutions controlled individuals with doctrines and practices that lacked credibility. At best, they kept the commoners in line, but they were unworthy of thinking people. As the French philosopher Voltaire remarked to Frederick the Great, king of Prussia, "Your majesty will do the human race an eternal service in extirpating this infamous superstition [Christianity], I do not say among the rabble, who are not worthy of being enlightened and who are apt for every yoke; I say among the well-bred, among those who wish to think."[5] French Enlightenment thinkers such as Voltaire, Rousseau, and Diderot were particularly critical of Christianity and fiercely anticlerical. Other Deists had a more benign posture toward Christianity, such as those in the American colonies, including giants like Thomas Paine, George Washington, Benjamin Franklin, and Thomas Jefferson. Not all of these figures thought the same. Jefferson, for example, believed that America ought to be a great, moral country so that God would bless it, that is, intervene in its affairs positively. Nonetheless, they all shared a fundamental Deist framing of religion.

FAITH IN HUMANITY

One of the greatest distinctions between a classical Christian framework and that of the Enlightenment is the very nature of the person. Most people in both camps believe that the human being is inherently valuable. Most Christians would say that this comes from the fact that humans have souls made in the image and likeness of God. Non-Christian Enlightenment figures might have phrased it in terms of human dignity or human potential that is self-evident.

But Christianity traditionally has also understood humans as born with something fundamentally corrupt regarding the state of the soul. Most Enlightenment thinkers disagreed, arguing that humans are naturally good. If they act immorally, it is because they are ignorant or bound by political and/or religious tyrannies.

Enlightenment confidence in the power of reason and human progress imagined a future of widespread education, the dismissal of religion, and scientific advances that would progressively move toward the perfection of humanity. One of the outcomes of Enlightenment thinking was the rather novel separation between church and state, and another was representative government. These have proven to be some of the greatest achievements of the Enlightenment, along with religious toleration, premised on the idea that one's individual conscience should be supreme in such matters. John Locke's political and human rights theories set the stage for the French Revolution beginning in 1789, in which *liberté, égalité, fraternité* (liberty, equality, fraternity) became a central slogan.

Unfortunately and ironically, Enlightenment confidence in human nature and the intrinsic goodness of human beings did not keep the French Revolution from executing thousands of French citizens—many for being religious—in the late eighteenth century. Nor has the same secular confidence prevented the death of tens of millions of Europeans in the secular wars of the twentieth century. One might pause at the modern degradation of the Earth, the progressive division between rich and poor, and the neocolonization of developing countries that mark the twentieth and twenty-first centuries. For many, this Enlightenment confidence in reason has not been realized. Even in its heyday, Enlightenment approaches were challenged by the philosophical school of Romanticism, which argued that the exclusive reliance on scientific reason ignores other ways of knowing truth, such as that which can be found in beauty, wisdom, intuition, and so on.

The Enlightenment was a prelude to modern-day secularism or naturalism. Today, religious faith is imagined by most, even among religious believers themselves, as something private. Further, locating meaning, truth, value, and so on are less grounded in religious sensibilities as they are in secular assumptions. John Hick, a noted philosopher of religion, has observed, "In our western world, beginning around the seventeenth century, the earlier pervasive religious outlook has increasingly been replaced by an equally pervasive naturalistic outlook, and during the twentieth century this replacement has become almost complete. Naturalism has created a *consensus reality* of our culture. It has become so ingrained that we no longer see it, but see everything through it."[6] And philosopher John Lucas has recognized the same thing in terms of scholarly discourse: "Philosophical naturalism is now the orthodoxy of the Western intellectual world."[7]

CONCLUSIONS

As noted in previous chapters, Christian just war theory framed violence as a last resort and only necessary to remove despots or protect innocent peoples from being conquered by invading foreign armies. While there were indeed political and social grievances that inflamed the violence of the sixteenth and seventeenth centuries, it is hardly possible to imagine much of it as just. Particularly troubling for Christianity was that *all* of it was led by Christians against other Christians. Augustine's distinction between the city of man and the city of God remained a daunting reminder that political institutions—really all institutions, including the church—are human and can suffer the delusions of what Augustine would call false loves. Power, riches, and control have marked many movements of the human race through all civilizations, including the early modern European one. The Enlightenment proved to be a double-edged sword for Christianity. Founded on scientific discoveries, it extended itself toward cultural values that the modern world, particularly the West, would embrace, then and now. Science, human rights, the primacy of one's conscience, and many other marks of the modern world have their foundation in the Enlightenment. As noted previously, however, this era's faith in progress and in the natural human condition seems fraught with counterevidence. It too seems to have suffered the consequences of being part of the city of man.

SUMMARY QUESTIONS

- The Wars of Religion were largely driven by many nonreligious factors. List some of the background conditions in Europe as well as immediate nonreligious factors that drove the wars.
- The Thirty Years' War ended with the Peace of Westphalia in 1648, marking the beginning of the modern era. What were the effects of Westphalia on political and religious entities? What were some of the political and religious ideas being challenged around this time, and what new ideas were emerging?

- What were the features and values of the Enlightenment? Explain the schools of rationalism and empiricism and the challenges that both posed to traditional sources of knowledge.
- What were the societal outcomes of the Enlightenment? What do you see as Enlightenment values, historically and philosophically?
- What were some roles that Christianity played in the pursuits of the major figures of the scientific revolution?

DISCUSSION QUESTIONS

- Do you think the Thirty Years' War succeeded in satisfying the criteria of just war theory? Explain your answer.
- The author claims that the Wars of Religion were less interested in religion as they were in politics and economics. What are his arguments and do you think that they are persuasive?
- The author believes that the church has principally supported science throughout history. What are his arguments and do you think he is persuasive?

KEY TERMS

Copernicus, Nicholas	Hapsburgs	Rationalism
Cromwell, Oliver	Heliocentrism	Scientific revolution
Deism	Huguenot	Thirty Years' War
Empiricism	King James Bible	Wars of Religion
Enlightenment	Presbyterian	
Galilei, Galileo	Puritan	

BIBLIOGRAPHY

- Appleby, Scott. 2000. *The Ambivalence of the Sacred: Religion, Violence, and Reconciliation.* Lanham, MD: Rowman & Littlefield.
- Armstrong, Karen. 2009. *The Case for God.* New York: Alfred A. Knopf.
- Balnshard, Brand. 1974. *Reason and Belief.* New Haven, CT: Yale University Press.
- Barbour, Ian. 2000. *When Science Meets Religion.* New York: HarperCollins.
- Bradley, James, and Dale Van Kley. 2001. *Religion and Politics in Enlightenment Europe.* Notre Dame, IN: University of Notre Dame Press.
- Buckley, Michael. 1987. *At the Origins of Modern Atheism.* New Haven, CT: Yale University Press.
- Buckley, Michael. 2004. *Denying and Disclosing God: The Ambitious Progress of Modern Atheism.* New Haven, CT: Yale University Press.
- Byrne, James. 1997. *Religion and the Enlightenment: From Descartes to Kant.* Louisville, KY: Westminster John Knox Press.
- Cavanaugh, William. 2010. *The Myth of Religious Violence: Secular Ideology and the Roots of Modern Conflict.* Oxford: Oxford University Press.
- Gragg, Gerald, ed. 1974. *The Church and the Age of Reason,* rev. ed. Harmonsworth, UK: Penguin.
- Haught, John. 2012. *Science and Faith: A New Introduction.* Mahwah, NJ: Paulist Press.
- Heal, Felicity. 2003. *Reformation in Britain and Ireland.* Oxford: Clarendon Press.
- Hick, John. 1999. *The Fifth Dimension.* Oxford: OneWorld.
- Jastrow, Robert. 1992. *God and the Astronomers.* New York: W. W. Norton & Company.
- Louthan, Howard, and Randall Zachman. 2004. *Conciliation and Confession: The Struggle for Unity in the Age of Reform, 1415–1648.* Notre Dame, IN: University of Notre Dame Press.
- MacCulloch, Diarmaid. 2003. *Reformation: Europe's House Divided, 1490–1700.* London: Allen Lane.
- Waldron, Jeremy. 2002. *God, Locke, and Equality: Christian Foundations of John Locke's Political Thought.* Cambridge: Cambridge University Press.

NOTES

1. "Nicholas Copernicus," *Calendars Through the Ages,* accessed at http://www.webexhibits.org/calendars/year-text-Copernicus.html.
2. Cited in Buckley, *Denying and Disclosing God,* 8.
3. Ibid., 35.
4. Cited in Catherine Cory and Michael Hollerich, eds., *The Christian Theological Tradition,* 3rd ed. (Upper Saddle River, NJ: Pearson Prentice Hall, 2009), 383.
5. Gragg, *Church and the Age of Reason,* 241.
6. Hick, *Fifth Dimension,* 14.
7. As cited in Alvin Plantinga, "Dennett's Dangerous Idea: Evolution and the Meanings of Life," *Books and Culture* 2 (May/June 1996): 16–18.

17

Colonization and Missions

Timeline

1491 CE	Missions sent to the Congo
1492 CE	Christopher Columbus lands in the Americas
1498 CE	Portuguese reach the Indies
1500 CE	Discovery of Brazil by the Portuguese
1519 CE	Conquest of Mexico by Hernán Cortés
1521 CE	Magellan establishes Christianity in the Philippines
1531 CE	Appearance of the Virgin Mary to Juan Diego in Mexico
1542–1552 CE	Francis Xavier leads missions in India and Japan
1582 CE	Matteo Ricci brings missions to China
1622 CE	Pope Gregory XV creates the Congregation for the Propagation of Faith, with the aim of supporting missions and protecting indigenous peoples
1622–1644 CE	Guinea Coast, Sierra Leone, and Angola embrace Christianity

WHAT TO EXPECT

The Christian drive to convert souls to Christ has been a long-standing agenda for the church. Until the modern period, the vast majority of Christians believed non-Christians would be eternally damned without the faith. This chapter investigates the massive European initiative of missions and colonization in Central and South America, Africa, and the Far East. Most of the colonial agenda had little to do with religion, however. The European states were far more interested in exploiting the natural resources of indigenous lands, and, indeed, exploiting indigenous peoples; something frequently framed as **colonialism**. The Christian faith did grow, particularly Catholicism in the Americas, where a sizeable percentage of Christians live today. Yet, as this chapter will recount, the moral costs of colonization were substantial, and its results were tragic for many native peoples.

 ## THE CHRISTIAN IMPERATIVE TO CONVERT SOULS

Some religions understand themselves as fundamentally aligned to a given culture or people. Hinduism is intrinsically connected to the Indian culture and caste system. Daoism and Confucianism are highly integrated into the Chinese spirit and the cultural mentality of the Orient. Shinto's cosmology, myths, and rites concern themselves solely with the Japanese. Buddhism sees its message as a universal one and generally believes embracing its eightfold path is necessary for ultimate liberation. Still, Buddhists widely believe that humans undergo millions, if not billions, of rebirths. Thus, belonging to another religion is not problematic and could even be spiritually advantageous in a given lifetime. In the West, Judaism locates itself with the people of Israel. Jews welcome converts, but the faith has never seen itself as a **proselytizing** religion, nor do Jews believe one has to be Jewish to be in God's favor. Islam, is convinced that Muhammad's message is both universal and constitutes the highest revelation. Thus, it is a proselytizing religion. But Muslims historically and today believe that non-Muslims can be saved through their own religious traditions, particularly if these are monotheistic. Christianity perhaps stands alone as a religion that has historically believed that membership in the church is necessary for salvation. "I am the way, the truth, and the life," Jesus said. "No one comes to the father except through me" (John 14:6). Are we to believe that all non-Christians will be damned?

Broadly, the church fathers believed that devout Jews and Gentiles who lived before Christ were saved by Christ's grace because the preexistent Word (*Logos*) spoke to them in the depths of their souls. Justin Martyr spoke of the seeds of the Word (*Logos spermatikos*) planted in the hearts of these pious souls. Other patristic thinkers shared the same belief. They presumed that God was benevolent and even in choosing Israel did not reject others. Once the gospel had been proclaimed, however, not believing in Christ was assumed to be an intentional choice to reject God's explicit offer of salvation. So while many church fathers taught that non-Christians who lived before Christ could be saved, most believed that non-Christians who lived after Christ could not be saved. The greatest articulator of this position was Augustine, who believed in predestination: those who were not part of the church, even if they had not explicitly rejected the faith, were not predestined to heaven.

In the West, the medieval church adopted Augustine's position. The Fourth Lateran Council (1215) declared, "There is only one universal church of the faithful, outside which none can be saved." The schisms in the church throughout the medieval period were imagined as a break in love, communion, and the authority Christ had invested in bishops as successors to the apostles. The church was the body of Christ, and it was inconceivable that one could stand outside his body and still experience his saving grace. Thomas Aquinas argued that non-Christians could not be damned for what they could not avoid, and that in cooperating with God's grace in their hearts, they evidenced a kind of implicit desire for baptism. But Aquinas also believed that, through God's providence, God would eventually lead them to explicit baptism. Centuries later, theologians would extend Aquinas's intuitions and recognize God's saving grace as implicitly working through the souls of non-Christians, even without their eventual baptism. Today, this is the theological assumption of most Christians. However, it is a modern idea. Given the imperative of baptism for salvation, Christians have assumed that it is their responsibility to share the faith in order to save as many souls as possible. Christianity has, through its history, thus become the most insistent proselytizing religion in the world.

Christian missions to evangelize non-Christians could be understood in terms of stages. The apostles of the early church spread the faith to whomever would listen, particularly throughout the Roman Empire. Although Christians of this era were persecuted and the faith was illegal, they still believed it was their responsibility to spread the saving message. Eventually, Christianity became a legal religion, the favored religion, and finally the only recognized religion of the empire. Consider these events collectively as the first stage. The second stage of evangelization was directed to non-Christians north and east of the empire. Christianity sought and gained converts in the Middle East, northern countries from the Balkans to Russia, modern-day Germany, England, Ireland, and Scandinavia. This chapter concerns itself with the third stage, which was perhaps the most ambitious, that is, the conversion of peoples throughout the world, from Africa to the Americas to Asia.

For centuries, Christians in Europe knew about Asian peoples. Following the Silk Road, Persian Christians had traveled to China as early as the sixth century. Roman explorers had a modest trade with India, following routes down the Red Sea and across the Arabian Sea. Still, these were not decisive encounters. The greatest surge in medieval interest in Asia came from the accounts of the Italian explorer Marco Polo (1254–1324), who visited lands of the East and found great wealth in spices, perfumes, and cloth. A century later the Islamic Moroccan explorer Ibn Battuta (1304–1369) traveled throughout much of the Islamic world, the interior and

east and west coasts of Africa, Southeast Asia, and China. He published his memoirs, *Rihla* (*Journey*), to wide acclaim and a great deal of European interest, particularly among the Portuguese and Spanish. What most impressed the Portuguese and Spanish was not initially the possibilities of converts to the faith, but rather opportunities for trade. Eventually, their interest degraded into the pursuit of colonies and the exploitation of native peoples.

AFRICA

As noted in Chapter Ten, Egypt, Nubia, and Ethiopia were all Christian from the late patristic period on. After the Islamic invasion of North Africa, only a remnant of the Coptic Church survived in Egypt, but Ethiopia remained a thoroughly Christian country. Ethiopia was under the patronage of the Coptic patriarch in Alexandria, but it also strove to maintain good relations with Rome. Even as late as the Renaissance period, it managed to retain a presence in the West. For example, Ethiopians sent representatives to both the Council of Constance and the Council of Florence, and Pope Nicholas V in 1451 sent a permanent representative to Ethiopia. The rest of Africa, however, remained outside the sphere of Christianity.

Portugal's Prince **Henry "The Navigator"** (1394–1460) expanded Western interest in Africa. After Henry's conquest of Morocco in 1415, he sent ships south to explore Africa's west coast. Many of the islands along the coast became colonized by Portugal and were used as part of that country's trading routes. By the time of Henry's death, Portuguese explorers and traders had reached as far as modern-day Sierra Leone. Expeditions also reached the Canary and Cape Verde Islands.

The most important base for Portuguese colonization and eventual missions was São Tomé, discovered in 1470. Over a decade later, 1482 became a decisive year for Portuguese exploration. Not only did they explore Ghana in this year, but from their São Tomé base they reached the mouth of the Congo River. There they encountered the king of Congo (modern-day Angola), Nzinga of Nkouwou. Nzinga accepted the Catholic faith, and the Portuguese allied themselves to him. Missionaries arrived in 1491 and were warmly welcomed. However, not all of Nzinga's family converted, and there was religiously related tension over who would replace Nzinga. The Portuguese backed his eldest son, **Afonso**, who had become a devout Christian. Afonso ruled the Congolese throne from 1506 to 1543 and was enthusiastic about the faith. He created a Christian capital, São Salvador, learned Portuguese, built churches, promoted missions, and created essentially a Christian monarchy. However, uniting his subjects to the agenda of the Portuguese turned out to be disastrous for the Congolese. Quickly, the Portuguese involved themselves in the slave trade, initially attacking Congo's neighbors but all too soon turning to Afonso's own people. Afonso appealed to the Portuguese monarchy to relent: "We cannot reckon how great the damage is, since the mentioned merchants are taking every day our natives, sons of the land and sons of our noblemen and vassals and our relatives. . . . So great is the corruption and licentiousness that our country is being depopulated."[1]

The Portuguese king, Manuel I, had earlier sent missionaries from Lisbon to the Congo. These were Augustinian canons, priests who lived the common life under the Rule of Saint Augustine. Some of these priests were exemplary and self-sacrificing, but a number were not. Many of them gave up the common life, openly lived with African concubines, and even themselves trafficked in the slave trade. Afonso was appalled. In yet another letter to the Portuguese monarchy, he pled, "In this kingdom the faith is still as fragile as glass on account of the bad examples of those who came to teach it. Today the Lord is crucified anew by the very ministers of his body and blood."[2] Strikingly, neither Manuel I (1495–1521) nor his successor Joao III (1521–1557) took any action.

Despite the scandalous Christian witness of the missionaries, Afonso sent his son Henrique to Lisbon to study for the priesthood. Henrique was consecrated a bishop and served in the Madeira Islands. He eventually returned home to the Congo and supported the mission work there until his death as the only native clergy of the Congo in this period. What could explain Lisbon's lack of response and the scandalous behavior of many of the missionary priests? Likely, the Portuguese Crown was unwilling to intervene in the missions because the slave trade was just too lucrative to undermine.

A semblance of Christianity in the Congo was restored only a century later when Jesuit missionaries came in the mid-sixteenth century and formed Christian villages. In 1595, Rome established the diocese of São Salvador for the Congolese kingdom, and the Jesuits formed a college there in 1624. Capuchin priests became part of the Congolese mission in the mid-seventeenth century, establishing schools in São Salvador and Soyo, and began systematic evangelization in the rural areas. They also started religious fraternities among Africans, which became forums for promoting African rights. Between 1672 and 1700, Capuchin missionaries recorded 341,000 baptisms. They also established themselves on the Guinea Coast and in Sierra Leone in 1644. Queen Nzinga of Matamba, in eastern Angola, embraced Christianity in 1622. She subsequently lapsed from the faith and only returned to it in 1656, though this time with greater gusto. She and a great number among her army and nobles converted, forming a Christian state.

After the Portuguese rounded the Cape of Good Hope, they set up colonies in East Africa. The island nation of Mozambique was the main administrative center for the eastern seaboard. Dominican priests entered the Mutapa Empire in Zimbabwe in the seventeenth century, and its kings accepted the faith. There was great hope among Catholic Christians in Europe that much of Africa would soon become Christian as an increasing number of African kings and other ruling elites converted to the faith. But Christianity's close ties to Portugal's colonial and exploitive agenda undermined these hopes. An

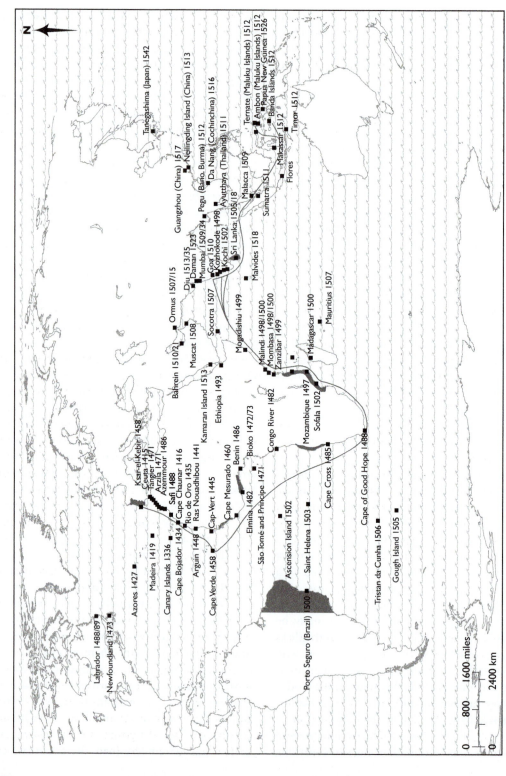

FIGURE 17-1 Portuguese exploration: Map detailing the Portuguese trade routes and areas of colonization.

anti-Portuguese civil war, for example, broke out in the Congo in 1678, after which São Salvador was deserted for a quarter-century. By 1750, there was only one Capuchin missionary in the land, the heroic Cherubina da Savona, who traversed the country many times from 1758 to 1774. He baptized as many as 700,000 people, but when he died, and without a regular priesthood, those Christians and Christian communities he had supported lapsed from the faith. It was a telling example of what occurred in much of Africa.

Other Christians also came to Africa for colonization, trade, and missions. In 1634, the French created a colony on the Ivory Coast and supported missions there. English clergymen were commissioned at the request of the Royal African Company in the Gold Coast. The Danes also created a fort at Christianborg in today's Accra, Ghana. The Dutch set up a colony in South Africa in the area of modern-day Cape Town in the mid-seventeenth century. They were forced to move inland when in 1795 the British seized power there, ultimately leading to the Boer War in the 1890s.

 THE NEW WORLD

In 1492, the Italian sailor and explorer Christopher Columbus, searching for a western route to the Indies on behalf of the Spanish, sighted a small island, which he named San Salvador. He also explored the islands of Cuba and Hispaniola, the latter of which today comprises Haiti and the Dominican Republic; in Hispaniola, he established a fort. When he returned one year later, he discovered that the natives had destroyed the fort and killed its Spanish inhabitants. While it is unclear why they killed the Spanish, it is widely assumed that the natives were mistreated from the very beginning. Columbus's response was to "pacify" the island by force. Thus began the subjugation of the peoples of Mexico, Central America, and South America. The aim of the Spanish and Portuguese was threefold: gold, glory, and God, in that order.

In 1493, Pope Alexander VI issued a series of papal bulls outlining a policy decision agreed to between the papacy, Spain, and Portugal. In his papal bull, *Inter Caetera*, he established a dividing line whereby the colonies in and missions to the lands across the Atlantic would belong to Spain, while Portugal would be left unencumbered in Africa. Brazil was the exception, and an odd one. The Portuguese had yet to "discover" Brazil, but when a Portuguese squadron attempted to sail south of the Americas for Asia, it came upon Brazil. Quickly Portuguese traders and settlers came to that land and began enslaving the natives to work on sugar plantations. Eventually, when it became too difficult to enslave them, the Portuguese imported slaves from Africa. Jesuit missionaries did their best to protect both the indigenous Brazilians and the African slaves, but they were fighting an uphill battle against the Portuguese colonialists.

The deal that Rome made with Spain and Portugal was intended to create the possibility for authentic missionary activity. The sheer size of the mission activity and its distance from Europe made normal independent mission work impossible. The system that was created to solve this problem was called **royal patronage**. The idea was that the Spanish and Portuguese Crowns would facilitate mission work alongside their colonization efforts. The two seemed to go hand in hand. The Crown's representatives would create forts and towns, build churches, and direct the missionaries, all at their own expense. Soon they set up dioceses, named bishops, hired priests, and controlled the church within their given jurisdictions.

Within the Spanish territories, *conquistadores* (literally, "conquerors") organized a system of pueblos or communities. This was called the *encomienda-doctrina* **system**, in which the *encomendero*, or leader, would run a given territory and missionaries would build a base from which to spread the gospel. By 1557, some 9,000 *encomienda* stations had been set up in Latin America, and the population of the collective pueblos was well into the millions. Even the most sincere preachers of the gospel did not distinguish their message from the Spanish culture or from other colonial interests. They saw the natives as "savages" who needed to be civilized. In their schools they taught Christian doctrine, Spanish literacy, and even liberal arts such as arithmetic and music.

Like the Portuguese's disdain for the Africans they encountered, the Spanish naturally thought of the American natives as barbaric and believed that their religious sensibilities were worse than idolatry. Contempt for the natives' religious practices went hand in hand with ignoring their inherent human dignity. Spanish theologian Juan Ginés de Sepúlveda (1489–1573) argued that "useful terror" could be legitimate in helping "the light of truth scatter the darkness of error . . . [and] break bad habits."[3]

When the conquistador **Hernán Cortés** observed the religion of the Aztecs in Mexico, he was appalled with their human sacrifices and thought their religion literally demonic. In 1519, with his own Spanish soldiers and a few thousand Mayans who were enemies of the Aztecs, he marched on Cholula, the second-largest city in Mexico. In less than two years he captured the city of Cuauhtémoc, the capital of the Aztec peoples, and renamed it Mexico City, ultimately imposing the *encomienda* system throughout much of Mexico.

How were the Spanish so easily able to conquer the natives of the Americas? Consider the first encounter between the Spanish conquistador **Francisco Pizarro** and the Inca emperor Atahuallpa at the Peruvian highland town of Cajamarca in 1532. At the time, Atahuallpa was the absolute monarch of an empire of millions, was considered the sun god by his people, and was surrounded by 80,000 soldiers, while Pizarro was the leader of 168 soldiers who were unfamiliar with both the terrain and the peoples there. Even so, Pizarro was able to capture Atahuallpa, hold him prisoner for eight months, and extract a ransom of enough gold to fill a room twenty-two feet long by seventeen feet wide, with a height of eight feet. Ultimately, after having sent this ransom back to Spain, he reneged on his promise and killed Atahuallpa anyway.

FIGURE 17-2   The execution of the last Incan emperor Atahuallpa by the Spanish conquistador Francisco Pizarro.

The accounts of the battle come from actual participants in it. Pizarro wanted intelligence on Atahuallpa and tortured some Incans, finding out that Atahuallpa was waiting for him at Cajamarca. His squadron came to Cajamarca and faced tens of thousands of Incan soldiers. He then sent an Incan messenger to the Incan king with this assurance: "Tell your lord to come when and how he pleases, and that, in what way soever he may come I will receive him as a friend and brother. I pray that he may come quickly, for I desire to see him. No harm or insult will befall him." As Atahuallpa advanced, with 2,000 Incans sweeping the road before him and surrounded by warriors, Pizarro fired a cannon and ordered his infantry to blow trumpets. Already, the Incas were somewhat in awe. Nevertheless, Atahuallpa came on, carried on a platform by warriors, while other chiefs and nobles followed him, also carried on platforms.

> Governor Pizarro now sent Friar Vicente de Valverde to go speak to Atahuallpa, and to require Atahuallpa in the name of God and the King of Spain that Atahuallpa subject himself to the law of our Lord Jesus Christ and to the service of His Majesty the King of Spain. Advancing with a cross in one hand and the Bible in the other hand, and going among the Indian troops up to the place where Atahuallpa was, the Friar thus addressed him: "I am a Priest of God, and I teach Christians the things of God, and in like manner I come to teach you. What I teach is that which God says to us in this Book. Therefore, on the part of God and of the Christians, I beseech you to be their friend, for such is God's will, and it will be good for you."

Atahuallpa took the Bible and threw it down. The friar then shouted, "Come out! Come out, Christians! Come at these enemy dogs who reject the things of God. That tyrant has thrown my book of holy law to the ground. . . . March out against him, for I absolve you!" At this point Pizarro's men attacked and mowed down thousands of Incan soldiers, taking Atahuallpa prisoner. This last action kept the rest of the Incan army at bay.

Atahuallpa was succeeded by Quizo Yupanqui, who in 1536 besieged the Spaniards in Lima. Two squadrons of Spanish cavalry charged a significantly larger Incan army and routed them in the first charge. A similar cavalry charge of twenty-six horsemen overran the Incans in Cuzco. Quickly, the Incan Empire collapsed.

What led to such fantastic successes among the Spanish against such overwhelming odds and the subsequent dissolution of a great empire in the matter of a few years? One answer is that the very centralization of the Incan leadership left it vulnerable. Once the emperor was killed, Incan society had little means to unite. The Incans also grossly underestimated the Spanish, whose arms and armor were vastly superior to their own. In addition, the Incans did not have the communication streams that the Spanish had. While the Spaniards had already been

successful in conquering the natives and shared that information among themselves, the natives knew virtually nothing about the Spanish, a situation that led to Atahuallpa's falling into such an easy trap. It was unimaginable to them that the Spanish would attempt violence, given his stature and army. The Incans were also simply stunned and intimidated by the Spanish use of horses. Incan soldiers, who were otherwise brave and intimidating, often froze in battle when confronted by the animals. Finally, the Incans, from the time of the first Spanish arrival, had often been overcome by illnesses their immune systems were unprepared to fight. Massive deaths from the smallpox epidemic alone destroyed a great deal of resistance.[4]

MARIAN INTERVENTION

Despite the abuses of the indigenous natives, many of them wholeheartedly embraced Christianity, and, in fact, many of the Franciscan and Dominican priests who arrived in the Americas came earnestly to share the gospel. While virtually all the missionaries accepted the *encomienda* system, many lived simply among those they served and witnessed authentically to the faith. Still, it was the faith of the conquerors.

A particular change in the religious ethos of the new Christians of the Americas happened through devotion to the Virgin Mary. As noted in earlier chapters, both Orthodoxy and Catholicism had a particular devotion to Mary from the patristic period on. In Catholicism, this devotion expanded dramatically in the medieval period. Mary was understood as the saint *par excellence*, as one who acted as a patroness of souls and actively intervened on their behalf.

Apparitions of Mary and miraculous interventions by her were reported throughout the Americas. She became a particular patron for the poor and marginalized natives. The most dramatic example of this affinity is the experience of **Juan Diego Cuauhtlatoatzin** in 1531. Mexico had just been conquered, and the Catholic faith was expanding. It did so, however, at the expense of the dignity of the Aztec people. The Spanish in the Americas, like the Portuguese in Africa, thought little of the native culture and had nothing but disdain for the Aztec's original religious practices or intuitions. This was the context for the events that occurred to Juan Diego, whose story is somewhat historically controversial. As fifty-seven-year-old Aztec widower Juan Diego approached Tepeyac Hill on his fifteen-mile walk to Mass, he heard music and someone softly calling his name: *Juanito! Juanito Dieguito!* (Little Johnny, Little Johnny Diego). On the hill he encountered a young Indian woman wearing traditional Aztec garb, including the black sash around her waist indicating that she was pregnant. She told him that she was the Virgin Mary and wanted a church built there, a place where she could hear her people's weeping and sorrows and could console them.

Mary instructed Juan Diego to inform the bishop of Mexico City. When he did, Bishop Zumárraga dismissed him and his vision. Mary sent him back to the bishop, who now demanded proof of the Marian apparition. Juan Diego had no idea of what kind of proof he might provide. During his third encounter with Mary on Tepeyac Hill, she instructed him to pick roses there and deliver them to the bishop. It should be noted that it was winter and not the time that roses would bloom, and further, that these roses themselves were not indigenous to Mexico. Juan Diego had nothing to hold them in, so he bundled them into the side of his cloak. When he arrived at the bishop's residence the third time, he opened his cloak to show the roses he had picked from Tepeyac's snowy rocks. On the cloak itself was the very image of the lady he had met on the hill, an image preserved to this day in the basilica dedicated to her outside Mexico City. Fascinatingly, his hemp cloak ought to have disintegrated within his lifetime, but both it and the image have been preserved intact to this day.

There are other interesting elements to this story. Mary came to Juan Diego speaking his native language as well as Spanish. When Juan Diego initially reported this, Bishop Zumárraga found it difficult to believe that Mary would

FIGURE 17-3   Modern painting on the chapel wall at Tepeyac Hill depicting Mary, the Lady of Guadalupe, giving Juan Diego roses as a sign for the bishop.

speak the pagan Nahuatl language. Further, Mary appeared on the small mountain of Tepeyac, the site of veneration of the Aztec goddess Tonantzin, the mother goddess who regenerates life. There are also striking features of the figure on the cloak. In the image, the sun radiates out from behind her. The sun was the symbol of the Aztec high god, and the image suggests symbolically that Mary is greater than the Aztec god and that she covers him, but that he is not extinguished. Rather, he seems to illuminate her from behind. The image of Mary also shows her standing on the moon, which was a lesser Aztec deity. She does not crush it, but stands above it. In Juan Diego's experience, Mary came from heaven, yet he saw her as familiar. In his dialogue with Mary, Juan Diego called her *nina mia* (my daughter), and Mary said that she was the Mother of the God of Great Truth (*Teotl*). This was the name for the local god of the Nahuatls, who had a different designation for the God of Christianity. Thus, Juan Diego's mystical experience provided a link for the original spiritual life of the Aztecs with the God of Christianity.

What does one make of such a claimed mystical experience? For the Aztec Christians it meant that God did not demand they abandon their past or utterly reject every part of their Aztec spirituality. Juan Diego was a Christian and Mary was the Mother of Jesus, but only in the context of the religious sensibilities of the people. Juan Diego's mystical experience showed the natives that they could reclaim their past spiritual intuitions even while being wholly Christian. Further, they believed that Mary also demanded a new kind of partnership with the Spanish Catholic Church, one in which both Aztecs and Spanish could join together to build a church for the Aztec Christian mother of everyone. The bishop represented the new religion, the religion of Juan Diego, as well as something of the oppressive power of the conquering Spanish. Embracing this mystical experience enabled the natives to reemerge as partners with the Spanish. They had the faith of Catholicism, but that faith had a wholly Aztec ethos. They understood this to mean that God was on their side.

Other miraculous apparitions or *Marian miracles* occurred throughout the Americas, including Brazil's *Virgin Aparecida*, Costa Rica's *La Negrita*, Argentina's *Our Lady of Luján*, Bolivia's *Our Lady of Copacubana*, Cuba's *Our Lady of Charity*, Ecuador's *Our Lady of Quinche*, Peru's *Our Lady of Mercy*, and Venezuela's *Our Lady of Cormoto*. In every case, she appeared to the poor and marginalized natives as a sign of dignity and hope.

◉ REACTIONS AGAINST THE SLAVE TRADE

Slavery is a complicated issue in the history of the West. In the ancient world, holding slaves was considered simply part of society, and the Bible offers no challenge to this aspect of the culture. In fact, it appears to support the institution. Consider: "Slaves obey your earthly masters with fear and trembling, in singleness of heart, as you obey Christ, not only while being watched, and in order to please them, but as slaves of Christ, doing the will of God from the heart" (Eph. 6:5).[5]

The Catholic Church's position on slavery had been adapted from Roman law and the writings of Aristotle. Accordingly, one could legitimately own slaves for the following reasons: (1) captivity as a result of war, (2) criminal punishment (as a substitute for capital punishment), (3) debt repayment as a limited period of servitude, (4) selling one's children out of destitution, (5) selling oneself out of destitution, and (6) retaining children born of a slave mother. Until the later modern era, slavery for Orthodox, Catholic, and Protestant Christians was simply part of society. Masters were supposed to act kindly toward slaves, but the institution was not condemned. For some Europeans, the slave trade in Africa had an oddly imagined particular biblical support. This was the story of Noah cursing Ham's son Canaan in the ninth chapter of Genesis: "Cursed be Canaan; lowest of slaves shall he be to his brothers." While the Genesis text was probably created as a justification for despising and conquering the Canaanites in ancient Israel, many European Christians took it as a condemnation of Africans, the supposed genealogical race coming from Canaan.

Portugal began the slave trade of African natives as early as 1442, and the Spanish Crown gave permission for this practice in the Americas in 1511. This policy, however, was not without religious challenge. One of the greatest early opponents of the slave trade was the Dominican priest Antonio de Montesinos, who in 1511 railed against the practice. One of the *encomenderos* at the time, **Bartolomé de las Casas** (1447–1566), was converted to Montesinos's defense of the natives. He soon became a Dominican and spent the rest of his adult life pleading on behalf of the native Americans. In 1544, he eventually became bishop of Chiapas, Mexico. De las Casas traveled extensively between the Americas and Europe arguing against the immorality of the slave trade and trying to protect the natives under his realm. At times his approach was one of moral persuasion: "Whatever we find that we may offer a first example of ourselves, by word and works, let it be peace. And let it be no different with Indians, Gentiles, Greeks, or barbarians: for there is one Lord of all, who died for all without distinction."[6] At other times he used the power of his office. For example, immediately after he became a bishop, he ordered the priests of his diocese not to absolve slaveholders in the sacrament of penance until they freed their native slaves. According to the beliefs of the time, this threat made their souls vulnerable to damnation. Within a year, a riot broke out among the colonists, and eventually de las Casas returned to Spain to continue to plead the natives' cause there. Other missionaries complained as well. In 1610, Jesuit Alonso de Sandoval, in order to awaken European lethargy, published accounts of the slave trade and even of the broken consciences of slave owners. In it he wrote, "Among human possessions, none is more valuable and beautiful than liberty. All the gold in the world and all the goods of the earth are not sufficient price for human liberty. God created man free. Slavery is not only exile, but also subjection, hunger, sorrow, nakedness, insult, prison, perpetual persecution, and, in short, is a Pandora's Box of all the evils."[7]

These moral voices had the support of Rome and the Spanish Crown. Pope Paul III issued the bull *Sublimis Deus* in 1537 that set forth the rights of native Americans and challenged their forced enslavement. In 1542, King Charles V of Spain also passed the "New Laws of the Indies" limiting the power of Spanish settlers over the natives. The Spanish colonists paid little attention to any of these measures. Interestingly, neither Pope Paul nor de las Casas challenged the institution of slavery itself. They continued to assume its potential legitimacy as a social institution, but saw it abused in the Americas.

 THE CONGREGATION FOR THE PROPAGATION OF THE FAITH

The royal patronage system was premised on the fact that the Crowns of Portugal and Spain were the only institutions capable of dealing with such massive foreign missions in such far distant lands. The colonies were under their control, and it was reasonable that they would know how best to create dioceses and send out missionaries. Further, it seemed ideal that the Crowns themselves would finance the development of the church there. The system was also premised on the assumption of good will, that is, that the Portuguese and Spanish cared about the very people and lands they colonized. When it became obvious to Rome that neither Portugal nor Spain had much concern for the peoples they had conquered, and were in fact abusing them, Rome canceled the royal patronage system and regained control of the missionary agenda. In 1622, Pope Gregory XV created the Congregation for the Propagation of the Faith. Within five years Gregory's successor, Pope Urban VIII, had created the *Collegium Urban* as a seminary to train priests for missionary work. One of the early policy statements of the Congregation reads:

> Do not regard it as your task and do not bring any pressure to bear on the peoples, to change their manners, customs, and uses, unless they are evidently contrary to religion and sound morals. What could be more absurd than to transport France, Spain, Italy, or some other European country to China? Do not introduce all that to them, but only the faith, which does not despise or destroy the manners and customs of any people, always supposing that they are not evil, but rather wishes to see them preserved unharmed.[8]

The principles of the Congregation for the Propagation of the Faith could be summarized as follows: (1) mission work is to be free from the colonial country; (2) the bishop of any new diocese would be appointed by Rome; (3) diocesan clergy would seek to balance the presence of religious orders; (4) indigenous clergy should be employed as soon as possible; and (5) it is necessary to affirm and preserve the native culture and all customs that were not intrinsically contrary to faith and morals. These principles could be unpacked. The first is easy to understand. Since the royal patronage system did not work, the missionaries had to be free from colonial control. They were to be agents of the church and not part of any government agenda. The second principle returned control of naming bishops to the papacy, thereby allowing it to regain its missionary authority and preventing bishops from being unduly influenced by the Crown's colonization agenda. The third principle sought to address the problem of missions being controlled by religious orders. The normal way the church had run since the patristic age was to create a local church (diocese) with priests whose life-long ministry would be to that local church. Standardizing these missions with stable priests who were accountable to a stable bishop was critical. The fourth principle argued for any given local church to be run by indigenous peoples. And finally, Christianity was not to be conflated with European culture. Rather, as a universal religion, it would engage with and **inculturate** itself into any society it evangelized.

These principles are rather foresighted for the time. They intended to honor the peoples and cultures of the lands the church sought to evangelize and to create local, stable, and self-authorizing Christians wherever the church went. Did this program work? In some respects it did not. The Americas continued to look and feel like mission countries even into the twentieth century. Spain and especially Portugal fought, often covertly, against Rome's policies well into the late seventeenth century. The Congo never did become self-sustaining. Further, the Congregation's policy affirming cultures is more complicated than it looks. Most cultures integrate religious, civil, and social conventions; they are all apiece. As we shall see later, parsing culture from religion is inherently problematic. Consider polygamy in Africa: Is it inherently evil or un-Christian? What about the caste system in

India? Ought one to condemn the Chinese veneration of ancestors or celebrate it? On a final note, it was not until 1839, with Pope Gregory XVI's encyclical *Supremo Apostolatus*, that all slavery was condemned as intrinsically evil, just two decades before the American Civil War.

ASIA

INDIA

As noted in Chapter Ten, the tradition among Indian Christians is that Thomas the apostle brought Christianity to India in the first century. While historically doubtful, certainly by the late third century the Church of the East had small Christian communities in both northern and southern India. Still, Indian Christianity was always a fledgling endeavor, and Christians there were dubbed the "Thomas Christians." The West was probably ignorant of Thomas Christians, as the Portuguese explorer and trader Vasco da Gama was surprised to find them when he traveled to India in 1498. Da Gama was, however, alarmed that these were Christians who represented the tradition of the Church of the East, that is, those Christians who rejected the Council of Chalcedon. Further, they had also taken on some of the religious/cultural practices of the Hindus and Muslims. For example, they washed their feet at the door of the church and entered it barefoot. They also took on the practice of kissing the floor twice before worship. Worship was long, and it often included Hindu rituals. Services on feast days lasted up to ten hours, and communion typically involved not bread and grape-wine, but rice-cakes and palm wine.

In 1507, the Portuguese took Goa on the west coast of India as the principle colonial port. Soon Franciscans, Dominicans, and later Jesuits came as missionaries. Indian Christians had either absorbed or tolerated the caste system, a rigid system of divisions in the Indian culture. According to the earliest Hindu writings, the Rig Vedas, the first spiritual being, *Purusha*, was incarnated into different castes. His mouth became the Brahmin, or priestly, caste; his arms became the noble caste; his legs became the merchant caste; and his feet became the peasant caste. The other group of Indian society was the untouchables, now called the *Dalit*, and not technically a caste at all. For Hindus, keeping caste distinctions was related to maintaining right social order and even cosmic order. Indian Christians reflected caste separations, but this offended the theological sensibilities of the early Portuguese Christian missionaries, who attempted to establish an Indian Christianity that was casteless.

In 1542, the Jesuit missionary **Francis Xavier** (1506–1552) came to Goa and spent several years preaching to any Hindu who would listen. He won vast converts among the Dalits, but few among the regular castes, and particularly few among the Brahmins. In his letters back to the newly formed Jesuit order he urged that more missionaries be sent. He wrote that he was overwhelmed with converts who were hungry for the faith. While many were wasting their time in scholarly debate in Paris, he argued, thousands of souls were being lost who could be saved if only Christian charity and courage could be mustered.

One of Xavier's greatest pains was the way the Portuguese dealt with the natives. Though they were not involved in the slave trade there, trade and colonial domination were their prime objectives. It was, for Xavier, a personal martyrdom to see the authentic mission work undermined by Portuguese greed: "Everywhere and at all times, it is rapine, hoarding and robbery. . . . I never cease wondering at the number of new inflections which, in addition to all the usual forms, have been added in this language to the avarice of conjugation of that ill-omened verb *to rob*."[9]

The Portuguese Christian mission also demanded that the Thomas Christians conform to Roman Catholic beliefs. They launched an inquisition to investigate these Christians' practices and theology, and in 1599 they called all local Christians to the Synod of Diamper, at which they demanded a full submission to Catholic Christianity. They also burned all the ancient writings of the Indian Christian community to prevent any backsliding. During the period of this inquisition, more than 16,000 Indian Christians were investigated and arrested, and around 100 were sentenced to death. While the Portuguese demanded strict Catholic orthodoxy, they did allow for a number of local customs, the so-called *Malabar Rites*, to continue; these themselves were debated in Rome for the next two centuries.

Xavier traveled to southern India and Sri Lanka, with continued success among those who were most marginal in society. A great contrast to Xavier's missionary style was that of Jesuit Roberto de Nobili (1577–1656), who served as a missionary in the southern state of Tamil Nadu. De Nobili became a Sanskrit scholar and wrote a number of vernacular texts for his Indian followers. Unlike Xavier, whose mission appealed to the lowest classes of Indian society, de Nobili strove to appeal to the Brahmin caste, allotting the task of converting the lower castes to a separate mission group. De Nobili was convinced that not only was inculturation of the faith necessary, but it was also crucial to win over the upper castes. He made it clear to his listeners that he was not a *parangi* (Portuguese), but a *sanyasi* (noble) born of a great family from Rome. De Nobili was something of an ideal witness to the faith for the Brahmins. He lived ascetically, like the great sages of India, but also evidenced great learning and an aristocratic style, adopting Hindu dress and conforming to the social norms of the culture, that impressed the Brahmins he ministered to.

Working with the caste system in India confounded Christians from the start. While missionaries believed the caste system was antithetical to the gospel, it was entrenched in the Indian mindset. Catholics mostly ordained native priests from the Brahmin caste, and when Lutherans finally made their way into India, they were unable to overcome the system they publicly opposed. The first Protestant Indian pastor was ordained in 1733 in a Protestant Danish colony. After he fell ill, the mission wrote that they wanted to replace him with a Dalit, but simply could not: "We desired to ordain him priest, which we would if his work were confined to the pariahs [Dalits]. But the Christians of highest caste avoid coming into contact with such people. We take great pains to lessen these prejudices among Christians, but to a certain degree they must be taken into consideration. But we should hesitate to have the Lord's Supper administered by him lest it diminish the regard of Christians of higher caste for that sacrament itself."[10]

Other Christian missionaries clearly broke lines with the caste system. **William Carey** (1761–1834) was a Baptist missionary in northern India. Because of the caste consciousness of his community, he moved to the Danish missionary outpost in Serampore. There he learned Bengali and ultimately produced the first Bengali Bible. Carey preached the gospel among the native community, and the daughter of his first convert, a peasant-caste woman, married a Brahmin. Carey's missionary work also included the building of hospitals and clinics. Eventually, he became a professor of Oriental languages at the University of Calcutta.

JAPAN

The Christian mission to Japan began when Francis Xavier and two Jesuit colleagues left South Asia. Xavier had spent a brief time in the Malay Peninsula and decided to make a Christian beachhead in Japan. They arrived in 1549 at Kagoshima, a town on the coast of the island of Kyushu. Japan was a divided nation, and the feudal lords the missionaries encountered were taken with the new religion. As in India, there were massive conversions. Within a half-century Catholics had established 200 missions and church schools. Xavier had clearly learned the lesson of inculturation well. Now, instead of dressing and living like the poor ascetics of India, he took on the dress and lifestyle that the Japanese thought appropriate for spiritual guides. Because of the Christians' great initial success in converts, one of their biggest problems was the lack of priests. In 1588, the ratio of priests to lay men was 1 to 422, but by 1614, it had risen to 1 to 3,061. As a result, many Japanese catechists or lay teachers took on much of the role of leadership. By the mid-seventeenth century, there were over 500 lay catechists in Japan.

The "Christian century" ended when Japan united under the Tokugawa Shogunate. The new government proclaimed Christianity a dangerous religion and expelled foreign missionaries, issuing its first edict in 1587. When the Japanese saw that these measures did not completely deter the faith, they tried and executed twenty-six Christians, who were crucified on Mount Tateyama, near Nagasaki. The martyrs included six Franciscans, three Jesuits, and seventeen lay men. That same site was used again in 1627 when twenty-three Christians were burned at the stake and another twenty-two beheaded. Between 1627 and 1636 up to 6,000 Christians were martyred. The Japanese policy was to have Buddhist priests control birth, marriage, and death certificates, and each year every citizen would have to attest at their local Buddhist monastery that he or she was not Christian; often, this was ascertained by the ritual of *e-fumi*, requiring individuals to step on a picture of Christ or the Virgin Mary. Eventually, Christianity was essentially wiped out. It took two and a half centuries of national isolation before Japan was forced by Commodore Perry of the United States to open up its borders for trade in 1854. Christian missions, whether Catholic, Protestant, or Russian Orthodox, then again became possible. After this time, Christian conversions were relatively light, only reaching a very small percentage of Japanese.

CHINA

Francis Xavier had intended to enter China in 1552, but died just before sailing from Japan. As noted in Chapter Ten, the earliest missions in China arrived in the sixth century, when a Persian priest and monk brought the faith to the land. Christianity did not spread widely, but was warmly welcomed by the T'ang dynasty. In 845, the emperor Wuzhong clamped down on both Buddhism and Christianity, and the latter disappeared for 400 years. In the thirteenth century the Mongol Genghis Khan established his empire across parts of Asia and Western Europe, and

Catholic Franciscans returned to the Chinese mission fields. Their activity again was interrupted when the Mongol empire was dissolved.

In 1582, Jesuit **Matteo Ricci** (1552–1610) came to China and, like Xavier in Japan, robed himself in garments that reflected the Chinese expectation of holy men and scholars. Initially he donned the garb of a Buddhist monk, and by 1585 he and his companion had dedicated a church in Chaoking. Later, he robed himself in garments that corresponded to those worn by Confucian scholars. Of course, Ricci was in no way pretending to be either a Buddhist or a Confucian scholar. Rather, he took on the lifestyle and cultural expectation that matched the Chinese culture. He was widely respected among the Chinese and was given the title "Doctor for the Great West Ocean." In 1601, Ricci presented the faith to the throne in Beijing and was granted residence. It is unclear if the emperor was impressed by the faith he represented or the Western scholarship he evidenced, as he was given an imperial subsidy to teach mathematics and astronomy.

Ricci and the Jesuits took on the culture, dress, and lifestyle of the Chinese. They were fully convinced that Christian faith had to be an inculturated one. Tensions eventually arose not from the Chinese, but from Rome, which became concerned with Christian participation in Chinese religious rites and even the incorporation of such rites into the church. One such example was the veneration of ancestors. While Catholicism embraced the practices of praying for the dead and veneration of saints, the veneration of ancestors looked to Rome like ancestor worship, and was thus deemed idolatrous. Rome had a point here: the distinction between veneration of ancestors and veneration of spirits was a blurred one in the Chinese mind, and ancestors worked something like minor gods who could bless those who venerated them and curse those who did not. The Jesuit missionaries insisted that such practices were functionally civil and not religious, but in 1715 Pope Clement XI issued a decree condemning Christian participation in ancestor veneration as well as the veneration of Confucius.

FIGURE 17-4 Bronze statue of Matteo Ricci, who in 1582 reintroduced Christianity to China. He is dressed as a Confucian scholar, which was one way he strove to inculturate the faith.

Because of the practice of Western colonization and its exploitation of natives and the fact that Christianity fell short of full integration in Chinese society, the emperor Yung-Cheng reversed his father's openness to the missionaries. Meeting with Jesuits in Beijing in 1724 he challenged them:

> You say that your law is not a false law. I believe you. If I thought it was false, what would prevent me from destroying your churches and driving you away from them? What would you say if I sent a troop of Bonzes and Lamas into your country to preach their doctrines? You want all Chinese to become Christians. Your law demands it, I know. But in that case what will become of us? Shall we become subjects to your King? . . . The emperor, my father, lost a great

deal of reputation among scholars by the condescension with which he let you establish yourselves here. The laws of our ancient sages will permit no change, and I will not allow my reign to be laid open to such a change.[11]

The emperor then issued the **Edict of Expulsion and Confiscation**. Some 300,000 Christians were affected, and churches were either destroyed or converted into public buildings. The emperor had a legitimate concern, and it was realized when the British East India Trading Company demanded that China open up its ports to trading in the nineteenth century, sparking the so-called Opium Wars. The British saw China as a great possibility for trade, particularly in opium. China resisted and was crushed by a British military invasion. China and Britain signed a treaty in 1842 giving the British control of Hong Kong and five "treaty ports" on the Chinese coast. The first Protestant church was built in China in Amoy in 1848. The terms of the 1842 treaty, however, were so high-handed that a second war broke out in 1856, which the British again won. It did not help matters that the Christian missionaries declared universal support for the Taiping Rebellion in 1854, which was eventually put down in 1864, but at the cost of 20 million Chinese. In voicing support for the rebellion, a London Missionary Society spokesman said that he was convinced the rebellion was a sign that God had intervened in China to uproot idolatry and prepare to establish China as a Christian country.

ASIAN ISLANDS

The first Catholic church in Indonesia was built by the Portuguese in 1534, but by 1605 the Dutch had conquered the country. They soon made Catholicism illegal and advanced a modest Protestant presence. It was only in 1807 that Catholics were again allowed to worship in Indonesia, but Christianity never fared well there. Malaysia was different. The Malay Islands had a Christian presence as far back as the seventh century, when Persian Christians settled in the northern parts of the peninsula. By the fifteenth century, Christian communities dotted much of the northern part of the country. When the Portuguese conquered the peninsula, they brought in eight priests, who soon engaged in missionary activity. Francis Xavier spent time there and built its first school, St. Paul's College. As in Indonesia, however, the Dutch eventually captured the port and suppressed Catholicism. When the British came to power in the nineteenth century, they allowed Protestant and Catholic missions to work alongside each other. Malaysia never did become robustly Christian. The Malays considered the faith *agama orang putih* (the white man's religion), and thus a foreign intrusion. Historically, the islands have had influences from Hinduism, Buddhism, Islam, and even Chinese Confucianism and Daoism, all of which are foreign to the native population. But to the Malays, Christianity stood alone as the religious and cultural other.

In contrast to the rather weak conversions in Indonesia and Malaysia, the Philippines became robustly Christian. In 1521, Ferdinand Magellan established a settlement in Cebu, and the Spanish subsequently established settlements throughout the archipelago. These outposts operated under the royal patronage system, but this expression of the policy was not exploitative as it was in the Americas, even though it conflated Spanish culture with the Christian faith. The Spanish created towns that replicated the grids in Spanish cities, including a central plaza surrounded by churches, civic buildings, and prominent residences. By the mid-seventeenth century Augustinian missionaries had founded over 100 towns along these lines. Often, the parish priest was de facto the church and colonial authority, and priests built roads, taught agricultural practices, and created orphanages, hospitals, and schools. Jesuits founded schools as well, including the Colegio de Manila for the training of priests and the Colegio de San Jose for other students. Dominican missionaries also founded the Colegio San Juan de Latran and Colegio de Santo Thomas, which became a university in 1611. They also established a school for girls in 1636, the Colegio de Sta. Isabel. Today, 91 percent of the Philippines is Christian, with the vast majority being Roman Catholic.

CONCLUSIONS

What does one make of this third wave of missionary activity? Christians were, at the time, convinced that one had to be baptized to be saved. When they discovered such masses of peoples in Africa, the Americas, and Asia, they believed it their absolute duty to convert the indigenous peoples, lest their souls be lost. The conversions of the Africans had initial but less long-term success. The conversions in Asia, while far more earnestly pursued, were modest. Statistically speaking, the conversions in the Americas were, however, a fantastic success. Millions of native Indians from Mexico down to Cape Horn became Christian. From the theological perspective of historical Christianity, their souls could be saved and God could be glorified. It would only be later that Christians, from Catholic, Orthodox, and Protestant communities, broadly came to believe that God could and does save souls who align themselves with his grace, even without explicit Christian membership.

It should be obvious, however, that the conversions of many of these peoples came at the staggering price of exploitation. One need not romanticize the societies or religions the Europeans met. They warred among themselves and often advanced their own interests in dominating and even enslaving their neighbors. Even so, their subjugation, particularly by the Portuguese and Spanish, in the name of God and Crown was little more than naked greed. Many of the missionaries acted authentically and even heroically, but many others were simply part of the colonial machinations of their respective country's expansion of power and wealth. Ironically, the European economy itself experienced mixed results from this colonization period. The flooding of silver and gold into Europe created huge inflation in prices, ultimately compromising the very countries that were so greedily expanding. Worse still, the Christian message was often advanced by the sword, and hardly as the witness of Jesus the Prince of Peace. And the colonization of Africa, much of which was not reversed until the 1960s, would create the political instability that still characterizes Africa today.

British economist Adam Smith, in his groundbreaking *Wealth of Nations* (1776), describes the impact of the colonial period, and particularly the development of the passage to the East Indies, as among the most important events in human history:

> Their consequences have already been very great; but in the short period of between two and three centuries which has elapsed since those discoveries were made, it is impossible that the whole extent of their consequences can have been seen. By uniting, in some measure, the most distant parts of the world . . . their general tendency would seem to be beneficial. To the natives, however, both of the East and West Indies, all the commercial benefits which can have resulted from those events have been sunk and lost in the dreadful misfortunes which they have occasioned.[12]

SUMMARY QUESTIONS

- What are the characteristics of Christianity that make it a proselytizing religion?
- How have views on salvation outside the church changed throughout church history?
- How did Christianity both lend itself to and restrict the exploitation of colonized peoples?

- What were the reasons for instituting the royal patronage system, and what assumptions was it founded on? How was the system different from the later revision by the Congregation for the Propagation of the Faith?

DISCUSSION QUESTIONS

- Thinking within a Christian framework, make an argument about the requirements for salvation.
- The Congregation for the Propagation of the Faith held five principles for missionary activity. Do you think they represent a respectable position even today? Why or why not?

- Discuss examples of the ways Christianity was able to inculturate itself among different peoples. What difficulties arise from trying to separate culture from religion?

KEY TERMS

Afonso
Carey, William
Casas, Bartolomé de las
Colonialism
Conquistadores
Cortés, Hernán
Cuauhtlatoatzin, Juan Diego

Edict of Expulsion and Confiscation
Encomienda-doctrina system
Henry the Navigator
Inculturation
Inter Caetera
Pizarro, Francisco

Proselytizing
Ricci, Matteo
Royal patronage
Supremo Apostolatus
Xavier, Francis

BIBLIOGRAPHY

- Brockey, Liam Matthew. 2007. *Journey to the East: The Jesuit Mission to China, 1579–1724.* Cambridge: Harvard University Press.
- Casas, Bartolomé de las. 1992. *The Devastation of the Indies: A Brief Account.* Trans. Herma Briffault. Baltimore: Johns Hopkins University Press.
- Diamond, Jared. 1997. *Guns, Germs and Steel: The Fates of Human Society.* New York: W. W. Norton & Company.
- Elizondo, Virgil. 1998. *Guadalupe: Mother of the New Creation.* Maryknoll, NY: Orbis.
- Jacobson, Douglas. 2011. *The World's Christians: Who They Are, Where They Are, and How They Got There.* Chichester, UK: Wiley-Blackwell.

- Neil, Stephen. 1984. *A History of Christian Missions.* New York: Penguin.
- Newbigin, Lesslie. 1986. *Foolishness of the Greeks: The Gospel and Western Culture.* Geneva: World Council of Churches.
- Phan, Peter, ed. 2011. *Christianities in Asia.* Chichester, UK: Wiley-Blackwell.
- Sanneh, Lamin. 2008. *Disciples of All Nations: Pillars of World Christianity.* Oxford: Oxford University Press.
- Smith, Adam. 1994. *The Wealth of Nations.* Ed. Edwin Cannan. New York: Modern Library.
- Williams, Eric. 1984. *From Columbus to Castro: The History of the Caribbean, 1492–1969.* New York: Vintage.

NOTES

1. Cited in Sanneh, *Disciples of All Nations*, 103.
2. Ibid., 99.
3. Cited in Jacobson, *World's Christians*, 360.
4. Diamond, *Guns, Germs, and Steel*, 67–81.
5. See also Colossians 3:22–25; 1 Timothy 6:1–2; and Titus 2:9–10.
6. Casas, *Devastation of the Indies*, 1.17.
7. Williams, *From Columbus to Castro*, 107.
8. Neil, *History of Christian Missions*, 174.
9. Cited in Sanneh, *Disciples of All Nations*, 95.
10. Cited in Phan, *Christianities in Asia*, 20.
11. Cited in Sanneh, *Disciples of All Nations*, 245.
12. Smith, *Wealth of Nations*, 675.

18

Christianity in the United States to the Civil War

Timeline

1606 CE	King James grants the charter for the colony of Virginia
1620 CE	Puritans arrive in North America on the *Mayflower* and establish a colony at Plymouth
1636 CE	Roger Williams founds the colony of Providence (Rhode Island), the first American colony with religious liberty
1642 CE	Beginning of English Civil War
1650s CE	Lutherans from Germany, Austria, and the Netherlands begin to emigrate to America
1652 CE	George Fox founds Quakerism
1675 CE	Philipp Jakob Spener publishes *Pia Desideria*; beginnings of Pietism
1681 CE	William Penn founds Pennsylvania as a colony of religious tolerance
1703–1758 CE	Life of Jonathan Edwards, the central figure of the First Great Awakening
1703–1791 CE	Life of John Wesley, the evangelist whose followers created the Methodist Church
1726 CE	Beginning of the First Great Awakening in America
1775 CE	Beginning of American Revolution
1787 CE	Richard Allen founds the African Methodist Episcopal Church
1789 CE	John Carroll is made first Catholic bishop in America

1801 CE	Beginning of the Second Great Awakening at Cane Ridge, Kentucky
1830 CE	Joseph Smith founds the Mormon faith
c. 1860 CE	Ellen White founds the Seventh Day Adventist Church
1861 CE	Charles Taze Russell founds Zion's Watchtower Society, which later becomes the Jehovah's Witnesses

WHAT TO EXPECT

In the last chapter we saw that the aim of many colonial projects was to exploit both the land and its peoples; this was particularly the case in Central and South America, as well as in Africa. The colonization of the eastern seaboard of the United States, that is, the thirteen colonies, was quite different. This chapter discusses the various visions of colonial leaders who came to America, from farming and trade to religious experimentation. The colonies were quite distinct from each other: some were theocracies, thoroughly uniting society, politics, and the church, and others were experiments in religious toleration. This chapter also discusses a particular breakthrough that separated the religious leanings of the various colonies, that is, revivalism and the American Evangelical movement. This movement privileged inner faith and the priority of one's conscience to institutional loyalties and united the colonists, even contributing to the American Revolution.

THE AMERICAN COLONIES

It would be politically foolish today for someone seeking a high civil office to suggest that the United States is not much different or not better than other developed countries. Americans have, from the earliest times of colonization, believed themselves special. This **American exceptionalism** is so much a part of the American self-understanding that to challenge it is to be considered anti-patriotic. The idea was first articulated by John Winthrop, the first governor of Massachusetts, on board the flagship *Arbella* as it approached the American mainland in 1630: "We must consider that we shall be a city on a hill, the eyes of all nations will be upon us."[1] Puritan theologian Peter Bulkeley in 1650 expanded this image further:

> We are as a city set upon a hill, in open view of all the earth, the eyes of the world are upon us, because we profess ourselves to be a people in covenant with God, and therefore not only the Lord our God, with whom we have made covenant, but heaven and earth, angels and men, that we witness to our profession, will cry shame upon us if we walk contrary to the covenant which we have professed and promised to walk in.[2]

Noted Puritan theologian Increase Mather in 1675 even referred to the growing society as the "New Jerusalem come down from heaven." These images grounded the early American ethos and have remained part of American religious and political discourse to this day.

VIRGINIA

In 1578, Queen Elizabeth instructed her explorers "to discover and take possession of such remote, heathen, and barbarous lands, as were not actually possessed by any Christian prince of people." English colonization represented beliefs about entitlement to land. Although the English colonists discovered American Indians living on the land, they also believed it was available to them since the Indians had not cultivated it. Explorer Thomas Harriot observed in 1585 that the

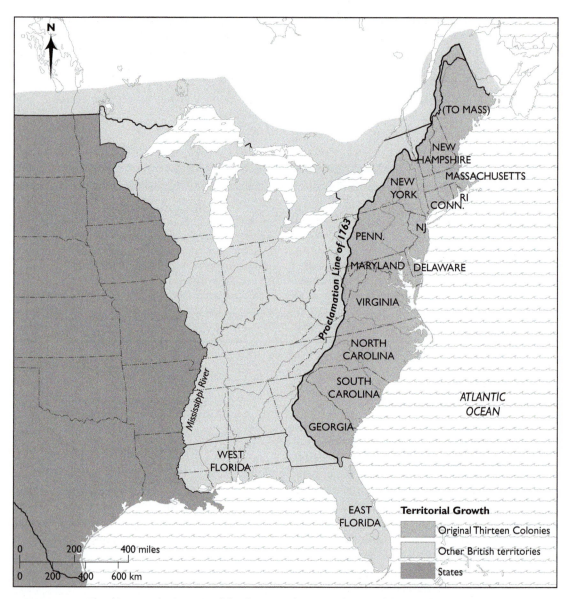

FIGURE 18-1 The thirteen colonies: Map of the thirteen colonies on the eve of the American Revolution.

English were free to "the ground they [Indians] never fatten with muck, dung, or any other thing, neither plough nor did it as we in England." Later, Puritan John Cotton would explain, "It is a principle of nature that in vacant soil, he that takes possession of it, and bestows culture and husbandry upon it, his right it is."[3]

In 1606, King James issued a charter for Virginia, seeing the territory as an opportunity for mission. Virginia was to promote Christianity to those living "in darkness and miserable ignorance of the true knowledge and worship of God."[4] Actually, Virginian colonists were never really much interested in missions, but they were interested in establishing residence on Virginia's fertile fields. In 1611, the Virginia Company set Lord Thomas De La Warr and Thomas Dale the task of creating a society based on trade and the Anglican Church. De La Warr and Dale quickly issued a set of laws to bring order to Virginia, partially through required religious practice. The new "Laws Divine, Morall, and Martiall" were strict, including mandated worship twice on Sunday. Failure to follow the Sabbath laws would result in losing one's daily allowance (first offense), being whipped (second offense), and being put in the galleys at sea for six months (third offense).

MASSACHUSETTS

As noted in Chapter Sixteen, Puritanism had a complicated relationship with the English Crown. Puritanism continued to develop under the reigns of James I and Charles I, fueled by resentment toward their autocratic rule. For the Puritans, the "divine right of kings" had no biblical warrant and contrasted with the virtues of the republican rule in Calvin's Geneva. In 1607, a Puritan congregation from Nottinghamshire migrated to Amsterdam, which was at the time the center of the Calvinist world. In 1609, the members moved to Leiden, but they never really integrated with the Dutch culture. So, in 1620, they decided to travel to the American colony of Virginia and establish a separate settlement. Due to a navigation error, however, they ended up landing at Cape Cod, and a month later they descended on Plymouth Rock, where they set up a community. Between 1627 and 1640, 4,000 Puritan pilgrims made the Atlantic crossing, settling on the coastline of Massachusetts Bay. America was seen as the land of freedom where they could build their New Jerusalem, a city upon a hill.

The Puritans in America were not like those in England who tried to reform the English Church; these colonists were decidedly **separatists**. As early as the 1630s they had abandoned the European presbyterian understanding of church government, and they became known as **Congregationalists**, for their organization into communities that were relatively autonomous. Eventually, this autonomy would allow for greater exploration of religious possibilities, but at the time it was something more along the lines of freedom from outside political control. This is not to say, however, that within each community there was a great deal of freedom. Puritans were among the most rigid religious believers in the Americas. In 1644, the Massachusetts General Court banned Baptists and Catholics from the colony. As Puritan leader Nathaniel Ward declared, "as far as to proclaim to the world in the name of our colony, that all Familists, Antinomians, Anabaptists, and other enthusiasts shall have the liberty to keep away from us; and such as will come, to be gone as fast as they can, the sooner the better."[5] It was their goal to create a kingdom of God on earth, and thus they believed it was necessary to purge the church of heretics. **Theocracy**, as John Cotton and other Puritan leaders held, was the best form of government for the commonwealth. With the most earnest intentions, the practices of exclusion, public humiliation, confinement, banishment, and even execution became common forms of keeping the community religiously pure.

There was something of a missionary spirit among the Puritans. They set up "praying towns" for American Indians, where natives could live in English-style houses, learn the faith, and cultivate the land. Working hard and adopting English customs, such as wearing English clothing, having short hair, and walking in cobbled shoes, were considered outer signs of inner religious conversion. By 1676, however, most of the "praying towns" had been dismantled after the outcome of the so-called King Philip's War, in which the Christian Native Americans allied themselves with other Native American forces against the Puritan colonists. After King Philip's War, the Puritans showed little interest in converting the Indians.

Following John Calvin's understanding of election, Puritans looked for two signs that one had been authentically called by God. The first was some palpable experience of the Holy Spirit in one's life, and the second was an exemplary life that evidenced this new existence in the Spirit. The latter sign was expressed by disciplined and productive work. The former was revealed by a practice that became standard in Puritan churches in which Christians would give an account of their personal experience of God's grace in their hearts—the more dramatic, the better. If the community was satisfied with the testimony, then one was admitted into the community with full rights to the sacraments and full civil voting rights.

One of the great problems that the second generation of colonists faced was a shrinking number of people who could claim such palpable experiences. These individuals had been baptized as infants, but as adults they were unable to provide a dramatic testimony of God clearly working in their hearts. At a general council in 1662 a compromise was worked out, known as the Half-Way Covenant. Under this agreement, members who could not give a satisfying dramatic witness to conversion were eligible for partial membership in the church. Consider the swift change: In the 1630s, 70 to 80 percent of taxpayers were full members of the Puritan Church. By 1670, only about 40 percent were. In Salem, infamous for its "witch trials," only about 30 percent were full members of the Puritan Church. Demand for this public testimony severely weakened Puritan hopes in America. Enthusiasm was further weakened by more European immigration, which brought to the colony Baptists, Presbyterians, French Protestants, Scots-Irish, and Welsh. In 1684, King Charles II decided that Anglicans could also be allowed to freely settle and worship in Massachusetts.

RHODE ISLAND AND PENNSYLVANIA

Puritan **Roger Williams** (1603–1684) was a leading proponent of a pure separatist church. Along with other Puritans he believed that the Church of England was heretical. But he was also alarmed by Massachusetts' commitment to the integration of church and state. For religion to be authentic and pure, he believed, it had to be free from any government intrusions. Ultimately,

Williams left Massachusetts and established the colony of Rhode Island. Governor John Winthrop had called Rhode Island the "cess pool of the world," but for Williams it was a place of great possibility, where inhabitants could enjoy complete religious liberty.

Others were also disenchanted with the Puritan religious–civic project. One member of the church, Ann Hutchinson, was a mystic who claimed a number of direct encounters with God. She gave lectures at her home to other women and argued that she only knew two Puritan clergymen who were actually saved. The rest, she insisted, were damned for trying to be saved by their good works. During her trial on charges of heresy, she declared, "God will ruin you and your posterity and your whole state." Winthrop asked her at her trial, "How do you know that it was God that did reveal these things to you, and not Satan?" She claimed as evidence the assurance in her soul. Ironically, the very palpable experiences of the Holy Spirit that the Puritans demanded ended up challenging them directly. They excommunicated her and banished her and her followers to Rhode Island.

Another Christian leader was **George Fox** (1624–1691), who also had many direct encounters with God. Fox preached throughout England a theology of rejecting rituals and church order so as to allow for such direct experiences. For this he was imprisoned. In 1652, he formed the Society of Friends, dedicated to experiencing the simple inner light of God's grace. Members of the Society were known as Quakers, and being a Quaker in Massachusetts was a crime. Quaker missionaries Mary Fisher and Ann Austin were arrested in Boston, stripped, searched for marks of witchcraft, and then deported. Other missionaries, however, continued to enter New England, which drafted a series of anti-Quaker laws. King Charles ultimately had to formally prohibit corporal punishment of Quakers in the English colonies, but it was still a trying time. Some Quakers migrated to Rhode Island, but others followed William Penn, who established his own colony of religious toleration: Pennsylvania.

COLONIAL ALIGNMENTS

The New England colonies of Massachusetts, Connecticut, and New Hampshire were dominated by Puritans and other Congregational churches. They did not much like the Anglicans. Virginia, North Carolina, and South Carolina, on the other hand, were dominated by Anglicans, and they did not much like the Puritans. New York had been originally founded by Dutch settlers, who named it New Amsterdam. In Europe, Amsterdam had already embraced religious tolerance, and the Dutch who emigrated to North America retained this value. The Dutch Reformed Church was the official church of the colony, but it was quite tolerant. Rhode Island likewise was religiously tolerant, though Jews who emigrated there still were not granted full legal rights. The most expansive expression of religious multiplicity was Pennsylvania, considered the "holy experiment." As one traveler wrote in 1750, "sects of every belief are tolerated. You meet here Lutherans, Reformed, Catholics, Quakers, Mennonites, Herrnhutur or Moravian Brethren, Seventh Day Baptists, Dunkers, Presbyterians, the New Born, Free Masons, Separatists, Free Thinkers, Negroes, and Indians."[6]

 PIETISM, METHODISM, AND THE EVANGELICAL MOVEMENT

PIETISM

During the time of North American colonization, a movement was spreading across European Christianity that would significantly affect the American religious scene: **Pietism**. By the mid-seventeenth century, many German Lutherans had become dissatisfied with their state religion. Lutheran orthodoxy was being experienced by many as austere and lacking warmth. After the Thirty Years' War a revivalist movement emerged. Its beliefs are best illustrated by Philipp Jakob Spener's *Pia Desideria* (Pious Desires), published in 1675. *Pia Desideria*, which quickly became a European sensation, challenged Lutheranism's obsession with theological orthodoxy and argued for a devotional life centered on a personal relationship with Jesus. Later, Nikolaus Ludwig von Zinzendorf (1700–1760) founded a Pietist community known as the "Herrnhuter," named after the village of Herrnhut in Saxony, Germany. The Herrnhuter believed that faith had little to do with the mere acceptance of doctrine, or even what Luther understood as absolute trust in Christ. Rather, faith was about a personal, transforming encounter with God. Inner transformation was the key for the Pietists.

Almost simultaneously with the printing of Spener's *Pia Desideria*, **John Bunyan** of England published *Pilgrim's Progress* in 1678. It too became an international sensation. In this text Bunyan provides an allegory of the Christian struggle to overcome sin and find salvation. *Pilgrim's Progress* translates the truths of Protestant theology, particularly Swiss Calvinism, into the subjective experience of the Pilgrim, who represents every Christian. Further, it communicates the message that doctrine and church institution matter little, while one's individual relationship with God matters completely. It is a story of inward repentance, the assurance of Christ's forgiveness, and the grace-filled way to live a holy life. In contrast to Luther and Calvin's church-centered faith, the story emphasizes individual faith, a religion that is essentially a private affair of the heart. Bunyan wrote:

> Now I saw in my dream, that the highway up which Christian was to go, was fenced on either side with a Wall, and that Wall is called Salvation. Up this way therefore did burdened Christian run, but not without great difficulty, because of the load on his back.
>
> He ran thus till he came to a place somewhat ascending; and upon that place stood a Cross, and a little below in the bottom, a sepulchre. So I saw in my dream, that just as Christian came up with the Cross, his burden loosed from off his shoulders, and fell from off his back; and began to tumble, and so continued to do so till it came to the mouth of the sepulchre, where it fell in, and I saw it no more.

Then was Christian glad and lightsome, and said with a merry heart, "He hath given me rest, by his sorrow, and life, by his death." Then he stood a while, to look and wonder; for it was very surprising to him that the sight of the Cross would thus ease him of his burden. He looked therefore, and asked again, even till the springs that were in his head sent the waters down his cheeks. . . . Then Christian gave three leaps for joy, and went on singing.[7]

We see in this small segment what exemplifies for Bunyan the deeply heartfelt religious experience and the individualized expression of faith. The Pilgrim walks the path of faith alone, personally walking the path of salvation. There he finds Christ's redemption, which frees him from his burden.

METHODISM

Pietism marks the initial movement to relocate the essence of Christian faith and revitalize the Protestant Reformation. This twofold agenda was furthered by the work of **John Wesley (1703–1791)**, his brother **Charles Wesley (1707–1788)**, and **George Whitefield (1714–1770)**, all of whom were members of the Church of England. These three, along with many others, bemoaned the religious culture of England, which they believed was geared toward upper-class sensitivities and lacked any real transforming power. As students at Oxford University, they founded a "Holy Club," where they met regularly and developed a rigorous schedule of spiritual practices. They came to be known as **Methodists** because of their methodical means for spiritual growth. John Wesley later traveled to Herrnhut to see how the German Pietist movement worked, and he came home inspired to make this movement part of his ministry. Wesley described his own powerful religious experience as follows:

In the evening I went very unwillingly to a society in Aldersgate Street [London], where one was reading Luther's Preface to the Epistle to the Romans. About a quarter before nine, while he was describing the change which God works in the heart through faith in Christ, I felt my heart

FIGURE 18-2 John Wesley (1703–1791) reinvigorated the Church of England and was part of the English and American religious revival.

strangely warmed. I felt I did trust Christ—Christ alone for salvation; and an assurance was given to me that He had taken away my sins, even mine, and saved me from the law of sin and death.[8]

What is particularly striking about this passage is that Wesley was, by this time, a very serious Christian. Still, for him this was his moment of inner conversion. For Wesley, conversion meant more than merely believing in the gospel or embracing the moral demands of the faith. Rather, it served as a "second baptism" in which he knew Christ in his heart and experienced him powerfully.

As the Methodist movement grew, members of the Church of England came to gather midweek for prayer, Bible reading, and fellowship. Itinerant preachers would travel around the circuit of these Methodist groups to give them ongoing support. Wesley himself preached throughout the English countryside, particularly to common laborers, and provided an experiential form of

Christian faith. Methodism's emphasis on experience raised criticisms among the upper-class Christian culture and was derided in the press, which referred to it as "enthusiasm," and critiqued the "faintings and swoonings" that frequently accompanied such deeply enlivened faith. Wesley himself was concerned that his movement was becoming overly emotional, and, as an Anglican priest, he hoped to provide something of a middle ground between formal high church and excessively emotional religious faith. He wanted to infuse the Church of England with dramatic inner life, not provide an alternative religious denomination. Ultimately, after his death, the movement did break away from the Anglican Church and formed itself as a new denomination: Methodism.

AMERICAN REVIVALISM AND EVANGELICALISM

Evangelical is a term that connotes a number of things. For some, it refers to a nondenominational Christian or church—if one is not a Lutheran, Catholic, Presbyterian, and so on, then one is an Evangelical. For others, it refers to specific denominational churches, such as the Evangelical Free churches or even denominations that sociologically fall under a large Evangelical umbrella, including Pentecostal denominations and the Southern Baptist Convention. Still, for others, it represents a *way* of being Christian. Originally the term "evangelical" was used in the Reformation period to refer to Christians who accepted the reformers' insistence on biblical faith with an emphasis on the preached word. By the seventeenth century, it was being used to refer to the German Pietistic movement and some forms of English Puritanism that advocated a life-transforming piety over a rational, rule-based Protestant faith.

The history of Evangelicalism in America is marked by **revivals** and "**awakenings**." In the 1670s, Puritan leaders were calling for an outpouring of the Holy Spirit to reinvigorate waning church life. Samuel Torrey, a pastor in Weymouth,

Massachusetts, is usually regarded as the first American Evangelical. Torrey was a prominent figure and was twice offered the presidency of Harvard University, which he declined. Torrey believed that Christianity in the colonies was languishing, and he was certain that merely calling people to greater moral zeal and faithful church attendance would not achieve real transformation. Rather, the Holy Spirit had to revive them. In 1674, he challenged other pastors to support a Christian revival.

Among those who took Torrey's call seriously was Solomon Stoddard, a pastor in Northampton, Massachusetts. Between 1679 and 1718 Stoddard held five revivals, which he called "harvests." These several-day gatherings were designed to infuse Christians with deeper faith through singing, dramatic preaching, and calls for new or renewed conversions. Stoddard encouraged other pastors to preach a double message: the real threat of damnation and the beautiful hope of salvation. For him, the threat of damnation was the most effective part of the message. He would not have framed this as a scare tactic, but rather that which would lead sinners to true "humiliation," or an utter sense of dread before God's holiness.

Revivals were held throughout New England. The first major revival was in Connecticut (1722) and boasted of hundreds of new conversions. The greatest one was held five years later, in 1727, in the aftermath of an earthquake that rocked New England. After the earthquake, churches filled with Christians utterly unnerved about the state of their souls. Pastors interpreted the event as a divine sign demanding repentance. In the 1720s and 1730s revival initiatives spread to the middle colonies of New Jersey, Pennsylvania, and New York. And, as more clergy with Pietist leanings arrived from the continent, the "religion of the heart" took off full force.

JONATHAN EDWARDS AND THE FIRST GREAT AWAKENING

Jonathan Edwards (1703–1758), Stoddard's grandson, led the greatest expression of revivalism, referred to as the *First Great Awakening*. Edwards held

FIGURE 18-3 Jonathan Edwards (1703–1758) was instrumental in the First Great Awakening that occurred in the American colonies.

outdoor revivals that attracted as many as 20,000 souls. His most important revival was in 1734–1735 in Northampton, where he had taken over his grandfather's pulpit. It is just one example of a much broader movement. Edwards's own writings note thirty-two communities besides Northampton that experienced dramatic awakenings, often in response to threats of damnation. Consider the following passage from his famous sermon "Sinners in the Hands of an Angry God":

> The bow of God's wrath is bent, and the arrow made ready on the string, and justice bends the arrow at your heart, and strains the bow, and it is nothing but the mere pleasure of God, and that of an angry God, without any promise or obligation at all, that keeps the arrow one moment from being made drunk with your blood. . . . The God that holds you over the pit of hell, much as one holds a spider, or some loathsome insect over the

fire, abhors you, and is dreadfully provoked: his wrath towards you burns like fire; he looks upon you as worthy of nothing else, but to be cast into the fire; he is of purer eyes than to bear to have you in his sight; you are ten thousand times more abominable in his eyes, than the most hateful venomous serpent is in ours. You have offended him infinitely more than ever a stubborn rebel did his prince; and yet it is nothing but his hand that holds you from falling into the fire every moment. It is to be ascribed to nothing else that you did not go to hell the last night; that you suffered to awake again in this world, after you closed your eyes to sleep. And there is no other reason to be given why you have not dropped into hell since you arose in the morning, but that God's hand has held you up. There is no other reason to be given why you have not gone to hell, since you have sat here in the house of God, provoking his pure eyes by your sinful wicked manner of attending his solemn worship. Yea, there is nothing else that is to be given as a reason why you do not this very moment drop down into hell.[9]

Even though Edwards was a powerful preacher and an excellent pastor, the revival in Northampton eventually waned. By this point, however, revivalism had become part of the American religious ethos, partly as a result of the publication of Edwards's memoirs, *Faithful Narrative*, which became a new literary genre: the conversion story.

GEORGE WHITEFIELD

George Whitefield (1714–1770) was a friend of the Wesley brothers and certainly America's first religious celebrity. Although he was an Anglican, one key to his success was his ability to work across denominational lines. For Whitefield, religious loyalty had little to do with institutional membership and everything to do with new birth in the Spirit. He grew up in England and began his preaching ministry there as soon as he became a deacon. Gatherings to hear him preach were massive, and, unlike the Wesleys, Whitefield was a media darling. Eventually, he widened his ministry by preaching to large outdoor crowds. Ben Franklin once heard him preach in

England and estimated the crowd at 25,000. Whitefield also published his sermons, which proved to be wildly popular.

In 1738, Whitefield received an invitation from the Wesley brothers, who had moved to the colonies to spread their Methodist style of faith. They had settled in Georgia and asked him to help with their mission. By the time he arrived, however, the Wesleys had already departed amid a good deal of anger from the Georgian Christians toward their demanding morality, an anger exacerbated by a public romance of a local young woman by John Wesley that went sour. After three months in Georgia, Whitefield returned briefly to England to be ordained a priest. Despite his ordination, Whitefield considered his brother priests to be different from him: their faith, he believed, was an outward faith and not an inner lived one.

In 1739, Whitefield returned to the colonies. Edwards, a Congregationalist, even had the Anglican Whitefield preach in his Northampton church, and he later noted that he wept throughout the entire sermon, struck by the elegance, grandeur, and deep faith Whitefield witnessed to. From Massachusetts, Whitefield went to Delaware and began his first major preaching tour of the colonies, which would include North and South Carolina and then Boston. In 1740, he returned to England.

One can hardly overestimate the change in the religious landscape brought on by the Great Awakening. For the revivalists, the institutional loyalties that separated Christians did not matter; it was all about dramatic faith. In this context, Christians began to feel free to leave their home churches and form their own. Such a movement was alarming to established congregations, so much so that Connecticut even passed a law intended to stop the activity of itinerant preachers and the congregations they inadvertently created. But this was to little avail. The freedom of conscience that the great Reformation heroes had heralded had become central to what became known as "radical evangelicalism." New England alone saw literally hundreds of new congregations spring up that had no direct institutional loyalties. Private judgment and the freedom to separate from established powers ended up not only becoming central to the Evangelical cause, but also creating a culture of populism and democratization in America.

THE SECOND GREAT AWAKENING

The years from 1800 to 1830 witnessed a Second Great Awakening in America, one that produced a tenfold increase in church attendance, easily outstripping the growth in population in the newly formed United States. The first revival happened in Cane Ridge, Kentucky, in 1801. It lasted a week and was attended by 10,000 persons. This is an extraordinary number, given that Kentucky did not have the dense population of New England. Like previous revivals, these events appealed to Christians' emotions and stressed the individual commitment to Christ over church membership. The Second Great Awakening also brought about the emergence of the **Bible Belt**—ranging from Missouri, Kentucky, and North Carolina in the north to Texas through Georgia in the south—and formed the basis for the Southern Baptist Convention.

Unlike the First Great Awakening, which was led by highly educated pastors, the Second Great Awakening was far more egalitarian. Since the intellect was minimized in favor of a more emotional faith, little difference was seen between the authority of scholars and that of common laborers. The Second Great Awakening stressed the spiritual impulses of ordinary people embracing a simple yet enthusiastic faith, which one could define for oneself and personally witness to.

An important figure in the Second Great Awakening was **Charles Grandison Finney** (1792–1875). Key to his revival techniques was the "altar call," an invitation to come forward and publicly accept the faith in the midst of the crowd. Twentieth-century revivals would later adopt this method. Finney also developed what he called the "anxious seat," where those inspired to become Christians would sit while others prayed over them. Like the Wesleys,

EXHORTATION AND PREACHING AT THE CAMP MEETING AT EASTHAM.

FIGURE 18-4 This watercolor from 1839 depicts a revival of the Second Great Awakening.

Finney was a strict moralist; he believed that Christian life ought to be completely free from sin. He also advocated the abolition of slavery, and he championed the rights of women. Faith was marked by moral purity and freedom for all. Ultimately, Evangelical Christianity has been strongly influenced by the Second Great Awakening. Even today, it represents a Christianity that is decidedly personal, relatively emotional, strictly moral, and less than robustly interested in scholarship.

THE AMERICAN REVOLUTION AND THE SEPARATION OF CHURCH AND STATE

The First Great Awakening gave American colonists three particular assets that supported the American Revolution. The first was a greater sense of national unity. Initially, the colonies were religiously separate. Virginian Anglicans, for example, thought New England Puritans were heretics and wanted little to do with them. The Puritans likewise believed the Virginians subscribed to a Christianity of apostates, those who had abandoned the true faith. The First

Great Awakening reworked the religious landscape. In its wake, denominations mattered little, and there was a great sense of shared faith among all. Simply put, the First Great Awakening bonded the colonists. The second asset was that the colonists came to deeply believe in the priority of their own conscience and their own personal right to self-authorize their lives. The third asset was that the colonists became increasingly suspicious of uniting religion and government. Collectively, these three shifts formed the backdrop not only for the Revolution, but also for the separation between church and state.

The vast majority of the founding fathers believed that religion was crucial to society. Article III of the Constitutional Convention's Northwest Ordinance of 1787 states: "Religion, morality, and knowledge, being necessary to good government and the happiness of mankind, schools and the means of education shall forever be encouraged." On the other hand, many of the founding fathers disliked organized religion and wanted to distance the government from it. A great exception was John Adams, who had a deep, pious Puritan background and believed that the government ought to commit itself to advancing religion. Others, however, like George

Washington, James Madison, and Thomas Jefferson, were strict separatists. Many were not Christians at all but subscribed to some version of Deism, as described in Chapter Sixteen. While most believed that God could intervene in a country's affairs—a belief that departs from a central Deist claim—they did not think much of the specific claims of Christianity.

The Declaration of Independence only mentions God once as a premise for human dignity, and the Constitution of the United States does not mention God or religion whatsoever. The First Amendment of the Constitution, which was ratified in 1791, reads: "Congress shall make no law respecting an establishment of religion, or prohibiting the free exercise thereof." This was a federal law and did not impede states' rights to regulate or support a given religion. These rights were only changed in the late nineteenth century. Still, the federal separation of church and state marks the American experience. Jefferson called it a "fair experiment," noting, "We have solved by fair experiment, the great and interesting question whether freedom of religion is compatible with order in government, and obedience to the laws. And we have experienced the quiet comfort which results from leaving everyone to profess freely and openly those principles of religion which are inductions of his own reason, and the serious convictions of his own inquiries."[10] America thus became the first country in the known history of the world to legislate the separation of church and state.

For many Americans today, the separation of church and state means that the government cannot acknowledge religion and that religion must be kept out of the public square. In no way, however, did the founding fathers intend this. It would be more accurate to say that they aimed to leave the government free to accommodate religion as long as one religion is not privileged. Their revolutionary formula could be condensed to the following three principles: religion is essential to public morality and the full flourishing of the republic; to thrive, religion works best with less help and not more from the state; and

God gave all humans the right to full religious freedom, according to which the primacy of one's conscience must be honored.

One of the most interesting dynamics in the public debate at the time of the American Revolution is that many religious leaders were themselves pleading for the separation of church and state. For some of the founding fathers, such a separation would free government for more authentic self-expression. For others, as well as many Christian ministers, the separation would free them from the tyranny of a religious state. For them, the American Revolution was a defining moment that offered the possibility of religious purification, whereby the privileges and also excesses of a state church could be eliminated. Shortly after the War of Independence, in 1789 in Philadelphia, the Church of England in the American colonies became the Episcopal Church. Members still saw themselves as part of the Anglican communion, but this communion was now divorced from loyalty to the English Crown. In an interesting historical note, on New Year's Day 1802, men on two horses pulling a wagon came up to the White House to present Thomas Jefferson a gift. On the wagon was a 1,235-pound cake of cheese, the work of 900 cows. The cheese was four feet in diameter and seventeen inches in height. Painted on the red crust was the inscription: REBELLION TO TYRANTS IS OBEDIENCE TO GOD. The cheese was a gift from a Baptist church in western Massachusetts.

CATHOLICS IN AMERICA

There was little Catholic presence in the colonies. The one exception was Maryland, which was founded in 1634 by the Catholic family of the Calverts and was therefore tolerant to Catholics. They also enjoyed religious freedom in Rhode Island and Pennsylvania, although one had to be a Quaker in Pennsylvania to have full civil and voting rights. The first American bishop was John Carroll of Baltimore, appointed in 1789. Most of the initial Catholic colonial efforts took place in Louisiana, where French missionaries created the city of New Orleans, and in Maine, where Cardinal Richelieu in the 1630s had sent Capuchin friars. Capuchins and later Jesuits also sent missions to Quebec. Unlike the Portuguese and Spanish colonial interests, however, there would be no royal patronage system or exploitation of the natives in the French missions. The Spanish Catholic presence was in the south, which was not yet part of the United States. From Florida to Texas to the Southwest to the Californian coast, the Spanish established a chain of missions, with some success.

Much of the rest of the history of Catholicism in the United States follows the waves of immigrants from Catholic countries, such as Italy, Germany, and Ireland from western Europe and Poland, Croatia, and Lithuania from eastern Europe, between the early nineteenth and the early twentieth centuries. Catholic immigrants were typically distrusted by the Protestant majority. While Protestants were learning to get along with each other, they hardly intended to maintain friendly relations with "papists." Many also wondered whether Catholics' loyalty to the pope would trump their loyalty to the state. Even as late as 1960, when Catholic John F. Kennedy was running for president, he had to formally assure the American people that his primary loyalty as president was to country and not to Rome.

Catholics endeavored to prove their patriotism. They served in American wars in far greater numbers than their percentage of the population, but they were widely considered the religious other, as were Jews. Because of their immigrant status and need for church support, many Catholics became more religious upon arriving in the United States than they had been in their home countries. Catholic fraternities, such as the Knights of Columbus, became core centers of support. The Catholic Church was the center not only of faith but also socialization. Distrusting public schooling, which often overtly taught Protestant theology, Catholics developed a parochial school system that is still robust today.

There was something to the Protestant suspicion of Catholics, at least in theory. The Catholic Church continued to teach that the preferred model of society was one that unified church, state, and public morality. While civil and ecclesiastical powers were separate, a religious state was considered a complete social whole. This had, in fact, been the assumption of every country and municipality throughout the history of Christendom, and given the anti-Catholic, anticlerical experience of the French Revolution starting in 1789—in which France became the second country to proclaim a separation of church and state—the Catholic Church was suspicious of such a break. American bishops had argued that the separation was a religious boon for church and society, but Rome rejected this position; it was considered by Pope Leo XII as *Americanism* and rebuffed. It would only be in the twentieth century that Catholic theologians such as **John Courtney Murray** (1904–1967) would argue compellingly for the good of a mixed civil society. Even at this late date, Roman authorities refused to allow Murray to publish his ideas, though eventually his position on religious liberty and primacy of the conscience became the backbone of modern Catholic thought.

 MILLENNIALISM AND NEW DENOMINATIONS

Christians broadly believe that Christ will return at the end of time. What this exactly constitutes and how it will play out, however, are matters of great debate. Throughout Christian history, particularly during times of great upheaval, some Christians have predicted the imminent end of the world and return of Christ. The sacking of Rome in the fourth century was such a time of popular conjecture, as was the late medieval period, the Protestant Reformation, and even the First Great Awakening. Today, few theologians or biblical scholars believe that the Book of Revelation is a future-telling book. Rather, for them, it depicts a securing of the faith in the context of persecution through an apocalyptic genre. But this is a modern idea. For most of the history of

Christianity the Book of Revelation was seen as an authentic account of the final days, with the arising of the anti-Christ, the battle at Armageddon, and the return of Christ. Revelation also says that at the second coming the bodies of the saints will be raised up, and they will reign with Christ for 1,000 years before the final judgment (Rev. 20:1–10). Those who take this text literally are known as millennialists. A *dispensational millennialist* is one who believes that the current period is the final period of history. The idea here is that there are eras of human history, or dispensations. The final dispensation represents the absolute imminent second coming of Christ. We will use here the term **millennialism** to refer to both the 1,000-year reign and the imminent second coming.

Several American Christian movements emerged as decidedly millennialist, with the expectation that Christ was soon coming. William Miller (1782–1849) interpreted a number of prophesies in the Bible to clearly show that the end of the world would be in 1843. When this did not occur he revised his prediction to 1844. After Christ still did not return—a nonevent known as the Great Disappointment—Miller's ideas were continued by **Ellen White** (1827–1915), who founded the Seventh Day Adventist Church. White herself made a number of prophecies and underwent many dramatic religious experiences that came to guide the Seventh Day Adventists, the most dramatic of which was that Christ had indeed returned, but invisibly.

Another Christian millennial group formed around **Charles Taze Russell** (1852–1916), founder of the Zion's Watchtower Society in 1861. This group was also premised on the invisible return of Christ. His successor, Joseph Franklin Rutherford (1869–1941), declared the official date of Christ's public return to be 1914, and he renamed the community the Jehovah's Witnesses.

One of the most fascinating Christian movements that united millennialism with American exceptionalism was that of the Church of Jesus Christ of the Latter-Day Saints (LDS), also known as the **Mormons**, which was founded in

1830 in upstate New York by **Joseph Smith** (1805–1844). The tenth of Smith's Articles of Faith says, "We believe in the literal gathering of Israel and the restoration of the Ten Tribes; that Zion (the New Jerusalem) will be built upon the American continent; that Christ will reign personally on the earth; and, that the earth will be renewed and receive its paradisiacal glory."[11]

Smith proclaimed that the "ten lost tribes of Israel" (from the time of the Assyrian conquest in 721 BCE) had actually emigrated to the Americas. Further, he claimed to have found golden plates revealed to him by the angel Moroni, which he translated into the Book of Mormon. For Mormons, this text, along with the Bible, constitutes the full revelation of God in Christ. Smith was driven from New York and brought his followers west. After trying to establish a community in Kirtland, Ohio, Smith's community settled in Nauvoo, Illinois, where he became both the civil and spiritual leader. In 1844, Smith and the Nauvoo city council angered non-Mormons by destroying a newspaper that had criticized their beliefs and practice of polygamy. Smith was imprisoned in Carthage, Illinois, and eventually killed when a mob stormed the jailhouse. His followers continued westward, led by Brigham Young (1801–1877), who succeeded Smith as leader of the faith. The majority of Mormons eventually settled in Salt Lake City, Utah, which continues to be the center of their faith today. Mormons are famous for their strict morality, including abstinence from alcohol, tobacco, and caffeine. They are also extraordinarily devout and committed to missions. The vast majority of Mormon young men and women serve stints as missionaries, either locally proselytizing or joining one of over 400 missions worldwide, with men typically expected to serve for two years and women for eighteen months. No doubt this helps solidify their faith.

Currently, the Church of the Latter-Day Saints has around 15 million members and is one of the fastest-growing denominations in Christianity. Their very presence returns us to the discussions in Chapter Five about what exactly constitutes Christianity. There, we distinguished between gnostic and proto-orthodox Christianity. At the time of the early church, each camp imagined it represented the authentic faith, and both camps would have had intelligent and highly moral representatives. Mormons believe that Jesus is the savior of the world, a fundamental claim in Christianity. They have also challenged most of the central dogmas created by the early ecumenical councils and added dogmas not shared by any other Christians. Perhaps we might ask two rhetorical questions: (1) Who gets to say what is authentically Christian? (2) What is legitimately up for grabs in marking Christianity?

BLACK CHURCHES

One of the great moral curses on American history is slavery. By 1790, America had 700,000 slaves in the southern states, along with 59,000 free Africans in the United States collectively. Many Americans, particularly in the north, were opposed to the slave trade. The first antislavery society was founded in 1775, and in 1785 Benjamin Franklin became its president.

Both free and enslaved African Americans were evangelized by Protestant churches, but full participation in those churches was not available to them. Given the American experience of starting denominations, many black churches were organized soon after the War of Independence. In 1787, Richard Allen (1760–1831) railed against the lack of full black participation in the Methodist church in Philadelphia.

When it was clear no reforms were in sight, he started the African Methodist Episcopal (AME) Church. In 1796, African Americans in New York also started a spin-off denomination called the African Methodist Episcopal Zion Church, whose membership included many black abolitionists, such as Sojourner Truth and Frederick Douglass.

Many white Evangelical Christians called for the emancipation of slaves as part of their understanding of the Christian faith. As noted earlier, Charles Grandison Finney, the great revivalist, believed in both black abolition and women's rights. Other Evangelical Christians joined the crusade. Catholics, who had very little presence in the American south, imagined themselves not implicated in slavery and tended to be uninvolved in the issue. Still, these Evangelical voices went fundamentally unheeded in the southern states, and the great moral curse Americans brought upon themselves would not be exorcised until the Civil War. Further, as discussed in Chapter Seventeen, many supporters of slavery drew on biblical texts that seemed to support slavery. In these scripture verses, slaves are called to obey their earthly masters (Eph. 6:5; Col. 3:22), to honor them (1 Tim. 6:1–2), and to be submissive to them (Titus 2.9). As will be discussed in Chapter Twenty-One, racism and the ongoing struggle for a truly free and equal society would continue in the civil rights movement of the 1960s and beyond, a movement that was fundamentally framed as religious.

◎ CONCLUSIONS

The United States became the first country in the world to legislate the separation of church and state, a decision broadly supported by both political and religious leaders. What might seem paradoxical is that today the United States is the most religious country in Western culture, which may very well have been the result of that separation. Europeans came to America for

trade, adventure, and religious freedom. There, they carved out a civil program that was less a compromise than a new vision of society, one in which religious tolerance created the conditions for religious flourishing. As the British Catholic author G. K. Chesterton once noted about America, it is "a nation with the soul of a Church."

SUMMARY QUESTIONS

- What is American exceptionalism, and what early colonial ideals contributed to its origination?
- How was the Puritans' desire for freedom theocratic? In contrast, what relation between religion and government was sought in Rhode Island and Pennsylvania?
- What was Pietism challenging, and what did it emphasize instead? How did the Wesleys originally seek to reform Anglicanism, and what was the result?

- How were Evangelical expressions through revivals and awakenings Pietistic? In what key way did the Second Great Awakening differ from the First?
- What three assets of the First Great Awakening contributed to the American Revolution and the legal separation of church and state? For what reasons did clergy support separation?

DISCUSSION QUESTIONS

- Given that many of the founding fathers of the United States were more sympathetic to Deism than they were to Christianity, do you think the assumption that the United States was grounded in the Judeo-Christian tradition is warranted? Why or why not? Considering the events discussed in this chapter, in what ways may the United States be historically unique? What challenges does any claim of exceptionalism face?
- Think about the differing positions expressed in the chapter and your own views

regarding the relationship between religion and government or public life. What do you see as a proper role (if any) of religion in the public sphere? Provide reasoning for your answer.
- Pietism worked to re-center the faith to the individual soul and its relationship to Christ. Does such a refocus provide assets? Describe what you think they are and why. Does such a refocus provide any liabilities? Describe what you think they are and why.

KEY TERMS

American exceptionalism
Awakening
Bible Belt
Bunyan, John
Congregationalism
Edwards, Jonathan
Evangelical
Finney, Charles Grandison

Fox, George
Methodism
Millennialism
Mormonism
Murray, John Courtney
Pietism
Revivalism
Russell, Charles Taze

Separatists
Smith, Joseph
Theocracy
Wesley, Charles
Wesley, John
White, Ellen
Whitefield, George
Williams, Roger

BIBLIOGRAPHY

- Bebbington, David. 1989. *Evangelicalism in Modern Britain*. London: Unwin Hyman.
- Bremer, Francis. 1995. *The Puritan Experiment: New England Society from Bradford to Edwards*,

rev ed. Hanover, NH: University Press of New England.
- Bunyan, John. 1987. *The Pilgrim's Progress*. Ed. Roger Sharrock. London: Penguin.

- Cherry, Conrad, ed. 1998. *God's New Israel: Religious Interpretations of American History*, rev. ed. Chapel Hill: University of North Carolina Press.
- Chidester, David. 2000. *Christianity: A Global History*. New York: HarperOne.
- Collinson, Patrick. 1986. *The Birthpangs of Protestant England: Religious and Cultural Change in the Sixteenth and Seventeenth Centuries*. Basingstoke, UK: Macmillan.
- Curry, Thomas. 1986. *The First Freedoms: Church and State in America to the Passage of the First Amendment*. New York: Oxford University Press.
- Hennesey, James. 1983. *American Catholics: A History of the Roman Catholic Community in the United States*. New York: Oxford University Press.
- Kidd, Thomas. 2007. *The Great Awakening: The Roots of Christianity in Colonial America*. New Haven, CT: Yale University Press.
- Marsden, George. 1991. *Understanding Fundamentalism and Evangelicalism*. Grand Rapids, MI: Eerdmans.
- Marsden, George. 2006. *Fundamentalism and American Culture, 1875–1925*, 2nd ed. New York: Oxford University Press.
- Mead, Sidney. 1963. *The Lively Experiment: The Shaping of Christianity in America*. New York: Harper and Row.
- Miller, Donald. 1997. *Reinventing American Protestantism: Christianity in the New Millennium*. Berkeley: University of California Press.
- Noll, Mark. 2002. *America's God: From Jonathan Edwards to Abraham Lincoln*. New York: Oxford University.
- Noll, Mark. 2011. *American Evangelical Christianity: An Introduction*. Oxford: Blackwell.
- Waldman, Steven. 2008. *Founding Faith: How Our Founding Fathers Forged a Radical New Approach to Religious Liberty*. New York: Random House.
- Whaling, Frank, ed. 1981. *John and Charles Wesley: Selected Prayers, Hymns, Journal Notes, Sermons, Letters and Treatises*. Mahwah, NJ: Paulist Press.

NOTES

1. Cited in Cherry, *God's New Israel*, 40.
2. Cited in Chidester, *Christianity*, 392–393.
3. Ibid., 389.
4. Cited in Waldman, *Founding Faith*, 4.
5. Cited in Chidester, *Christianity*, 395.
6. Cited in Waldman, *Founding Faith*, 24.
7. Bunyan, *Pilgrim's Progress*, 35–36.
8. John and Charles Wesley, *John and Charles Wesley: Selected Prayers, Hymns, Journal Notes, Sermons, Letters and Treatises*, ed. Frank Whaling (Mahwah, NJ: Paulist Press, 1981), 107.
9. John Edwards, "Sinners in the Hands of an Angry God," accessed at http://voicesofdemocracy.umd.edu/edwards-sinners-in-the-hands-speech-text.
10. Cited in Mead, *Lively Experiment*, 59.
11. Joseph Smith, "Mormon Articles of Faith," accessed at http://www.mormon.org/beliefs/articles-of-faith.

Modern Challenges to Christianity

Timeline

1789 CE	Beginning of French Revolution
1795 CE	Separation of church and state in France
1848 CE	Karl Marx publishes the *Communist Manifesto*
1859 CE	Charles Darwin publishes *On the Origin of Species*, describing evolution
1869–1870 CE	Vatican I declares papal infallibility
1870 CE	Papal States are lost to a new Kingdom of Italy
1919 CE	William Riley founds the Christian Fundamentals Association
1962–1965 CE	Vatican II updates the Catholic Church
1990 CE	Russia allows for freedom of religion

WHAT TO EXPECT

Religions and their great leaders have always been controversial. They have been central in the making and remaking of cultures. They have inspired great movements of justice and peace, as well as provided resources for conflict. Questions as to whether a given religious movement is good or bad, right or wrong, have always been raised. The modern age, however, is unique in that it is the first time in history when religion itself has been called into question. This development has already been noted in Chapter Sixteen, on the Enlightenment, and the modern post-Enlightenment era became even more challenging to the very idea of religion. This chapter reviews some of the political and intellectual developments that have fostered these great challenges to religion itself, and how Christianity has responded.

THE FRENCH REVOLUTION
AND THE ITALIAN *RISORGIMENTO*

FRANCE

In the late eighteenth century, France had such political dominance in Europe that French was the common language spoken by elites from England to Russia. By the end of the eighteenth century, however, it was an economically broken country. France had never established a proper banking and credit system, and, given its over-reaching support of the American Revolution, it was heavily in debt. It had also suffered a number of successive years of bad harvests, exacerbating the problem. Nevertheless, the royal house of King Louis XVI continued to live in a style beyond extravagance at this time of severe poverty, creating a great deal of resentment. In 1789, King Louis summoned the Estates General to reform the tax system. France at this time had what was known as "Three Estates": the first was the monarchy and nobles, the second the Catholic Church, and the third the middle class and commoners. For a century, Europeans had been feeding on the ideas of Enlightenment thinkers, from John Locke to Jean-Jacques Rousseau to François-Marie Arouet, who wrote under the name Voltaire. Skepticism about anything that represented the *ancien régime* was thoroughly entrenched in the minds of many, particularly those of the "Third Estate."

The delegates who were summoned by the king not only refused to cooperate with him, but declared social and financial reforms the king was unwilling to accept. That same year, they issued the **Rights of Man**, a charter of human rights resembling the American Bill of Rights, which was simultaneously being introduced across the Atlantic. Later that year, a mob stormed the Bastille, a fortress used by the government to incarcerate political prisoners. The takeover of the Bastille and the freeing of its political prisoners remains one of the great icons of the French Revolution. In 1790, the Assembly passed the Civil Constitution of the Clergy, by which bishops and priests would have

to swear allegiance to the emerging democracy and disavow allegiance to the pope. French Catholicism would be a national church. Only four bishops and a modest minority of priests signed the Civil Constitution. Those who did became known as the *abjurors*, or constitutional clergy, while those who refused to sign were called the *nonjurors*, or refractory clergy. To further worsen the tensions, in 1792 provincial rebellions in the name of the king and church sparked a vicious response by the newly formed government. In retaliation, members of the royal family, as well as many clerics, were arrested, and most were executed. At Nantes, Assembly officials killed political prisoners by mass drowning, beginning with priests. In Paris, a mob stormed a Carmelite church where 150 bishops and priests were being held while awaiting forced deportation. They were all executed. Violence against priests and religious orders became widespread, and most convents, monasteries, and other religious houses were seized.

The irony of the French Revolution is that until the Revolution itself, there was not much widespread hostility toward the Catholic Church. The Revolution created something of its own self-driven antagonism. If it was not implicitly atheistic, it was certainly at least Deistic. In 1793 the Festival of Reason was declared. As part of its elaborate ceremonies at the seized Notre Dame Cathedral in Paris, an actress representing the "goddess of reason" was lowered and enthroned on the cathedral's altar, not far from the site of mass executions of Catholic clerics and other imagined enemies of the state. Refugee priests and monks flooded England and were welcomed as victims, a response that would have been inconceivable earlier. Pope Pius VI (r. 1775–1799) strenuously objected to the French Revolution, and in 1798 the French invaded the Papal States and exiled Pius to France, where he died the next year. One of most troubling social ills that resulted from the Revolution was the languishing of the sick and poor whose institutional support had in the past come almost entirely from the Catholic Church.

FIGURE 19-1 Napoleon Bonaparte staged a coup d'état and declared himself the emperor of the French. His massive military victories throughout Europe were, however, short-lived.

In 1799, **Napoleon Bonaparte**, one of France's most successful generals, staged a coup d'état and declared himself the emperor of the French. In 1801, he and Pope Pius VII (r. 1800–1823) reached an agreement, or Concordat, to restore the Catholic Church in France. This is not to say that all was now well or that there was a great deal of mutual trust between the papacy and the French ruler. In 1804, Pius agreed to go to Paris for Napoleon's coronation as emperor of the French at the Notre Dame Cathedral. Before leaving, he wrote a resignation letter, which was only to be opened if he had been imprisoned by Napoleon. During the ceremony, as the pope was about to bestow the emperor's crown, Napoleon took it out of the pope's hand and put it on his head himself. It was an omen of things to come. In 1809, Napoleon seized the Papal States

and effectively imprisoned Pius VII for the next four years.

Napoleon was a warrior and led France through invasions of much of Europe, from the Iberian Peninsula of Spain and Portugal to Poland and Russia. Through all of these campaigns, he deposed monarchies and replaced them, in part, with institutions and laws based on the kinds of representative governments that France and the United States were creating. His victories were short-lived, however, as France soon overextended itself. In 1812, Napoleon's army had to withdraw from Moscow and was defeated in 1813 at the Battle of Leipzig. Napoleon was forced to abdicate the throne and go into exile on the Italian island of Elba. In 1815, he escaped and returned to power, only to be defeated that same year at the Battle of Waterloo. He was again exiled, this time to the island of Saint Helena.

While the French Revolution and the subsequently brief rule of Emperor Napoleon were responsible for massive violence in Europe, the aftermath of the French wars contributed to the creation of the Europe of the twentieth century. Along with the Wars of Religion, Napoleon's invasions undermined much of the remaining vestiges of medieval and Renaissance Europe. He not only replaced monarchies and established laws that would remain permanent throughout Europe, but also created the conditions for the establishment of further nation-states and an upsurge in **nationalism**. In 1814–1815, European representatives met in the Congress of Vienna to redraw national boundaries, which would remain in place for the next 100 years, and some even to today.

ITALY

A result of the upsurge in nationalism was that many Italians, including even high-ranking nobles in the Papal States in central Italy, demanded a unified Italy. The movement was known as *Risorgimento*, Italian for "resurgence." Pope Gregory XVI (r. 1831–1846) was so alarmed at the ferment that he had Austria assist him in putting down the many uprisings, creating additional animosity. His successor, Pius IX (r. 1846–1878), was welcomed as a reformer. He established a new constitution for the Papal States and released political prisoners. The turning point was in 1848, when leaders of the *Risorgimento* declared a complete Italian state. Pius IX fled Rome, and the leaders of the new republic seized church-owned land. Pius appealed for foreign help; ironically, he received it from the French, whose forces entered Rome and restored the pope. They would remain in the city until 1870. The *Risorgimento* continued to work for a single Italian state, but it would not achieve this aim until the breakout of the Franco-Prussian War (1870–1871). At that time, France withdrew its troops to defend itself against German invasion, and the vacuum allowed Italian armies, led by Victor Emmanuel II, to capture Rome as the capital city of the new Italian state, the Kingdom of Italy.

ATHEISM

Until the Enlightenment, virtually no one was an atheist; God's existence was considered a fact. Controversies about who or what God was, what God demanded, and how societies should be managed given religious beliefs dominated the consciousness of both ancient and modern humanity. One of the greatest challenges to religion in the late modern period was the emerging belief that there simply is no God. Four key thinkers developed the foundations of the modern expression of **atheism**: **Ludwig Feuerbach** (1804–1872), **Karl Marx** (1818–1883), **Friedrich Nietzsche** (1844–1900), and **Sigmund Freud** (1856–1939). Feuerbach ranks first among them, not only in history, but also because Marx and Nietzsche identify him as an important influence to their thought. Feuerbach believed that God is a projection of humanity's most cherished values, particularly its high moral norms. In placing these norms on a non-existent God, humans then see themselves as judged by God insofar as they live these values out. Positively, this projection can help people

be moral; God has expectations and is watching them. Negatively, he believed that the strategy ultimately divorces humanity from its own truth by projecting what is most noble about it onto a fictitious supernatural being. Such a projection also keeps humans in a childlike state of trying to please a supernatural father figure. In essence, it keeps humans immature.

Karl Marx famously declared that "religion is the opiate of the people." Marx is famous for his critique of the Industrial Revolution and its demeaning social conditions. Religion, he thought, gives people hope and comfort in their degraded lives, but that comfort both is an illusion—God does not exist—and does nothing to improve the cultural conditions that lead to abject poverty. In fact, he believed that religion is complicit in supporting a society that creates the culture of poverty. It teaches that if the people follow the rules that have been collectively sanctioned by church, state, and capitalists, they will please God and be assured paradise later. Along with Friedrich Engels, Marx created a socialist philosophy that was entirely committed to **materialism**, that is, the belief that the only thing that exists is matter. There is no God and nothing supernatural; everything can be explained by causes and effects of the physical world. As early as 1844, Marx was writing of the need to abolish religion. He and Engels took over a socialist organization called the League of the Just in 1847 and changed its name to the League of Communists. Not only was Marx's work a stinging challenge to both religion and economics, but it embraced the Enlightenment's confidence in humanity. If people were given real freedom, Marx assumed, they would naturally work for the common good.

No greater voice for an all-out atheism exists than that of Friedrich Nietzsche, whose clarion announcement that "God is dead" swept across Europe with serious impact, though mostly after his death. Voltaire and others had dismissed religions and their claims to revelation, but they did not imagine that this would undermine culture at all. Rather, one would simply be free from antirational beliefs. Nietzsche, much like

FIGURE 19-2 Friedrich Nietzsche (1844–1900) was one of the great articulators of atheism. To him, God was dead, and now culture had to reinvent itself based on the will to power.

Marx, recognized that the real implication of atheism was that it would undermine the very moral and societal constructs of society. We are "beyond good and evil," he maintained, and have to create a new world through courageous self-authorization: "Morality will gradually perish now: that great spectacle in a hundred acts that is reserved for Europe's next two centuries, the most terrible, most questionable, and perhaps the most hopeful of all spectacles."[1] Nietzsche imagined himself the prophet of a new age, the age of the *übermensch* (great man) whose "will to power" would construct a new kind of human race. He particularly challenged Christianity, which seemed to glory in the weakness of the cross.

Nietzsche did not have much toleration for Voltaire or other bourgeois atheists. They had yet to realize what was at stake. In his *Joyful Wisdom*, he tells of a "madman" in the marketplace who declares that God is dead:

> Have you ever heard of the madman who . . . ran into the market-place calling out unceasingly: "I seek God! I seek God!"—As there were many people standing about who did not believe in God, he caused a great deal of amusement. Why! Is he lost? said one. Has he strayed away like a child? . . . —the people cried out laughingly, all in a hubbub. The insane man jumped into their midst and transfixed them with his glances. "Where is God gone?" he called out. "I mean to tell you! *We have killed him,*—you and I! . . . How were we able to drink up the sea? Who gave us the sponge to wipe away the whole horizon? What did we do when we loosened this earth from its sun? . . . Do we not stray, as through infinite nothingness? . . . Has it not become colder? Does not night come on continually, darker and darker? . . . Is not the magnitude of this deed too great for us? Shall we not ourselves have to become Gods, merely to seem worthy of it?[2]

In this passage, the madman announces just what was at stake in unmooring society from its transcendental assumptions.

Sigmund Freud is another famous voice in the development of atheism. In virtually creating the separate discipline of psychology and the practice of psychoanalysis, his understanding of religion has carried a great deal of influence. Like Feuerbach, he believed that religion facilitates psychological immaturity. In his *Totem and Taboo* and *The Future of an Illusion*, he depicts religion as little more than a security blanket, which a fully actualized person must cast off if he or she is ever to hope for psychological freedom. Religious beliefs, to Freud, are "wish-fulfillments" of deeper needs in the subconscious. While they are beneficial in coercing the psyche not to act out in antisocial ways, they ultimately prevent full psychological integration.

During their day, the atheists discussed here were highly influential and believed to be prophets of a new kind of human society. In hindsight, their critiques of religion and the positive possibilities of atheism have not proven very compelling. Every communist experiment, such as the Soviet Union, China, Vietnam, and Cambodia, has evidenced massive social breakdown, poverty, corruption, and dictatorial leadership. Marx's optimism seems misplaced. Nietzsche, in his *Twilight of the Idols*, rails against the French Revolution's ideas of equality and justice, since these ideals presume that people have intrinsic value, rather than value self-created by power. He was a proponent of child labor and approved of eleven-hour workdays for children and twelve-hour workdays for adults. He opposed the education of workers and considered their treatment in terms of whether their "descendants also work for our descendants."

Atheism, both in its beginnings and as it appears today, often proclaims religion to be socially and politically pernicious, that is, it positively harms societies and is the fundamental cause of violence in the world. It turns out that religion usually has the opposite effect. As noted in Chapter One, social scientists have discovered that, generally speaking, the more religious one is, the more law abiding, socially generous, and religiously tolerant. In 2004, the BBC commissioned the University of Bradford's Department of Peace Studies to conduct a "war audit" for its program *What the World Thinks of God*. The study's conclusion was that no major war in the twentieth century had religion as a core cause. When one considers the many tens of millions of lives lost to "secular wars" in the twentieth century, as well as the over 60 million murders perpetrated by atheistic totalitarian states against their own people, including Stalinist Russia at 25 million and Maoist China at 35 million, it is difficult to respect atheism's critique.

◎ EVOLUTION AND THE SCIENTIFIC WORLDVIEW

As noted in Chapter Two, in 1650 the Anglican archbishop James Ussher analyzed the genealogies of the Old Testament and concluded that creation happened in 4004 BCE. Such a claim

would not stand up to the scientific scrutiny of the modern period. At the height of the French Revolution, Georges Cuvier was mapping out the strata of the Paris river basin and saw a long geological history, including evidence of extinct creatures. These geological findings pointed to an Earth far older than 6,000 years. This was not necessarily life-threatening to those Christians who relied on the Bible for revelation. Many Enlightenment era clergy assumed that the creation stories spoke figuratively about God's plan of creation. For them, the geological discoveries pointed to God's ongoing creative providence: God had provided replacement species when others died out.

This kind of speculation about species and their divine origins became much more difficult to sustain, however, with the work of **Charles Darwin** (1809–1882). In 1837, Darwin observed the natural phenomena of the Pacific islands of the Galapagos and concluded that what he had discovered were neither the relics of Eden nor spontaneously new species created by God to replace others. Rather, the data only made sense if they were correlated to his theory that species developed by adapting better to life's conditions. Instead of a benevolently provident God acting, he saw a cruel battle for survival via natural selection. In 1859, he published *On the Origin of Species* and later revised his work in *The Descent of Man* in 1871. What was particularly disturbing to some of his readers was that humanity was no longer framed as a special creation by God, but was merely depicted as part of a chain of evolution.

Darwin was not the first to espouse the theory of evolution, but he soon became its main spokesperson. From the 1860s on, the theory of evolution gained broad acceptance among the educated classes of the West. It even corresponded to the Enlightenment's confidence in human progress. Many Protestant intellectuals publicly embraced evolution as well. It became part of a new natural theology, one that interpreted evolution as part of God's providential guidance in the history of the world. In the late nineteenth century, Frederick Temple, the

FIGURE 19-3 Charles Darwin (1809–1882) was a scientist who decisively advanced the theory of evolution based on natural selection.

archbishop of Canterbury, presented a series of lectures at Oxford University on the relationship between science and religion. In these lectures, he simply assumed that evolution was a sound theory, as did his listeners. Since then, geological and zoological findings have continued to support evolution.

A scientific theory is not simply a hypothesis. In science, the word "theory" references a massive amount of data interpreted in a way that satisfactorily explains those data. Further, if a theory is to be sound, it has to be predictive, that is, ongoing discoveries have to continue to confirm it. Of course, any broad theory has to account for apparent counterevidence and compete with other theories that also seek to rationally explain the data. Even a theory that appears sound at one time may be displaced by another that later does a better job of interpreting the

data. To this day, evolution has far outdistanced any other interpretation of the facts.

From the late nineteenth century through the 1920s, debate raged among Protestant leaders. Some Protestant denominations, such as the Baptist and Presbyterian churches, split over whether to accept or reject evolution. The Catholic Church was slow to wholly embrace the theory. For example, Jesuit priest Pierre Teilhard de Chardin, one of the discoverers of "Peking Man" (a primitive version of humanity), was forbidden to publish books or articles that extrapolated theological ideas from evolutionary findings. Finally, Pope Pius XII (r. 1939–1958), in his encyclical *Humani Generis* (1950), acknowledged that evolution could well be true and that it did not conflict with Christian faith. Since him, every modern pope appears to have signed off on it. Consider Pope John Paul II's speech to the Pontifical Academy of Sciences:

> Today, more than a half-century after the appearance of that encyclical [*Humani Generis*], some new findings lead toward the recognition of evolution as more than a hypothesis. In fact, it is remarkable that this theory has had progressively greater influence on the spirit of researchers, following a series of discoveries in different scholarly disciplines. The convergence in the results of these independent studies—which was neither planned nor sought—constitutes in itself a significant argument in favor of the theory.[3]

SCIENCE AND SCIENTISM

In the nineteenth century, T. H. Huxley (1825–1895) coined the term **scientific naturalism** to insist that science ought never to appeal to anything other than natural phenomena to explain scientific causation or correlation. Everything in science should remain within the confines of the scientific method, itself devoted to physical properties, repeatable experimentation, and so on. Commitment to this method over the last several centuries has allowed science to develop extraordinarily in innumerable fields. In this view, everything has to be based on physical evidence, and rigorous attention to the evidence clearly produces the best results. In contrast, religion, which is based on revelation, seems to have lost its explanatory power. Atheistic philosopher Bertrand Russell once quipped, "The clergy have fought a losing battle against science."[4]

One of the most searing essays against a theological worldview, "The Ethics of Belief" by W. K. Clifford, appeared in 1877. Clifford framed his argument thus: Believing something without sufficient evidence is intellectually offensive as well as immoral. To hold a view without adequate evidence compromises one's duty to seek the truth and leads others astray. So it is not simply bad form, it's a moral and cultural evil. Given that, religions of revelation would obviously seem to be a problem. They rely on claims that one cannot easily investigate, and certainly not with the scientific method. Christians claim certain beliefs based on revelation, but other religions do as well. Following Clifford's argument, one could ask: Which set of beliefs is true, and how would you know?

Theists and other philosophers have responded to these challenges. One of the problems they point out is that some scientists and philosophers have fallen into the trap of **scientism**, a position that asserts that the *only* way to secure knowledge of any kind is through the scientific method. This position has not impressed philosophers, particularly philosophers of science. They point out that while the scientific method is the best way to do science—that is, to determine correlations and causation among physical things—it is not equipped to address issues that are not physical. To demand from the start that only physical things exist and therefore only the scientific method can secure knowledge is to argue in a circle. That the scientific method does not provide insight into spiritual things does not necessarily mean there are no spiritual things. Rather, this method is simply the wrong tool for the task. Scientism, it turns out, is not a scientific claim, but a philosophical one. And, ironically, it is not based on the scientific method, nor does the claim itself provide sufficient evidence that it is correct.

One famous responder to Clifford was William James, the late nineteenth- and early twentieth-century giant in philosophy and psychology. James's article "The Will to Believe" (1896) takes on some of Clifford's assumptions. In it, James argues that humans rightly believe many things they have not scrutinized. The vast majority of educated persons, for example, believe that the Periodic Table of Elements is accurate, though few know the evidence for it, and far fewer have scrutinized that evidence. James also argues that scientific evidence is not germane to some areas of inquiry, such as love, justice, truth, or morality. Can we not, he also argues, know something to be morally true without being able to adequately articulate reasons for it? Further, sometimes one begins with an intuition, and this drives one's beliefs long before the evidence comes in. This is often even how science works: a scientist has intuitive confidence that something is the case and only later confirms it by experimentation. Finally, James argues that in some cases, having faith is a necessary precondition to confirming it with evidence. New managers of an office have to start with some faith in their workers as a precondition for them to later evidence that they are competent. Human relationships, from friendships to marriage, are premised on some sense of faith in the other person and a lot of intuition. The evidence comes later and only progressively.

RELATIONSHIP BETWEEN SCIENCE AND RELIGION

In *Religion and Science*, physicist Ian Barbour proposes four types of possible relationships between science and religion. Barbour's first type is the "conflict model." Here science regards religion as an outmoded or prerational way of thinking, and attacking religion is an exercise in truth-telling, one that challenges religious believers to recognize their superstitions and become intellectually accountable. On the other side, religious believers in this model tend to see science as threatening to religious truth and as trying to replace that truth with a secular worldview.

Barbour's second type is the "independence model." Here religion and science are utterly distinct because they are invested in different kinds of issues. Science is about the *how* and the *what* of things, while religion is about the *why* and the *what does it mean* of things. Scientist Stephen Gould, who advocates this position, writes that "the net, or magisterium, of science covers the empirical realm: what the universe is made of (fact) and why it works this way (theory). The magisterium of religion extends over questions of ultimate meaning or moral value. These two magisteria do not overlap."[5]

Barbour's third type is the "dialogue model." Here science and religion are also believed to be distinct from each other and invested in different concerns, but they can influence each other. Physicist John Polkinghorne endorses this position. He thinks science is constructed to raise questions that its own methodology cannot answer, but which can be addressed by philosophy and theology. In this way religion works with scientific insights and makes judgments, not about the science itself, but about the implications of that science with regard to transcendental issues that go beyond science's purview, such as human dignity or what human flourishing entails.

Barbour's fourth type is the "integration model." Here both science and religion pool their resources to create a grand narrative about the nature of the universe, a master synthesis. Teilhard de Chardin, mentioned previously, seems to have advocated this position, at least in terms of evolutionary theory. A contemporary advocate of the integration model is Ken Wilber, whose books attempt to uncover an integral theory of everything, including evolution, health, spirituality, human development, and even physics.

SCIENCE AND THE ANTHROPIC PRINCIPLE

Some scientists and philosophers find that physics suggests a God who has intelligently provided the conditions for life against otherwise impossible odds. This is called the *anthropic principle*. In this view, the small number of total possible mass–energy interactions in the universe for all time reveals the extreme improbability of high degrees of complexity coming out of the universe by pure chance. According to leading mathematician and physicist Roger Penrose, the odds of the universe surviving as a universe without collapsing or failing to allow matter to form are 1 in 10 to the 10th to the 123rd. Philosopher of science Bruce Gordon concludes: "When the logical and metaphysical necessity of an efficient cause, the demonstrable absence of a material one, and the proof that there was an absolute beginning to any universe or multiverses are all conjoined with the fact that our universe exists and its conditions are fine-tuned immeasurably beyond the capacity of any mindless process, the scientific evidence points inexorably toward transcendent intelligent agency as the most plausible, if not the only reasonable explanation."[6]

BIBLICAL CRITICISM

Not all the challenges to traditional Christian faith in the nineteenth and twentieth centuries have come from outsiders. One of the most decisive challenges—**biblical criticism**—has come from within. As noted in Chapter Thirteen, Renaissance thinkers developed critical literary skills to gain insight into the meaning of ancient texts and to assess reliable manuscripts. In the modern period these methods were greatly enhanced, initially by German scholars. When applied to the Bible, and alongside developments in archeology in the Holy Land, this approach gave Christian scholars pause. They began to doubt the factual reliability of the Old Testament. Ancient Israel, they found, did not have the importance the Bible seems to presume, and some of the ideas in the Old Testament seemed to have come from outside sources. As noted in Chapter Two, for example, many of the elements of the second creation story in Genesis also appear in texts that precede the Old Testament, such as the creation-flood stories from Mesopotamia, Sumeria, and Egypt.

John William Colenso (1814–1883), a bishop of the Church of England, was one of an increasing number of scholars and churchmen to concede the problems in the Old Testament. For example, the Pentateuch, or first five books of the Old Testament, was traditionally assumed to have been written by Moses. But as new findings were uncovered, this assumption was challenged. These books contain various writing styles, different names for God, different theologies, and so on. Colenso would eventually declare, "Though imparting to us, as I fully believe it does, revelations of Divine Will and Character, it cannot be regarded as historically true."[7] Scholars also became more willing to concede contradictions in the biblical narrative (see box).

PROBLEMS LINING UP TEXTS

Samples of contradictions in the biblical text: creation stories won't align with the timing of the creation of animals compared to humans if they are imagined as literal; in Second Samuel 24 God incites David to take a census, while First Chronicles 21 says Satan incited David; the infancy narratives in Matthew and Luke cannot be reconciled, as Matthew has Jesus flee to Egypt while Luke has him return to Nazareth; Mark's quote "from Isaiah" (1:2–3) is initially from Malachi 3:1; Mark 2:26 misidentifies the priest Ahimelech as Abiathar from First Samuel 21:1-6; Matthew places Jesus's birth at the time of Herod, who died in 4 BCE, while Luke places it when Quirinius was governor of Syria, which only began in 6 CE; Jesus cleanses the Temple at the end of his ministry in the synoptic Gospels, but at the beginning of his ministry in John's Gospel; the synoptic Gospels identify the Last Supper as a Seder/Passover meal, while John says that Good Friday (after Jesus died) was the time for the Seder; Jesus's words at his trial do not align; the crucifixion narratives cannot be reconciled, as Mark says that both thieves mocked Jesus on the cross (15:32), while Luke says that only one thief mocked him, while the other refused and repented (23:39–43); the narratives of the death of Judas in Matthew 27:18 and Acts 1:18 cannot be aligned; the resurrection narratives cannot be reconciled; Luke says Jesus ascended on Easter Day (24:50), while Acts says that Jesus ascended forty days after his resurrection (1:3–11); Psalm 119 says that the Law is eternal (119:152), but Paul says that God intended the Law to be temporary (Gal. 3:19–29); the post-death union with God is inconsistently depicted as immediate (Luke 23:43; Phil. 1:23) and as all resting in peace in the grave until the day of judgment (1 Thess. 4:13–17); in one place Paul declares that God created some people with the divine intent of damnation (Rom. 9:13–23), but in another place Paul maintains that God desires all to be saved (1 Tim. 2:4).

Not only was the historical veracity of the Old Testament shaken, but that of the New Testament was as well. David F. Strauss (1808–1874), a young Lutheran pastor and lecturer at the University of Tubingen, Germany, challenged the historicity of the Gospel narratives. In his book *Leban Jesus* (Life of Jesus Critically Examined), he sees Jesus as a Jewish teacher whose followers created a hero's myth around him. These narrative events written in the New Testament, including all Jesus's miracles, are, for Strauss, theological symbols rather than facts. Other scholars followed suit and thought that they could get behind the symbolism of the New Testament accounts to discover the historical Jesus, one stripped of any supernaturalism.

This movement represented the first stage of the quest for the Jesus of history. It came to a close with Albert Schweitzer's classic *The Quest of the Historical Jesus*. In this work Schweitzer reviews the previous quests and argues that the Jesus "discovered" by these scholars actually reveals the biases and agendas of those given scholars. The Jesus they thought they found by a scientific study of the Bible, he claims, is little more than a mirror of their own theology. This did not keep Schweitzer from attempting his own quest. He decided that Jesus was not a savior per se, but an apocalyptic prophet who, it turns out, was wrong about the end of the world.

Church historians, such as Ernst Troeltsch (1865–1923) and Adolf von Harnack (1851–1930), also became important voices in the movement. They saw in the narrative a layer depicting the development of the early church, even departing from the original meaning of Jesus's message. For Harnack, the teachings *of* Jesus developed into a religion *about* Jesus.

The second quest for the historical Jesus, from the 1940s to the early 1970s, worked through some of the problems of the first quest, although it rejected the a priori assumption that Jesus would not have acted miraculously. The second quest focused on uncovering the authentic oral traditions that had been incorporated into the New Testament and distinguishing them from the layer representing the early church in order to find the pristine Jesus. One of the great distinctions scholars involved in this quest often made was that between the "Jesus of history" and the "Christ of faith." Eventually it came to a point at which some scholars would simply throw up their hands and say: "We know nothing of the Jesus of history. The Bible is only about the Christ of faith."

In the end, this conclusion seemed to satisfy few, but it gave rise to a third quest, one that is still ongoing today. In the intervening years between the first quest and this ongoing third quest, scholars have advanced their methods and expanded their knowledge base considerably. They have also come to look for other things that would give them the kind of confidence that historians broadly enjoy. Recall Chapter Three's discussion on historicity and the Bible and the worthy results that have come from this third quest, including John Maier's multivolume series *A Marginal Jew*.

Perhaps the most daring expression of the quest for the historical Jesus is the *Jesus Seminar*, which began in 1985 and functionally ended in 2006. In this seminar scholars gathered to debate about whether a certain saying of Jesus was historical or had been added by the Gospel writers. They ultimately voted with beads: the red bead represented a saying that came from Jesus directly; a pink one represented something like what Jesus said; a gray bead represented

something Jesus did not say, but that corresponded to ideas he shared; and a black bead represented something wholly manufactured by the Gospel writer. The beads were also weighted in the voting (red = 3; pink = 2; gray = 1; black = 0). Fewer than 20 percent of Jesus's sayings received either a red or a pink bead. The rest were believed to be barely or not at all associated with the historical Jesus. Critics of the Jesus Seminar charge that it is simply a more sophisticated version of the first quest, in which Jesus was interpreted along the theological lines the scholar held in the first place.

Today, many scholars think the historical quest for Jesus is something of a minor project. Virtually all scholars agree that the interests of the early church are intertwined with the Gospel narratives about Jesus. As noted in Chapter Two, authors prior to the modern period believed they had license in their descriptions. Thus, to apply to ancient texts the modern demand that every datum is only true if it was fact-checked or lacked any possibility of symbolism is to place a burden on ancient authors they would not have recognized and probably would have considered invalid. On the other hand, it is widely believed that the Gospel writers were very invested in telling the true story about Jesus as they understood it. To be sure, their accounts are interpretations, but so is every narrative, even in the modern period. Today, most Christian scholars would say that, without neglecting intellectual nuances or critical analysis, the Jesus of history *is* by and large the Christ of faith.

 ## CHURCH RESPONSES TO THE MODERN CHALLENGES OF FAITH

LIBERAL PROTESTANTISM

One way to deal with some of the modern challenges of faith is to embrace many of them. While many Protestant denominations, such as the largest Lutheran, Methodist, Presbyterian, and Anglican bodies, are sometimes understood as "mainstream" Protestants, they also house what has been labeled **liberal Protestantism** or progressive Protestantism. These individuals have embraced modernity and its insights. Scientific analysis of the Bible has become an integral part of such ministers' seminary training, and it is presumed that such an analysis would be utilized or even articulated in their sermons. Following Barbour's "dialogue model," they see insights from the physical and social sciences as influencing the kinds of questions they pose to their faith and the Bible, and as one of the lenses through which to interpret their tradition. Taking feminist insights seriously has led them to reinterpret New Testament restrictions Paul seems to provide about female ministers. And taking social science insights about same-sex attraction seriously has led some to conclude that it is God's will to support same-sex unions.

NEO-ORTHODOXY

A second response to modernity is the **Neo-Orthodoxy** movement. Its most important articulator was Reformed theologian **Karl Barth** (1886–1968), who almost single-handedly revived Calvinist theology for the twentieth century. In his work he takes full sight of all the challenges of modernity and enters into dialogue with them without surrendering revelation to them. For Barth, liberal Protestantism fails to understand the very nature of revelation and its relationship to God. He argues that this project has resulted in a dilution of the faith, not the creation of a robust, relevant modern faith. Without rejecting the insights of critical biblical analysis or developments in ways of knowing (epistemology), Barth refuses to accommodate or "sacrifice" the Christian message to modernity. Like Luther and Calvin, he sees Christian revelation as drawing its own logic from a God who transcends culture. The full Christian integration of modern philosophy, he argues, tends to reduce God to human categories of knowing and thinking. Barth's project was aimed at maintaining absolute submission to the revelatory word while being fully in dialogue with the modern world. He is most famous for his massive work

Dogmatic Theology, which in its English paperback series contains thirty-one volumes and almost 9,000 pages. Those who have embraced Barth's "dialectical theology" continue to advance a modern faith that aims to be in dialogue with the modern world without being reduced to it. It was from Barth on that the terms "conservative" and "liberal" started shaping theological camps.

FUNDAMENTALISM

If the liberal (and mainstream) Protestants and the Neo-Orthodox Protestants represent Barbour's dialogue model, other Christians chose to follow his conflict model. These are often dubbed "fundamentalists." Fundamentalists and modernists broke over a wide range of challenges in the modern world, from science to modern biblical analysis. For the former, such developments challenged the supernatural basis of the faith. From 1883 to 1897, a series of conferences were held yearly, with the most prominent being those held at Niagara-on-the-Lake in Ontario, Canada. These conferences gave rise to a resistance movement against evolution and the critical analysis of the Bible. The term **fundamentalism** comes from the movement itself. Between 1910 and 1915, a number of pamphlets were issued in the United States by a collection of British and American conservatives entitled *The Fundamentals*. These fundamentals represented nonnegotiable dogmas. The core fundamentals were the inerrancy of the Bible, the deity and virgin birth of Christ, the cross as a substitutionary atonement for sins, Christ's bodily resurrection, and Christ's miracles as reported in the Bible. In 1919, **William Riley** (1861–1947) founded the Christian Fundamentals Association.

In Chapter Eighteen, we discussed *millennialism* in terms of several groups, such as the Seventh Day Adventists, who believed that Christ either would return imminently or, as they eventually asserted, has already returned secretly. The fundamentalist movement is also decidedly millennialistic. To them, these are the end times, and the Rapture is virtually upon us. For many in the fundamentalist movement, mainstream and liberal Protestants as well as Catholics are apostate Christians who have abandoned the true faith, along with the Bible. Because of this, they also tend to be hostile to the ecumenical movement or even dialogue with these churches.

ROMAN CATHOLICISM

REACTIONS AGAINST MODERNISM

No church has undergone greater changes in the last 150 years than Roman Catholicism. The French Revolution, the Italian Risorgimento, French philosophy, and the modern scientific study of the Bible and theology shook Roman Catholicism to its roots. The papacy reacted. In 1864, Pope Pius IX (r. 1846–1878) issued the encyclical *Quanta Cura* (Condemning Current Errors) that reacted against the modern celebration of the liberty of conscience, freedom of speech and religion, secular democracy, and secular socialism. He also attached to it a *Syllabus of Errors* to be repudiated by every Catholic. It was the first in a series of papal encyclicals condemning "modernism."

As the papacy was being shaken in Italy, the Catholic Church was being battered throughout Europe. Anything that represented the *ancien régime*, from monarchies to the Catholic Church, was resented by some of the populace and much of the European intelligentsia as holding culture back. In response, many Catholics looked to the pope as a sure sign of unity and stability. This position is known as **ultramontanism**, from a term meaning "over the mountains," and refers to Catholicism looking over the Alps to Rome for some sense of security. In 1869, Pope Pius IX convened the First Vatican Council, the first church council since Trent in the sixteenth century. It was supposed to be a robust response to the modern crisis, but it dispersed in 1870, when the French troops who had been protecting Rome from Italian revolutionaries withdrew to fight the Franco-Prussian War. Rome was invaded shortly after. One of the documents the bishops were working on was a Constitution

on the Church. It began with an overwhelming defense of the power and authority of the pope: chapter one declared the pope's primacy of jurisdiction over the whole church, chapter two asserted the permanence of that primacy, chapter three addressed the power of the papacy, and chapter four proclaimed the power of the pope to speak infallibly regarding faith and morals when speaking *ex cathedra* (from the Chair of Peter). The bishops attending, when voting on the first four chapters, had been assured that the subsequent chapters of the constitution would balance the papacy's authority with their own, but these chapters were never written. Rome was about to be attacked, and the bishops left hastily. Only two bishops voted against the document, but fifty-seven withdrew before the vote so as not to vote against it. The final outcome was the height of ultramontanism.

The Catholic reaction against modernism continued through the rules of subsequent popes. Influential Catholic theologians, such as Alfred Loisy and George Tyrrell, began to advance the kind of biblical and historical scholarship that had become part of the Protestant world. In 1907, the Vatican's Holy Office (formerly called the Inquisition) published *Lamentabili Sane* (Condemning the Errors of the Modernists), which declared that modernism had become an internal threat. That same year Pope Pius X (r. 1903–1914) published the encyclical *Pascendi Dominici Gregis* (Feeding the Lord's Flock) condemning modernism. By 1910, all clergy and seminary professors had to take an oath against modernism, an oath that the church continued to demand until 1967.

While the theological pressure against modernism ebbed at the death of Pius X and with the election of Benedict XV (r. 1914–1922), Roman Catholic theology fell under a kind of intellectual shadow. In 1879, Pope Leo XIII (r. 1878–1903) had published the encyclical *Aeternis Patris* (Eternal Father), which advocated a return to the theology of Thomas Aquinas. This reinvigorated Thomistic studies, but it was a rather meager theological diet.

The middle of the twentieth century saw two openings for Catholic theology. The first came from Pope Pius XII's 1943 encyclical *Divino Aflante Spiritu* (Inspired by the Holy Spirit), which opened up Catholic biblical scholarship to modern methods of interpretation. The second was the *ressourcement* (back to the origin) movement, which returned to the inspiration, theological style, and insights of the church fathers.

VATICAN II

From the late nineteenth century to the middle of the twentieth century, Roman Catholicism had its own version of Catholic fundamentalism, which reacted against liberal secular democracies, challenged the full freedom of religion and the primacy of the conscience—error has no rights—and rejected modern biblical and theological developments. The Catholic Church became a fortress against the rising tide of modernist thinking. But, unlike the Protestant fundamentalist movement, Roman Catholicism had a rich history of intellectuals, philosophers, and theologians. Its reactive stance could not be sustained. Well before Pius XII's 1943 *Divino Aflante Spiritu*, Catholic biblical scholars were reading Protestant works and discussing them among themselves. By the time Pope Pius's 1950 encyclical *Humani Generis* argued that evolution did not

undermine Christian faith, many Catholic intellectuals had already come to the same conclusion. While many theologians aligned themselves to a restrictive version of Thomistic thought, some greats, such as Karl Rahner and Bernard Lonergan, tried to take Aquinas's principles and align them with modern philosophy. And finally, much to the chagrin of Roman theologians and a number of high-ranking officials in Rome, some scholars, such as Henri de Lubac, Jean Daniélou, and Hans Urs von Balthasar, virtually abandoned a Thomistic framework for a modern appropriation of the patristic spirit.

The walls of the Catholic fortress finally fell when Pope **John XXIII** (r. 1958–1963) called the **Second Vatican Council**. It would be a council, he declared, that would "open up the windows to let in fresh air." The kind of fresh air Pope John had in mind was a dialogue with the modern world and a reconsideration of the Catholic tradition that would be relevant to the times. Pope John's key word for the Council was *aggiornamento*, an Italian word meaning "bringing up to date."

The council met over four sessions between 1962 and 1965. It included 2,000 bishops from across the world and many Protestant and Orthodox observers. Its agenda was massive, something along the lines of that of the Council of Trent. Unlike Trent or many other councils,

FIGURE 19-4 The Second Vatican Council (1962–1964) updated Roman Catholicism and opened it to dialogue with the world.

however, this council was not convened by a crisis or in order to defend Catholicism from schism or theological controversy. Thus, its very style was completely different. Many scholars believe the *spirit* of Vatican II was just as important as the specific claims its documents ultimately put forth. Recall, for example, the first four chapters in Vatican I's document on the church, which were solely devoted to the primacy of the papacy. Scripture was cited only three times, and always as a proof text for claims for the papacy. In contrast, the first three chapters of Vatican II's *Dogmatic Constitution on the Church* are meditations on the saving work of the Father, the Son, and the Holy Spirit. They characterize the church as a mystery, a sacrament of salvation in exile with the rest of humanity. Scripture is cited almost 100 times, rarely as a proof text, but as a way of entering the biblical imagination.

Some of the claims of Vatican II were complete reversals of previous teachings. The *Syllabus of Errors* (1864) had condemned the thesis that "every man is free to embrace and profess that religion, which guided by the light of reason, he shall consider true" (no. 15). Vatican II celebrated the right to religious freedom and personal conviction. It declared that one's conscience, properly searching for the true and the good, is the highest seat of moral authority. The Fourth Lateran Council (1215) asserted that all those outside the church could not be saved, and Pope Boniface VIII in 1302 declared that being subject to the pope was a necessary condition to being saved. Vatican II taught that God's will is for everyone to be saved, and they will be so if they cooperate with God's grace in their hearts, regardless of their specific religious affiliation. In 1832, Pope Gregory XVI rejected the notion that the church should be considered subject to defect, and Pius IX in his *Syllabus of Errors* rejected as heresy the belief that the pope should "come to terms with progress, liberalism, and modern civilization" (no. 80). Vatican II asserted that the church profits from the progress of the sciences and the riches hidden in cultures, and

that the church is always in need of purification, penance, and renewal.

Vatican II reformed the liturgy and allowed for the sacraments to be celebrated in the languages of the people. It empowered laity and bishops alike as mutually responsible for discerning revelation and pursuing holiness in the church as well as holiness in society. Protestants were no longer regarded as "heretics and schismatics," but as "separated brethren" who are truly Christian. In short, Vatican II was a complete reversal from the suspicion of modernism to a full engagement with the modern world. It was a thorough reconsideration of the Catholic Church. To be sure, most of what Vatican II taught reaffirmed long-taught doctrines, even as it reframed them. There was much continuity in Vatican II from what the Catholic Church had believed for centuries. Still, the council redirected the church outward to the world and inward to a vision of mutual responsibility.

EASTERN ORTHODOXY: RUSSIA AND THE OTTOMAN DECAY

The fall of the Ottoman Empire in 1922 led to a kind of renewal and redistribution of authority in the Orthodox Church. The patriarch of Constantinople was intimately tied to the Ottoman sultan. Ironically, under the Ottoman sultanate, broad administrative power within the church was given over to the Constantinople patriarch, who thereby attained more authority than he had enjoyed under the Orthodox Byzantine Empire. All Orthodox, whether Greeks, Bulgars, Serbs, or Arabs, were classified by the Ottomans as *millet-i-rum* (religion of the Roman Empire) and were taken to be under the authority of the patriarch of Constantinople. Orthodoxy thus experienced the Islamic Ottoman Empire as its protectorate.

When the Ottoman Empire finally collapsed, the future of Orthodoxy fell on the shoulders of the Russian Church, which was facing its own challenges with the czar's autocracy. In 1905, the government responded to one peaceful demonstration of unarmed workers, led by Georgii Gapon, a popular and charismatic priest in St. Petersburg, by calling in soldiers to shoot the whole mass. The sheer brutality of the czarist government left the church undecided as to how to proceed in the face of repression. The fall of the czarist government and the rise of communist Russia brought the Russian Church into even greater straits as religion itself was repressed as antithetical to communist ideology.

Key to Orthodox thinking was the concept of *sobornost*, the proposition that freedom is inseparable from unity and communion. Orthodox theologians believed that Catholicism represented something of a unity without freedom and Protestantism represented freedom without unity. Russian Orthodoxy was a pan-Slav community that tried to maintain itself through a new kind of inner freedom, a freedom *in* community. In short, its response to the Soviet Union's religious intolerance was one of community identification. Nonetheless, the community of the Russian Orthodox Church was one in which leaders were monitored, many churches were confiscated, and anyone who voiced any hint of objection to communist control was liable for arrest and imprisonment. This was devastating to the Russian Church. Relief came only in 1985, when Mikhail Gorbachev reversed the Soviet Union's religious policies under his larger cultural restructuring of *glasnost* (openness). In 1990, Russia granted a modest freedom of religion, which allowed the Orthodox Church to begin to heal. Russia at this time also allowed some Protestants and Catholics to enter its borders uninhibited. Orthodox leaders have since accused these groups of "sheep stealing." Today, Christianity is growing in Russia, and the Orthodox Church is regaining its bearings. Many who had not been "churched" are now returning to their family's religion, and one of the greatest challenges of the Orthodox Church is to educate its new members. In the past, church leaders could assume an Orthodox culture and knowledge base. This now has to be re-created from scratch.

 ## CONCLUSIONS

Movements in the modern world have given Christianity something of a beating in the last 200 years. The long-term results of the French Revolution and Italian Risorgimento have arguably led to these two stalwart Catholic countries now being relatively nonreligious. The atheistic thinkers of the late nineteenth and early twentieth centuries began a movement that has contributed not only to a larger atheism in the culture and parts of the scientific community, but also a kind of chic dismissal of religious faith. In his book *The Evolution of God*, Robert Wright argues that Western culture is shifting toward an antireligious attitude that is becoming public and aggressive:

Indeed, the first decade of the twenty-first century made god-talk an even greater breach of highbrow etiquette than it has been in the twentieth. . . . [An] anti-religious attitude was central to a slew of influential cultural products. . . . In the space of only a few years, the more-or-less official stance of intellectuals toward believers has moved from polite silence to open dismissal if not ridicule.[8]

Christianity has responded to these challenges. Some of the response looks defensive and anti-intellectual. But much of the response has been engagement in dialogue with science and the questions the modern mind needs to address.

SUMMARY QUESTIONS

- What is atheism, and how did the four influential atheists discussed in this chapter view religion?

- Geology, evolutionary biology, and archeology all posed challenges for Christianity in the modern era. What were those challenges, and how have Christians reconciled them with the faith?

- What are Barbour's four possible relationships between science and religion?

- Briefly explain the three Protestant responses to modernity that are discussed in the chapter.
- How did Catholicism initially respond to the challenges of modernity, and how did Vatican II reverse this response?

DISCUSSION QUESTIONS

- What do the events of the twentieth century show about the causes of conflict and religion's relationship to them?
- The author states that the optimism that atheists such as Marx and Nietzsche had for the future of humanity has not proven compelling.

Do you think that this then gives credence to a religious worldview?
- Among Barbour's four possible relationships between science and religion, what position is most plausible to you, and why?

KEY TERMS

Atheism
Barth, Karl
Biblical criticism
Bonaparte, Napoleon
Darwin, Charles
Feuerbach, Ludwig
Freud, Sigmund

Fundamentalism
John XXIII
Liberal Protestant
Marx, Karl
Materialism
Nationalism
Neo-Orthodoxy

Nietzsche, Friedrich
Rights of Man
Riley, William
Scientific naturalism
Scientism
Second Vatican Council
Ultramontanism

BIBLIOGRAPHY

- Barbour, Ian. 1997. *Religion and Science: Historical and Contemporary Issues.* San Francisco: Harper and Row.
- Brooke, John, and Ian McLean, eds. 2006. *Heterodoxy in Early Modern Science and Religion.* Oxford: Oxford University Press.
- Clifford, Catherine, and Richard Gaillardetz. 2012. *Keys to the Council: Unlocking the Teachings of Vatican II.* Collegeville, MN: Liturgical Press.
- Cragg, Gerald. 1974. *The Church and the Age of Reason,* rev. ed. Harmondsworth, UK: Penguin.
- Feldmeier, Peter. 2014. *The God Conflict: Faith in the Face of New Atheism.* Liguruori, MO: Liguouri Press.
- Flannery, Austin, ed. 1975. *Vatican Council II: The Conciliar and Post Conciliar Documents,* rev. ed. New York: Costello Publishing.
- Gould, Stephen Jay. 1999. *Rock of Ages: Science and Religion in the Fullness of Life.* New York: Ballantine.
- Hitchens, Christopher. 2007. *The Portable Atheist: Essential Readings for the Nonbeliever.* Philadelphia: Da Capo Press.
- John Paul II. 1996. "Messages to Pontifical Academy of Sciences on Evolution." *Origins* 26:350–352.
- Knox, Zoe Katrina. 2005. *Russian Society and the Orthodox Church: Religion in Russia after Communism.* London: Routledge.
- Linker, Damon. 2002. "Nietzsche's Truth." *First Things* 125 (August/September): 50–60.
- Miller, Donald. 1997. *Reinventing American Protestantism: Christianity in the New Millennium.* Berkeley: University of California Press.
- Miller, Kenneth. 1999. *Finding Darwin's God.* New York: HarperCollins.

- Nietzsche, Friedrich. 1960. *Joyful Wisdom.* Trans. Thomas Common. New York: Frederick Ungar Publishing.
- O'Malley, John. 1989. *Tradition and Transition: Historical Perspectives on Vatican II.* Collegeville, MN: Michael Glazier.
- O'Malley, John. 2008. *What Happened at Vatican II.* Cambridge: Harvard University Press.
- Polkinghorne, John. 1998. *Belief in God in the Age of Science.* New Haven, CT: Yale University Press.
- Putman, Robert, and David Campbell. 2010. *American Grace: How Religion Divides Us and Unites Us.* New York: Simon and Schuster.
- Schacht, R. 1994. *Nietzsche, Genealogy, Morality: Essays on Nietzsche's Genealogy of Morals.* Berkeley: University of California Press.
- Sullivan, Maureen. 1985. *The Road to Vatican II: Key Changes in Theology.* New York: Paulist Press.
- Wright, Robert. 2009. *The Evolution of God.* New York: Little, Brown and Company.

NOTES

1. Cited in Schacht, *Nietzsche, Genealogy, Morality*, 20.
2. Nietzsche, *Joyful Wisdom*, 167–168.
3. John Paul II, "Message to Pontifical Academy," 352.
4. Bertrand Russell, "An Outline of Intellectual Rubbish," in *The Portable Atheist: Essential Readings for the Nonbeliever*, ed. Christopher Hitchens (Philadelphia: Da Capo Press, 2007), 183.
5. Gould, *Rock of Ages*, 6.
6. See Feldmeier, *God Conflict*, 114–117.
7. John William Colenso, *The Pentateuch and the Book of Joshua Critically Examined* (1863) accessed in http://www.victorianweb.org/religion/colenso.html.
8. Wright, *Evolution of God*, 444–445.

The Rise of Evangelical and Pentecostal Christianity

Timeline

c. 1900 CE Social Gospel Movement becomes influential

1906 CE Azusa Street Revival; beginnings of the American Pentecostal movement

1919 CE William Riley founds the Christian Fundamentals Association

1925 CE Scopes "Monkey Trial" marks conflict between fundamentalist and modernist Christians

1948 CE World Council of Churches established in Amsterdam

1949 CE Billy Graham launches his national career with a three-month revival in Los Angeles

1966 CE Beginnings of charismatic renewal worldwide

1978 CE Religious Right emerges in U.S. political life

WHAT TO EXPECT

In terms of numbers, the most dramatic Christian movement in the United States is the Evangelical movement, which now represents about a quarter of all U.S. adults. The beginnings of the movement were discussed in Chapter Eighteen, and this chapter investigates its most recent expressions. In many ways Evangelicalism continues to embrace the assumptions of the Puritans and others who considered the United States a divinely elected society. Thus, not surprisingly, members of the movement have become highly involved in politics in order to advance the same sense of divine destiny. This chapter also explores the Pentecostal movement, which is changing the face of Christianity throughout the world. Recalling the charismatic nature of the early church, which evidenced dramatic gifts of the Holy Spirit, this movement aims to revive that same character in the modern world, though not without controversy.

THE MODERN EVANGELICAL MOVEMENT

WHAT IS AN EVANGELICAL CHRISTIAN?

Just over 70 percent of Americans identify themselves as Christian. Among them, about half claim to have been "born again," or to have "accepted Jesus Christ as their personal Lord and Savior." The term "born again" comes from John's Gospel, in which Jesus says, "Very truly, I tell you, no one can see the kingdom of God without being born from above" (3:3). The biblical phrase here is *gennaithai anōthen*, which is best translated "born from above," but can also be translated "born again." Acquiring a new spiritual identity and accepting Jesus as Lord are central to Christian baptism and would presumably apply to all Christians. Why, then, do only half of American Christians respond positively to this identification? One answer might be that many who identify themselves as Christians are merely culturally so, and have not really internalized their faith. Another answer is that the discrepancy arises from the language "born again" and "personal Lord and Savior," which is a style of speaking about faith associated with the Evangelical tradition.

The term *Evangelical*, as discussed in Chapter Eighteen, is hard to define. For some, to be an Evangelical is to belong to a nondenominational church. For others, the term encompasses specific denominations, such as the Southern Baptist Convention. For still others, it represents a *way* of being Christian. All of these understandings are valid, and each reflects something of the Evangelical movement, from its beginnings to its modern-day expressions.

As noted in Chapter Eighteen, the term "Evangelical" was used broadly during the seventeenth century to designate the German Pietistic movement and forms of English Puritanism. Members of these groups emphasized personal conversion and a faith infused with heart, focusing more on life-transforming piety than on a rational, rule-based, mainstream Protestant faith. They showed relatively little interest in dogma or liturgy, but great interest in an interpersonal life with Christ. These elements figure prominently among some strands of Lutheranism, Methodism, Congregationalism, Baptist, and Presbyterianism, and more universally among the Church of Christ and Disciples of Christ. Today, "Evangelical" also connotes a particular theological framing of the faith. Generally speaking, Evangelicals hold that the Bible is inerrant and that priority of biblical interpretation is granted to the believer rather than to church authority. Many Evangelicals believe in the imminent return of Jesus (the second coming) and place great emphasis on preaching, with little interest in sacraments, except baptism. They also tend to be suspicious of Roman Catholicism. In many ways, their theology and spirituality look a good deal like Zwingli's and Calvin's. Evangelical Christianity is also, in the modern period, wildly successful in terms of membership. John Vaughn, in *Church Growth Today*, reports that nine of the ten most rapidly growing non-Catholic churches in the United States self-identify under the Evangelical umbrella.[1]

The year 1846 saw the instigation of the Evangelical Alliance, which was formed to bring Christian energies to the service of converting American society. Other smaller Evangelical associations followed this lead. Drawing on the ever-present idea that America enjoys God's particular blessing, the movement intended to create a bona fide "Christian civilization" (meaning Protestant). Such aspirations have continued to be part of the American Evangelical view, in which Christianity is granted the role of sanctifying the social, political, and even economic interests of the United States.

Recall from Chapter Eighteen that Christianity experienced two awakenings rooted in revivalism. **Dwight L. Moody** (1837–1899) continued the spirit of revivalism with his own revival meetings and eventually started the Moody Bible Institute in Chicago. This and other Bible colleges were established to prepare ministers for evangelization. Moody was something of a feminist:

FIGURE 20-1   Billy Graham (b. 1918) was the twentieth century's greatest Christian Evangelist.

he advocated that women be allowed to assume leadership roles, and his college often enrolled as many women as men. He also applied business and advertising techniques to his religious revivalism and held large interdenominational meetings in urban areas. Unlike the Evangelical preachers of the eighteenth century, he presented his message through a virtually anti-intellectual platform. The gospel, for Moody, was about the love of God and the need for repentance. For him, revivalism facilitated a deeply emotional experience that led sinners to God.

Fueled by the new Evangelical energy of the nineteenth century, the Southern Baptist Convention, Assemblies of God, and Christian Missionary Alliance all grew rapidly. But the anti-intellectual leanings of both the revivalist movement and the fundamentalist movement created a battleground against more modern, mainstream Protestant and Catholic theological sensibilities. In 1925, The Scopes trial,

pitting evolution against a literal interpretation of Genesis, marked a watershed moment that revealed the intellectual unacceptability of biblical literalism to much of the American public. By the 1940s, Wheaton College near Chicago, Gordon College in Massachusetts, and Westmont College in California had ramped up their scholarly energies to try to address this intellectual gap between the Evangelical community and the theological mainstream. One important figure of the time was Carl F. H. Henry (1913–2003), whose book *Uneasy Conscience of Modern Fundamentalism* (1947) proposed a more rigorously intellectual message.

William Franklin (Billy) Graham Jr. (b. 1918) is assuredly the most important figure in modern American Evangelicalism. In 1949, he planned a revival meeting in Los Angeles, anticipating that it would last as long as three weeks. The revival was such a fantastic success that it went on for three months, with crowds of 6,000 cramming into his "canvas cathedral." Famous athletes and entertainers publicly converted during the revival, adding momentum to its success. The essence of Graham's message was simple: one needed to have faith in Christ. Although criticized by the more fundamentalist members of the Evangelical movement for being too ecumenical, Graham expanded his ministry to become fully interdenominational.

Graham's Evangelism appealed to the heart and focused almost entirely on personal salvation. He represented a highly individualistic faith, with little concern for institutional religion or theological divides. In one sense he offered a kind of generic Christianity. The Evangelism of Edwards, Whitefield, and the Wesleys was quite morally demanding and theologically specific. To be sure, Graham challenged sin, but in a relatively general manner, concentrating on examples such as neglect of one's family or alcohol abuse. In doing so, he retained a kind of broad acceptability that allowed him to preach widely. His broad-stroke approach also allowed his ministry to enjoy a robust **ecumenism**, or Christian unity. He broke down the walls that separated many Christians. Listening to his preaching, one clearly sees the influence of the fundamentalist movement. He regularly preached within the framework of biblical literalism and taught that the Rapture was virtually upon the world.

Graham has clearly been one of the most trusted voices of the American Evangelical experience. His preaching is seen as electrifying, and his ability to unite Christians is undeniable. He has crossed barriers and proved to be a consistent and long-thriving voice of Evangelicalism. His personal life has also been impressive. With never a hint of scandal or question of his personal integrity, he drew a modest salary and helped raise a family of ministers, who have continued his ministry.

American Evangelical Christianity takes two basic forms. One is the denominational association, such as the Southern Baptist Convention. The other is the independent free church. Many belong to the National Association of Evangelicals, which represents over 45,000 independent churches. Given their independence from each other, there is some theological variation. Generally speaking, they embrace the following: (1) the Bible is the infallible inspired word of God; (2) the Bible provides the content for all doctrines; (3) the Holy Spirit dwells in believers and can be palpably known; (4) it is imperative to preach the gospel and win conversions for the sake of others' salvation; (5) Christian life demands moral rectitude; (6) Christ will return visibly in the second coming and will institute a thousand year reign, which will precede the last judgment; and (7) Christian faith is primarily a matter of the heart, through which one finds friendship with Christ and the soul becomes transformed.

EVANGELICALISM AND THE AMERICAN RELIGIOUS RIGHT

Jerry Falwell (1933–2007), a conservative Southern Baptist pastor, was initially much like Graham in shying away from mixing the Evangelical message with politics. He even publicly criticized his more liberal Baptist ministers for taking part in the civil rights movement in the 1960s. But when the Supreme Court blocked prayer in public schools and legalized abortion in the 1970s, he had a change of heart. Falwell, Timothy LaHaye, James Dobson, Pat Robertson, and many others created the Evangelical Religious Right, forming lobbying groups such as the Christian Coalition and the Moral Majority. They aligned themselves with the Republican Party, which, from President Ronald Reagan on, promised a platform of traditional family values. Today, a sizeable majority of Evangelical Christians vote Republican. Consider the following trajectory: In the 1960s, 57 percent of Evangelicals in the north and 21 percent in the south were Republicans. By the 1980s, 72 percent of Evangelicals in the north and 39 percent in the south were Republicans. This support of the Republican Party continued in the following decades, with Evangelicals voting for Republican presidential candidates at an astounding rate: Bob Dole received 75 percent of the Evangelical vote in 1996, George W. Bush received roughly 80 percent in 2000 and 2004, John McCain received 71 percent in 2008, and Mitt Romney—a Mormon versus a Protestant—received 74 percent in 2012.

As we saw in Chapter Eighteen, modern American Evangelicals tend, much like the Evangelical leaders from the Great Awakenings to the early part of the twentieth century, to conflate Christianity with the interests of the United States. This outlook represents a new kind of **Manifest Destiny**, whereby the United States is somehow specially endowed as a Christian nation and responsible to this great endowment. Consider the following conversation that occurred between Reverends Jerry Falwell and Pat Robertson on the *700 Club*, a national Evangelical television show, two days after the September 11, 2001, terrorist attacks on the World Trade Center and Pentagon:

JERRY FALWELL: I've never sensed a togetherness, a burden, a broken heart as I do in the church today, and just 48 hours. I have a booklet I wrote ten years ago. I gave it away last night on the biblical position on fasting and prayer because I do believe that is what we've got to do right now—fast and pray. And I totally agree with you that the Lord has protected us so wonderfully these 225 years. And since 1812, this is the first time that we've been attacked on our soil, first time, and by far the worst results. And I fear, as Donald Rumsfeld, Secretary of Defense, said yesterday, that this is only the beginning. And with biological warfare available to these monsters; the Husseins, the Bin Ladens, the Arafats, what we saw on Tuesday, as terrible as it is, could be miniscule if in fact God continues to lift the curtain and allow the enemies of America to give us probably what we deserve.

PAT ROBERTSON: Jerry, that's my feeling. I think we've seen the antechamber of terror. We haven't even begun to see what they can do to the major population.

JERRY FALWELL: The ACLU [American Civil Liberties Union]'s got to take a lot of blame for this.

PAT ROBERTSON: Well, yes.

JERRY FALWELL: And, I know I'll hear from them for this. But throwing God out of the public square, out of the schools. The abortionists have got to bear some burden for this because God will not be mocked. And when we destroy 40 million little innocent babies, we make God mad. I really believe that the pagans, and the abortionists, and the feminists, and the gays and the lesbians who are actively trying to make that an alternative lifestyle, the ACLU, People for the American Way, all of them who have tried to secularize America. I point my finger in their face and say, "You helped this happen."

PAT ROBERTSON: Well, I totally concur, and the problem is that we have adopted that agenda at the highest levels of our government. And so we're responsible as a free society for what the top people do. And the top people, of course, is the court system.[2]

In this conversation, both prominent Evangelical ministers imagine that God has kept a providential and protective watch over America because it is somehow exceptional. Other European countries have had to deal with terrorist groups for decades, including the Irish Republican Army in Great Britain, the Basque separatists in Spain, and the Red Brigade in Italy, to name just a few. But America is understood by Falwell and Robertson to be different and protected by God. According to their dialogue, the increasing secularization of American culture has caused God to remove his protection from the nation. Note that they do not claim God is responsible for the attack. Rather, God had been keeping America's enemies at bay until now.

Missing from the conversation is any explanation detailing how, exactly, culturally liberal movements violate God's laws. Many mainstream Protestants are pro-choice. The ACLU is a nonprofit organization designed to protect civil liberties, something the founding fathers and religious leaders of that era thought crucially important. Feminism has produced everything from the right to vote to protections against job discrimination and, in Christianity, women's ordination. Further, court rulings separating church and state were often celebrated by Christians during the colonial period. Of course, many Christians believe that abortion is immoral and that civil liberties have become exaggerated, such as in the pornography industry. But the cultural critique by figures like Falwell and Robertson is strikingly overreaching and assumes that Christianity reflects their own social/political agenda.

Most importantly, absent from their dialogue is any critique of America's past, including its hundreds of years of slavery. Would these not be more egregious violations of God's law than, say, disallowing prayer from public schools? Even though it is obvious that Falwell and Robertson have swept many problems in their interpretation of the terrorist attack under the rug, and indeed have conflated their particular cultural interests with their theology, the fact remains that they are also channeling a theme as old as the colonial period: America is particularly God's country, with a unique responsibility to hold up the faith.

Today, there is something of a "liberal" American Evangelical movement, which has intentionally distanced itself from its identification with a political party or conservative politics. A significant minority of Evangelical pastors and churches has called for greater social reform, increased concern for the environment and the need to address climate change, and attention to world justice initiatives, regardless of their relationship to U.S. political interests.

THE MEGA-CHURCH MOVEMENT

A particularly interesting development in the Evangelical movement is the boom in "mega-churches." The Hartford Institute identifies a **mega-church** as a church having a sustained weekly attendance of at least 2,000 worshippers. Most mega-churches are located in the southern Sunbelt, with California, Texas, Florida, and Georgia having the highest concentrations. Typically, these churches are found in suburban areas of growing major cities, such as Atlanta, Dallas, Houston, Phoenix, and Los Angeles, occupying large tracts of land (50–100 acres) near major traffic thoroughfares. The mega-church movement began in the 1970s. In 1979, there were ten mega-churches in the United States. Just a year later there were fifty. This number grew to 300 by 1990 and 500 in the early 2000s; currently, there are about 1,600 mega-churches in the United States. Typically, the head pastor of a mega-church is largely responsible for its magnetic effect and large congregation; such figures are almost always experienced as superb preachers and storytellers.

Around half of all mega-churches are denominational, with the greatest number being Southern Baptist, at 16 percent of all mega-churches. Most of the largest mega-churches consider themselves Evangelical free churches or simply Christian communities with no labels. **Rick Warren**, who in 2002 was named by *Christianity Today* as "America's most influential pastor," discovered in focus groups that the term "Baptist" did not sit well with people in Southern California. So, in creating his church, Saddleback Valley Community Church, Warren decided to downplay its association with the Southern Baptist Convention.

Warren is clearly market-savvy, as is his church. Warren's book *The Purpose-Driven Life* has sold over 30 million copies. Rich Karlgaard, the publisher of *Forbes* magazine, called it "the best book in entrepreneurship, business, and investment in a long time . . . identify a consumer need—the religious consumer need—and fill it."[3] Donald Miller, a professor of religion at the University of Southern California, sees the same dynamic in the church itself: "Saddleback attends to the consumer demand by fine-tuning their worship and organizational style to today's culture, not the cultures of the past."[4] Warren does not apologize for creating a church and worship style that are market-driven; for him, this is simply a question of relevance. He also insists that formal members of Saddleback formally commit themselves to daily prayer, participate in small faith-sharing groups, and play active roles in at least one of the dozens of ministries to which Saddleback is committed. Today, Saddleback has 20,000 formal members.

The largest mega-church in the United States at present is Lakewood Church in Houston, founded by **John Osteen**, a Southern Baptist minister. Within a few years, Lakewood dropped "Baptist" from its name and became nondenominational. By 1979, the church had over 5,000 weekly worshippers and had begun to host a weekly television program. In 1999, John Osteen died of a heart attack, and his youngest son, Joel, became the pastor. Church attendance soared

REVEREND RICK WARREN'S PRESIDENTIAL INAUGURATION PRAYER, JANUARY 20, 2009

Almighty God, our Father, everything we see, and everything we can't see, exists because of you alone. It all comes from you, it all belongs to you, it all exists for your glory. History is your story. The Scripture tells us, "Hear, O Israel, the Lord is our God, the Lord is one." And you are the compassionate and merciful one. And you are loving to everyone you have made.

Now today, we rejoice not only in America's peaceful transfer of power for the 44th time, we celebrate a hinge point of history with the inauguration of our first African-American president of the United States. We are so grateful to live in this land, a land of unequaled possibility, where the son of an African immigrant can rise to the highest level of our leadership. And we know today that Dr. King and a great cloud of witnesses are shouting in heaven. Give to our new president, Barack Obama, the wisdom to lead us with humility, the courage to lead us with integrity, the compassion to lead us with generosity. Bless and protect him, his family, Vice President Biden, the Cabinet and every one of our freely elected leaders.

Help us, O God, to remember that we are Americans, united not by race or religion or blood, but to our commitment to freedom and justice for all. When we focus on ourselves, when we fight each other, when we forget you,

forgive us. When we presume that our greatness and our prosperity is ours alone, forgive us. When we fail to treat our fellow human beings and all the earth with the respect that they deserve, forgive us.

And as we face these difficult days ahead, may we have a new birth of clarity in our aims, responsibility in our actions, humility in our approaches and civility in our attitudes—even when we differ. Help us to share, to serve and to seek the common good of all. May all people of good will today join together to work for a more just, a more healthy, and a more prosperous nation and a peaceful planet. And may we never forget that one day, all nations, and all people, will stand accountable before you. We now commit our new president and his wife, Michelle, and his daughters, Malia and Sasha, into your loving care. I humbly ask this in the name of the one who changed my life—Yeshua, Isa, Jesus [Spanish pronunciation], Jesus—who taught us to pray: Our Father, who art in heaven, hallowed be Thy name. Thy kingdom come, thy will be done, on earth as it is in heaven. Give us this day our daily bread. And forgive us our trespasses, as we forgive those who trespass against us. And lead us not into temptation, but deliver us from evil, for Thine is the kingdom and the power and the glory forever. Amen.

---

so high that in 2003 Lakewood moved from its original mega-church location to the Compaq Center, a former sports arena. With Compaq Center's capacity to accommodate 16,800, Lakewood averages around 43,000 worshippers weekly, split over several Sunday services. The main weekly service is broadcast on the Trinity Broadcasting and Daystar Television networks, as well as local channels in most major markets. It is viewed in over 100 countries worldwide.

THE PENTECOSTAL EXPLOSION

Nothing has changed the landscape of the modern Christian world more than the **Pentecostal movement**. It represents Christianity's newest and fastest-growing expression by far. Recall that the early church was a *charismatic church*. The word "charism" derives from the Greek word

for "gift," and the early church seemed to be endowed with a great number of spiritual gifts. Paul describes them as follows:

> Now there are a variety of gifts, but the same Spirit; and there are varieties of services, but the same Lord; and there are a variety of activities, but it is the same God who activates all of them in everyone. To each is given the manifestation of the Spirit for the common good. To one is given through the Spirit the utterance of wisdom, and to another the utterance of knowledge according to the same Spirit, to another faith by the same Spirit, to another gifts of healing by the one Spirit, to another the working of miracles, to another prophecy, to another the discernment of spirits, to another various kinds of tongues, to another the interpretation of tongues. (1 Cor. 12:4–10)

Paul then goes on to rank these gifts: "And God has appointed in the church first apostles, second prophets, third teachers; then deeds of power, then gifts of healing, forms of assistance, forms of leadership, various kinds of tongues" (1 Cor. 12:28).

The church has always had leaders, wisdom figures, and extraordinary examples of faith. Some of the other gifts Paul mentions were expressed more rarely, such as prophecy or gifts of healing and miracles. The gift of **speaking in tongues** and its interpretation seems to have dropped out of Christianity quickly, certainly by the latter part of the first century.

Pentecostalism celebrates the resurgence of all these gifts, and particularly the gifts of healing, prophecy, and tongues, as well as an expectation that they have come as a prelude to the second coming of Christ. Today, worldwide there are as many as half a billion Pentecostals in the world, if we include charismatic Christians in mainstream churches. The movement spread so quickly that within ten years of its emergence in the early twentieth century, its message reached over fifty countries.

As noted in Chapter Eighteen, Evangelical Christianity swept across Europe and the United States initially through the Pietist and Methodist movements. These movements emphasized the heart and emotions. The great revivalists insisted that the hallmark of Christian faith was a dramatic experience of God transforming the soul and bringing new life in the Spirit. By the 1840s, the Methodist revival dominated the American Protestant scene, so much so that Methodists outnumbered Presbyterians, Congregationalists, Episcopalians, Lutherans, and Calvinist Reformed members combined.

During the second half of the nineteenth century, however, Methodism lost much of its Evangelical fervor and became a more mainstream Protestant church. Some Christians left Methodism and formed **Holiness churches**, small denominations that linked dramatic experiences of God with radical holiness. These churches include the Church of the Nazarene (1885), the Church of God (1886), the Christian and Missionary Alliance (1887), and the Pilgrim Holiness Church (1897). Many Protestants, especially those in Holiness churches, embraced what has been variously called the **fullness gospel**, the "fourfold gospel," or the "foursquare gospel." The fullness gospel centers on Jesus as Savior, baptizer in the Holy Spirit, healer, and soon-coming king. Representatives of Holiness churches claim that Christ promised gifts of healing, and that these would be widely available to the church (John 14:12–14). One can best understand the Holiness movement as a combination of Evangelicalism, revivalism, millennialism (the belief that Christ is returning soon), and the belief that radical holiness is a sign of one's new life in Christ. Further, members believe that this holiness will be expressed through prophecy, healing ministries, and the revival of the early church's experience of the gift of tongues.

THE EARLY MOVEMENT

Pandita Ramabai, an Evangelical Christian with ties to the Holiness movement, started a mission in Kedgaon, India, in 1895 to serve the needs of destitute adolescent and young adult women. It was called the Mukti Mission, from the Hindi word meaning "salvation." By 1900, 2,000 Indian residents lived at the Mukti Mission, and in 1906 a number of young women residing there began to spread the gospel to local Hindus. That same year these women began experiencing ecstatic phenomena, including receiving visions and speaking in tongues.

Similar events were taking place on the other side of the globe on Azusa Street in Los Angeles. **William J. Seymour** (1870–1922) came to Los Angeles to be the pastor of a Holiness congregation after spending six weeks at a Bible school in Houston run by Charles Fox Parham (1873–1929). At that session, Parham had made the connection between baptism in the Holy Spirit and speaking in tongues. Speaking in tongues was a necessary sign, Parham taught, of a true Spirit baptism. In April 1906, Seymour led a revival during which incidents of speaking in tongues broke out. Seymour and other leaders relocated to 312 Azusa Street, a two-story building that once served as an African Methodist Episcopal Church, and continued the revival there. While it was going on, San Francisco experienced its great earthquake of 1906. People participating in the Los Angeles revival interpreted this as a sign that the second coming was upon them. The mission ran around the clock, serving 1,500 persons a day. It first attracted people from the city, then from around the United States, and then from around the world; all came to receive their own Pentecostal baptism. Seymour also started a monthly newspaper, the *Apostolic Faith*, which had 50,000 subscribers at its height.

Within two years of the initial revival, missionaries from Azusa Street were working in twenty-five countries. Within ten years, they had spread the message to over fifty countries. One of the most inspiring qualities of the Azusa Street mission is that it transcended gender and class lines. William Seymour, a poor black man from the Ku Klux Klan–dominated Deep South, became the spiritual leader for blacks and whites, rich and poor. Even today, Pentecostalism tends to transcend classes and ethnicities.

In 1906, one of Ramabai's fellow missionaries, Minnie Abrams, published a booklet entitled *The Baptism of the Holy Spirit and Fire*, which sold 30,000 copies. While visiting her friend May Louise Hoover in Valparaiso, Chile, they disseminated the booklet there. In 1909, Methodist churches in Valparaiso and Santiago began holding Pentecostal revivals. At the same time, Korea too experienced a Pentecostal revival. At a convention in Pyongyang led by Sun Ju Kil, many in the audience began speaking in tongues. In 1908, in Gansu, China, a Chinese preacher named Brother Yong experienced Spirit baptism and started to speak in tongues. He was reportedly effective in healing, prophecy, and casting out demons.

These events highlight some of the more dramatic expressions of early Pentecostalism. The movement did not begin as an organized outgrowth of existing Protestant churches, but as a missionary enthusiasm for the common experience of Spirit baptism. Soon, however,

denominations arose and theological lines were drawn. Some maintained that spiritual transformation necessarily involved a three-stage conversion process, beginning with initial conversion and baptism, followed by Spirit baptism with the gifts of the Holy Spirit, and culminating in a sinless life of radical holiness. Others aligned Spirit baptism with sinlessness, a framework called the *Finished Work* program. Still others proclaimed the *oneness gospel*, according to which Jesus is the incarnation of the entire Trinity. This position constitutes a form of *modalism*, as discussed in Chapter Seven. About 10 percent of all Pentecostals embrace the oneness gospel. Adherents to the Finished Work theology are more numerous and include members of the Church of Christ and Assemblies of God. Some counts put the membership of today's Assemblies of God at 40 million around the globe.

CHARISMATIC RENEWAL

For decades, Pentecostal Christians isolated themselves from mainstream Christianity. The Holiness churches, many of whose members became Pentecostals, believed that Spirit baptism rendered them utterly sinless and thus distinct from the larger society and even from other Christians. They also widely believed that the gifts of the Holy Spirit, particularly speaking in tongues, represented an essential mark of one's authentic faith. And those who lacked such spiritual gifts were obviously not genuinely, or at least not fully, Christian. Finally, they believed in the imminent second coming of Christ. Given the approaching apocalypse, why participate in cultural or political initiatives? What was urgent was saving as many souls as possible before the Rapture.

By the middle of the twentieth century, however, the Pentecostal movement had become more mainstream. Many denominations joined the National Association of Evangelicals, and some of its leaders became prominent in the larger culture. **Oral Roberts** brought Pentecostalism into the homes of many Americans through his weekly television program, and his magazine

Abundant Life had a circulation of over a million at its height. In 1963, he built Oral Roberts University, and in 1968 he shocked the Pentecostal world by becoming ordained as a Methodist minister, thus bringing his ministry to mainstream Christianity. Earlier, in 1960, Roberts had joined Pat Robertson to begin the Christian Broadcasting Network. In 1977, Robertson also started a university, now named Regent University, which is arguably the most influential Pentecostal university in the United States.

Many mainstream Protestants and Catholics have been influenced by the Pentecostal movement but have remained in their respective denominations. These individuals are typically called *charismatic Christians*, and they meet regularly for fellowship and prayer during the week as well as join their fellow church members for standard Sunday services. In Catholicism, the Catholic Charismatic Renewal had as many as 300,000 members in the mid-1970s. By 2010, there were over 120 million Catholic charismatics in 220 countries, particularly in South America.

The Pentecostal movement still tends to embrace the fullness gospel, and many Pentecostals still await the imminent second coming, a view shared by many Evangelicals. But Pentecostalism today is somewhat of a tamer movement than it once was, and most Pentecostals have rejected the assumption that unless one speaks in tongues, one is not a Christian. In fact, currently, many Pentecostals—although still a minority—do not speak in tongues. It is a gift, they believe, given to some, but not all, as a sign of the Holy Spirit's presence.

PENTECOSTAL PIETY

Pentecostal spirituality is most clearly evident in revivalist-style worship services at which participants have great freedom to speak in tongues, proclaim a prophecy, or actively respond to the sermon. Worship services have a typical flow. They often begin with loud music, hand clapping, dancing, and hugging. These activities progressively move to softer prayer voices and

FIGURE 20-2 Pentecostal prayer is known for its exuberance and celebration of the gifts of the Holy Spirit, particularly prophecy and the gift of tongues.

quieter music. This quieting down of the congregation moves to a sermon. The service then continues with more vibrant praise.

Pentecostal spirituality is intense and dramatic; it expects prophecies to be given and miracles to be provided. Pentecostals are fond of telling miracle stories of healing or divine intervention. For many, it would not be out of place to talk about such experiences at family gatherings or even during casual conversations on the sidewalk. Pentecostals are convinced that God speaks to them regularly through prophecy, dreams, visions, and their own spiritual intuitions. They are, by far, more likely than any other Christians to report having received a direct revelation from God.

Pentecostals, even more than their Evangelical forerunners, tend toward biblical fundamentalism. "Believing in the Bible" constitutes a regular theme of their faith. The Bible is imagined by most to have been directly dictated by God, and Pentecostal sermons are often sprinkled with the phrase "God says . . . ," followed by a biblical reference. What is different about this approach from other forms of biblical fundamentalism, however, is that biblical texts principally serve as resources for storytelling. Pentecostals typically use the Bible to explain how the Holy Spirit works in their own lives, particularly regarding healing and prophecy. Stories often deal with supernatural power and spiritual warfare. In developing countries, many believe that the world is crowded with angels and demons. Pentecostal spirituality is uniquely suited to encompass numerous accounts of exorcism, and exorcism comprises a regular part of Pentecostal practice in South America, Africa, and Asia.

PROSPERITY PREACHING

One of the early leading Pentecostal revivalists, Smith Wigglesworth (1859–1947), advocated the controversial practice of **positive confession**, whereby one could claim a gift from God and have faith that God would bestow it. Throughout the Bible, God promises abundant life for those who follow him, and these passages seem to promise earthly as well as heavenly rewards. Wigglesworth and others who embraced this positive confession form of Pentecostalism fueled what is now known as **prosperity preaching**.

In its most modest form, prosperity preaching is a message that God cares about one's earthly life and wishes it to be abundant. By the 1980s, prosperity preaching had moved to a new level and became central in much of Pentecostal practice throughout the globe. Gloria Copeland and her husband Kenneth are among the foremost prosperity preachers in the United States. She promises that if you give $1 for the gospel's sake—meaning to their ministry—God will make sure you get $100 return. A gift of $10 gets you $1,000, and $1,000 ensures you $100,000. This message has been profitable for the Copelands, as they own a $6 million mansion and a $20 million jet. "Receive your miracle," she tells her listeners.

The spiritual agenda of prosperity preaching is simply this: God wants Christians to claim wealth, which provides an abundant life for the Christian and acts as a public witness to the possibilities of faith. The first step toward such a life is to "just claim it every day." The second step consists of thanking God in advance for already granting wealth while waiting until it comes to full fruition in one's bank account. Success

stories of Christians who trust this message abound in prosperity preaching.

Robert Tilton, an American prosperity preacher with a televangelistic infomercial called *Success-N-Life*, testified in court that he made $800,000 a month. As astounding as this figure is, in 1991, ABC's *Prime Time Live* reported that he actually brought in significantly more. Bruce Wilkenson's book *The Prayer of Jabez* is premised on the promise that Christians can become wealthy if they have enough faith. The book has sold over 20 million copies to date. Prosperity preaching has exploded all over the globe. Over 90 percent of Pentecostals in Nigeria, South Africa, India, and the Philippines believe in prosperity preaching, and it is the cornerstone of Brazil's Universal Church of God's Kingdom, which boasts a membership exceeding 10 million people and owns banks, radio stations, and Brazil's third-largest television network.

Some Pentecostals have attacked this expression of faith. The Assemblies of God Church, for example, has formally repudiated the positive confession formula. Other Pentecostals, such as Ron Sider, author of *Rich Christians in an Age of Hunger*, have challenged first-world Pentecostals to address the pressing global issues of hunger and poverty. While some Pentecostal initiatives do address social inequities, Pentecostalism tends to be a form of Christianity true to its roots of disinterest in political and social activism.

Widely, Pentecostal scholars distinguish themselves from some of their faith's popular theological sensibilities. Few are biblical fundamentalists, and many have raised concerns about exaggerated claims of miracles and the potentially naïve alignment between one's dreams or desires and God's will. It would be difficult to find a Pentecostal scholar who affirms the crass prosperity preaching described here. Pentecostalism is one of the most dynamic and certainly the fastest-growing movement in Christianity today. It will continue to be one of the dominant players in the future of the church.

CONCLUSIONS

As will be discussed in the next chapter, Evangelical and Pentecostal Christianity represent the most robust expressions of the growth of Christianity both in the United States and worldwide. From small, relatively informal communities to the mega-church movement, they have morphed and will continue to do so as they are transferred to new cultures. In the United States, while Roman Catholic and mainstream Protestant communities are experiencing a depletion of their traditional bases, these two forms of Christianity are at least holding their own, and increasingly seem likely to become even more dominant expressions of American Christianity.

SUMMARY QUESTIONS

- As discussed in Chapter Eighteen, the word "Evangelical" has a number of senses. What features does Evangelical theology tend to have? What features of the Second Great Awakening were picked up by Moody and other early Evangelicals?
- How has the tension between intellectualism and emotionalism played out in modern Evangelicalism?

- What are some ways, discussed in the chapter, in which Christianity has adapted to American culture since the second half of the twentieth century?
- How has American exceptionalism manifested itself through the Evangelical movement and the rise of the Religious Right?
- What are the features of Pentecostalism, and how have these led to its popularity, especially in the developing world?

DISCUSSION QUESTIONS

- What are the benefits and problems for Christians of tying theology to a particular political agenda or party? Defend your answer.
- What do you see as the assets and liabilities of mega-churches in terms of living out an authentic Christian faith?

- Given that the gift of tongues is part of the biblical witness and that it has risen in popularity worldwide today, what do you make of this experience?

KEY TERMS

Ecumenism
Falwell, Jerry
Fullness gospel
Graham, William Franklin, Jr.
Holiness churches
Manifest Destiny

Mega-church
Moody, Dwight L.
Osteen, John
Pentecostal movement
Positive confession
Prosperity preaching

Roberts, Oral
Seymour, William J.
Speaking in tongues
Warren, Rick

BIBLIOGRAPHY

- Alexander, Paul. 2009. *Signs and Wonders: Why Pentecostalism Is the World's Fastest Growing Faith.* San Francisco: Jossey-Bass.
- Anderson, Allan. 2004. *An Introduction to Pentecostalism.* Cambridge: Cambridge University Press.
- Anderson, Allan. 2013. *To the Ends of the Earth: Pentecostalism and the Transformation of World Christianity.* Oxford: Oxford University Press.
- Coleman, Simon. 2000. *The Globalisation of Christianity: Spreading the Gospel of Prosperity.* Cambridge: Cambridge University Press.
- Ellingson, Stephen. 2007. *The Megachurch and the Mainline: Remaking Religious Tradition in the Twenty-First Century.* Chicago: University of Chicago Press.
- Kay, William. 2011. *Pentecostalism: A Very Short Introduction.* Oxford: Oxford University Press.
- Mair, George. 2005. *A Life with Purpose: Reverend Rick Warren: The Most Inspiring Pastor of Our Time.* New York: Berkley Books.
- Mardsen, George. 1991. *Understanding Fundamentalism and Evangelicalism.* Grand Rapids, MI: Eerdmans.
- Miller, Donald. 1997. *Reinventing American Protestantism: Christianity in the New Millennium.* Berkeley: University of California Press.
- Miller, Donald, Kimon Sargeant, and Richard Flory, eds. 2013. *Spirit and Power: The Growth and Global Impact of Pentecostalism.* Oxford: Oxford University Press.
- Noll, Mark. 2001. *American Evangelical Christianity: An Introduction.* Oxford: Blackwell.
- Pew Forum on Religion and Public Life. 2006. *Spirit and Power: A 10-Country Survey of Pentecostals.* Washington, D.C.: Pew Forum on Religion and Public Life.
- Ruthven, Malise. 2004. *Fundamentalism: A Very Short Introduction.* Oxford: Oxford University Press.
- Smith, Christian. 2011. *The Bible Made Impossible: Why Biblicism Is Not a Truly Evangelical Reading of Scripture.* Grand Rapids, MI: Brazos Press.
- Sparks, Kenton. 2008. *God's Word in Human Words.* Grand Rapids, MI: Baker Academic.

NOTES

1. Noll, *American Evangelical Christianity*, 278.
2. Originally, I accessed the transcript from http://www.speakingoffaith.publicradio.org/programs/fundamentalism/falwell.html. As that link has since been broken, most of the dialogue can now be found accessed as https://www.truthorfiction.com/falwell-robertson-wtc/ along with youtube videos that carry most of the dialogue, e.g., http://www.bing.com/videos/search?q=pat+robertson+and+jerry+falwell+700+club+after+9%2f11&qpvt=pat+robertson+and+jerry+falwell+700+club+after+9%2f11&view=detail&mid=D511D8317172ABB44850D511D8317172ABB44850&FORM=VRDGAR.
3. Mair, *A Life with Purpose*, 82.
4. Ibid., 125.

21

Modern Faith and Future Trends

Timeline

1999 CE   Catholic Church and Lutheran World Federation sign Joint Declaration on the Doctrine of Justification; World Methodist Council adopts it in 2006

2005 CE   United Church of Christ allows same-sex marriages, followed by ELCA Lutheran Church in 2011 and Presbyterian Church U.S.A. in 2014

2015 CE   Anglican Church ordains Libby Lane as first woman bishop in the Church of England

2015 CE   Historic high killing of Christians at 7,100 that year with the highest tolls from Nigeria, Central African Republic, Syria, Kenya, and North Korea

2016 CE   First meeting in history between the bishop of Rome (Francis I) and the Moscow patriarch (Kirill I)

WHAT TO EXPECT

This chapter engages two issues. The first is descriptive of Christianity as it currently exists in the world. European Christianity is markedly weaker than it historically has been, and U.S. Christianity, while still strong, is becoming less so. But in Central and South America, as well as Africa and Korea, Christianity is a flourishing religion. The second regards the emergence in the late twentieth and early twenty-first centuries of theologies of liberation that strive to make the gospel more relevant to those who have been marginalized, whether in terms of society, gender, or race. Further advancements in Christianity include greater interest among Christians in dialoguing with each other and with other religions. A final ambition of this chapter focuses on modest prognosticating of where Christianity will take itself through the twenty-first century. Certainly the church in Latin American and Africa will dictate some of these trends.

LEAVING BEHIND EUROCENTRISM

In 1900, five of the world's ten most populous nations of Christians were in western Europe: Britain, Germany, France, Spain, and Italy. Three others were in eastern Europe: Russia, Poland, and the Ukraine. One hundred years later, only two European countries made that list: Italy and Germany, with Italy's association with Christianity being primarily one of cultural identity. Even as some Europeans still identify themselves as Christian, church attendance has fallen radically, often to under 10 percent of the population. It would be odd in Europe today to hear any reference to religion in public policy, and most modern social programs are civically run, a reversal from past cooperative ventures between church and state. Additionally, cultural knowledge of the basic doctrines of Christianity, particularly among the young, has diminished profoundly.

Mainstream Protestant Christianity in the United States is also in something of a decline. Throughout the 1950s the number of Christians belonging to traditional Protestant denominations surged. Episcopalians, Methodists, Lutherans, Presbyterians, and Congregationalists all reported membership gains. Protestants stayed in their denominations as well. In 1955, a Gallup poll showed that 96 percent of all adult Christians still belonged to the denomination in which they were raised. But the trend would not last long. By 1990, all of these memberships had dropped, with mainline denominations losing around a quarter of their members at a time when the population of the United States was surging. Further, as mentioned in Chapter One, most Christians in America are not well versed in their faith. In terms of basic literacy of the faith, sociologist Christian Smith found that Pentecostals fared the best, followed by Evangelicals, mainstream Protestants, and finally Catholics, although none is particularly impressive. Much of these groups' relative knowledge base can be correlated to the resources they allocate to youth and adult education, as well as the degree to which they make demands on their members.

Pentecostal churches are growing in the United States, and Evangelical churches are fundamentally holding their own, but mainstream Protestantism is shrinking. Catholicism would be shrinking dramatically as well if it were not for immigrants from Mexico and Central America, most of whom are Catholic. Some of these more traditional Christians—Protestant and Catholic—have left their churches to join Evangelical ones, and others have left the faith entirely. As noted previously, Europe is functionally a wholly secularized society. This is not true of the United States, but America is becoming more secularized. According to the Pew Research Center, between 2007 and 2014, mainstream Protestant churches went from 18.1 percent of the U.S. population to 14.7 percent, Evangelical Christians went from 26.3 percent to 25.4 percent, and Roman Catholics went from 23.9 percent to 20.8 percent. Most of those losses were accounted for by gains in the "unaffiliated" class, which went from 16.1 percent to 22.8 percent. The greatest growth in the unaffiliated comes from those who are often called by sociologists the "nones," that is, those who do not identify as atheists or agnostics, but simply as those

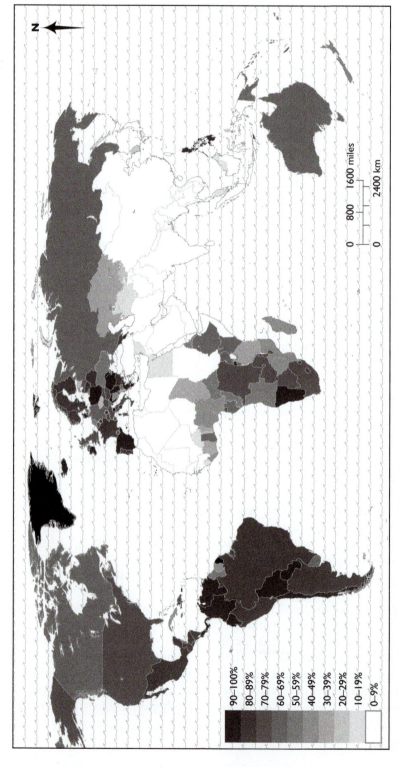

FIGURE 21-1 Christianity throughout the world: The percentage of the populace worldwide that self-identifies as Christian.

for whom no category fits. These are typically younger Americans for whom institutional religion was simply not part of their landscape growing up.[1]

THE GROWTH OF CHRISTIANITY WORLDWIDE

If Christianity is somewhat anemic in Europe and modestly struggling in the United States, it is flourishing elsewhere. In its earliest years, Christianity was identified as a Jewish sect, tied to the fate and theology of Judaism. Within a few centuries, it became the religion of the Roman Empire, a Mediterranean faith. As the church developed, it became predominantly a European and Slavic religion. Even in the colonial period, when missions went to the Americas, Africa, and Asia, it was still identified as the religion of Europe. Today, at least in terms of numbers, Christianity is predominantly a religion of the southern hemisphere, where the majority of Christians reside.

As noted in Chapter Seventeen, Christianity came to Central and South America through Spanish and Portuguese colonization in the sixteenth century. Natives broadly embraced the faith, and the Catholic Church came to dominate the region. Throughout the second half of the twentieth century, Evangelical and Pentecostal churches began to spread in these areas. Their appeal was a simpler faith of the heart and a style of emotional worship that seemed to suit the cultural temperament. Pentecostalism is by far the fastest-growing force in the southern Americas today. Not surprisingly, the Catholic Charismatic Movement has also grown dramatically in South America. This has less to do with an intentional, coordinated initiative by the Catholic institution and more to do with the religious intuitions of the people themselves.

The recent success of Evangelical and Pentecostal Christianity in Central and South America is also due to a shortage of priests to serve the Catholic population. The requirement of celibacy for priests, which is so odd to the native culture, has contributed mightily to the lack of clerical availability to serve the masses of Catholics. Evangelical and Pentecostal churches not only do not demand celibacy, but do not necessarily require much formal training of their leaders. Thus, they can adapt easily to more informal gatherings, and their smaller church communities with ready ministry have proven appealing. As noted in Chapter Twenty, the spirituality of Pentecostal Christianity, with its understanding of a highly active supernatural world and its emphasis on prosperity preaching, appeals to many in South America.

THE CHRISTIAN EXPLOSION IN AFRICA

In 1900, there were 7 million Christians in Africa, making up 5 percent of the total population. Today, there are 400 million Christians there, or about 53 percent of the total population. While the rise in this percentage has recently leveled off, the extraordinary population growth in Africa ensures that the total number of Christians will continue to rise. Christianity is now a majority religion in most countries of Africa, particularly south of the Sahara.

One of the most interesting developments in twentieth-century African Christianity is the rise of **African Initiated Churches** (AIC). Both Catholic and Protestant Christians sent missions to Africa, and throughout Africa we find Lutheran, Dutch Reformed, Anglican, Methodist, and Roman Catholic communities. However, one of the problems these missions faced, particularly in the Protestant communities, was their implicit assumption that to be Christian is to act and think like a European. Some African Christians responded by developing their own forms of worship and even theological sensibilities. Consequently, African Lutherans have more in common with African Methodists than they do with American or European Lutherans. Other African Christians simply left their original denominations and formed their own churches. AICs are the strongest and most numerous in

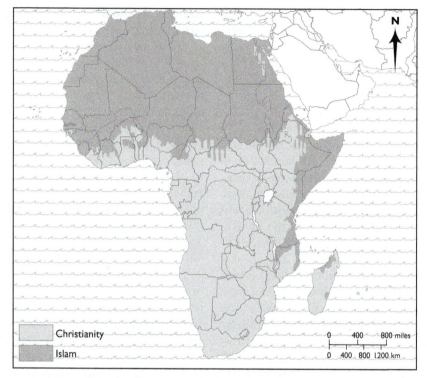

FIGURE 21-2 Religious distribution in Africa: One sees in this map the dominance of Christianity in the southern half of Africa, with Islam dominating the north.

Kenya, Congo, Zimbabwe, and southern Africa. Many of these are "prophet-healing," churches in the Pentecostal form. Here leadership is local, autonomous, and entirely African, with no institutional ties to Pentecostal denominations outside Africa. The exact number of African Christians who belong to AICs is very difficult to ascertain, but it could be as high as 90 million. One finds in these churches something of a union of traditional African beliefs and Pentecostalism.

The explosive growth in Nigerian Pentecostalism is a dramatic example of the AIC's success. Many of these churches are mega-churches, led by Spirit-filled charismatic preachers. So successful has Pentecostalism been in Nigeria that its followers are now engaged in world missions. The largest church in the Ukraine, for example, is pastored by a Nigerian Pentecostal. The Anglican

Church in Nigeria is also flourishing, with a membership of 18 million, which represents almost a quarter of the Anglicans in the world, and several missionary congregations in the United States.

Nigeria is the most populous Christian country in Africa, with 61 million Christians, and the Democratic Republic of Congo comes in second, with 53 million, an astounding 95 percent of the population. Congo became a royal colony of Catholic Belgium in 1885. The Belgian exploitation of the population in the colony's rubber plantations caused such alarm that the Belgian government seized control of the country and tried to turn it into a model colony. Protestant churches arrived in the Congo in the 1920s, and Simon Kimbangu, a Congolese Baptist catechist, launched an independent movement of evangelization and spirit healing. Belgian authorities arrested and imprisoned him, but his movement, the Church of Jesus Christ on Earth by His Special Envoy Simon Kimbangu, survived him. Today, it is the largest AIC in Africa, claiming 17 million members, 9 million of whom are in the Congo.

AFRICAN CHRISTIANITY AND VIOLENCE

Christians in South Africa and Rwanda represent conflicts connected to colonization. As noted in Chapter Seventeen, the Dutch colonized South Africa, though they would have to make room in the late eighteenth century for the British. It was the Dutch who devised the oppressive system of **apartheid**, the separation of blacks and whites in South Africa. While apartheid was not instigated by the Dutch Reformed Church, it became part and parcel of the Dutch presence. In 1912, the South African Native National Congress movement (SANNC) was formed at the Waaihoek Wesleyan Church in Bloemfontein in order to pursue civil rights for blacks in South Africa. It became the African National Congress (ANC) in 1923 and formed a military wing in 1961.

Many Christian leaders supported the justice aims of the ANC and sought political reforms, a support that was not very controversial. What was particularly controversial, however, was whether to support the armed resistance against oppressive government forces. Ordained ministers asked themselves, Could a Christian leader support violence? Was such support akin to a just war? Some Anglican priests worked tirelessly for reform, including Trevor Huddleston, an Anglican who worked alongside the ANC, and John Collins, who railed against apartheid in London's St. Paul's Cathedral and created the International Defense and Aid Fund for the South African poor. In the 1960s Collings also worked with the UN's Special Committee Against Apartheid and addressed the UN on three separate occasions. The most prominent representative of the religious response to apartheid was Desmond Tutu, an Anglican priest who became the archbishop of Cape Town. Tutu eventually won the Nobel Peace Prize and headed the Truth and Reconciliation Commission after apartheid was defeated in 1994.

Disastrous events unfolded in Rwanda, a Catholic country that was home to two tribes traditionally at odds with each other, the Tutsi and Hutu. After a massive wave of Tutsi conversions in the 1930s, Rwanda dedicated the country to Christ the King in 1947. But tensions were always high between the Tutsi leadership and the Hutu majority. From the 1950s on, Catholic leaders challenged the unjust discrimination against the Hutu. From 1990 to 1994 sporadic local attacks on Tutsi grew into larger uprisings. Vatican delegate Monsignor Giuseppe Bertello eventually published a forty-page booklet condemning the country's social and economic crisis and the tribal hatreds that fed most of their problems.

In 1994, a missile shot down a plane carrying Rwandan president Juvénal Habyarimana and the president of Burundi. The assassination triggered a genocide of the Tutsi. About 800,000 were killed, including hundreds of priests and nuns. Archbishops Vincent and Thaddée Nsengiyumva, along with Bishop Joseph Ruzindana, were later targeted and murdered. Most of these murders were performed by Catholics on Catholics. While some Tutsi were hidden and sheltered by Hutu, the massacres betrayed the Christian faith of a country dedicated to Christ the King.

SOUTH KOREA

Christianity is thoroughly grounded in South Korea, and its last four presidents have been Christian. Catholic missions were established in the 1880s but remained very small, while Protestant missionaries, particularly Presbyterians, who also arrived around the same time, enjoyed much greater success. Unlike Japan and China, which viewed Christianity as a foreign import connected to Western imperialism, Korea experienced Christianity as an institution that supported nationalism. Christians played an active role in winning Korean independence from Japan and developed relief programs following the Korean War, thus endearing themselves to the Korean public. After World War II, Pentecostals, such as the Assemblies of God, organized in Korea and opened their first Bible school there in 1954. Paul Yonggi Cho, who was one of its first students, became the founder to the Yoido Full Gospel Church, based in the Yoido district of Seoul. Today, its membership is 700,000, with a main worship space that holds 25,000 persons. The Yoido Full Gospel Church has numerous services on Sundays as well as a number of satellite centers.

Like Nigeria, Korean Christianity is flourishing so well that it sends out missions to other countries. In 1979, Korean churches sent ninety-three missionaries overseas. In 1990, that number was over 1,600. By 2000, they were sending over 6,000 missionaries around the world.

PROPHETIC LIBERATING THEOLOGIES

One of the greatest trends in modern Christianity is the effort to address the disparity between the kingdom of God proclaimed by Jesus and the status of many people in the world and in the church. Theologians working in the context of massive institutionalized poverty, sexism, and racism have responded by creating ways of engaging the gospel to explicitly reveal the problems of marginalization and posit possibilities for countering them. They all share the same impulse: Christ came to liberate people from every kind of oppression and institute a kingdom of justice and love. Where injustice exists, the imperative of the gospel is to rectify it. The theologies that have come out of this impulse are **liberation theology**, **feminist theology**, and **black theology**. Theologians working through these lenses often critique traditional theology as abstracting the message of the gospel and ultimately watering it down. Jesus's own call for a kingdom of justice, they point out, echoes a central theme in the prophetic tradition of the Old Testament, in which the prophets regularly link authentic worship of God to a just society.

LIBERATION THEOLOGY

Liberation theologian Gustavo Gutiérrez observes, "Everywhere we look, we see death. . . . [W]e are confronted with a reality contrary to the reign of life that the Lord proclaims."[2] Some have accused liberation theologians of being religiously dressed "leftists" in a culture war between socialism and free market capitalism. Liberation theologians, in turn, have responded that they merely take the witness of Jesus in the Bible, particularly his preaching on the kingdom of God, and apply it to the real-life situation of widespread poverty in the countries where they live.

According to the World Bank, 25,000 children die of starvation each day, and hundreds of millions live on less than $1 a day. Liberation theologians ask, Is justice served by merely encouraging the rich to be more charitable to the poor and the poor to accept their dismal circumstances? Is the kingdom now reduced to "going to heaven" with no relevance to issues of human dignity? For liberation theologians, assuaging the poor with the hope of a future eternal life while they suffer oppression in the present is tantamount to gutting the gospel message and twisting the very meaning of the kingdom of God.

Central and South America include countries with excellent natural resources, though these countries have historically lacked the social and economic infrastructure to take advantage of them. In the 1950s, companies from industrialized countries, such as the United States, made deals with governments and landowners to utilize these resources in the production of consumer goods. These companies vigorously exported Latin American resources, such as wood, coffee beans, and fruits. Such business was billed as advantageous for these countries, which would now be able to more fully participate in world markets and develop economically. By the 1960s, however, it had become clear to economists that what had been touted as a possibility for social advancement of Latin America amounted to little more than a blatant exploitation of the region's resources for the enrichment of already-developed countries. Between 1960 and 1970 developed countries dramatically increased their wealth, while the indigenous peoples of Latin America continued to suffer great poverty.

The Catholic Church spoke for the people, who in this case were clearly being brutalized by abject poverty. In 1955, the bishops of the Latin American Bishops Conference (CELAM) began to take a public stance against economic injustice in their land. In 1968, CELAM met in Medellin, Columbia, and called for a "preferential option for the poor." In this, they not only reflected Jesus's preaching about the kingdom of God as human flourishing, particularly for the poor, but also exposed "structural sin," that is, economic structures that inherently abuse, manipulate, or exploit others. In a pastoral letter issued following the meeting they wrote, "[T]o us, the Pastors of the Church, belongs the duty . . . to denounce everything which, opposing justice, destroys peace."[3] CELAM also met in 1979 in Puebla, Mexico, and in 2007 in Aparecida, Brazil, to reiterate the imperative for liberating the peoples of Latin America. The bishops of CELAM were bolstered by liberation theologians, who had been analyzing the cultural situation according to theological principles and, at times, socialist economic critiques.

CATHOLIC SOCIAL JUSTICE ENCYCLICALS

Popes in the Catholic Church have issued a number of encyclicals in the modern era regarding social justice. These started in 1891 with Leo XIII's *Rerum Novarum* (On the Condition of Labor), which argued for the rights of workers, their freedom to form unions, and the necessity of the government to ensure an equitable distribution of wealth. Other encyclicals followed throughout the twentieth century: Pius XI's 1931 *Quadregesimo Anno* (After Forty Years) strongly critiqued unrestrained capitalism. John XXIII's 1961 *Mater et Magistra* (Mother and Teacher) argued that Christians have the responsibility to eliminate excessive inequities, particularly among richer and poorer nations. Paul VI's 1967 *Populorum Progressio* (On the Development of Peoples) argued for the universal distribution of goods, just wages, security of employment, and fair working conditions. John Paul II's 1981 *Laborum Exercens* (On Human Work) examined the problem of capitalism's failure to fairly compensate those who contribute to labor. John Paul II's 1987 *Solicitudo Rei Socialis* (On Social Concern) surveyed the structures of sin in developing nations. John Paul II's 1991 *Centesimus Annus* (The Hundredth Year) emphasized the problems between rich and poor nations, environmental degradation resulting from unrestrained consumerism, and the relationship between the right to private property and the demand for equitable distribution. And Francis I's 2015 *Laudato Si* (On Care for Our Common Home) addressed global warming and the association between environmental degradation and poverty.

While CELAM fully embraced liberation theology, there has been a kind of tension between liberation theologians and the larger institutional church. Latin America went through several decades of violence, and Rome wanted to ensure that the Catholic Church was not identified with socialistic reformers or the revolutions they initiated. Rome literally feared that the gospel would become reduced to a Marxist-styled manifesto. On the other hand, many of the principles from liberation theology are reflected in numerous encyclicals issued by popes on economic justice over the past few decades.

Some bishops even spoke and acted like liberation theologians, prophetically challenging the status quo. Oscar Romero, archbishop of San Salvador, El Salvador, placed himself on the front line of social conflict on behalf of his people. Romero spoke out against widespread poverty, systematic injustice, and the torture and murder of citizens who criticized the government. During his three years as archbishop, more than fifty priests were attacked, and six assassinated. In February of 1980, the University of Louvain awarded Romero an honorary doctorate for his work for peace and justice. During his acceptance speech, he said,

> But it is important to note why [the Church] has been persecuted. Not any and every priest has been persecuted, not any and every institution has been attacked. That part of the church has been attacked and persecuted that put itself on the side of the people and went to the people's defense. Here again we find the same key to understanding the persecution of the church: the poor. . . . Now we realize what sin is. We realize that offences against God bring death to human beings. We realize that sin is truly death-dealing; not only does it bring the interior death of the one who commits it; it also produces objective death. We are thus reminded of a basic truth of our Christian faith. Sin caused the death of the Son of God; sin continues to cause the death of the children of God.[4]

Romero was assassinated on March 24, 1980, while celebrating Mass, just one day after ordering Salvadoran Christians in the army to disobey any order that violated human rights.

FEMINIST THEOLOGY

The cultural critique of Latin America in liberation theology has an analogue in the feminist ecclesiastical critique of **patriarchy**. The church, along with essentially every other historical institution, has traditionally been patriarchal. While there have been notable examples of holy, influential women throughout the church's history, particularly women mystics in Catholicism, these examples remain outliers to the dominant control of the church by men. For the most part, this was not controversial until the modern period. The feminist movement of the 1960s voiced a large-scale critique of Western culture's systematic marginalization of women, from restrictions on reproductive control to a lack of equal rights in the workplace. This movement gained momentum in the church in the 1970s and continues to exist today. Critique of the church's patriarchy has come in many forms, from challenges to masculine God-language and

dominantly masculine models of holiness to demands regarding access to leadership.

Feminists have asked, If males and females are both made in the image and likeness of God (Gen. 1:27), then why is God imagined as male? Of course, most everyone believes that God *as* God is not gendered at all. But if anthropomorphic language is useful, why is it always masculine? Such a practice makes the spiritual norm male and relegates females to a secondary status. Many feminist theologians have rethought biblical studies by both highlighting feminine models and language that are part of the Bible and critiquing patriarchal cultural assumptions on which the Bible was written. Just as the many biblical passages that seem to support slavery are now understood as culturally specific, so too, these thinkers argue, should these patriarchal assumptions be viewed.

The most crucial and controversial element of feminist theology has to do with ordained leadership. Many women (and men) have argued that leadership is a gift from the Holy Spirit. If some women clearly have this gift, then it is an insult to God not to exercise it. Further, many argue that the *kind* of leadership women could offer would balance the style of leadership the church has known. A feminist perspective, they argue, tends to emphasize wholeness and interconnections. Leadership incorporating this element would be less autocratic and would involve greater dialogue.

In the New Testament, Paul seems to limit the role of women in the church. We find in First Corinthians, "Women should be silent in the churches. For they are not permitted to speak, but should be subordinate, as the law also says. If there is anything they desire to know, let them ask their husbands at home. For it is shameful for a woman to speak in church" (14:34–35). And First Timothy reads: "Let a woman learn in silence with full submission. I permit no woman to teach or to have authority over a man; she is to keep silent" (2:11–12). Catholic Church leaders have also added the argument that while Jesus had women followers, he only chose men to be his apostles.

Given that Jesus regularly broke cultural norms, they argue, if he had wanted women leaders, he certainly would have chosen women for those roles. The issue here is that apostles are seen as the forerunners to bishops, who now take over their role, directly supported by priests. Finally, the Catholic Church has argued that in the Eucharist, the priest acts in the person of Christ, and that gender is intrinsically tied to the natural association between the male priest and male Christ.

Feminists are undaunted by these arguments. They point out that Paul's assumptions about women reflect exactly the same cultural limitations that are seen in the biblical passages regarding slavery. Further, they point out that the early church did indeed have women leaders. At the end of Romans, Paul offers greetings to those in Rome he knows personally. They include "Phoebe, the deacon of the church at Cenchreae"; Prisca, who, with her husband, Paul identifies as "fellow workers"; and even "Andronicus [male] and Junia [female], my relatives who were in prison with me; they are prominent among the apostles" (Rom. 16:1–7). To the argument that Christ only chose men among his apostles, feminists respond that while Christ was free from the culture in some ways, he did not dislocate himself entirely from it, nor was he intentionally ordaining a primitive version of the Catholic priesthood in choosing apostles. Finally, they find the argument that priests resemble Christ in the Eucharist to be flawed. What resembles Christ, they argue, is not gender, but authentic life in the Spirit, something available to both men and women.

Women's full leadership in the church probably had its first expression in the Salvation Army, which when constituted in 1878 had forty-one female and forty-nine male "officers." The first ordination of a woman in the Anglican communion was in 1944, under the Japanese occupation of China, when the bishop of Hong Kong ordained Florence Li Tim Oi to the priesthood. The Anglican Church at large balked, and she voluntarily ceased to exercise her priesthood without renouncing it. In 1974, eleven women in Philadelphia were ordained by the Episcopal Church, the American expression of the Anglican Church, and a year later four were ordained in Washington, D.C. The Anglican Church in England initially declared these ordinations to be both "irregular" (illegal) and "invalid" (sacramental nonevents) but eventually consented to label them valid, though irregular. Today, about half of the ordinations in the Episcopalian Church are for women, now all both legal and valid. In 2015, the Anglican Church in England ordained Reverend Libby Lane as a bishop. In doing so, it joined other churches that ordain women, including the Lutheran, Presbyterian, Methodist, and United Church of Christ churches. Other Christian churches have held out, including the Roman Catholic, Eastern Orthodox, Southern Baptist, and Wisconsin and Missouri Synod Lutheran Churches.

BLACK THEOLOGY

Black theology arose from the civil rights movement. Martin Luther King Jr., the foremost leader of the movement and a Baptist minister, saw civil rights as a religious imperative. In his "Letter from a Birmingham Jail," King identifies the civil rights struggle as one following the prophets of the Old Testament in their religious quest against injustice. He wrote in this famous letter that he felt commanded by God to do his holy work of justice, and that God's judgment would be upon the church if it failed to address this curse. In his great "I Have a Dream" speech before the Lincoln Memorial, King himself spoke like an Old Testament prophet:

> Now is the time to make justice a reality for all God's children. It would be a fatal mistake for the nation to overlook the urgency of the moment. This sweltering summer of the Negro's legitimate discontent will not pass until there is an invigorating autumn of freedom and equality. . . . [W]e are not satisfied nor will be satisfied until justice rolls down like waters and righteousness like a mighty stream. . . . I have a dream that one day on the red hills of Georgia the sons of former slaves and the sons of former slave owners will be able to sit down together at the table of brotherhood. I have

a dream that one day even the state of Mississippi, a state sweltering with the heat of injustice, sweltering with the heat of oppression, will be transformed into an oasis of freedom and justice. I have a dream that my four little children will one day live in a nation where they will not be judged by the color of their skin but by the content of their character. . . . I have a dream that one day every valley shall be exalted, and every hill and mountain shall be made low, the rough places will be made plain, and the crooked places will be made straight, and the glory of the Lord shall be revealed and all flesh shall see it together.[5]

While there are many forms of sin, both personal and institutional, black theology uses the category of racism as its lens. It works from the presupposition that African Americans are those most marginalized in the United States and looks to the Bible and other theological resources to challenge this sin. James Cone, one of the great articulators of black theology, has written:

The task of black theology, then, is to analyze the nature of the gospel of Jesus Christ in light of oppressed blacks so that they will see the gospel as inseparable from their humiliated condition and as bestowing on them the necessary power to break the chains of oppression. This means that it is a theology of and for the black community, seeking to interpret the religious dimensions of the forces of liberation in that community. . . . There can be no theology of the gospel which does not arise from an oppressed community. This is so because God is revealed in Jesus as God whose righteousness is inseparable from the weak and helpless in society. The goal of black theology is to interpret God's activity as related to the oppressed black community. . . . The Jesus-event in the twentieth century America is a black-event.[6]

THE ECUMENICAL MOVEMENT

Engaging in "polite society" has often meant that one must avoid the issues of religion and politics, as these topics are believed to be simply too contentious. Christian differences have indeed been historically controversial. The patristic church broke up over dogmas in its early councils. Rome and Constantinople mutually excommunicated each other's patriarch in the eleventh century. Protestants broke from Roman Catholics in the sixteenth century. Further, after the Protestant Reformation, not only did Catholics widely think of Protestants as "schismatics" and "heretics," but some Protestants have refused to believe that Catholics are even Christian. Protestants also often quarreled mightily among themselves.

It is also the case, however, that inter-Christian quarrelling can be overstated. Constantinople remained in dialogue with Rome, and both made several formal attempts at reconciliation throughout the Middle Ages. And, as the Wars of Religion died down, for the most part Christians learned to get along with each other. In the United States, Evangelical revivals, from the First Great Awakening on, have downplayed denominational loyalties and emphasized a personal faith that transcends congregational or doctrinal particularities. As noted in Chapter Twenty, Evangelical preacher Billy Graham was especially important in bringing denominations together.

In 1948, the World Council of Churches (WWC) was formed. This was the first great experiment with the **ecumenical movement**. The term "ecumenical" comes from the Greek word *oikoumene*, which means "the world" or "totality." The WWC was a Protestant gathering of Christians from throughout the world designed to work for Christian unity. It was not intended to promote a reunification of a single church, but aimed to establish a "fellowship of churches" that could work together. The organization's website notes, "All activities of the WCC are rooted in a threefold vision for transformation of the church and world. This vision is to live out Christian unity more fully, live as churches being neighbours to all while addressing threats to the human community and encouraging churches to take greater care of creation through protection of the earth and its people."[7] Its current membership includes virtually all large Christian bodies, including representation from Rome and from the patriarchs of Eastern Orthodoxy.

The World Council of Churches is but one initiative in a larger ecumenical movement. Pastors in cities and towns regularly join ministers' groups for fellowship and joint service projects. On a higher level, some Christian communities have more dramatic unity. Since 2009, the Evangelical Lutheran Church in American and the United Methodist Church have been in full communion and share Eucharistic fellowship with each other. Their ministers, despite having been ordained in one denomination, can even serve as pastors in the other. Pope John Paul II (r. 1978–2005) in his 1995 encyclical *Ut Unam Sint* (That They May Be One) called Christian unity one of the highest imperatives of the gospel, and in 1999 the Catholic Church and the World Federation of Lutheran Churches signed a joint declaration of agreement on the doctrine of justification. In 2006, the World Methodist Council even adopted this document as an expression of its own faith regarding justification. As noted in Chapter Eight, Pope John Paul II and representatives of the Coptic Church and Church of the East signed the Vienna Christological Formula declaring themselves of fundamental accord in the very issues that split the church in the fifth century. Finally, in 2016, Pope Francis I and Moscow patriarch Kirill met in Havana, Cuba, to discuss further collaboration in church unity and response to the Christian crisis in the Middle East.

 ## RECONSIDERING THE RELIGIOUS OTHER

THEOLOGIES OF RELIGION

As noted in Chapter Seventeen, Christianity has traditionally considered other religious traditions to be tragically flawed. Some Christians still view other religious traditions negatively. In their opinion, these religions are at best worthy expressions of the moral life, but not salvific. These Christians adhere to what is regularly called **exclusivism**. While not necessarily arrogant or self-righteous, the exclusivist position expresses a foundational belief that there is no salvation outside of a Christian confession. It draws on such biblical warrants as "I am the way, and the truth, and the life. No one comes to the Father except through me" (John 14:6) and "There is salvation in no one else, for there is no other name under heaven given among mortals by which we must be saved" (Acts 4:12). Exclusivists are most often found in Evangelical and Pentecostal communities.

Other Christians believe that God's grace extends beyond the borders of Christianity. They consider Christ the absolute savior but believe that his saving grace operates in and through the souls of all people, and that their implicit but real participation in that grace allows them to be saved. Often called **inclusivism**, this position affirms the priority of Christianity, believing God's revelation is most clearly expressed in that faith. Inclusivists typically argue that other religions are in some respects authentic responses to God, infused in some way by Christ's grace. Thus, they contend that not only can the soul of a non-Christian cooperate with grace, but various non-Christian religions can as well. They would affirm the previously mentioned scriptural citations, since they do consider Christ the savior of all, but they would also draw on other texts, such as "Whoever loves a brother or sister lives in the light" (1 John 2:10) and "God is love, and those who abide in love abide in God, and God abides in them" (1 John 4:16). If God "desires everyone to be saved" (1 Tim. 2:4), then, they argue, God has to make such salvation possible by his grace working outside of formal Christianity. Inclusivists are more likely to be found in mainstream Protestant churches, as well as the Roman Catholic and Eastern Orthodox traditions.

A third Christian response to the religious other is called **pluralism**. Pluralist Christians believe that God transcends all boundaries, categories, and conceptualizations, making any articulation of belief, by its very nature, relative to human considerations. Pluralists see the many religions as addressing God variously, but believe that they all share the same God, the same Absolute Reality, known through different religious expressions. Some pluralists focus on different religions as the means for the same salvation, while others highlight the same fundamental religious experiences that they see expressed in various traditions. These Christians believe in the Bible but think that the exclusivist claims in the Bible were meant to inculcate an absolute faith in Jesus, not address the larger issue of grace and non-Christians. Although no Christian church formally embraces the pluralist position, a decent number of individual Christians along with some Christian scholars, consider themselves pluralists.

A final position that has taken hold in recent years is the **mutualism** position. Christians who take this stance believe that religions are unique and differ enough from each other that they cannot be compared easily. They also critique pluralists as naïvely imagining golden threads among religions that under scrutiny they believe disappear. The mutualist stance has taken hold among some scholars, though still as a minority position in academic circles, but it is virtually nonexistent outside of academia.

Among scholars, even Evangelical scholars, an absolute exclusivist position has few adherents. For the vast majority of scholars, this position closes off the possibility of salvation to whole swaths of people who in many cases had no chance to become Christian; further, they believe, its understanding of grace seems restrictive, and it does not seem to look at the phenomena of religious experience or religious transformation very objectively. Most scholars believe that many of the kinds of religious experience and transformation that Christians report are the same reported in other religions. The vast majority of Christians and Christian scholars take the inclusivist position, which they see as faithful to the doctrine of absolute salvation proclaimed in Christianity while still respectful of authentic practice in other religions.

INTERRELIGIOUS DIALOGUE

In 1984, the Vatican's Pontifical Council for Interreligious Dialogue published a document titled *The Attitude of the Church Towards the Followers of Other Religions*. This text provides a good template to describe various ways that Christians interact with other religions. First, it assumes that true dialogue involves mutual learning and enrichment. Thus, one has to believe that the religious other has something of value to bring to the encounter, something that one's own religious outlook could find helpful. Second, the document explores several forms of dialogue, each with its own agenda: the *dialogue of life* concentrates on how each religion uniquely expresses our common humanity; the *dialogue of deed and collaboration* focuses on how different religions can cooperate to further the common good; *theological dialogue* seeks better understanding of the religious other, and even oneself, in the context of dialogue; and the *dialogue of religious experience* involves sharing one's spiritual life and even considering the possibility for corporate religious experience, such as prayer.

Many scholars in interreligious work focus on the last two types of dialogue. Among other things, they believe that encountering the religious other may help them understand their own religious faith better. This discipline is called *comparative theology*. In comparative theology, scholars try to enter into the religious worldview of another religion so as to return to their own religion with a different perspective. They think of the process in terms of *passing over* and *coming back*. One passes over into the texts and religious imagination of other faiths and returns to one's own asking new questions or bringing new insights into one's theological thinking. The point of this kind of comparative work is not to create new theological truths or a melding of various traditions. Rather, by reflecting on insights from other traditions, one approaches one's own anew.

Interreligious encounters can also offer insights unknown in one's religious tradition. Pope John Paul II touched on the possibility of new religious learning in his reflection on the interreligious experience of the 1986 Assisi Day of Prayer, to which he had invited representatives from many religious traditions to pray for peace, when he said, "There are undeniably differences [in religions] that reflect the genius and spiritual 'riches' that God has given to the peoples."[8]

FIGURE 21-3 Pope Benedict XVI gathers world religious leaders in Assisi, Italy, to pray for peace in 2011.

THE FUTURE OF CHRISTIANITY

While no one can divine the future, it is not impossible to confidently imagine developments in Christianity through the twenty-first century. In terms of sheer numbers, Christianity is becoming increasingly a southern hemisphere religion. The African explosion of Christians alone will remake the face of Christian history. Both Africa and South America are cultures where an enthusiastic faith is thriving. Culturally, they are likely to resist moves to liberalize the church.

Some Christian communities have decided to liberalize, and there is no reason to think they will not continue to do so. Consider the issue of same-sex unions. In 2004 the United Church of Christ began allowing same-sex union. They were followed by ELCA Lutherans in 2011 and the Presbyterian Church U.S.A. in 2014. Currently, the United Methodists are debating the issue. Influenced by the social sciences and a basic sense of fairness and inclusion, they are convinced that such a move is right and that it has been necessary to simply proceed. The Episcopalian Church also ordains ministers from same-sex unions and even raised a firestorm in 2003 when it ordained Gene Robinson, a gay priest in a public same-sex union, a bishop. This has caused a deep rift in the Anglican Communion, of which the Episcopal Church is the American expression. This hot-button issue

is emblematic for how some Protestant denominations will continue into the twenty-first century. That is to say, some Protestant denominations appear to continue to press for changes in their church that they believe represent emerging, less traditional cultural patterns. While one might sympathize with their decisions and even regard these changes as courageous, such denominations will likely become smaller. None of this is to say that mainstream or liberal Protestantism is on a course of collapse. However, in terms of numbers, these churches appear to be on the ebb. America continues to be a very Christian-identified society, but it is a Christianity that will have less and less impact on the culture, and whose members will be less and less religiously literate.

The face of the twenty-first-century church will likely be increasingly non-Western, non-white, and non-affluent. It will also be more morally conservative and more biblically fundamentalist. Secularism, which is a dominant concern for European and American Christians, will likely not draw the same concern of the church worldwide. As Catholic scholar John Allen reports, "secularism doesn't have a terribly large footprint anywhere outside the West, particularly outside Europe."[9] The mentality shift from north to south will highlight the developing world's critique of Western political and military dominance and its patterns of consumption and waste. Finally, Christianity in the southern hemisphere seems set to see a resurgence in young membership and energy. Southern hemisphere Catholicism, Evangelicalism, and Pentecostalism strike many American and European visitors today as Christian communities that are innovative and dynamic. This trend will almost certainly continue.

A final dimension to be considered is the advancement of technology. The printing press transformed the Renaissance church and was instrumental in advancing the Protestant Reformation. The modern analogue is cyberspace. Christians today not only can get their Bibles on their phones, but they also have access to lectures, sermons, podcasts, and so on throughout the world. An inspiring preacher can build a global audience without leaving his or her congregation, and mega-churches can now exist online. While these developments are highly promising for access to religious resources, some have also decried the loss of physical community. Christianity, from its beginnings, has been a religion of a gathered community. The

word "church" (*ekklesia*) means "assembly," and Christianity historically was convinced that uniting together in worship was crucial to actually experiencing the faith.

In some ways the issue of Internet-focused religiosity versus congregational worship and fellowship has an analogue in the difference between online courses and those taught in a classroom; the data may be the same, but the experience is not. John Henry Newman, one of the great voices of the nineteenth-century Anglican Church and then later the Roman Catholic Church, once reflected that one of the greatest gifts university professors give to their students is a "philosophical habit of mind." Newman wrote, "General principles of any study you can learn by books at home; but the detail, the colour, the tone, aire, the *life* which makes it live in us, you must *catch* all these from those in whom it lives already."[10] If this is true in education, it would seem to be all the more true in religion. One *catches* it from direct human relationships, something the Internet and *cyber-faith* cannot provide.

 ## CONCLUSIONS

Christianity claims about a third of the world population and a sizeable majority of the U.S. population. We began this study by noting that it is culturally imperative to understand Christianity. Its history implicates the histories and cultures of nations throughout the world, particularly in Europe and North and South America. Art, literature, architecture, civil law, and many other cultural expressions can only make sense if one

understands the religious values that premised much of them. If one is a Christian or particularly interested in Christianity, a solid grounding in its history and theology is simply necessary to understand it. Yet, even if one belongs to another religion or identifies as nonreligious, agnostic, or atheist, understanding Christianity is crucial to understanding the culture in which we live. Its history and assumptions are part of the air we breathe.

SUMMARY QUESTIONS

- Where is Christianity becoming the most widespread today, and what types of Christianity appear to be most successful?
- Briefly explain each of the prophetic liberating theologies discussed in the chapter.

- Define each of the four theologies of religion discussed in the chapter.
- What is the aim of comparative theology, and by what methods does it attempt to realize that aim?

DISCUSSION QUESTIONS

- Which theology of religion sounds most reasonable to you theologically? Defend your answer.
- Do you think it is valuable for one religion to consult other religions in order to rethink its own beliefs? Explain your answer.
- The author describes liberation theology, feminist theology, and black theology. In each of these theologies, there is a clear intent to provide theological underpinnings for cultural reform. Do you think Christianity ought to be invested in this? Why or why not?

KEY TERMS

African Initiated churches
Apartheid
Black theology
Ecumenical movement

Exclusivism
Feminist theology
Inclusivism
Liberation theology

Mutualism
Patriarchy
Pluralism

BIBLIOGRAPHY

- Allen, John. 2009. *The Future Church: How Ten Trends Are Revolutionizing the Catholic Church.* New York: Doubleday.
- Anderson, Allan. 2013. *To the Ends of the Earth: Pentecostalism and the Transformation of World Christianity.* Oxford: Oxford University Press.
- Armstrong, Karen. 2001. *The Battle for God: A History of Fundamentalism.* New York: Random House.
- Boff, Leonardo. 1982. *Saint Francis: A Model for Human Liberation.* Trans. John Dierchsmeier. New York: Crossroad.
- Boff, Leonardo, and Clodovis Boff. 1986. *Introducing Liberation Theology.* Maryknoll, NY: Orbis Books.
- Centro de Estudios y Publicaciones. 1983. *Signos de vida y fidelidad: testimonios de la Iglesia en américa Latina, 1978-1982.* Lima: Centro de Estudios y Publicaciones.
- Clooney, Francis X. 2010. *Comparative Theology: Deep Learning Across Religious Borders.* Chichester, UK: Wiley-Blackwell.
- Conn, Joann Wolski, ed. 1986. *Women's Spirituality: Resources for Christian Development.* Mahwah, NJ: Paulist Press.
- Feldmeier, Peter. 2008. "Is the Theology of Religions an Exhausted Project?" *Horizons* 35(2): 253–270.
- Feldmeier, Peter. 2011. *Encounters in Faith: Christianity in Interreligious Dialogue.* Winona, MN: Anselm Academic.
- Fredriksen, Paula. 1988. *From Jesus to Christ: The Origins of the New Testament Images of Jesus.* New Haven, CT: Yale University Press.
- Gutiérrez, Gustavo. 1984. *We Drink from Our Own Wells: The Spiritual Journey of a People.* Trans. Matthew O'Connell. Maryknoll, NY: Orbis Books.
- Gutiérrez, Gustavo. 1988. *A Theology of Liberation: History, Politics, and Salvation,* rev. ed. Trans. Caridad Inda and John Eagleson. Maryknoll, NY: Orbis Books.
- Hays, Michael, and David Tombs, eds. 2001. *Truth and Memory: The Church and Human Rights in El Salvador and Guatemala.* Leominster, UK: Gracewing Publishing.
- Hick John. 1995. *A Christian Theology of Religions.* Louisville, KY: Westminster.
- Jenkins, Philip. 2002. *The Next Christendom: The Rise of Global Christianity.* New York: Oxford University Press.
- John Paul II. 1987. "The Meaning of the Assisi Day of Prayer." *Origins* 16 (31): 561–563.
- Johnson, Elizabeth. 2002. *She Who Is: The Mystery of God in Feminist Theological Discourse.* New York: Crossroad.

- Johnson, Elizabeth. 2008. *Quest for the Living God: Mapping Frontiers in the Theology of God.* New York: Continuum.
- Kay, William. 2011. *Pentecostalism: A Very Short Introduction.* Oxford: Oxford University Press.
- Knitter, Paul. 1994. *No Other Name?: A Critical Survey of Christian Attitudes Toward the World's Religions.* Maryknoll, NY: Orbis, 1994.
- Knitter, Paul. 2005. *Introducing Theologies of Religions.* Maryknoll, NY: Orbis.
- Lassalle-Klein, Robert, ed. 2011. *Jesus of Galilee: Contextual Christology for the 21st Century.* Maryknoll, NY: Orbis Books.
- Light, Aimée Upjohn. 2014. *God at the Margins: Making Theological Sense of Religious Plurality.* Winona, MN: Anselm Academic.
- Miller, Donald, Kimon Sargeant, and Richard Flory, eds. 2013. *Spirit and Power: The Growth and Global Impact of Pentecostalism.* Oxford: Oxford University Press.
- Phan, Peter. 2004. *Doing Theology Interreligiously in the Postmodern Age.* Maryknoll, NY: Orbis.
- Race, Alan. 1983. *Christians and Religious Pluralism: Patterns in the Christian Theology of Religions.* Maryknoll, NY: Orbis Books.
- Radford Ruether, Rosemary. 1983. *Sexism and God Talk: Toward a Feminist Theology.* Boston: Beacon Press.
- Ruffing, Janet, ed. 2001. *Mysticism and Social Transformation.* Syracuse, NY: Syracuse University Press.
- Schneiders, Sandra. 2011. *Prophets in Their Own Country: Women Religious Bearing Witness to the Gospel in a Troubled Church.* Maryknoll, NY: Orbis Books.
- Segundo, Juan Luis. 1976. *The Liberation of Theology.* Maryknoll, NY: Orbis Books.
- Segundo, Juan Luis. 1985. *The Historical Jesus of the Synoptics*, Vol. 2. Trans. John Drury. Maryknoll, NY: Orbis Books.
- Sobrino, Jon. 1978. *Christology at the Crossroads: A Latin American Approach.* Maryknoll, NY: Orbis Books.
- Sobrino, Jon. 1993. *Jesus the Liberator: A Historical Theological Reading of Jesus of Nazareth.* Trans. Paul Burns and Francis McDonagh. Maryknoll, NY: Orbis Books.
- Soelle, Dorothee. 2001. *The Silent Cry: Mysticism and Resistance.* Trans. Barbara and Martin Rumscheidt. Minneapolis, MN: Fortress Press.
- Sullivan, Francis. 1992. *No Salvation Outside the Church?: Tracing the History of the Catholic Response.* New York: Paulist.

NOTES

1. "America's Changing Religious Landscape," Pew Research Center, May 12, 2015, accessed at http://www.pewforum.org/2015/05/12/americas-changing-religious-landscape/.
2. Gutiérrez, *We Drink from Our Own Wells*, 10.
3. CELAM, *Peace*, no. 20, in *Renewing the Earth: Catholic Documents on Peace, Justice and Liberation*, ed. David O'Brien and Thomas Shannon (New York: Doubleday, 1977), 569.
4. See Centro de Estudios y Publicaciones, *Signos de vida y fidelidad: testimonios de la Iglesia en américa Latina, 1978–1982*: 2.
5. "Full Text of King's 'I Have a Dream' Speech," *Chicago Tribune*, January 3, 2013, accessed at http://www.chicagotribune.com/news/nationworld/sns-mlk-ihaveadream,0,36081.story.
6. James Cone, *A Black Theology of Revelation* (Maryknoll, NY: Orbis Books, 1986), 5.
7. World Council of Churches, "What We Do," accessed at http://www.oikoumene.org/en/what-we-do.
8. John Paul II, "Meaning of the Assisi Day," 562.
9. Allen, *Future Church*, 434.
10. John Henry Cardinal Newman, "Rise and Progress of Universities," in *Historical Sketches* (London: Longmans, Green, & Co., 1888), 3:8.

GLOSSARY OF KEY TERMS

ABBA Male spiritual guide, typically regarding monastics.

ABBESS Leader of a monastery of women.

ABBOT Leader of a monastery of men.

ABELARD, PETER (1079–1142) Influential forerunner to medieval scholasticism, whose book *Sic et Non* (Yes and No) challenged readers to greater theological synthesis.

ABRAHAM (c. 1850–1750 BCE) First patriarch of the people of Israel and known as the father of the Jewish people and faith.

ADAM AND EVE According to Genesis, the first humans created and the parents of the human race.

AFONSO Congolese king (r. 1506–1543) who advanced Christianity in the Congo (modern-day Angola), and who vigorously objected to the slave trade.

AFRICAN INITIATED CHURCHES (AIC) Christian communities created by Africans that reflect African cultural and theological sensibilities. They often have a Pentecostal style and are most popular in Kenya, Congo, Zimbabwe, and South Africa.

ALIGHIERI, DANTE (1265–1321) Florentine poet whose *Divine Comedy* and other writings represent cultural seeds for the emergence of the Renaissance.

AMBROSE OF MILAN (337–397) Influential patristic bishop whose works included theological texts, guidance in Christian virtue, and hymns for religious service. He was instrumental in converting Augustine to Christianity.

AMERICAN EXCEPTIONALISM The idea that the United States is different from or superior to other nations. It is often coupled with the belief that America has some special relationship with God.

AMMA Female spiritual guide, typically regarding monastics.

ANABAPTISTS Radical reformers who subscribe to the ideas of believers' baptism, restorationalism, and separatism.

ANCHORITIC MONASTICISM Monasticism characterized by the solitary lifestyle of hermits.

ANTHROPOCENTRISM Literally, "human centered"; a mindset that places humans as the norm or point of focus.

ANTHROPOMORPHISM The act of ascribing human characteristics to nonhumans.

ANTONY OF EGYPT (251–356) The most famous model of early anchoritic monasticism (hermits), whose biography by Athanasius became a model for other monks.

APARTHEID South African system of legalized racial segregation created by Dutch colonial rulers.

APATHEIA Literally "no-suffering"; refers to the state of being freed from inordinate desires.

APOCALYPTIC Term used to describe a genre of literature growing out of Second Temple Judaism in the context of persecution. Apocalyptic writing related the current situation to a larger fight between cosmic good and evil.

APOCRYPHA From the Greek meaning "hidden" or "false"; refers to Old Testament biblical texts whose authenticity was rejected by Protestants.

APOLOGIST   Literally "defender"; refers to Christian intellectual defenders of the faith in the Roman world.

APOSTLE   From the Greek *apostelein*, meaning "to send out"; refers to the twelve apostles who closely followed Jesus, as well as to missionaries in the early church.

APOSTOLIC CHURCH   Refers to the historical development of the church from the original apostles to the early second century.

AQUINAS, THOMAS (1225–1274)   Greatest scholastic theologian of the thirteenth century whose *Summa Theologiae* became one of the most impressive theological syntheses produced in Western scholarship.

ARIUS (256–336)   Priest and theologian from Alexandria, Egypt. He taught that Jesus's divine nature was not fully divine, but a lesser emanation of God.

ARMINIANISM   Named after Jacob Arminius (1560–1609); refers to the movement among Calvinists that challenged some Reform beliefs, such as double predestination.

ARMINIUS, JACOB (1560–1609)   Foundational figure who challenged Calvin's doctrines on free will, irresistible grace, and the lack of biblical clarity about the certain perseverance of faith.

ASCETICISM   Literally "discipline"; characterizes a lifestyle of limitations and restraint in order to rid oneself of disordered desires.

ATHANASIUS (300–373)   Great bishop of Alexandria, Egypt, whose theology included the insistence that Jesus had a fully divine nature as well as a human nature.

ATHEISM   Belief that no deity exists.

AUGSBURG CONFESSION   The primary expression of Lutheran faith at the time of the Reformation.

AUGUSTINE OF HIPPO (354–430)   The most influential theologian in the Western church. He was foundational for Western theology's understanding of human nature, original sin, how sacraments work, and the relationship between grace and the soul.

AWAKENING   Term used for periods of American history when religious consciences dramatically grew in fervor in response to revivals.

BAPTISM   A ritual of initiation, designating "dying" to the old self and being "reborn" as a Christian.

BARTH, KARL (1886–1968)   Most important Protestant theologian in the Neo-Orthodoxy movement of the twentieth century. His monumental *Church Dogmatics* (9,000 pages and thirty-one volumes in the English paperback edition) continues to influence Protestant theology today.

BASIL OF CAESAREA (330–379)   One of the Cappadocian Fathers, important for his contributions to Trinitarian dogmas and his monastic Rule, which is the standard Rule for the Eastern Church.

BASILICA   Modeled after Roman public buildings, eventually referring to churches of special significance.

BEGUINES   Unofficial religious communities of women devoted to prayer and ministry.

BENEDICT OF NURSIA (480–543)   Most important figure in early Western monasticism. His Rule of Benedict ended up becoming the standard Rule in the West.

BERNARD OF CLAIRVAUX (1090–1153)   Fundamental figure in the Cistercian reform movement, known for his mystical theology and his support of the Second Crusade.

BIBLE BELT   Region in the southern United States where Evangelicalism holds a strong cultural sway and has since the Second Great Awakening.

BIBLICAL CRITICISM   Application of modern literary analysis to the biblical text.

BIBLICISM   The view that the Bible was essentially dictated by God. Adherents embrace a number of central tenets, including the beliefs that the Bible answers every religious question and is assessable by all in a commonsense way.

BLACK THEOLOGY   Prophetic theology in the United States, coming out of the civil rights movement, that focuses on remedying the sins of racism in America.

BONAPARTE, NAPOLEON (1769–1821)   Staged a coup d'état in 1799 and declared himself emperor of France. He reunited France and Catholicism after the French Revolution, and waged wars throughout Europe.

BONIFACE VIII (r. 1294–1303)   Pope whose *Unam Sanctam* declared that salvation was dependent on obedience to the pope.

BOOK OF COMMON PRAYER   Liturgical guide for the Church of England, originally created by Archbishop of Canterbury Thomas Cranmer.

BUNYAN, JOHN (1628–1688)   Early Pietist leader whose *Pilgrim's Progress* became an international best-seller.

CALVIN, JOHN (1509–1564)   Part of the Swiss Reform movement in Geneva. His *Institutes for* *the Christian Religion* became foundational for Reform Christianity.

CANON Literally "rule" or "measuring stick"; typically refers to the authoritative texts in a given religion or discipline.

CAPPADOCIAN FATHERS Basil of Caesarea (330–379), Gregory of Nyssa (335–395), and Gregory of Nazianzus (329–390). These three theologians and bishops were central in shaping the theological outcomes of the Council of Constantinople in 381.

CAREY, WILLIAM (1761–1834) Baptist missionary to northern India and Bengal who tried to break Indian Christianity from the caste system.

CARMELITES Religious order founded in Palestine in the twelfth century; its members emigrated to Europe in the thirteenth century.

CARTHUSIANS Monastic order founded by Bruno of Cologne in 1084, in which monks lived semi-hermetic lives away from urban centers.

CASAS, BARTOLOMÉ DE LAS (1447–1566) Spanish bishop who railed against the enslavement of indigenous peoples in Mexico.

CASSIAN, JOHN (360–435) Important figure in the development of Western monasticism. His *Conferences* and *Institutes* brought insights of Eastern monasticism to the West.

CATECHUMEN Literally, "hearer" or "learner"; designates initiates to Christianity who undergo formal instruction and tests of moral disposition before baptism.

CATHARS French ascetic religious group that was opposed to materialism and the body.

CATHERINE OF SIENA (1347–1380) Third Order Dominican lay woman whose mystical writings and spiritual authority influenced fourteenth-century Italy.

CATHOLIC REFORMATION Movement within the Catholic Church before, during, and after the Protest Reformation that sought decisive reform in the Catholic Church.

CHARLEMAGNE Charles the Great (r. 768–814), who ruled the Franks and ultimately conquered and united much of Western Europe. In 800 he was consecrated emperor of the Holy Roman Empire.

CLEMENT OF ROME (d. 99) A late first-century Christian leader in Rome whose letter to the Corinthian church explained the nature of church offices.

CLIMACUS, JOHN (525–606) Late patristic theologian whose *Ladder of Divine Ascent* was influential in describing spiritual development in the monastic life.

COENOBITIC MONASTICISM Monasticism characterized by communal life within a larger monastery.

COLONIALISM Historical practice of European nations wherein people from other nations would settle in foreign territories to exploit the land and people of that territory for the benefit of the colonizing nation.

CONCILIARISM Position within the Catholic Church that claimed that ultimate authority was held by councils of bishops rather than the pope.

CONFESSOR A Christian who suffered severe persecution for the faith.

CONGREGATIONALISM Form of church government in which individual congregations largely hold authority over themselves.

CONQUISTADORES Spanish word for conquerors. They took control of American lands from the people living there and set up Spanish-run communities under the *encomienda-doctrina* system.

CONSTANTINE Roman emperor who ruled as a single emperor from 324 to 337, and publicly supported Christianity.

COPERNICUS, NICHOLAS (1473–1543) Astronomer and first to articulate the theory of heliocentrism, according to which the planets revolve around the sun.

CORTÉS, HERNÁN (1485–1547) Spanish explorer and conquistador who conquered the Aztec people.

COSMOGONIES Stories of how the world or universe was created.

COSMOLOGY An overarching theory of reality, usually entailing the creation of the universe, its members, and the structure of the universe.

COUNCIL OF CHALCEDON (451) Council that declared Jesus was fully divine and fully human, that his divine nature was eternally begotten of the Father, and that he ought to be understood as a singular person (with two natures).

COUNCIL OF CONSTANCE (1414–1418) Council that ended the Avignon papacy crisis by affirming conciliarism and appointing a new pope (Martin V).

COUNCIL OF CONSTANTINOPLE (381) Council that reasserted Nicaea and formulated a fuller creed.

COUNCIL OF EPHESUS (431) Council that declared Jesus had two full natures—human and divine—and that these did not intermix. It also proclaimed Mary as *Theotokos*, or God-bearer.

COUNCIL OF JERUSALEM (c. 50) Gathering of Christian leaders in Jerusalem to decide whether Gentile converts had to follow the Jewish Law (Torah). They decided that Gentiles did not, with the exception of sexual purity and modest dietary restrictions.

COUNCIL OF NICAEA (325) Council that declared that Jesus Christ had a fully divine nature.

COUNCIL OF TRENT (1545–1563) The most important event in the Catholic Reformation. In it the church cleaned up abuses, created a uniform liturgy, and articulated its theology, thereby creating a separating wall between itself and Protestant traditions that would last until Vatican II (1962–1965).

COUNTER-REFORMATION The Catholic Church's direct reaction to the Protestant Reformation.

COVENANT Compact made between two parties that bound them to each other.

CRANMER, THOMAS (1489–1556) Appointed by Henry VIII as the first archbishop of the Church of England. He created the Book of Common Prayer and was foundational in the creation of the Thirty-Nine Articles, which articulated the Anglican Church's theology.

CREED A concise statement of core beliefs.

CROMWELL, OLIVER (1599–1688) Puritan member of Parliament who took political power as Lord Protector in England and instituted strict Puritan reforms in the Church of England.

CRUSADES A series of religiously motivated wars against heresy, schism, and perceived occupation of Christian lands by Muslims. Most often references four wars launched in the Middle East by Europeans from 1069 to 1204.

CUAUHTLATOATZIN, JUAN DIEGO (1474–1548) Aztec peasant whose mystical experience of Our Lady of Guadalupe marked a shift in Spanish–Aztec relations and theology.

CYRIL (826–869) Along with his brother Methodius, he converted the Slavs and was instrumental in bringing literacy to Slavic culture.

DAMIAN, PETER (1007–1072) Leader of an eremitical (hermit) movement in the Middle Ages.

DARWIN, CHARLES (1809–1882) Greatest early articulator of the theory of evolution, particularly in his book *On the Origin of Species*.

DAVID (r. 1000–961 BCE) Second national king of the people of Israel. Often, the Bible sees his rule as the golden age of the monarchy.

DEISM Founded by Lord Herbert of Cherbury (1583–1638), it proclaimed that God did not intervene in history, religions of revelation were not possible, and humans were morally responsible and would be judged by God after they died.

DIET OF WORMS Formal meeting at which Luther was excommunicated in 1521.

DOCETISM Literally "to seem"; represents a gnostic commitment that Jesus only seemed to be human or to have a human body.

DOCTRINE Important religious teachings.

DOCUMENTARY HYPOTHESIS Theory regarding the authorship or oral editing of the material from of the Old Testament; these are the Yahwist, Elohist, Deuteronomist, and Priestly sources.

DOGMA Core religious teachings that constitute essential beliefs in the faith.

DOMINICANS Formally known as the Order of Preachers, an order of Catholic priests and brothers begun by Dominic Guzmán in 1216 as a response to heretical movements in Europe and the perceived wealth of the institutional church.

DOUBLE PREDESTINATION Theological position that God predestined from eternity those who would be saved and those who would be damned.

DYNAMIC MONARCHIANISM A rejected view that the Father was the absolute God, while the Son and Spirit were lesser emanations of God.

ECUMENICAL COUNCIL Large gathering of bishops representing the whole church that decides church teaching, practice, and administration.

ECUMENICAL MOVEMENT Organized movement by churches to promote Christian unity, especially through the World Council of Churches (WCC).

ECUMENISM Christian action aimed at promoting greater Christian unity.

EDICT OF EXPULSION AND CONFISCATION Act by the Chinese emperor Yung-Cheng that suppressed Christianity in China for fear that continued mission work would introduce too great a European influence.

EDWARDS, JONATHAN (1703–1758) The most famous figure of the First Great Awakening, whose sermons became classics and whose memoirs, *Faithful Narrative*, became a new literary genre: the conversion story.

EMPIRICISM Philosophical school that views sense experience as the best method for attaining knowledge.

ENCOMIENDA-DOCTRINA SYSTEM System by which colonized communities were run by officials put in place by the Spanish state and in which religious organizations worked to spread Christian doctrine.

ENLIGHTENMENT Period marking the transition from the Renaissance to modernity; characterized by a questioning of traditional modes of authority and an emphasis on the use of reason rather than revelation or institutional authority.

ERASMUS OF ROTTERDAM (1466–1536) Great humanist of the late Renaissance who sought to reform the church through lay piety.

ESCHATON The end time. Christians saw themselves as instruments of God as world history neared its final conclusion.

ESSENES Jewish sect that arose during the late Second Temple Period. They withdrew from society and awaited a divinely led messianic era.

EUCHARIST Literally, "thanksgiving"; designates the central ritual of Christian life commemorating the Last Supper, the crucifixion of Jesus, and communion with the risen Jesus, with the bread and wine being identified in some way with the body and blood of Christ.

EVANGELICAL A term used to describe public witnessing to the gospel, a Christian lifestyle marked by a form of Pietism, or specific nondenominational churches.

EXCLUSIVISM Traditionally popular Christian theological position that holds to the belief that salvation can only come through Christian confession.

FALWELL, JERRY (1933–2007) Southern Baptism minister who was foundational in the Religious Right movement, which aligned conservative Christian values to political causes.

FEMINIST THEOLOGY Theology that critiques the historical and ongoing patriarchy in Christianity. Of special interest are the exclusively male images of God and the exclusion of women from leadership positions in churches.

FEUDALISM Social system built around notions of honor and of labor in exchange for protection. Legal power of property was controlled by a lord, who was expected to manage upkeep of, defend, and support the religious and social customs of the land.

FEUERBACH, LUDWIG (1804–1883) Atheistic philosopher who taught that God was really a projection of human virtues.

FINNEY, CHARLES GRANDISON (1792–1875) Most important figure in the Second Great Awakening and famous for trying to eliminate gender and racial divides.

FOURFOLD METHOD OF INTERPRETATION Approach to biblical interpretation that posits four possible layers of understanding: literal, moral, analogical, and anagogical.

FOX, GEORGE (1624–1691) Founder of the Society of Friends (Quakers), a Puritan offshoot that downplayed institutional authority and focused on egalitarian Christianity led by the Holy Spirit.

FRANCIS OF ASSISI (1181–1226) Founder of the Franciscan Order and known for his love of poverty and care of the poor, particularly lepers.

FRANCISCANS Formally known as the Order of Friars Minor (Little Brothers), a group begun by Francis of Assisi in 1209 to preach the gospel of simplicity and to serve the poor and ill.

FREUD, SIGMUND (1855–1939) Pioneer in psychoanalytic theory. He taught that religion was a form of wish fulfillment.

FULLNESS GOSPEL Also called the "fourfold gospel" or "foursquare gospel"; emphasizes Jesus as the savior, baptizer, healer, and soon-to-be-returning king.

FUNDAMENTALISM Religious stance that rejects modernity insofar as it is opposed to fundamental beliefs such as the inerrancy of the Bible, the virgin birth, bodily resurrection, and the miracles of Christ.

GALILEI, GALILEO (1564–1642) Astronomer who secured greater evidence for Copernicus's theory of heliocentrism. He was found guilty by an ecclesiastical court of heresy.

GELASIUS I (r. 492–496) Pope who first coined the term "Vicar of Christ" for the pope and articulator of the two-swords theory, whereby the pope was understood as having absolute authority over the church while the civil leader has absolute authority over civil matters.

GIFT ECONOMY Economic system in which power, prestige, and honor are communicated with gifts, which that in turn oblige recipients to bestow counter-gifts.

GNOSTIC Literally "knower"; designates a variant of Christianity that taught salvation came principally through secret knowledge and insight.

GOD-FEARERS Gentiles who adhered to much of Judaism during the Second Temple Period, despite not being fully members of Judaism. Reasons for not fully converting included the difficulty of embracing every aspect of the Torah, particularly kosher laws and adult male circumcision.

GOSPEL Literally "good news"; refers to Jesus and his message at large (gospel) or to biographies of Jesus (Gospel). In the New Testament, the latter are Matthew, Mark, Luke, and John.

GRACE Refers to God's unmerited saving presence in the soul that both saves the soul and continues to spiritually animate it.

GRAHAM, WILLIAM FRANKLIN, JR. (b. 1918) The most influential Christian Evangelist of the twentieth century.

GREGORY I (r. 590–604) Pope and defender of Rome, known for his care of the poor, missions to England and Saxony, theological tracts, and coinage of the phrase *servus servorum Dei* (servant of the servants of God) for the pope.

GREGORY VII (r. 1073–1085) Pope who reformed the church, particularly regarding issues of simony, nepotism, and lay investiture. He published the *Dictatus Papae*, which declared the papacy's right to universal sovereignty of the church.

GREGORY OF NAZIANZUS (325–390) One of the Cappadocian Fathers, important for distinguishing the various relations in the Trinity.

GREGORY OF NYSSA (335–394) One of the Cappadocian Fathers, whose mystical theology and advancement of the fourfold method of biblical interpretation became highly influential.

GRIEVANCE LITERATURE Texts during the time of the Reformation that criticized the church's leadership and policies.

GUTENBERG, JOHANNES (1398–1468) Inventor of the moveable-type printing press, which was instrumental in flooding Europe with books.

GUZMÁN, DOMINIC, (1170–1221) Founder of the Dominican order, which focused on evangelical poverty, education, and the ministry of preaching.

HAPSBURGS Family that came to power in the twelfth century and was able to gain ruling control of much of Europe through intermarriage. They were especially powerful during the Thirty Years' War.

HASMONEANS Ruling Jewish dynasty from 167 to 63 BCE, also known as the Maccabees.

HELIOCENTRISM Theory that the planets of the solar system revolved around the sun.

HELLENIZATION After the conquests of Alexander the Great, the spread of Greek language, culture, and political organization across the ancient Near East.

HENRY VIII (r. 1509–1547) Creator of the Church of England, of which he declared himself the head.

HENRY THE NAVIGATOR (1394–1460) Portuguese explorer, particularly of the west coast of Africa.

HERESY Holding beliefs that are contrary to established doctrines.

HESYCHASM Literally "inner stillness"; refers to silent contemplation.

HIPPOLYTUS OF ROME (170–235) Christian leader and disputed pope whose writings describe the rites of the early church.

HOFFMAN, MELCHIOR (1495–1543) Led the Radical Reformation in Strasbourg and Munster.

HOLINESS CHURCHES Nineteenth-century Congregational forerunners to Pentecostalism that saw dramatic experiences of God as signs of radical holiness and embraced the fullness gospel.

HUGUENOT Name given to French Calvinists.

HUMANISM Mindset that celebrated the human subject and was particularly enthusiastic about liberal arts, such as philosophy, literature, art, and rhetoric.

HUMILIATI Religious group of priests and laity who traveled through Italy preaching simplicity and support of the poor as a reaction against the emerging market economy.

HUS, JAN (1369–1384) Bohemian reformer who challenged indulgences and some doctrines in Roman Catholicism.

IBN RUSHD (AVERROES) (1126–1198) Islamic intellectual who combined Greek philosophy with Islamic scholarship.

IBN SINA (AVICENNA) (980–1037) Islamic intellectual who united Aristotelian philosophy with Islam.

ICON Literally "image"; refers to images of Christ, angels, and saints.

ICONOCLAST Literally "image breaker"; refers to a Christian who believes that icons are idols.

ICONODULE Literally "image venerator"; refers to a Christian who supports the use of icons.

ICONOSTASIS Row of icons partitioning the sanctuary from the nave in Eastern Orthodox churches.

IGNATIUS OF ANTIOCH (d. 107) An articulator of early church teachings about ministry, church structure, and the sacraments.

IGNATIUS OF LOYOLA (1491–1556) Catholic reformer who, with his companions, began the Society of Jesus (Jesuits), which became known for its missionary and educational efforts.

INCLUSIVISM Christian theological position that sees the presence of God in other religions and/or religious believers, and holds that salvation is available to non-Christians.

INCULTURATION Process by which Christian life adapts itself to new cultures.

INDULGENCES Practice by which the pope could give out proclamations that were believed to reduce the experience of purgatory or even annul it.

INNOCENT III (r. 1198–1216) Pope known for expanding the papacy's influence over the Western church.

INQUISITION Church instrument beginning in the twelfth century involving investigators who systematically sought to expose and reform those whose views were considered heretical.

INTER CAETERA Papal bull given by Pope Alexander VI in 1493 that gave Spain claim to colonize the Americas and Portugal claim to Africa.

INTERDICT Penalty meant to realign offenders with the church by prohibiting their participation in the sacraments.

IRENAEUS OF LYONS (130–202) Author of *Against Heresies*, in which he describes authentic Christian theology and contrasts it with Christian beliefs (mostly gnostic) that deviated from it.

ISAAC Second patriarch, son of Abraham and father of Jacob.

ISRAEL Literally "one who wrestles with God"; refers to Jacob, who is renamed "Israel" after wrestling with a heavenly figure; also refers to the Jewish people or the northern Jewish kingdom that existed from 922 to 721 BCE.

JACOB Also known as Israel, the third patriarch who fathered twelve sons, creating the foundations for the twelve tribes of Israel.

JESUITS Short for "Society of Jesus," a group founded by Ignatius of Loyola and his companions, which became a dynamic order in the Catholic Reformation, education, and missionary work.

JESUS PRAYER Popular prayer practice involving ongoing repetition of the words, "Lord Jesus Christ, have mercy on me."

JOHN OF THE CROSS (1542–1591) Carmelite monk whose mystical theology is considered by many to be one of the greatest articulations of Christian mysticism.

JOHN XXIII (r. 1958–1963) Pope who instigated the Second Vatican Council, the most important reform of Catholicism in 400 years.

JUDAIZERS Early Christians who taught that Gentile converts had to take on the Mosaic Law.

JUDGES Refers to the tribal leaders who led Israel to greater faithfulness and also in battle against its neighbors. Also refers to the early period of Israel in the land of Canaan, when the Israelites functioned as a loose federation of the twelve tribes (1220–1020 BCE).

JULIAN OF NORWICH (1342–1416) English mystic whose *Showings* expresses insight into the Christian faith and the nature of God.

JUST WAR THEORY Any theory stipulating conditions for a war to be morally justified. It is usually traced to Saint Augustine in the Christian tradition.

JUSTIFICATION The condition of being aligned with or made righteous before God.

JUSTIN (d. 165) An important apologist (defender) of Christianity, whose writings were part of the formation of Christian theology.

JUSTINIAN (r. 527–565) Roman emperor whose legal code (*Codex Juris Civilis*) united Roman legal principles with Christian virtues.

KERYGMA Central message of the Christian gospel, including Jesus's fulfillment of Old Testament prophecies, his miracles and preaching about the kingdom of God, his saving death on the cross, his resurrection, and the necessity to repent and be baptized.

KING JAMES BIBLE The definitively authorized Bible of the Church of England in the early seventeenth century. It was considered the finest translation of the Bible in the English language to date, and remains a favorite of some Protestants today.

KOSHER RULES Jewish dietary regulations, including prescribed permissible animals for consumption as well as slaughtering and consumption rules.

LAY INVESTITURE The appointment of lay persons as church officials by secular political figures.

LEO I (r. 440–461) Pope who was a great defender of Rome against barbarian attacks, and who is known for his *Tome of Leo*, which was influential in the Council of Chalcedon.

LIBERAL PROTESTANT Protestant denominations that have reevaluated doctrine to conform to the insights of modernity.

LIBERATION THEOLOGY Prophetic theology, most common in Central and South America, that sees the gospel as advocating social justice and works to enact change to promote economic equality and end extreme poverty and exploitation.

LITERARY CRITICISM Analyzing texts and using contextual information to better understand the nature and meaning of written material.

LITURGY Public worship performed by the church; can also specifically reference the Eucharist.

LOMBARD, PETER (1100–1160) First great scholastic theologian, whose *Four Books of the Sentences* attempts to synthesize theology.

LUTHER, MARTIN (1483–1546) First great figure of the Protestant Reformation and founder of the Lutheran faith.

MANIFEST DESTINY Doctrine connected to American exceptionalism, which views it as God's will that the United States take a particularly important hand in carrying out God's global interests.

MARTYR Literally "witness"; denotes a Christian who was killed for the faith.

MARX, KARL (1818–1883) Philosopher who argued that all facets of society, including religion, are complicit in the economic enslavement of the masses.

MATERIALISM Metaphysical position that material things are all that exist.

MEGA-CHURCHES Churches with a weekly congregation of at least 2,000 participants. They are most common in suburbs of major cities, particularly in the Sunbelt.

MESSIAH Literally "anointed"; typically referred to the anointing of ancient Israel's kings. Christians understood Jesus to be a messiah who inaugurated a new kingdom.

MESSIANIC SECRET Term used by scholars to describe Jesus's resistance to being identified as the messiah publicly, particularly in Mark's Gospel.

METHODISM A religious denomination started by the efforts of John and Charles Wesley and George Whitefield. Methodists emphasize spiritual practices that promote individual communion with God, rather than focus on ritual.

METHODIUS (815–885) Along with his brother Cyril, he converted the Slavs and was instrumental in bringing literacy to Slavic culture.

METROPOLITAN The bishop of the capital of a province of the Roman Empire. Churches were grouped into church provinces whose boundaries coincided with the empire's, with the metropolitan bishop overseeing those within his province.

MIAPHYSIS Literally "one nature"; a technical term used by the Coptic (Egyptian) Church to refer to the whole of the person of Christ, though he is still seen as possessing distinct human and divine natures.

MILLENNIALISM Belief that the present period of history is the final one before the second coming of Christ and that Christ will reign for 1,000 years after the second coming.

MODALISTIC MONARCHIANISM A rejected view that each person of the Trinity was simply a mask or mode of the singular God. Each activity of God was imagined to fall under one of the three masks or modes.

MONOPHYSITE Literally "one-nature"; a pejorative term designating Christians who believed Jesus had only one complete nature, a combination of divinity and humanity.

MOODY, DWIGHT L. (1873–1899) An important figure in the nineteenth-century Evangelical movement who continued the spirit of revivalism and founded the Moody Bible Institute.

MORMONISM A Christian denomination started by Joseph Smith, based on his discovery of golden tablets that chronicled the ten lost tribes of Israel who had migrated to the Americas.

MOSES (13TH CENT. BCE) The greatest prophet of the Jewish faith, who led the Israelites out of slavery in Egypt and received the Law on Mount Sinai.

MOSES MAIMONIDES (1135–1204) Jewish intellectual who united Aristotelian philosophy and Jewish theology.

MUHAMMAD (570–632) Prophet who founded Islam and united Arabia under it.

MÜNTZER, THOMAS (1489–1525) Part of the Radical Reformation in Germany, where he led a group in the Peasants' War.

MURRAY, JOHN COURTNEY (1904–1967) Catholic priest and intellectual who argued for the separation of church and state as well as the primacy of conscience.

MUTUALISM Christian theological position that holds that different religions differ too greatly to compare.

NATIONALISM Ideology wherein individuals primarily identify themselves in terms of and alongside the interests of their nation.

NEO-ORTHODOXY Response to modernity largely driven by the ideas of Karl Barth, who sought to address the challenges of modernity while maintaining traditional doctrine.

NEPOTISM The practice of favoring relatives for placement in positions of political or religious power.

NIETZSCHE, FRIEDRICH (1844–1900) Atheistic philosopher who argued for a new kind of culture that celebrated self-authorization and the "will to power."

NINETY-FIVE THESES Series of statements posted by Martin Luther on the door of Wittenberg Castle, which constituted a challenge for public debate concerning some practices and doctrines held by the church, particularly indulgences.

NOMINALISM Position that universals, such as truth, justice, and the good, exist in name only and do not refer to real entities.

ORATORY Association of clergy committed to prayer and mutual support.

ORDER OF PENITENTS Members of the church body in the patristic period who underwent a lengthy period of penance for serious sins.

ORIGEN (185–254) One of the most influential theologians of the patristic church who united Platonic philosophy and Christian theology.

ORIGINAL SIN The theological doctrine in the West that the human will is trapped by sin without God's grace. The origins of original sin were Adam and Eve.

ORTHODOX Pertaining to right teaching.

OSTEEN, JOHN (1921–1999) Creator of the Lakewood Community Church outside Houston, Texas. Now headed by his son Joel, this mega-church boasts of 43,000 worshippers weekly and broadcasts its services on local channels viewed by 100 countries.

PACHOMIUS (290–346) Leader in the early coenobitic monastic movement (communities of monks), whose rule and monastic structures became a model for Eastern monasticism.

PACIFISM The belief that violence cannot be morally justified under any circumstances and that disputes must be settled by peaceful means.

PAPAL BULL Official decree made by the pope and named for its lead seal (*bulla*).

PATRIARCH Literally "father"; refers to the heads of the first three generations of the people of Israel: Abraham, Isaac, and Jacob.

PATRIARCHAL SEES These cities and their bishops governed groups of provinces and held authority over them. There were five of them, known as *patriarchates*: Antioch (Syria), Alexandria (Egypt), Jerusalem (Palestine), Rome (Italy), and Constantinople (Turkey).

PATRIARCHY Social and/or ecclesiastical structures that privilege males.

PATRICK (c. 390–460) Missionary of the faith to Ireland, baptizing thousands and setting up the institutional church there.

PATRISTIC CHURCH Refers to the historical development of the church from the early second century to the sixth century.

PAUL Also known by Saul, his Jewish name, the most celebrated evangelist in the early Christian movement and author of many of the letters of the New Testament.

PEACE OF AUGSBURG Decision that each German prince could establish the Lutheran or Roman Catholic faith in his realm, and that their citizens must also follow this faith or emigrate.

PENANCE Sacrament for the forgiveness of sins involving contrition, confession, absolution, and satisfaction.

PENTECOSTAL MOVEMENT The modern expression of the early charismatic church that looked for spiritual gifts among its members. The most celebrated gifts in Pentecostalism are healing, prophecy, and speaking in tongues. The movement is characterized by a sort of Pietism, which has made it extremely popular in South America, Africa, and Asia.

PETER One of Jesus's first apostles and often regarded as the most important of the twelve apostles.

PHARISEES Religious party in late Second Temple Period that emphasized the role of the Torah in everyday life and insisted on the Tanakh as representing the canon.

PIETISM Religious movement seeking to move the heart of Christianity from doctrine to the experience of the Holy Spirit.

PIZZARO, FRANCISCO (1471–1541) Spanish conquistador whose decisive victory over the Incas became the beginning of the Spanish conquest in South America.

PLURALISM Christian theological position that holds that all different religions are culturally bound expressions of the same God, thus refusing to give any a unique privileged position.

POPE Literally "father"; typically refers to the bishop of Rome.

POSITIVE CONFESSION Belief that as a follower of God, one can claim earthly gifts with the faith that God will bestow them.

PREMONSTRATENSIANS Semi-monastic order of priests who performed priestly duties in parishes while living austere communal lives without private property.

PRESBYTERIAN System of church governance in which the church is ruled by a council of elders.

PRIESTHOOD OF THE BAPTIZED View held by Martin Luther that the spiritual gift of priesthood was given to all believers at baptism and that ordination did not confer a unique kind of priesthood.

PROFIT ECONOMY Economic system in which goods and services are traded in markets with regard to calculated monetary value.

PROPHET One called by God to speak on behalf of God, principally regarding authentic worship, covenant fidelity, and care of those most neglected.

PROSELYTIZING Attempts by members of a religion to convert others to that religion.

PROSPERITY PREACHING Belief that God desires Christians to have materially abundant lives. It is often used by predatory televangelists to derive personal donations with promises of a larger financial return.

PROTESTANT Initially a term for those who protested the decision of the Second Diet of Speyer, but came to represent all Western Christians who were not Roman Catholic.

PURGATIVE WAY/ILLUMINATIVE WAY/UNITIVE WAY Stages of the spiritual life, starting with moral purity and the discovery of God as mediated through created things (purgative way), moving to more immediate experience of God within the soul (illuminative way), and culminating with direct union with God and a life of perpetual knowledge of God's presence in the soul (unitive way).

PURGATORY Realm in the afterlife where souls who were saved continued to be purged of imperfections before entering into heaven.

PURITAN Name given to Anglican reformers who sought to "purify" the English Church of its remaining Roman Catholic elements. In America, a separatist religious immigrant group seeking religious freedom from the Church of England.

Q (QUELLE) Source of the sayings of Jesus, drawn on by Matthew and Luke.

RABBINIC JUDAISM Form of Judaism that arose after the destruction of the Second Temple in 70 CE. It is oriented around Torah and synagogue-centered meetings.

RATIONALISM Philosophical school that holds that reason is the only method of establishing certainty with knowledge.

RENAISSANCE French for "rebirth"; designates a massive cultural shift marked by the reemergence of classical culture, a shifting of concern toward humanism and the individual, and increased rigor and precision in the sciences.

REVIVALISM Movement in American Christianity that sought transformation by the Holy Spirit. This often occurred at revivals, which were large gatherings seeking to promote deeper faith.

RICCI, MATTEO (1552–1610) Jesuit missionary to China who exemplified inculturation by taking on the cultural habits of Chinese scholars and religious figures.

RIGHTS OF MAN French statement of human rights made around the time of the American Bill of Rights.

RILEY, WILLIAM (1861–1947) Founder of the Christian Fundamentals Association in 1919.

ROBERTS, ORAL (1938–2005) Important figure in Pentecostalism and Evangelicalism who had a weekly television program, founded *Abundant Life* Magazine in the mid-twentieth century, and was co-creator of the Christian Broadcasting Network and founder of Oral Roberts University.

ROYAL PATRONAGE Name of the system established by *Inter Caetera* that sought to use the expansion of colonial powers as a means for conducting mission work in colonized territories.

RUSSELL, CHARLES TAZE (1852–1916) Prophet of Christ's imminent second coming and founder of the Zion's Watchtower Society, a forerunner of the Jehovah's Witnesses.

SACRAMENTS Symbolic rituals that serve as intermediaries between God and humans.

SACRIFICIAL ATONEMENT Belief that Jesus died on the cross as a sacrifice that atoned for the sins of the world, according to Jewish understanding of Temple sacrifice.

SADDUCEES Religious party in the late Second Temple Period that emphasized Temple worship and insisted on the Torah (first five books) as representing the canon.

SAUL (r. 1020–1000 BCE) First national king of the people of Israel.

SCIENTIFIC NATURALISM Interpretation of the scientific method that asserts that the method must only appeal to empirical, intersubjective, natural phenomena for explanation.

SCIENTIFIC REVOLUTION The historical change in the Western worldview toward modernism. Its beginning is usually marked by the Copernican revolution and is regarded as culminating with Isaac Newton.

SCIENTISM Belief that knowledge can only come from employment of the scientific method.

SECOND TEMPLE PERIOD (530 BCE–70CE) Period in Jewish history corresponding to the second Jewish Temple.

SECOND VATICAN COUNCIL (1962–1965) Most recent council of the Catholic Church, which modernized the Catholic Church and opened it up to dialogue with the world.

SEPARATISTS Term used for religious adherents wishing to formally separate from, rather than reform, a religious institution.

SEPTUAGINT Greek translation of the Old Testament whose canonical choices included texts that were ultimately rejected by Judaism and Christian Protestants.

SEYMOUR, WILLIAM J. (1870–1922) Foundational of the Pentecostal movement in the United States and leader of the Azusa Street Revival in Los Angeles, California, in 1906.

SHEOL Place of afterlife dwelling depicted in the Old Testament that precedes belief in heaven and hell; depicted as a place of watery darkness where all people go.

SIMONY The practice of buying and selling positions of power in the church, named after Simon, who tried to buy spiritual power from Peter and John (Acts 8:18).

SMITH, JOSEPH (1805–1844) Founder of the Church of Jesus Christ of Latter-Day Saints (Mormons).

SOLA SCRIPTURA Position held by many Reformers that the Bible alone held all theological authority.

SOLOMON (r. 961–922) Son of David and third national king of the people of Israel. He expanded the capital of Jerusalem and built the Temple. Known initially for his wisdom, his rule also degenerated as a result of his foreign wives, pagan worship, and forced labor of his people.

SON OF DAVID A messianic reference that appealed to a reconstitution of David's monarchy.

SON OF MAN Apocalyptic figure often used by Jesus to describe himself.

SOTERIOLOGY Having to do with how Christians are saved and what constitutes that salvation.

SPEAKING IN TONGUES The practice of praising God or prophesying in a language given directly by the Holy Spirit.

SPIRITUAL EXERCISES An extended month-long retreat created by Ignatius of Loyola and focused on identifying one's life and ministry with that of Jesus.

STIGMATA The miraculous appearance on the bodies of some Christians of wounds of Christ that did not heal throughout their lives. Francis of Assisi is the first to have received the stigmata.

SUPREMO APOSTOLATUS Papal bull issued by Pope Gregory XVI in 1839 that formally condemned slavery.

SYNOPTIC GOSPELS Literally "same eye"; refers to the similarities among Matthew, Mark, and Luke.

T.U.L.I.P. Acronym for the five points of Calvinism: total depravity of the soul, unconditional election, limited atonement, irresistible grace, and perseverance of the saints.

TANAKH Hebrew acronym for the three parts of the Jewish scriptures: *Torah* (first five books), *Nevi'im* (Prophets), and *Khetuvim* (Writings).

TERESA OF AVILA (1515–1582) Carmelite reformer whose writings on the mystical life have had perennial importance in the Catholic Church.

THEOCRACY A form of government based around a religion.

THEODOSIUS I (r. 379–395) Roman emperor who declared the necessity for all Christians to adhere to the Nicene Creed, and who eventually made Christianity the official religion of the state.

THEOSIS Literally "becoming God"; refers to the Christian belief that eternal life consists of living God's life with God, although still as human beings.

THIRTY-NINE ARTICLES Created by Archbishop of Canterbury Thomas Cranmer, a document that lists fundamental doctrine for the Church of England.

THIRTY YEARS' WAR Conflict involving much of Europe in the seventeenth century that devastated the populations and economies of those countries involved. Its resolution with the Peace of Westphalia in 1648 marks the beginning of the modern era.

TORAH Literally "law" or "teaching"; can refer to the first five books of the Old Testament, Jewish law and interpretation, or God's revelation.

TRANSUBSTANTIATION Doctrine that the essence of the bread and wine consecrated in the Eucharist is changed into the body and blood of Jesus Christ, while the "accidents" or physical properties remain bread and wine.

TRINITY The term Christians use to refer to a singular God, with three relations or persons in the singular God-head.

TRI-THEISM The belief that God is rightly represented by three separate beings—the Father, the Son, and the Holy Spirit—each of whom have the same divine nature.

ULFILAS Known as "apostle of the Goths," his missionary work led to widespread conversion among Germanic tribes in the late fourth century.

ULTRAMONTANISM Literally, "over the mountains"; refers to European Catholicism looking over the Alps to the pope in Rome for a sense of security and leadership.

VLADIMIR (r. 980–1015) Russian monarch who converted to Christianity and helped advance the faith throughout his realm.

VULGATE Jerome's (347–420) Latin translation of the Bible. It was long regarded as the standard Bible by the Western Church.

WALDENSIANS Lay religious group that began in 1184 and preached radical poverty and opposition to the authority of the clergy and sacraments.

WARREN, RICK (b. 1954) Creator of what is often considered the model of the successful megachurch, the Saddleback Valley Community Church in Orange County, California.

WARS OF RELIGION Name used to describe the European conflicts from the Reformation through the mid-seventeenth century.

WESLEY, CHARLES (1707–1788) One of the founders of Methodism.

WESLEY, JOHN (1703–1791) The most famous founder of Methodism, whose preaching and hymnody continue to influence Christianity today.

WESLEYAN QUADRILATERAL The interplay of reason, experience, tradition, and scripture in understanding Christian faith.

WHITE, ELLEN (1827–1916) Prophet and founder of the Seventh Day Adventist movement.

WHITEFIELD, GEORGE (1714–1770) Famous preacher in England and the American colonies who had little interest in denominational alliances and preached a form of Christianity from the heart.

WILLIAMS, ROGER (1603–1684) American Puritan leader who sought the separation of church and state.

WYCLIFFE, JOHN (1320–1384) English reformer who argued for a national church and the translation of the Bible into the vernacular, and challenged the authority of church offices.

XAVIER, FRANCIS (1506–1552) Jesuit missionary to India and Japan, whose great success came from his evangelical poverty.

XIMENES DE CISNEROS (1436–1517) Spanish cardinal who was instrumental in reforming the Spanish church.

ZEALOTS Jewish party that arose during the late Second Temple Period and were intent on overthrowing the Roman occupation.

ZWINGLI, ULRICH (1484–1531) First great Swiss reformer, known for his insistence on the Bible as the only source of doctrine, his iconoclasm, and his rejection of the objective quality of the sacraments, except for baptism.

CREDITS

Chapter 1
1.1 iamfree007/Shutterstock.com

Chapter 2
2.1 lian_2011/Shutterstock.com
2.2 Renata Sedmakova/Shutterstock.com
2.3 Nicku/Shutterstock.com

Chapter 3
3.1 Michal Szymanski/Shutterstock.com
3.2 Courtesy of Wikimedia Commons.

Chapter 4
4.1 Renata Sedmakova/Shutterstock.com
4.2 Renata Sedmakova/Shutterstock.com

Chapter 5
5.1 Andreas Zerndl/Shutterstock.com
5.2 Tupungato/Shutterstock.com

Chapter 6
6.1 lian_2011/Shutterstock.com
6.2 Renata Sedmakova/Shutterstock.com

Chapter 7
7.1 SimonHS/Shutterstock.com
7.2 Renata Sedmakova/Shutterstock.com
7.3 Iosif Chezan/Shutterstock.com

Chapter 8
8.1 Eileen McGuckin emcguckin@excite.com
8.2 Renata Sedmakova/Shutterstock.com
8.3 Paul Brennan/Shutterstock.com

Chapter 9
9.1 Sergey Kamshylin/Shutterstock.com
9.2 Maxim Tarasyugin/Shutterstock.com
9.3 Nancy Bauer/Shutterstock.com
9.4 perspectivestock/Shutterstock.com
9.5 OlegDoroshin/Shutterstock.com
9.6 Antony McAulay/Shutterstock.com

Chapter 10
10.3 © VPC Travel Photo / Alamy Stock Photo

Chapter 11
11.2 Panaspics/Shutterstock.com
11.3 Patryk Kosmider/Shutterstock.com
11.4 Everett Historical/Shutterstock.com
11.6 Darryl Brooks/Shutterstock.com
11.7 SEF/Art Resource, NY
11.8 Marzolino/Shutterstock.com

Chapter 12
12.1 Everett Historical/Shutterstock.com
12.2 Zvonimir Atletic/Shutterstock.com
12.3 Zvonimir Atletic/Shutterstock.com
12.4 Courtesy of Wikimedia Commons.
12.5 Pecold/Shutterstock.com
12.6 imagedb.com/Shutterstock.com
12.7 ©Interfoto/Alamy Stock Photo

Chapter 13
13.1 Courtesy of Wikimedia Commons.
13.2 Janis Lacis/Shutterstock.com
13.3 Oleg Golovnev/Shutterstock.com
13.4 Matej Kastelic/Shutterstock.com

13.5   Georgios Kollidas/Shutterstock.com
13.6   Only Fabrizio/Shutterstock.com

Chapter 14

14.1   Georgios Kollidas/Shutterstock.com
14.2   Courtesy of Wikimedia Commons.
14.3   Nicku/Shutterstock.com
14.4   Georgios Kollidas/Shutterstock.com
14.5   Georgios Kollidas/Shutterstock.com

Chapter 15

15.1   StockPhotosArt/Shutterstock.com
15.2   FXEGS Javier Espuny/Shutterstock.com
15.3   Georgios Kollidas/Shutterstock.com
15.4   Marzolino/Shutterstock.com

Chapter 16

16.2   Oleg Golovnev/Shutterstock.com
16.3   Georgios Kollidas/Shutterstock.com

Chapter 17

17.2   Everett Historical/Shutterstock.com
17.3   Chad Zuber/Shutterstock.com
17.4   qian/Shutterstock.com

Chapter 18

18.2   Georgios Kollidas/Shutterstock.com
18.3   Everett Historical/Shutterstock.com
18.4   Courtesy of the Library of Congress.

Chapter 19

19.1   Everett Historical/Shutterstock.com
19.2   Everett Historical/Shutterstock.com
19.3   Everett Historical/Shutterstock.com
19.4   giulio napolitano/Shutterstock.com

Chapter 20

20.1   Anthony Correia/Shutterstock.com
20.2   John Wollwerth/Shutterstock.com

Chapter 21

21.3   Courtesy of Wikimedia Commons.

INDEX